THE japanese house

THE japanese house

A TRADITION FOR CONTEMPORARY ARCHITECTURE

BY **heinrich engel**

charles e. tuttle company: publishers

RUTLAND, VERMONT / TOKYO, JAPAN

Published by the Charles E. Tuttle Company, Inc.
of Rutland, Vermont and Tokyo, Japan
with editorial offices at
Suido 1-chome, 2-6, Bunkyo-ku, Tokyo, Japan

© 1964 by Charles E. Tuttle Company, Inc.

Library of Congress Catalog Card No. 63-20587
International Standard Book No. 0-8048-0304-8

First edition, 1964
Fourteenth printing, 1991

Book design and typography by Kaoru Ogimi
Printed in Japan

THE GIRL shoko hashimoto

table of contents

PART THREE environment

PART FOUR aesthetics

list of illustrations

list of figures

list of plates

PART THREE environment

ᴛʜɪs ɪs a difficult book, partly because of its complex intent and partly too because of the author's unusual style. At one time we urged that, in the interest of greater clarity, the manuscript be completely rewritten either by the author or else by a professional editor. But the author, pointing to the inevitable inadequacy of old words when having to use them to approach new concepts, has argued that such a rewriting would inevitably sacrifice something of his closely reasoned meaning and much of the imprint of the writer's personality, without which any book becomes a dull recital rather than a communion of minds. Perhaps no amount of editorial primping can ever make a book more or less than what it is. At any rate, we have exercised only a minimum amount of editorial discretion, limiting ourselves to problems of punctuation, consistency in the use of italics and capitalization, and a few considerations on matters of style. The text, however, remains essentially as it was handed to us in manuscript, and the decision to leave it as such was based on our conviction that this book is something important, something well worth the effort of understanding—an amazingly thorough analysis and interpretation of the Japanese house and a sincere attempt to arrive thereby at certain universal architectural truths.

foreword

by WALTER GROPIUS

THIS BOOK should help to build a bridge between East and West. It is apt to abate the notorious presumption of Western man towards the older and deeper culture of the Orient.

The author concentrates particularly on those features of the Japanese architectural tradition that appeal so strongly to the modern architect of the Western world. He shows that this is not just the result of a fashionable trend toward Oriental design motives, but that it is based on the recognition that certain discoveries in the realm of form creation have permanent significance for all branches of human society.

In revealing the meaningful cultural aims and the high craftsmanship of the Japanese domestic architecture as it evolved through the centuries and in laying bare the compelling motives that directed its development, the author never contents himself with offering a historical study only, but brings, instead, the traditional values alive for the present. The Japanese example of the dedication of a whole nation to the task of giving form and substance to recognized spiritual values comes here as an eye-opener to all those who doubted that such unity of purpose could ever exist. Zen Buddhism, the great, moving power of Japanese thought and action, succeeded in creating an identity of matter and spirit such that we can understand one only by embracing the other.

When I was so fortunate to be invited for an extensive visit to Japan in 1954, I found myself overwhelmed by a new and fundamental experience, namely, to see, at first hand, in the Japanese domestic architecture the results of an extraordinarily consistent attempt at creating a cultural pattern so basically homogeneous, yet, at the same time, so strikingly varied and rich in its elements that it stands unchallenged among history's most notable architectural achievements. The traditional domestic architecture embodied the general principles and ideals of the Japanese society in such a perfect manner that even now, in our day and age, its impact is strong and its cultural influence ubiquitous.

Of course, many of its features that seem related to our Western modern architecture have developed from entirely different premises. But our modern architectural requirements of simplicity, of outdoor-indoor relation, of flexibility, of modular coordination and prefabrication, and, most importantly, of variety of expression have found such fascinating answers in the classic domestic architecture of Japan that no architect should neglect its stimulating study. For me, it held the additional surprise of discovering how closely some of the Japanese attitudes and methods of approach corresponded to certain basic convictions held at the Bauhaus in Germany, which I founded in 1919. In the Japanese house the spiritual links between man and his house had been made apparent by a humanized technique, consistently related to both the mental and emotional needs of man. The design conception had started from the very bones of the building and not merely at its skin as a cosmetic play. Spiritual and practical requirements of living had been coordinated into an artistic approach that represents one of the most valuable contributions to a universal philosophy of architecture.

This book offers the key to the understanding of this profound approach to design. It will interest every teacher and student of architecture and architectural history, every creative architect and designer in East and West alike. To the Western architect it will show up the missing ingredient in our own civilization, the coherent effort at attaining *unity in diversity*. It will make him conscious of the necessity to develop a philosophy of common purpose, able to absorb and give focus to the manifold experiments in technique and aesthetics as they bewilder him today. To the Japanese architects it will give support to their new outburst of creativity, the fruits of which must already now be considered to be contributions to modern architecture of the highest rank.

Walter Gropius

acknowledgments

THIS WORK owes much to the assistance rendered by individuals and institutions. Their role in the pursuit of the project was diverse; their contribution to its materialization was essential; their part in the final product cannot really be estimated in words. Therefore, stating the bare facts of their participation in the project is the best possible tribute to them; and stating these facts in chronological order not only resolves the impossible task of establishing a scale of priority, but also gives hard evidence, how much the history of the project is indeed the history of inspiration, advice, and assistance which individuals and institutions gave toward the realization of this work.

Professor Ernst Neufert	inspired interest in Japanese architecture and encouraged research
the Hashimoto family in Ōtsu	offered home for living; provided platform for learning; allowed direct experience with, and participation in, the culture of the Japanese
Professor Walter Gropius	provoked realization of the significance of Japanese culture and sparked the idea of starting the project
Professors Keiichi Morita and Tomoya Masuda	assisted in programming research and advised in initial studies
the Architectural Research Institute of Kyoto University with Professor Ryō Tanahashi	granted fellowship to support studies
Mr. Gary Cook	examined original draft and made suggestions; secured some of the illustrations; negotiated with the publishers on behalf of the author
Mr. Kazuo Matsubayashi	assisted in the delineation of drawings
Mrs. Evelyn Zimmerman	edited and typed the manuscript
the Institute of Technology of the University of Minnesota with its Dean, Professor Athelstan Spilhaus, and the Head of the School of Architecture, Professor Ralph Rapson	granted funds for completion of the study
the Japan Society, New York, with Mr. Douglas W. Overton and Mr. Louis W. Hill, Jr.	granted funds to aid publication of the work
the Faculty of Architecture of the Technische Hochschule Darmstadt, with Professors Ernst Neufert and Rolf Romero as sponsors	accepted the first chapter of the work as Ph.D. dissertation
the Charles E. Tuttle Company, the publishers, with Mr. Meredith Weatherby, their former Editor-in-Chief, and the successor to this project, Mr. Kaoru Ogimi	showed broad understanding for deviations from editorial standards; made suggestions for improvement; gave the work its final shape

THE CHARACTERISTIC phenomenon of the contemporary epoch is this:

Scientific-technical advancement is no longer anteceded, even less induced, by new spiritual-philosophic cognitions as in previous ages. Instead, science and technique advance autonomously, without the moral control and intellectual preparation that religion and philosophy provide. Each new phase in the rapid transformation of the contemporary physical environment meets man unprepared and hence remains outside his full control.

As a result, new scientific-technical achievements no longer address human sentiment. Consequently, they no longer assume the role of art as in previous ages, when all creative manifestations of man were within popular conception. That is to say, science and technique—the two major forces that shape the contemporary environment—are without art and without the humanizing force that art gives.

This alienation is evident in man's emotional indifference to the forms created by science and technique. It is also apparent in his failure to grasp the new dimensions conquered in space and energy or to imagine their meaning for the human race on this planet. Indeed, science and technique—the two most efficient instruments of human progress—now virtually endanger the very existence of mankind.

The challenge of the present, thus, is not discovery of the new but the total comprehension of the existing and its integration into contemporary ethics; hence, its human application and aesthetic appreciation. The tragedy of the present is that any such spiritual search for the meaning of man's existence in the contemporary epoch is no longer a noble expression of man's inner desire for enlightenment, but a necessity forced upon him by technical-scientific progress.

The challenge exists also for the architecture in the industrial society. For even though building technically lags far behind other industries, it has, nevertheless, progressed so far that its forms remain largely neutral to human emotions. Not being incorporated into a universal order of contemporary thought, architecture constitutes still another alien and inhuman element among man's scientific and technical creations and, especially in residential architecture, revives an unrealistic escape to romanticism.

Therefore, it is not the improvement of technical, economical, functional, hygienic or visual factors of building, but the establishment of organic relationships between man, society, technique, and shelter within the total framework of contemporary ethics that is the vital task of contemporary architecture.

For this universal theme the residential architecture of Japan, more than any other, holds instructive comparisons and discloses basic problems. For in Japan the spiritual order of the epoch was successful in a unique way:

it brought man into intimate emotional relationship to most simple shelter and most humble living;

it gave aesthetic meaning to an architecture that was a pure expression of necessity;

it humanized an environment that was largely standardized and prefabricated;

it established an accord between feeling and thinking.

introduction

idea

The idea of any study is best understood and consequently best pursued when expressed through a series of questions. For the question is not only the origin of all intellectual endeavor of man but also, if precisely formulated, indicates the sphere that encircles the answer.

The idea of this paper has been prompted by such questions as:

What are the distinct qualities of the ordinary residential architecture in Japan?

What correlations do these qualities have to contemporary architectural creation?

What universal values for residential architecture are contained in these correlations?

What bearing, then, do these values have upon the solution of problems in contemporary architecture?

The idea of this paper, thus, is a confrontation of the characteristics of Japanese residential architecture with the respective phenomena in contemporary architecture. As any fair comparison should show the values of both sides in distinct contours, such a confrontation by means of either analogous or contrasting results will show the Japanese achievement in a realistic light. It will also uncover the problems of contemporary living and building and directly inspire their solution. This task cannot be accomplished through reasoning based merely on visual aspects, but requires a thorough study of the total formative and circumstantial factors. As the trends in contemporary architecture are obvious, it is a matter of course that the larger part, though not the final importance, is given to analyzing Japanese residential architecture.

The subject matter is the ordinary Japanese dwelling as it has evolved in the 17th and 18th centuries. The architecture of monastic residences, aristocratic mansions, military houses, farm dwellings, or tea huts will not be discussed in full, but only insofar as they influenced the development of the commoner's residence. Too much confusion has been created by essays that do not make a clear distinction between the various forms of Japanese residential architecture, with their different backgrounds, different philosophies, and, consequently, different meanings.

The subject matter is but a scale for judging contemporary affairs and is, therefore, of only secondary importance. Yet, the choice of this "scale" was not at all accidental. In fact, the choice was prompted by the belief that there is no other architecture equally suited to demonstrate the principles of cultured living and building and to stimulate contemporary design as is the dwelling of the common people in Japan.

The singular significance of the Japanese house for contemporary architecture is evident in many ways:

1. Its unique characteristic is spiritual and physical order that stands in contrast to contemporary disorder in residential building.
2. Its comprehensive standardization of detail and system has effected principles in design and construction that bear direct analogies to contemporary building.
3. Its formative forces are essentially determined by economic factors, as is the case in contemporary architectural creation.

4. Its individual diversity, in spite of rigid standardization, differs favorably from the uniformity of contemporary housing developments.

5. Its representation of family morals and social ethics discloses relationships hardly ever found in contemporary housing.

6. Its aestheticism of simplicity and restraint stands out against the modern simplicity brought about by economization and mechanization of building.

7. Its organization of the total interior space is unique because of a highly efficient flexibility, which in principle is also desirable for contemporary houses.

8. Its relationship to the garden is distinct, manifesting spatial principles that contrast with contemporary confusion in space interpretation.

The Japanese dwelling itself, however, unmistakably belongs to the past, for it no longer meets the physical and psychological requirements of contemporary man, Oriental and Occidental alike. Measured with life, thought, and technique of the era, it reached a rare architectural perfection in the 19th century, a culmination, however, that already signaled the end. Although traditional houses are still dominant, the incorporation of Western conveniences such as glass, electricity, furniture, metal fixtures, etc. has falsified the original purity. Also, ideally, owing to the fast-changing attitude toward life and the dissolution of the family system, the traditional house no longer manifests the actual spiritual values to which the contemporary Japanese adhere. Thus, all architectural trends toward revival of form and motif of the traditional Japanese house, both in Japan and the West, are merely imitative and eclectic in spite of an apparent "modern look."

purpose

The purpose should justify the idea. This treatise thus aims at making an architecture of the past seizable for the contemporary. It is an attempt to interpret the outstanding achievements of a prior architecture, not as forms with obscure causes and motivations, but as forms that actively state a particular order of values. By discussing architectural causes rather than merely comparing architectural forms, the analysis of Japanese residential architecture will deal with the very core of the problems in contemporary architecture:

1. Contemporary architecture reflects the conception of contemporary living: absence of universal standards, vagueness of principles, confusion of aims. An analysis of the individual formative factors of Japanese building and living will show the contributive forces of architectural creation in general and is apt to directly stimulate the reinstallment of universal fundamentals for building, which the rapid change in technique, society, and philosophy has obscured.

2. A survey of contemporary architectural literature reveals the following tendencies: studies on historical subjects do not establish a relationship with contemporary building and no longer act as architectural stimuli; studies on contemporary subjects lack philosophic orientation and have failed in their mission of making architectural achievement attainable other than by mere imitation of form. The disclosure of causes and motives of one of the architectural achievements of Japanese civilization will show that it is the discussion of architectural cause rather than of form that will establish links between past and present and produce ideas in contemporary design.

3. Many Western publications on Japanese architecture are strongly biased by the wish to find affirmation of current theories in architecture and do not show serious attempts to uncover the real backgrounds. They have misinterpreted both the merits and defects in Japanese architecture and have fostered imitative usage. This treatise will attempt to dissolve existing misconceptions and to bring to light those values of Japanese residential architecture that have a timeless significance for architectural creation.

4. Contemporary architecture does not possess qualitative standards other than those applied to any industrial product: efficiency, economy, and visual beauty. Research into the spiritual backgrounds of Japanese residential architecture will

show how philosophy, religion, ethics of family, and individuality are manifested in the Japanese house, in spite of standardization and prefabrication, and will uncover those properties that distinguish architecture from mere industrial products.

5. Japan's relationship with other countries after her emergence as a modern world power was, and in fact still is, prone to tensions, owing to the inability of the outside world to comprehend Japan, her culture, and her people. Since residential architecture is the most honest, because the most unconscious, expression of a people's temperament, ideals, and intellect, a study of the Japanese dwelling will provide a more profound insight into the character of the Japanese nation and the formative factors in her cultural growth.

6. The training of the student at Western universities in architectural history is mainly concerned with monumental architecture of Western cultures, less with residential architecture, except for palaces, and least of all with the houses of common people. The high qualitative standard of Japanese residential architecture, plus the many features that directly relate to contemporary building in any locality, make Japanese residential architecture a very suitable subject for study at universities. For such a purpose, this treatise will provide valuable data and will act as a stimulus for further investigation and evaluation.

7. The words that the architect employs in describing and defining his work are inarticulate and vague, and so is their usage. This absence of a common vocabulary of architectural concepts, which in fact is closely related to the lack of a common vocabulary of expression in contemporary architecture, reflects the absence of a universal philosophy of architecture. As a result, the importance of architecture as the art and science of building, and the shelter for society and man, is not acknowledged by the people. The architect himself is little respected and is largely unsuccessful in making his work understood and appreciated. This treatise, therefore, attempts to establish definitions for basic architectural terms to enable precise understanding and to stimulate similar attempts.

method

The method should emphasize purpose and idea. The method, then, of evaluating a past architecture for contemporary architectural work cannot content itself with the description and depiction of external-visible features alone, because then only form would be conveyed and not the motives that produced the form—a situation only too appropriate for stimulating imitation. It would be equally unsuccessful to single out only certain aspects, for such an approach would place undue emphasis on these aspects, thereby producing a one-sided evaluation.

Only a comprehensive study of all the factors involved in the evolution of the Japanese house can lay the basis for comprehension, interpretation, and final utilization. As wrong as the overestimation of mere analytical recording is, it would be equally wrong to do away altogether with any methodical investigation and depend alone on intuitive assumption.

Though it is agreed that architecture is the combined result of many forces and that any analytical separation of subjects will obstruct the immediate grasp of the total idea, the belief is that a subdivision into individual aspects still is the only method consistent to the purpose and idea of this paper:

1. The research was carried out through the investigation of primary and secondary sources: studying traditional building practice, measuring existing buildings, conferring with traditional carpenter families, participating in Japanese home life, reading original documents, examining old depictions on paper scrolls and screens, and also comparing these evidences with the contemporary literature on the same subject, both Japanese and foreign.

2. In view of the lack of a concise and universal architectural terminology, each chapter is introduced by definitions of title and content of the chapter.

3. The individual subject is analyzed, brought into relationship with the respective

contemporary problem, and examined for its potential in contemporary design.

4. Historical antecedence has been mentioned only if the understanding of a particular feature required it.

5. In view of the numerous and excellent photographic illustrations in literature already existing on Japanese dwellings, only those photographs are included which either show new aspects or substitute for extensive verbal explanation.

6. However, reproductions of important Japanese documents and drawings in exact scale (with Japanese, metric, and foot-inch measurements) are furnished extensively because both sectional drawings and historical documents are essential for understanding architecture.

7. In conclusion, the total effort of the research is reviewed and linked to the contemporary architectural scene. An attempt is made to contribute to the discussion of, and to the work for, the establishment of contemporary culture.

limitations

This treatise possesses the limitations inherent in any investigation on a historical subject: interval in time with resulting inadequacy in thinking in terms of the past and of constructing a complete picture with but documentary fragments. In the case of Japanese residential architecture many phases of evolution are still in the dark because individual studies of documentary evidence have not yet been pieced together; there is also reason to believe that even more documentary material is yet unknown— worm-eaten paper scrolls perhaps hidden and forgotten somewhere in the storehouse of a former nobleman or carefully stored away in secret by the craftsmen themselves or their decendants.

In addition, in order to concentrate the volume of research materials, certain limitations were intentionally exercised:

1. An independent historical treatise on the successive stages of residential evolution is not presented. Instead, the necessary historical comments are given in context with the particular subject of study, since a thorough historical study beyond those comments would have, in fact, required a volume of its own.

2. Though the quality of architectural technique and structure, today as in the past, is in direct relationship to type and quality of the tools of its time, no particular space is provided for listing the many excellent tools of the Japanese carpenter nor for describing his methods in attaining therewith a craftsmanship of such precision that it can be called unique in the world.

3. Also, a particular treatise on the development and transformation of the carpenter profession throughout the Middle Ages of Japan has been omitted even though those changes were in close affinity with the development of architecture as a whole.

readers

This treatise does not attempt to catch the fancy of the one who looks for exotic information or novel forms directly applicable in either his home or his design. It differs, therefore, from most of the current tendency of architectural literature, which, owing to its primary pictorial presentation, serves as the architect's copybook from which to get "ideas" or as the art lover's picture book with which to demonstrate his "culture." Instead, the treatise is directed toward those readers who take a serious interest in Japanese and contemporary architecture and do not shy away from strenuous reading and tedious studying.

PART ONE structure

fabric
measure
design
construction

definition

FABRIC IN BUILDING is the material which, when assembled with others into an organism, constitutes architecture. Dominance of one fabric in the organism can characterize the building and may even become the distinctive feature of an architectural region or period.

FABRIC IN BUILDING is in close interdependence with construction. Some materials forbid certain construction systems just as others may stimulate them. Disclosure of fabric's inherent possibilities, therefore, effects architectural advance.

FABRIC IN BUILDING is apt to disclose national traits and standards of civilization. Identical materials have been differently employed by different peoples and thus distinctly reflect the skill, taste, and thought of their builders.

FABRIC IN BUILDING possesses an innate quality, i.e., a characteristic substance that determines proportion, scale, and expression of fabric, as these in turn influence the entire building structure. Interdependence of material consistency and architectural expression, therefore, is a legality to which building and its design are subjected.

FABRIC IN BUILDING is the total of many materials, each with its own distinct qualities. Harmonious composition of these properties is architectural design, while mere restriction in number of materials employed has no architectural importance.

FABRIC IN BUILDING depends on natural resources. Abundance of particular natural materials can stimulate the growth of architectural features just as lack of all ordinary materials can instigate the development of new products.

FABRIC IN BUILDING is but one component in the entirety of forces that constitute architectural creation. Subordination of all component elements to an encompassing architectural idea is an important principle that establishes unity in building.

FABRIC IN BUILDING, then, embodies an innate order of architecture. Its principles have been the determining factors of early architecture everywhere; they were for some time neglected and are newly interpreted in contemporary architecture.

In view of the countless building materials that crowd the market today, it may appear of little significance here to gain detailed information as to consistency, quality, and usage of the comparatively few individual fabrics that form Japanese architecture; the more so since, at first sight, those materials hardly seem qualified to meet the exacting requirements of modern living.

It is obvious, however, that no proper evaluation for contemporary building can be made unless the Japanese house itself is thoroughly explained in its physical form and in the causes that effected this form. Since architectural form is directly dependent on the materials employed, an aquaintance with those various fabrics that determined Japanese form and expression is prerequisite to any understanding. That is to say, any interpretation as to what significance Japanese architecture has for the present requires detailed knowledge of its constituent materials.

And it is equally essential to list all the materials, both major and minor. For not only do the major constituent fabrics decide building, but minor building materials also often decisively affect the total quality of building, either positively or negatively. For thorough understanding of each fabric it is further necessary to know not only its functional, structural, and aesthetic qualities, but also its share in the entire composition, its interdependence with others, and its potential for development.

In this light, the often used and commonly accepted assumption that the Japanese house is made of "wood, paper, and bamboo" has but the poetic value of a proverb. It distracts from the very fact that there are other fabrics, sometimes less in proportion but not in importance. All of them, though with different intonations, play their part in the ensemble, and all of them have to be taken into account in order to comprehend what the Japanese house does represent.

stone

The use of stone in the Japanese house is limited and has not altered throughout history, although the technique of treatment may have improved. In India, and even in China, stone and brick superseded wood in architecture, but Japan, though in close interchange (or rather cultural dependence) with these countries, did not follow suit. Japan possesses good stone material, but there is no record of any concerted attempts to build residences of stone. The reasons are generally said to be the hot summer climate and frequent earthquakes. Entirely ignored are the facts that the winter is rather severe in large parts of the country and that stone sometimes was used in the construction of the storehouses for valuables (kura), which are linked to the dwelling and need to be structurally very firm. It is also interesting to note that another country in similar geological circumstances, Greece, progressed from wooden buildings to a stone architecture unsurpassed in its eternal beauty.

These facts strongly indicate that neither lack of suitable material, ignorance of its technique, nor compelling natural conditions adverse to stone usage were the actual circumstances that prevented adoption of stone as an important constructional constituent for residential building. Instead, it appears that the decisive factors were, first, a religion that effected a passive, non-creative attitude towards life and, secondly, the country's low economic capacity throughout history. Both factors have indeed influenced every component of the Japanese house and have decisively affected its evolution. Their mention here is meant to give but a hint of the variety of forces at work, without yet entering into their analysis.

As limited as the use of stone is in the house, its importance in the total organization increases with its distance from the house. While stone is used in the house construction itself only as foundation stone or slab, just outside the house it plays the role of an important mediator, connecting as a neutral stage the levels of room and veranda with the lower level of the garden. These steppingstones, though they are both part of the building as well as components of the environment, do not efface clear separation or distinction between inside and outside (Plate 37). Rather, by bridging the gap between interior and exterior space, they manifest awareness of the basic contrast between house and environment. In the garden, then, stone plays not only the role of decoration (stone lanterns), but frequently becomes its sole content and essence.

Japan possesses stone of igneous rock, sedimentary rock, and metamorphic rock. Granite is found throughout Japan but mainly along the Inland Sea. Hard and resilient against weather, beautiful and varying in structure and appearance, it is used for foundation, pavement, steppingstones and fences; but difficulty in treatment, together with lack of fire resistance, prevents universal application. Instead andesite, a material available throughout Japan, is used not only because it is capable of being split and is therefore very workable but also because it is fire resistant. Pumice, due to its lightness and fire resistibility, is frequently used in the construction of storehouses attached to residences. Sandstone varies in color and quality and is used accordingly. Tuffstone, too, is sometimes used in storehouses, but because of poor workability its use is limited as a rule to site enclosure fences.

glass

Glass, long an important component in Western residential architecture, is said not to have entered the residential architecture of Japan before the beginning of the 19th century. As the evolution of the Japanese residence dates from a much earlier time, the validity of considering glass a component fabric of the Japanese house must be doubted. Moreover, glass is certainly not a fabric possessing the common denominator which characteristically coordinates the ensemble of Japanese building materials, for it is neither a natural product nor is it shaped by hand. True, it stresses its inherent substance, which is faultless technicality and intellectual transparency, but these particular characteristics are in diametric opposition to the uneven naturalness and emotional semitransparency of the paper and other materials (Plates 24–25).

Nevertheless, all houses now have incorporated glass to a varying extent, a fact which demonstrates either neglect or non-existence of that unique aesthetic sense which allegedly guided the Japanese in their choice, technique, and treatment of fabric. In this instance, one of the astonishing contrasts of Japanese residential architecture appears. Harmony of composition has been sacrificed in favor of a certain practicality, i.e., architectural taste has failed to assert itself. This is all the more difficult to understand since the practical merits of glass, compared with those of the translucent paper used in the outer doors, are not that overwhelming; because the Japanese home is never heated and the paper-covered sliding doors can be opened to the garden without adverse effects at any time of the year if a view to the outside is desired.

In other instances Western achievements of comparatively superior merits were simply rejected, allegedly in order to maintain the purity of atmosphere. At this point it suffices to note only the inconsistency of attitude; its interpretation will be subject to separate study.

Glass in the common dwelling house is used in movable parts of outside walls, i.e., in the following instances:

glass *shōji* (outside sliding panels)
glass doors for entrance or veranda enclosure
glass windows of various types

bamboo

In the fabric of the Japanese house bamboo plays an extraordinary role. Its particular structure achieves high stability with a minimum of weight, and its hollowness makes it an ideal medium for any form of water transport. As such it has served for ages as eaves, gutters, water pipes, etc. and has fulfilled a distinct functional purpose until sheet metal and ceramics offered, not more beauty, but longer durability and higher efficiency. The substitution can be called complete, and only teahouses, ancient buildings, or remote farmhouses still occasionally preserve this simple and romantic piping system which nature had provided.

Yet, one kind of bamboo still serves a functional purpose. It forms the interwoven latticework that supports the clay wall between the horizontal and vertical members of the house framework (Plate 46). In this instance the bamboo is concealed. When, however, bamboo is visible, its usage is decidedly decorative (Plates 44–45). This does not mean that it is mere decoration in the Western sense where décor either is additive or, if incorporated in the structure, hardly performs any other function than decoration. Rather, it substitutes for purely structural fabrics where accentuation is desired. Being used in its natural state, the roundness of its stem and glossiness of its structure constitute an attractive contrast to the usual squareness of material, planes, parts, and their organization.

It is with this decorative purpose that bamboo may be used as the post of the *tokono-ma* (picture recess) or as a vertical member in reception rooms, but its principal use is in the teahouse, where it often substitutes for beams, crossbeams, rafters, and other visible structural members. Furthermore, bamboo frequently is used for window lattice, fence, or ceiling. More seldom it serves as flooring, principally where the floor is exposed to rain such as on the veranda, stepping platform, and the like.

There are about ten different varieties of bamboo native to Japan, and some scholars maintain that most of them once were imported from China. There is no proof, but the mere possibility is noteworthy, for it indicates that contact with the Asian continent at certain ancient times must have been extremely close. The following are the main varieties used in building:

mōsō-chiku (phyllostachys miti), mainly for constructional parts
ma-dake (phyllostachys bambusoides)
ha-chiku (phyllostachys puberula)
me-dake (arundinaria simoni)

Bamboo, which reaches a height of 60 feet and more, is sold in bundles of a constant circumference of 1.8 *shaku* (545 mm. = 21.6 in.) measured at a height of 3 *shaku* and 6 *shaku* (1 *shaku* = 1 English foot = 303 mm.). Having no annular rings, the bamboo can easily be split and thus allows for almost universal use with little labor. Moreover, it has great elasticity and strength and, in comparison with ordinary wood, there is the advantage that it contracts and expands very little with changing humidity. The latter makes bamboo particularly suitable as a decorative structural member in the clay wall.

clay

Though clay has been found hardly worthy of mention by Western writers on Japanese architecture, this fabric, nevertheless, performs an important role as the basic material for the manufacture of roof tiles, as the joinery for the laying of roof tiles, and finally as the dominant component of the Japanese wall. Moreover, clay is a distinct component in Japanese architecture in general because of its quantity of participation, universalness of application, and quality of expression.

While roof tiles and the laying of them will be discussed later, the following concerns only the clay that constitutes the Japanese wall *(komai-kabe)*. Hardly any other component in the ensemble of fabric offers such a variety of expression and manifests Japan's particular aestheticism so strikingly as does the Japanese wall. Western interpretations often deny its very existence by claiming that the Japanese house actually has no walls, but only movable partitions. The fact is that every Japanese house has walls, not as solid and not as many as in the Western house, but certainly of no less importance.

In all areas of the world where modernization has taken place, synthetic building materials have replaced clay as a fabric directly applied in the house and have made its role secondary, i.e., as an ingredient (sometimes a basic one) for the manufacture of building materials. Japan, though being the most industrialized and developed country in Asia, and in spite of having wholeheartedly adopted everything new, still avoids abolishment of the traditional clay wall. Even modern houses of steel or concrete construction still prefer the Japanese wall as it was evolved in early dwellings and refined in the Japanese Middle Ages under the influence of the tea cult. The chief reason for this preference is beauty of texture. Warmth of natural color, plasticity of texture, economy of usage, and stability during climatic changes make it a definite challenge to any wood panel. Though not too resistant to wear and tear, its qualities are yet such that they may lead to a rediscovery of clay as a directly applicable modern building material.

In Western architecture the substance of the wall itself is hardly expressive. In order for the wall to lose its anonymity it needs another factor in the form of additional colors, panels, veneers, pictures, paintings or, in terms of proportion as a whole, contrast to another fabric, ornamentation, or sculpturesque treatment. In the Japanese wall the two factors are one. Substance *is* color, proportion, texture, and decoration in itself. No doubt this phenomenon resembles a trend in contemporary architecture of giving self-expression to walls by exposing their constituent fabrics, such as brick or concrete. However, this resemblance hardly has any value for a judgment of contemporary features in architecture. As will be seen later, the motivating backgrounds of the Japanese symptom were essentially different from those that effected their contemporary counterpart, and it is only on this level of cause and motivation that a comparative study has any value.

The wall material, i.e., clay with admixtures, is applied in three, four, or five layers on both sides of a bamboo latticework (Plates 46–48).

shita-nuri   first coat
mura-naoshi   second coat
shita-zuke   third coat
naka-nuri   middle coat
uwa-nuri   finish coat

Of these sometimes the second or third coat or both, are omitted. The coats from *shita-nuri* to *naka-nuri* are called *ara-kabe* (rough wall), and the *uwa-nuri* is also called *shiage-kabe* (wall with finish).

For the rough wall ordinary yellow-ochre or blue-black clay is seasoned by exposure to the open air for two to three weeks with a water additive. During this period two to three batches of chopped straw are added at intervals. The clay called *arakida-tsuchi* from the tributary of the river Arakawa in the Tokyo area has been recognized for its quality since olden times. The length of the chopped straw is about 1–2 *sun* (30–60 mm. = 1.2–2.5 in.).

The method and mixture vary locally according to available products, but the following example of mixture for the rough wall *(ara-kabe)* appears to be widely applied:

shita-nuri, first coat: 100 l. (106 qts.) well-seasoned clay
    + 0.6 kg. (1.3 lbs.) chopped straw
naka-nuri, middle coat: 100 l. (106 qts.) well-seasoned filtered clay
    + 30 kg. (6.6 lbs.) river sand
    + 0.4 kg. (0.88 lbs.) fine-chopped straw

Volume required for a wall area of 1 *tsubo* (about 3.3 sq. m. = 36 sq. ft.):
First coat: 3–3.5 *ka* (1 *ka* = 0.6 cu. m. = 2.16 cu. ft.)
Middle coat: 1 *ka*

With regard to a possible application of clay in modern building, the consistency of the interior wall finish *(shiage-nuri)* is more important. Different combinations of ingredients produce an infinite variety of color, grain, and structure, which, however, owing to a common denominator in choice, technique, and treatment, never lose cohesion with any of the other materials used in the house.

There are about fifty different kinds of clay used for the interior wall finish. Some of them are:

bishū-matsuba-zuchi   black-blue
tokiwa-matsuba-zuchi   blue
iwashiro-matsuba-zuchi   dark blue
enshū-matsuba-zuchi   blue
kyōto-asaki-zuchi   gray-blue
bishū-sabi-zuchi   iron-colored
kodai-zuchi   dark iron-colored
kakiiro-zuchi   red-iron-colored

In some instances fine sand or plaster is used for the wall finish instead of the fine clay material in natural colors. The color of sand varies enormously. It is mixed with glue of seaweed, and sometimes crushed pearl shell is added. For example:

ōgasawara-zuna   green
suishō-zuna   white
morokoshi-zuna   brown
tetsu-zuna   gray

The consistency of the plaster finish also varies widely and usually it is selected, together with color, according to the particular taste of the owner.

Because of their applicability in contemporary architecture, some consistencies of the Japanese wall finish are listed in detail:

1. *doro-ōtsu-tsuchi-kabe* (mud-colored clay wall)

80–100 l.	(84.8–106 qts.)	sea-shell powder
40–50 l.	(42.4–53 qts.)	river clay
18 l.	(19.1 qts.)	any kind of cellulose *(susa)*; used to prevent shrinkage

2. *ki-ōtsu-tsuchi-kabe* (yellow-colored clay wall)

28 kg.	(61.5 lbs.)	yellow brown clay
100–150 l.	(106–159 qts.)	sea-shell powder
18 l.	(19.1 qts.)	cellulose *(susa)*

3. *cha-ōtsu-tsuchi-kabe* (light-brown-finish clay wall)

16 kg.	(36.3 lbs.)	yellow-brown clay
100–150 l.	(106–159 qts.)	sea-shell powder
20 l.	(21.2 qts.)	river clay
18 l.	(19.0 qts.)	cellulose *(susa)*

4. Ordinary plaster

55 l.	(58.3 qts.)	lime
130 l.	(137.8 qts.)	sea-shell powder
3.5 kg.	(7.7 lbs.)	glue of seaweed
2.6 kg.	(5.7 lbs.)	cellulose of hemp *(hamazusa)*

5. White (clay) plaster

22 l.	(23.3 qts.)	lime
0.23 kg.	(0.51 lbs.)	glue of seaweed
1.1 kg.	(2.42 lbs.)	cellulose of hemp *(hamazusa)*

6. Egg-colored plaster

0.6 kg.	(1.32 lbs.)	yellow-brown clay
36 l.	(38.2 qts.)	lime
150 l.	(159 qts.)	sea-shell powder
3 kg.	(6.6 lbs.)	seaweed

7. Fine sand finish

45 l.	(47.7 qts.)	colored sand
0.6 kg.	(7.32 lbs.)	seaweed

The exterior wall finish is treated differently according to the local climate or tradition. Yet, its consistency does not differ from the material used as interior wall finish. White or bright colors predominate and the surface is smooth. Of course, with clay as its basic material, the Japanese wall lacks not only insulation against transmission of heat but also durability against weather. Therefore, in areas with heavy rainfall, this surface is protected with a covering of thin wooden boards.

paper

It is understood that the component fabrics of the Japanese residence do not differ in substance nor in their positioning in the total composition from those of many other countries. The distinction lies less in the individual fabric than in the singular atmosphere created through the summary of all the elements. Still, paper occupies a place in the Japanese house that is in itself distinct and characteristic, because paper functions as an indispensable and basic fabric. In any other architecture, paper never emerged from a secondary role as decoration, and its intrinsic potential was never fully exploited. It is the merit of the Japanese to have uncovered the inherent architectural qualities of paper, the equivalents of which have not yet been found in new building materials.

Actually, paper was an import from China by way of Korea sometime in the 6th century, and at that time served as an expensive decoration in the houses of the nobility. But after a lapse of another six centuries, an essentially different type of paper had evolved from this: the translucent door paper *(shōji-gami)*, which thereafter basically influenced the evolution of the Japanese house. Paper in its decorative meaning, though, still continued to serve as wall cover or as panel for the inside sliding doors. Yet, the translucent form constituted a new and primary material in the home and effected a distinct architectural form and essential changes in plan. The achievement itself, however, is of less importance than the process whereby it was attained. The instigating impulse came from abroad. A foreign cultural achievement was taken over and, in a process that lasted for centuries, was not materially changed, but was methodically and distinctly altered in its application.

This evolution of paper as a fabric in the Japanese home manifests a tendency of architectural growth that repeated itself throughout Japanese history: adoption of things foreign, penetration of the adopted, and, lastly, transmutation of the penetrated or occasionally even perfection of the adopted such as was never achieved in the country of origin. This particular Japanese trait has provoked much argument about the question of inventiveness or imitativeness. However, of much more importance is a study of the qualifications and motivations that made this trait so advantageous for the Japanese throughout history. As will be noted later, a study of these backgrounds will disclose those prerequisites and essentials that make a cultural exchange bear fruits.

The papers used in the Japanese house are classified as follows:

1. Japanese paper, also called "hand-filtered paper." Its main materials are bast fiber of:
    kōzo (broussonetia papyrifera), mulberry tree
    mitsumata (edgeworthia papyrifera), a thyme shrub
    gampi (wickstroemia canescens), a thyme shrub
2. Foreign paper, also called "machine-filtered paper." Its main materials are:
    rag pulp of cotton, linen, or cannabis fiber
    straw pulp of rice-straw fiber
    wood pulp of the fiber of pine such as:
    karamatsu (larix), larch
    ezomatsu (picae), spruce
    todomatsu, momi (abies), fir
    tsuga (tsuga), hemlock spruce

The functions of paper in the house can be summarized as follows:
shōji-gami, paper for translucent sliding panels
fusuma-gami, paper for opaque sliding panels
kabe-gami, wallpaper (rarely used since the influence of the tea cult)

Shōji-gami (paper for the translucent sliding panels) is a thin paper that is pasted on the exterior side of the light latticework of doors or windows. The thin spars of the latticework are spaced to correspond to the standard size of the paper.

Shōji paper is the "glass" of the Japanese house. Its qualities, however, are of a different nature, and, thus, also are its effects. The light, broken already by the broad overhang of the eaves, is diffused by the paper and creates a characteristic light condition comparable to twilight (Plate 49). This situation does not change basically even if the evening or winter sun hits the paper directly. No glare, no shadows; a general gloom creates a soft, emotional atmosphere. With artificial light in use, the *shōji* paper shows its reflective-diffusing ability, and at night with lights turned out, might even offer an interesting shadow play the moon has staged with the old weather-worn pine tree. As time passes, the paper darkens. Here and there, a torn piece is carefully cut out and replaced by new, lighter paper. The paper pattern becomes, though irregular, more interesting and lively. The paper ages, as does man.

Such an aesthetic quality, of course, has not been the motivation for development of the translucent paper, and therefore cannot be termed a manifestation of Japanese aesthetic disposition, as interpretations tend to infer. This quality was an accidental result of paper's use at first, but then its superior beauty over glass became fully understood, as proven by the preference for paper today, even in houses of the wealthy. Definitely, architectural development took place first, and aesthetic realization and appreciation followed much later.

The following sorts of *shōji* paper are on sale:

1. *Mino-gami* or *shōin-gami* *(gami* or *kami* means paper):
   hand-filtered paper—made of *kōzo* fiber
   machine-filtered paper—made of *mitsumata* fiber or pulp

The standard size of a single sheet is 9 × 13 *sun* (273 × 394 mm. = 10.8 × 15.6 in.), the actual width being 9.2 *sun*. The sheets are pasted together at their short sides until a length of 65 *shaku* is reached. About 50 sheets are needed to cover a typical door area of one *jō* (1.65 sq. m. = 18 sq. ft.).

2. *Hanshi* (literally, half paper):
   kōzo-banshi—main material *kōzo* fiber; pulp added
   mozō-banshi—main material pulp; *kōzo* fiber added
   ryū-banshi—main material is *mitsumata* fiber; pulp added
   parupu-banshi—main material pulp

The standard size of the single sheet is 8 × 11 *sun* (242 × 333 mm. = 9.6 × 13.2 in.), the actual width being 8.3 *sun;* the sheets are pasted together to a length of 65 *shaku*.

3. *Tokushu-gami* (literally, special paper):
   ito-iri—main material pulp or manila hemp

In this paper a thread is interwoven. It is used for special rooms like the reception room, guest room, etc. Its standard size is the same as *mino-gami* in rolls of 31 *shaku* length.

   toshimon-iri—material like *mino-gami*

While filtering, a mark in the form of a leaf or the like is impressed. It is used for the study place *(shoin)*. The standard size is the same as *mino-gami*.

Fusuma-gami (paper for the opaque sliding panels) is a thick paper made of bast fibers and is pasted on both sides of the light wooden frame of the interior sliding panels called *fusuma*. As it is rarely used other than decoratively, it has served, since its introduction from China, as a canvas for paintings and has thus preserved its original meaning (Plate 158). Influence of the tea cult in the 17th and 18th centuries, however, moderated the previously very colorful and gorgeous style of painting and finally effected a shift in emphasis from applied colors to the inherent texture of the paper itself.

There are various kinds of *fusuma* paper, both in method of fabrication (hand filtered and machine filtered) and in size. Yet the standard size of the paper sheets is 30 *sun* (also, 22, 40, and 45 *sun)* × 60 *sun*. Some *fusuma* papers are sold in rolls of 3 × 24 *shaku*. Though there are papers with flashing colors, bold patterns, and strong contrasts, the design of *fusuma* papers as a rule is quiet and restrained and thus blends well with the general expression of the house interior. The basic colors are white, yellow, cream, gray, or light brown. Most frequently they are printed in an all-over pattern derived from natural models such as leaves, bamboo, or grass. Paper with plain colors may receive a pictorial or calligraphic work, which is best when done with definite restraint.

The main kinds of *fusuma* paper (for component materials see also *shōji* paper) are the following:

1. *Torinoko*—main materials *gampi* or *mitsumata*

The paper is sold in plain colors such as cream, beige, light brown, yellow. A pattern is usually applied after purchase, but ready printed patterns are also available.

2. *Michinoku-gami*—main material *kozō,* occasionally, pulp added

The paper is very thick and is preferred in ceremonial buildings. It is frequently printed with a heraldic pattern.

3. *Maniai-gami*—main material *mitsumata*

As the surface is not glossy, it does not rank as a first-class paper. Sometimes gold

column centers, but sometimes not. Here, the discrepancy between center distance and clear width, a problem of modern standardization, clearly reveals itself.

As a fabric that should equally facilitate walking, sitting, and sleeping, the *tatami* demanded both stiffness and resiliency. Limited to the use of natural materials, this demand could be met only by accepting a fabric with high porosity, i.e., with a consistency impractical and unhygienic for a floor, because as such it is susceptible to accumulation of dust and penetration of humidity from the damp ground. It does facilitate ventilation. This summertime advantage, however, is a wintertime nuisance. Having originated as an implement to serve a particular way of life, once it had emerged in the present form, it began to counterinfluence the manners of living of its users.

With the mat a fabric of the Japanese home has evolved that constitutes an important junction where many opposing movements have met, have been moderated, and have been coordinated. The *tatami,* as distinct as it is for the Japanese house, is not distinct in itself. It functions as moderator and unifier of architectural contrasts and thus is, in its nature, the product of a compromise between human and structural scale, between vertical and horizontal order, and between climatic and habitual demands. As such it fulfills the demands of none of them completely, and consequently is manifold in its meaning. This indistinctness of the nature of the *tatami* also explains the frequent misinterpretations it is subject to.

The word *tatami* stems from *tatamu,* meaning to fold, to pile up; for the early form of the object, as depicted in early scroll paintings illustrating the *Kojiki* and *Manyō-shū,* was but a thin skin cover or a grass mat that could be easily folded. It might also be possible that several layers, one upon the other, were used simultaneously. In the Kamakura period (1185–1336) thickly knit straw mats, called *tsuka-nami,* appeared for the first time in the residences of the nobility. Yet, they did not cover the whole surface but were carried to a desired place. The size of this mat, as is evident in picture scrolls, corresponds to a space occupied by two men sitting, and was already fairly standardized. At the beginning of the Muromachi period (1393–1573) the entire floor was covered for the first time. Thus *tatami* had become floor itself. The spreading of the *shoin* style markedly helped its propagation, but economic circumstances prevented general use among the people before the 18th century.

The three main constituent parts of the *tatami* are:

　　toko (floor), thick straw underpart
　　omote (surface), thin reed cover
　　fuchi or *heri* (edge), cloth tape binding

The *tatami-doko* (mat underpart) is made either by hand or by machine, the latter method now being prevalent.

Handmade mats: The straw material is arranged in successive transverse layers and then stitched with hemp strings. The sewing work can be done in two ways: with the stitched rows closed, *kake-nui,* or with the stitched rows parted, *suji-nui.* The *kake-nui* mat has 11–18 stitch rows, the *suji-nui* mat 8–15 stitch rows.

Machine-made mats: Though techniques differ, the order is similar to that of the handmade ones. The distinction lies in the number of stitch rows and not in the number of stitches. The machine-made underpart is 22–30 stitches in width, 40–80 stitches in length.

The thickness of the underpart of the mat is officially standardized at 45, 50, and 57 mm. (about 1.8–2.2 in.), but there are many local differences.

The *tatami-omote* (mat cover) consists of a reed *igusa* (juncus effesus) knitted around a pattern of cotton or hemp strings. When the strings are single it is called *meseki,* when double, *morome.* The reed is used in two forms: *maru-igusa,* when the reed has not been split, and *shichito-igusa,* when it has been split lengthwise. The mat cover consisting of *maru-igusa* is called *bingo-omote.* The mat cover of *shichito-igusa* is called *ryūkyū-omote.* Most common is the *morome-tatami* (double string), but *ryūkyū-omote* has only the *meseki* type (single string).

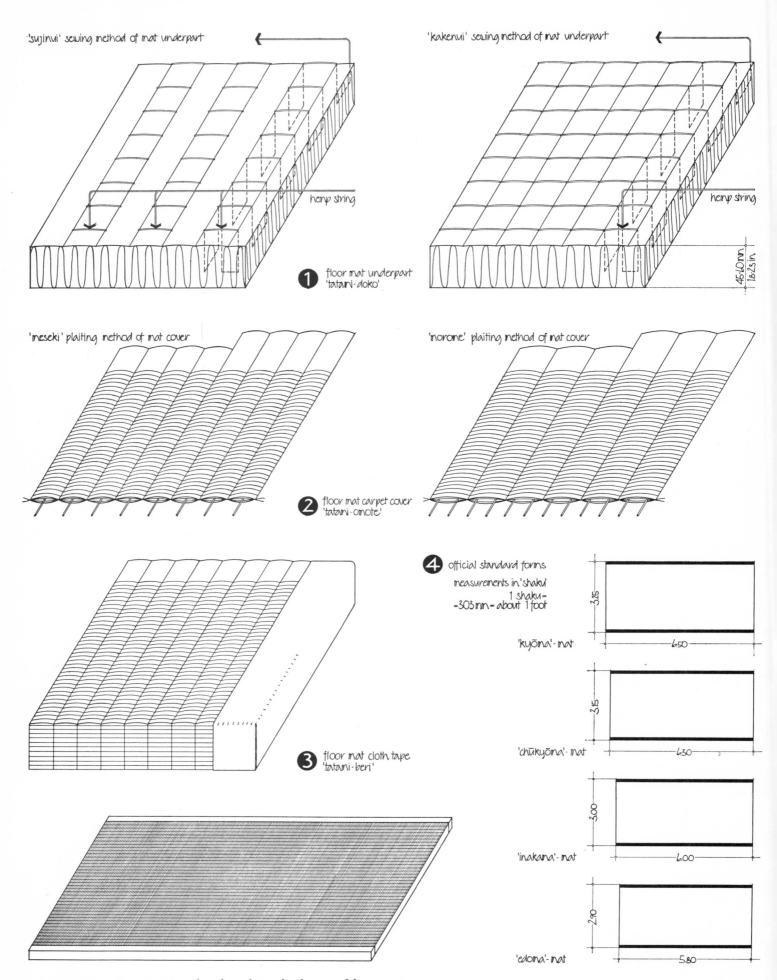

'sujinui' sewing method of mat underpart

'kakenui' sewing method of mat underpart

hemp string

hemp string

45-60mm
1.8-2.5 in

1 floor mat underpart 'tatami-doko'

'meseki' plaiting method of mat cover

'morone' plaiting method of mat cover

2 floor mat carpet cover 'tatami-omote'

3 floor mat cloth tape 'tatami-beri'

4 official standard forms

measurements in 'shaku'
1 shaku =
= 303mm = about 1 foot

3.15	6.50

'kyōma'-mat

3.15	6.30

'chūkyōma'-mat

3.00	6.00

'inakama'-mat

2.90	5.80

'edoma'-mat

FIGURE 2: Construction details and standard sizes of the *tatami*.

Reed material is applied in three different ways:

hiki-tōshi, in which the stalks extend over the whole width without intermediate connection.

naka-tsugi, in which stalks shorter than the width of mat are used and connected at the underface of the cover.

tobi-komi, which is similar to *naka-tsugi,* but in which the stalks are connected at both the surface and the underface of the cover; thus, the connections are hardly visible.

There are many standard sizes for the mat cover and they correspond with the local mat size. For example:

homma-omote, 66 × 31.5 *sun* (2,000 × 955 mm. = 79.2 × 37.8 in.) for a mat of 63 × 31.5 *sun* (1,909 × 955 mm. = 75.6 × 37.8 in.)

go-hachi-hiki-tōshi, 61 × 29 *sun* (1,848 × 879 mm. = 69.6 × 34.8 in.) for a mat of 58 × 29 *sun* (1.758 × 879 mm. = 69.2 × 34.6 in.)

The *tatami* usually is bordered on its long side with a dark cloth tape, the *tatami-beri.* Mats without these bindings are rare. They are called *bōzuberi-tatami,* literally meaning "mat with a monk tape." Materials for the tape are silk, linen, or cotton. The colors are black, brown, indigo, gray, or their intermediates, and there are numerous special designs for the tape. Only a few tapes are listed here:

matsuida-beri—indigo-colored tape commonly used in residences, usually of linen cloth, but recently also of cotton or synthetic fabrics.

koyaku-beri—another commonly used tape in various colors made of cotton.

takamiya-beri—rarely used in recent times; a tape of hemp thread for particular rooms such as reception rooms, guest rooms.

kōrai-beri—an elaborate tape of varying design and material, used for shrines, temples, and palaces and frequently in residences as cover for the picture recess *tokonoma.*

The multitude of existing "standard" sizes of *tatami* proves more than anything else the inadequacy of *tatami* as a module. However, official standardization lists only four main sizes:

kyōma-tatami 65 × 32.5 *sun* (1,970 × 985 mm. = 78 × 39 in.)

chūkyōma-tatami 63 × 31.5 *sun* (1,909 × 955 m. = 75.6 × 37.8 in.)

inakama-tatami 60 × 30 *sun* (1,818 × 909 mm. = 72 × 36 in.)

edo-tatami 58 × 29 *sun* (1,757 × 879 mm. = 69.6 × 34.8 in.)

wood

Hardly any other architecture reveals so convincingly the inherent characteristics of wood, both structurally and aesthetically, as does that of the Japanese (Plates 40–41; Plates 156–157). Yet, the actual discovery of wood's potential certainly was not a manifestation of an inherent aesthetic taste of the Japanese. Extreme poverty of all lower classes and rigid feudalistic control of those citizens who could afford more were the reasons why the common people did not, and could not, follow (even though they really wanted to) the decorative, colorful usage of wood in the buildings of nobility and clergy, and, therefore, had to apply wood in the most economical manner. The tea cult responded to these prevailing circumstances. It created the aestheticism of simplicity and restraint and thus refined an unwanted architectural situation. While providing for the wealthiest of the lower classes an area in which to satisfy material ambitions, it helped the poorest, if not to enjoy their poverty, at least to find some meaning to the pitiful life they were leading.

Three factors, poverty, feudalism, and tea cult, all of them in close affinity to each other, then, provided the situation that produced the Japanese awareness of the intrinsic quality in wood. The growth of this sensitivity was not inherent but environmental and is only a little more than three hundred years old.

Consequently, wood in the Japanese house is used without paint or surface treatment other than that which will stress its inherent nature. Thus, having renounced all additional methods of décor, the inbred consistency of wood in terms of color, gloss, grain, and texture has become the sole medium of expression and therefore plays an important part in the aesthetic effect of the Japanese house.

Moreover, as construction parts, as a rule, are visible both from outside and inside, their scale and proportion are the dominant factors in the appearance of the house. Scale of wood in the Japanese house is interrelated with density of grain, construction, and market size. However, as construction (in terms of technique) and market size (in terms of economy and practicality) are strongly related to each other, as well as to density of texture, the scale of wood in fact is basically determined only by the innate nature of wood.

An identical affinity exists in the relationship of individual wood pieces to each other. As the single parts are each subjected to a common scale, when fitted together their interdependent proportion expresses even more convincingly the common order they embody. Nevertheless, it appears that this order was unconsciously followed rather than thoroughly comprehended and purposely applied, for substance is never displayed in a decorative calculation, nor are textural contrasts of woods combined for an artistic effect. It is not man's intentional order, but the inbred order of wood, as gradually brought forth in the attempt to economize.

Never does man's visual-aesthetic consideration interfere with this order. True, at the end of Japan's Middle Ages certain proportions, based on a former module of aesthetics, the *kiwari-hō* (literally, canon of how to proportion wood), were taken from residences of the warrior class. However, at that time this canon had already largely deteriorated into an economic, practical scale, and only as such did it function in the house of the common man.

The ignoring of visual-aesthetic principles in deciding the scale and proportion of wood manifests conscious neglect of form, and thus leads to concentration on inherent essence. What finally appears to the eye and thereby becomes "form" is just the barest necessity. Thus the word "form" in the Western sense is hardly applicable to the Japanese residence. Whereas architectural form in the West is conceived as something given to a material and therefore remains attributive, in Japan form evolved from the material itself and is essentially its own substance.

In this application wood reveals an order distinct from the ordinary Western conception of aesthetics. Wood in the Japanese house actually has no form, or it might be said that its form is disregard of form. Though this trait is apparent not only in architecture but also in Japanese art in general, it constitutes more a phenomenon than a conception. That is to say, the resulting visual appearance of simplicity, austerity, and honesty is not an intended and calculated one, as Western architecture preconceives aesthetic effect, but has originated as the result of the environmental conditions previously mentioned. Only much later was this form intentionally sought after, stimulated mainly by Zen Buddhism's teaching, which renounces formalism, conventionalism, or ritualism.

Commonly used types of wood are the following:

Hinoki (chamaecyparis obtusa), a kind of Japanese cypress. It is neither too hard nor too soft. Thus, it combines both easy workability and high resistance to decay, features that make it an excellent fabric. A fine grain, a color that soon after use becomes beige-gray, and finally a pleasing odor make it aesthetically very expressive. The cost is high, however, so that it is more frequently used in mansions, palaces, and ecclesiastical architecture than in common dwellings. In the latter it serves mainly for columns and those parts liable to decay.

Asunaro (thujopsis dolobrata), also called *asuhi* and *hiba,* another kind of Japanese cypress. It resembles *hinoki* in quality and appearance, yet susceptibility to splitting makes it inferior.

Akamatsu (pinus densiflora), also called *mematsu* (literally, female pine), red pine. With normal strength it displays high elasticity. Being very resinous and therefore not subject to decay, it is used in its frequently curved form for such irreplaceable parts as roof beams or those liable to rapid decay such as the ground sills.

Kuromatsu (pinus thunbergii), also called *omatsu* (literally, male pine), black pine. Its features resemble those of the red pine, but quality is generally inferior.

Tsuga (tsuga sieboldii), a kind of hemlock spruce. Unlike the pine tree, its trunk is straight and hard. The structure is dense and firm with a fine grain. The new wood has a yellow-brown color, which turns, in time, into a yellow-gray. Resembling in many ways *hinoki,* it has become the chief wood material of the ordinary dwelling house.

Sugi (cryptomeria Japonica), Japanese cedar. It is a fast- and straight-growing tree. Consequently, its percentage of water is high and firmness low. Its texture is soft, and it is very workable. Its color, usually a reddish brown, varies from the darker center to the lighter outside, and its straight or only lightly curved grain makes it decoratively very expressive. Its qualities thus allow an almost universal application both as constructional and ornamental fabric. Young *sugi* is frequently used in its natural round form for the constructional-decorative column of the picture recess or for the sculptural-ornamental column in the tearoom. In this case the only treatment given is to peel off the bark and polish the wavy surface.

Keyaki (abelicea serrata), zelkova. A hard, elastic-durable consistency makes this wood particularly suitable for use as posts and beams. Its texture is lively and contrasty and thus it is highly decorative.

Kiri (paulownia tomentosa), paulownia. It is structurally and aesthetically an excellent building wood, but expensiveness prevents its general use. With a fine grain and a light silver-blueish color, it is extremely decorative in its expression. Resistance to moisture makes it a good material for ground sill. Further, it is often used in cabinet work.

Additional woods used in the Japanese house are:

Momiji (acer palmatus) also called *kaede,* maple.

Kuwa (morus alba), mulberry.

Indian and Indo-Chinese wood such as sandalwood, red sandalwood, ebony, etc., introduced to Japan via China.

But, as the costs of these additional woods are either high or their treatment is difficult, their proportional use is small.

Technical means were primitive during the early stages of residential building and consequently they set limits for the size and weight of building components. Thus, the first use of wood in building was immediately followed by preference for certain lengths and forms that constituted at the time the optimum of practicality and function. Wood was standardized. Being an essential fabric of life, next to food and clothing, wood simultaneously became a trading article, and as such, even more required standard sizes. Feudalistic control of the lower classes in the Middle Ages of Japan and rigid curtailment of house size further contributed to standardization. However, due to lack of technical skill, the standard scales in use *(sumi-gake-sumpō)* and the copies made from them, show strong local deviations. A tendency toward sectionalism on the part of the local rulers, the daimyo, further deepened regional differences. But in general, the market size is based on the standard length of a *ken* (about 1,800 or 2,000 mm. or 6 or 6 1/2 ft.,). In turn, once the market sizes were set, they influenced the work of the builder and helped achieve an extreme refinement on the one hand, but no doubt also strangled technical improvement in many cases.

for contemporary architecture

Interpretation and evaluation of a past architecture presupposes a comprehensive and thorough understanding of that architecture. Therefore, it has been considered necessary to investigate the component materials of the ordinary Japanese dwelling analytically, individually, functionally, and aesthetically, and to give, if not a complete historical background, at least some hints as to how their evolution was interwoven with politics, social structure, and other environmental factors. In doing so, it has become clear that already the mere discussion of each individual material has revealed the factors that determine choice, form, and treatment of fabric in building independent of time and place.

Such disclosure is especially valuable because, in contemporary architecture, extreme and opposing viewpoints characterize the discussion of the role of fabric in building and account largely for the ideological and physical discord in present architecture. One trend in contemporary architectural design is the striving for the "honest use of material." Being originally but a concept of opposition to the formalism of the 19th century, this idea claims that each material is beautiful in itself and should never be covered up, but should be "honestly" displayed, i.e., mere display of the substance of each and every material is held to be the essence of aesthetic effect through fabric.

However, against this trend of indiscriminate and ostentatious "honesty" another theory has already crystallized. It contends that the characteristic form expression of modern material is determined by synthetic consistency, productional method, and structural necessity, and therefore propagates geometric rectangularity of form, evenness of surface, primary colors, unreserved transparency of enclosure, and floating lightness of structure. Yet, such expression is not only unscrupulously imposed upon each constituent fabric and its assemblage, but has also become the principle for the design of plan and façade, or even of décor and furniture, as alleged form expression of the new technical age. Indeed, this latest trend possesses all the characteristics of the eclectic formalism of the 19th century, except that the outward form has changed.

Common to both ideas are two symptoms: their preoccupation with external form and finish treatment, and their academic, dogmatic application. In the one case, individual material itself is the imposing element in the composition, being almost beyond the influence of being designed; in the other case, material is subjected to the alleged expression of the "new technicality" both as single components and as composition. It seems that the individual, as well as society, is in a continuous search for certain styles or recipes, is permanently entangled in the question of an intolerant "either or" rather than of a tolerant "as well as." Certainly, since both conceptions are dogmas based on reaction rather than recognition, they will be followed by others in the not too distant future, as is always the case when styles are concerned with external things and not with the underlying matter.

In this regard, the role of fabric in the Japanese house is very instructive. Here, a unique and convincing expression in all constituent materials is achieved without any dogmatic approach. The Japanese, hardly being concerned with visual-external factors of the art of building, never made form and treatment of individual material a matter of intellectual decision a priori. Low economic capacity and low technical standards were the conditions that generally effected geometric form of material and its unfinished appearance. But it is characteristic of the tolerance of attitude that there are also wooden components in the house (picture recess, *tokonoma;* opaque paper panel, *fusuma;* Buddhist altar, *butsu-dan)* which for architectural accentuation are painted and lacquered, just as the strict rectangular form (though only rarely) is given up when there is reason for its abandonment and none for its strict maintenance.

This does not imply that the exercise of any principle for the use of material in building is altogether deplorable, but it is to be interpreted as a suggestion to establish principles on a more profound level than that which deals with visual unity only. Such a principle could be the simple imperative to use and treat fabric only in full awareness of *all* factors involved: inherent aesthetic quality of fabric itself, its functional role in the building, and its logical form as dependent on material consistency and productional method. The decision then, as to which of the factors in each instance should be pronounced or restrained, or whether there should be individual differentiation at all, would be a matter of artistic composition that would give the creator an enormous potential of varied expression in building, even if only a very limited variety of materials were at his disposal.

Through such a principle, form and treatment of individual fabrics in building would lose its stigma of being a uniform manifestation of a dogma or rule. Through simultaneous use of all possibilities in fabrics and their juxtapositioning or contrapositioning in a conscious composition, an awareness could be raised in the beholder of each conditioning quality of the fabrics: beauty, purpose, and origin.

Investigation of individual fabrics has further disclosed that the material expression of the Japanese house is actually not determined by the distinctiveness or dominance of one or two particular materials as is commonly assumed. True, structurally it is a wooden house, but what distinguishes it from other wooden architectures of the world is not the wood itself but how this material has been used, has been put together, and has been decoratively exploited. It becomes evident that, though each material basically invites certain architectural usage and thereby initiates distinctiveness, there still remains an enormous range where creative instinct can assert itself.

The contemporary age, with its quick and hasty judgments, only too often has limited the full exploitation of fabric. Each fabric soon after its emergence is labeled with certain qualities that appear finite. The architect takes them for granted and the building industry follows, running very soon in deep tracks that obstruct any later alteration, or, because of economic reasons, make alterations impossible altogether. Japanese post-lintel construction has experienced this, as has also the stud-wall construction in America. The fact that a material of such distinct properties as wood can produce two styles so very much different in every aspect, evidently suggests that the traditional usage of material should not be accepted as finite, but that the potential in material should be continuously investigated. There is no end to the exploitation of material, both traditional and modern.

Observation also revealed that the causes for the expressional unity of the Japanese house do not lie in the fewness of its constituent fabrics. Instead, harmony is established through dependence of fabric on encompassing factors, i.e., the choice of fabric relies on natural products, its technique on handicraft, its treatment on stress of inherent characteristics. Though this unity was due to chance rather than intention, it nevertheless refutes a theory in modern design that shortsightedly identifies unity or simplicity of fabric's expression in building with the number of materials used.

Additional evidence is produced also by the negative results of Japanese residential design. The incorporation of glass, mechanical fixtures, modern furniture, etc., shows that any deviations from a universal denomination of fabric will not only disturb this harmony, but will also reduce the convincibility of each individual fabric. The source and production of modern materials is widely divergent, and their variety is abundant. Yet, no limitation of their number in a building can ever achieve a unique expression. This can only be accomplished by conscious selection of materials according to their expressional relationship.

And finally, the Japanese house provides distinct proof that aesthetic quality of fabric is absolute and inherent and is not related to its monetary value. The Western conception is still largely entangled in the fallacy of interpreting quality of building with quality of component fabric and quality of fabric with expensiveness of material. In Japan, the house of the wealthy differs from that of the poor not in the material, its form, or treatment (though more resistant types of wood may be chosen), but in the number of space units and the subsequent wider range of composing spaces.

This Japanese order of fabric is universally practiced throughout the country. It originated physically as a logical response to existing conditions of technical means and natural resources and not in compliance with aesthetic taste a priori. Later, however, its aesthetic meaning was interpreted and, consequently, refinement was focused. The result was a unique material harmony, the study of which is apt to throw light on the important question of the role of fabric in building, past and present.

CHAPTER TWO **measure**

definition

MEASURE IN BUILDING is the order that controls the scale, proportion, and form of the building. It relates the parts to the whole and in turn makes the whole dependent on its parts.

MEASURE IN BUILDING means standard. The standard of man's body was the earliest measure. Incorporation of various standard units of the body into one system by relating them in simple ratios effected the first measure system.

MEASURE IN BUILDING precedes construction. Before man could build, he had to conceive of measuring. Measuring is one of man's first intellectual achievements. It distinguished man's house from the animal's den.

MEASURE IN BUILDING is the essential means by which man brings building into precise relationship with himself. Measure is the element which humanizes man's environment.

MEASURE IN BUILDING thus is manifestation of culture. For standard of culture is determined by the variety and depth of emotional intercommunication of man and man-made environment, i.e., by the degree of human measure in his environment.

MEASURE IN BUILDING also contains measures of aesthetics, fabric, and technique and thus constitutes in itself a compromise between these frequently opposite forces. The character of this compromise reflects the purpose of a building.

MEASURE IN BUILDING manifests the skill, taste, and thought of builders. Ancient cultures possessed an elaborate order of measure that determined building. This order was based primarily on visual aesthetic principles.

MEASURE IN BUILDING, then, is the instrument by which man masters the basic fabric of building. Thus, it is his "measure" to organize the elements of building into an entirety and to create the human environment called architecture.

The question of measure in building is as old as building itself. In fact, the history of architecture is but the history of man's quest for the secret of measure, in proportion, number, scale, and form. Not only architects, but artists, mathematicians, and philosophers as well, have participated throughout the ages in the search for a "measure" that would both physically and spiritually establish the complete harmony between man and the world.

This striving for the appropriate measure is evidenced by the many geometric as well as arithmetic methods that architects of various periods developed in order to determine the proportions of their buildings. Usually simple grids (square, rectangular, triangular, or circular) or more complex geometric patterns were employed as a reference system for the dimensioning of the building. Numbers themselves were thought of as possessing mystical and aesthetic significance. The golden number, the golden section, the divine proportion, all representing the irrational number which is the positive root of the equation $x^2 = x + 1$ and whose value is approximately 1.618, essentially controlled such modular design.

Whereas these traditional efforts were prompted by man's search for visual beauty and not by an immediate necessity for living, the problem of measure in the contemporary industrial society is concerned with the very substance of building. Even though increased mechanization in most industries has initiated mass production of most of the important goods and has thus raised the standard of living, the building industries have yet to emerge from the medieval method of handicraft production. Therefore, assimilation of building to the machine industry is one of the main tasks of contemporary architecture and the first step toward this goal is the establishment of standard measures that are all based upon one single common measure, the module. The module should fulfill the practical demands of both building and living and should control design and production of building whatever be its purpose or size. Coordination of all activities connected with building and of all building components in accordance with the module, i.e., modular coordination, is a necessity in the machine age.

Especially in the face of the largely unchecked and impersonal authority of the machine industry over the production of building elements and the dehumanized environment created by their assemblage, the control of measures in the building industry is one means of re-establishing the emotional accord of man to his creations, without which there is no true culture.

Concern with measures in the contemporary age is also important because of the existence of two major measure ideologies in the industrialized societies: the foot-inch system and the metric system. Since there is no direct relationship between the two, either in their build-up or in the actual size of their units, international cooperation in technique—and partially still in science—is essentially obstructed, which is always the case when means of communication are essentially different.

There is no doubt that only the metric system has an international claim, yet, the foot-inch system not only has definite merits of its own, but, being the measure in common use in the Anglo-American sphere, whose products exert great influence in the world economy, also carries considerable practical importance. Because of the urgent need for measure coordination on an international plane, a comparative study of the consistency, growth, effect, and potential of measure in the Japanese dwelling should have value beyond the scope of completing the analysis of Japanese residential architecture; for it should directly provide material for a more profound insight into the matter of measure, standard, and module of contemporary building in general. Indeed, the Japanese house, more than any other architecture, past and present, provides a unique example of comprehensive and thorough standardization which surpasses the most progressive ideas of contemporary modular coordination.

building measures

Though in Japan the metric system has been in use since 1891, the ordinary residence is still controlled by the traditional measure system. Its basic unit is the Japanese foot called *shaku,* almost identical with the English foot. The structure of measures was taken over from China and in its original subdivision was consistently decimal.

1 *ri* = 150 *jō* = 1500 *shaku*
1 *jō* = 10 *shaku* = 100 *sun*
1 *shaku** = 10 *sun* = 100 *bu*
1 *sun* = 10 *bu* = 100 *rin*
1 *bu* = 10 *rin*

In the latter half of Japan's Middle Ages another length unit, the *ken,* appeared. *Ken* originally designated the interval between two columns of any wooden structure and varied in size. However, it became standardized in residential architecture very early and was used as a measure unit in the cities. After various transformations the *ken* finally emerged as the unique design module, although in two essentially different applications: the *kyō-ma* method and the *inaka-ma* method (see Chapter III). Both have affected the measures in residential architecture up to the present time, but

---

* The *shaku* measurement in use at that time was probably the *kōrai-shaku,* which is 1.17 times the size of present *shaku* measurement (approximately 355 mm. or 14 in.).

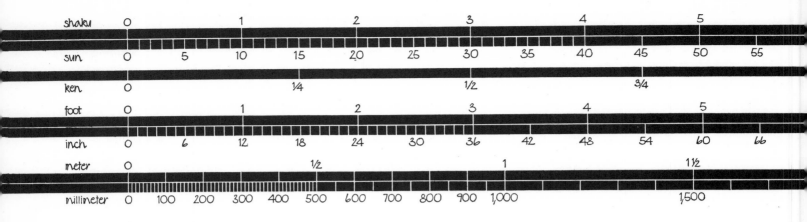

comparison of traditional japanese length units with foot/inch-system and metric system. 1 shaku = 10 sun = 303 mm. = 11.93 in. 1 foot = 12 in. = 1.01 shaku = 10.1 sun = 305

only the *ken* of the *inaka-ma* method of 6 *shaku* (1,818 mm. = 6.0 ft.), which relates to center-to-center distance between columns, eventually replaced the *jō* unit of 10 *shaku* used in handicraft and for common use and was incorporated as the official unit of the Japanese system of measures. The primary reasons for this development were the *ken* measure's intimacy with daily life, its close relationship to human measurements, and its practicality in use.

The Japanese system of length measures is comparatively simple:

1 *ri* = 36 *chō* = 2160 *ken* = 3,927,165.12 mm. = 12,884.40 ft. = 2.44 mi.
1 *chō* = 60 *ken* = 36 *jō* = 109,087.92 mm. = 357.90 ft.
1 *jō* = 10 *shaku* = 3,030.22 mm. = 9.94 ft.
1 *ken (inaka-ma)* = 6 *shaku* = 1,818.13 mm. = 5.97 ft.
1 *shaku* = 10 *sun* = 303.02 mm. = 11.93 in.
1 *sun* = 10 *bu* = 30.30 mm. = 1.19 in.
1 *bu* = 10 *rin* = 3.03 mm. = 0.12 in.

The units *ri, chō,* and *jō* are applied only in field measurements and city planning. Yet, as the construction of cities systematically subjected blocks, streets, and houses to a common order, these large units also affected the single residential site and therefore, though indirectly, the houses too.

While the above length units constitute exact measurements, the Japanese square measures for residences are conspicuous by their vagueness. Two units are used to denote room area, but neither can be expressed in exact measurement.

The one unit, *jō* (not to be mistaken for the length unit *jō,* which has a different Chinese ideograph), is actually the area covered by one mat. The latter, however, being dependent on the standard *ken* unit with its two design methods, varies not only with different room sizes but also with local practice. In spite of this, *jō* denotes room areas corresponding to the number of mats, e.g., 3, 4, 4 1/2, 6, 8, and 10 *jō.* The only correct identification of *jō,* then, is that it is the area covered by one mat, which may be anywhere between 6.5 × 3.25 and 5.8 × 2.9 *shaku* (approximately 2.00–1.54 sq. m. = 21.1–16.8 sq. ft.).

The other unit for architectural square measurement is *tsubo.* Being the area of one square-*ken,* it also has inherited all those differences that characterize the two methods of the *ken* module. Moreover, since the *ken* of 6 *shaku* is a center-to-center column distance, the *tsubo* only gives the amount of the area as marked by the constructional *ken* grid. It does not denote the actual floor area because walls are placed on center of this grid and their thickness subtracts from the floor area. Still *tsubo* is used indis-

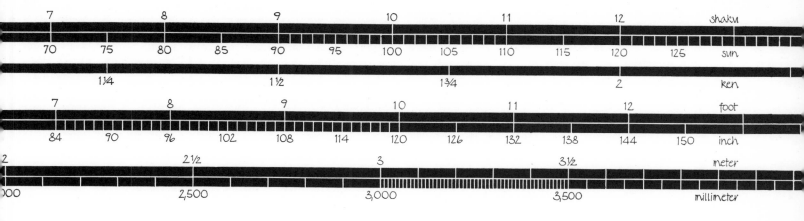

7		8		9		10		11		12		shaku
70	75	80	85	90	95	100	105	110	115	120	125	sun
	1¼			1½			1¾			2		ken
7		8		9		10		11		12		foot
84	90	96	102	108	114	120	126	132	138	144	150	inch
2		2½			3			3½				meter
)00		2,500			3,000			3,500				millimeter

eter = 1,000 mm = 3.30 shaku = 33.0 sun = 3.28 foot = 39.37 in.   scale of reduction 1:10

FIGURE 3: Comparative scales for *shaku*, foot-inch, and metric systems.

criminately for both interior and exterior areas of residential sites, taking into account neither the different sizes and methods of the application of the *ken* nor the discrepancy between constructional distance and open width. The actual size of 1 *tsubo*, thus, may vary from 6.50 × 6.50 to 6.00 × 6.00 *shaku* (3.9–3.3 sq. m. = 42.3–36.0 sq. ft.).

These, then, are the measure units which have exerted an influence upon, and also have emerged from, Japanese living and building. Among them certainly *shaku* and *ken* are the most important and therefore are given closer examination in the succeeding pages.

early measures and shaku

The outset of humanity can well be identified with man's intellectual achievement of measuring. For any creative human activity is in fact but the imposing of a human scale upon the environment—upon stone to become a tool or weapon, upon water to become electricity. Thus, building as much as any intellectual creation presupposes awareness of measure.

Measure (in the original meaning denoting dimension) and its employment, measurement, are in essence but comparison. To measure is to compare, and the resulting measurement is the difference of that comparison. The first standard of comparison was man himself. Since man could not count—certainly not beyond two or three—a variety of human units was needed. Thus, the finger, hand, arm, span, foot, step, were the first standards of measurement throughout the world.

Early Japanese measurements do not differ essentially from those of China and the rest of the world. There is reason to believe that some were taken over from China and others were replaced by their Chinese equivalents.

arm span	*hiro*	approx.	6 ft. = 1,650 mm.
double step-pace	*po*	„	6 ft. = 1,650 mm.
finger span	*ata*	„	2/3 ft. = 183 mm.
palm	*tsuka*	„	1/3 ft. = 92 mm.
foot*	*shaku*	„	1 ft. = 275 mm.

Because there was not yet any relation between counting and measuring in early times, a ratio between the different units did not exist. Consequently building measure in the primitive ages was concerned with subdivision of a larger unit rather than

* It is assumed here that the early foot measure was smaller than in later history—about 275 mm. or 11 in.

combining smaller ones, especially because divisions into halves and the halves again into halves, even division into thirds, could easily be accomplished with fair control of accuracy. Thus, the first architectural order, being based on divisions of 1/2 (1/4, 1/8 etc.) combined with 1/2, was in structure a duodecimal system. Conceivably it was already well in use before man possessed any consciousness of numbers.*

Independently from this, man gradually learned to count. Being endowed by nature with ten fingers, he counted in groups of ten and the decimal system of counting was established. But counting was not at first applied to measuring. The different units, as derived from the human figure, had no constant relationship to each other and were not yet absolute measurements. Rather, they were adopted for the duration of the task and were then subdivided. The inconvenience of using the body for each measurement later prompted the invention of a measuring stick. Thus the word "measure" received its second meaning of an instrument, and it was only thereafter that counting was used in building.

As a result ratios between the various units were discovered, which because of their derivation from the human body were predominantly relations of three to one (examples: 1 arm span = 6 feet; 1 step = 3 feet; 1 foot = 3 palms). Interrelated then with the craftsman's technical subdivisions into 1/2, 1/4, 1/8, 1/16, a measuring system of twelve units, essentially different from the counting system of ten units, was produced.

These, then, are the deeper roots of the controversy that exists about the metric and the foot-inch system—the inherent contrasts of measurement and computation. The discrepancy between the two systems is especially disadvantageous in technique and consequently also in architecture, both of which increasingly have to work on an international level. Though science in the Anglo-American countries has largely adopted the metric system as international language, it still is handicapped because of the overlapping of technique and science and the continuance of traditional measures in certain branches. The rapid progress of industrialization in the world will reinforce the gap between the two systems and will increase the obstructions to international collaboration.

This inability of the industrial-scientific world of the present to establish an integrated measure system is merely a continuation of an old "tradition" of civilization. For among all of man's efforts to control his environment and to organize his life, none have been so unsuccessful as his continuous attempts to bring order to his system of measures. As in the case of the "foot" in the Western world, the story of the *shaku* is a record of error, confusion, subversion, and revision—a testimonial to the noble aspirations and petty failures of man.

It is not certain when the *shaku* was first used in Japan but it is likely that it was imported from China, probably in the 1st century at the time of the earliest recorded cultural exchange with the continent. The oldest known measures in Japan are:

shu-shaku = 1.64 *shaku* (present measurement)**

shinzen-shaku = 1.80 *shaku*   ,,   ,,

kōrai-shaku = 1.1735 *shaku*   ,,   ,,

Probably these were only a part of the many scales in use. Having been brought over from various parts of China and Korea at different times, they were used simultaneously. As yet there was no central government as in China and consequently no single power that could enforce a common measure. However, after the first unification of the country in the 6th century according to Chinese model, an attempt was made to bring order into the confusion of existing measures. This is documented in the first Japanese law script of the 8th century, the *Taihō-ritsuryō*. As in China, two different *shaku,* in ratio 5:6, are mentioned, a so-called big *shaku* and a small *shaku,* the latter actually being the big *shaku* of the T'ang dynasty in China.

1 *dai-shaku* (big *shaku*) = 1.2 *shō-shaku*

* These theories are based on the findings of John Perry (see Bibliography).
** 1 *shaku* in present measurement is 303 mm. or 11.93 in.

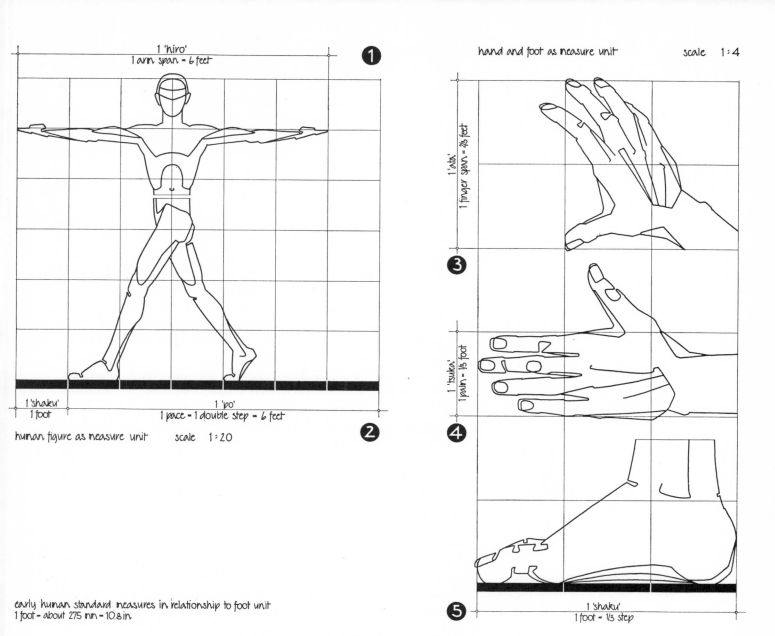

1 'hiro'
1 arm span = 6 feet

①

1 finger span = 2/3 feet
1 'ata'

③

1 palm = 1/3 foot
1 'tsuka'

1 'shaku'
1 foot

1 'po'
1 pace = 1 double step = 6 feet

②

human figure as measure unit   scale   1:20

④

early human standard measures in relationship to foot unit
1 foot = about 275 mm = 10.8 in.

⑤

1 'shaku'
1 foot = 1/3 step

FIGURE 4: The human figure as standard for measure units.

1 *shō-shaku* (small *shaku)* = 1 *tō-no-dai-shaku* (big *shaku* of the T'ang dynasty)
= 0.978 *shaku* (present measurement)

Accordingly, the absolute size of the big *shaku* was:

1 *dai-shaku* = 0.978 × 1.2 = 1.1736 *shaku* (present measurement)

This measurement is exactly the *kōrai-shaku,* suggesting that the latter was in use as big *shaku.* Other measures mentioned are:

1 *jō* = 2 *po* (step) = 10 *dai-shaku* (big *shaku)*

1 *po* = 5 *dai-shaku* = 6 *shō-shaku*

Here already a 6-foot unit is mentioned within a decimal measure system, but there is no archeological evidence linking the *po* unit in any way with the *ken* unit that many centuries later was to control measure and design in the Japanese house.

In the same 8th century the *shō-shaku* (small *shaku)* of the *Taihō-ritsuryō* system became the *dai-shaku* (big *shaku)* of a new system called *wadō* after the name of the era at that time. As the length of the new *dai-shaku* was 0.978 *shaku* (present measurement), the new *shō-shaku* became 0.815 *shaku* because of the 5:6 ratio between the two.

It is noteworthy that not only absolute dimensions of foot measurement were changed, but that this change was often followed by a new relationship of the smaller unit to the larger.

Taihō-ritsuryō system = 1 *ri* = 150 *jō* = 300 *po*

Wadō system = 1 *ri* = 180 *jō* = 300 *po* (dimension of *jō* changed)

Present system = 1 *ri* = 1,296 *jō* = 2160 *ken* (dimension of *ri* changed)

From the 8th century on, then, the former *dai-shaku* of *Taihō-ritsuryō,* i.e., the *kōrai-shaku,* functioned only as a unit of measure for clothing while undergoing several changes in name and size.

kōrai-shaku 1.173 *shaku* (present measurement)

gōfuku-shaku 1.2 *shaku* (present measurement)

kujira-shaku 1.25 *shaku* (present measurement)

The *dai-shaku* of the *wadō* system, i.e., the *dai-shaku* from the Chinese T'ang dynasty, is the predecessor of the *kane-shaku,* the present official Japanese foot measurement. Its lineage, though, was not at all steady. With every new ruler, new measures were issued, but the power of the ruling men was not strong enough to completely extinguish the previous measures. Therefore, the number of existing *shaku* increased. Further, as professions were hereditary, the convenient measures for each group were transmitted from generation to generation, as they also were in Europe, and powerful monasteries possessed and used their own ancient measures.

Even the establishment of a particular department for measure control under the rule of the ruthless Tokugawa family (1600–1867) proved unsuccessful against the proud landlords and powerful monasteries. In fact, it was not before the 8th year of Emperor Meiji (1890), in the course of the great Japanese reformation, that the whole measure system was re-examined and coordinated. At that time the former *setchū-shaku* became the standard length and was called *kane-shaku.* All other *shaku,* with the exception of the *kujira-shaku,* were declared invalid and for the first time were successfully barred from any further use.

ken measure and module

The term "module" stems from the Latin "modulus" (little measure) and has been used in building ever since the time of Vitruvius (1st century B.C.). It denotes a basic length unit in building from which all other dimensions of measurements are derived. In the classical Greco-Roman temple the module was the diameter of the column and in the Chinese temple it was the width of the rafter. In Classic architecture the module was not an absolute measurement but varied according to the size of each building. It was meant to control aesthetic-visual proportions and was conspicuous by its independence from any other material or human-utilitarian measurement.

Industrialization of contemporary building has again prompted the search for a single measurement that would at the same time be a convenient unit for architectual design and a practical unit for industrial production. Because of its analogy with the Classical "order," this measurement is called "module"; the comprehensive coordination of all building activities and building components according to this unit is called modular coordination. It differs from the past module in that it is not an aesthetical but a practical-functional measure and in that it is no longer relative to the size of each building but is an absolute measurement.

This modern meaning of module, however, has an outstanding precedence in Japan, where for the last two to three hundred years the ordinary houses of the entire nation have been built on the basis of a modular order which is unique in the history of world architecture. Indeed, the Japanese *ken* module is an extraordinary phenomenon in architecture without equivalent elsewhere; and, though its complicated past is anything but clear, its uniqueness among all architectural measures, modules, and standards, past and present, cannot be contested.

The history of the Japanese residence is the history of the *ken.* When the *ken* was consciously applied for the first time, Japanese architecture struck one of its most distinct features, order. What contemporary architecture hitherto has striven for so unsuccessfully emerged in Japan logically: a unit universally applied in living as in building, a standard distance for construction and economy, a module for aesthetic order, a six-fractioned measurement in decimal system, a length related to human proportions, even a link between city and domestic planning. Even though other forces may have contributed to its evolution, the *ken* is mainly the carpenter's achievement. No other feature in the Japanese house is likely to better demonstrate his mastership of the total range of his profession.

The Chinese ideograph *ken* means "distance" or "interval," and major column distance was the original meaning of the *ken* as used in house construction. Remains of the earliest dwellings confirm that this distance was fairly well fixed even before a regular system of measures existed. But it was only after organization of the feudalistic society, patterned after the Chinese, that the rise of cities and the growth of artisan professions effected more systematic residential building in the city. There is no doubt that this early standardization was based on economic-constructional considerations rather than on man's exact spatial requirements. Definitely, no visual-aesthetical considerations were involved. Logically, the typical column distance was the decisive measurement and it is, therefore, probable that the *ken* measurement came into being as an independent dimension of residential construction and not as the multiple of an existing smaller length unit.

Accordingly, this *ken* must have been applied predominantly in the cities, a theory that is supported by the fact that early records always refer to the *"kyō-ma ken,"* which literally means "column distance in metropolis measurement." Apparently this denotation of the *ken* was made to distinguish it from *ken* as employed outside the towns, where residential building was not yet a matter of a particular and organized craft and also where residential design was not limited by a rigid street and block pattern. Thus, the column distance *ken* that previously had varied between 7 1/2 and 6 ft. was established at 6 1/2 ft.; the changeable constructional distance *ken* became exact measurement.

Doubtless, in the design of buildings, the increasing influence of the carpenter himself played a decisive part in the evolution of the *ken*. In pace with the social transformations that took place at the end of the Middle Ages in Japan, the carpenter also began to design temples and aristocratic mansions, a privilege that previously had been limited to the priest and nobleman. Conceivably, stimulated by ancient proportional rules of Buddhist architecture as inherited from China, the carpenter also developed a canon of aesthetics for the various buildings of the influential warrior class for whom he had to work. The essential and, as it proved, decisive change in this order was that all measurements were brought into direct ratio to one unit, the *ken* of the cities, the *ken* in *kyō-ma* measurement of 6.5 *shaku* (1,970 mm. = 6.5 ft.); the constructional measurement *ken* became aesthetic module.

In the meantime a different *ken* unit emerged outside the cities and towns, the *ken* in *inaka-ma* measurement (column distance in countryside measurement).

  1 *ken* in *kyō-ma* measurement (original) = 6.5 *shaku* (1,970 mm. = 6.5 ft.)
  1 *ken* in *inaka-ma* measurement = 6.0 *shaku* (1,818 mm. = 6.0 ft.)

Many theories have been set forth about the origin of the *ken* of 6 *shaku* and how the difference in measurement between *kyō-ma* and *inaka-ma* came about. All of them lack evidence, but there is much probability in the theory that in areas outside the influence of the organized towns, an independent system of design evolved which was different from the urban pattern. For building in rural areas was not tied to city planning nor subjected to aesthetic-conventional rules of guilds, and therefore could develop strictly along economical-practical lines. Certainly an even unit of 6 *shaku* is a more practical standard length for design and constructional layout with divisions into halves and quarters than the odd *ken* of *kyō-ma* measurement of 6.5 *shaku*.

Because of such advantages, the employment of *ken* in *inaka-ma* measurement also gradually spread into the cities. A governmental regulation of March and August 1657 concerning reconstruction and building in Edo (Tokyo) mentions both *ken*

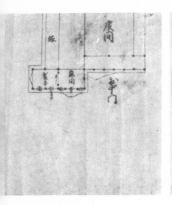 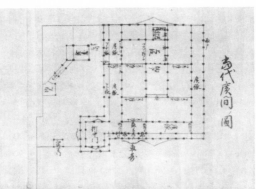 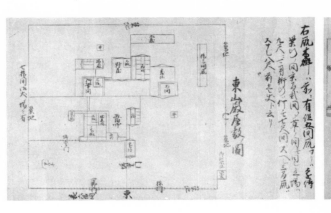

measurements; yet, later on, the *ken* of 6 *shaku* became dominant in the entire northern part of Japan. Because of its practical advantages rather than its functional appropriateness as length, the 6-foot *ken* was incorporated into the existing measure system; the architectural measurement *ken* became official unit of length.

The architectural advantage gained was extraordinary. The consistent sequence of decimal subdivisions was interrupted at a decisive point, thereby permitting an important multi-divisibility into 2, 3, and 4 (room width is usually 2 *ken* or 12 *shaku*) without sacrificing the merits of the decimal system. Moreover, the intimate relationship between living and building effected complete adoption of this architectural measurement in everyday living, replacing the former *jō* of 10 *shaku*.

Nevertheless, the use of the *ken* in *kyō-ma* measurement continued regardless of its odd subdivision. The former imperial capital, Kyoto, as well as the major part of Japan, still uses *ken* in *kyō-ma* measurement. It is used even in Hokkaidō, the most northern island, which was settled in more recent times. The reason for this preference is the greater absolute length of the *ken* in *kyō-ma;* for the *ken* standard of 6 feet has the disadvantage that its half, the 3-feet fraction, is slightly too small for minimum spaces such as corridor, veranda, toilet, and bath. In the *inaka-ma* system, therefore, the 1/2-*ken* module is frequently not applied for the small rooms, in favor of either 3.5 *shaku* or even 4 *shaku*.

The differences in the two *ken* measurements had further consequences. After both constructional standard distances had established themselves as exact measurements. usage of the rigid floor mat gradually became common among the lower classes. Since the mat was prefabricated and often was taken along with change of domicile. it became necessary to standardize floor area instead of structural interval. Thus in the *kyō-ma* method of design, the system of measuring column distance *ken* from center to center was upset and spacing of columns was determined by the standard mat size, measurements of which originally had been subjected to the regular center-to-center distance of the columns.

Whereas *ken* in *inaka-ma* maintained its congruity with constructional distances, from this time on, the measurement of *ken* in *kyō-ma* was no longer constant, but was variable depending on the interior room width which was determined by the mat units. As will be explained later, due to this transformation, the two measures of *ken* came to denote particular systems of plan technique; the length unit *ken* became a method of design.

With this the *ken* terminated a rather complicated development: transmutation and differentiation from varying column distance to two different but exact measurements—to aesthetic module in the one case and to official length unit in the other; dissolution of the original meaning of the *ken* as actual column distance; and, finally, emergence of two essentially different design methods, one of which even nullified the role of the *ken* as absolute measurement. These transformations, then, are the source

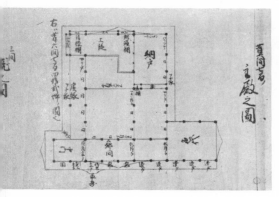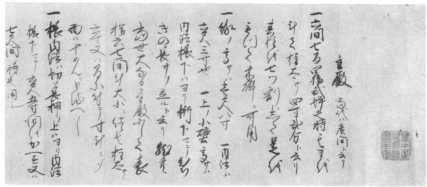

FIGURE 5 (right to left): The *Shōmei* scroll, 1608, by Masanobu Heinouchi. The part depicted shows plans of standard structures and layout of the Higashiyama Palace.

of the many misinterpretations of the architectural meaning of *ken*. At different times *ken* meant different things, just as it does at present in different areas of Japan.

order of kiwari

The Buddhist architecture of China was introduced in the 7th and 8th centuries in the form of scripts brought back by returning Japanese scholars—priests, merchants, artists, and craftsmen—who had studied and traveled on the continent. These scripts contained exact procedural regulations of building in terms of measure, construction, orientation, and ceremony to be observed when laying out and erecting the various building types of the temple compound. In the course of centuries, these imported canons were basically altered, were combined with existing techniques, and were further developed. They finally reached a stage of perfection as modular order for residential building that is a definite challenge to any modular system of contemporary architecture. The order encompasses the wooden architecture of the entire nation; it is unique because of the following reasons:

1. It acknowledges economy and practicality as important factors,
2. It subjects form to structural and utilitarian requirements,
3. It functions by means of a constant module that is not relative to size of building,
4. It has evolved as independent module for residential architecture in particular, and
5. It is applied universally over and above differences of wealth or social standing.

It is generally assumed that the modular order in the Japanese residence originated in the early Momoyama period, i.e., at the end of the 16th century. This belief is based on the fact that the word *kiwari* (literally, proportion of wood allotment) appeared for the first time in a carpenter's manual in the form of five paper scrolls, called *Shōmei* and written in 1608, and that the type of building described, the *shuden-zukuri* architecture, was dominant at that time. It is as fallacious, however, to identify the origin of this architectural order with the first appearance of the word *kiwari* in a certain script as it is to assume that the Japanese module *kiwari* was without precedence. In fact, before the *Shōmei* was written many *shahon* (copy scripts) existed that contained exact rules for measure and procedure in the construction of the various building types in the Buddhist temple compound, including the mansions of the priests. One of those scrolls called *Banshō-shiki-shaku* (literally, master builder's ceremony and measure) explains the "holy art" of building as follows:

1. Origin: Mystic bestowal of the *Banshō-shiki-shaku* by Shōtoku, Prince Regent (570–621?).
2. Situation: Orientation of building and superstitious relation to sun, moon, wind, and water.
3. Ceremony: Prayers, services, and festivals at the various stages of building.
4. Process: Measure, proportion, construction, and erection of building.

The latter rules for the actual structure are given separately for temple, pagoda, and a so-called *yashiki* (literally, a spread of rooms). Assumably the *yashiki* is a residential type that served as dwelling for the priests. Though there is no clue as to the probable shape of the building, the measures and proportions given resemble very closely those of a building which the *Shōmei* script refers to as "the *kiwari* of former days." This resemblance certainly was not accidental and it can be concluded that there is a very close, if not essential, link between the Buddhist building rules adopted from China and the later Japanese modular order.

Banshō-shiki-shaku: The column distance *ken* measured center to center is 7 *shaku*, and the whole building seems to have an extent of 6 × 7 *ken* because the width of column is moduled with 6 × 7 = 42 *bu* (128 mm. = 5 in.). This is the same method by which the so-called "former *kiwari*" of the *Shōmei* script computes the dimension of column: namely, length times depth of building in *ken* equals column dimension in *bu*. Accord exists not only in extent of building, which is 6 × 7 *ken* or 42 *tsubo*, but also in the subdivision of the column face into 7 parts, according to which the other wood sections are usually moduled. But, whatever dimensions *Banshō-shiki-shaku* mentions for individual components, they do not relate to this column subdivision as they do in *kiwari* of *Shōmei*. Instead, horizontal brace, *nuki;* rafter, *taruki;* hanging door, *shitomiyose;* papered sliding door, *shōji;* wooden sliding door, *yarido;* column brackets, *hijiki;* etc., not mentioned in the old *kiwari* of *Shōmei*, have measurements unrelated to each other.

However, these absolute measurements seem to have originally stemmed from a common system of numbers or proportions because the text states that temples are to be measured in 9-part counting, pagodas in 8-part, and mansions in 6-part counting. This is also confirmed by the theoretical subdivision of the column face into 7 parts. But whether and how, then, this order was applied is not clear, making the whole text appear to be a mere collection of measurements of a former canon.

Former *kiwari* (according to the *Shōmei* script): Though this rule is essentially the same as the *Banshō-shiki-shaku* of the Buddhist priest's residence, *yashiki*, it nevertheless is accepted as first evidence of, and proof for, the independent rise of Japan's residential standardization. The rule describes the prototype for the warrior's residence, the *shuden* style house, which indeed marks the beginning of the modular order in Japanese residential architecture. The column distance *ken* has changed to 6.5 *shaku*. No ratios, but only absolute measurements are given. They are, however, comparatively few and are confined to veranda height above ground level, door opening, and the upper small wall, *kokabe*.

Kiwari (according to *Shōmei* script): In this set of rules, which the author of the 1608 script calls the "present-day *kiwari*," an important deviation from the previous rules is evident, which indicates the beginning of a basic transmutation of what most likely was an adopted system, a Japanization, so to speak, as so often has been the case in Japan's evolution. In this new system all measures are brought into direct ratio to the column distance of 6.5 *shaku*. Owing to this ratio, aesthetic proportions determined by timber length are significantly linked with constructional-economical standard distance, whereas wood sections of individual members are moduled after the major column section which, however, is derived from the column distance in a ratio of 1:10. Though the column distance *ken* in city measurement (*kyō-ma*) already was an exact length of 6.5 *shaku* and was the same as the column distance in the *Shōmei* script, there is no indication that the latter was also an absolute measurement. Rather, it can be assumed that all wood members changed in length and section according to every change of column interval.

Buke-hinagata (literally, model for samurai house): From about 1670 many books of *hinagata* (model miniature) were woodblock-printed and circulated among the carpenters (Plates 124 & 127). One of these scripts was the *Buke-hinagata*, which describes a later form of *kiwari* for a building called *hiro-ma* (wide hall). The content shows that the carpenter had lapsed back into a set pattern of formalistic technique with absolute measurements as in the "former-*kiwari*" of the *Shōmei* script. Also, the

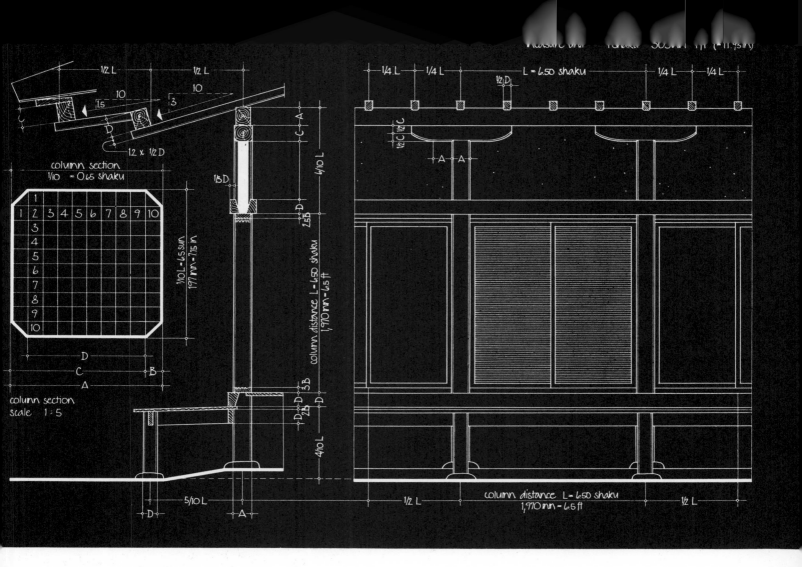

FIGURE 6: The order of *kiwari* according to the *Shōmei* scroll.

module for the individual wood sections is again derived from subdividing the column face into four parts. But at this time, in the wake of the commercialization of building components, column distance as well as column section was probably a constant measurement and was no longer relative to the size of building.

Kōjō-in temple (in Otsu at Lake Biwa): The practical performance of *kiwari* is exemplified in various buildings of the so-called *shuden-zukuri* architecture of that time. Among them the *kyaku-den* (guest hall) of the Kōjō-in temple built in 1601 very closely resembles the *shuden* of the "former *kiwari*" and the *hiro-ma* of the *Buke-hinagata* (Plates 123–125). There are differences of ratio, but it is evident that a *kiwari* module was consistently used, though with many individual deviations.

Present *kiwari*: With the increasing wealth and influence of the merchants and artisans, certain features of the warrior's dwelling were incorporated into that of the citizen, as were also the proportional rules of *kiwari*. However, in the course of adaptation, these rules finally deviated so decisively from the previous module of the warrior residence that they justly can be considered as a new *kiwari* for the residences of the commoners. The proportions of building components were no longer determined by the actual column spacing, but by an exact measurement, the *ken*. The columns then could be spaced 1/2, 1, 1 1/2, 2, *ken,* etc. without influencing other measurements.

Comparison of various 'kiwari' modules   front elevation   scale 1:40
                                          column section   scale 1:5

column section = 7 × 6 = 42 bu = 0.42 shaku

measure unit: 1 shaku = 305mm = 1ft (-1.19 in)

column section A = 1/10 L
                = 0.65 shaku = 197mm = 0.75 in

1/10 L = 0.65 sun = 197mm = 7.75 in

A — column in 'shomei' script (late form)

A — column in 'shomei' script (earlier form)

A — column in 'bansho shiki shaku' script

0.42 shaku   42 sun   127mm = 50 in

L = 650 shaku

L = 700 shaku

L = 650 shaku

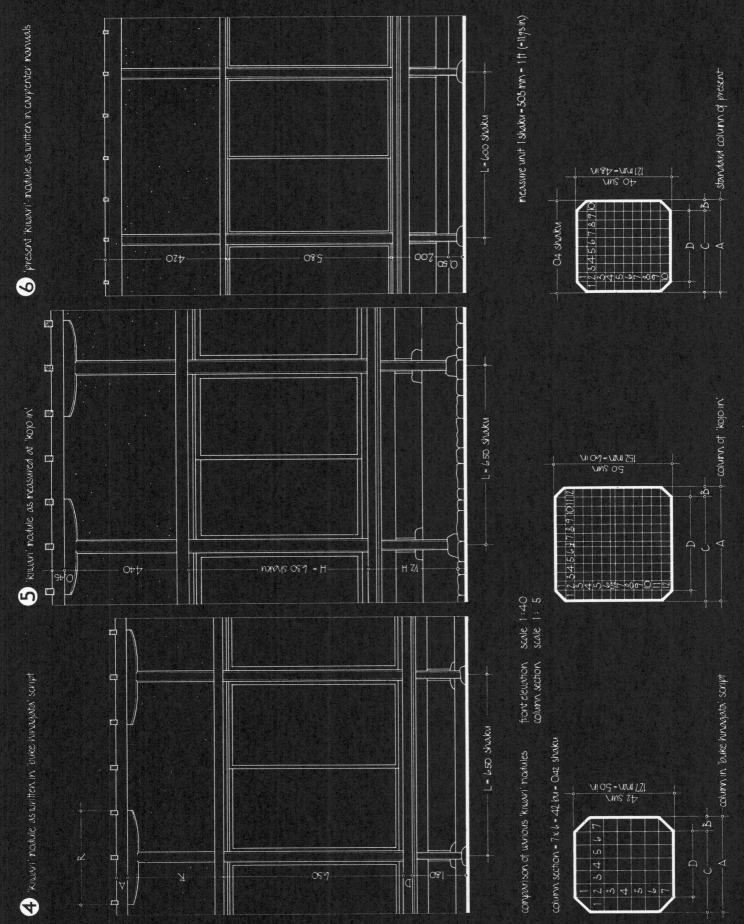

④ 'kiwari' module as written in 'buke hinagata' script

⑤ 'kiwari' module as measured at 'kojo in'

⑥ present 'kiwari' module as written in carpenter manuals

comparison of various 'kiwari' modules   front elevation   scale 1:40
                                          column section   scale 1:5

column section = 7 x 6 = 42 bu = 0.42 shaku

measure unit 1 shaku = 305 mm = 1 ft (=11.95 in)

column in 'buke hinagata' script

column of 'kojo in'

standard column of present

FIGURE 7 (continued): A comparison of various *kiwari* orders.

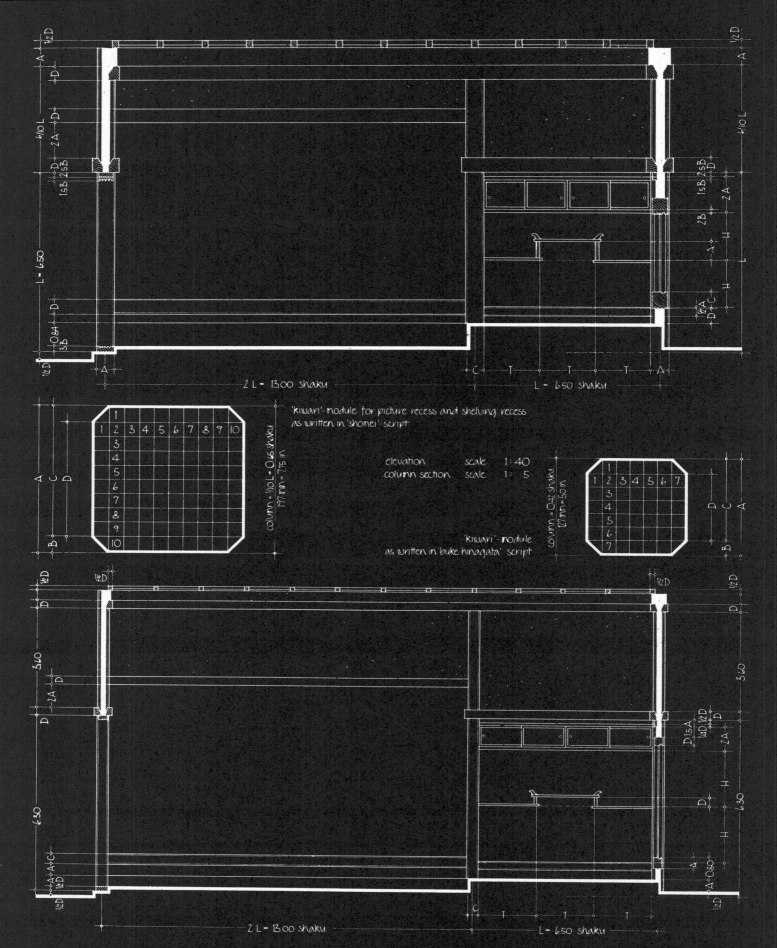

'kiwari'-module for picture recess and shelving recess
as written in 'shomei' script

| elevation | scale | 1:40 |
| column section | scale | 1:5 |

'kiwari'-module
as written in 'buke hinagata' script

FIGURE 8: A comparison of *kiwari* orders for the picture recess, *tokonoma*.

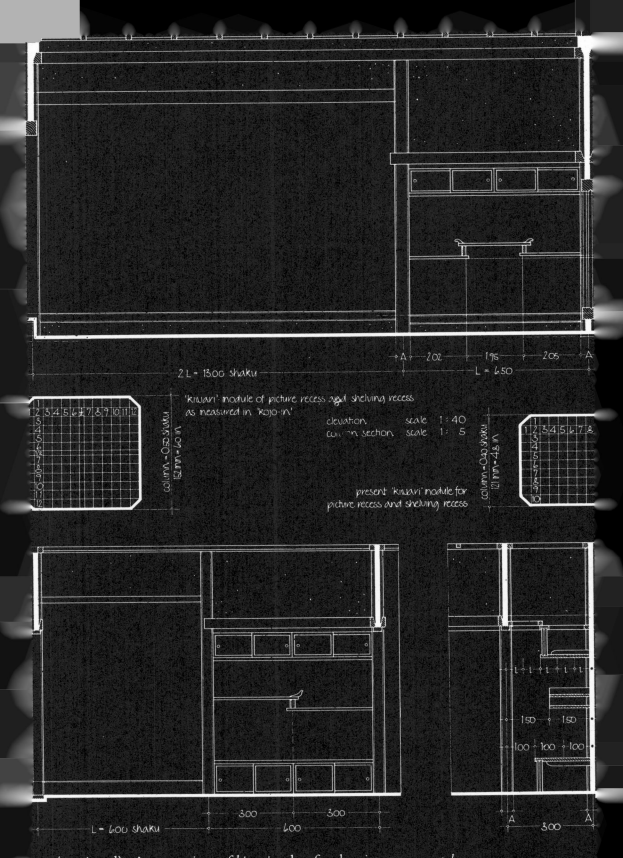

'kiwari' module of picture recess and shelving recess
as measured in 'kojo-in'

elevation   scale   1: 40
column section   scale   1: 5

present 'kiwari' module for
picture recess and shelving recess

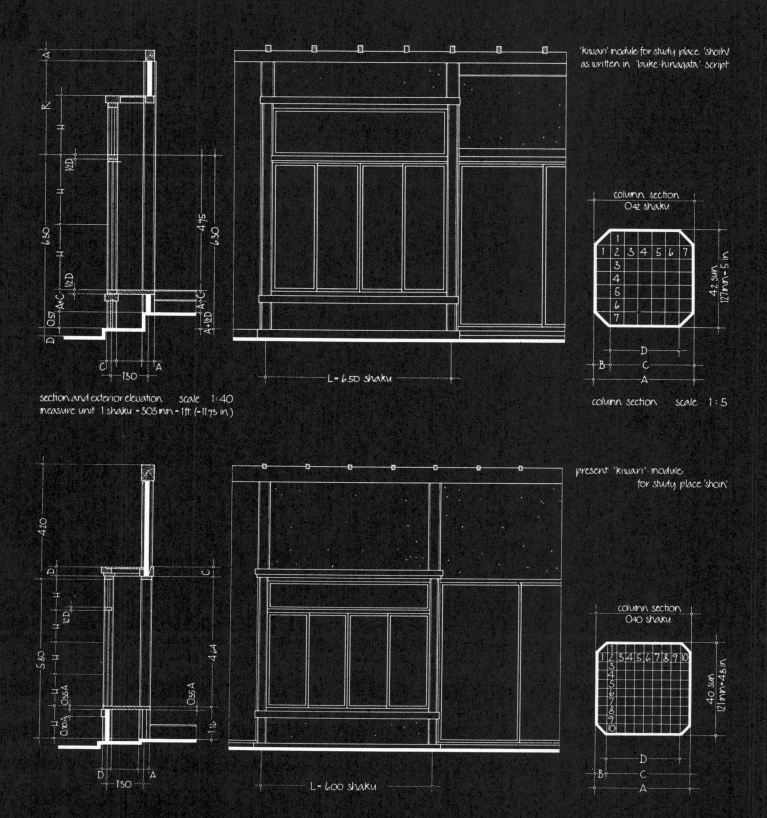

'kiwari' module for study place 'shoin'
as written in 'buke-hinagata' script

column section
0.42 shaku

column section   scale 1 : 5

section and exterior elevation   scale 1 : 40
measure unit 1 shaku = 303 mm = 1 ft (= 11.93 in.)

present 'kiwari' module
for study place 'shoin'

column section
0.40 shaku

FIGURE 9: A comparison of *kiwari* orders for the study place, *shoin*.

Since column section is also standardized at 4 *sun* (121 mm. = 4.8 in.), the *kiwari* of the ordinary dwelling is determined by two modular keynotes: the measure unit *ken* for wood lengths and construction; the thickness of the standard column (which also is an absolute measurement) for dimensions of all wood sections. Thus *kiwari* of the ordinary dwellings is a system of related measurements that are dependent on material and construction and through *ken* are related to human requirements. As such, it is basically different from the previous *kiwari* systems, and for the same reason is essentially identical to the character of module used in the industrial society.

Evidence of *kiwari* in scripts and buildings, then, shows that this order had its roots in the Buddhist architecture imported from China. Originally it was a modular system for aesthetic proportions that changed relative to size of building. However, the frequent use of certain sizes in this order brought about several standard measures. The repeated phrase "there should not be any personal willfulness at all" characterizes the inalterable and impersonal nature of the measurements given. It is in this meaning that the measures appear in both the old priest's mansion, *yashiki,* and the early form of the warrior's residence, *shuden.* Early in the 17th century, however, the *kiwari* underwent an essential transformation. No longer were the major proportions determined by a comparatively small material element (the column section). Instead, all measurements were made dependent on the most important, though still variable, structural interval—the center-to-center distance between columns. Characteristically, this distance is called "the greatest common measure," thereby manifesting a conception that does not basically differ from that of contemporary modular standardization.

Yet, it was only after the development of *kiwari* for the ordinary dwellings that Japanese modular coordination achieved historic significance. Now a constant measurement, the *ken* (simultaneously the standard for material, construction, and living) directly and indirectly controlled length and section of all wood members. As a result, the actual column spacing has no influence on the modular order; extent of building, shape of plan, and size of room (all of course within the order of the *ken* grid) do not modulate any wood member. Thus a great freedom for design was achieved and the way was free for standard market sizes of timber and prefabrication of building components.

However, there also is reason to suppose that standardization of timber was not only a result of, but also to no small degree an incentive for, this physical order in building. For with the commercialization of many essential goods in the 17th century, a wholesale-retail system came into being that also increasingly handled building components. Thus, on the timber market *kiba* in Kyoto 4-*sun* (121 mm. = 4.8 in.) standard timber called *kyō-kaku* (wood section of the metropolis) was sold in definite lengths. It is conceivable that this economical-practical cut of wood, together with other sections resulting from it, prompted a modular system very similar to contemporary ideas.

kyō-kaku	(section of metropolis)	4 × 4 *sun*	for column *(hashira)*
futatsu-wari	(cut into two)	4 × 2 *sun*	for lower sliding track *(shikii)*
yotsu-wari	(cut into four)	2 × 2 *sun*	for rafter *(taruki)*
mutsu-wari	(cut into six)	2 × 1.3 *sun*	for upper sliding track *(kamoi)*
jūni-wari	(cut into twelve)	2 × 0.66 *sun*	for ceiling, doors, and other
		1 × 1.3 *sun*	components of house interior

It is apparent that the ratio to the standard column is no longer a matter of aesthetic proportion but relates to the most economical wood section. In the course of further differentiation, more finely graded wood sections were derived from the standard column, and possibly some dimensions were taken directly from the *kiwari* of the warrior mansions, but as to basic build-up, the *kiwari* of the ordinary houses had very little in common with the previous modules of *kiwari.* That is to say, *kiwari* became an indigenous Japanese module.

Many local differences have emerged; they consist of slight changes in certain measurements, but they are not basic. A major local difference developed only in the method of using the *ken* in design, the *kyō-ma* method and the *inaka-ma* method. Yet, again, this difference is not one of modular system but of design technique, and, therefore, is examined in the respective chapter.

This system, then, undoubtedly accounts for the high refinement of the domestic architecture. On the other hand, as it was tightly knit into the social organism, the productional methods, and the commercial practice, it was difficult to change and thus essentially hindered architectural progress or improvement. It did not act as stimulus for the new but functioned to preserve the old, its merits and defects alike.

traditional standards

Since the unforeseen onset of the machine revolutionized the basis of architectural creation, the standardization of building elements on a modular basis has become a matter of increasing importance in contemporary architecture. Agreement exists that standardization, i.e., the finding and determining of large and small units of excellence in contemporary architecture, is inevitable not only because of the need for economic use and control of the mass-productional machine, but also because it constitutes a creative medium in architectural expression. However, opposing viewpoints and vague conceptions exist about the possible consequences of standardization upon architectural creation, as well as upon life in general, because the West, throughout its history, has not produced an architecture with a comprehensive physical standardization that would allow a study of the effects of standardization.

On the other hand, since the early Middle Ages the East (India, China, and Japan) possessed an elaborate standardization that controlled residential architecture. Only in Japan has this standardization survived to the present. It penetrates the universal range of architectural work to a degree paralleled as yet by no other modular system of residential building in the contemporary West. In fact, everything that is a component of, or contributive to, the erection of a Japanese house is standardized: fabric, measure, design, and construction; even the garden. The integral unit is standardized as is the total organism. That is to say, they all have been developed to a level of excellence that from the viewpoint of the traditional Japanese life does not ask for further improvement. This comprehensive standardization, then, not only holds the value of instructive comparison with contemporary architecture, but also should remove many misconceptions and thereby promote a better understanding of the potential of standardization and prefabrication in building. For in its history of more than three hundred years, Japanese modular coordination has produced certain results that have immediate relationship to modern standardization:

1. Since architectural creation is no longer concerned with individual room, material, construction, detail, façade, not even with the dominating silhouette of the roof, design is concentrated on that which is solely decisive for architecture in general: organization of space by means of composing rooms of fixed sizes, choosing among a limited number of materials and techniques, and interrelating outdoors and indoors. Free from the entanglement of constantly developing anew individual units of space, form, or construction, and given cohesiveness by the discipline of the *ken* grid, architectural creation becomes an immensely free play with spaces in space.

2. Since the house is decided in all its components, everyone is familiar with both design and construction of a building, even in detail. Therefore, residential architecture is not a particular craft or art to the Japanese, but is just a part of daily life of which everyone has sufficient knowledge to be his own architect. Consequently, the professional architect, as he emerged with the introduction of the West's new materials and constructions, is as recent as he is little respected, and he is not at all necessary for the design of traditional residences.

3. Since residences of any size and room arrangement are built with identical units, the component parts are prefabricated at the carpenter's workshop. As a result,

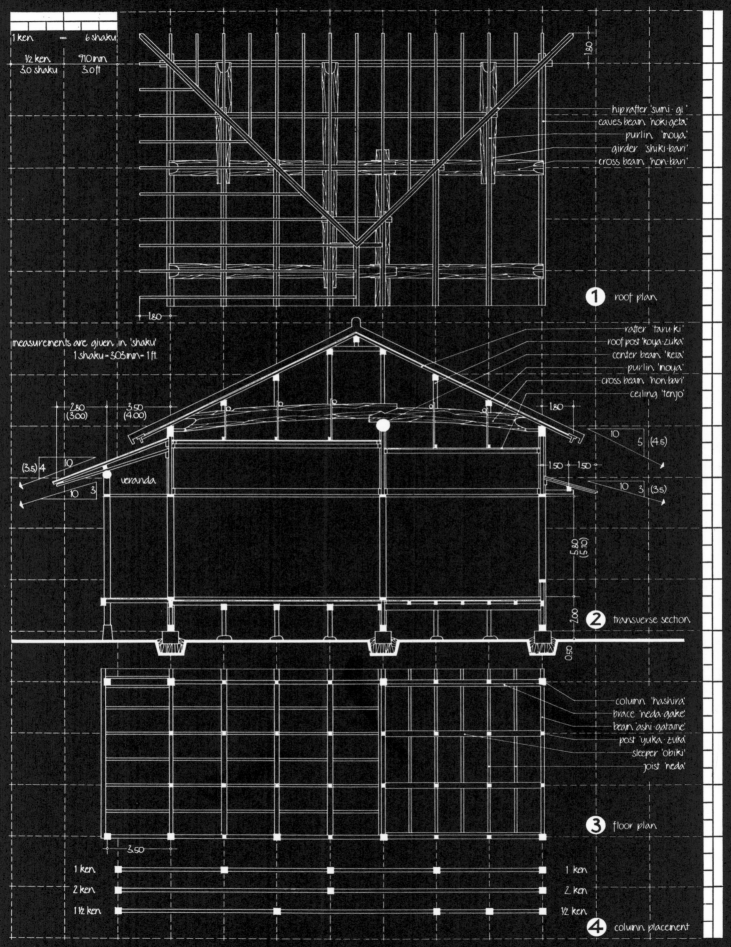

1.80

hip rafter 'sumi-gi'
eaves beam 'noki-geta'
purlin 'moya'
girder 'shiki-bari'
cross beam 'hon-bari'

① roof plan

1.80

measurements are given in 'shaku'
1 shaku = 303mm = 1 ft.

2.80
(3.00)

3.50
(4.00)

1.80

rafter 'taru-ki'
roof post 'koya-zuka'
center beam 'keta'
purlin 'moya'
cross beam 'hon-bari'
ceiling 'tenjo'

10   5   (4.5)

(3.5) 4   10

10   3

veranda

1.50   1.50

10   3   (3.5)

5.80
(5.70)

2.00

② transverse section

0.50

column 'hashira'
brace 'neda-gake'
beam 'ashi-gatame'
post 'yuka-zuka'
sleeper 'obiki'
joist 'neda'

③ floor plan

3.50

1 ken   1 ken
2 ken   2 ken
1½ ken   ½ ken

④ column placement

FIGURE 10: The modular order of the Japanese house.

the actual building process consists of merely assembling the various units, and requires a minimum of time and labor. Removable building parts such as windows, doors, mats, and ceiling components can readily be bought on the market so that deteriorated parts can easily be replaced. With equal simplicity the house can be extended as old parts can be used for new construction.

4. Since in his work the carpenter is confined to only a few standard forms and methods, he attains exacting technical precision and skill and accomplishes highly qualified work with a minimum of time and material. He does not need working drawings, nor is he concerned with constructional problems. Instead, he concentrates his creative instinct solely on the refinement of that which standardization has not yet reached. This accounts for the extreme refinement of the Japanese residence, which, by the same reason, is more evident in detail than in entirety.

5. Since on the other hand, the carpenter is subjected to an order, the alteration of which both social environment and his own professional belief forbid, he does not attempt to improve the standards his forefathers creatively developed. Throughout centuries, therefore, method and construction have remained stagnant at a primitive stage and have essentially strangled progress in building and living. Thus the present residence constitutes a strange contrast of primitivity in essence and perfection in performance. In this instance, the Japanese house clearly demonstrates a defective tendency caused by standardization.

Though standardization in the Japanese residence actually covers all phases of architectural work, only the standard measurements of the house anatomy will be studied. Among them the absolute measurements are of less interest than those which are incorporated into a particular order or system such as the dimensions that are in ratio to either the *ken* or the column section of 4 *sun*. If the *ken* is the basis of such an order, actually two groups of standards have to be considered, i. e. the standards based on:

ken in *kyō-ma* measurement = 6.5 *shaku* (on the average), and
ken in *inaka-ma* measurement = 6.0 *shaku*.

Only the *inaka-ma* system is exemplified in the drawings, since the *kyō-ma* measurements are more complicated and also are somewhat modified by different design methods.

It is evident that all horizontal structural distances are in direct ratio to the standard length *ken*. This modular order of *ken* is then consistently subdivided into fractions of 1/2 or 1/4, i. e., into smaller intervals of 3 or 1 1/2 *shaku*. Thus the order of *ken* also controls the details. Yet, this order is not slavishly adhered to in all instances. As the standard unit of 1/2 *ken* (3 *shaku* = 909 mm. = approx. 3 ft.) is rather small for the width of corridors, toilets, and verandas, the width of these minimum spaces is frequently enlarged to 3.5 or 4.0 *shaku*, the adjustment being easily accomplished by the handicraft technique.

The standard heights in the Japanese house show greater variety, yet the mere fact that they are standardized is of interest rather than the actual length, which may differ very slightly from one carpenter to the other. In the drawings, measurements most frequently used are listed, while those used less frequently are set in brackets. Deviations are given in percentages. The measurements of roof projections show the greatest local deviations, probably due to particular climatic circumstances. However, they are strictly observed within the particular locale. Most of them are not in ratio to any basic unit, but are absolute measurements.

Actually, the organization of the ceiling exemplifies the only module in the composition of standards that changes relative to room size. But here too, the former flexible ceiling height has become constant measurement in many areas, and so has the market size of the ceiling board. Present carpenter manuals contain only absolute measures.

The module for the ceiling, both in its height above floor and its subdivision, is

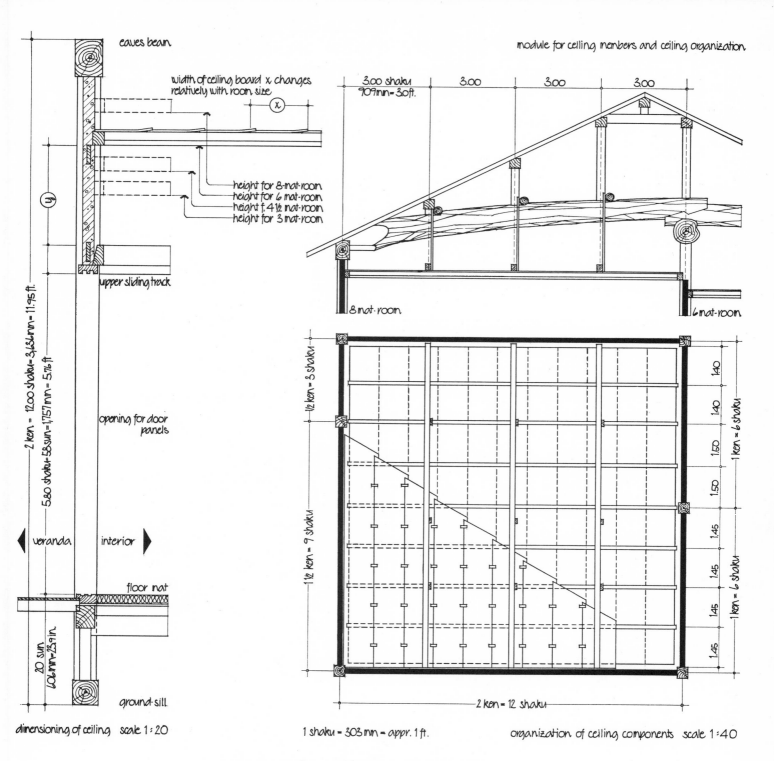

eaves beam

width of ceiling board x changes relatively with room size

(x)

height for 8-mat-room
height for 6 mat-room
height f. 4½ mat-room
height for 3 mat-room

upper sliding track

2 ken = 1200 shaku = 3,635mm = 11.95 ft.

5.80 shaku = 58 sun = 1,757 mm = 5.76 ft.

(y)

opening for door panels

veranda   interior

floor mat

20 sun
606 mm = 23.9 in.

ground sill.

dimensioning of ceiling   scale 1:20

3.00 shaku 909mm = 3.0ft.   3.00   3.00   3.00

8 mat-room   6 mat-room

1½ ken = 3 shaku

1½ ken = 9 shaku

2 ken = 12 shaku

140
140
1.50
1.50
1.45
1.45
1.45
1.45

1 ken = 6 shaku

1 ken = 6 shaku

1 shaku = 303 mm = appr. 1 ft.   organization of ceiling components   scale 1:40

FIGURE 11: The modular order of the ceiling.

the floor mat *tatami*. However, the mat itself does not function as module, but only the number of mats contained in each room; i.e., room size determines ceiling height and organization. As the ceiling is suspended by perpendicular ties to the main beams above, these height variations within a single house can be accomplished without additional time, work, or material.

Ceiling height from top of frieze rail *(nageshi)* to underside of ceiling ledge *(tenjō-mawaribuchi)*, i.e., height of upper wall *(kokabe)*:

height measured in *shaku* = number of mats × 0.3 (0.25)

Dimension of ceiling boards, *tenjō-ita*, i.e., board width:

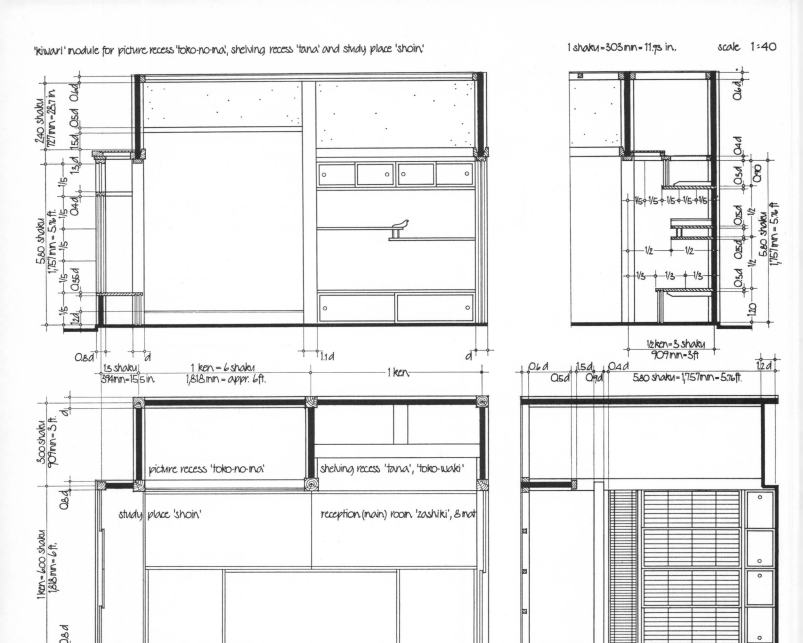

'kiwari' module for picture recess 'toko-no-ma', shelving recess 'tana' and study place 'shoin'   1 shaku = 303 mm = 11.93 in.   scale 1:40

FIGURE 12: The modular order of the picture recess, *tokonoma*.

width for 4 1/2- and 6-mat rooms = 1.0 *shaku* (303 mm. = 11.9 in.)
width for 8-mat room = 1.2 *shaku* (364 mm. = 14.3 in.)
width for 10-mat room = 1.5 *shaku* (455 mm. = 17.9 in.)

The ceiling parts, then, are arranged so that they correspond with the position of the columns. That is to say, a ceiling rod is centered above each column whereas the other rods are evenly distributed in between on an average interval of 1/4 *ken* = 1.5 *shaku*. The drawings show that, even though the column centers themselves are exactly placed upon the *ken* grid, three or even more different intervals may result, which differences, however, are hardly noticeable.

Here, then, the great problem of standardization is revealed: discrepancy between clear distance and center-to-center distance. Since the Japanese house is based entirely on handicraft, this discrepancy can easily be adjusted, but modern standardization requires an order that integrates both the clear distance and the center-to-center distance into a common system. Only if the thickness of structural members or partition elements follow the same modular order as is set up by the structural center-to-center distances, will the clear width also become a modular measurement.

Though the standard sizes of all wood sections in residential construction are generally determined by the most economical cut of the standard timber of 4 *sun* (121 mm. = 4.8 in.), certain ratios and proportions have been directly adopted from the *kiwari* of the warrior residence, where the module was predominantly based on visual-geometric, i.e., aesthetic, principles.

This visual-aesthetic meaning of *kiwari* can still be observed in the proportions set up for picture recess, *tokonoma;* shelving recess, *tana;* and study place, *shoin*—elements that are all organizationally, spiritually, and historically interrelated and have maintained their decorative function. Again, the basic module for the dimensioning of the wood members is the standard column section (d).

d = 4 *sun* (121 mm. = 4.8 in.)

Recess column, *toko-bashira:*
    for dressed column the facia *menuchi* without bevelings = 1.1 d
    for round log the entire diameter   = 1.0 d

Threshold, *toko-gamachi:*
    thickness = 0.8–1.0 d   width = 1.0 d
    height above floor = 1.0–1.2 d

Crossbeam, *otoshi-gake:*
    thickness = 0.5 d   width = 0.7–0.8 d
    elevation from top of frieze rail = 1.5–3.0 d

Polished facia at the lower part of round recess column, *takenokomen:*
    height = 2.5–3.0 d

Ceiling ledge, *tenjō-mawaribuchi:*
    thickness = 0.6 d   width = 0.5 d

Baseboard of upper cabinet, *fukurodana-ita (fukuro to-tana):*
    thickness = 0.3–0.35 d   width = 3/5 of recess depth
    distance from frieze rail = 9.3–9.5 *sun* (appr. 285 mm. = 11.4 in.)

Cover board of lower cabinet, *jibukuro-ita (ji-ita):*
    thickness = 0.3–0.35 d   width = 2/3 of recess depth
    height above floor = 12.0 *sun* (364 mm. = 14.3 in.)

Board of displaced shelves, *chigaidana-ita:*
    thickness = 0.2–0.25 d   width = 1/2 recess depth
    clear distance between upper and lower shelves = 1 d

Support between shelves, *ebizuka:*
    square section = 1.5–1.7 × thickness of shelf boards, *chigaidana-ita,* or = 0.4 d
    beveling = 1/7 of section

Cornice of upper shelves board, *fude-kaeshi:*
    thickness = 1.5–2.0 × thickness of shelf boards, *chigaidana-ita*
    projection = 1.0–1.5 × thickness of shelf boards

Reading bay post, *shoin-bashira:*
    square section = 0.7–0.8 d

Table board (sill), *shoin-jiita:*
    thickness = 0.35 d   width = about 1.3 *shaku* (394 mm. = 15.5 in.)
    height from floor = 1/5 of standard door height

Intermediate cross piece, *chū-gamoi:*
    thickness = 0.4 d   width = 0.8 (facia *menuchi*)
    distance from upper track = 1/5 of standard door height

Sliding panel, *shoin-shōji:*
    height = 3/5 of standard door height

Exterior cornice, *daiwa:*
    thickness = 0.5 of *shoin* post; width = 1.2 of *shoin* post
    projection = 1/4 of width

In the awareness that the inherited standardization basically would be suitable for industrial mass production, an attempt was made after World War II to unify the locally varying standards of measure and to establish the prerequisite for production of residences on a broad industrial basis, as was intended for social housing projects. In these new standards, distinction was made between one- and two-story houses and between two major climatic areas in Japan, resulting in standard sizes for four different types.

However, neither were the proposed measurements adopted nor did the industrialization in social housing become reality. This outcome could be expected with good reason. The inherited problems of Japanese standardization, previously described, cannot be solved by the mere introduction of a few new measurements; furthermore, since labor is cheap in Japan, machine-production afforded little economical advantage, at least not in the existing socio-economic state; and, finally, with constructional standardization being based entirely on handicraft, a shift to machine production would create additional problems requiring entirely new solutions.

Yet, aside from these technical-practical reasons, the real crux of the matter is that this house has meant a realistic architectural solution only for the society of the past. Except for inherited basic constructional defects, the Japanese house had reached a level of perfection that did not demand improvement if considered from the standpoint of living modes and requirements of the past. However, the word "perfection" implies not only the quality of being superb, but also the state of being completed and finished; and indeed the development of Japanese residential architecture has long since come to a standstill; its culmination is over. New technical impediments such as electricity, furniture, glass, metal, radio, etc. adopted from the West have degraded the quality and standard of the traditional Japanese residence; gradual Westernization of living manners has rendered inadequate what formerly was spatially convenient; and dissolution of the traditional family system has removed the philosophical basis that underlies the Japanese house. Once again it is apparent that the traditional dwelling belongs to the past, and that not only spatial requirements of contemporary living in Japan, but also measures and standards of her contemporary residential architecture are in dire need of radical change.

for contemporary architecture

In the Japanese house, then, is manifested an order of measure that because of its comprehensive influence upon building and living is unequaled in the history of civilization. Its distinction is not so much due to the particular relationship of measure units or to the appropriateness of the basic dimensions, but to the fact that it integrates all those advantages that have evolved separately in other systems. For the Japanese system of length measurement is:

standard measure of man,
standard measure of building material and construction,
standard measure with decimal subdivision, and
standard measure with duo-decimal relationship.

As in other measure systems, Japanese architectural measures have been determined by general measures that were based on the standard measures of the human figure. However, one architectural measure, the constructional standard distance, reversely effected a measure unit for general use. Indeed, it was by this influence of architectural structure that an otherwise consistent decimal system of measurements integrated a unit that was made of six parts and thus achieved the architectural advantage also of the duo-decimal system with its divisibility into 2, 3, 4 and 6.

A comparison of the two current systems, metric and foot-inch, clearly shows the advantage of the Japanese order of measure; i.e., it uncovers the main defects of the two major measures of the present. The Anglo-American system, while possessing the merits of human scale and of duo-decimal subdivision, is impractical and non-rational because it is without decimal structure on which mathematics and, consequently, science and technology are based. The metric system, while being of decimal structure with direct relationship in measurements of area, volume, weight, etc., is non-human and non-organic because it does not have a direct ratio to human measurements.

Unquestionably, there is only one international measure, the metric system. It is replacing the old systems in Asia. It is gaining ground even in the Commonwealth countries. Also, in North America certain industries have had to adopt the metric system, whereas the foot-inch system in its present form is certainly doomed to lose ground, never to gain. Nevertheless, the major industries in the Anglo-American countries have meanwhile committed themselves to the foot-inch measure to such a degree that it would cost the nation concerned billions of dollars to make any industrial transformation to the metric system. Of course, for building, by comparison still a non-precision industry, the system of fractions 1/2, 1/4 and 1/3 is very convenient, but where computation is required fractions become laborious in comparison to decimals, as is apparent in structural calculations, material specifications, mechanical computations, etc.

The unmatched superiority of the decimal order on the one hand, and the probable continuation of the foot-inch measure for the Anglo-American industries on the other, strongly suggests the need of probing the possibility of a measure system that would combine the convenient with the inevitable. Since the inch rather than the foot is important for the machine industry in Anglo-American countries, a possibility exists in a decimal usage of the inch-unit, i.e., in the establishment of a deca-inch system, with complete abolishment of the traditional foot measurement.

It is probably this necessary abolishment of the familiar foot that has so far prevented the introduction of a system as simple, convenient, and advantageous as the deca-inch system. But, upon closer examination, it becomes evident that most of the objections raised from an architectural viewpoint are emotional rather than intellectual:

1. The human relationship of foot measure, if precise and real, would assert itself in the consistent use of round foot measurements for interior spaces. The fact, however, is that deviations occur more often than not, because the foot measurement is insufficient as module for all spatial and structural requirements of building.

2. The familiarity of foot measure as length or area unit is actually a matter of usage and training, not of dimension. With equal ease it could be achieved for deca-inch units such as 10, 25 or 50 in., as can be observed in the effortless change to new dimensions in usage and thought by nations that adopted the metric system.

3. The suitability of foot measure for larger distances is actually unfounded, because this unit is too small for both urban and regional planning. Man conceives urban distances in yards rather than feet, and the ratios of the foot to larger units such as furlong, mile, and square measures are complicated and not consistent.

4. The appropriateness of foot measure for technical module is irrational because it is too large a unit to be used as basic measurement for standardization of the smaller building elements, as is proven by present U.S. standardization on basis of 1/3 ft. (4 in.), which has an absolute value of 0.333 ft.

5. Divisibility of foot measure into 3 and 4 (also 2 and 6), if found to be important enough, could be achieved by adopting standard measures in inches that are multiples of 3 and 4 without upsetting decimal computations.

The advantages of using inch measurements in the deca-inch system for architectural work are simply enormous:

1. Building industry and science would work on the basis of a single unit in the convenient decimal system, and their instruments and technical equipment would remain unaffected by this change.

2. Computation of volumes, areas, and lengths would be simplified as would the computation of structural engineer, mechanical engineer, specifier, and others.

3. By introducing new architectural scales such as 1:1, 1:5, 1:10, 1:20, 1:50, a direct arithmetical ratio would exist between these scales of reduction.

4. Scales in architectural drawings would immediately give the exact ratio of reduction from actual size and would facilitate the visualization of that which is represented.

5. It would be possible to read actual dimensions directly from drawings of any scale with only a single inch-ruler.

6. No designations as to foot or inch, nor the latter's 1/16 fractions, would be required, but only numerals that always indicate quantity in inches in a decimal order.

7. By means of a single index, inch measurements could be translated into metric system, as length, area or volume.

8. Conversely, metric measurements could be read directly with one centimeter rule from drawings of any scale.

9. Based only on the inch, a more homogeneous standardization could be established, integrating both small elements and large components of building.

Unquestionably, by decimalization of the inch the Anglo-American building measures could easily be made accessible to metric countries. In fact, it would reduce the international measure barrier to a single index that would state the ratio between the two units, inch and meter.

A study of the Japanese order of measure does not only provide suggestions for Anglo-American measures in building, but is also revealing for the discussion of standard measurements in countries with the metric system. A comparison of both decimal systems discloses that the meter, decimeter, and centimeter themselves do not bear a direct relationship to human measures and thus are not likely to serve as modules either for design or for the interrelated production of building components.

The Japanese measure system in its role as a human measurement with a decimal structure, which is simultaneously functional module for design and constructional standard distance, is strongly akin to the German modular coordination which is not based upon the deca-metric numbers of 100, 200, 300, 400, 500, etc. but upon the octa-metric numbers of 125, 250, 375, 500, etc., as elaborated by the architect Ernst Neufert. For these octa-metric measurements combine the advantages of being used only as decimals, of adding up always to round numbers, of being related to human measurements, and of providing practical sizes for standardization of building material.

It is interesting to note that this modular coordination of material and design (material on 125 mm., design on 1,250 mm. or 1,250/2 = 625 mm.) establishes a somewhat larger foot measure system within the metric system,* and even meets the deca-inch units with an exact difference of 10 mm. (less 55/1,000,000 mm.).

25 in. = 635 mm.	octa-meter module for residential design	= 625 mm.
(634.999945)		
50 in. = 1,270 mm.	octa-meter module for industrial design	= 1,250 mm.
(1,269.99989)		

Of course, the deca-inch system would also permit continuation of the present module of 4 and 48 in.; but such a modular order, though by comparison very simple, would deprive the deca-inch system of one important potential; namely, to serve as a module in its decimal structure—an advantage that would grant a maximum simplicity. Also, as a large part of the building industry in the United States still works with the old brick sizes of 4×8 in., the question of a new module is still open. Indeed, it must seem curious that instead of changing the standard brick format, apparently no attempt has been made to find a convenient system under which the existing standard material could be used within the existing order of measure. And the possibility of such a system does exist, because three lengths of the old 4 × 8 in. brick plus three joints of 1/3 in., equals exactly 25 in. (as 1 1/2 brick length would be 12.5 in.), which

---

* 2 Engl. ft. = 610 mm. versus 625 mm. of residential design standard, i.e., about 0.6 inch difference.

would permit a modular coordination on the basis of 50 in., which, in fact, is the deca-inch system.

It is even more difficult to understand why, in dimensioning the modular brick, a simplification of the impractical 3/8 in. joint was not sought, which would also have solved the complexity of dimensioning brick courses. Presently, three courses of the modular brick (plus three joints) measure 8 in., one brick height plus one joint being 2 2/3 in. Since the joint itself is supposed to be 3/8 in., the resulting exact brick height is 2 7/24 in., the latter figure being then "adjusted" to 2 6/24 = 2 1/4 in. Or, if the brick height is taken to be exactly 2 1/4 in., the resulting joint will measure 5/12 (10/24) in., again being "adjusted" to 9/24 = 3/8 in.

These "adjustments" are the source of many errors in the architectural practice. They obstruct simple height dimensioning and, in addition, result in continuous discrepancies between center-to-center dimensions and face-to-face dimensions, which, if the "adjustments" are not done to the proper direction, will add up to considerable differences. For example, if a wall opening would extend over eight brick courses, the grid dimension (measured center-to-center joint) will be given as 21 1/3 in. The actual clearance, however, according to which the man on the job works, is not simply this grid dimension plus one joint (21 1/3 + 3/8 = 21 17/24 in.), but is an "adjusted" figure of 21 16/24 = 21 2/3 in. This means that in this case, the difference between grid dimension and actual clearance is *not* equal to one joint (3/8 in.), but is only 1/3 in.

These discrepancies, the dire consequences of which go far beyond those indicated here, would not occur with a deca-inch brick format, i.e., a format based on 10 in. Requisite for simplification would be that a decision be made whether the standard joint for masonry be 1/2 or 1/4 in., if not actually, then, at least nominally for ease of dimensioning. If the standard joint is 1/2 in., the resulting brick format would be 7 × 3 1/4 × 2 in., with resulting decimal dimensions of coursing 2.5–5.0–7.5–10.0 in., etc. Accordingly, all wall openings in such masonry would have dimensions in both height and width of multiples of 2 1/2 in. For dimensioning the actual openings and solids of the wall, the only thing required would be to add or subtract another 1/2 in. from the grid dimension.

For elements with 1/4-in. joints, the resulting dimensions for the individual component would be the grid dimension minus one joint, i.e., 2.25–(3.5)–4.75–7.25–9.75 in., etc. The important advantage is that all horizontal and vertical grid dimensions would be multiples of 2.5 in. and that actual dimensions can simply be derived therefrom through the difference of one joint, be it 1/2 or 1/4 in.

The Japanese order of measure, therefore, provides material to better judge the problems of measure and standard in contemporary building and consequently is apt to confirm or refute existing theories and to instigate new ones. Characteristically, Japanese measures were determined not only by relationship with human measures and decimal partition, but also by the inherent scale of the major building fabric, wood. As little significance as this affiliation with construction seems to have for modern fabric with its infinite methods of spanning space, it yet discloses the very truth that the "technical" building and "human" dwelling actually are submitted to the same measure. This affinity is semantically confirmed by the common background of the two German words "to build," *bauen,* and "to dwell," *wohnen,* both of which at one time had the single form of *"buan."* Japanese measures have preserved this interrelationship up to the present time. The human scale and the practical unit for daily use are, together, the module for design, the standard distance for construction, and the official measurement.

On the other hand, the Japanese order of measure and the resulting comprehensive standardization of technique, construction, and form, both in detail and system, undoubtedly also had their negative effects. As the rules of guilds and the decrees of government made these standards obligatory on all and declared them sacrosanct, the standards became stagnant, blocking development and finally arresting progress altogether. The significance for contemporary architecture, however, is no less valuable. For it discloses that in a society with a standardized production, such as the Japanese in the past and the industrial society in the present, the professional mission and social responsibility of the architect is no longer the design of individual buildings. Instead, the emphasis of the architect's task has shifted to the control and inventive design of new standards, the influence of which on society is likely to be more profound, lasting, and comprehensive than the creation of a single building. These architectural efforts, however, encompass not only standards of measure, material, and form, but are also concerned with the standards for tool, technique, construction, and design. They even include the formation of standards for taste that have value for society as a whole beyond the individual. And all of these efforts aim at raising the quality of another standard, the "standard" of living.

It is true that, owing to comprehensive standardization of design and construction, no architect is needed for Japanese residential building. However, curtailment of all progressive development of the Japanese house, once it was standardized, convincingly demonstrates the real need for an architect. For standards are not a static finality but should be as dynamic as life and its material manifestation through architecture, and thus demand continuous and inventive improvement along with the progress of mankind.

definition

DESIGN IN BUILDING is the creative process of intellectually developing the building. It is the gradual organization of individual factors under an encompassing idea, thereby establishing artistic unity.

DESIGN IN BUILDING is pictorial representation of an architectural idea. As such, it is the controlling agent through which the architect puts his conception under test, removes defects, and derives new ideas.

DESIGN IN BUILDING is the abstract symbolization of all experience and study preceding the actual building. It is not the mere manual work of a designer but is the creative act of the architect.

DESIGN IN BUILDING is the medium through which the architect conveys his idea to patron and builder. It embodies the whole range of building activity and expresses itself in prescriptions for fabric, measure, and method.

DESIGN IN BUILDING is not boundless imagination but is tied to the realities of locality and time. Thus, it reflects technical level, social structure, and cultural background of the people.

DESIGN IN BUILDING not only confirms the existing but is also the very instrument by means of which the visionary idea of architecture finds its first substantiation. As such, it is an essential means for architectural progress.

DESIGN IN BUILDING possesses tools, techniques, and procedures of its own. Pencil, triangle, compass, and T-square, just as much as the organization of design work, leave their distinct imprint on the appearance of a building.

DESIGN IN BUILDING, then, is an integral stage of architectural creation. It "de-signs" construction, form, space, and idea of a building and thus is the only medium that can translate architectural conception into material form.

Though architectural design is concerned with all the factors determining or influencing building and also reflects their individual role in the total architectural genesis, this chapter on "structure" deals only with design in its more narrow, though more original meaning: "de-signing," i.e., marking out the building physique. Accordingly, only the methods and characteristics of Japanese residential design will be examined here because the actual themes of this design, such as utilization of space, structural system, environmental conditions, or aesthetic conceptions, in fact, comprehend the entire volume of this book.

Such analysis of the mere practical-technical aspect of Japanese residential design should give definite clues as to how architectural design is likely to develop in an age of standardization. For just as building, both the manufacture of its components and the procedure of its construction, has undergone decisive changes owing to increased mechanization and standardization (though not comprehensive as yet), so too a major transformation can be expected in design technique.

In fact, certain changes in the role of design in architectural creation are already evident. But these changes have come about without the architect, sometimes in spite of him. The architect seems to be unaware that his activity must adapt itself precisely to the two activities of the building industry for which his design provides the essential link: the manufacture of building materials and components and the procedure of building construction. Due to his unrealistic attitude, further changes in his design technique are likely to happen beyond his control, and there is even danger that he may no longer be able to exercise his initiative of determining the form and character of his profession.

This unchecked development itself, and not the architect, has already expanded the range of architectural work by compelling the building industry to incorporate science, business, and politics as essential elements of building. Indeed, this vigorous development simply overran the now inert architect who formerly was the professional that could control and basically influence all phases of architectural creation. It has confined him to the role of a so-called designer who takes care of the utilitarian aspect of building and who eventually may apply beauty for a better appearance.

Yet even in this limited range of activity, the architect's designing methods are still based upon the individualistic handicraft techniques of the past, which easily could adjust to any individualistic design detail. His methods do not in the least make allowances for the fact that the building components are to become ever larger and seem to ignore altogether the increasing mechanization of building construction. No doubt, the detrimental alienation of architectural execution from architectural design, together with the increasing subjugation of the architect's spatial-aesthetic ideas to technological, financial, or other practical aspects of building, is due in no small degree to his obsolete and non-adjusted notions of the role and method of design in contemporary building.

Therefore, it is vital and imminent to study the procedure and aim of contemporary architectural design. For such endeavor, the comparison with other design techniques should produce valuable information. The Japanese method is particularly instructive because it has maintained its unity with the manufacture and construction of building. Here, design is based strictly on a modular order and is essentially concerned with the creative organization of standard forms of fabric, construction, and space. Significantly, two distinct methods of design have emerged, and the differences between them illuminates one major difficulty in contemporary standardization and modular design. Indeed, the Japanese method of design is likely to demonstrate both the effects and consequences of a comprehensive modular design in domestic architecture, and hence should be of particular interest for an architecture whose method of design lacks unity as does the resulting architecture itself.

kyo-ma method

It is generally assumed that the *ken* in *kyō-ma* measurement is a definite length of 6.5 *shaku* (1,970 mm. = 6.5 ft.) as the *ken* in *inaka-ma* measurement is a definite length of 6 *shaku* (1,818 mm. = 6.0 ft.). Yet, this assumption holds true only for the period prior to the end of the 18th century, when the floor mat, *tatami,* was not yet in common use among the lower classes and also did not yet cover the entire floor area.

When thereafter the mat became indispensable, it also became a commercial article just as other goods had done before that time and, as such, required an exact size. This fixation of size also was necessary because it was customary for tenants and even house owners to take the mats along with them when moving to another residence. Naturally, the mats had to fit in the new domicile as well. Finally, the tearooms *(sukiya* architecture) also demanded a single-mat format because the mats were frequently rearranged according to the season or to a particular occasion. It is obvious, therefore, that the mat had to be of universal size; *tatami* was standardized. That is to say, when the mat became the covering for the entire floor area, its standard size in return controlled the intercolumniation.

Thus, it seems appropriate to consider *kyō-ma* from this time on no longer a measurement or a measure system with definite units, but rather a method of designing and a method for deciding exact column distance. As consistent as this method is in itself,

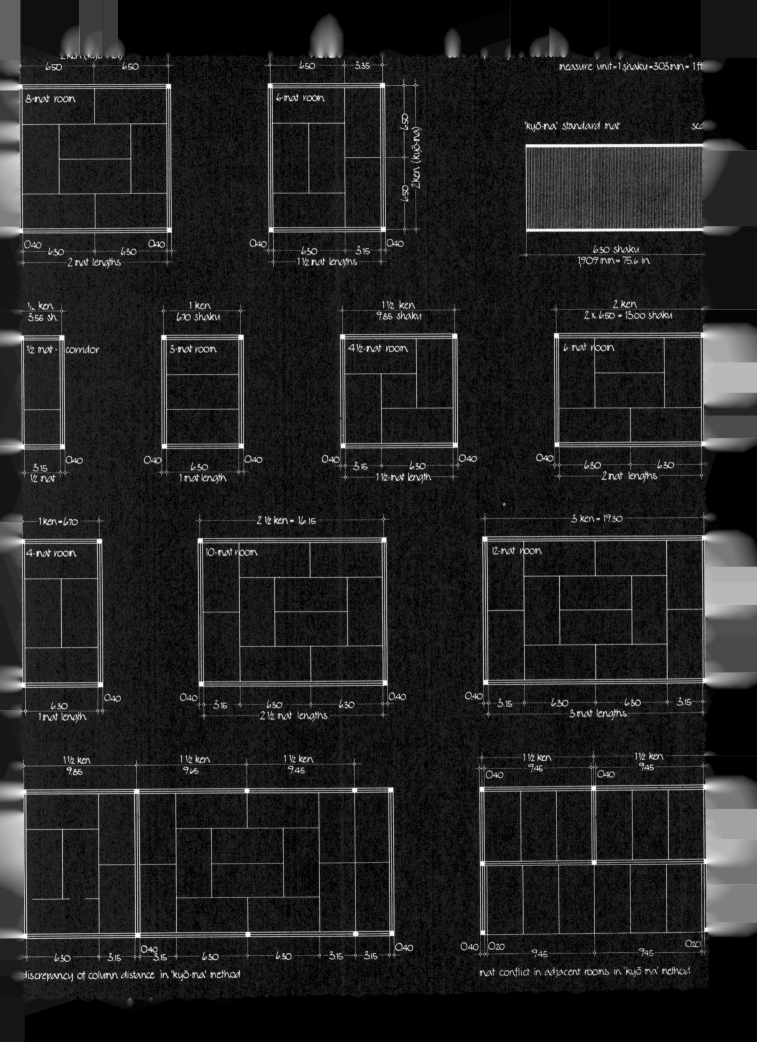

discrepancy of column distance in 'kyō-ma' method

mat conflict in adjacent rooms in 'kyō-ma' method

the resulting constructional distances are no longer consistently multiples or fractions of the former ken of 6.5 shaku, but also show in one and the same structure deviations that forbid the identification of ken in kyō-ma measurement as a fixed length. Rather the ken in kyō-ma again regained its original meaning as a column interval, a distance, however, measured from face to face of two columns instead of from center to center.

The mat size for the kyō-ma system was derived from the mat dimensions in room sizes most frequently used. These were rooms of 6 or 8 mats with a long side column center distance of 2 ken in kyō-ma measurement ($2 \times 6.5 = 13.0$ shaku). With a standard column section of 0.4 shaku (4 sun = 121 mm. = 4.8 in.) the resulting length of the standard mat became:

$13.0 - 0.4 = 12.6$ shaku (clear width of 2 ken in kyō-ma)

1 mat length $= 12.6/2 = 6.3$ shaku

Standard mat, kyō-ma system: 6.3×3.15 shaku ($1,909 \times 954.5$ mm. $= 75.6 \times 37.8$ in.)

Prefabrication of the standard mat and its consistent use for all different-sized rooms then brought about a deviation from the previous strict use of multiples or fractions of the ken of 6.5 shaku. Standardization of constructional center distance had finally given way to standardization of intercolumniate clearance.

It is evident that the post center distances correspond to the former kyō-ma measurement only in the 6- or 8-mat rooms, i.e., rooms with length of 2 ken, while all others show slight differences.

Center-to-center column distances, ken, in the kyō-ma method:

Room width = 1 mat $\quad$ $(6.30 + 0.40) \div 1 \quad = 6.70$ shaku

$\quad\quad\quad\quad$ 1 1/2 mats $\quad$ $(9.45 + 0.40) \div 1.5 = 6.57$ shaku

$\quad\quad\quad\quad$ 2 mats $\quad$ $(12.60 + 0.40) \div 2 \quad = 6.50$ shaku

$\quad\quad\quad\quad\quad\quad\quad\quad$ (this is the original ken in kyō-ma measurement)

$\quad\quad\quad\quad$ 2 1/2 mats $\quad$ $(15.75 + 0.40) \div 2.5 = 6.46$ shaku

$\quad\quad\quad\quad$ 3 mats $\quad$ $(18.90 + 0.40) \div 3 \quad = 6.43$ shaku

$\quad\quad\quad\quad$ 4 mats $\quad$ $(25.20 + 0.40) \div 4 \quad = 6.40$ shaku

With standardization of column clearance, the entire constructional measuring that always relates to center of structural member is no longer consistent. But, as the technique of construction is handicraft, slight variations are not a problem as they would be with machine craft and can be resolved without additional labor or material.

Difficulties, however, still arise in determining the standard measurements necessary for prefabrication of sliding panels between the columns. In fact, in spite of standardization of clear room width, discrepancies in intercolumn distance do occur in certain cases (as is evident in the illustration of kyō-ma method of design). Accordingly, sliding elements for wall openings are prefabricated only for the most common cases and frequently are manufactured separately for each house, very clearly demonstrating that even standardization of clear room width does not necessarily guarantee simple standardization of intercolumniate panels.

Another problem is the discrepancy that results when two smaller rooms are backed up to one larger room. In practice, this problem is solved by one of two methods. Either the mats of the two small rooms determine the outside walls and the difference appearing in the large room is compensated by additional wood boards; or the mats of the large room determine the outside walls, requiring special sizes for the mats of the two small rooms.

The kyō-ma method, then, constitutes design of constructional members around the standardized unit of the room interior, the mat, tatami. The disadvantages for systematic measuring and designing of the structure are obvious. Nevertheless, the fact that the kyō-ma method is still being used, even predominantly so (contrary to the opinion of many writers), does prove that the economical advantage gained by standardizing interior units, and the generally larger room sizes, must have outweighed all the other defects. That these defects can be overcome only by handicraft methods is as obvious as is the fact that contemporary architecture based on machine-craft production cannot work on such a basis.

inaka-ma method

Contrary to the inconsistent column distance in the *kyō-ma* method, intercolumnia-tion in the *inaka-ma* method is strictly based on a square grid of 1 *ken* (6 *shaku*), and is not dependent on interior mat or panel size. Consequently, all constructional dis-tances are either a fraction or a multiple of 6 *shaku*. However, as the unit 1/2 *ken* (3 *shaku*), functionally speaking, is slightly too small for minimum spaces such as the veranda, corridor, bath, and toilet, frequently the direct ratio to *ken* is unhesitatingly deserted and instead, distances like 3.5 or 4 *shaku* are used.

Abolishment of the grid system in such a decisive matter as minimum spaces is interesting, since standardization in terms of length should begin with the finding of a common denominator for minimum rooms, which would then be the largest com-mon measure. The larger rooms, then, should be subjected to the order of the smaller ones and not vice versa. It appears that the *ken* of 6 *shaku* is a standard of material economy and practicality rather than one of spatial adequacy, and is abandoned each time utilitarian demands are endangered. This also explains the distinct preference for the *kyō-ma* measurement (not as method but as a larger *ken* unit), for the resulting room sizes are considered more appropriate than those of the *ken* of 6 *shaku*.

From the viewpoint of contemporary architecture with its standardization, such conscious tolerance toward a self-imposed order is significant. For it shows that even the most unique standardization that architecture has produced still does not com-pletely fulfill all the demands of structure, function, economy, and aesthetics. Certainly a larger *shaku* unit could solve the problem to a certain degree, but it is certain then that other disadvantages will arise. It demonstrates that requirements of man, material, and technique are oftentimes opposed to each other and that the standard establishes the optimum of compromise between them. It contradicts the opinion that economi-cal construction necessarily satisfies utilitarian requirements or that perfect compliance with these requirements produces beauty.

Evidently, the Japanese builder-architect, the carpenter, followed this compromis-ing nature of modular design, if not consciously, then instinctively. Though he based his plan essentially upon the *ken* grid, his unique mastership of both design technique and building construction qualified him to know precisely in which cases he had to deviate from the modular grid.

While in the *kyō-ma* method there is only one standard mat, the dimensions of which do not correspond with the on-center constructional distance, in the *inaka-ma* method, several standard mat sizes exist: the norm mat being 3×6 *shaku* (909 $\times$ 1,818 mm. = 3×6 ft.) whose dimensions are derived directly from center-to-center column distance, and several variational types that are smaller in order to com-pensate for differences at the outside wall. As the column width in the ordinary dwelling is always 4 *sun* (121 mm. = 4.8 in.), the deviation of the variational types from the norm mat is 1/2 column width or 2 *sun* (60 mm. = 2.4 in.), i.e., the length is reduced to 5.80 *shaku* and the width to 2.80 *shaku*.

The illustration of *inaka-ma* method shows that no less than five variational mat types, (a) to (e), are necessary in addition to the norm mat (n), in order toa ccurately cover any floor space without additional members. Among the five variational types, two sizes only, (a) and (b), are used in the 3-mat room, a space comparatively rare in the ordinary house. Another type (d) appears only when the 4 1/2-mat room is arranged in the unusual manner of the half mat on the outside. That is to say, only two variational mat types, (c) and (e), are usually required in addition to the norm mat (n). These three mat sizes, then, (n), (c), and (e), are standardized and are usually kept in stock.

Yet, in another area of Japan where the *inaka-ma* method is applied, the norm mat (n) measures not 3.00×6.00 *shaku*, but 5.80×2.90 *shaku*. No additional standard mats are in use. Consequently, for rooms of 3, 4, and 4 1/2 mats, special sizes smaller than the norm mat are needed. Also, the 6-mat room still requires, in addition to the

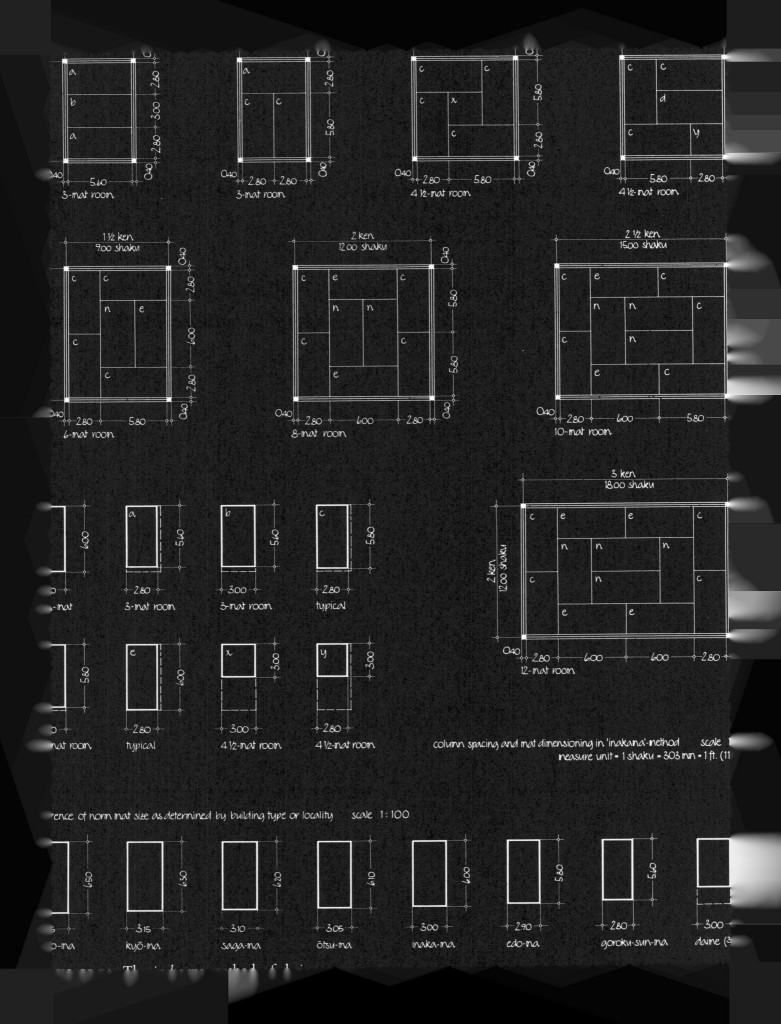

3-mat room

3-mat room

4½-mat room

4½-mat room

1½ ken
9.00 shaku

6-mat room

2 ken
12.00 shaku

8-mat room

2½ ken
15.00 shaku

10-mat room

3 ken
18.00 shaku

2 ken
12.00 shaku

12-mat room

-mat

3-mat room

3-mat room

typical

nat room

typical

4½-mat room

4½-mat room

column spacing and mat dimensioning in 'inakana'-method   scale 1
measure unit = 1 shaku = 303 mm = 1 ft. (11

rence of norm mat size as determined by building type or locality   scale 1 : 100

ō-ma

kyō-ma

saga-ma

ōtsu-ma

inaka-ma

edo-ma

goroku-sun-ma

daime (3

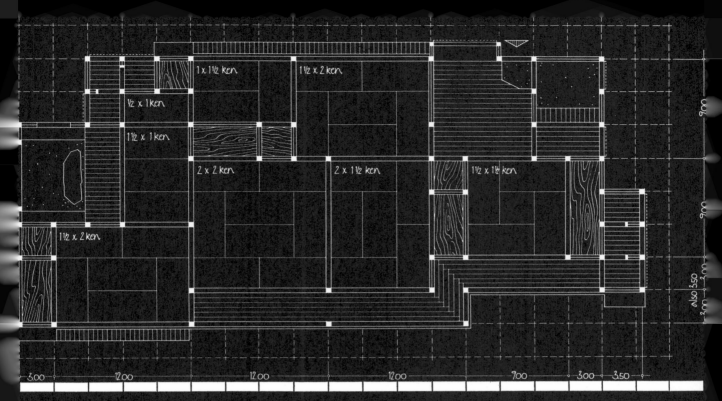

1 x 1½ ken   1½ x 2 ken

½ x 1 ken

1½ x 1 ken

2 x 2 ken   2 x 1½ ken   1½ x 1½ ken

1½ x 2 ken

also 3.50

| 3.00 | 12.00 | 12.00 | 12.00 | 9.00 | 3.00 | 3.50 |

…sign in 'inaka-ma'-method: column spacing on grid pattern with columns placed on grid center   measure unit = 1 shaku = 303 mm = 1 ft (11.93 in
…dule for grid pattern = 3.00 shaku = 910 mm = 3.0 ft   total floor area = 32.75 tsubo = 108.2 sq.m. = 1,165.2 sq.f

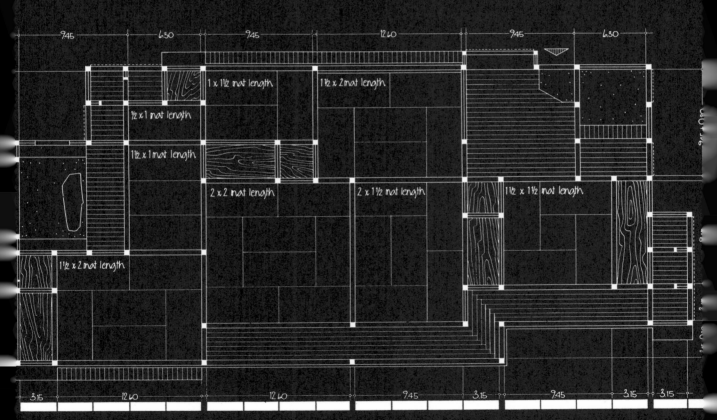

| 9.45 | 6.30 | 9.45 | 12.60 | 9.45 | 6.30 |

1 x 1½ mat length   1½ x 2 mat length

½ x 1 mat length

1½ x 1 mat length

2 x 2 mat length   2 x 1½ mat length   1½ x 1½ mat length

1½ x 2 mat length

| 3.15 | 12.60 | 12.60 | 9.45 | 3.15 | 9.45 | 3.15 | 3.15 |

…sign in 'kyō-ma'-method: column spacing according standardized clear width of mat covered space   measure unit = 1 shaku = 303 mm = 1 ft (11.93 in
…dule for clear width = 3.15 shaku = 955 mm = 3.15 ft   total floor area = 32.75 tsubo = 128.1 sq.m. = 1,378.7 sq.f

norm mat, a special size, while the 8-mat room is covered solely by the norm mats. If the room exceeds a width of 2 *ken* (3,636 mm. = 12 ft.), the spaces left between the mat edges and the partition are filled with small wood boards.

The *inaka-ma* method, then, constitutes design on a square grid system of 1 *ken* (6 *shaku*), in which the center line of construction or partition corresponds with the grid line. The mat, *tatami*, being an element of clear room width, is unconditionally subordinated to this system. Even with set standard mat sizes, the present practice of the matmaker is to take the measurements of the completed house framework before delivering the single mat units. In spite of all standardization, then, differences and inaccuracies owing to handicraft technique and irregularity of natural fabric are inevitable, and require special handling.

Design itself, however, in the *inaka-ma* method is an easy arranging of standardized space units on the *ken* grid, and in essence is no different from contemporary modular design. Yet, in the Japanese residence, even though the manual design is limited only to the floor plan in scale 1:100 or 1:50, the actual modular coordination is far more comprehensive than in contemporary design. It penetrates the detail and system, the material and the spiritual substance of building and, in a century-long process, has coordinated the market size and the production of fabric. Deviations from this elaborate system are easily accomplished in the handicraft system of the time, but would not be so easily done under the machine-conditioned standardization of the industrial society.

process of design

If the word "design," in its contemporary definition, is at all appropriate for that which is drawn with a brush or frequently with a pencil on a single wooden board and which serves as a working drawing, then no architect is needed to "design" a house, or else both patron and carpenter are the architects. Due to the close relationship of standardization to both living and building, the layman is familiar with all room units in dimension, form, equipment, and arrangement, and it is therefore easy for everyone to be his own architect. Moreover, since there is a very intimate relationship between indoors and outdoors at all times of the year, even the children are familiar with the orientation of the rooms to the compass.

Thus, preliminary ideas are transformed into two-dimensional plans by the client himself. Based on a consistent *ken* grid (significantly also in the case of the *kyō-ma* method with 1 *ken* = 6.5 *shaku*) simple mat sketches are drawn without any scale other than the mat unit (Plate 10).

Once the room requirement is decided, the separate rooms are sometimes cut out in paper and children and parents individually try to achieve the best room arrangement on the *ken* grid. One mat arrangement is finally decided upon and wall openings, picture recess *(tokonoma)*, closets, etc., are listed. No measurements are given. Everything is controlled merely by the *ken* grid and the mat arrangement.

Present building codes require that a plan be submitted for governmental or municipal approval; and if the carpenter does not feel himself a skillful enough draftsman, he merely asks an architect to transfer to paper the room arrangement that has already been decided upon. Such, then, is the role of the "architect" in residential architecture of traditional style, and likewise is his reputation. Not being too familiar with the details of the carpenter's practice, he draws the plan strictly on a *ken* grid, i.e., 6 *shaku* in the *inaka-ma* method and 6.5 *shaku* in the *kyō-ma* method. The practice of the latter method probably accounts for the widespread, yet erroneous, belief that the *kyō-ma* grid in present usage is still based on a fixed measurement of 6.5 *shaku*, as it used to be.

The difference in square footage between the two design methods is remarkable. In identical designs it averages 15% and in houses with many small rooms there is an even greater difference. For example, the 4 1/2-mat room in the *inaka-ma* method is

17.5% smaller than that in the *kyō-ma* method, yet both floor areas denote an area of 2 1/4 *tsubo* (sq. *ken*).

The carpenter, then, draws an exact ground plan on a wooden board to the scale of 1:50 or 1:20, which, except for column placement, contains only brief indications as to location and kind of wall openings (Plate 11). If the *kyō-ma* method is used, he adjusts column distance according to standard size of the mat, and lists exact measurements. While the actual creative work in the designing process, i.e., adding and grouping space, is accomplished by the client, the carpenter's part is confined solely to placement of the columns. Imperative for this placement is primarily room division and secondarily construction, but not visual-geometric considerations. Thus intermediate columns in opposite walls, produced by the partitioning of other adjacent rooms, need not correspond either in number or in placement. Since columns are exposed on both sides of the wall, the irregularity of arrangement is both obvious and striking. The same blunt neglect of external orderliness is evident in the arrangement of doors in two adjoining rooms of different widths, for example, rooms of 2 *ken* and 1 1/2 *ken*. Separated only by a slender column, these two markedly different wall openings are each furnished with four panels, which distinctly differ in proportion. This lack of concern with visual effect is evidenced even more in the fact that only three sliding units in the 1 1/2 *ken* span would have permitted identical doors and thus continuity of identical proportion for both openings.

No other instance shows the Japanese basic disregard for form more convincingly. Though at first sight this disposition appears irregular, even disorderly, at second glance the logical and uncompromising arrangement creates an atmosphere of intimacy between object and beholder more convincingly than if regularity had prevailed. The differences in column distances, whatever are the reasons, are not covered up, but are clearly stated by using different-sized units for each interval. Though in appearance this irregularity is in direct contrast to the continuity of geometric order which usually dominates, in essence it is so logical and natural that one hesitates to identify it with Japanese taste in particular. Rather, Western striving for uniformity and symmetry must appear in this light unnatural and therefore questionable.

Another distinct feature of Japanese design is universality. For design is not only concerned with structure but also with the garden; and equal effort is put on organizing both interior and exterior spaces. In fact, in planning houses, the garden-view is oftentimes the primary consideration. Since both the garden and the structure as a whole are standardized in feature and arrangement and are classified as to type, it is not difficult to be one's own landscape designer. The two Chinese ideographs that stand for home, *ka-tei,* actually mean "house" and "garden," and thus the Japanese consider it. A house without a garden is not a home. However, as the garden in the common residence is hardly a space to be walked through as it is in the houses of the aristocracy, but is more an ever changing picture to be looked upon, the plan of the house is shifted around until its position offers the most varied and interesting vista and makes the best and fullest use of the site.

present building regulations

It could be expected that the inherited comprehensive order of the Japanese dwelling would have inspired the state or city to guide, if not to control, contemporary residential architecture with the latest tools offered by science and technique. For in the late Middle Ages of Japan, the shogunate of the Tokugawa family, though for different reasons, had strictly controlled or even suppressed residential building in the city to a degree that proved decisive in the evolution of the characteristics of the Japanese house. Yet, what is written in the present building code hardly seems likely to produce as distinctive an architecture as the feudalistic regulations did in the past. In fact, the code is primarily concerned with minimum requirements for building site, street setback, construction, wood preservation, fire security, hygiene, etc., and merely aims at confirming the existing rather than creating new standards of living. There is neither city planning in the Western sense, nor an official body that would extend its concern to aesthetics.

To the contrary, some of the regulations in force prevent the use of architectural features that are generally lauded by Western architects. For example, in the present houses, for more stable construction of the framework, not only angle ties must be applied at the corners in the horizontal plane both in the ground sill *(hiuchi-dodai)* and in the eaves beam *(hiuchi-bari),* but also diagonal struts in the vertical plane *(sujikai),* i.e., in the outside wall. Since the latter members are frequently exposed on both the inside and outside, the dominant geometric order of horizontal and vertical members is badly upset. Such measures again demonstrate the lack of concern for external form and contradict the general opinion that all external expressions of the Japanese house are calculated and intended.

Of even more regrettable consequences is the law which, for security's sake, prohibits exposure of wood to the outside in particular zones of the city. As understandable as such a fire-preventive measure might be, on the other hand it shows a lack of understanding for one of the important expressional merits and distinct features of Japanese residential architecture. In houses governed by this restriction, structural members are no longer visible from the outside, and the elaborate woodwork of the eaves is covered by a clumsily plastered box. The transformation of architectural expression resulting from this regulation once again confirms that the house that is being analyzed belongs to the past. The houses of the present, both in feature and expression, are losing more and more of their original distinction and show a trend of Westernization or internationalization to which the Japanese culture as a whole is subjected.

One change for the better, however, has been the abolishment of the earthen floor. The kitchen, bath, toilet, and entrance, which frequently had nothing but stamped earth as a floor, must now be covered by concrete or tile material for health purposes. The minimum requirements for lighting and ventilation also improve the quality of living. Window and door areas in exterior walls must together amount to 1/7th of the floor area of the house for lighting purposes and to 1/20th for ventilation purposes, interior paper panels, *fusuma,* not included.

Especially interesting are the minimum requirements for living space mentioned in the code, for the data given shed light on the marked difference in Western and Japanese thought as to how much space is needed for decent human living. Differing standards of living may well account for this phenomenon, yet, it seems more probable that the particular mode of Japanese living can simply do with far less space than can the Western. For four people to live in a house of not more than 9 *tsubo* (appr. 30 sq. m. = 325 sq. ft.) with actual living space of only 5 1/2 *tsubo* (appr. 18 sq. m. = 200 sq. ft.) may be conceivable to the Western mind and even may be considered appropriate for certain emergency conditions. But to declare such a toy-sized area as the official minimum standard for living area is another thing. It shows not only that there did exist the possibility of living in smaller areas—otherwise no minimum standard would be required—but also that the spatial requirements of the average Japanese must be distinctly lower than those of the Westerner. Indeed, without thorough knowledge of the particular manners of the inhabitants, such a low existence minimum must appear incredible.

This difference is further brought to the open by the data published in the *Standards for Residences.* Since rooms are used for both sleeping and living, minimum areas for the living-sleeping area are listed:

1 person	3-mat room	= 6 × 9	*shaku* (appr. 4.9 sq.m.	= 54 sq. ft.)
2 persons	4 1/2-mat room	= 9 × 9	*shaku* (appr. 7.4 sq.m.	= 81 sq. ft.)
3 persons	6-mat room	= 9 × 12	*shaku* (appr. 9.8 sq.m.	= 108 sq. ft.)
4 persons	8-mat room	= 12 × 12	*shaku* (appr. 13.2 sq.m.	= 124 sq. ft.)

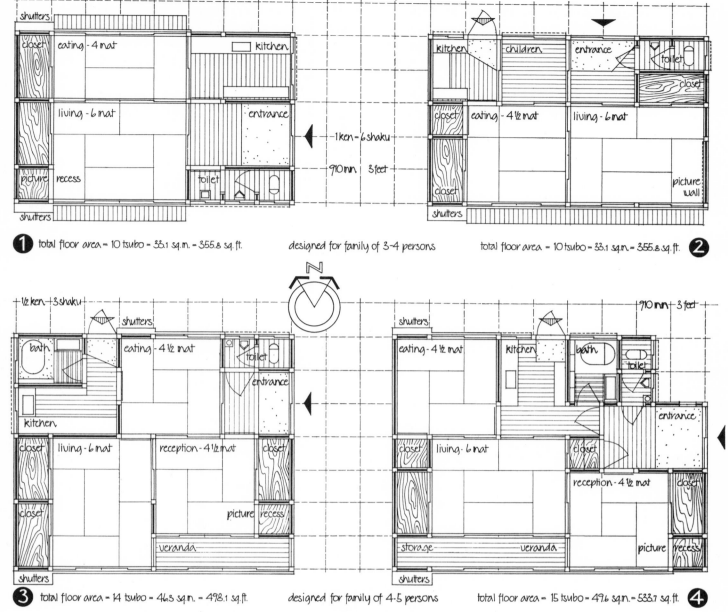

① total floor area = 10 tsubo = 33.1 sq.m. = 355.8 sq. ft.　designed for family of 3-4 persons　total floor area = 10 tsubo = 33.1 sq.m. = 355.8 sq. ft. ②

③ total floor area = 14 tsubo = 46.3 sq.m. = 498.1 sq. ft.　designed for family of 4-5 persons　total floor area = 15 tsubo = 49.6 sq.m. = 533.7 sq. ft. ④

FIGURE 16: Select examples of typical residences.

Because bedding must be stored away during the day, the proportion of closet space to living space in the Japanese house surpasses by far that in the Western residence. The minimum requirement is listed as 15% of the total area for smaller houses and as 10% for larger ones. There are other standards mentioned, both constructional and functional, but these constitute no other purpose than to set the minimum standards and do not by any means attempt to stimulate or even foster progress.

distinctions

Japanese residential design is distinct in many ways. The distinctions are interrelated very intimately with the mode of living, as architectural design always encompasses the total range of factors that comprehend human living both physically and spiritually. Yet, the distinctions of the mere technique of design are striking and important enough to justify particular mention. For they show that even the method of design itself can produce characteristics in architecture.

Design on the grid basis, no doubt, has been instrumental in producing a strictly

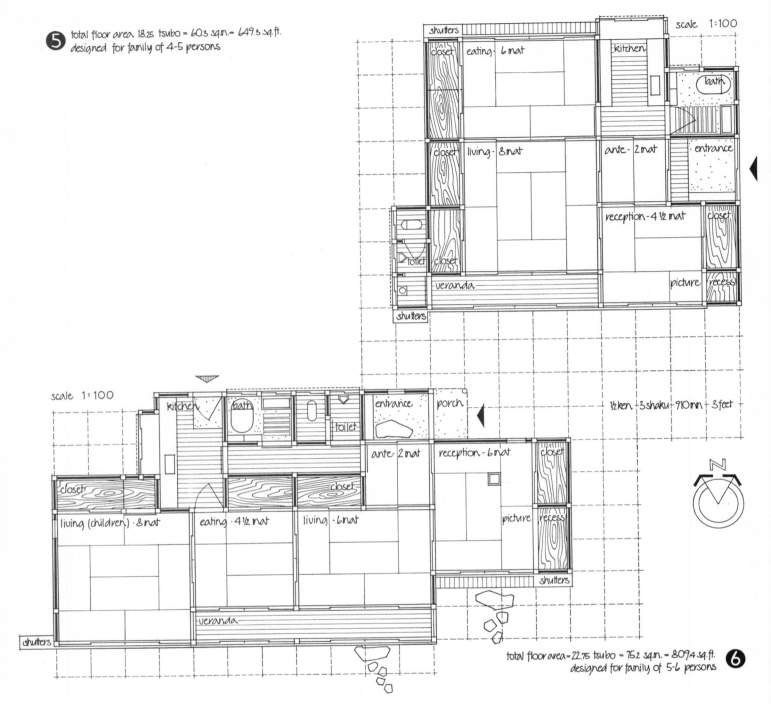

5 total floor area 18.25 tsubo = 60.3 sq.m. = 649.3 sq.ft.
designed for family of 4-5 persons

scale 1:100

shutters
closet | eating · 6 mat | kitchen
closet | living · 8 mat | ante · 2 mat | entrance
toilet | closet | reception · 4½ mat | closet
veranda | picture | recess
shutters

scale 1:100

kitchen | bath | toilet | entrance | porch
closet
closet | closet | ante · 2 mat | reception · 6 mat | closet
living (children) · 8 mat | eating · 4½ mat | living · 6 mat | picture | recess
veranda | shutters
shutters

½ ken · 3 shaku · 910mm · 3 feet

N

total floor area = 22.75 tsubo = 75.2 sq.m. = 809.4 sq.ft.
designed for family of 5-6 persons **6**

FIGURE 16 (continued): Select examples of typical residences.

rectangular plan. Yet, the rectangle is indeed the logical geometry of floor area, as it is the only form which allows free addition of individual room units that in turn result in another rectangular shape, at the same time providing the basis for a most economical and simple construction. Indeed, to deviate from the rectangular pattern requires sound and valid reason, and the Japanese "designer," though in certain instances departing from the exact *ken* grid pattern of 6 *shaku* (1,818 mm.=6 ft.), even occasionally using curved forms, apparently never did find any reason to search for another form in the ground plan other than the rectangular.

Thus, standardized room units are shifted as easily as they are connected along the grid system of the *ken,* which in turn facilitates design pattern of steplike, staggered room units for which Japanese building is noted; because each of the units, being tied to the grid, never loses its cohesiveness with other units in spite of total freedom of

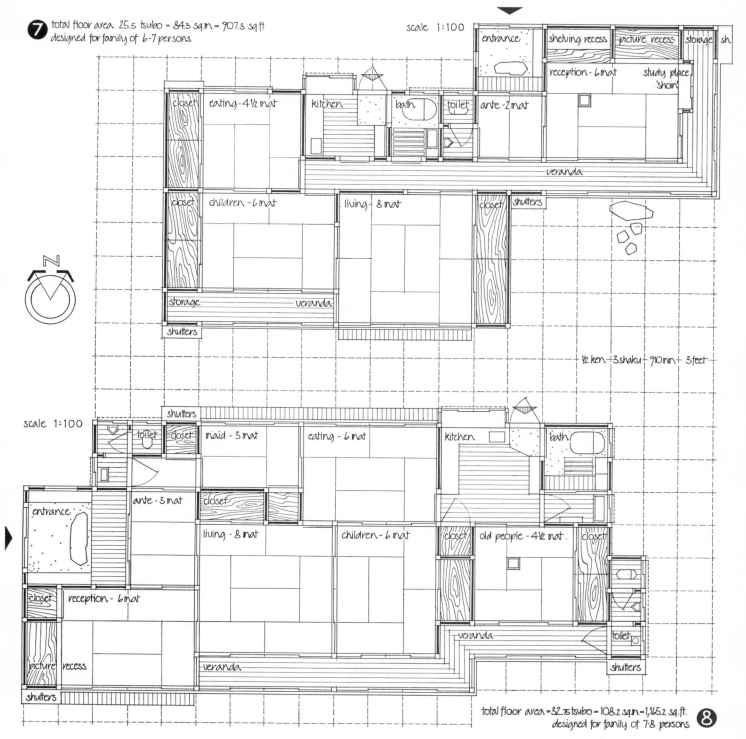

7 total floor area 25.5 tsubo = 84.3 sq.m. = 907.3 sq.ft
designed for family of 6-7 persons

scale 1:100

entrance | shelving recess | picture recess | storage | sh.

reception - 6 mat | study place 'shoin'

closet | eating - 4½ mat | kitchen | bath | toilet | ante - 2 mat

veranda

closet | children - 6 mat | living - 8 mat | closet | shutters

storage | veranda

shutters

½ ken = 3 shaku = 910 mm = 3 feet

scale 1:100

shutters

toilet | closet | maid - 3 mat | eating - 6 mat | kitchen | bath

ante - 3 mat | closet

entrance | living - 8 mat | children - 6 mat | closet | old people - 4½ mat. | closet

closet | reception - 6 mat | veranda | toilet

picture recess | veranda | shutters

shutters

total floor area = 32.75 tsubo = 108.2 sq.m. = 1,165.2 sq.ft.
designed for family of 7-8 persons **8**

FIGURE 16 (continued): Select examples of typical residences.

placement. On the other hand, the structural system undoubtedly has also contributed
to making the "casualness" of room disposition possible. The roof load is transmitted
by heavy crossbeams (1 *ken* on center) to strong longitudinal members whose maximum span is 3 *ken* (5,454 mm.= 18 ft.), a distance hardly required in the common
house. Moreover, additional supporting beams can be used without disadvantageous
visual-constructional consequences because of the suspended ceiling and plenty of constructional height. Thus, placement of supporting columns is done freely and follows
room organization rather than constructional necessity.

Room is added to room, and space has become additive, a sequence of single room

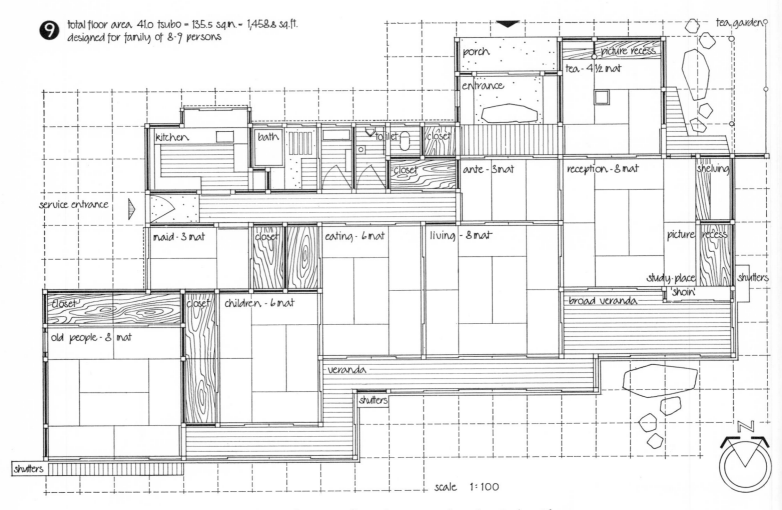

FIGURE 16 (continued): Select examples of typical residences.

demarcations without distinct beginning or end, constituting no finality but only a state of organic growth. Design is never really completed, nor is the construction of the house itself. With an increase in either children or wealth, another unit is simply added as long as any space on the lot remains; and the house, like its design, becomes dynamic.

Problems in circulation do not arise as they do in the West, for as a rule the room is provided with a veranda-like corridor at the outside or may serve as a corridor itself. Though as time progresses some houses may finally cover the whole site and may reach considerable length, corridors in the Western sense, i.e., as mere means of circulation, are actually not necessary. Here again, a particular mode of living effected a distinct method of design, which in turn, then, enabled a continuous organic growth of building that could not be so simply achieved under the different conditions of Western living and building.

The same factors actually also allow the steplike dislocation of adjoining rooms because there are no corridors to demand a linear lineup of adjoining rooms. This steplike pattern is used as long as the site permits and is very much liked because it also affords the opportunity of seeing the outside of one's own house from the inside. This no doubt was a factor that in many cases determined the layout of more extensive houses. But of more architectural importance is the fact that it creates exterior spaces each attached to and marked by two perpendicular outside walls.

This disposition, then, is characteristic of Japanese design: addition of individual spaces with equal value, without particular spatial accentuation, culmination, or

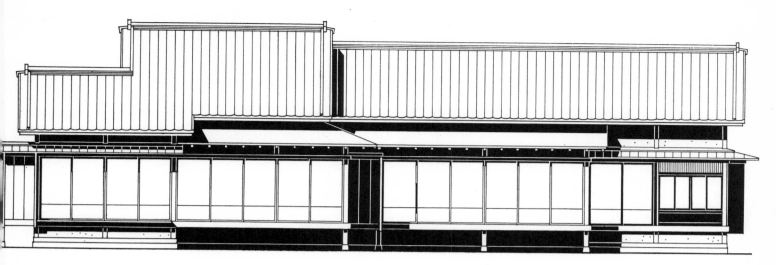

south elevation

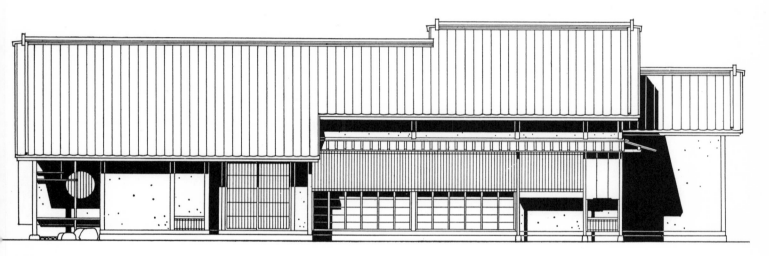

north elevation

9 one-family residence
designed for 8-9 persons

scale 1:100   east elevation

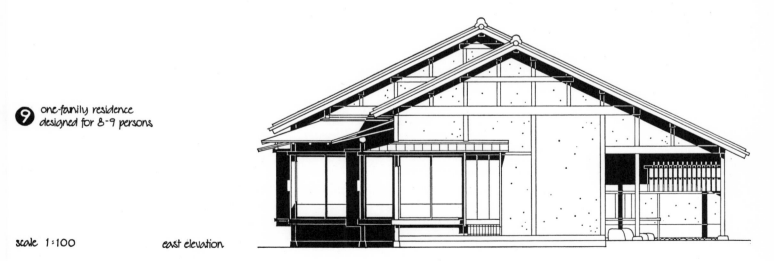

FIGURE 16 (continued): Select examples of typical residences.

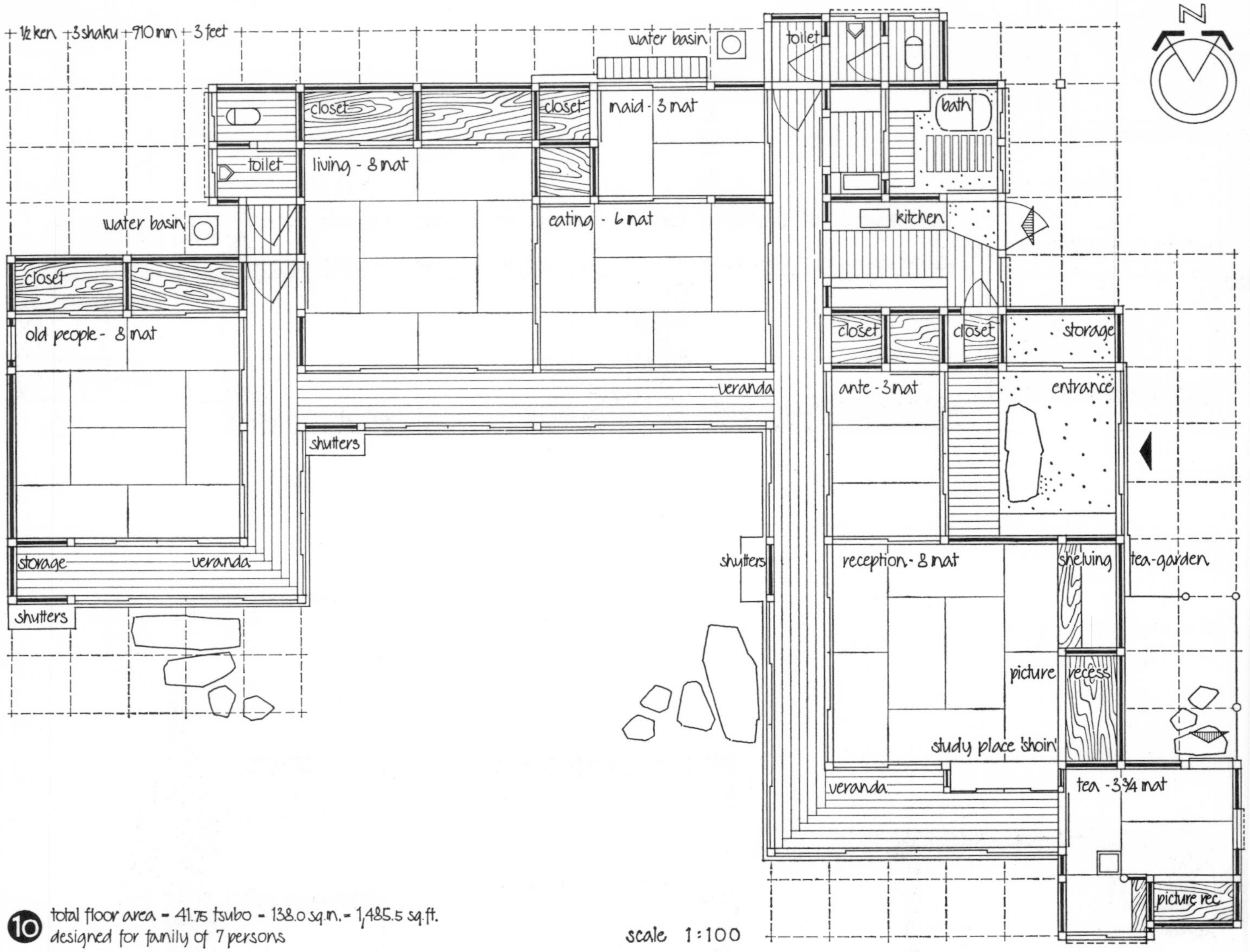

½ ken - 3 shaku - 910 mm - 3 feet
water basin
toilet
closet
closet
maid - 3 mat
bath
toilet
living - 8 mat
water basin
eating - 6 mat
kitchen
closet
old people - 8 mat
closet
closet
storage
veranda
ante - 3 mat
entrance
shutters
shutters
reception - 8 mat
shelving
tea-garden
storage
veranda
shutters
picture
recess
study place 'shoin'
veranda
tea - 3¾ mat
picture rec.
10
total floor area - 41.75 tsubo - 138.0 sq.m. - 1,485.5 sq.ft.
designed for family of 7 persons
scale 1:100

FIGURE 16 (continued): Select examples of typical residences.

finality. Space units, though distinct in themselves, are design-wise not graded into major and minor or into exterior and interior. Rather, the space-marking elements enclose both indoor and outdoor spaces, resulting in a sequence of crisply defined spaces, so different from both the rigid indoor-outdoor separation of traditional Western architecture and the amorphous dissolution of house-garden distinction in contemporary residential architecture.

superstition

The layout and orientation of the house plan, however, is not entirely done on the basis of practical and logical considerations. Even at the present time, the client usually insists on observance of certain rules in the design that would guarantee the help of the good spirits and would not provoke the antagonism of the evil ones.

Although the carpenter, as architect and builder, usually is familiar with the basics of these rules, the wise man would not take any chances, but would have the plan checked by an expert in this mystic art, by a professional soothsayer, so that the orientation of rooms, the location of important features of the house, and the organization of the total site would not be in contrast to the mysterious instructions handed down from the past.

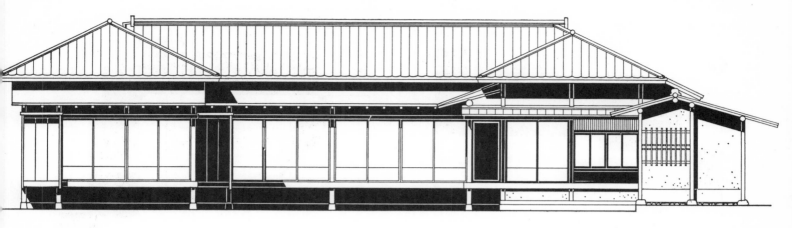

south elevation

scale 1:100

⑩ one-family residence designed for 7 persons

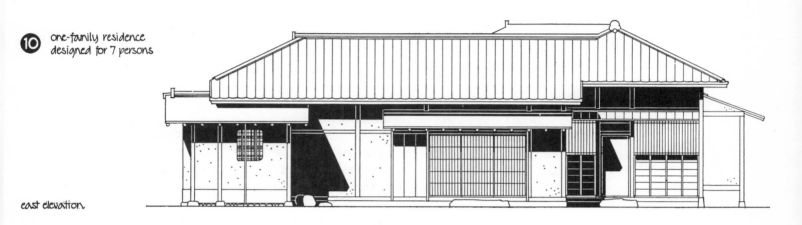

east elevation

north elevation

FIGURE 16 (continued): Select examples of typical residences.

A compass rose serves as a reference pattern. It is divided into eight major parts corresponding to north, northeast, east, south, southeast, etc.

North	*kan:*	unhappiness (danger)	
Northeast	*gon:*	limitation (stay)	"gate of demon"
East	*shin:*	fear (thunder)	
Southeast	*son:*	modesty	"gate of wind"

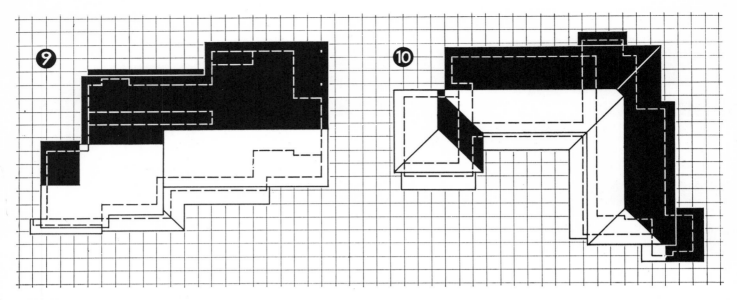

roof plans of designs 9 and 10   scale 1:250

FIGURE 16 (continued): Select examples of typical residences.

South	*ri:*	departure (separation)	
Southwest	*kon:*	obedience (female, earth)	"gate of man"
West	*da:*	joy (pleasure)	
Northwest	*ken:*	heaven (lord, emperor, male)	"gate of heaven"

The intervals between these eight major sectors have each two sectors with names of animals, thus all adding up to twenty-four sectors.

There is no single way of applying this compass rose to the floor plan. The general idea is to superimpose the rose and check the locations of rooms and house features with regard to the meaning implied by the symbols of the rose and elaborated in written instructions that are the basis for the interpretation of the symbols. Usually the rose is centered on the house, but sometimes it is placed on the center of the site. At other times it may be placed on the living room of the head of the house or on the sacred center pillar, *daikoku-bashira*. Also, the interpretation of the various symbols with regard to rooms, house features, and site may differ slightly from case to case, but there is fair unanimity regarding the major implications of the mystic meaning of the rose and its instructions.

The northeast-southwest axis with "gate of demon" and "gate of man" as opposites seems to be given prime attention. Toilet or dirt in this axis will bring diseases and misfortune to the inhabitants as will a gate or a storehouse. A firestead in northeast will cause infantile diseases and an extension of the homestead in this direction will bring outright destruction. However, a garden hill in northeast is likely to ward off all the demons and will guarantee good luck, while a well in southwest will assure nothing less than continuous wealth for everyone in the family.

Other instructions concern the configuration of the total floor plan, i.e., the major projections and recesses of the house. Naturally, a simple rectangular plan without such projections or recesses will not be affected by these instructions.

SIDE OF PROJECTION: IMPLICATIONS		SIDE OF RECESS: IMPLICATIONS	
N:	(no mention)	N:	(no mention)
NE:	(no mention)	NE:	(no mention)
E:	favor of superiors, luck	E:	hindrance to fulfillment of hopes
SE:	prosperity in business, assurance of peace	SE:	bad luck
S:	no harm	S:	first wealth, later ruin

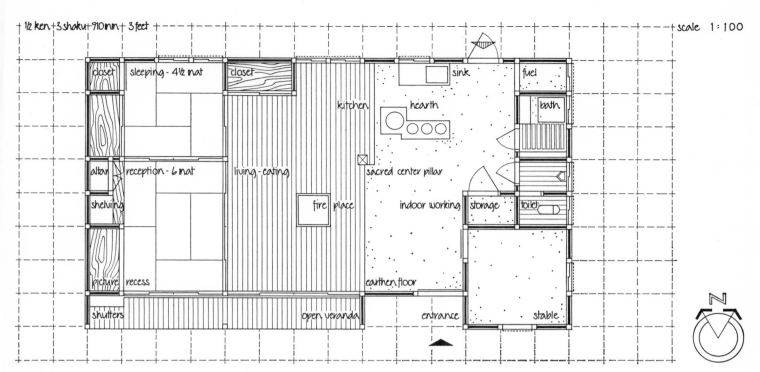

1 floor plan of typical farm house
area with flooring 16.00 tsubo = 52.88 sq.m. = 569.3 sq.ft.   area without flooring 11.25 tsubo = 37.2 sq.m. = 400.3 sq.ft.

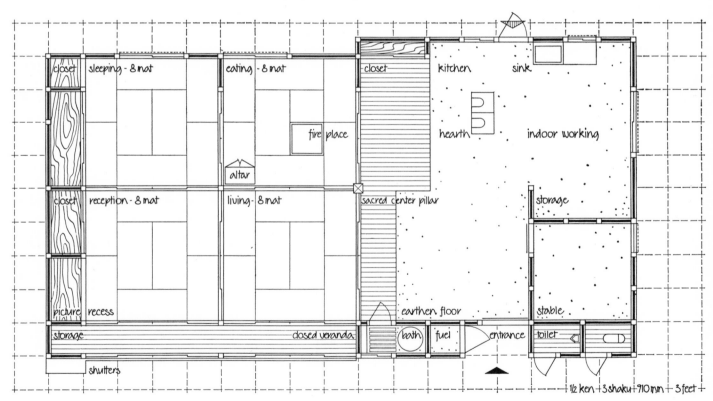

2 floor plan of typical farm house
area with flooring 23.75 tsubo = 78.5 sq.m. = 845.0 sq.ft.   area without flooring 15.5 tsubo = 51.2 sq.m. = 551.5 sq.ft.   scale 1:100

FIGURE 17: Select examples of typical farmhouses.

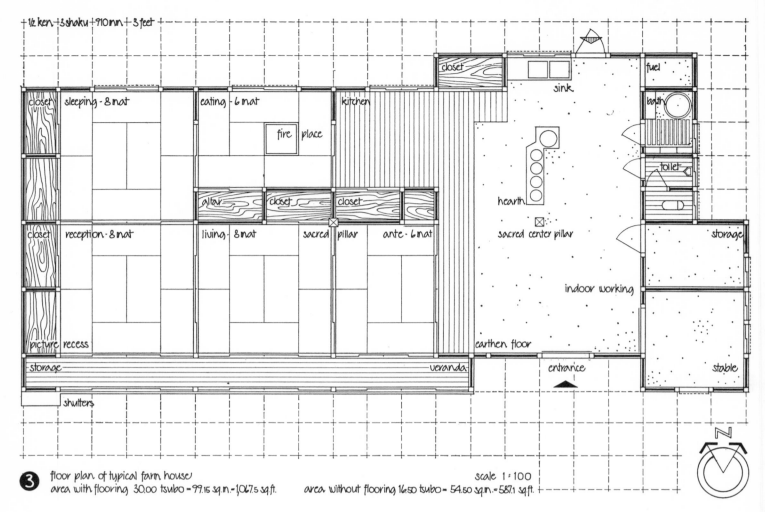

½ ken = 3 shaku = 910mm = 3 feet

closet | sleeping - 8 mat | eating - 6 mat | kitchen | closet | sink | fuel

fire | place | bath

altar | closet | closet | toilet

closet | reception - 8 mat | living - 8 mat | sacred | pillar | ante - 6 mat | hearth | storage

sacred center pillar

picture | recess | indoor working

storage | veranda | earthen floor | entrance | stable

shutters | N

③ floor plan of typical farm house
area with flooring 30.00 tsubo = 99.15 sq.m. = 1,067.5 sq.ft.

scale 1:100

area without flooring 16.50 tsubo = 54.50 sq.m. = 587.1 sq.ft.

FIGURE 17 (continued): Select examples of typical farmhouses.

SW:	predominance of feminine power, early death of master	SW:	(no mention)
W:	bad luck	W:	prosperity, tenderness of heart
NW:	success in business	NW:	(no mention)

In addition, these instructions specify good and bad locations for wells, Buddha altar, god shelf, toilet, kitchen, and doors. They also concern the garden layout, the appropriate location for rocks and waters, and the arrangement of gates. They may even determine succession of rooms, number and arrangement of mats, and location of the hearth.

Considering the strange interweaving of practical and mystical implications, it seems certain that these rules had come from China. In a land in which directions of winds and water courses are distinct and the climate fairly uniform, and in which the practical always was interlocked with the mystical, it was quite reasonable to set up practical rules for adjusting the house design to the prevailing climate and to lend force to those rules by linking them with consequences of both material and spiritual nature. It is very likely that Japan adopted these rules developed in China, some of which also apply to Japanese conditions. But among them there were certainly many that needed to be adjusted for Japanese application, and it is possible that in doing so a number of inconsistencies entered the formerly unique compass guide for the house layout.

Since the general observance of these rules is less due to an acknowledgment of their reasonableness than to fear of the unknown and to belief in magic, the rules must properly be called superstitious. On the other hand, although the instructions

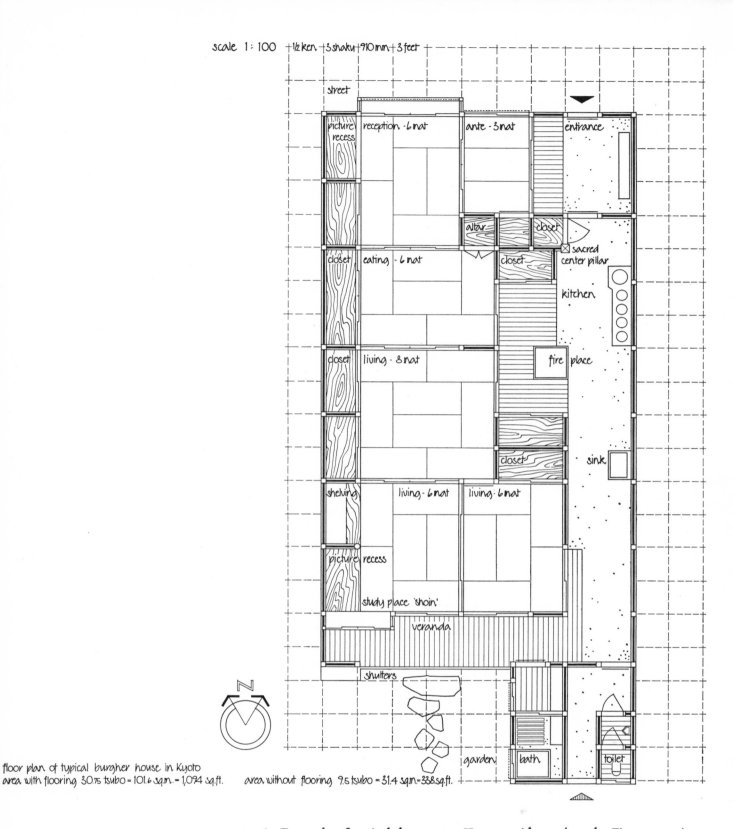

scale 1:100 ⊢½ ken⊣3 shaku⊦910 mm⊦3 feet⊣

street

picture recess
reception · 6 mat
ante · 3 mat
entrance

altar
closet
sacred center pillar

closet
eating · 6 mat
closet
kitchen

closet
living · 8 mat
fire place

closet
sink

shelving
living · 6 mat
living · 6 mat

picture recess

study place 'shoin'
veranda

shutters
garden
bath
toilet

N

floor plan of typical burgher house in Kyoto area with flooring 30.75 tsubo = 101.6 sq.m. = 1,094 sq.ft.   area without flooring 9.5 tsubo = 31.4 sq.m. = 338 sq.ft.

FIGURE 18: Example of typical downtown Kyoto residence (*see also* Figure 59–3).

contain gross and inexplicable contradictions and may obstruct the exploitation of a good design idea, there are many of them that do make sense, especially with regard to the climate. The climatic implication is also evident in the dependence of these rules on the cardinal points of the compass, and, indeed, if considered from the viewpoint of sun exposure, wind direction, bad weatherside, etc., the rules seem to be quite reasonable and helpful.

Thus, it rightly can be assumed that the basis of these superstitious rules is the concern with the health of the inhabitants. Their purpose is to give the "designers" of the house a handy rule of thumb, the observance of which would avoid errors in design; and the carpenter manuals suggest that in designing a house, though one need not strictly follow these rules, one should by no means ignore them.

for contemporary architecture

What distinguishes the design method of the Japanese house, then, is the plain fact that there does exist a distinct technique of design for residences. The history of Western architecture can hardly claim to have produced a distinct order of residential design such as the Japanese—an order primarily concerned with the houses of the common classes, an order universally applied, an order encompassing both system and detail. It is true that contemporary architecture also employs modular design methods in compliance with standardized building components. But, not only are these techniques employed in a comparatively small portion of cases, but they are also often applied without understanding the full impact that mere method of design can have upon architectural expression.

An often-heard definition is that modular design technique would be "but" a tool in the hand of the designer—an interpretation, however, that is used more as an excuse for the many deviations from the module whenever problems arise. No doubt modular design is an obstacle rather than a help, even to the versed architect if he is still unexperienced in those techniques; and it takes a long period of consistent practice to gain the mastership necessary to make the modular grid a truly creative instrument. Indeed, no tool of any form can be used efficiently without the experience gained by long practice; and in this sense, modular design does constitute a real "tool" after all.

Such supreme mastership has been achieved by the Japanese carpenter because of his simultaneous control of both material production and building construction. It is rooted in his comprehensive knowledge of the triad of manufacturing, designing, and building, which in fact are but different phases of the same creative process, one requiring the others to become meaningful. It qualifies him to use modular design as a "tool," it enables him to employ the modular grid creatively, and it permits him to deviate from it when better judgment, and not compelling circumstance, so dictates.

Such integrity of design method in Japanese building has a direct meaning for contemporary architecture, where the increasing complexity and specialization in all fields of architecture, has irrevocably separated the formerly integral activities of manufacturing, designing, and building. For, whereas both the manufacture of components and the procedure of construction have largely been adapted to the efficient methods of the mechanical age, the decisive link between the two, design (which in fact gives meaning to both), has remained unaffected and still works with the same techniques, tools, and terms that were established when handicraft controlled the manufacture and erection of building. Not the breakdown of a unique architectural creation into specialized functions, but the increasing lag of design methods behind the "adjacent" activities of manufacture and construction, is the dilemma in contemporary architecture. It has caused the manufacture of building materials to go largely its own way, while development of efficient building methods has often been held back. Thus, design, being alienated from the factors that gave it its birthright, has become a separate and oftentimes unrealistic activity, with which the influence of the architect has waned.

These dire consequences unmistakably affirm the necessity of employing design methods that work on the same terms as manufacture and building construction: a modular coordination. Especially in the present industrial civilization, where the material potential is represented by mass-productive machine craft and not by flexible handicraft, modular technique of design is the only appropriate method for linking together all phases of building. Through such an adaptation of design technique to the facts of the mechanical age, the present gap between design and manufacture and between design and building construction can be narrowed to such a degree that it may re-establish the stimulating role of design and reinstall the influence of the architect in all matters of building.

Japanese residential design also very clearly disproves the commonly held opinion that modular coordination limits the free and creative design of a single building. Actually, the opposite is true, for it is the modular grid that assures the Japanese carpenter that each move along the grid lines during the process of design is within material possibility, grants economical usage of prefabricated parts, affords adequate functional space, is constructionally feasible, and, above all, results in harmonious relationships of form and proportion and maintains aesthetic unity. Thus, residential design has been truly liberated from the many stifling and merely practical difficulties and has become a matter of spatial organization and material composition.

Again, the significance for contemporary architecture is obvious. In a building industry that produces infinite types and forms of material, and with a technology that actually does not know any limitations, the modular design technique is a helpful restraint. Even more important, since that same industry and technology is producing larger and larger elements with an ever increasing precision and since those components cannot be adapted to individualistic designs, only modular coordination can integrate the two initial phases of building, manufacture and design, in a meaningful way.

However, the acceptance of these modular design methods as sacrosanct rules by the Japanese carpenters, as much as it accounts for the outstanding refinement of architectural form and for the efficiency of architectural work, was a circumstance that finally arrested all progressive tendency. This defective result of Japanese modular coordination leaves no doubt that in standardized building there is a distinct temptation to accept existing standards as finite, an attitude that hinders the rise and spread of new ideas and methods. To counteract such a trend, it is evident that a major and very important part of design effort must be directed toward the control and development of standards, be they of form, material, space, type, or design method itself.

Here, the consequences of the Japanese carpenter's failure to keep standards alive show the deficiency of the contemporary architect, who is either indifferent or is simply unwilling to concern himself with the new area of architectural design— development of component units. Doubtless, the major responsibility of the architect in the industrial society is no longer the design of individual buildings. It is true the progressive idea of one building might possibly spark a distinct architectural language, but the expression of most buildings is increasingly determined by the individual elements as provided by the industry. Therefore, one major part of creative design efforts needs to be focused on the component media of building, i.e., on the development of individual building components. As long as these remain neglected by the architect, even the best design will fail to establish unity in building.

And, finally, the Japanese design technique has shown that even the technique of design per se directly influences the physical appearance of building just as the media of communication always have bearing upon the content of the message itself. (Indeed, the decimal structure of numbers or the character of a national language has influenced human thought and action to an extent that men are hardly aware of.) The intimate relationship between design technique and architectural form is evidenced by the fact that the architect can only conceive and build what he is actually able to draw, to describe, or to mold with his own hands, i.e., the conceiving of architectural form presupposes the ability of delineating or substantiating this form, a physical talent that most likely is also the hidden source of what is vaguely termed "imagination" and "intuition."

Thus, the multiform creations of prior architectures were not the abstract imaginations of designers, but were conceived by men who were well qualified to execute those forms in practice. However, the contemporary architect can no longer rely on his direct experience with innumerable materials and, hence, probably without being aware of it, derives his architectural forms from those shapes he is able to achieve with his design technique and tools. Thus, it is by no means a mere coincidence that contemporary architectural form is predominantly composed of straight lines, rectangular planes, square cubes, or geometric forms as a whole, because such is the result when triangles, T-square, and compass are used. Evidently, the imagination of the architect for form is no longer stirred through experience in the workshop or at the job site but rather by experience on the drafting board. That is to say, the expression of contemporary building is closely linked with the mere practical-technical aspect of draftsmanship.

The modular design technique of the Japanese house, though employing but rectangles as geometric forms, indicates that geometric drawing, in addition to its aesthetic meaning, stands in direct affinity to structural principles. This is confirmed by the fact that contemporary design preferably employs constructional principles of spheric dome, paraboloid, hyperboloid, elliptoid, cylinder, etc. And still it may be open to question whether those forms were actually developed because of their superior constructional potential, or whether they had been structurally examined because those were the only forms that could be precisely measured, precisely drawn, and therefore conceived at all. To withdraw from the geometric pattern of design requires men with the stature of Le Corbusier, and even then economic restrictions may ask for retreat to geometric design patterns again.

Even more obvious is the influence that design technique exerts upon the functional organization of the architectural plan. It is true the rectangular form is the logical architectural plan-geometry because it allows multiple combinations that then again assume rectangular form. But also, such preference must be closely related with the simplicity of architectural drafting. Design with irregularly curved shapes is structurally as feasible as that with a rectangular pattern and might even have distinct functional advantages. However, depiction would be much more difficult and inaccurate and therefore would complicate the calculation and construction of building and render them uneconomical, without in the end assuring the precise conformity of building with the original design.

Such interrelationship between design technique and interior organism is strikingly evident in the examples of Japanese residential floor plans. Their pictorial-aesthetic quality even suggests that there is also a distinct connection between functional-spatial adequacy of building and the beauty of its abstract representation in plan, just as the floor plan drawing of a spatially ill-organized building will lack the quality of a painting.

Here, relationship between painting and architectural design drawing is intimated, which so far has hardly been examined, since comparisons with painting usually are drawn from the actual building and not its plan. As multiple as all these affiliations and influences of design might be, they constitute probabilities rather than factual proof. The only thing factually proven is that technique of architectural design, the very instrument of the architect's "language," has never been considered a subject for thorough investigation and consequently is not understood as to the influential and often decisive role it performs in architectural creation—another paradox in an age that claims to investigate comprehensively and utilize exhaustively the vehicles of progress.

CHAPTER FOUR construction

definition

CONSTRUCTION IN BUILDING is both the act of building and the structural system, translating into reality what theretofore has been idea, conception, or design. Construction in building, therefore, is a means rather than an end.

CONSTRUCTION IN BUILDING, thus, is the materialization of design. As such it comprehends the total range of factors that condition design—the practical, technical, functional, environmental, and spiritual aspects of architecture.

CONSTRUCTION IN BUILDING demonstrates architectural growth in its transformation and evolution. Architecture began with purposeful construction of human shelter and developed in direct interdependence with technical improvement.

CONSTRUCTION IN BUILDING reflects the level of civilization and thereby gives clues as to the conditioning society and the philosophic background. Thus, construction marks cultural epochs as distinctly as does literature, painting, or music.

CONSTRUCTION IN BUILDING is closely interrelated with form, expression, and sensation of building. Stimulating certain forms and preventing others, it is an element that gives character and substance to architectural space and thus renders architecture distinctive.

CONSTRUCTION IN BUILDING also influences the psyche of man. Influencing architectural form and space, it invites a particular mode of living. Thus, it not only orientates the taste and customs of the inhabitant but also influences the ethics and morals of family and society.

CONSTRUCTION IN BUILDING is dependent on various factors. Utilitarian purpose of building, distinct idea of design, climatic-geological conditions, also traditional methods and thoughts, all decisively influence construction in building.

CONSTRUCTION IN BUILDING, then, is an essential element in both building process and building structure. Though it is not architecture itself, yet, it is the decisively formative medium in the earliest shelter as well as in contemporary building.

Not only has the system and form of construction undergone essential changes throughout the ages, but the proportional contribution of construction in the ensemble of architectural factors has been a subject of widely different interpretations. Some epochs unconditionally subjugated construction to spatial ideas, while others indiscriminately adopted the form dictated by construction. Such extreme and opposing conceptions also characterize contemporary architectural work. After the period of eclecticism in the 19th century, characterized by an alienation of architectural form from construction, contemporary architecture obviously tends toward constructivism. Under the watchword "structural integrity" construction is ostentatiously displayed and architectural idea often is no longer primary conception but mere constructional result.

In the light of such extreme tendencies, an analysis of the role of construction in the Japanese dwelling should be attributed more importance than that of mere record, because Japanese residential architecture throughout its evolution has preserved a unique balance between form, space, and construction. Indeed, construction in the

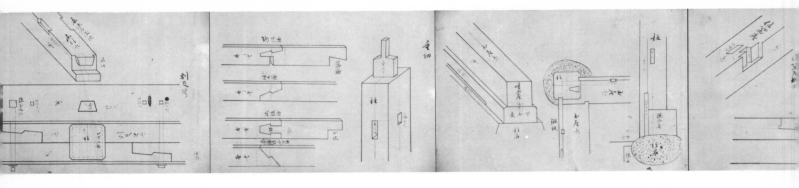

Japanese house is an essential component of space, as well as the major source of form. Architectural accentuation is attained mainly through constructional means, and architectural décor is derived from constructional device.

Although for an assessment of the structural qualities of the Japanese house it should suffice to analyze only the overall system of construction, a study of constructional detail is also required in order to gain that broad understanding which alone can become the basis for a substantial evaluation. Studying the details of one house without forsaking their general validity for the total domestic architecture of Japan is possible only because all constructional features are employed uniformly throughout the nation. In fact, with the description of a single house, the entire residential architecture of Japan is covered, both in system and detail, a unique phenomenon in the history of architecture.

But it is both unnecessary and impossible to describe every constructional detail and its variations. Basically, they are the same all over Japan. However, local differences, especially climatic adaptations, even carpenters' personal preferences, have emerged. Moreover, Western methods have effected modifications through use of metal. The original construction, however, that is to say, the classic performance (the subject matter of this book), was constructionally free of any metal support or joinery.

Such general application was possible only because of the particular order of the feudalistic society. Constructional procedure, dimension, and detail were written down on paper scrolls and kept by the master carpenter. As the profession was hereditary, the scripts were handed down from father to son. In the Tokugawa period (1600–1867) they were woodblock printed and thus provided an exchange of new methods as well as universal dispersion (Plates 8–9). The measurements as they appear in these rules are not absolute, but are moduled by column distance and column

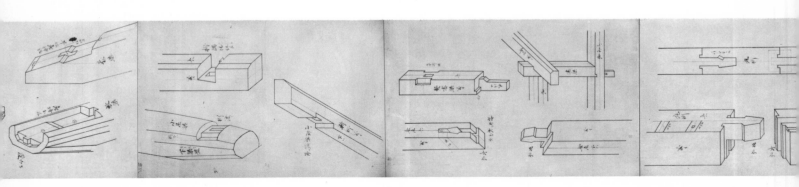

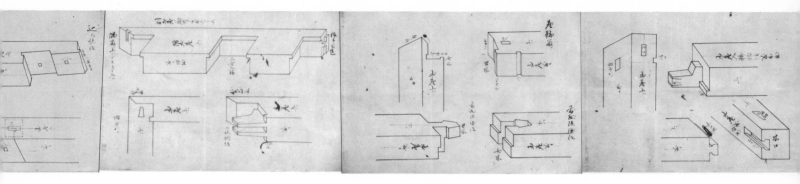

FIGURE 19: Carpenter's scroll (right to left). The scroll, reproduced
in total, depicts construction details for residential building.

section. Since both are standardized, measurements of constructional detail for
residences have become fairly fixed.

In describing constructional detail, this book employs the same depictive methods
as those that appear in the traditional carpenter manuals, for there is hardly another
method so simply executed and so easily comprehended as is the illustrative technique
of the Japanese carpenter.

This analysis, then, with a short description of historic precedence and architectural
evolution, is intended to.provide a scale for better judgment of contemporary affairs.
It should also shed light on the role of construction in the creation of architecture,
which is so much disputed and so much abused in contemporary building.

process

The construction of the Japanese house, both the act and the system, albeit very
refined in detail, has in fact never quite left its original primitive stage. When, during
the first and second centuries, dwellings with elevated floor, *taka-yuka,* first appeared,
Japanese residential architecture not only found one of its distinct constructional-
organizational features, but also made its first and last, though major, technical
achievement (Plates 113–114). All fundamental constructional distinctions of the
Japanese residence already existed in the *taka-yuka* and no essential change took place
thereafter.

While in the constructional system of the earliest "house," the pit dwelling,
tate-ana, the slanting rafters rose directly from the ground and were themselves the
major members forming both the framework and roof, in the system of the dwelling
with elevated floor, *taka-yuka,* the vertical columns became the major supporting
members (Plates 108–112). The resistant qualities of this house, however, were
less than adequate in bearing horizontal stresses provoked by seasonal typhoons and

FIGURE 19 (continued): Carpenter's scroll (right to left).

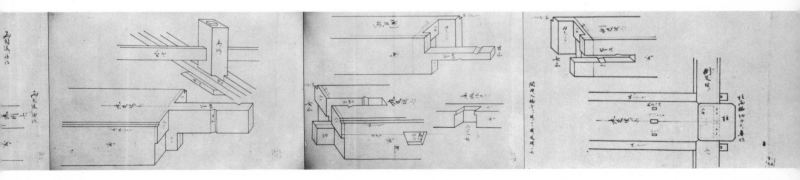

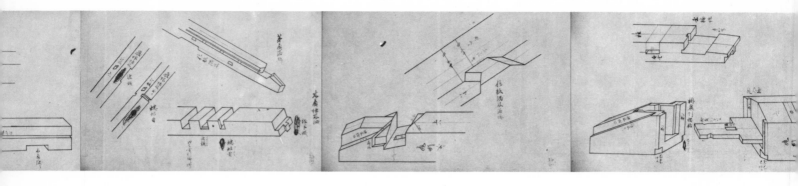

frequent earthquakes, and in this regard were also inferior to the original pit dwelling construction.

This constructional deficiency of the prototype of the Japanese house has given rise to many a speculation as to the underlying reasons. The most simple, though least convincing, explanation is that the diagonal members of construction were distasteful to the Japanese sense of form. Yet, the foregoing study does not convey the slightest clue that such a visual-sensational concept had ever been instrumental in the formation of architectural features, but rather proves the contrary, a distinct disregard of form. Also, in the case of construction, it seems improbable that during the feudalistic society, when the mass of people hardly had enough to sustain themselves, man would concern himself with formalistic ideas, and even less would intentionally sacrifice security, durability, and economy for a visual effect. This seems all the more certain because, after introduction of the suspended ceiling, diagonal members in the roof construction would have been no longer visible. Moreover, with regard to the wall framework, the carpenter already knew very well how to conceal the constructional members in the upright framework. Instead, all evidence shows that obstacles such as arresting restrictions of the rulers, minute standardization of methods, traditional attitude of the guilds, submissive teaching of Buddhism, stagnating influence of Confucianism, and also, no doubt, historic lack of inventiveness proved to be too strong to overcome.

And it is no contradiction to the aforesaid that in detail Japanese construction displays high elaborateness and a refinement that has reached perfection in method, economy, and form. For constructional detail was the only architectural sphere that neither could be controlled by man or law nor required innate inventiveness for improvement. Indeed, it appears that the very reason for Japan's famous refinement in constructional detail was the immutability of the basic constructional system which

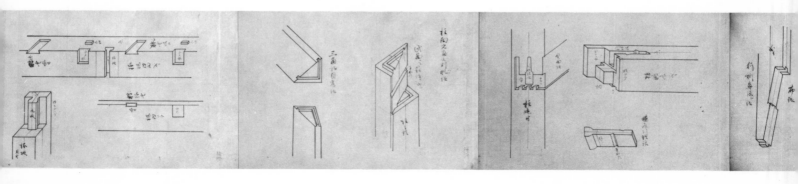

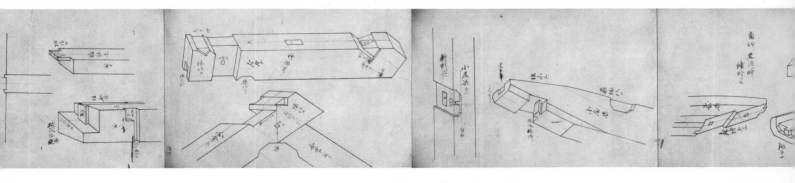

FIGURE 19 (continued): Carpenter's scroll (right to left).

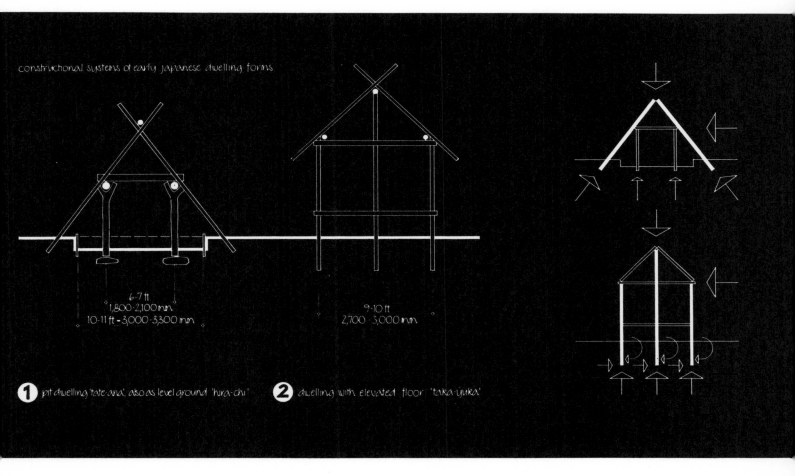

constructional systems of early japanese dwelling forms

6-7 ft
1,800-2,100 mm
10-11 ft = 3,000-3,300 mm

9-10 ft
2,700-3,000 mm

1 pit dwelling 'tate-ana', also as level ground 'hira-chi'   **2** dwelling with elevated floor 'taka-yuka'

FIGURE 20: Constructional systems of early Japanese dwellings.

FIGURE 19 (continued): Carpenter's scroll (right to left).

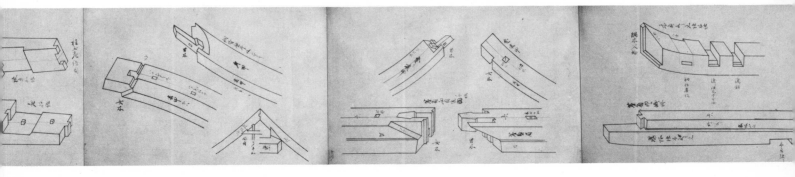

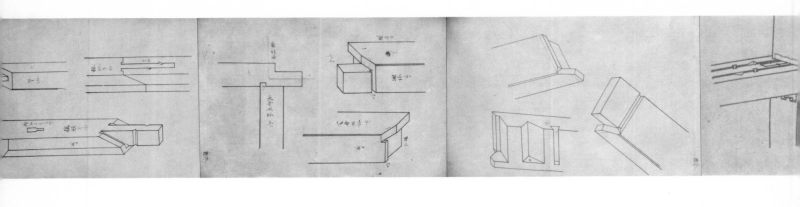

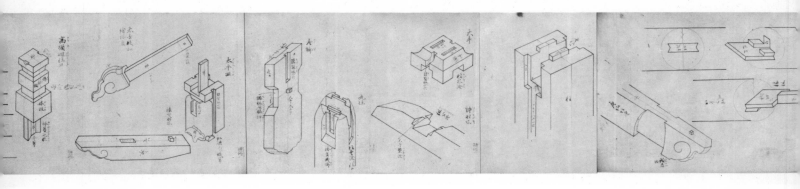

End of carpenter's scroll.

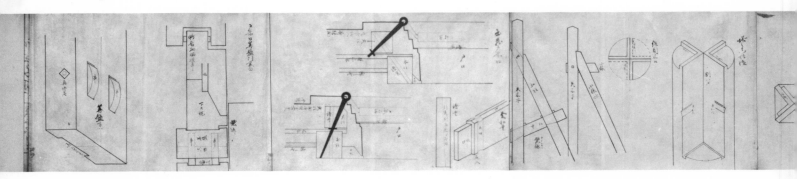

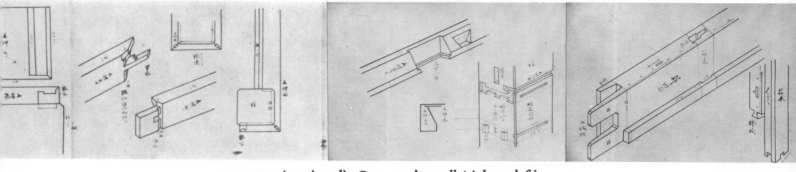

FIGURE 19 (continued): Carpenter's scroll (right to left).

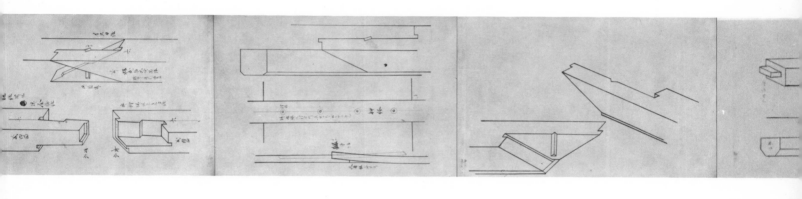

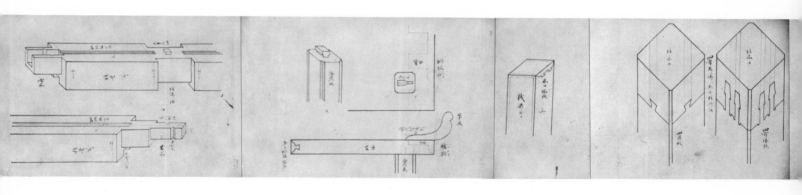

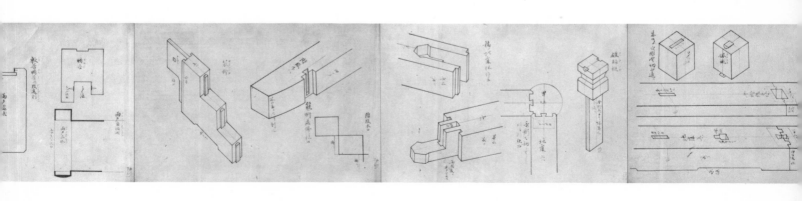

directed the handicraftsman's imaginative spirit to detail and provided centuries for gradual empirical improvement. While primitiveness of structural system might at first sight appear contradictory to the refinement of constructional detail, it becomes evident that one was only the logical consequence of the other.

Because the structure is a simple post-beam framework without any braces or struts, the wall planes in between those structural members support only themselves and do not require foundations. Only at places of actual structural supports, i.e., at columns, is the groundsill provided with a simple foundation of natural or hewn stone that raises the whole wooden framework above the damp ground. In present construction concrete has largely replaced slab stone.

The upright members, *hashira,* are erected upon the groundsill's frame in standard distances and connected to each other by horizontal tie members. Simultaneously, the floor beam, *ashigatame,* is set in and the top is then held together by eaves beams, thus completing the upright framework which, except for elaborateness of joint detail, lacks any constructional stability.

This primitiveness is more obvious in the roof construction. Heavy and untreated logs are simply dropped from eaves beam to center beam, and at their joint in the middle are hardly more than just laid upon each other. Preference for entire trunks, roughly hewn with archlike shape to gain some additional strength, stresses this primeval character. Upon these transverse beams, posts are erected and onto them purlins and rafters are finally laid. Part is put onto part, member upon member, a system of horizontals and verticals capable only of sustaining vertical pressure and possessing nothing to resist horizontal stress other than its own weight (Plates 15–18). Until the advent of Western methods, diagonal ties or struts were not used, or, if known of at all, certainly their structural value in saving material and granting firmness and durability was not realized.

Yet, this form of setting up the framework is surprisingly fast. As the components have previously been dressed, the assemblage itself takes but a few days (Plates 21–23). With hardly more accomplished than what appears to be circumscription of space by fragile timbers, the roof will already be covered and heavily loaded with tiles that are traditionally inbedded in clay or, as is often done today, laid upon latticework. The roof, then, is the first component of the Japanese residence to be completed in the construction process, and it appears as if the preceding work is primarily orientated to achieve that aim in the quickest way possible. Once material and man is protected against the frequent rains, the carpenter can continue his work with more ease and leisure.

This change of pace seems to be almost symbolic of the distinct difference in constructional quality, for the succeeding work displays high elaborateness, structural sense, and sophisticated refinement to a degree comparable to a cabinetmaker's sensitive exactness. Floor boards are laid upon a sleeper-joint construction which is elevated on posts perching on foundation stones; at the top and bottom wooden tracks for sliding panels are fixed between the uprights; the ceiling is suspended from the beams above; clay mixed with chopped straw is applied on both sides of the latticework between the uprights to form the wall; interior elements are minutely joined and set in; and finally the Japanese residence's most unique ingredient, the floor mat, *tatami,* is laid.

Constructional work is done entirely by the master carpenter and his assistants. Yet, the mats, sliding panels, and other interior elements in more recent times are frequently manufactured at different places due to the specialization of trades. While in the West the specialization of the building industry has alienated the architect from many fields in building, in Japan the master carpenter, owing to standardization and limitation of architectural work, still fully masters and controls every phase of residential construction.

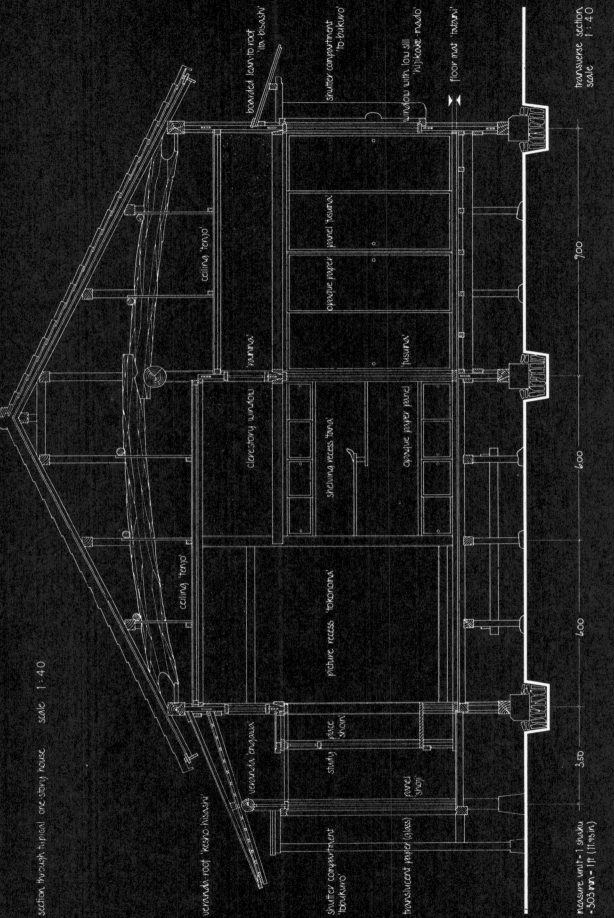

section through typical one-story house   scale 1:40

braided lean-to roof "ita-bisashi"

shutter compartment "to-bukuro"

window with low sill "hijikake-mado"

floor mat "tatami"

ceiling "tenjo"

opaque paper panel "fusuma"

clerestory window "ranma"

shelving recess "tana"

opaque paper panel "fusuma"

picture recess "tokonoma"

ceiling "tenjo"

veranda-roof "kesho-hisashi"

veranda engawa

study place "shoin"

shutter compartment "to-bukuro"

translucent paper (glass)

panel "shoji"

transverse section
scale 1:40

900

600

600

3.50

measure unit = 1 shaku
= 303 mm = 1ft (11.93 in.)

FIGURE 2I: Section of typical one-story residence.

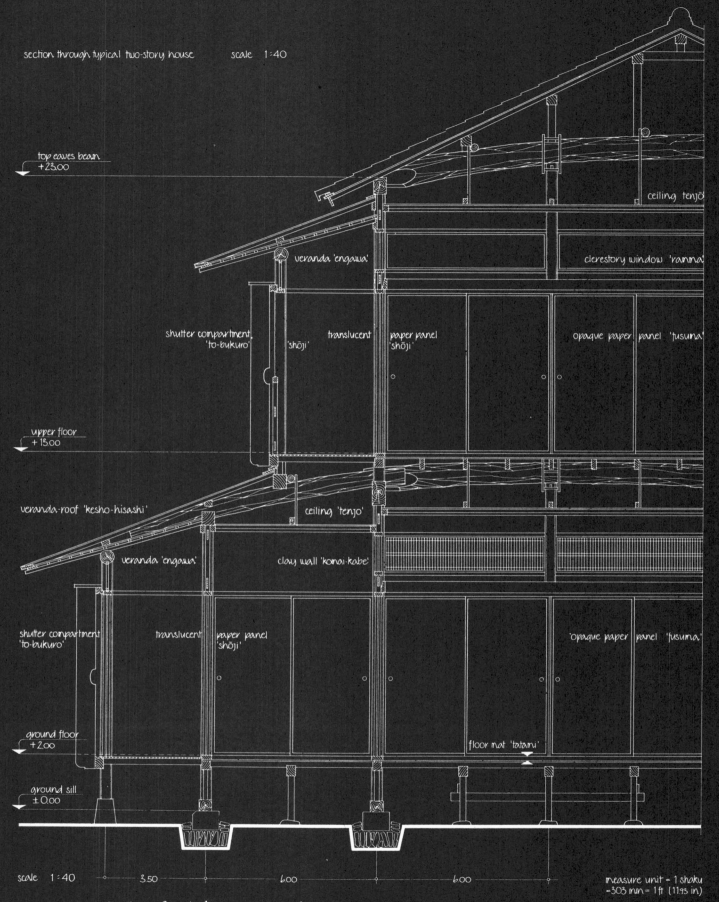

section through typical two-story house   scale   1:40

top eaves beam
+23.00

ceiling tenjō

veranda 'engawa'

clerestory window 'ranma'

shutter compartment   'shōji'   translucent   paper panel   opaque paper panel 'fusuma'
'to-bukuro'   'shōji'

upper floor
+ 15.00

veranda-roof 'kesho-hisashi'   ceiling 'tenjo'

veranda 'engawa'   clay wall 'komai-kabe'

shutter compartment   translucent   paper panel   'opaque paper panel 'fusuma'
'to-bukuro'   'shōji'

ground floor
+ 2.00   floor mat 'tatami'

ground sill
± 0.00

scale   1:40   3.50   6.00   6.00   measure unit = 1 shaku
                                                                             =303 mm = 1 ft (11.93 in)

FIGURE 22: Section of typical two-story residence.

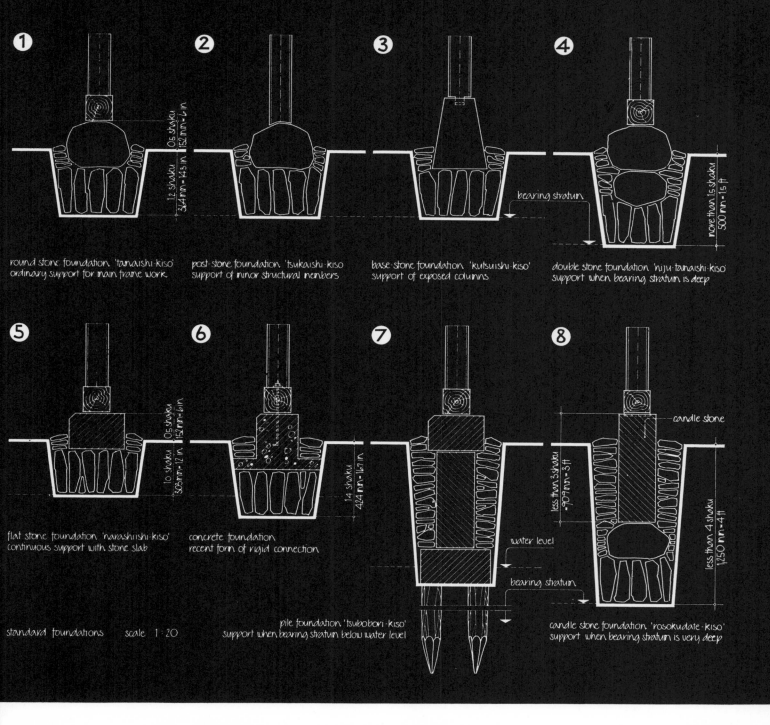

① round stone foundation 'tamaishi-kiso'
ordinary support for main frame work.

② post-stone foundation 'tsukaishi-kiso'
support of minor structural members

③ base-stone foundation 'kutsuishi-kiso'
support of exposed columns

④ double stone foundation 'niju-tamaishi-kiso'
support when bearing stratum is deep

⑤ flat stone foundation 'narashiishi-kiso'
continuous support with stone slab

⑥ concrete foundation
recent form of rigid connection

⑦ pile foundation 'tsubobori-kiso'
support when bearing stratum below water level

⑧ candle stone foundation 'rosokudate-kiso'
support when bearing stratum is very deep

standard foundations   scale 1:20

FIGURE 23: Details of typical foundations.

foundation

If there is some truth in the overemphasized architectural saying that the simplest response to a problem is also its most appropriate solution, then, the foundation of the Japanese house seems to prove such theory. For there is hardly anything as simple and logical as the organization of the foundation. As may be expected, the foundation, both in type and performance, is also standardized and classified as to its particular constructional function and as to the varying ground conditions prevailing. Since there is no basement and the floor is elevated about 2 1/2 feet (750 mm.) above ground level, the sole function of the foundation is to keep the wood parts clear from the usually damp ground, rather than to tie construction solidly to the ground. Further,

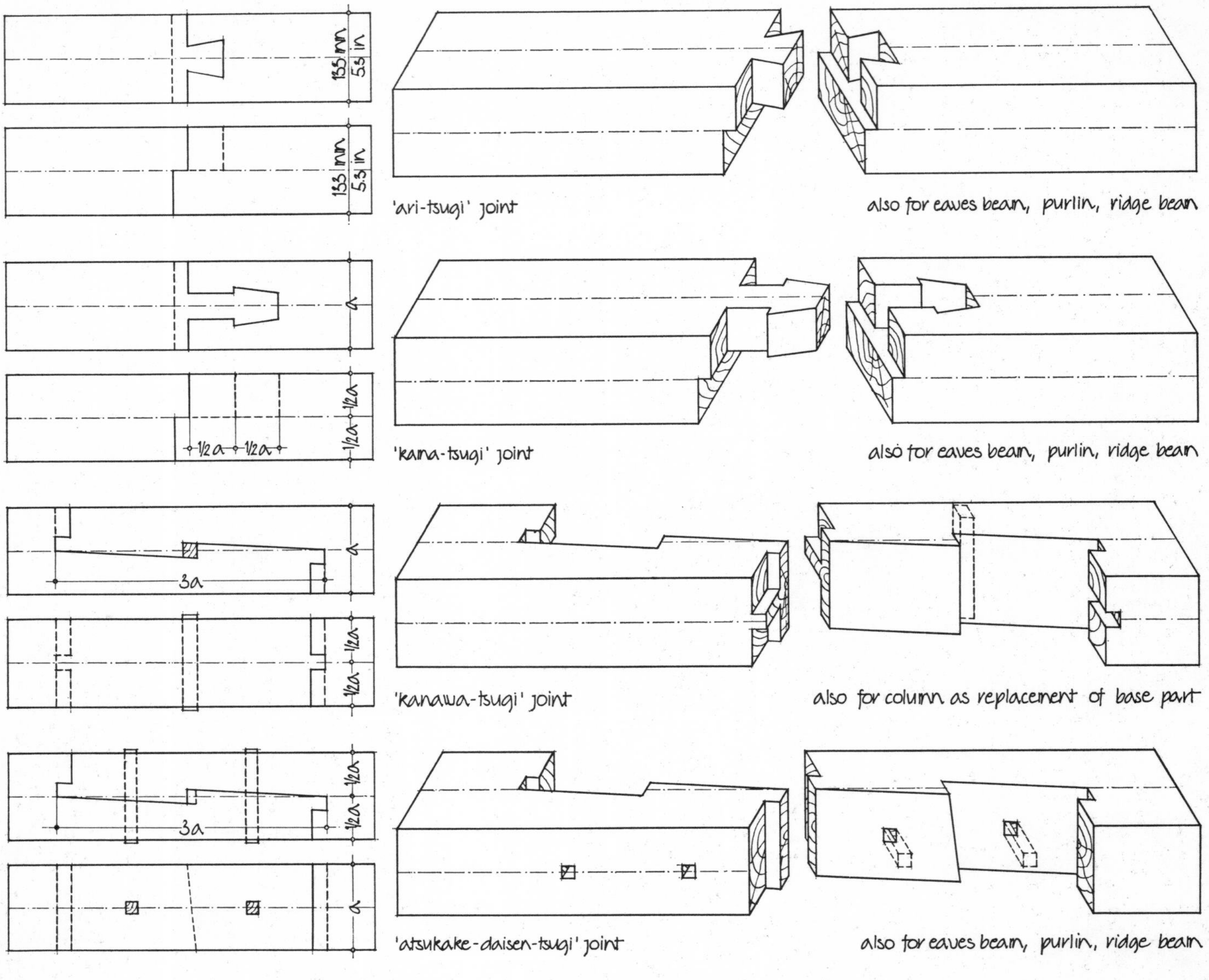

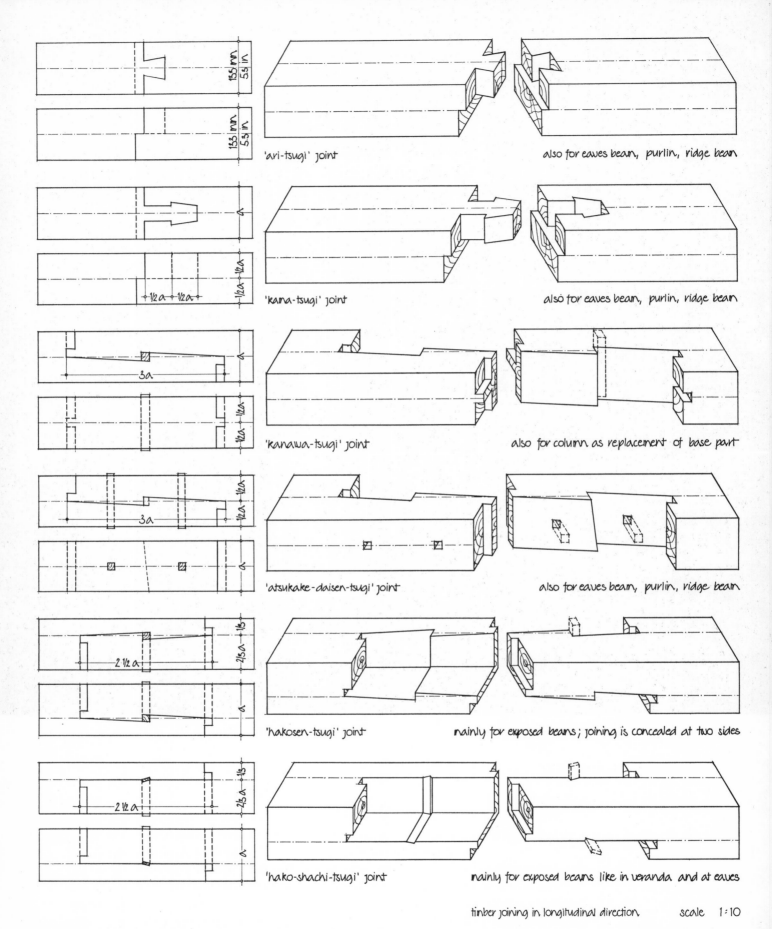

133 mm
5.3 in
133 mm
5.3 in
'ari-tsugi' joint
also for eaves beam, purlin, ridge beam
a
1/2 a
1/2 a
1/2 a
1/2 a
'kama-tsugi' joint
also for eaves beam, purlin, ridge beam
a
3a
1/2 a
1/2 a
'kanawa-tsugi' joint
also for column as replacement of base part
1/2 a
1/2 a
3a
a
'atsukake-daisen-tsugi' joint
also for eaves beam, purlin, ridge beam
1/3
2/3 a
2 1/2 a
a
'hakosen-tsugi' joint
mainly for exposed beams; joining is concealed at two sides
1/3
2/3 a
2 1/2 a
a
'hako-shachi-tsugi' joint
mainly for exposed beams like in veranda and at eaves
timber joining in longitudinal direction
scale 1:10
dimensioning of ground sill 'dodai' according 'kiwari' module: height - width - 1.1 x column section (- 4 sun) - 4.4/4.4 sun - 133/133 mm - 5.25/5.25 in

FIGURE 24: Some standard longitudinal joints.

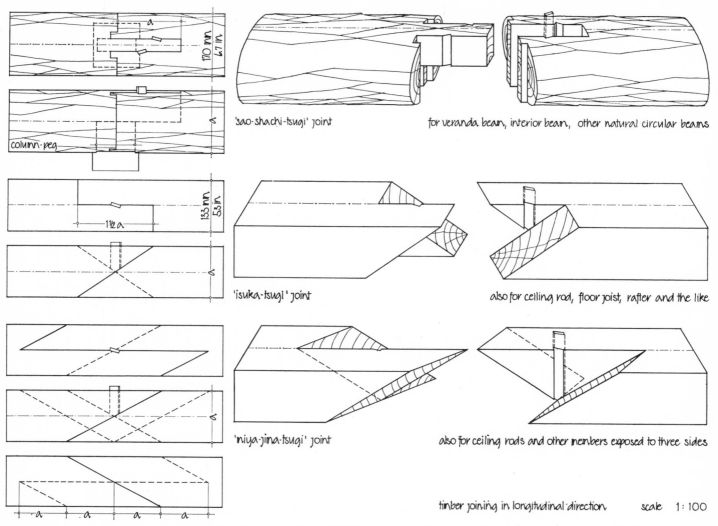

'sao-shachi-tsugi' joint — for veranda beam, interior beam, other natural circular beams

column-peg

'isuka-tsugi' joint — also for ceiling rod, floor joist, rafter and the like

'niya-jina-tsugi' joint — also for ceiling rods and other members exposed to three sides

timber joining in longitudinal direction   scale   1 : 100

dimensioning of veranda beam 'engeta' according 'kiwari' module :   radius = 1.4 (1.5) x column section (~4 sun) = 5.6 (6.0) sun = 170mm (182mm) = 6.7 in (7.2 in)

dimensioning of floor joist 'neda', ceiling rod 'saobuchi', rafter 'taruki' :   height = width = 0.5 x column section (~4 sun = 121 mm = 4.7 in) = 2/2 sun = 60/60 mm = 2.4/2.4 in

FIGURE 24 (continued): Some standard longitudinal joints.

with the wall itself not bearing any weight other than its own, only the structurally bearing members, the columns, are provided with foundations, either directly as in the veranda, porch, or interior, or otherwise via the groundsill.

Thus, the whole structure does not gain any additional stability or firmness from the foundation, but achieves, constructionally, protection of its most important parts and obtains, visually, accentuation of constructional lightness through the egg-shaped stones upon which the column and framework rest. Frequently, in order to prevent not only shelter-seeking animal creatures but also human creatures with less modest intentions from entering all too easily, the foundation facing to the street, or sometimes the entire outside foundation, is closed up by laying a continuous layer of stone slabs, or more recently concrete, underneath the groundsill.

In view of the frequent earthquakes, this loose connection between the foundation stone and framework is doubtlessly very appropriate constructionally, especially for a house with such deficient framework as that of the Japanese. However, the fact that in more recent times the groundsill is tied by strong bolts to the concrete foundation does raise doubt as to whether the Japanese actually were fully aware of the advantage of countering horizontal stress with flexibility rather than rigidity.

wall framework

The appropriateness of using the word "wall" for what vertically encloses space in the Japanese house is generally questioned by scholars, for the wall in the Western sense has in the past achieved the meaning of something solid. On the other hand, contemporary architecture, although attempting to clearly distinguish the wall's supporting elements from its screening elements, as did the Japanese, still uses as a general term "wall," or as specific terms "bearing wall" and "non-bearing wall" (curtain wall), not only for lack of a more appropriate word but also because originally in Western residential architecture wooden structures were based on similar construction principles.

Although the greater portion of the wall's screening members are movable and removable, in the ensemble of space-forming members the solid wall plays an important role, and its functional, proportional, and aesthetical significance is generally underestimated. Not only is the entire section above the upper track for the sliding doors made solid, but there is no house without at least one entire solid clay wall.

The wall framework is composed of conspicuously short members, and joinings of members in longitudinal direction are frequent. The probable reason for this is that wood fabric is floated down small and often shallow rivers from the mountains and is easier to handle in small pieces in the river as well as at the job site (Plates 38–39). The standard details for joinery are multiple. Some are so elaborate that they weaken the timber unduly, while others are striking in their simplicity.

The framing of the wall once more demonstrates primitiveness in system and refinement in detail. Upon the prepared foundation, the groundsill, *dodai,* is leveled and connected at the corners and junctions with standard methods, special joinery being provided for corners, which remain exposed. Then, the columns, *hashira,* are erected at standard distances and connected with each other by five, or as in the case of door openings, two (three) horizontal tie members, *nuki.* The tie members penetrate the column at standardized vertical distances of about 2 feet. Fastened only by wedges, the tie members function to keep the column upright and to sustain the solid wall, but contribute very little to the stability of the framework.

Therefore, in more recent times, under Western influence, diagonal struts are applied at the corners in the vertical plane, the groundsill plane, and the beam plane. These diagonal members are usually covered up, but in the case of the wall framework, they sometimes are left visible to the outside. This clearly contradicts the widespread opinion that the absence of diagonals would be the result of a formalistic taste.

Although the floor beam, *ashigatame,* is inserted into the column simultaneously with the horizontal tie members, constructionally it is an element of floor construction rather than of framework and therefore is mentioned in context with floor. At their top the columns have pegs by which they are joined to the eaves beam, *noki-geta,* interior beam, *keta,* and veranda beam, *en-geta.* As the latter two are usually round logs, the column head is shaped accordingly. In case the column distance exceeds 1 1/2 *ken* (2,727 mm. = 9 ft.), a hanging post, *tsuri-zuka,* is tied to the beams, holding the upper sliding track, *kamoi,* for the paper panels and receiving the horizontal tie members, *nuki,* which sustain the solid wall. Until this stage the framework is called *jiku-bu* (literally, vertical part).

roof

The roof construction of the Japanese house has been the subject of many controversies, less as to its constructional inadequacy, which in fact cannot be disputed, than to the factors that were instrumental in preventing its improvement. Though Western influence has taught the structural merits of triangulation, it did not succeed in replacing the heavy, rough-treated trunks that, albeit delicately joined, are simply laid from eaves beam to center beam and carry the entire roof load, equally distributed on their

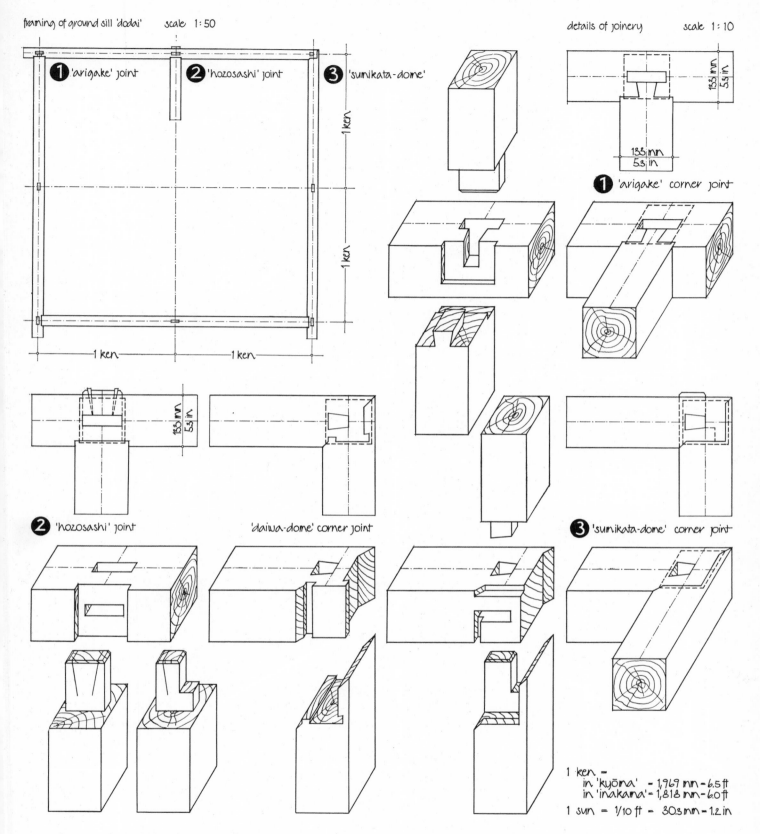

framing of ground sill 'dodai'   scale 1:50

details of joinery   scale 1:10

① 'arigake' joint   ② 'hozosashi' joint   ③ 'sumikata-dome'

1 ken   1 ken   1 ken   1 ken

133 mm 5.3 in

133 mm 5.3 in

① 'arigake' corner joint

133 mm 5.3 in

② 'hozosashi' joint   'daiwa-dome' corner joint   ③ 'sumikata-dome' corner joint

1 ken =
  in 'kyōma' = 1,969 mm = 6.5 ft
  in 'inakama' = 1,818 mm = 6.0 ft

1 sun = 1/10 ft = 30.3 mm = 1.2 in

dimensioning of ground sill 'dodai' according 'kiwari' module: height = width = 1.1 x column section (=4 sun) = 4.4/4.4 sun = 133/133 mm = 5.25/5.25 in

FIGURE 25: Framing of ground sill and joint details.

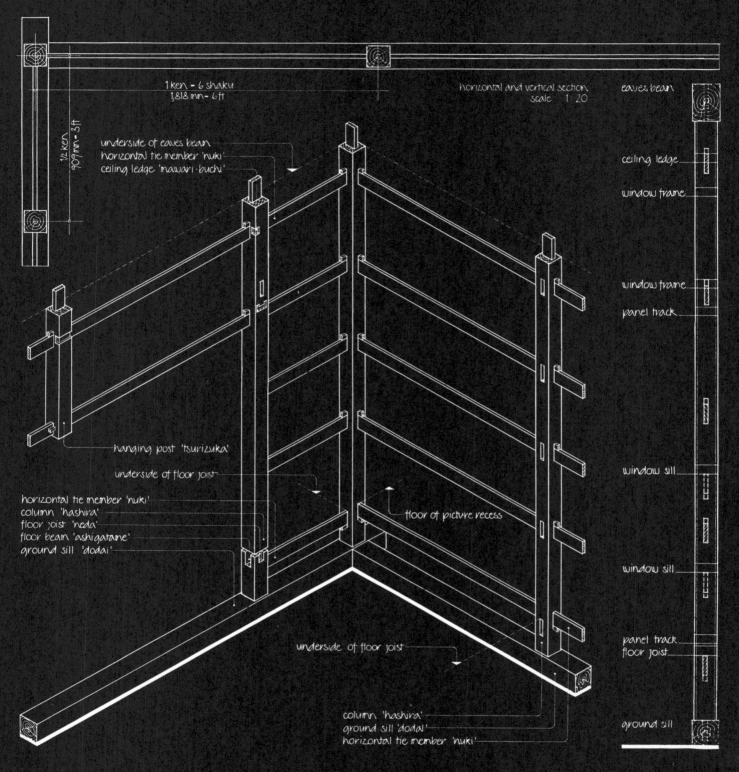

1 ken = 6 shaku
1,818 mm = 6 ft

½ ken
909 mm = 3 ft

horizontal and vertical section
scale 1:20

underside of eaves beam
horizontal tie member 'nuki'
ceiling ledge 'mawari-buchi'

hanging post 'tsurizuka'

underside of floor joist

horizontal tie member 'nuki'
column 'hashira'
floor joist 'neda'
floor beam 'ashigatane'
ground sill 'dodai'

floor of picture recess

underside of floor joist

column 'hashira'
ground sill 'dodai'
horizontal tie member 'nuki'

eaves beam

ceiling ledge

window frame

window frame

panel track

window sill

window sill

panel track
floor joist

ground sill

FIGURE 26: Wall framework construction.

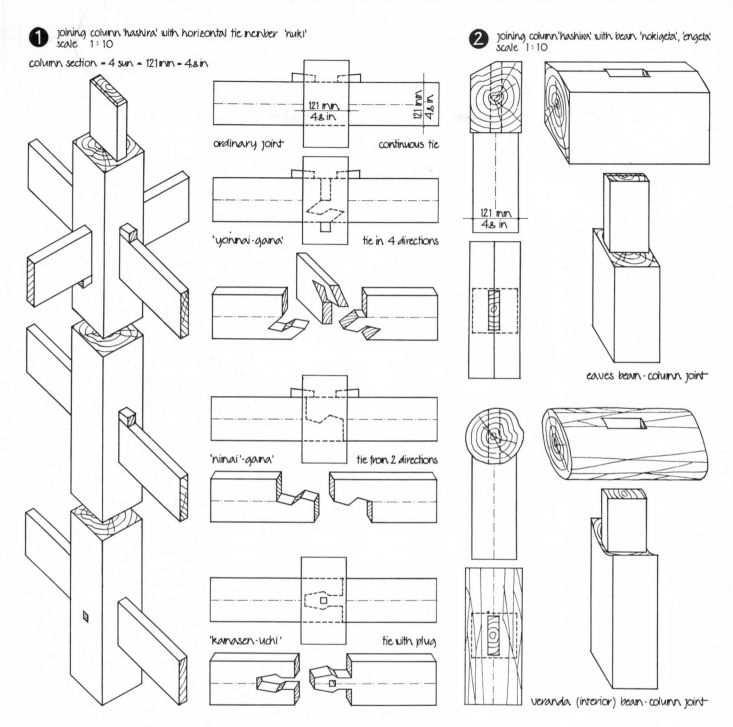

① joining column 'hashira' with horizontal tie member 'nuki'
scale 1:10

② joining column 'hashira' with beam 'nokigeta', 'engeta'
scale 1:10

column section = 4 sun = 121 mm = 4.8 in

121 mm / 4.8 in

121 mm / 4.8 in

ordinary joint   continuous tie

'yoirnai-gana'   tie in 4 directions

121 mm / 4.8 in

'ninai'-gana   tie from 2 directions

eaves beam · column joint

'kamasen-uchi'   tie with plug

veranda (interior) beam · column joint

dimensioning of tie member 'nuki' according 'kiwari' module: height/width = 1.0/0.2 x column section (=4 sun) = 4.0/0.8 sun = 121/24 mm = 4.8/1.0 in

FIGURE 27: Column, beam, and tie joinings.

full length. It appears that until the present both tradition and simpleness of method proved to be stronger than did constructional reasoning (Plates 15–18).

Upon these crossbeams, *hari,* posts, *koya-zuka,* stand in standard distance supporting the purlins, *moya,* and the rafters, *taruki,* above. As the rafters need not be very strong, it is easy to curve the roof slightly. Upon the rafters a layer of butted boards encloses the roof construction and provides support for either the clay or lattice-work which receives the final tile cover.

Three roof shapes have emerged in the Japanese residential architecture:

kiri-zuma   gabled roof

yose-mune   hipped roof (All carpenter manuals refer to it as *hōgyō,* and call the square pyramidal roof *yose-mune,* while historians seem to have decided just the opposite.)

iri-moya   hipped gable roof

Formally speaking, the hipped gable roof constitutes a combination of the other two simple forms, but it seems probable that this roof was introduced from China as an independent form. On the other hand, its distinct shape strongly resembles the roof of the old farmhouse, which is derived directly from the early pit dwelling, *tate-ana.* Presumably China also took this roof form from its own prehistoric pit dwelling.

While the roof shape itself is hardly characteristic of Japan, certainly the use of separate lean-to roofs, *hisashi,* for the veranda and above all the wall openings is a characteristic feature of the Japanese dwelling. Their lineage goes back to the *shinden-*style mansions of the nobility in the 10th–12th centuries, which were patterned after Chinese model (Plates 119–120). In these mansions the open, veranda-like rooms attached at all four sides to the enclosed main room, *moya,* yet under one and the same roof, were called *hisashi.* Thereafter, in the process of adding these veranda rooms into the enclosed space, the newly screened-in areas received a separate lean-to roof. Contradictory as the incorporation of a room into the house enclosure and the simultaneous differentiation by separation of roofs appear, it actually was a very reasonable and necessary change. For since the separation between outdoors and indoors had moved further to the outside, the heavy rainfalls demanded low roof eaves for protection. It is likely that owing to both the particular roof construction and the fairly steep roof slope, this requirement could not be met with a single roof slope even though the main supporting members still remained inside at the periphery of the main room, the *moya.* Also, such use of a separate roof must have been very practical for the common people, who in early times neither could afford, nor were allowed, to provide a *hisashi* space in the original construction, as this was a distinction of the architecture of the aristocracy. In a word, the lean-to roof was the simplest method of later adding covered space such as veranda, toilet, bath, or the like to an existing house.

Actually, the historical precedence is of less significance than an interesting phenomenon that went with it. Since those two early rooms in Japanese architecture, *moya* and *hisashi,* could be identified by their different roofs, these definitions were gradually attributed to the roof itself. As roof definitions, the terms *moya* and *hisashi* are still used in the traditional houses, while their original usage as room definition has been extinguished by the growth of rooms with more distinct denominations.

In this unconscious transfer of designation from room to roof, an important architectural causation is restated: the roof is the most basic requirement for protection against weather, it is the earliest element of man's space designation in architecture (a profound meaning that is still preserved in the German word for "shelter," the "Ob-Dach," i.e., the "roof above"). This twofold use of the word appears to be especially characteristic of Japanese architecture. While in Western architecture solid walls or, in warmer areas, columns of a particular order distinctly create the "indoor" feeling and even do so without necessarily requiring a cover above—a roof—Japanese "indoor" feeling is primarily dependent on the roof. This significance of the roof in Japanese architecture is confirmed by the word for roof itself. For the two Chinese

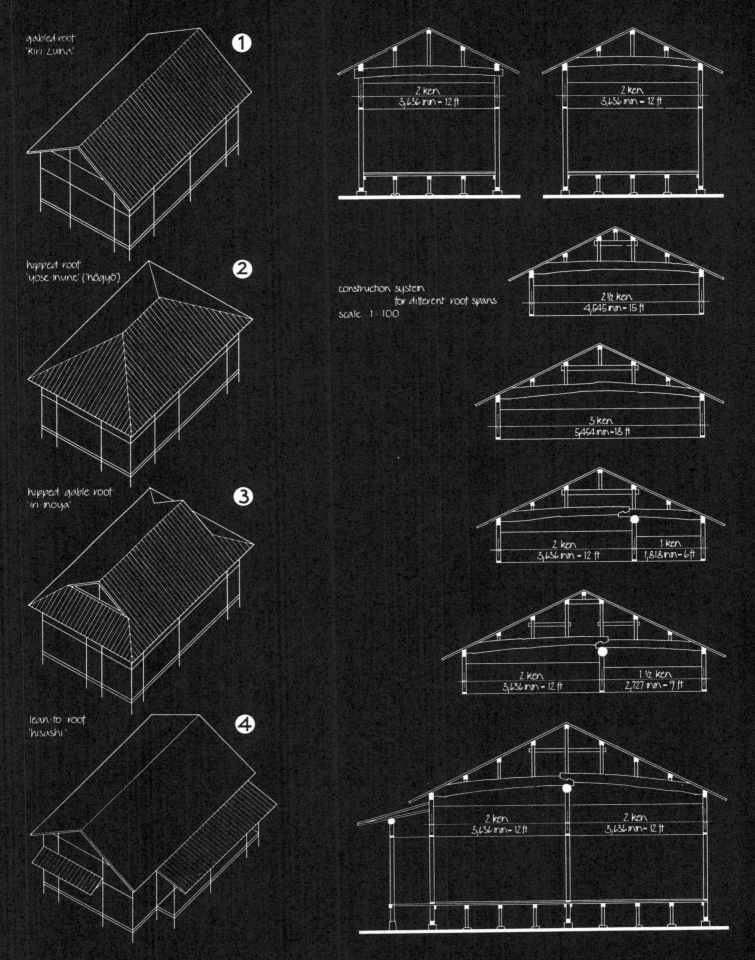

gabled roof
'kiri-zuma'

①

2 ken
3,636 mm = 12 ft

2 ken
3,636 mm = 12 ft

hipped roof
'yose-mune' ('hōgyō')

②

construction system
    for different roof spans
scale 1:100

2½ ken
4,545 mm = 15 ft

3 ken
5454 mm = 18 ft

hipped gable roof
'iri-moya'

③

2 ken
3,636 mm = 12 ft

1 ken
1,818 mm = 6 ft

2 ken
3,636 mm = 12 ft

1½ ken
2,727 mm = 9 ft

lean-to roof
'hisashi'

④

2 ken
3,636 mm = 12 ft

2 ken
3,636 mm = 12 ft

FIGURE 28: Roof types and framing systems for different roof spans.

ideographs, *ya-ne,* for the Japanese word for roof mean nothing but "house" (interior) and "root" (source). Roof is the very root of house.

The system of framing the roof skeleton, as defective as it is constructionally, still has many advantages. Within a basic construction system, all different lengths can be spanned with equal-sized members. Naturally, in the case of crossbeams the length may vary according to the depth of the building, but otherwise the size of the building does not affect the stress on any member and consequently does not demand separate dimensioning for each structure. Since the maximum free span is 2 1/2 or 3 *ken* (4,500 or 5,400 mm. = 15 or 18 ft.) such a system allows, without abnormal constructional measures, free room areas of 18 × 18 ft. or 18 mats, an exceptional room size in the ordinary residences. That is to say, this constructional system permits practically any desired column placement for any possible room arrangement without constructional disadvantages. Also, visual problems do not arise because the suspended ceiling conceals the roof construction, which in the process may have become quite complex and unsightly. It is for this reason that in designing a house, both the patron, in arranging rooms, and the carpenter, in placing posts along the *ken* grid, need not pay attention to visual or constructional consequences and, therefore, can design freely.

The early method of tying roof tile to roof skeleton was with clay, a form even now widely preferred in the building of traditional houses because of its simplicity (Plate 42). The rafters are boarded or covered with bark, which provides a base for the roof plaster, a mixture of seasoned clay and chopped straw, in which the tiles are imbedded. It seems probable that this simple and appropriate method has survived from a time when tool and technique were not developed far enough to guarantee an exact and even roof plane. For by using clay any unevenness can be leveled and any difference in dimension can be compensated for more easily than by other methods.

Although clay in conjunction with tiles adds rigidity to an otherwise weak framework, the disproportionate increase in the roof load makes the house even more susceptible to collapse in case of horizontal stress. There is no evidence to sustain the belief that the disproportionately heavy weight of the Japanese roof was by its sheer mass meant to resist sudden earthquake shocks or the continuous pressure of seasonal storms. Nor are there any instances other than exceptional ones where top weight has shown constructional merits at the time of strong horizontal stress.

Thus, the practice of placing tiles on lathwork has increased. In this system the rafters are boarded as in the clay-bed method, but instead of applying clay to the boards lathwork is used. This however, has not proved overly effective in resisting storms. The wind easily grips under the tile, and at times after a typhoon roofs can be seen practically devoid of tile. In this respect, the clay-imbedded roofing shows more resistance.

The method used to protect the ridge against rain is quite remarkable. While Western architecture felt it adequate to cover this important and endangered joint between two roof planes by one row of tiles with a particular shape, the Japanese ridge roofing seems to manifest more concern for its safe insulation. As the illustrations of tile fabric have shown, the joint between two roof planes is not merely covered at the top with ridge tiles, but receives several layers of flat tiles, called *noshi-gawara,* which lift the final ridge tiles to a considerable height and give the ridge a heavy and dominant appearance. It appears almost as if in this instance for once visual concern triumphed over reason, for any layers beyond three of these flat tiles hardly add anything to the watertightness. It might also be possible that the Japanese builders simply followed the Chinese from whom they had originally learned the tile roofing or, more likely, that they felt the need for emphasizing security measures at this very vulnerable part of the roof.

Heavy wind ridges along the gable side, accentuated roof hips, particularly shaped tiles at the end of the ridge cover (the so-called demon heads to ward off evil spirits), curving of the roof slope, and other elements of the roof that differ from Western forms do not constitute distinct Japanese features, but confirm only how manifold

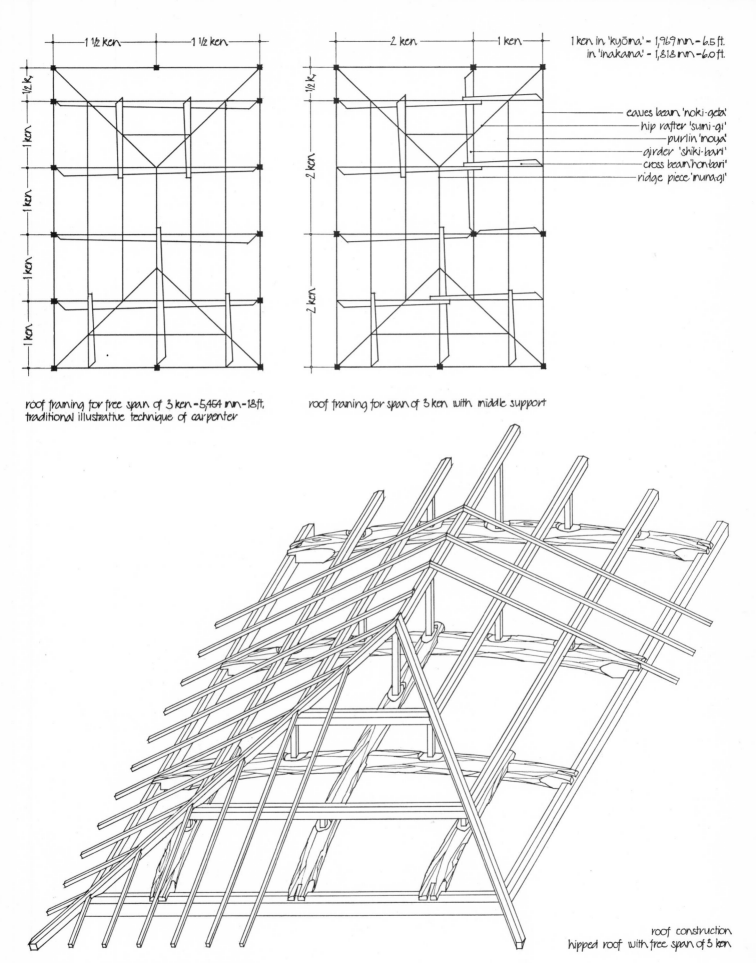

1½ ken | 1½ ken

½ k.
1 ken
1 ken
1 ken
1 ken

2 ken | 1 ken

½ k.
2 ken
2 ken

1 ken in 'kyōma' = 1,969 mm = 6.5 ft.
in 'inakama' = 1,818 mm = 6.0 ft.

eaves beam 'noki-geta'
hip rafter 'sumi-gi'
purlin 'moya'
girder 'shiki-bari'
cross beam 'hon-bari'
ridge piece 'muna-gi'

roof framing for free span of 3 ken = 5,454 mm = 18 ft.
traditional illustrative technique of carpenter

roof framing for span of 3 ken with middle support

roof construction
hipped roof with free span of 3 ken

FIGURE 29: Hipped-roof construction.

dimensioning of eaves beam 'nokigeta' according 'kiwari∙module: height/width = 1.6/1.1 x column section (= 4 sun) = 6.4/4.4 sun = 194/ 133 mn = 7.7/5.25 in

1 scale 1:10

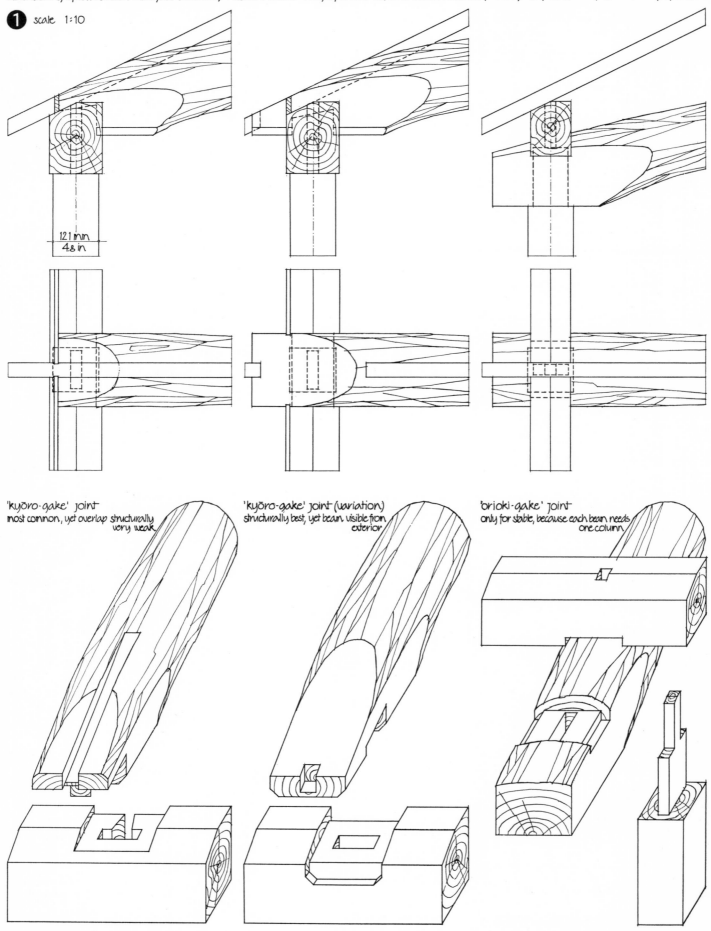

121 mm
4.8 in

'kyōro∙gake' joint
most common, yet overlap structurally
very weak

'kyōro-gake' joint (variation)
structurally best, yet beam visible from
exterior

'orioki∙gake' joint
only for stable, because each beam needs
one column

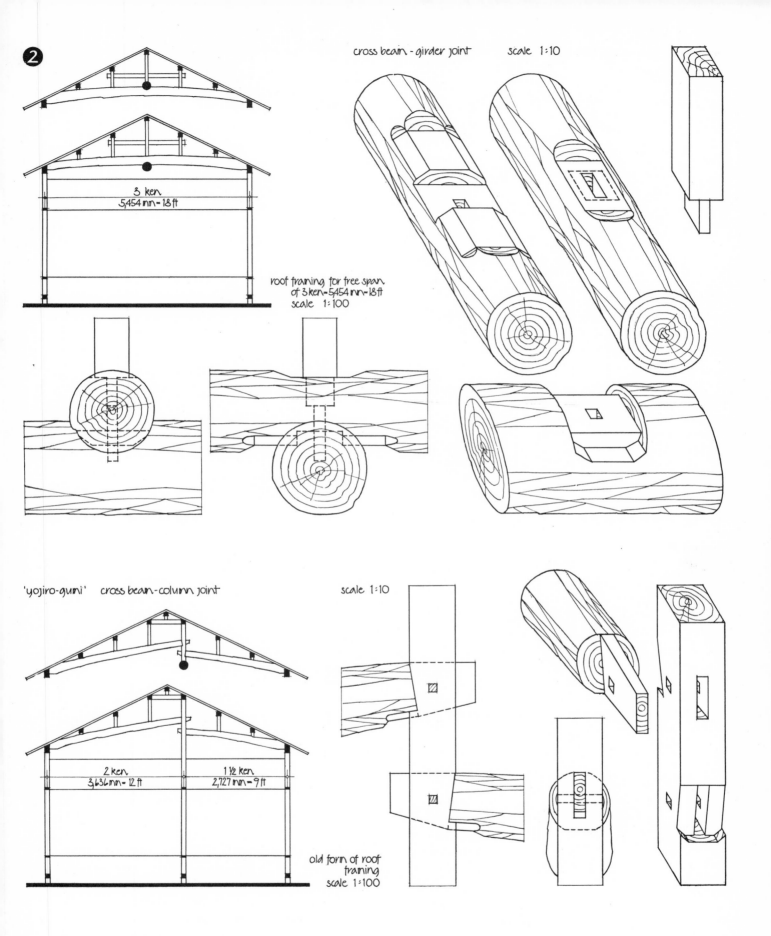

cross beam - girder joint   scale 1:10

3 ken
5,454 mm - 18 ft

roof framing for free span
of 3 ken - 5,454 mm - 18 ft
scale 1:100

'yojiro-guni'   cross beam-column joint   scale 1:10

2 ken
3,636 mm - 12 ft

1½ ken
2,727 mm - 9 ft

old form of roof
framing
scale 1:100

FIGURE 30 Details of roof structure.

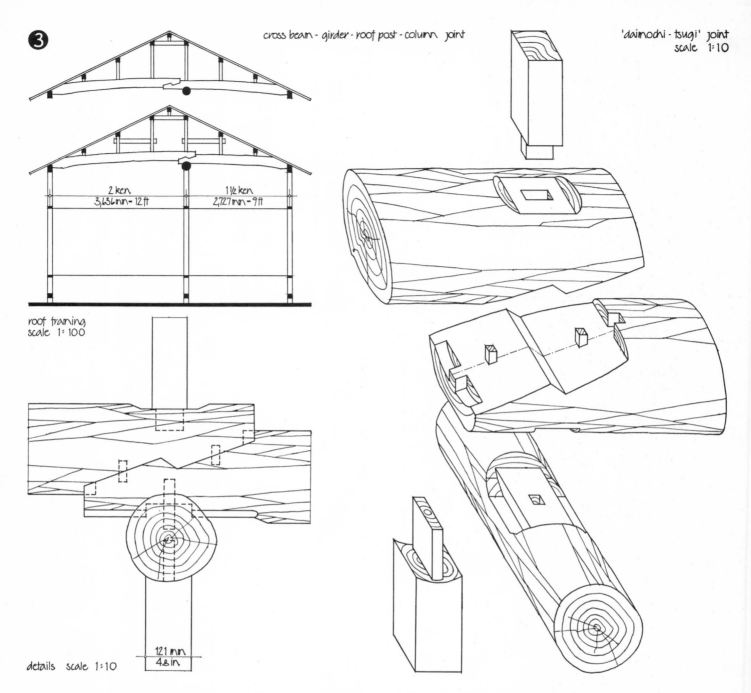

③ cross beam · girder · roof post · column joint

'daimochi · tsugi' joint
scale 1:10

2 ken
3,636mm = 12 ft

1½ ken
2,727mm = 9 ft

roof framing
scale 1:100

details   scale 1:10

121 mm
4.8 in

dimensioning of roof post 'koyazuka' according 'kiwari' module: width = breadth = 0.8 x column section = 0.8 x 4.0 sun = 3.2/3.2 sun = 97/97 mm = 3.8/3.8 in.

FIGURE 30 (continued): Details of roof structure.

the architectural motifs and features were that Japan took over from China (Plate 43).

However, the lean-to roof, *hisashi* (or less frequently *kiri-yoke)*, does constitute a characteristic feature of the Japanese residence. Its function is to protect the individual wall openings with their paper-covered sliding panels against rain and sun. Yet, such function concerns not only the doors, windows, or verandas, but also such exterior building elements as the shutter compartment, the attached bath, or the toilet. Here, as will become increasingly apparent, a practical device of construction did not remain strictly within the limits of necessity, but in addition became a medium of decorative expression.

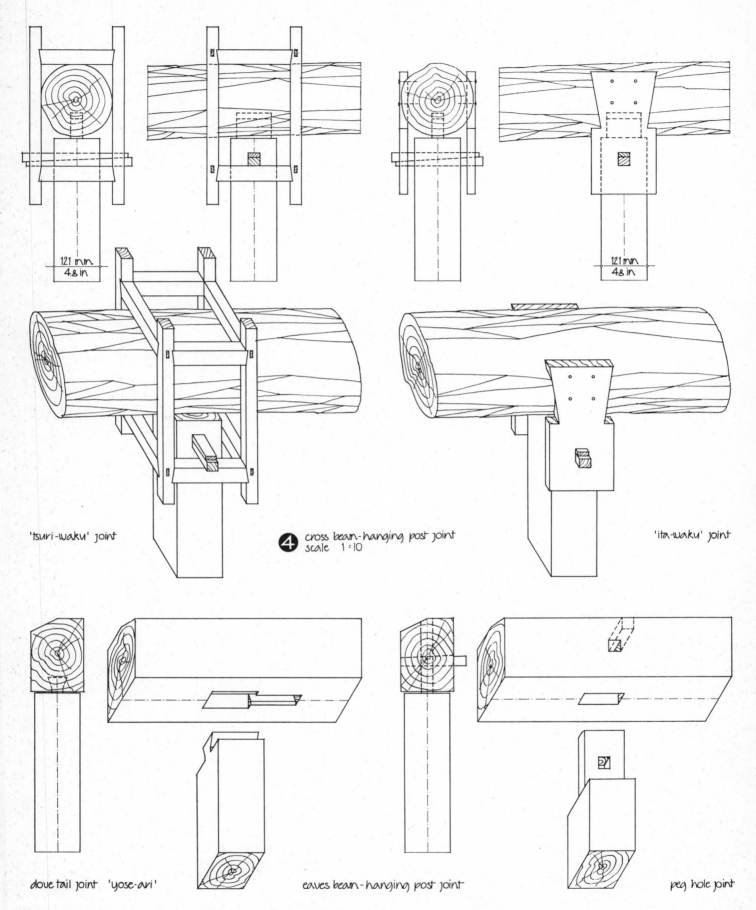

121 mm
4.8 in

121 mm
4.8 in

'tsuri-waku' joint

④ cross beam-hanging post joint
scale 1:10

'ita-waku' joint

dove tail joint 'yose-ari'

eaves beam-hanging post joint

peg hole joint

dimensioning of eaves beam 'nokigeta' according 'kiwari' module: height/width - 1.6/1.1 x column section (-4 sun) - 6.4/4.4 sun - 194/133 mm - 7.6/5.25 in

FIGURE 30 (continued): Details of roof structure.

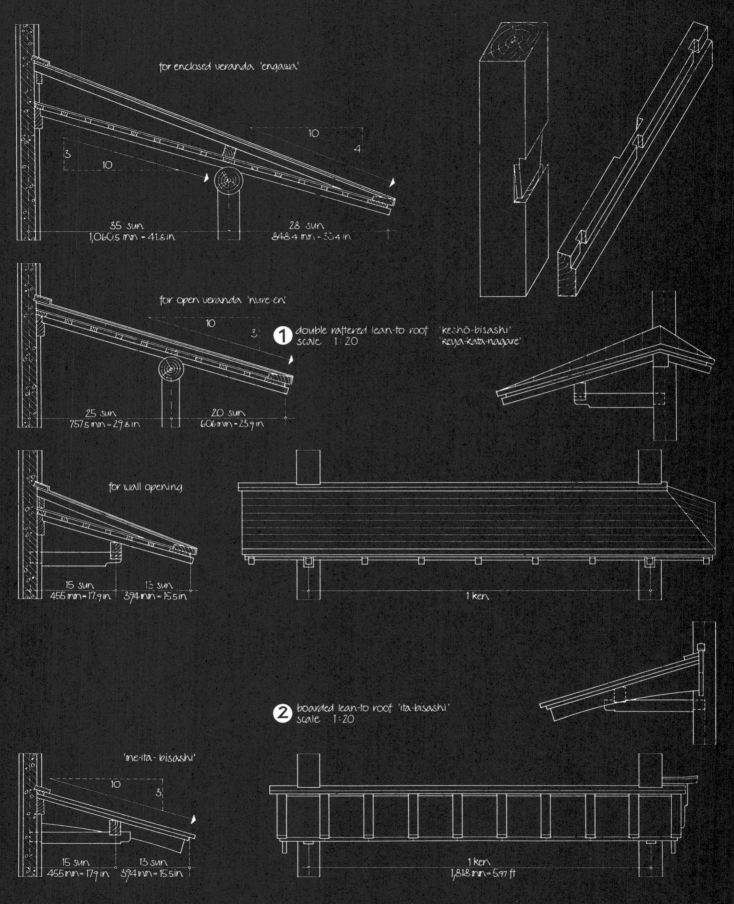

for enclosed veranda 'engawa'

3
10

10
4

35 sun
1,060.5 mm = 41.8 in

28 sun
848.4 mm = 33.4 in

for open veranda 'nure-en'

10

3

① double raftered lean-to roof 'keshō-bisashi'
scale 1:20   'keya-kata-nagare'

25 sun
757.5 mm = 29.8 in

20 sun
606 mm = 23.9 in

for wall opening

15 sun
455 mm = 17.9 in

13 sun
394 mm = 15.5 in

1 ken

② boarded lean-to roof 'ita-bisashi'
scale 1:20

'ne-ita- bisashi'

10
3

15 sun
455 mm = 17.9 in

13 sun
394 mm = 15.5 in

1 ken
1,818 mm = 5.97 ft

dimensioning of upper rafter set 'nodaruki' according 'kiwari'-module : height = width = 0.35 × column section = 0.35 × 4 = 14/14 sun = 42.4/42.4 mm = 1.7/1.7 in
dimensioning of lower rafter set 'keshodaruki'   : height/width = 0.3/0.25 × column section (4 sun) = 12/10 sun = 36.4/30.3 mm = 1.4/1.2 in

FIGURE 31: Typical forms of lean-to roofs, *hisashi*.

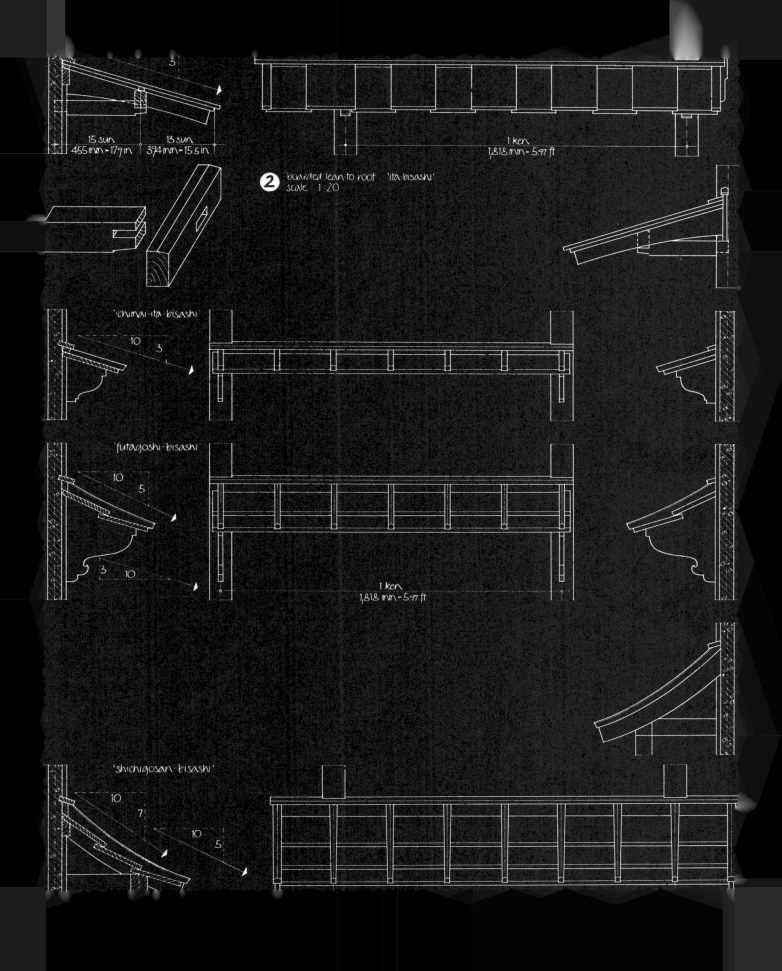

15 sun
455 mm = 17.9 in

13 sun
374 mm = 15.5 in

3

1 ken
1,818 mm = 5.97 ft

② boarded lean-to roof 'ita-bisashi'
scale 1:20

'ichimai-ita-bisashi'

10   3

'futagoshi-bisashi'

10   5

3   10

1 ken
1,818 mm = 5.97 ft

'shichigosan-bisashi'

10

7

10   5

For each of the many distinct uses of the lean-to roof a standard type developed, and the number of such types increased with later decorative differentiation. Among them, the double raftered lean-to roof, *keshō-bisashi,* became a dominant feature in the external expression of the Japanese dwelling. Its two sets of rafters have been the subject of much dispute. Since the roof cover could very well have been laid upon the boards of the lower set, the upper set of rafters is superfluous, at least constructionally (Plates 19–20). Thus it is generally professed that a certain visual intention (though never clearly defined) had effected this additional element. However, since in many cases both rafter sets have an identical inclination or, if not, differ only slightly, neither the presence of the second rafter set nor the difference in appearance is actually recognizable from the normal standpoint of a pedestrian. The assumption that the second set of rafters has a visual purpose is therefore dubious. Instead, it is more likely that the second set of rafters originally served to conceal an unsightly structural member. Such probability also is supported by the fact that in the warrior's house, built in the *shuden* style, the broad roof overhang is achieved by a sloped beam, *hanegi,* carrying a set of rafters on purlins above and concealed from underneath by a second set of rafters. Supposedly this feature, with many others, was introduced into the ordinary dwelling, but since here the rafters themselves took over the constructional function of the sloped beam, the concealment no longer had any meaning. Yet, instead of reconsidering and redesigning according to the new situation, the Japanese carpenter, as in many other instances, apparently submitted himself to habit and tradition.

Another feature of the lean-to roof construction, the intersection of the round veranda beams, *engeta,* at the corners seems to contradict earlier statements that visual concern never had been an instrumental factor in producing features of the Japanese residence. For here a third piece, a round log with no apparent constructional function whatever, is inserted, obviously to make the two beams appear as if they were penetrating each other. It is true such a measure must at first sight appear formalistic in cause. However, referring back to earlier stages of development, it becomes plain that this device does not actually owe its existence to a creation of pleasing form but rather to a reasonable endeavor to preserve by illusion the architectural form of two overlapping members—the more primitive, though constructionally more logical, method of the past.

This tendency is distinctive of decorative elements in the Japanese dwelling as a whole. For in the Japanese residential evolution, whenever one or another feature shifted its purpose from a utilitarian to a decorative one, an abstraction of form was never resorted to. Instead, an architectural anatomy was developed that maintained the basic expression or even more distinctly manifested what had been the original cause.

japanese wall

One of the most expressive features in the Japanese house, though the least regarded as such by Western writers, is the solid wall. In technique and consistency it does not differ much from the old clay wall used in Central European wood-frame buildings, and yet, expressing color, texture, and proportion through its own substance and thus being decorative by itself, it has a character all its own. Thus, it is well justified to use the term "Japanese wall" instead of the more exact Japanese term, *komai-kabe,* literally meaning "wall with small (bamboo) laces."

The aesthetic and cohesive qualities of the solid wall by far outweigh its constructional and resistive qualities. But, as most of its parts are either above the sliding panels or at places hardly exposed to much abuse, such as the picture recess or tearoom, there was no real requirement for constructional permanence, especially as the children in Japan do not consider the house interior a suitable place for strength-testing games. If carelessness does cause damage, repairs can easily be made. And it does not offend the Japanese eye if the repaired part of the wall differs from the adjacent parts (Plate 47). Indeed, the constructional quality of the Japanese wall seems to be consistent with all the other measures taken in constructing the house. For they hardly give the

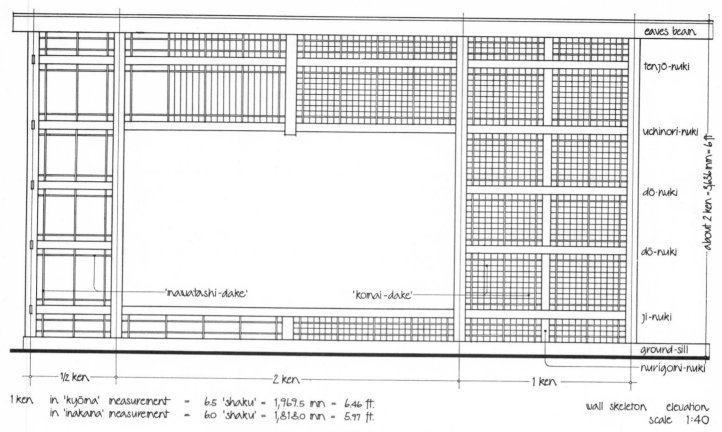

eaves beam
tenjō-nuki
uchinori-nuki
dō-nuki
dō-nuki
ji-nuki
ground-sill
nurigomi-nuki

about 2 ken = 3636 mm = 6 ft.

'mawatashi-dake'   'komai-dake'

½ ken   2 ken   1 ken

1 ken   in 'kyōma' measurement = 6.5 'shaku' = 1,969.5 mm = 6.46 ft.
        in 'inakama' measurement = 6.0 'shaku' = 1,818.0 mm = 5.97 ft.

wall skeleton elevation
scale 1:40

FIGURE 32: Details of wall-skeleton construction.

impression of any intention to erect an imperishable monument, but rather manifest the architectural idea of a temporary shelter in those changeable times.

As the columns of the vertical framework are the only bearing members, the wall's sole constructional function is to sustain itself. This is achieved by a wood-bamboo skeleton in which the main horizontal tie members, *nuki,* extend their functional range to keeping the columns in their upright position. While these horizontal members, at an average distance of 2 feet (600 mm.), provide adequate support for the wall skeleton, additional members, *nurigomi-nuki,* need to be inserted vertically in between the columns. The preferred distance is 1/2 *ken* (909 mm. = 3 ft.), according to the *ken* grid, creating a skeleton pattern of 2 × 3 foot rectangles. Into each opening is tied a bamboo lathwork, consisting of a major frame, *mawatashi-dake* (literally, spanning bamboo), and a grid of bamboo strips, *komai-dake* (literally, bamboo in small laces). They are individually fastened either with rice-straw fiber or rope.

The order of this intermediate skeleton is seemingly insignificant, as it will be covered up later. Yet, it is descriptive of the system that prevails in the overall constructional method. Major order is subdivided into minor, and minor again into minor. Small units are not added, but large units are subdivided again and again into minor orders of continuous subordination.

With this skeleton completed, the wall clay is applied on either side in two, three, or four coats of slightly different consistency, constituting the so-called *arakabe,* the rough wall. Its thickness is about a half to two-thirds of the column thickness, i.e., 2–3 *sun* (60–90 mm. = 2.4–3.6 in.). After its curing process, the finish coat, *uwa-nuri* or *shiage,* is laid on in a very even layer of about 1/16 in., with an infinite variety of color, consistency, and texture and thus with infinite expressional possibilities.

Yet, constructionally speaking, the most amazing feature of the wall is not the extreme refinement of a basically primitive wall construction but the way the solid wall

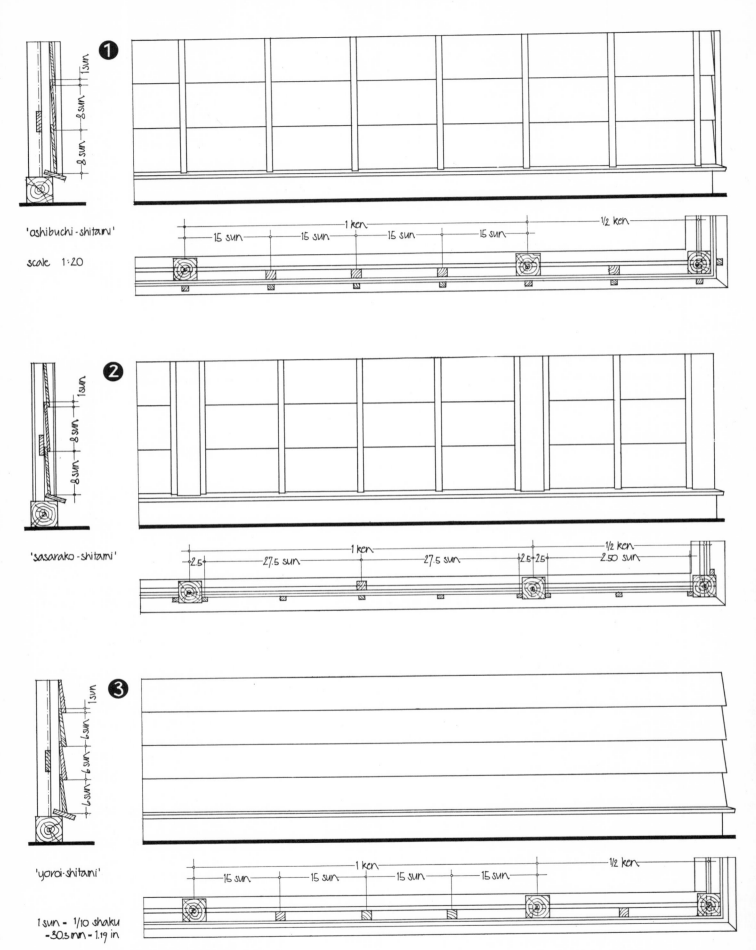

'ashibuchi-shitami'

scale 1:20

1 ken

15 sun · 15 sun · 15 sun · 15 sun · ½ ken

'sasarako-shitami'

1 ken

2.5 · 27.5 sun · 27.5 sun · 2.5 · 25 · ½ ken 2.50 sun

'yoroi-shitami'

1 ken

15 sun · 15 sun · 15 sun · 15 sun · ½ ken

1 sun = 1/10 shaku
= 30.3 mm = 1.19 in

FIGURE 33: Typical forms of exterior wood siding.

and column are joined. Although the plaster is simply butted to the wood, no wooden cover detail is used to provide a clean joint or to hide the minute connections which even trained craftsmen find difficult to execute properly (Plate 58). Here, the Japanese carpenter has renounced all trim details that in Western architecture are so necessary and has thus preserved an austere purity of distinction between supporting and non-supporting members.

However, it is certainly too far-fetched to ascribe this method to an active concept that refused the use of members that were liable to efface clarity of constructional definition. The fact is that there simply was nothing that demanded countermeasures with trim details, for there is no shrinkage of either wood or wall clay that could be compared to that in average continental conditions. The reasons for this architecturally favorable circumstance are constructional, climatic, and insulational. The curtain skeleton is tightly connected with the column, thus granting constructional homogeneity; the local climate throughout the year is fairly humid, thus eliminating excessive movement of material; and, finally, the house is neither insulated against temperature or humidity nor is it heated in the winter, thus providing identical climatic conditions for both the interior and exterior. Difference of environmental circumstances, then, is the final reason for this favorable distinction of the Japanese house as compared to its traditional Western counterpart.

Since the wall material is not very resistant to weather, exterior wall parts particularly exposed to rain are frequently covered by thin wooden boards. Characteristically, this cover does not extend over the clay wall's entire height, as aesthetic consideration would suggest, but begins 2 to 3 feet below the roof projection, be it gable or eave. And this is very understandable, because the upper part of the wall, being sufficiently protected by the roof overhang, does not require additional sheathing as does the rest of the wall down to the groundsill.

As a rule, the boards are arranged horizontally, overlapping each other from above in a pattern called *shitami-bari* (literally, underview boarding), which again is performed in several standard methods. In the houses of the wealthier class, boarding is used also for decorative purposes. It usually has a vertical order, *tateita-bari,* and is constructed in the same manner as the shutter compartments, *tobukuro.*

floor

Floor in the Japanese single-storied house is clearly differentiated into three planes. This difference is basic and is more obviously marked than in the usual Western case. For the distinction between the planes is not a mere difference in elevation but a clear definition of the purpose that each of those three planes serves, both in its construction and its utilization. Actually, the height-level difference is only the logical result of the latter. Clarity of definition is further stressed by the three different materials used for floor covering, earth, wood, and mat, which again reflect but the difference of purpose. Among them, the matted floor occupies the largest area, living space; the boarded floor is provided for communicative and utilitarian space; and the earthen floor forms transitional space between interior and exterior. A floor covered with bamboo or particularly shaped logs may occasionally be used, yet indicating no other motive than that of decorative concern.

Like all constructional systems in the Japanese residence, the build-up of the floor framework is a succession of subimposed orders, i.e., the constructional system is not derived from the addition of small units as in brick architecture, but is organized in repeated subdivisions of a dominating structural unit. Such a major order is established by the floor beam, *ashigatame.* The floor beam, being inserted between room-circumferential columns, designates the area to be floored. It is additionally supported by short posts erected upon the groundsill. At the sides where there is no veranda or at interior room partitions, instead of a floor beam, continuous braces, *nedagake,* are tied to the columns. They are in the same height with the floor sleepers, *obiki,* that form the second order. The sleepers are spanned in the direction of the room width

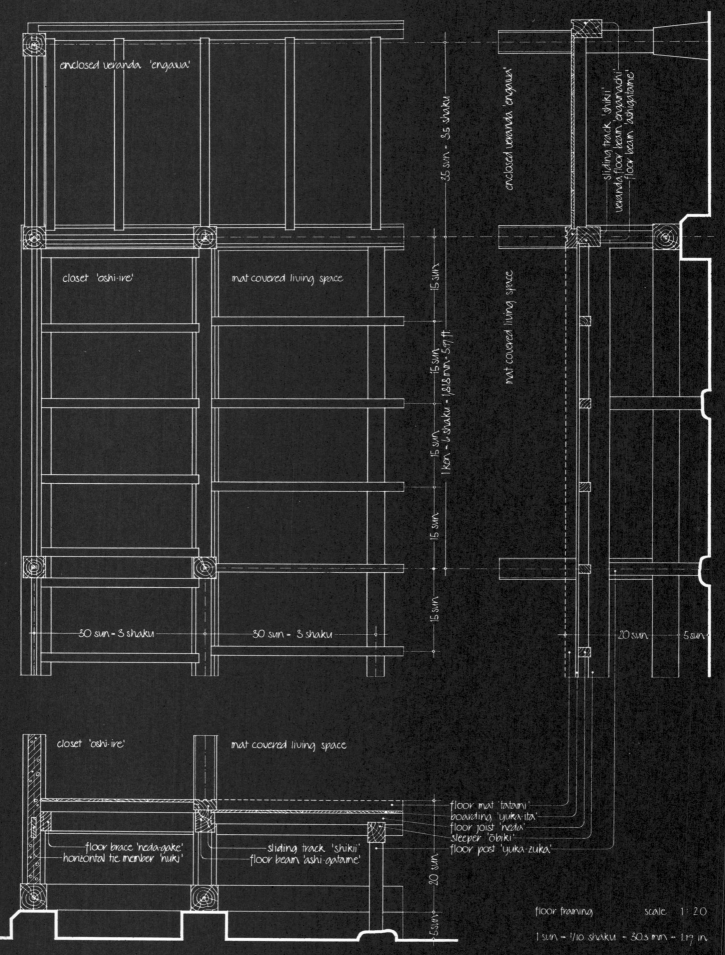

enclosed veranda 'engawa'

closet 'oshi-ire'

mat covered living space

35 sun - 3.5 shaku

15 sun

15 sun

15 sun

1 ken - 6 shaku - 1,818 mm - 5.97 ft

15 sun

15 sun

15 sun

30 sun - 3 shaku

30 sun - 3 shaku

enclosed veranda 'engawa'

mat covered living space

sliding track 'shikii'
veranda floor beam 'engawanachi'
floor beam 'ashigatame'

20 sun

5 sun

closet 'oshi-ire'

mat covered living space

floor brace 'neda-gake'
horizontal tie member 'nuki'

sliding track 'shikii'
floor beam 'ashi-gatame'

floor mat 'tatami'
boarding 'yuka-ita'
floor joist 'neda'
sleeper 'ōbiki'
floor post 'yuka-zuka'

20 sun

5 sun

floor framing   scale 1 : 20

1 sun - 1/10 shaku - 30.3 mm - 1.19 in

FIGURE 34: Details of floor construction.

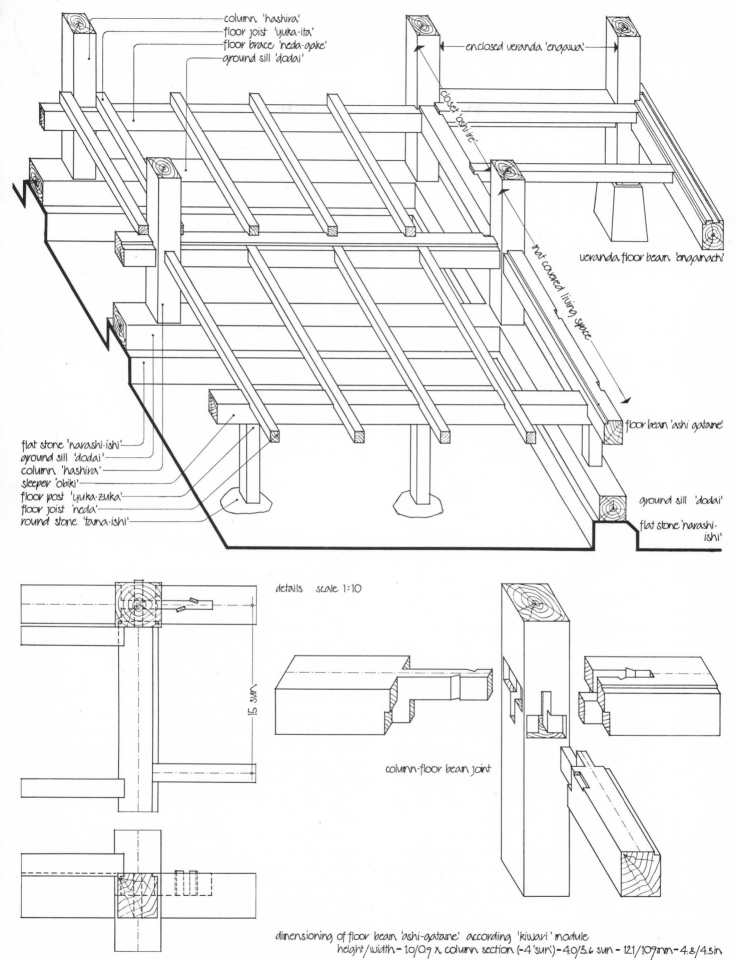

column 'hashira'
floor joist 'yuka-ita'
floor brace 'neda-gake'
ground sill 'dodai'

enclosed veranda 'engawa'

closet 'oshiire'

veranda floor beam 'engawachi'

mat covered living space

floor beam 'ashi gatane'

flat stone 'narashi-ishi'
ground sill 'dodai'
column 'hashira'
sleeper 'obiki'
floor post 'yuka-zuka'
floor joist 'neda'
round stone 'tama-ishi'

ground sill 'dodai'

flat stone 'narashi-ishi'

details   scale 1:10

15 sun

column-floor beam joint

dimensioning of floor beam 'ashi-gataine' according 'kiwari' module
height/width = 1.0/0.9 x column section (=4 'sun') = 4.0/3.6 sun = 121/109mm = 4.8/4.3in

FIGURE 34 (continued): Details of floor construction.

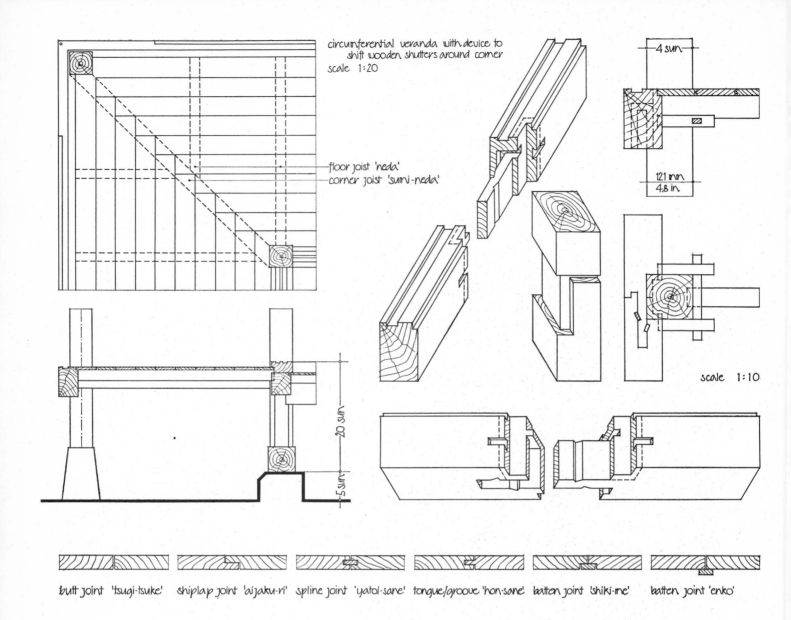

circumferential veranda with device to
shift wooden shutters around corner
scale 1:20

floor joist 'neda'
corner joist 'sumi-neda'

4 sun

121 mm
4.8 in

20 sun

5 sun

scale 1:10

butt joint 'tsugi-tsuke'   shiplap joint 'aijaku-ri'   spline joint 'yatoi-sane'   tongue/groove 'hon-sane'   batten joint 'shiki-ne'   batten joint 'enko'

dimensioning of floor joist 'neda' according 'kiwari' module: height/width - 0.5/0.4 x column section (= 4.0 'sun') = 2.0/1.6 'sun' = 60.5/48.5 mm = 2.4/1.9 in.
dimensioning of floor board 'yuka-ita'   thickness/width - 0.15/0.9 x column section   = 0.6/3.6 'sun' = 18.0/109.0 mm = 0.7/4.3 in.

FIGURE 34 (continued): Details of floor construction.

and are supported by short posts at standard intervals. The top of the sleeper is lower than that of the floor beam and thus provides space for the third order consisting of joists, *neda,* which again are laid in modular distances. Then follows the last order of floor-supporting members, the boards that are laid transversely upon the joists. They, finally, are in one level with the floor beam and thus combine major and minor orders, providing a uniform level for the mat cover.

Construction of the floors in the second plane (kitchen, veranda, corridor, toilet, etc.). is somewhat more simple because the span is rather small. For example, in the veranda the forementioned interior floor beam provides support for the transverse joists at the inside, while at the outside another floor beam, *engamachi,* is notched into the veranda post and receives the other end of the floor joists. The joists again are laid at standard distances, providing the base for the floor boards.

The boards of the exposed floor are planed but otherwise are left untreated or only rubbed with a vegetable oil for protection. Continuous use by bare feet or with *tabi,* the cloth footwear, together with an occasional sweeping (and, no doubt, the aging process too) effects the noted contrasting appearance of the wood's natural texture (Plate 51). In both floor planes, the matted and the boarded, one or two of the boards, *age-ita,* are left loose so that it is possible to get under the floor if repairs become necessary. The boards in this case are only butted, whereas usually they have overlapping joints.

The floor of the third level, as in the kitchen and in the entrance hall, *genkan,* was traditionally an earthen floor, a simple, though not too hygienic, surface that required no other treatment and care outside of being stamped and occasionally broomed. Today, however, concrete, stone, tiles, and other more resistant fabrics have largely replaced earth in the cities, while rural areas have not as yet parted with this primitive material.

ceiling

The foregoing analysis has already shown that the components of the Japanese house, whether in their origin and evolution or in their treatment and final form, do not manifest a primary concern for visual forms. They have been motivated and determined by constructional-utilitarian purpose, environmental adaptation, and fabric limitation, the latter two, no doubt, in the Japanese case, manifesting passive yielding rather than active response. Realization of their aesthetic qualities followed much later, as did their appreciation and conscious application.

The ceiling in the Japanese house seems to contradict this statement because, clearly, it was prompted by the visual purpose of concealing the roof construction. And yet, the ceiling is no real exception. For concealing the unsightly is one thing and playing with visual forms is quite another. Nevertheless, the stress of the optical purpose of the ceiling was a logical consequence and the step toward decorative treatment was not too great. This is evidenced by the fact that the ceiling is the only component among all elements of the dwelling in which dimensions and organization are still moduled by room size and orientation. The height of the ceiling varies according to number of mats, as does the width of the ceiling boards, which are the main constituent parts (Figure 16). Placement of the rods underneath is determined by the location of columns, and the whole is arranged according to the room orientation.

It is true the ceiling functions as an insulator against temperature and also as a protector from dust, but since the thin boards are not very tightly connected, and frequently even chink open, both functions are more imagined than real. Its function is to conceal and this aim has been achieved with the least means possible. The purity of this response to a functional demand is décor in itself, and in such simple type of ceiling no additional trim is needed to make it aesthetically pleasing. This is significant insofar as it shows that even the most simple constructional device, if it is approached with austere discipline, possesses distinct expressional-aesthetic potentialities.

The increasing wealth of the townspeople was the reason that the ceiling, until then used only in residences of the nobility, found entry into the ordinary houses —at first only in the reception room, but gradually also spreading into the other living rooms. Yet, there still are many houses in which the kitchen has no ceiling. This somewhat belated appearance of the ceiling in the dwelling, long after all other features had established themselves, has relegated the ceiling to a part that is added rather than incorporated into the constructional anatomy. It thus granted a convenient independence from the total organism that allowed visual adjustment to room size and orientation without additional labor or material. It is noteworthy that now, with roof construction being no longer visible, constructional improvement through use of diagonal truss members did not take place. For it clearly contradicts the common assumption that a particular, inherited Japanese taste prevented the use of structural members other than the horizontal and vertical.

The constructional system of the ceiling is simple. In the ordinary case, the ceiling boards, *tenjō-ita,* are laid upon slender rods, *saobuchi,* which are inserted by their ends

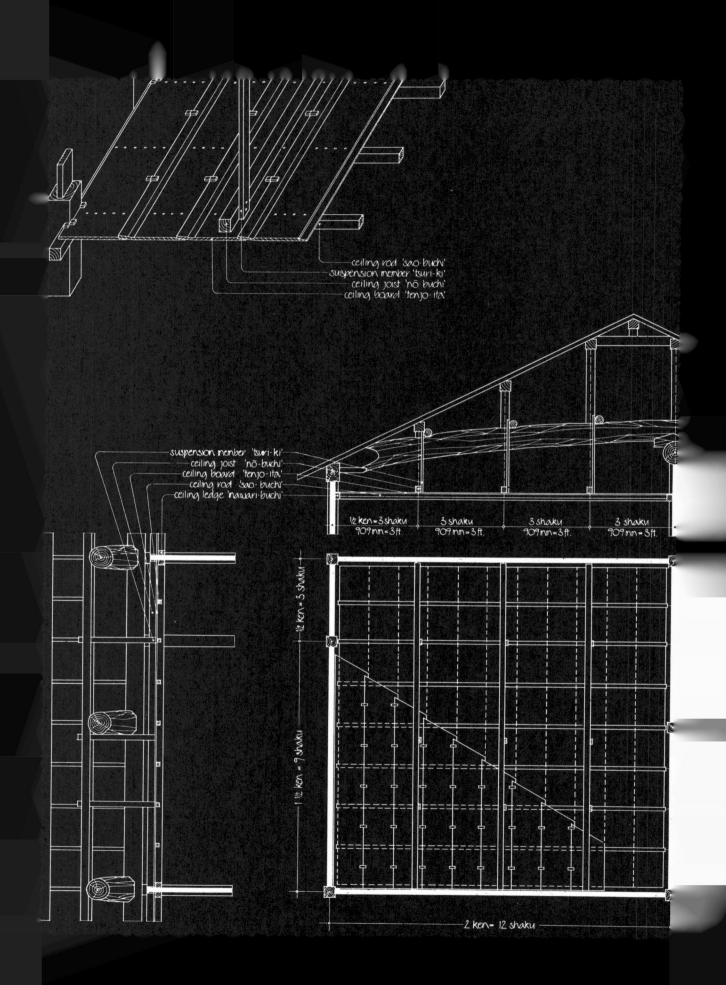

ceiling rod 'sao-buchi'
suspension member 'tsuri-ki'
ceiling joist 'nō-buchi'
ceiling board 'tenjo-ita'

suspension member 'tsuri-ki'
ceiling joist 'nō-buchi'
ceiling board 'tenjo-ita'
ceiling rod 'sao-buchi'
ceiling ledge 'nawari-buchi'

| ½ ken = 3 shaku | 3 shaku | 3 shaku | 3 shaku |
| 909mm = 3 ft. | 909mm = 3 ft. | 909mm = 3 ft. | 909mm = 3 ft. |

½ ken = 3 shaku

1 ½ ken = 9 shaku

2 ken = 12 shaku

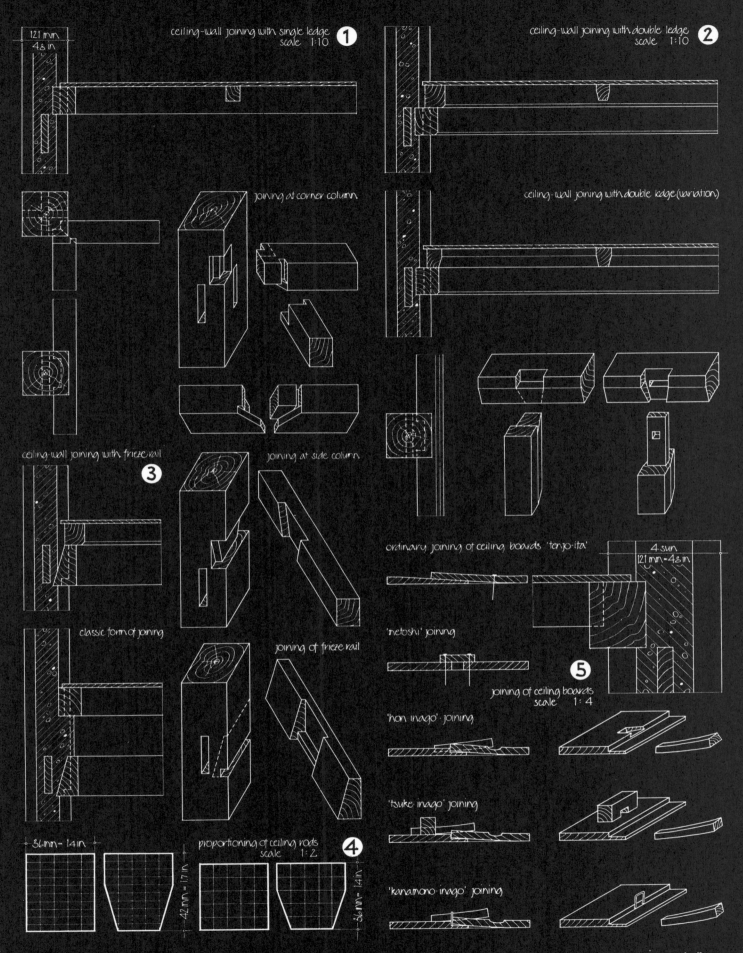

121 mm
4.8 in

ceiling-wall joining with single ledge ①
scale 1:10

ceiling-wall joining with double ledge ②
scale 1:10

joining at corner column

ceiling-wall joining with double ledge (variation)

ceiling-wall joining with frieze rail ③

joining at side column

classic form of joining

joining of frieze rail

ordinary joining of ceiling boards 'tenjo-ita'

4 sun
121 mm – 4.8 in

'netoshi' joining

⑤

joining of ceiling boards
scale 1:4

'hon-inago' joining

'tsuke-inago' joining

36 mm – 1.4 in

proportioning of ceiling rods
scale 1:2

④

42 mm – 1.7 in

36 mm – 1.4 in

'kanamono-inago' joining

dimensioning of ceiling ledge 'mawari-buchi' according 'kiwari' module: height/width = 0.6/0.5 × column section (=4 sun) = 2.4/2.0 sun = 72/60 mm = 2.9/2.4 in
dimensioning of ceiling rod 'sao-buchi'   height/width = 0.3 (0.35)/0.3 × column section (=4 sun)= 1.2 (1.4)/1.2 sun = 36 (42)/36 mm = 1.4 (1.7)/1.4 in

FIGURE 36: Details of ceiling construction.

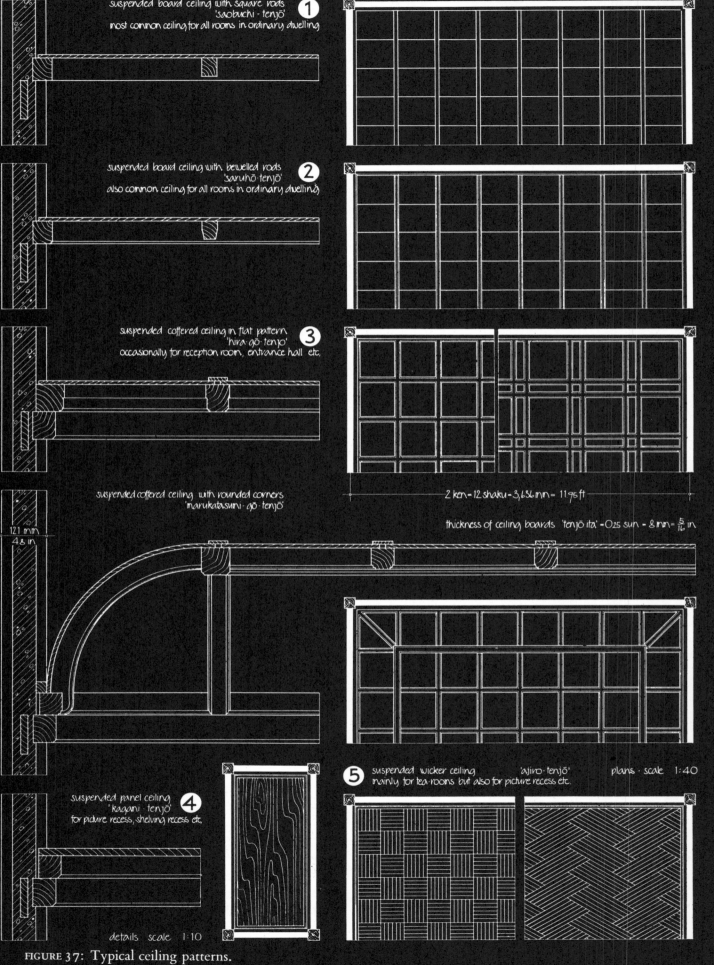

suspended board ceiling with square rods
'saobuchi - tenjō'
most common ceiling for all rooms in ordinary dwelling ①

suspended board ceiling with bevelled rods
'saruhō · tenjō'
also common ceiling for all rooms in ordinary dwelling ②

suspended coffered ceiling in flat pattern
'hira·gō·tenjō'
occasionally for reception room, entrance hall etc. ③

suspended coffered ceiling with rounded corners
'marukatasumi· gō · tenjō'

121 mm
4·8 in

2 ken = 12 shaku = 3,636 mm = 11·95 ft

thickness of ceiling boards 'tenjō ita' = 0·25 sun = 8 mm = $\frac{5}{16}$ in

suspended panel ceiling
'kagami · tenjō' ④
for picture recess, shelving recess etc.

⑤ suspended wicker ceiling   'ajiro·tenjō'   plans · scale 1:40
mainly for tea·rooms but also for picture recess etc.

details scale 1:10

FIGURE 37: Typical ceiling patterns.

into a ledge at the wall, *mawaribuchi,* and are secured by nails along their entire length to another set of transverse joists, *nobuchi,* above the boards. These joists are connected to perpendicular members, *tsuriki,* that suspend the ceiling from the beams above. Usually, the center of the ceiling is lifted about 8 to 9 *bu* (approx. 25 mm. = 1 in.) in order to compensate for eventual sagging of the beams.

The second set of ceiling joists *(nobuchi)* as well as the suspension members *(tsuriki)* are not visible, creating an impression as if the ceiling boards would rest entirely on the square rods *(saobuchi)* which are dimensioned only about 1 1/2 × 1 1/2 in. (40 × 40 mm.). Since these rods would indeed sag by their dead weight alone in the case of a normal span of 12 ft. (3,636 mm.), a twofold illusion is produced: extreme lightness of the ceiling boards and extraordinary strength of the slender ceiling rods. Still it must be doubted whether this unquestionably strong effect was actually anticipated and intentionally sought, or whether this effect was but the result of quite reasonable methods to construct a light suspended ceiling under the given circumstances.

Though the structural principle does not change essentially, both the organization of ceiling pattern and its detailing may show slight variations which in turn may reflect the wealth of the owner. In general, Japanese residential architecture characteristically does not display material wealth through scale, form, organization, construction, or decoration, except for the quality of fabric and size of enclosed space. But in the case of the ceiling, a difference in monetary wealth is more clearly expressed than in other instances, again demonstrating the decorative implication of the ceiling.

Thus, several types of ceiling patterns have evolved, which again are standardized. Among them, the one with square rods, *saobuchi-tenjō,* is the most frequently used. Besides those already depicted, the oblique veranda ceiling, *keshōyane-ura* (literally, underside of the disguise roof), needs mention. This type, which is also called *keshōbi-sashi-ura,* is not employed in the ordinary interior rooms, but only as a component of the lean-to roof, *hisashi,* and as such, has been treated earlier in the study of the lean-to roof.

Each of these ceiling types again has its variations, both locally and monetarily, but standardization and distribution of carpenter manuals during the Tokugawa era (1600–1867) resulted in uniform application. The wood dimension of each component member is a ratio of the column section, but since the column section in the ordinary house, as a rule, is standardized at 4 *sun* square (121 mm. = 4.8 in.), component members of the ceiling have also become fairly standardized.

Since the main components of the ceiling plane, the ceiling boards, are very thin (1/10 of column section = 40/10 = 4 *bu* = approx. 7/16 in = 12 mm.) and thus are liable to curl and chink open, the overlapping edges require additional joinery to at least prevent any major dislocation. The most ordinary procedure is to nail the overlapping board upon the underlying rod, but, in general, additional clips are employed.

Dimensioning and organizing of ceiling elements follows certain rules according to the room size and column placement. In addition, their orientation is decided by visual factors:

1. As the profile of the ceiling is most obvious if the overlapping edges of the boards are seen, the boards are laid with their overlapping edges facing the main direction of approach.
2. If the room has a picture recess, *tokonoma,* the main direction of approach becomes of less importance because it is imperative that the arrangement of ceiling rods, *saobuchi,* be parallel to the opening of the picture recess.
3. In the latter case the overlapping edges of the boards have to face the place of honor, *kamiza,* in front of the picture recess where the guests are seated.

In arranging the boards, there are cases in which the latter rule is ignored. The ceiling is then called *mikaeshi* (literally, reverse facing), indicating that the average Japanese is very well aware of the visual effect of the ceiling's simple order.

fittings

In the course of civilization, the development of technology was the reason that increasingly small and convenient metal elements took over the functions of joining, strengthening, and fastening of structural parts, functions that were formerly fulfilled by structural parts of wood, stone, or brick themselves. Accordingly, the word "fittings" in Western architecture has achieved the meaning of additional metal fixtures rather than components that are integrated into, and are part of, the structure. Yet, as "fittings" were originally those structural parts that were shaped "to make fit" the movable parts in the house (the doors, windows, etc.), the designation "fitting" is applicable in the instances discussed below. For all movable parts in the Japanese house, especially the interior and exterior sliding doors and windows, are held in position and kept under control by "fittings" in their original meaning.

In most forms of early architecture, wall openings such as doors and windows were furnished with removable panel-like units that would merely be set in place. But while the West, in defense against the cold, soon took to the more appropriate swinging variety, Japan, favored by a relatively mild climate, retained the original form, and through the centuries, refined what at first had been a simple standing screen imported from China. In the course of this refinement, the screen was set into wooden tracks below, *shikii,* and above, *kamoi.* The lower tracks were sunk into the floor, and the upper tracks were tied to a pair of braces, *nageshi,* which already existed as a constructionally important element even before the advent of sliding panels. Dimensions of the components of the sliding panel were reduced to the minimum and its features exploited as a decorative medium. Of course, the step from portable screen to sliding panel was, technologically speaking, a remarkable achievement. Yet, considering its practical purpose, it was only refinement of what already existed rather than invention of something essentially new. Again in this instance the Japanese house manifests one of its unique characteristics: utmost refinement of what is principally primitive.

Since columns are the only supporting members, the entire space between two columns could easily be furnished with these sliding panels, *shōji* at the outside wall and *fusuma* at the interior wall, or their window-like variations. Minute grooves in a wooden track hold the bottom of these panels in place; they are exposed to the same wear as the floor itself, a circumstance that certainly must have been one of the many motives for the Japanese removing their shoes before entering the interior rooms. For the contours of even the hardest wood could not successfully withstand wear by shoes, especially if they were but 1/8 in. (3 mm.) deep.

As a rule, the sliding tracks have two adjacent grooves, each of which holds one or two sliding panels. Two subsequent panels, therefore, can be slid over each other, reaching a complete overlap. For a two-part sliding wall, this allows an opening of about 1/2 *ken* width (909 mm. = 3 ft.) and for a four-part sliding wall, an opening of about 1 *ken* (1,818 mm. = 6 ft.). The upper sliding grooves have a height tolerance slightly greater than the depth of the lower grooves. Thus, the sliding panels can be easily removed from the wall merely by lifting them from the lower tracks and swinging the bottom out.

The merits of this method of enclosing space have been sufficiently lauded by Western architects. Since the sliding panels can easily be opened as well as entirely removed, stored, and exchanged, interior room partitioning gains a highly desirable flexibility for dwellings with a minimum of space, such as the Japanese house. Moreover, it grants excellent ventilation during the humid summer months and even allows an effortless exchange of sliding panels if season or damage ask for it. Finally, the operation of these panels does not require additional space as in the case of a swinging door, an advantage of which contemporary architecture has become again aware.

On the other hand, there are numerous defects, such as lack of insulation against cold and heat, sound, and dirt and the incapacity to provide privacy for the individual.

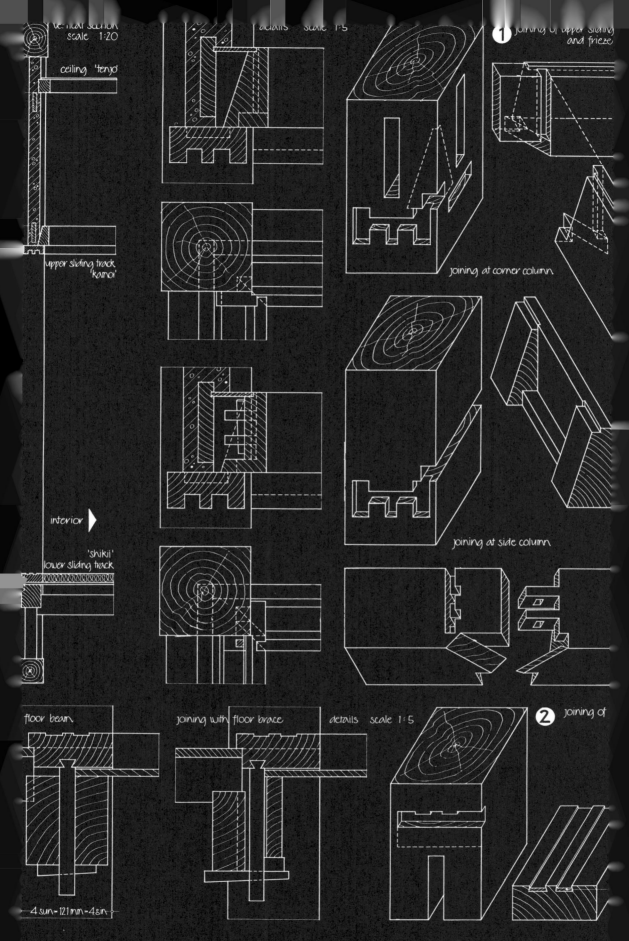

vertical section
scale 1:20

details   scale 1:5

① joining of upper sliding
and frieze

ceiling 'tenjo'

upper sliding track
'kamoi'

interior ▶

'shikii'
lower sliding track

floor beam

joining at corner column

joining at side column

joining with floor brace   details   scale 1:5

② joining of

4 sun = 121 mm = 4 sin

of upper sliding track 'kamoi' according 'kiwari' - module :   height/width = 0.4/0.85 x column section (=4 sun) = 1.6/3.4 sun = 48/103
of frieze rail 'nageshi'   height/width = 0.9/0.5 x column section (=4 sun) = 3.6/2.0 sun = 109/605

Though they seriously affect life in many ways, they are hardly mentioned by writers on Japanese architecture—another circumstance that has added to the general confusion of opinion that exists about the potential of Japanese motifs in contemporary architecture. The increasing use of this type of room partitioning in contemporary building is not due to a somewhat belated recognition of the advantages of this system, but is to be attributed to the technical improvement that enables partitioning with sliding units without having to accept the multiple defects mentioned above.

A very controversial part among the components of fittings is the frieze rail, *uchi-nori-nageshi,* which braces the columns just above the upper wooden track, *kamoi,* at a height of about 1 *ken* (1,818 mm. = 6 ft.) and reinforces the latter. Doubtlessly, its origin was due to the necessity of providing lateral bracing to the columns as can be evidenced in many old buildings where these strong lateral bracings are firmly tied to the column in various heights. Yet, since the introduction of concealed horizontal tie members, *nuki* (from 17th-century Sung period architecture of the Chinese), these lateral bracings were no longer constructionally needed for the main framework and instead were only put to reinforcing—quite unnecessarily—the upper sliding track, *kamoi,* at certain points. Thus, controversy exists as to why the frieze rail, *nageshi,* is still used, even in solid walls that do not have sliding panels, and why, upon remaining, it did not follow the general tendency to economize by reducing wood dimensions, but instead retained its original, somewhat heavy appearance.

Since apparently neither constructional logic nor economic reason can account for its continued presence, it is reasonable to believe that visual-aesthetic considerations were instrumental. This assumption seems to be supported by the fact that, optically speaking, the wall above the doors, *kokabe* (literally, little wall), which ranges from 1.8–3.0 ft. (560–900 mm.) in height, needs a beamlike element that would appear to carry the load above. Also, in the case of a solid wall plane without doors, the division of the whole wall height by an intermediate frieze rail in a ratio of 1:2 to 1:3, combined with the frequently irregular column placement of 1 *ken,* 1 1/2 *ken,* or 2 *ken,* actually does create a harmonious, though asymmetrical, pattern of white wall rectangles, which in its entirety reaches artistic quality.

However, as logical as the previous assumptions may seem, it appears improbable that the ordinary carpenter in building for the lower classes and being provided with a minimum of means, would have concerned himself with such visual effects. Rather it must be assumed that he willingly would have made changes if he could have reduced the costs; and indeed this he has done. There are many houses that do not have a frieze rail, and others wherein the frieze rail has been reduced in size to a bare minimum necessary for reinforcing the upper sliding track, *kamoi.* The only conclusion then is that the retention of the frieze rail and its dimension in the ordinary dwelling is due to traditional custom.

Cases where real structural elements were concealed and instead superfluous ones introduced in order to create a particular visual-aesthetic effect, cannot, even as an exceptional case, be professed to be a feature of the Japanese house in spite of such claims by many Western writers. These cases owe their existence usually to a misunderstood attempt to revive the former *sukiya* architecture in the current so-called new *sukiya* style. The latter, however, is lacking that very structural directness and honesty of the original *sukiya* style, of which an essential component was the *shin-kabe* (literally, genuine or honest wall), a wall that honestly shows structural systems.

translucent paper panel

There are two different types of sliding paper panels in the Japanese house: *shōji* and *fusuma.* Both possess a structural skeleton of light wooden strips arranged in a rectangular pattern and framed by somewhat stronger struts. But, while the *shōji* is pasted with translucent paper only on one side, the *fusuma* is covered on both sides with heavy opaque paper. The translucent variety, *shōji,* as a rule furnishes walls either facing directly to the outside or facing across the veranda or corridor. As this panel type is

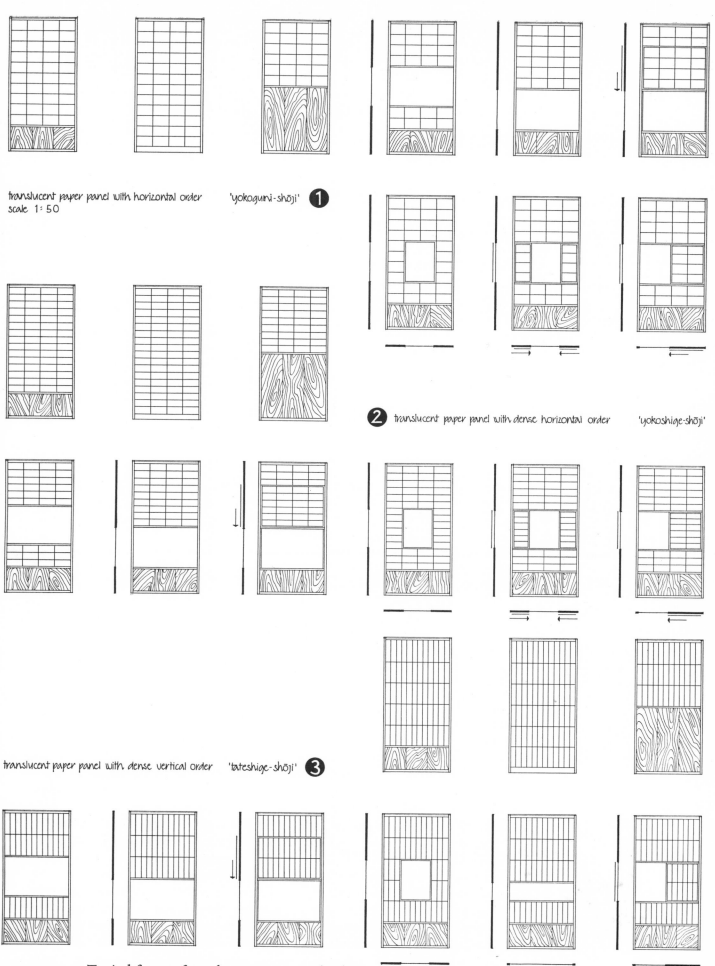

translucent paper panel with horizontal order   'yokogumi-shōji' **1**
scale 1:50

2 translucent paper panel with dense horizontal order   'yokoshige-shōji'

translucent paper panel with dense vertical order   'tateshige-shōji' **3**

FIGURE 39: Typical forms of translucent paper panels, *shōji*.

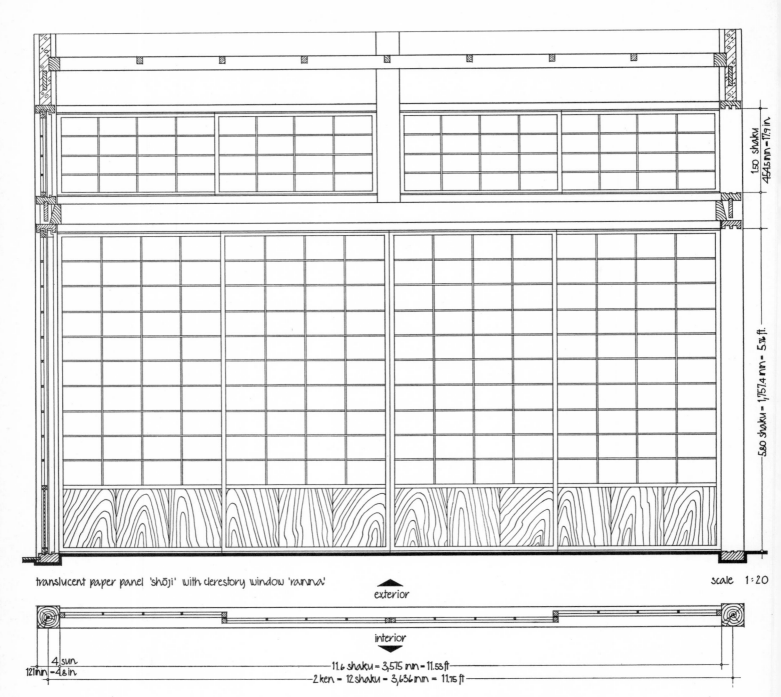

translucent paper panel 'shōji' with clerestory window 'ramma'

exterior

interior

scale 1:20

1.50 shaku
4545 mm = 17.9 in

5.80 shaku = 1,757.4 mm = 5.76 ft.

4 sun
121mm - 4.8 in

11.6 shaku = 3,575 mm = 11.53 ft
2 ken = 12 shaku = 3,636 mm = 11.75 ft

FIGURE 40: Translucent paper panels, *shōji,* in wall opening.

sometimes used also on interior walls where light is wanted, the translation "translucent paper panel" for *shōji* is actually a more appropriate definition than "exterior sliding door," which it is usually called.

The literal meaning of *shōji* is "interceptor," a word very appropriate to indicate its original role in the house organism. The word was first used to designate the portable standing screen, which was the earliest room partition and room enclosure. Then, after being put into tracks, the sliding variety was generally called *fusuma-no-shōji,* *fusuma* literally meaning bedquilt because its pattern resembles the latter (Plate 53). Yet, after the evolution of the translucent sliding door, *fusuma-no-shōji* was applied only to the opaque variety while the new translucent variety was given the name *akari-shōji* (literally, light interceptor). In the process of simplification, *akari-shōji* became just *shōji* while *fusuma-no-shōji* became *fusuma.*

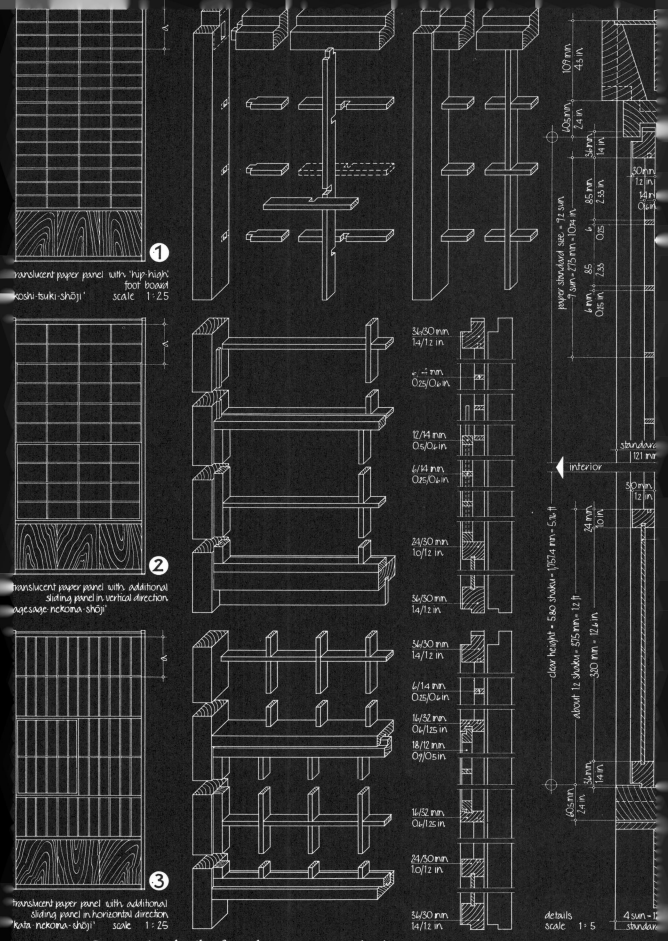

①
translucent paper panel with 'hip-high'
foot board
'koshi-tsuki-shōji'   scale 1:25

②
translucent paper panel with additional
sliding panel in vertical direction
'agesage-nekoma-shōji'

③
translucent paper panel with additional
sliding panel in horizontal direction
'kata-nekoma-shōji'   scale 1:25

36/30 mm
14/12 in

6/14 mm
0.25/0.6 in

12/14 mm
0.5/0.6 in

6/14 mm
0.25/0.6 in

24/30 mm
1.0/1.2 in

36/30 mm
14/12 in

36/30 mm
14/12 in

6/14 mm
0.25/0.6 in

16/32 mm
0.6/1.25 in

18/12 mm
0.9/0.5 in

16/32 mm
0.6/1.25 in

24/30 mm
1.0/1.2 in

36/30 mm
14/12 in

details
scale   1:5

109 mm
4.3 in

605 mm
2.4 in

36 mm
1.4 in

85 mm
2.33 in

6
0.25

85
2.33

6 mm
0.25 in

paper standard size = 7.2 sun
9 sun = 273 mm = 10.74 in

clear height = 580 shaku = 1,757.4 mm = 5.76 ft

about 1.2 shaku = 375 mm = 1.2 ft

320 mm = 12.6 in

34 mm
1.4 in

605 mm
2.4 in

interior

30 mm
1.2 in
1.4 in
0.16 in

standard
121 mm

310 mm
1.2 in

24 mm
1.0 in

4 sun = 12
standard

FIGURE 41: Construction details of translucent paper panels shōji

It is understood that *shōji,* like all other components of the Japanese house, has standard measurements. Its width is determined by column distance and its height by distance between upper and lower track, both of which are subject to the horizontal and vertical modular order of the house. Organization of the wood-strip skeleton of the *shōji* is, as a rule, determined horizontally by a process of halving the panel width and vertically by the market size of the translucent *shōji* paper, commonly 9 *sun* (nominal size; actual size 9.2 *sun* = 279 mm. = 11 in.). The paper strips are pasted horizontally on the outside starting from the bottom and continuing upwards, to keep dust from entering if the paper becomes loose. According to the organization of the skeleton of the *shōji,* three major types have emerged (see drawings), each of which has several variations.

In better houses additional wood strips are provided for the frame, and members are beveled. Yet, the simple form, used in the ordinary dwelling, is not only aesthetically better but can also be composed in a greater variety of patterns.

Constructionally, the most astounding feature of both the translucent and opaque sliding panels *(shōji* and *fusuma)* is their extreme lightness. In the case of *shōji,* the horizontal members of the frame measure no more than 12 × 10 bu (36 × 30 mm. = 1.4 × 1.2 in.), whereas the vertical frame members are only 8 × 10 *bu* (24 × 30 mm. = 1.0 × 1.2 in.). The skeleton inside the frame then consists of wood strips 2 × 5 *bu* or even 2 × 4 *bu* (6 × 12 mm. = 1/4 × 1/2 in.), and the wooden plate inserted below at the base is but 1.5 *bu* (4.5 mm. = 3/16 in.) thick. The single sliding unit weighs but ounces and is so light that rollers to reduce friction in the lower track would be superfluous. All members have rectangular sections, and, as a rule, the edges are not even beveled; no decorative effect is striven for, and expediency and restraint are the only prevailing factors.

And yet, an intimate aesthetic sensation is effected. It is true that the proportions of the *shōji* pattern and the harmony of expression between wood and the translucent paper are partly responsible for this effect, but they only emphasize the actual source of this aesthetic quality: display of the fabric's structural potentialities through the utmost restraint in dimensioning.

To render possible the reduction of fabric to the minimum, excellent craftsmanship was required, especially since none of the components receive any surface treatment after their assemblage. Yet, even more instrumental for this extraordinary lightness were the prevailing climatic conditions. Without the noted high humidity throughout the year any craftsmanship, however excellent, would prove futile, for unsealed wood of such dimensions would certainly deform in the climatic conditions common to the West. But even with the favorable climate, the wood-strip skeleton, which actually gives the rigidity to the frame, needs preventive measures against deformation, since the members are no stronger than 2 × 4 *bu* (6 × 12 mm. = 1/4 × 1/2 in.). Thus, the wooden strips are notched into each other from alternate sides and thereby effect unexpected rigidity.

Simplicity of response to the constructional problem is demonstrated in each detail. Friction from sliding is reduced by having only the sides of the struts in contact with the upper track, and by having the grooves in the lower track just deep enough to keep the panel in position. Additional sliding panels that run in the vertical tracks of the *shōji* frame are joined so exactly that the smaller ones are held at any height by mere friction and do not require more than a light touch of a finger to be moved up or down. Larger units are provided with a simple bamboo spring to increase the friction. Of course, with age and use the minutely dressed joinings wear out; door panels chink open and shake in their track at the slightest breeze. But it is as inexpensive as it is simple to buy a replacement on the market, and there are Japanese who feel emotionally attracted, even touched, at the sight of an old, wornout, and fragile *shōji* (Plate 50).

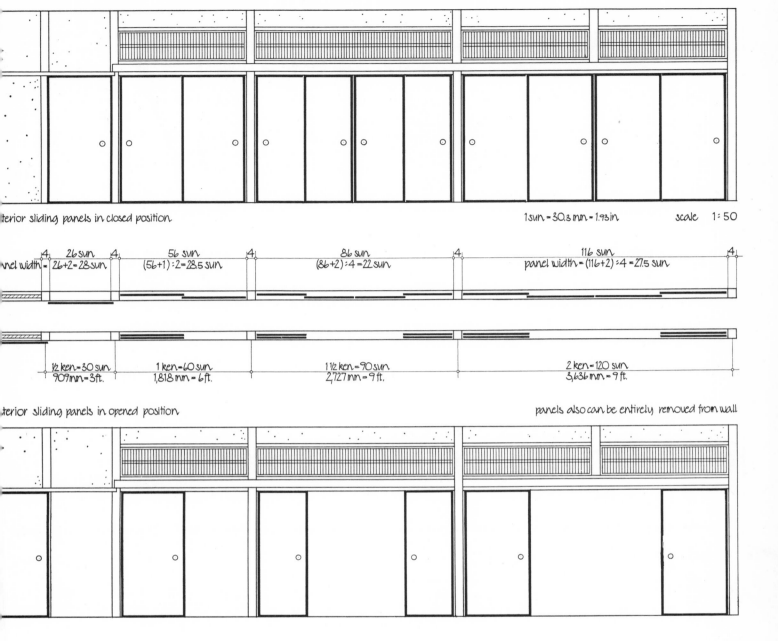

interior sliding panels in closed position

1 sun = 30.3 mm = 1.93 in   scale   1:50

panel width = 26+2 = 28 sun   56 sun   86 sun   panel width = (116+2) ÷ 4 = 27.5 sun
26 sun   (56+1) ÷ 2 = 28.5 sun   (86+2) ÷ 4 = 22 sun   116 sun

½ ken = 30 sun   1 ken = 60 sun   1½ ken = 90 sun   2 ken = 120 sun
909 mm = 3 ft.   1,818 mm = 6 ft.   2,727 mm = 9 ft.   3,636 mm = 9 ft.

interior sliding panels in opened position

panels also can be entirely removed from wall

arrangement of interior sliding panels for different column spacing on 'ken'-grid

elevations show wall facing to room of major importance

FIGURE 42: Arrangements of sliding panels for different column spacings.

opaque paper panel

The opaque paper panel which constitutes both room partition and room door in the house organism is called *fusuma*. Its constructional system closely resembles that of the translucent paper panel, *shōji,* in that it consists of a light wooden frame stiffened by thin wooden strips that are arranged in a rectangular pattern. Yet, while in the case of *shōji* this structural skeleton is pasted only on one side with translucent paper, the *fusuma* wood grid is covered on both sides by heavy opaque paper and additionally framed all the way around by a delicate wooden ledge that is frequently lacquered.

Since both *shōji,* the translucent sliding panel, and *fusuma,* the opaque sliding panel, have a common origin, the latter's evolution from standing screen to sliding panel, as mentioned before, does not differ in essence from the translucent variety. But,

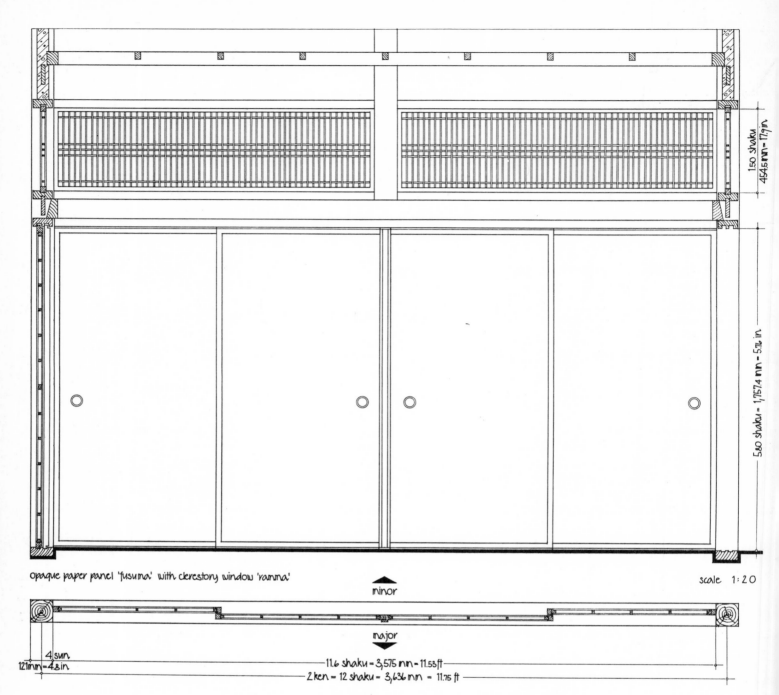

opaque paper panel 'fusuma' with clerestory window 'ramma'

scale 1:20

150 shaku = 4,545 mm = 17.9 in

5.80 shaku = 1,757.4 mm = 5.76 in

minor

major

4 sun
121mm = 4.8 in

11.6 shaku = 3,575 mm = 11.53 ft

2 ken = 12 shaku = 3,636 mm = 11.75 ft

FIGURE 43: Opaque paper panels, *fusuma*, in wall opening.

whereas the translucent paper panel underwent an essential metamorphosis in regard to function and application (and has gained a quality that proved decisive in the evolution of many distinct features of the Japanese residence), the opaque sliding panel, *fusuma,* because of its utilitarian function and decorative role, has preserved the original nature it had at the time it was imported from China. Otherwise, as to standardization of panels, dimensioning of wood, organization of panels together, etc., *fusuma* is modeled after the same factors as is the translucent paper panel, *shōji.*

Outstanding again is the extreme lightness of the structural skeleton. The frame, as a rule, is only 5.5 × 6.0 *bu* but there are also skeletons with frames of only 4.5 × 5.5 *bu* (14 × 17 mm. = 8/16 × 11/16 in.). Rigidity of this light frame is achieved by the same type of interior wooden grid that is used in the *shōji.* The wooden strips are no stronger than 5.5 × 3 *bu* (17 × 9 mm. = 10/16 × 6/16 in.), sometimes even only 4.5 × 3 *bu.* In

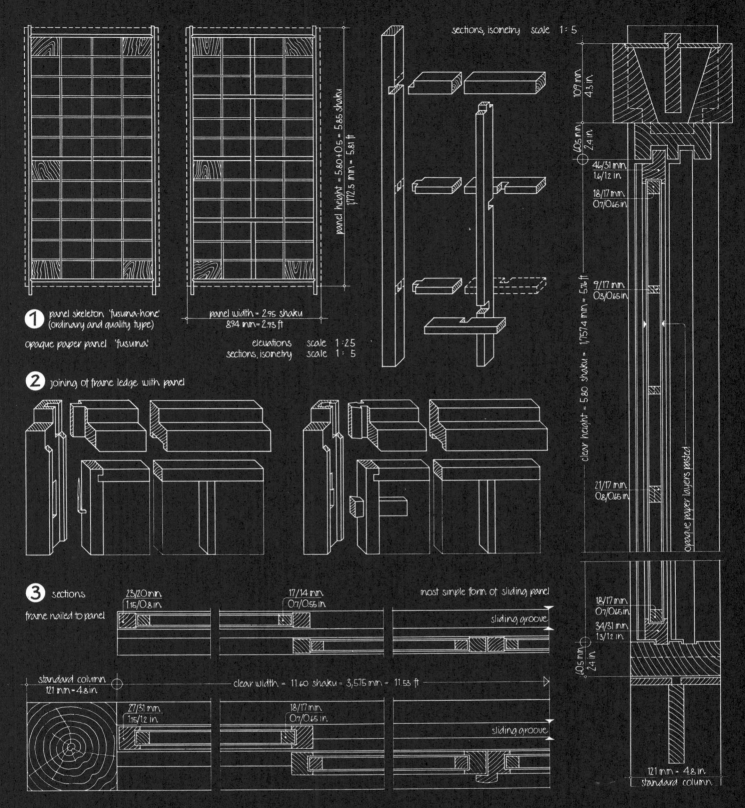

sections, isometry   scale 1 : 5

1 panel skeleton 'fusuma-hone'
(ordinary and quality type)

opaque paper panel 'fusuma'

panel width = 2.95 shaku
894 mm = 2.93 ft

elevations   scale 1 : 25
sections, isometry   scale 1 : 5

panel height = 5.80+0.5 = 5.85 shaku
1,772.5 mm = 5.81 ft

2 joining of frame ledge with panel

3 sections
frame nailed to panel

23/20 mm
1.15/0.8 in

17/14 mm
0.7/0.55 in

most simple form of sliding panel

sliding groove

standard column
121 mm = 4.8 in

clear width = 11.60 shaku = 3,575 mm = 11.53 ft

27/31 mm
1.15/1.2 in

18/17 mm
0.7/0.65 in

sliding groove

109 mm
4.3 in

.05 mm
2.4 in

46/31 mm
1.6/1.2 in

18/17 mm
0.7/0.65 in

9/17 mm
0.3/0.65 in

clear height = 5.80 shaku = 1,757.4 mm = 5.76 ft

opaque paper layers pasted

21/17 mm
0.8/0.65 in

18/17 mm
0.7/0.65 in

34/31 mm
1.3/1.2 in

.05 mm
2.4 in

121 mm = 4.8 in
standard column

FIGURE 44: Construction details of opaque paper panels, *fusuma*.

better-quality panels, rigidity is improved by using stronger members in the middle, both horizontally and vertically. The number of those members is the only means of distinguishing the constructional quality of *fusuma,* a difference hardly worth mentioning as far as Western architecture is concerned, where difference in personal wealth is much more clearly manifested in the quality of construction.

The sliding panels in the Japanese house characteristically demonstrate an unstable state of equilibrium of architectural fundamentals, a compromise between factors opposed to each other in their requirements but again depending on each other for their effects: constructional stability, utilitarian convenience, aesthetic proportion, material economy. Optimum exploitation of each factor has produced a state of unstable equilibrium so liable to topple if one factor just slightly leaves the area dictated by the ensemble of all the others. If, for example, constructional stability were improved, not only utilitarian convenience would suffer because of increased weight, but also aesthetic proportion and material economy would fade. Or if too much consideration were given to utilitarian convenience by reducing the panel weight, then conversely, the quality of all other factors would be encroached upon many times. The highest possible exploitation of all factors concerned and the resulting fragile state of harmony are true refinement for which the Japanese house is justly famed.

As the Japanese also cannot entirely escape the general human ambition of displaying monetary wealth in their dwellings, the *fusuma* offers an opportunity to do so with its thick paper capable of receiving a printed pattern, a mural, or calligraphic work, or through the color of the wooden ledge (Plate 158). In this instance, the Japanese house, which in general lacks any manifestation of wealth distinction other than by the quality of material and the size of building, clearly permits a clue as to the wealth of the owner.

windows

Since *shōji,* the translucent paper panel, principally fulfills the functions ordinarily performed in Western architecture by windows, the relative amount of actual window area, *mado,* is small in the Japanese house. Yet, there are numerous standard types, each of which plays a definite, and occasionally necessary, role in the whole organism, thus contradicting the allegation that the window is but an inferior component. Rather, it might be said that because of its quantitative limitation, it attracts marked attention when used and thus is frequently applied where architectural accentuation is desired. Therefore, in addition to its role as an architectural medium to facilitate ventilation, to provide light, and to allow view to the outside, as the Western window does, it constitutes an architectural feature in its own right, to be seen and appreciated as an object of aesthetic quality rather than as a mere expression of architectural necessity (Plates 58–60).

The window with low sill, *hijikake-mado* (literally, elbow-rest window), is used on the exterior walls of living rooms and does not differ essentially in construction, organization, appearance, and purpose from the translucent paper panel, *shōji,* except that it does not serve as a passage.

As the interior of the Japanese house is short in providing space (such as shelving) for storing continuously used utensils, bay windows, *de-mado* (literally, projected window) are arranged in the kitchen or living room in order to provide additional surface as table or shelf. The extent of projection varies from 1.5 *shaku* to a mere doubling of the width of the lower wooden track beyond the wall plane, and also the height of the lower track is not fixed but ranges from 1.2 *shaku* to 3.5 *shaku.*

The function of the window with high sill, *taka-mado* (literally, high window), is limited to ventilation and illumination. As such, it is used mainly in utility rooms such as the kitchen, bath, toilet, etc., usually on the outside walls but also sometimes on walls toward the corridor. Though much smaller than the *hijikake-mado,* the constructional-organizational system of these translucent sliding panels in tracks is quite similar to that of the *shōji.*

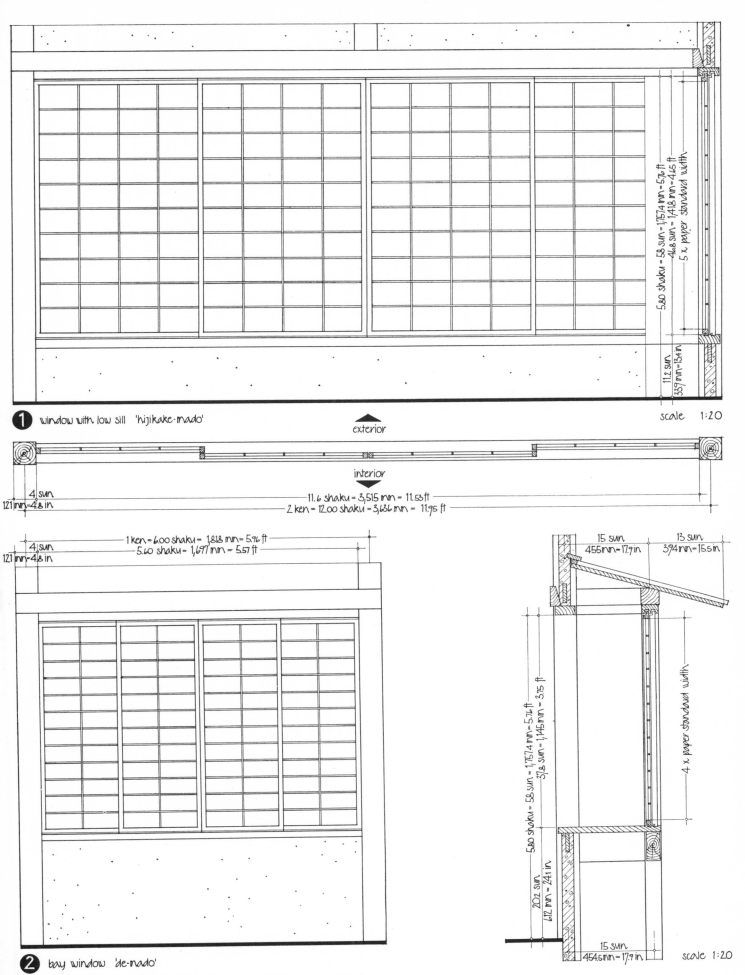

1 window with low sill 'hijikake-mado'

scale 1:20

5.80 shaku = 58 sun = 1,757.4 mm = 5.76 ft
4.68 sun = 1,418 mm = 4.65 in
5 × paper standard width

11.2 sun
339 mm = 13.4 in

▲
exterior
▼
interior

4 sun
121 mm = 4.8 in

11.6 shaku = 3,515 mm = 11.53 ft
2 ken = 12.00 shaku = 3,636 mm = 11.95 ft

4 sun
121 mm = 4.8 in

1 ken = 6.00 shaku = 1,818 mm = 5.96 ft
5.60 shaku = 1,697 mm = 5.57 ft

15 sun   13 sun
455 mm = 17.9 in   394 mm = 15.5 in

5.80 shaku = 58 sun = 1,757.4 mm = 5.76 ft
37.8 sun = 1,145 mm = 3.75 ft
4 × paper standard width

2 bay window 'de-mado'

20.2 sun
612 mm = 24.1 in

15 sun
454.5 mm = 17.9 in

scale 1:20

FIGURE 45: Window types and their construction details.

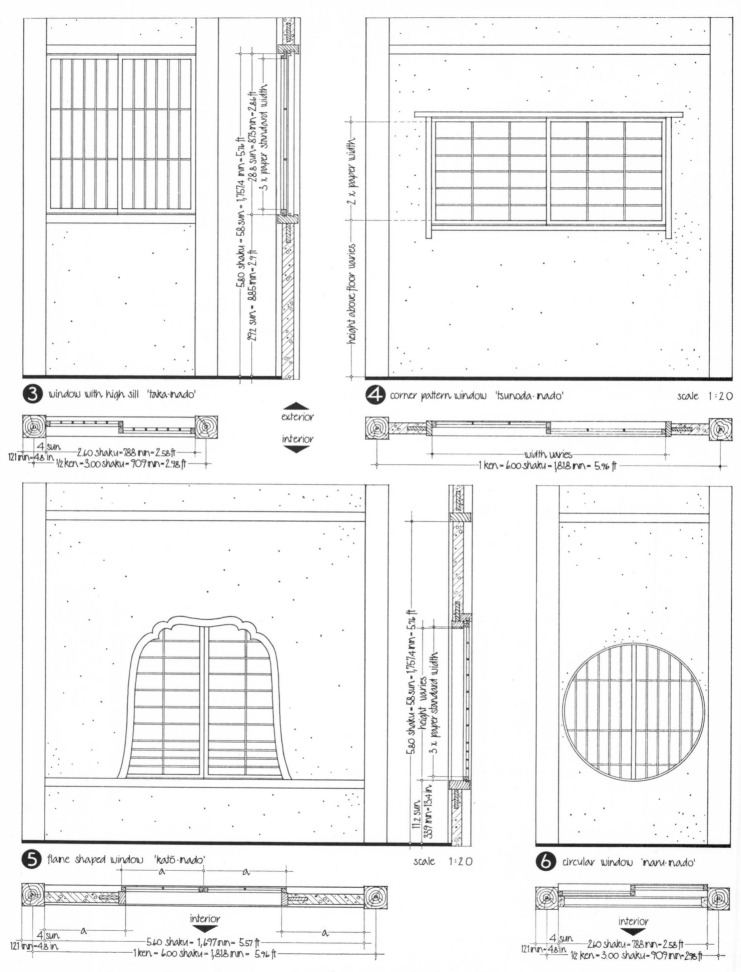

③ window with high sill 'taka-mado'

⑤ flame shaped window 'katō-mado'

④ corner pattern window 'tsunoda-mado'   scale 1:20

⑥ circular window 'maru-mado'

exterior
interior

5.80 shaku = 58 sun = 1,757.4 mm = 5.76 ft
28.8 sun = 873 mm = 2.86 ft
3 x paper standard width
29.2 sun = 885 mm = 2.9 ft

height above floor varies
2 x paper width

4 sun
121 mm = 4.8 in
2.60 shaku = 788 mm = 2.58 ft
1/2 ken = 3.00 shaku = 909 mm = 2.98 ft

width varies
1 ken = 6.00 shaku = 1,818 mm = 5.96 ft

5.80 shaku = 58 sun = 1,757.4 mm = 5.76 ft
height varies
3 x paper standard width
11.2 sun
339 mm = 13.4 in

scale 1:20

a   a

interior

4 sun
121 mm = 4.8 in
a
a
5.60 shaku = 1,697 mm = 5.57 ft
1 ken = 6.00 shaku = 1,818 mm = 5.96 ft

interior

4 sun
121 mm = 4.8 in
2.60 shaku = 788 mm = 2.58 ft
1/2 ken = 3.00 shaku = 909 mm = 2.98 ft

FIGURE 45 (continued): Window types and their construction details.

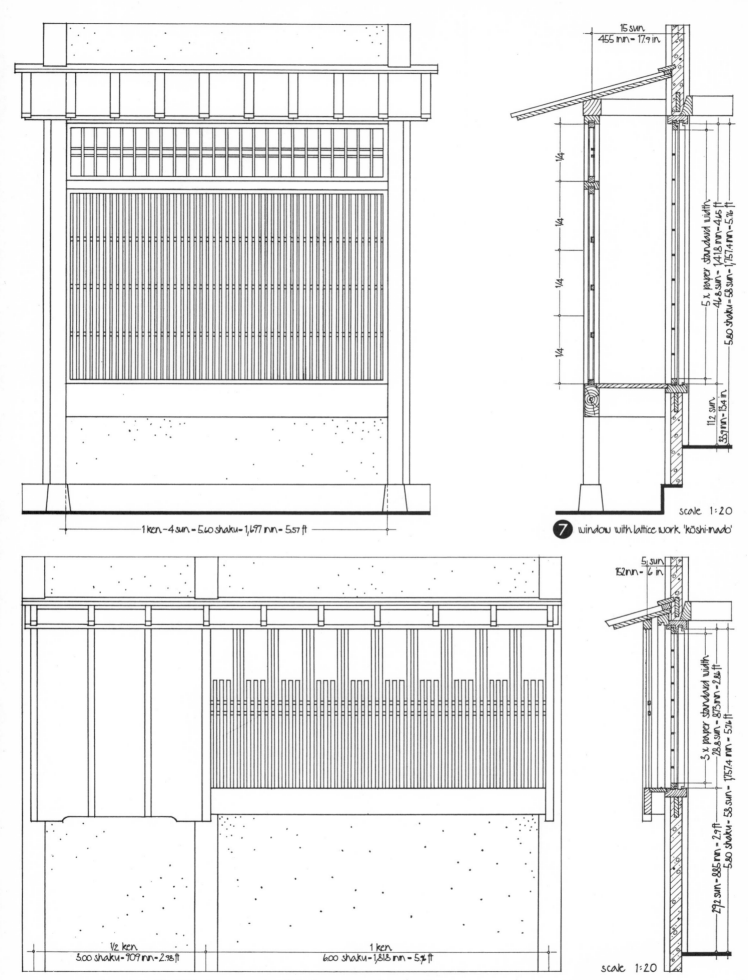

1 ken - 4 sun - 5.60 shaku - 1,697 mm - 5.57 ft

15 sun
455 mm - 17.9 in

1/4
1/4
1/4
1/4

1.12 sun
359 mm - 13.4 in

5 x. paper standard width.
41.8 sun - 1,418 mm - 4.65 ft
5.80 shaku - 58 sun - 1,757.4 mm - 5.76 ft

scale 1:20

7 window with lattice work. 'kōshi-mado'

1/2 ken
3.00 shaku - 909 mm - 2.98 ft

1 ken
6.00 shaku - 1,818 mm - 5.97 ft

5 sun
152 mm - 6 in

3 x. paper standard width.
28.8 sun - 873 mm - 2.86 ft
5.80 shaku - 58 sun - 1,757.4 mm - 5.76 ft

29.2 sun - 885 mm - 2.9 ft
5.80 shaku - 58 sun - 1,757.4 mm - 5.76 ft

scale 1:20

FIGURE 45 (continued): Window types and their construction details.

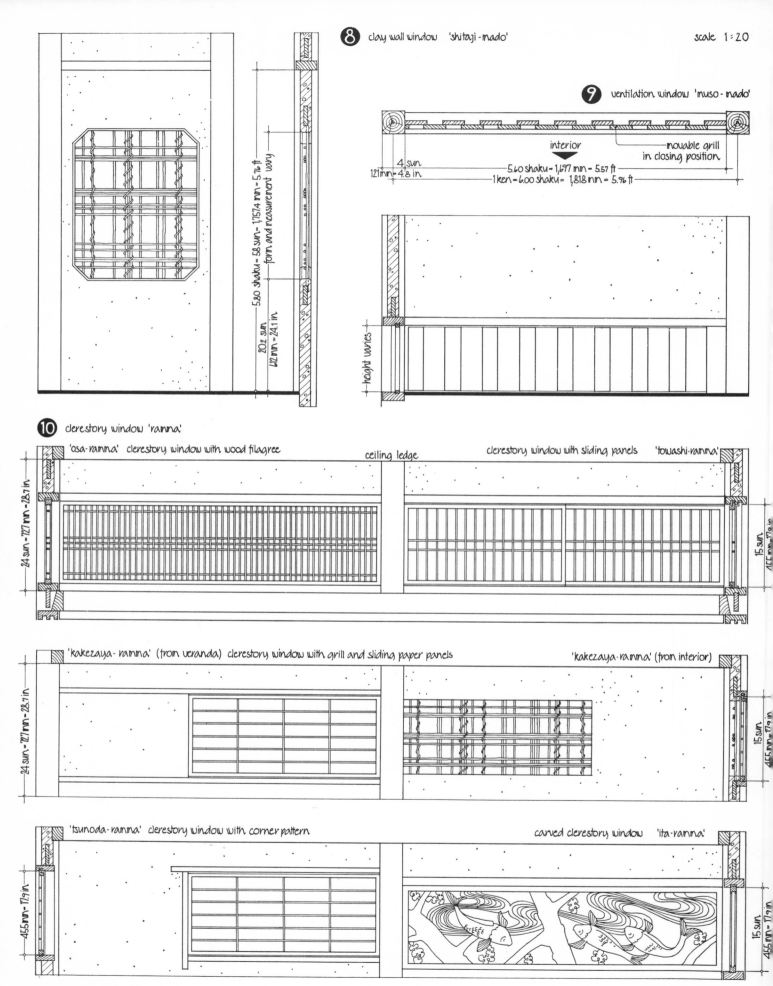

8 clay wall window 'shitaji-mado'   scale 1:20

9 ventilation window 'muso-mado'

interior ▼ — movable grill in closing position

4 sun
121 mm = 4.8 in
5.60 shaku = 1,697 mm = 5.57 ft
1 ken = 6.00 shaku = 1,818 mm = 5.96 ft

5.80 shaku = 58 sun = 1,757.4 mm = 5.76 ft
form and measurement vary

20.2 sun
612 mm = 24.1 in

height varies

10 clerestory window 'ranma'

'osa-ranma' clerestory window with wood filagree   ceiling ledge   clerestory window with sliding panels   'towashi-ranma'

24 sun = 727 mm = 28.7 in

15 sun
455 mm = 17.9 in

'kakezaya-ranma' (from veranda) clerestory window with grill and sliding paper panels   'kakezaya-ranma' (from interior)

24 sun = 727 mm = 28.7 in

15 sun
455 mm = 17.9 in

'tsunoda-ranma' clerestory window with corner pattern   carved clerestory window   'ita-ranma'

455 mm = 17.9 in

15 sun
455 mm = 17.9 in

FIGURE 45 (continued): Window types and their construction details.

The form of the flame-shaped window, *katō-mado* (literally, firelight window), which is also called *andon-mado,* is almost alien to the whole composition of rectangular planes, linear construction, and geometrically simple forms, and suggests that its major function is of a decorative nature. It is a rather common sight in shrines and temples, while its use in the residence is confined to the wealthier class who can afford to accentuate the place of the picture recess, *tokonoma,* by an ornamental window and a more effective light source than could be provided by a simple sliding door, *shōji.*

The corner pattern window, *tsunogara-mado,* and the circular window, *maru-mado,* also obtained their names because of their distinctive shapes. The shape of the former is a very characteristic feature of Japanese architecture, and with its clear distinction of horizontal and vertical frame members, reflects a very fine sense of structure and proportion. Both these window forms are primarily used in tearooms and sometimes in the entrance hall and reception room.

The lattice window, *koshi-mado* (literally, grating window), exists in three different forms: flush with the wall surface like *hijikake-mado;* projected on cantilevers like *demado;* or projected on stilts that perch on foundation stones. Its characteristic feature is a wooden latticework which permits the removal of the translucent sliding panels behind it for ventilation purposes or for viewing, yet without permitting sight from the outside in. This window type therefore is used in living rooms facing the street and, therefore, mainly in the city houses where living rooms often must face a very close roadside.

The clay-wall window, *shitaji-mado* (literally, under the earth window), is modeled into the solid clay wall; the choice of its form is left up to the personal taste of the owner. Geometrically pure forms have evolved that are supplied with an elaborate grill of bamboo, reed, or young branches. It is said that the famous tea master, Sen-no-Rikyu (1518–91), developed this type of window for the tearoom after having been stimulated by the sight of a farm hut where the wall openings simply had been broken into the clay wall, exposing the wall's bamboo skeleton. The window is used preferably in tearooms or, with strong decorative accent, next to the picture recess, *tokonoma.*

The functional system of the ventilation window, *musō-mado* (literally, unequal window), also called *renji-mado* (window with parallel batons) or *musha-mado* (soldier window) is based on two grills with vertical wooden strips, the clear space between the strips being equal to the width of each strip. While the exterior grid is stationary in the frame, the interior one can be moved in tracks of the same frame either to the left or right, thereby either closing or opening the slits of the exterior grid. It serves mainly as ventilation in toilet, bath, and storage space, but if used in the exterior shutters, *amado,* it also permits a view to the outside without having to open the protective shutter, an advisable precaution if the night is late and the caller unknown.

Primarily in order to permit air circulation, but also to provide additional light to the farther side of the room, the wall portion between the frieze rail, *uchinori-nageshi,* and the ceiling is frequently left open and provided with a wooden grill pattern, *ramma* (literally, space for *ran,* a type of wood), similar to a clerestory window. Here a constructional, practical device stimulated decorative utilization, and the many forms and formations in which the clerestory window has emerged suggest that the decorative quality is no longer a secondary attribute.

Ramma is employed above the opaque paper panels between two rooms, above the translucent paper panels between living room and veranda, above the main door of the entrance hall, above the glass panels of the enclosed veranda, and above the translucent paper panels of the study-place window. Frequently, in addition to a wooden grill, the opening is furnished with translucent paper panels to check excessive air circulation. Sometimes the clerestory window fills the entire space between the frieze rail and the ceiling, but normally it is inserted into the clay wall.

In addition to the "study-place window," *shoin-mado,* and the "chicken-heart window" of the wooden shutter, *okubyō-mado,* which will be mentioned later at the respective places, there are still other window forms. But they constitute variations of the forementioned basic types rather than variety. The interesting and almost paradoxical fact is that though the application of windows in the Japanese house is limited in proportion to other features, they nevertheless have emerged in so many essentially different types. The reason for this somehow astonishing phenomenon is that the window's function is neither dictated by mere necessity nor is it in each case clearly defined and singular. Rather, its purpose changes with location and produces, together with frequently dominating decorative functions, many differing states of architectural demand, each eliciting a different response.

picture recess

It has been stated that the Japanese room, like the house as a whole, lacks accentuation of one side or one direction other than that effected through orientation to sun and environment. Unlike Western residences, rooms are not axially organized by obvious location of entrance-exit and by placement of furniture, nor is the sequence of rooms defined by a gradation from minor to major. Such will certainly be the impression received while passing through a sequence of several rooms, all controlled by sameness of scale, material, feature, and treatment. Yet, to the Japanese the spiritual center of the house is the picture recess, *tokonoma,* or abbreviated, *toko.* Not only does such a focusing of esteem exist psychologically, but as is evidenced in the construction of the ceiling, this orientation of room and house to *tokonoma* is also physically manifested through spatial organization and constructional detail. Here, as a single instance in the Japanese house, additive decoration is displayed in the form of a hanging picture scroll, *kakejiku,* and a flower in a simple vase below it, giving an excellent example of the increase in effect through limitation of motif (Plates 75–79).

While the undisputed aesthetic significance of the picture recess and its controversial historic background will be examined later, at this time it only needs to be mentioned that *tokonoma* is not a mere form of décor with a questionable architectural integrity, but is simply a part of the basic stuff of which the Japanese residence is composed. Indeed, it is a strong statement of the spiritual-aesthetic significance of building and dwelling, which is unique for Japan. Just as the origin of *tokonoma* is multiple—varying with the eager opinion of the scholar—so too its conclusive meaning in the ordinary dwelling is not but one. Display place for a piece of art, sacred place of an admittedly uncertain relation to Buddhism, honorable place for defining the seat of the distinguished guest, all of these have supposedly in the past had their separate architectural expressions but have streamed together and, each of them contributing its own significant distinction to one singular statement, have resulted in one of the most dynamic achievements of Japanese residential architecture.

The *tokonoma* is also subjected to the modular order of design (based on 1 *ken* = 1,818 mm. = 6 ft.). It is usually recessed 1/2 *ken* and extends over a length of 1 *ken,* thus occupying a bay of 3 × 6 feet (909 × 1,818 mm.). The floor of this recess is differentiated from the room's mat floor either by a separate level or a different material, or both. In case the difference is in level, the recessed space is marked by a raised threshold, *tokogamachi,* which in its traditional execution is lacquered in black. Since the floor area behind the threshold corresponds with the standard mat size, the flooring may consist of a single mat, but more frequently a boarded floor, *ita-datami,* slightly lower than the threshold, is provided, which is covered with a thin straw carpet, *usuberi;* or the boarding itself remains the final floor surface, either in one single piece or several joined together. The height of the crossbeam above, *otoshigake,* differs markedly from the standard height of all the other wall openings, sharply interrupting the circumferential frieze rail, *uchinori-nageshi,* and effecting through a bold break of continuity an architectural accentuation which could not be stronger if more elaborate and extensive means were employed. It supports the wall above and has, as a rule, a square section.

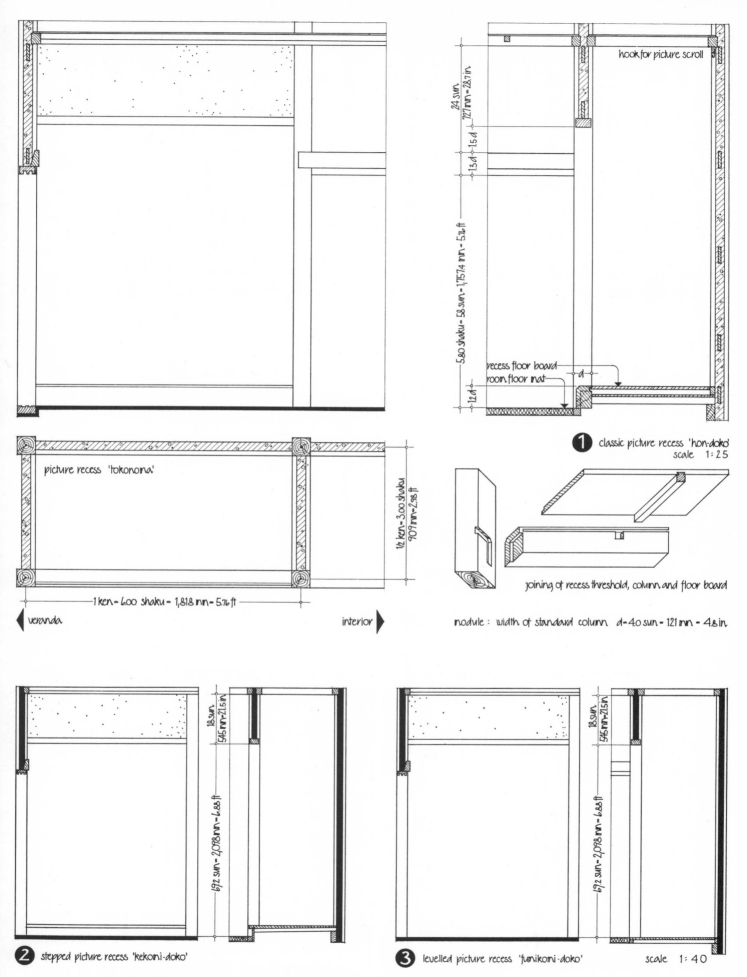

hook for picture scroll

24 sun
727 mm = 28.7 in

1.3 d - 1.5 d

5.80 shaku = 58 sun = 1,757.4 mm = 5.76 ft

recess floor board
room floor mat
12 d
d

1 classic picture recess 'hon-doko'
scale 1 : 25

picture recess 'tokonoma'

1/2 ken = 3.00 shaku
909 mm = 2.98 ft

1 ken = 6.00 shaku = 1,818 mm = 5.76 ft

◀ veranda

interior ▶

joining of recess threshold, column and floor board

module : width of standard column d = 4.0 sun = 121 mm = 4.8 in

18 sun
545 mm = 21.5 in

672 sun = 2,078 mm = 6.88 ft

2 stepped picture recess 'kekomi-doko'

18 sun
545 mm = 21.5 in

672 sun = 2,078 mm = 6.88 ft

3 levelled picture recess 'fumikomi-doko'

scale 1 : 40

FIGURE 46: Typical forms of picture recess, *tokonoma*, and their construction.

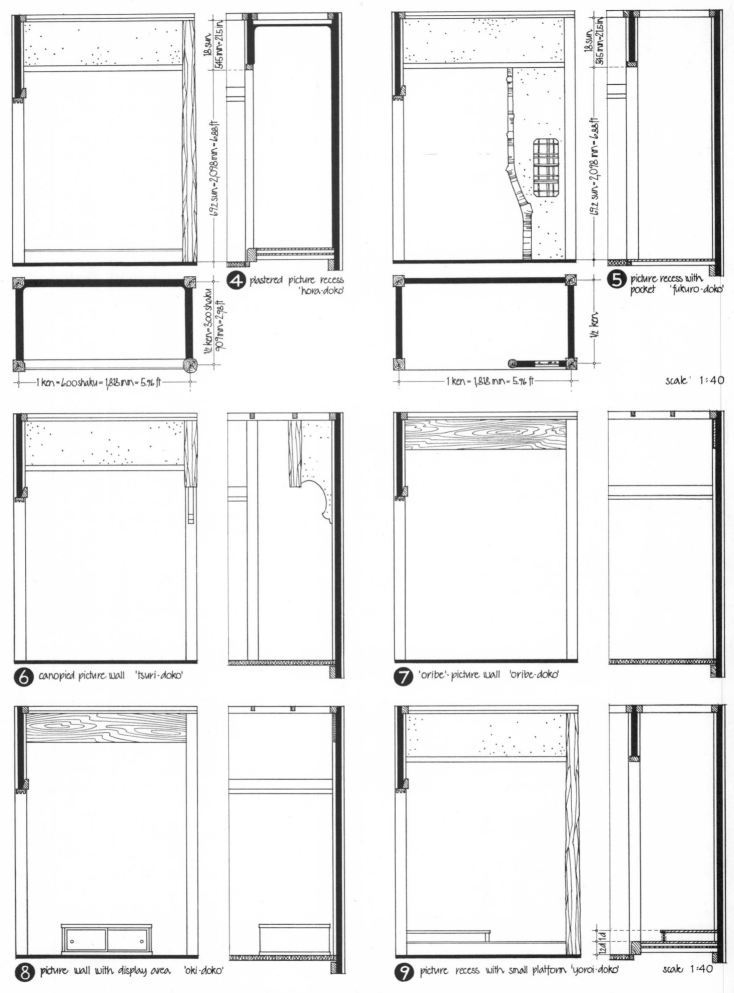

4 plastered picture recess 'hora·doko'

18 sun
545 mm = 21.5 in

19.2 sun = 2,078 mm = 6.88 ft

1/2 ken = 3.00 shaku
909 mm = 2.98 ft

1 ken = 6.00 shaku = 1,818 mm = 5.96 ft

5 picture recess with pocket 'fukuro·doko'

18 sun
545 mm = 21.5 in

19.2 sun = 2,078 mm = 6.88 ft

1/2 ken

1 ken = 1,818 mm = 5.96 ft

scale 1:40

6 canopied picture wall 'tsuri·doko'

7 'oribe'·picture wall 'oribe·doko'

8 picture wall with display area 'oki·doko'

9 picture recess with small platform 'yoroi·doko'

12 da

scale 1:40

FIGURE 46 (continued): Typical forms of picture recess, *tokonoma*.

One side of the recess borders the outside wall of the room through which light enters, while on the interior side another recess, *tana* or *tokowaki,* which contains wall shelves and cabinets arranged in various ways, is aligned. The partition between the two recesses consists of a solid wall piece with a column, *tokobashira,* at the front. In the archaic performance, the section of this recess column is square and is of identical material and appearance to that of the other columns in the room. However, occasionally this member, like many another in the *tokonoma,* is altered for satisfaction of a personal liking, although hardly to the improvement of expression; and exquisite woods of particular grain and shape are widely used. At the back wall directly under the ceiling ledge, a minute wooden strip is attached which contains a metal hook for hanging the picture scroll, *kakejiku.* While the walls of the recess are formed by materials and methods identical to those of the solid walls of the room, the ceiling of the *tokonoma* is distinct from the room ceiling, thus completing the multiple measures taken to distinguish this place from the rest of the room.

Like all components in the Japanese house that have a certain optical-decorative implication, such as the window and the ceiling, so too the *tokonoma* has emerged in various forms. Again, all the variations, as could be expected, have been largely standardized, although the *tokonoma* in the tearoom has always remained the object of invention and innovation.

In addition to the types depicted, there are also many other variations which may produce new details, but hardly new aspects. However, the archaic, and probably most pure, design of the *tokonoma* employed materials and forms of a kind not different from those used in the entire dwelling. The architectural task, so to speak, was to create additional space reserved solely for a piece of art and to distinguish the spiritual importance of its location. The immediate and bold-simple way of responding to this demand in the classic way without any elaborate artistic means was architectural accentuation in its best and strongest form. Yet, man's wish for individuality and his inclination toward extravagance wherever means permit did not exempt the Japanese, and the use of exquisite woods along with a preference for odd shapes has somewhat falsified that pure effect of the classic *tokonoma.*

shelving recess

Since the picture recess, *tokonoma,* as a rule does not occupy the entire room width, another recess, which is usually furnished with decorative shelves and cabinets, is placed to one side. Adjoining the *tokonoma* at the end toward the house interior, this shelving recess is to be interpreted as an integral part of the picture recess rather than as an independent architectural feature. Yet, there are houses in which the decorative shelving recess is replaced by the more useful closet, the *oshiire.*

The decorative shelving recess is called *tana,* a name that was given to it because the recess contains built-in shelves called *tana* in Japanese. Frequently the name *chigaidana* is also used. This, however, refers to a particular order of shelving most commonly used in the ordinary houses. Another identification, *tokowaki* (literally, side of the *toko*), designates its adjoining location to the picture recess. It is separated from the latter by a shieldlike solid wall of clay which is defined at the front by the previously mentioned column, the *tokobashira.* The parting wall has, as a rule, a bamboo grid window admitting light from the outside across the picture recess and into the shelving alcove, which otherwise would be left quite dark.

It is said that the origin of the *tana* dates back to the 10th and 11th centuries, at the time of the *shinden* style, when a similar kind of cabinet which was not yet built-in but was designed as a portable unit was already in use. Although utilitarian in origin, the shelf arrangement, by being placed at the picture recess and by becoming combined with the latter, inevitably changed into a decorative element, while its original function as a container for utensils was no longer of primary concern.

Thus, having changed not in form but in function to a decorative piece, the shelving recess, *tana,* has produced more organizational varieties than any other feature in the

adjacent picture recess 'tokonoma'

1 ken = 1,818 mm = 6 ft

1/2

1/2

3/4

1/4

1/2

1/2

1/3   1/3   1/3

1/2

1/4

1/4

1/3   1/3   1/3

3/5

2/5

1,757 mm = 5.8 ft

1/2

1/4

1/4

1/2

1/3   1/3   1/3

1/4

1/4

1/2

1/2

examples of standardized order for
shelving recess 'tana' ('tokowaki')

upper cabinet

2/5   3/5

shelves

1/2   1/2

1/3   2/3

lower cabinet

5.80 shaku
1,757 mm = 5.7 ft

scale 1:50   909 mm = 3 ft

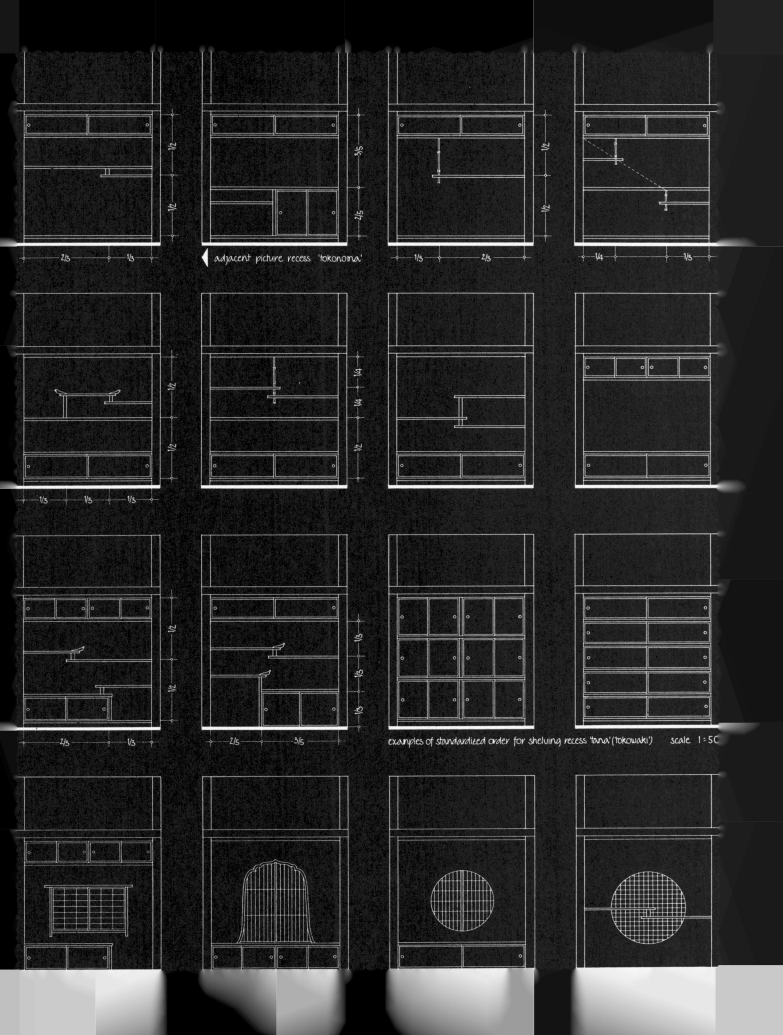

adjacent picture recess 'tokonoma'

examples of standardized order for shelving recess 'tana' ('tokowaki')   scale 1:50

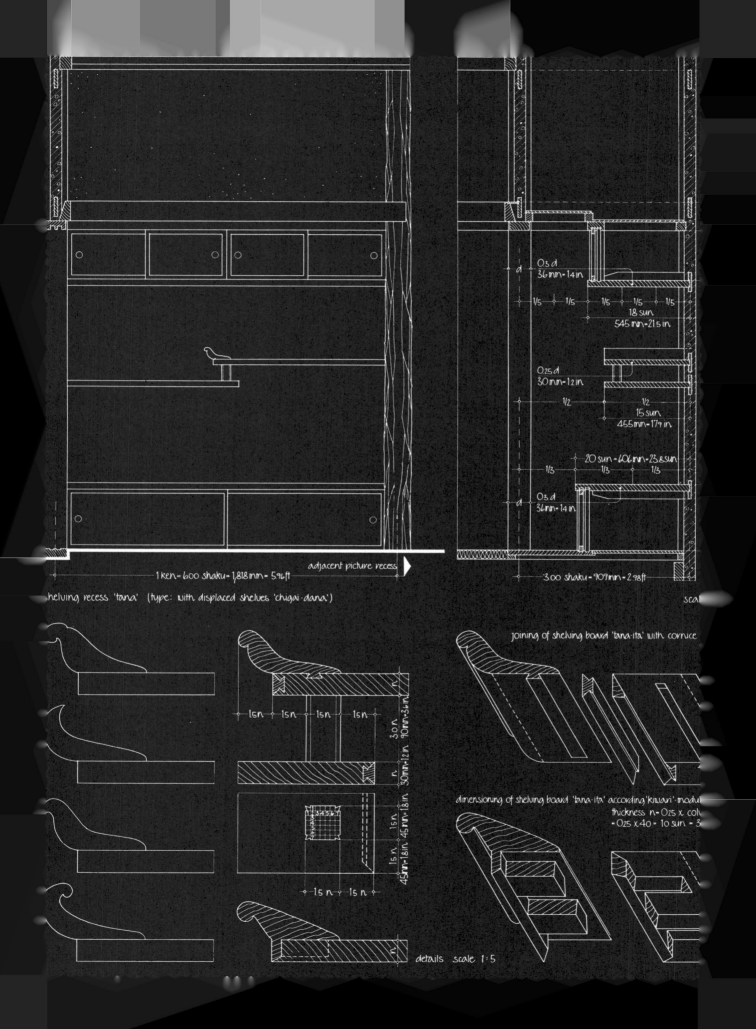

1 ken = 6.00 shaku = 1,818 mm = 5.96 ft

adjacent picture recess ▶

shelving recess 'tana' (type: with displaced shelves 'chigai-dana')

scale

0.3 d
36 mm = 1.4 in

1/5 1/5 1/5 1/5 1/5
18 sun
545 mm = 21.5 in

0.25 d
30 mm = 1.2 in

1/2 1/2
15 sun
455 mm = 17.9 in

20 sun = 606 mm = 23.8 sun
1/3 1/3 1/3

0.3 d
36 mm = 1.4 in

3.00 shaku = 909 mm = 2.98 ft

joining of shelving board 'tana-ita' with cornice

1.5 n 1.5 n 1.5 n 1.5 n

3.0 n 90 mm = 3.5 in
n 30 mm = 1.2 in
1.5 n 45 mm = 1.8 in
45 mm = 1.8 in

1 2 3 4 5 6 7

1.5 n 1.5 n

1.5 n 1.5 n

dimensioning of shelving board 'tana-ita' according 'kiwari'-modul
thickness n = 0.25 x col
= 0.25 x 40 = 10 sun = 3

details scale 1:5

house. All of them have been classified, denominated, and put into woodblock prints at the disposal of every carpenter in the country. Yet, such a particular concern for the *tana* does not necessarily imply an affirmation of its architectural quality. On the contrary, in many cases the wish for originality led design to petty absurdities which harmed the unity of expression that distinguished the interior of the Japanese dwelling.

The shelving recess, usually covering an area of 3 × 6 ft. (909× 1,818 mm.), is, like the picture recess, incorporated into the house organization by being synchronized with the universal beat of the *ken* module. Yet, contrary to the picture recess, it is tied to the room order by being assimilated into the circumferential frieze rail, which also braces the top of the door and window tracks. Thus, the *tana,* as a physical feature, is to be considered a component adjusted to its neighborhood rather than a component contrasting to it as some *tana* patterns tend to suggest.

Both floor and ceiling consist of a wooden plank, the latter at the same height as the frieze rail, while the back and side walls consist of the same clay used in the room itself. Constituent parts of *tana* are cantilevered shelves attached to the back wall. If cabinets with sliding panels are incorporated, they are fixed in height of the frieze rail above or below at the floor, or both. These members extend to only a part of the depth of the recess, thus preserving the effect of one niche. Their dimensions and relationship to each other are standardized to the minutest detail in a precise ratio to the standard column section (4 *sun* = 121 mm. = 4.8 in.) and are coordinated with the *ken* module. Exactness and accuracy of joinery ranks with the finest cabinetwork. Sculptural treatment is given in particular to the wooden cornice, *fude-kaeshi* (literally, writing brush returner), which accentuates the end of the upper shelf when the freely projecting form is employed. Here also the profiles have become standardized, and the carpenter makes use of them rather than engaging in the development of new forms.

The most distinct and probably most frequently employed type of *tana* is the *chigai-dana,* the recess with displaced shelves. More than one hundred different types of *tana* have emerged, all catalogued, yet hardly requiring complete recording at this place. It suffices to state that in spite of austere limitation of space, motif, and means such a variety of standard forms could be produced, for such a phenomenon surely contradicts the commonly held opinion that standardization strangles creative design and renders narrow the scope of architectural possibilities. On the contrary, it is evident that standardization of a basic feature and the resulting clear definition of its architectural role in the house organism was the very requisite for freeing all creative forces from entanglement with mere practical-constructional factors, thus allowing full exploitation of architectural potential and development of new form.

However, it must be pointed out that once standardization had exerted its eliminative and sobering effect and had encompassed the entire house the Japanese failed completely in developing new standards, both for living and building, leaving the standards in a medieval state, too perfected and too remote to permit organic transfer to contemporary living and building. Western civilization and technology, although bringing conveniences into the house in the form of electric and sanitary installations, furniture, and the like, only created architectural discrepancies in the formerly unique expression and could not satisfactorily bridge the gap between the past and present. On the other hand, the same technology also provided the means for enabling a radically new approach to a contemporary form of dwelling, which Japan's domestic architecture has yet to see.

study place

As utilitarian or even indispensable as devices and components generally are in the Japanese house, some of them have not remained true to their original functional motive. As the picture recess, *tokonoma,* and shelving alcove, *tana,* have exemplified, the Japanese, also, could not quite escape the common architectural trend to decoratively exploit a constructional-utilitarian necessity, gradually bringing about a shift

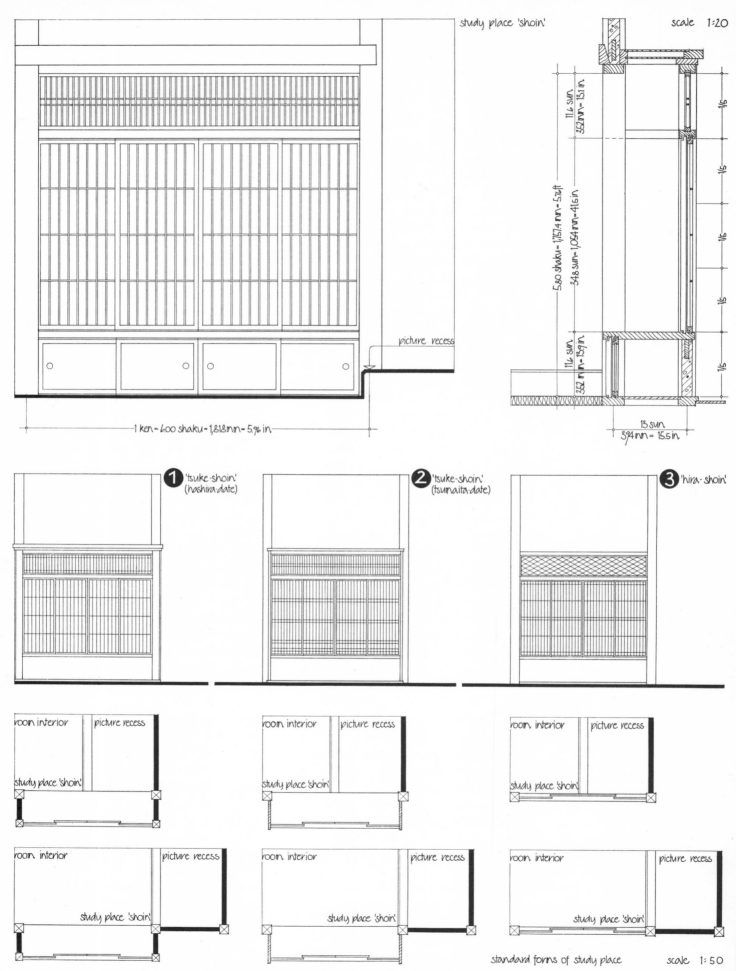

study place 'shoin'   scale   1:20

picture recess

1 ken = 6.00 shaku = 1,818 mm = 5.96 in

11.6 sun
352 mm = 13.1 in

5.80 shaku = 1,757.4 mm = 5.74 ft

34.8 sun = 1,054 mm = 41.5 in

11.6 sun
352 mm = 13.9 in

13 sun
394 mm = 15.5 in

1 'tsuke-shoin' (hashira-date)   **2** 'tsuke-shoin' (tsunaita-date)   **3** 'hira-shoin'

room interior | picture recess
study place 'shoin'

room interior | picture recess
study place 'shoin'

room interior | picture recess
study place 'shoin'

room interior | picture recess
study place 'shoin'

room interior | picture recess
study place 'shoin'

room interior | picture recess
study place 'shoin'

standard forms of study place   scale   1:50

FIGURE 49: Typical forms and construction details of the study place, *shoin*.

of emphasis from utilitarian to decorative in a manner that preserved the original meaning only in form, but not in function.

A similar transformation can be observed also in another distinctive component in the Japanese residence, the study place, *shoin*. Also here a formerly practical device has become a decorative feature without essentially changing its form. As is the case in the picture recess and shelving alcove, the evolution of the *shoin* reflects the close architectural interchange between the various social strata—nobility, clergy, warrior, and commoner—which distinguishes the growth of the Japanese residence, and plainly manifests the various backgrounds to which the Japanese house owes its extraordinary character.

Originally a reading place in the house of Buddhist priests of the Zen sect, the *shoin* was projected into the veranda for better light conditions and was elevated for convenient reading. But when re-enacted in the mansions of the nobility and the military, the *shoin* left the private sphere of the house and was performed in the reception room which was reserved for official occasions. With the effacement of the feudal rank distinction in buildings, the merchants adopted this feature for their own representative space in the house and thus made it accessible for the houses of the common people. Here, *shoin* is but a window attached at right angles to the picture recess, *tokonoma*, to which it provides light, and being harmoniously incorporated into the spiritual, decorative organism of *tokonoma* and *tana* (the two recesses) it no longer primarily serves its original purpose as a study place. Still, one can occasionally see the master of the family sitting at the bay and contemplating life while viewing the garden, not unlike the priest who hundreds of years ago wrote his scripts in the *shoin* (Plates 88–89).

Although exposed to many influences and resulting alterations, the study place, *shoin,* has essentially preserved its original features. The modular grid of *ken* determines the main dimensions of height and width, whereas the baseboard is elevated approximately 1.2 ft. above the floor. The upper frame piece, then, corresponds to the circumferential frieze rail and integrates the bay into the room composition. The upper fourth of the opening is provided with a lattice grill, *ramma,* while the remaining three-fourths of the opening is furnished with four translucent sliding panels, *shōji.* In case the *shoin* is projected as was its original form, the side wall consists of clay or of a thick wooden board, while the space under the table board serves as storage with access through wooden sliding panels either from the inside or from the veranda. In the simplified execution, the *shoin* window is in the same plane as the rest of the wall. Usually it adjoins the picture recess, *tokonoma,* directly in front of the latter's opening to the room, but often the opening of the study place begins at the back wall of the recess and extends $1/2$ *ken* (3 ft.) into the room. Another variation consists in reduction of width; thus, the opening is occasionally only $1/2$ *ken,* with only two sliding panels.

wooden shutters

Since the translucent paper panels, *shōji,* which close the various forms of the outside wall openings, actually constitute only a screen against sight but do not extend their shielding function to other unwanted exterior elements, be it wind, cold, and dust, or man with his not always respectable intentions, each opening that leads directly to the outside has, in addition, wooden shutters, *amado* (literally, rain door), which safely and efficiently lock the entire house.

The smallest of the shutters are used for individual windows and during the day are swung up to the rafters if they are hinged, or if suspended by hooks, are simply hung onto other hooks adjacent to the opening. Larger openings are furnished with shutters that run in a single groove next to the translucent paper panels. During the day these shutters, *amado,* are slid back and kept in wooden compartments, *tobukuro* (literally, door container), which are arranged conveniently at one side of the wall opening or at the end of a panel sequence. With fading daylight, these units are drawn from the compartment and are slid along the tracks, sometimes even shifted around

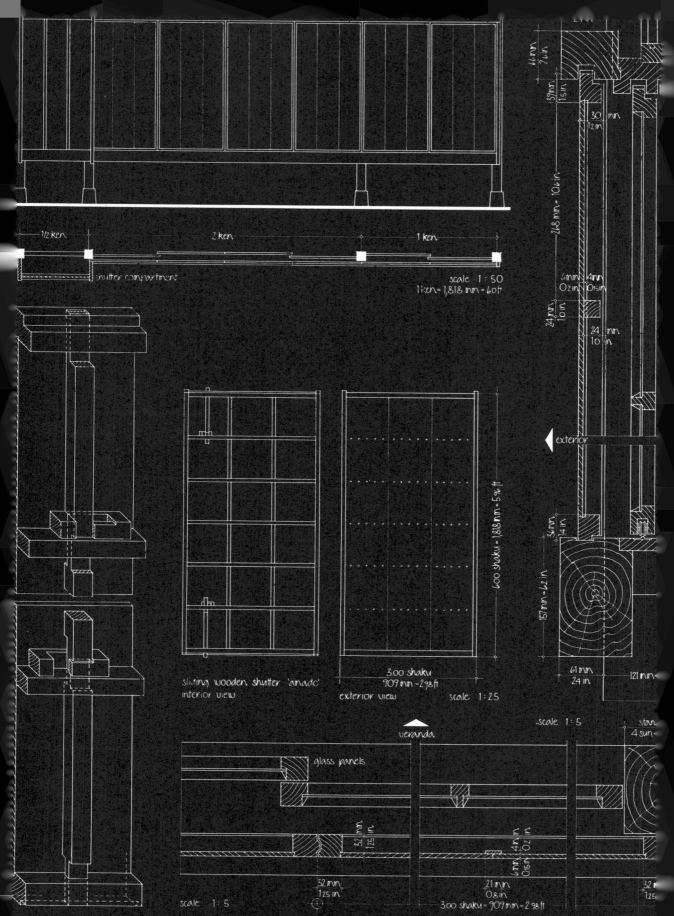

1/2 ken 2 ken 1 ken

shutter compartment

scale 1 : 50
1 ken = 1,818 mm = 6.0 ft

exterior

44 mm / 2 in
39 mm / 1.5 in
30 mm / 1.2 in
248 mm = 10.6 in
6 mm / 0.2 in   4 mm / 0.15 in
24 mm / 1 in
24 mm / 1.0 in
3 mm / 1.4 in
157 mm = 6.2 in

61 mm / 2.4 in   121 mm

sliding wooden shutter 'amado'
interior view

exterior view   scale 1 : 25

300 shaku
909 mm = 2.98 ft

600 shaku = 1,818 mm = 5.96 ft

scale 1 : 5   stan
4 sun

veranda

glass panels

32 mm / 1.25 in

4 mm / 0.15 in

scale 1 : 5   32 mm / 1.25 in   21 mm / 0.8 in   32 mm / 1.25 in

300 shaku = 909 mm = 2.98 ft

FIGURE 50: Arrangement and construction details of typical shutters, amado

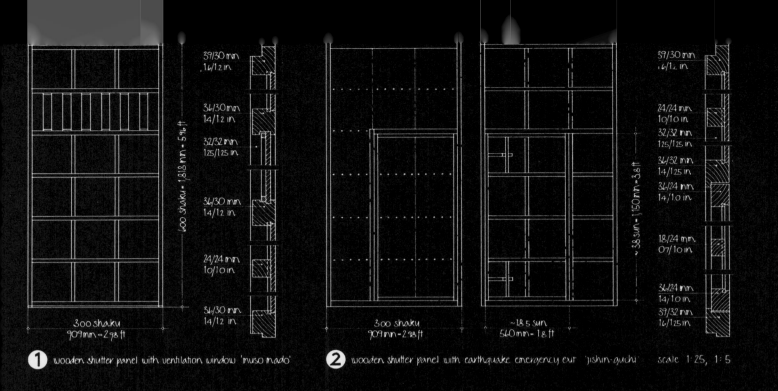

FIGURE 51: Special forms of shutters, *amado*.

corners, to again close the opening. Since they run in a single groove and are all in one plane, the entire wall can be closed by manipulating the panels from the storage space. To lock the panels safely in place, only the last unit taken from the container needs to be bolted into the tracks above and below, thereby arresting the entire sequence of panels. But, since the panels are light and actually could be lifted individually out of their grooves from the outside, they are frequently all bolted to each other.

This is especially advisable in the case of the simple application, when the panels are merely butted to each other. In a better execution, the joining has either a shallow profile or is slightly overlapped. At the bottom, the panels run in grooves of hardwood, and, in the ordinary type, no other means are utilized for reducing friction than an occasional waxing of the grooves. But since the introduction of Western methods, rollers of hard rubber or metal are very common, permitting heavier and stronger shutter construction without affecting maneuverability.

Since in the summer months even at night there is hardly any relief from the moist heat, some of the wooden shutters are provided with a ventilation window, *musō-mado,* which can be opened and closed at will. Another device is a square opening of less than 1 foot width, arranged about 2 feet above the floor level and provided with a wooden sliding panel at the inside. It is called *okubyō-mado,* meaning "chicken-heart window." Being inserted into the entrance shutter and into the panel next to the interior toilet and exterior handwash basin, it is welcomed by the timid who at night do not like to leave the protection of the locked house, whether to see a caller or to wash the hands after having used the toilet. Provision has also been made for leaving the enclosed house during the night without undergoing the fussy and noisy process of unlocking the shutter panels. Especially in traditional houses, where toilet and bath often are under a different roof, such a device in the form of a swinging door of 2× 3 ft. (610 × 1,068 mm.) inserted in the first shutter next ot the shutter compartment, has proven very convenient. Its name, *jishin-guchi* (literally, earthquake exit), suggests that it was originally a kind of emergency exit for leaving as quickly as possible a place that was not safe against the frequent earthquakes.

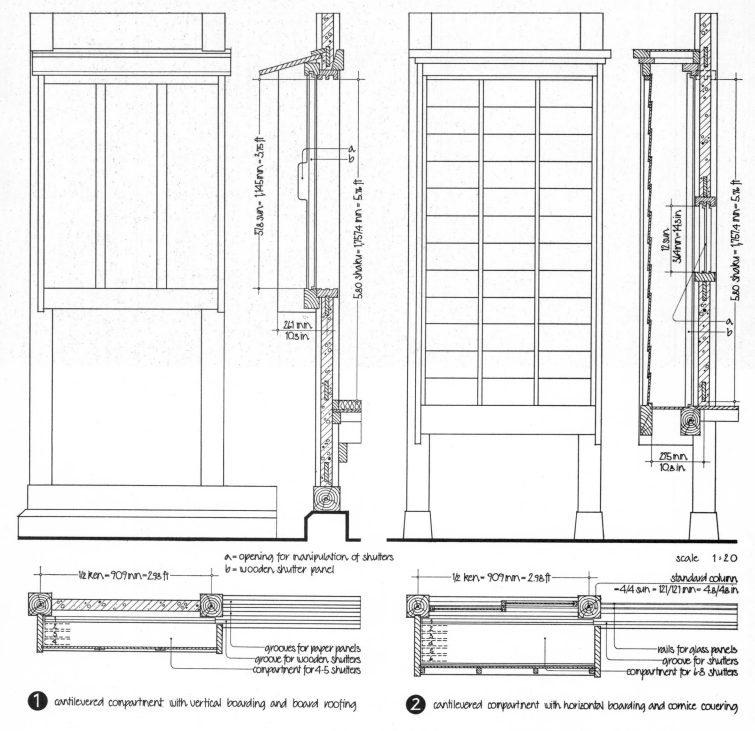

a = opening for manipulation of shutters
b = wooden shutter panel

scale   1:20

½ ken = 909 mm = 2.98 ft

grooves for paper panels
groove for wooden shutters
compartment for 4-5 shutters

1 cantilevered compartment with vertical boarding and board roofing

½ ken = 909 mm = 2.98 ft

standard column
= 4/4 sun = 121/121 mm = 4.8/4.8 in

rails for glass panels
groove for shutters
compartment for 6-8 shutters

2 cantilevered compartment with horizontal boarding and cornice covering

FIGURE 52: Typical forms and construction details of shutter compartments, *tobukuro*.

shutter compartment

The method of how to secure the extensive openings of the Japanese house—and for that matter the opening of any building—against the possibility of forcible impact by weather or man is not so much a constructional-static problem as it is a functional-dynamic one. That is to say, the architectural challenge is less a question of how to join solid wooden panels with openings and how to keep them in their position, than it is a problem of how to move them to and from an opening (which might be the entire house front itself) and how to store them in the simplest way possible.

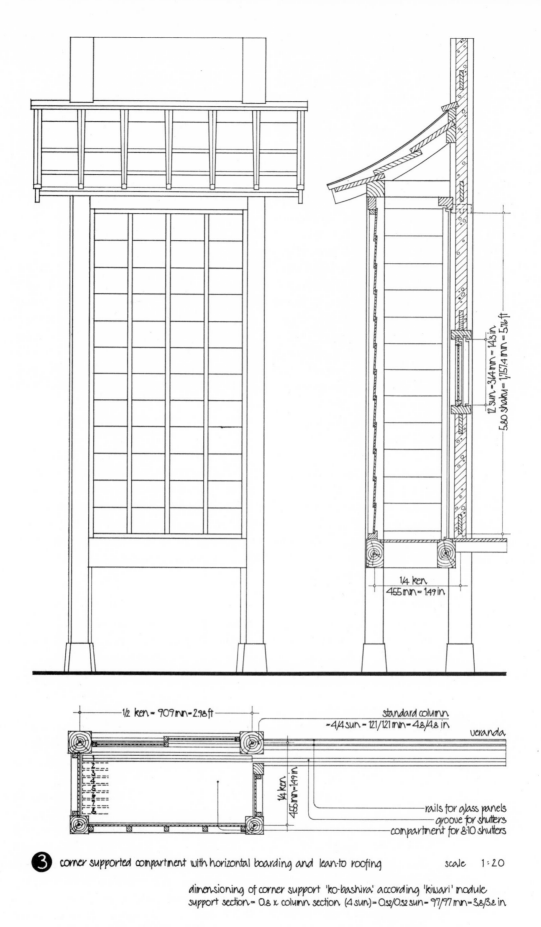

12 sun = 364 mm = 14.3 in
5.80 shaku = 1757.4 mm = 5¼ ft

1/4 ken
455 mm = 1.49 in

1/2 ken = 909 mm = 2.98 ft

standard column
= 4/4 sun = 121/121 mm = 4.8/4.8 in

veranda

1/4 ken
455 mm = 1.49 in

rails for glass panels
groove for shutters
compartment for 8-10 shutters

③ corner supported compartment with horizontal boarding and lean-to roofing   scale   1:20

dimensioning of corner support 'ko-bashira' according 'kiwari' module
support section = 0.8 x column section (4 sun) = 0.32/0.32 sun = 97/97 mm = 3.8/3.8 in

FIGURE 52: Typical forms and construction details of shutter compartments, *tobukuro*.

The task of enclosing a front of 36 feet would present the Western architect with quite some difficulties in regard to the constructional system and functional manipulation, not to mention the economic or aesthetic aspects. The problem is solved by the Japanese very ingeniously. At the end of each shutter sequence a boxlike door compartment, *tobukuro,* is provided where all shutters can easily be slid to and fro. Naturally the size of this compartment corresponds to the height, width, and number of shutter panels, this being the only matter that actually requires some thought, since the length of front to be enclosed is of no direct concern. In cases where placement of the shutter compartment, *tobukuro,* on either side of the house front would be detrimental to the view, a particular construction at the house corner is provided which permits shifting of shutters around the corner.

The constructional-functional system of the shutter compartment, *tobukuro,* is as appropriate as it is simple. The high part of the upper and lower sliding track on the exterior side is taken away inside of the compartment so that the shutters, after being led into it, bend over to the outside, so they can be pushed aside by the following panel, thus gradually filling the compartment. In taking out the shutters, each panel must be set into the upper and lower tracks and the whole sequence moved along, one panel pushing all the rest. Since the width of the entry into the compartment is just the thickness of a single panel, a particular opening needs to be provided so that one can reach into the compartment. It takes either the form of a widening of the entry slit at its center or else a small sliding window at the interior wall of the shutter compartment. Since both upper and lower track are attached from the outside to the veranda post, shutters can be moved and arranged independently of placement of exterior column.

The shutter compartment is but a device of necessity and thus differences in performance are limited to systems of construction, means of boarding, and methods of roofing. These differences can be applied in various combinations and are defined each by their respective names. For openings of up to eight shutter panels, the compartment is simply projected from the veranda and suspended by two vertical flanking boards, which simultaneously constitute the side walls of the compartment; if more panels are used, the compartment requires additional posts at its corners, which rest on foundation stones.

doors

Besides the translucent and opaque paper panels, *shōji* and *fusuma,* two other types of sliding doors are employed in the house. One of them, the glass sliding panel, *garasu-shōji,* though but recently introduced into the house composition, has achieved increasing popularity. Being a better insulator against cold and more resistant to weather, it gradually has replaced the translucent paper panel, which was the original device for closing all exterior openings such as in toilet, bath, veranda, etc. Yet, in spite of this popularity it should be understood that glass is actually alien to the Japanese house. Its texture and consistency do not possess the common denominator that encompasses all other constituent fabrics, and its weight makes the panel's sliding system, with its simple grooves, inappropriate and difficult.

As doubtful as the integrity of the glass sliding door must be in the pure performance of the Japanese house, just as unequivocal is the homogeneity of the wooden doors in the fabric of the traditional house. They are used in the ordinary houses mainly for practical purposes in utilitarian rooms and serve as door panel from corridor to closet, kitchen, bath, etc., but also perform a refined aesthetic task as the main entrance to the house, *genkan-iriguchi,* as a partition between the entrance hall and the interior of the house, *genkan-agariguchi,* and as an access from the corridor to veranda, *engawa-totsuatari.* In these instances, the wooden door is not only a practical device but accentuates the importance of the place and thereby constitutes decoration.

The panel's dimensioning is submitted to the same controlling factors as are all the other sliding units described previously. Outstanding again is the extreme lightness

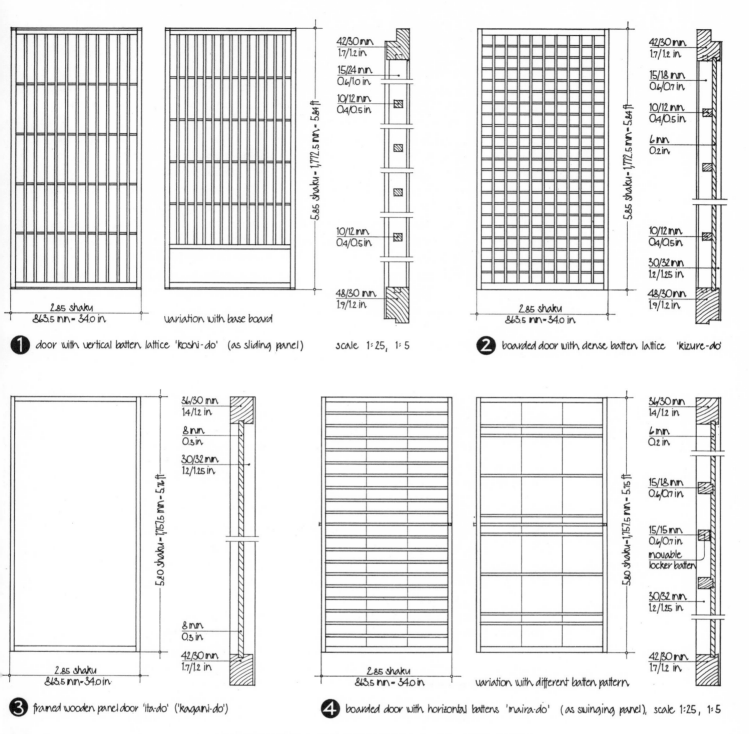

1 door with vertical batten lattice 'koshi-do' (as sliding panel)

variation with base board

scale 1:25, 1:5

42/30 mm
1.7/1.2 in

15/24 mm
0.6/1.0 in

10/12 mm
0.4/0.5 in

10/12 mm
0.4/0.5 in

48/30 mm
1.9/1.2 in

5.85 shaku = 1,772.5 mm = 5.84 ft

2.85 shaku
863.5 mm = 34.0 in

2 boarded door with dense batten lattice 'kizure-do'

42/30 mm
1.7/1.2 in

15/18 mm
0.6/0.7 in

10/12 mm
0.4/0.5 in

6 mm
0.2 in

10/12 mm
0.4/0.5 in

30/32 mm
1.2/1.25 in

48/30 mm
1.9/1.2 in

5.85 shaku = 1,772.5 mm = 5.84 ft

2.85 shaku
863.5 mm = 34.0 in

3 framed wooden panel door 'ita-do' ('kagami-do')

36/30 mm
1.4/1.2 in

8 mm
0.3 in

30/32 mm
1.2/1.25 in

8 mm
0.3 in

42/30 mm
1.7/1.2 in

5.80 shaku = 1,757.5 mm = 5.76 ft

2.85 shaku
863.5 mm = 34.0 in

4 boarded door with horizontal battens 'maira-do' (as swinging panel), scale 1:25, 1:5

variation with different batten pattern

36/30 mm
1.4/1.2 in

6 mm
0.2 in

15/18 mm
0.6/0.7 in

15/15 mm
0.6/0.7 in
movable
locker batten

30/32 mm
1.2/1.25 in

42/30 mm
1.7/1.2 in

5.80 shaku = 1,757.5 mm = 5.76 ft

2.85 shaku
863.5 mm = 34.0 in

FIGURE 53: Typical forms and construction details of doors.

so essential to the whole functioning of the Japanese house mechanisms. In connection with the entrance hall, panels are used as sliding doors, framed and joined into the fittings in the same way as all the other sliding units in the house. Yet, the swinging type is frequently employed for toilet, bath, corridor, etc. In this case, the panel is butted and hinged in simple pin fittings of metal. The frame is made rigid by wooden lattice, or by boards, or by both, giving rise to multiple patterns of form and system, of which only the major types are depicted.

for contemporary architecture

The development of technology in the last century has brought about revolutionary changes, not only technically but also socially and hence politically. To architecture, it meant a change from handicraft methods to machine-craft methods for the manufacture of materials and components and also for the procedure of construction. This transformation however, was not confined to the mere technical-practical aspect of building. Just as civilization as a whole entered a basically new phase, each architectural factor, its content and its proportional contribution in the total creation, is drawn into the whirlpool of this revolution.

It is true that both the manufacture of materials and the procedure of construction have for a long time realized the potential of machinery and are largely, though far from completely, following the principles of technology in their activities. But it is erroneous to assume that with this the period of technical transformation belongs to the past. Instead, as the conflicting viewpoints regarding the meaning of technology in building prove, the intellectual argumentation and ideological discussion among those who actually design and control all this building, the architects, is only in its very early stages. Thus, a portion of them works on the basis of the theory that modern technology has changed only the productional method and not the product itself, its entity, its function, and its expression. Whereas the other group indiscriminately surrenders to technology and does not consider architectural form and space the primary aim, but only a secondary consequence dictated by structure: constructivism. Common to both the first underestimation of technology and the second overestimation, is the dogmatic interpretation of construction in building, and thus its very narrow leeway. The result is that the transformation of building by technology so far has remained but a physical affair, outside of human comprehension or sympathy, and therefore frequently with inhuman tendencies.

Against this trend of oversimplification and intolerance, the role of construction in Japanese building is a favorable, and therefore instructive, contrast. Far from affirming constructivism, it nevertheless states clearly that the very medium of creating architectural form and space is construction. With construction, space is spanned, is enclosed, and enriched; and human space is created. With construction, human emotions are also addressed. Yet, never is the spatial-utilitarian requirement encroached upon by constructional dogma, and never is the expression of building dictated by constructional demonstrativeness and structural exhibitionism, as so often is the case in contemporary building, where either ignorance or indifference on the part of the architect has obstructed full intellectual comprehension and hence excludes the full mastership of handling structure in building.

The value for contemporary architecture lies in the realization of the fact that a residential architecture—standardized in element and system as no other before and after —still succeeded in exercising a tolerance, both physically and conceptually, in the application of construction. For it can be concluded that even mechanized and industrialized building does not necessarily mean constructivism. Certainly, constructional systems, such as thin shells or post-lintel construction, do impose their respective orders upon the plan, space, and form of building. But if they thereby obstruct or limit human requirements, both physically and emotionally, the construction itself is not at fault, but its initial choice. There is an infinity of constructional systems and forms available in contemporary technology, assuring a ready and exact constructional answer for any possible human requirement. There is no justification for ever limiting utilitarian, visual, or even emotional needs of man because of the constructional system.

The Japanese residence reveals most of its constructional members to the inside and outside and distinguishes the component parts of building, support and non-support, crisply and without cover pieces or unnecessary detail. The structural system, except that of the roof, is therefore exposed to the eye of the beholder and, no doubt, effects a strong intimacy with the anatomy of house, both from within and without. However, such an aesthetic expression is not a conception in the sense of something previously conceived, but is a logical result of architectural methods to enclose human space in the simplest way, with the least means possible. The Japanese have by no means intended to make their dwelling a constructional showpiece, as the frequent identification with contemporary trends suggest. Exposure of construction in the Japanese house was never a matter of intellectual principle, but was the result of very reasonable architectural measures that suggested themselves. In fact, previous analysis has not given the slightest evidence that constructional regularity, though seemingly the inevitable result of modular design, has ever been considered by the Japanese more important than man's comfort.

Still, there is no question that the structural system is likely to become the dominant source of form expression in contemporary architecture. Because increasingly building will become an assembling of prefabricated parts, as effected by the industrialization of building; and consequently physical distinction between structural and non-structural screening members will be inevitable, as is also the case in Japanese residential architecture.

Yet, in the Japanese house the function of construction is not confined to spanning space or to revealing the structural forces of the building or, as in the best examples of contemporary architecture, to displaying pleasant proportion and texture of material. Its range extends also to areas that are still occupied in Western architecture by other agencies. Thus, construction also constitutes decoration itself. Structural members are employed in awareness of their aesthetic meaning. Constructional device is exploited as ornamental form. And even non-functional construction is introduced to serve as décor. It is by this reason that decoration in the Japanese house is essentially architectural, i.e., it is not additive but is structurally integrated. Form (in the sense of color, shape, and texture), therefore, the mediatory element of décor, is a derivative of construction, i.e., it is not alienated from its *raison d'être,* as was the trend in each architectural period in the West, and therefore has not taken to abstraction. Even the spiritual center of the house, the picture recess, *tokonoma,* is but a niche differentiated from all other room components by change of floor level and a bold interruption of the frieze rail that horizontally circumscribes the Japanese room.

Furthermore, Japanese construction functions as the interpreter of religious-philosophic values that characterized the epoch. As the succeeding chapters will show, the aestheticism of the tea cult and the religion-philosophy of Buddhism recognized, in the unsophisticated and humble construction of the ordinary dwelling, a singular opportunity to demonstrate their own spiritual values and bring them to the consciousness of the common people. It may even be that both tea cult and Buddhism obtained decisive motifs and stimuli from a constructional order which, better than any words, directly stated life, the simple life of man in its basic and true meaning. Through such linking of physical structure with the spiritual values of the epoch, the cultural standard of the lowest classes was elevated to a level that shows a keen awareness as to the presence of art and religion in living and thus contrasts favorably with that of the comparable social class in the West.

This successful employment of construction for the multiple functions which architecture performs as a necessity of life, as a symbol of era and as a form of art, is of revelation for contemporary architecture. For not only does the Japanese example show that the medium for all architectural efforts is construction, but it also unveils the enormous potential of structure in building. Just as art and philosophy, the one through material means, the other through intellect, are apt to interpret the life of the contemporary epoch, to establish the relationship of the individual to the universal, and thus to stimulate cognitions as to the ethical values of the epoch, so too the physical structure of a building does possess the potential of being an artistic and philosophical instrument that identifies architecture, symbolizes era, and interprets life.

Yet, this intellectual recognition would remain without purpose and meaning, if not followed by a plan for action. The practical conclusion to be drawn, then, is the imperative of employing structure in building not only as medium of spanning space but also as medium of substantiating man and his time. Through such spiritual interpretation of structure, the intellectual basis would be established for concealing obtrusive structure, changing ill-sized (although economical) structure, employing decorative structure, and inserting symbolic structure. That is to say, justification would be gained for breaking the mere technical-dogmatic supremacy of constructivism in contemporary building to pave the way for a more universal, more tolerant, and more valid application of construction in building—a prime requisite for making building a true expression of the total meaning of technique, as it determines the contemporary epoch not only physically, but even more so spiritually.

While this would be primarily the task of the architect-designer, the other imperative would concern the architect-educator. For it could hardly be expected that the general public is sensitive a priori to this multiple and profound significance of construction in building. Rather, an education of the general public is required in the form of an introduction to the vocabulary of contemporary architecture, and the symbolic, aesthetic, and anatomic meaning therein occupied by construction. While admittedly it is the architect's privilege to address society directly with his buildings and not with words, it must be questioned whether in the present state of alienation —between man and art, man and science, man and architecture—the advanced performance of any individual architect can still reach the sentiment of the masses.

Rather, as the increasing emotional indifference of the general public to contemporary art, science, and architecture proves, there is an urgent need for basic intellectual education. In the case of building, this task has to be performed by those who actually carry the social responsibility in matters of the physical environment, the architects. And it is due in no small part to either the architects' ignorance of the cultural mission of architecture or to their inertness in matters of public opinion, that the level of culture, characterized by the psychological relationship of man to the man-made environment, is at such an all-time low.

Although the constructional system of the Japanese house has never really evolved from its primitive pattern and is defective in many ways, it nevertheless reaffirms the truth, which is also apparent in all architectures of the past, that no period has built less skillfully than it knew how, regardless of the current taste. Thus, if it is accepted that regularity in the historic occurrence of a distinct feature proves that this feature is an essential and characteristic quality, then, contemporary building can only make the claim of being true architecture if it consciously and consistently applies the latest recognitions provided by science. There is no excuse for designing and building unscientifically because of an obsolete preference of the general public for the form expressions of backward beliefs, thoughts, or methods.

To build scientifically, yet, does not only concern the technical-mechanical aspect of building, but distinctly means use of, and strict compliance with, the scientific facts of sociology, hygienics, optics, and psychology. With such intellectual foundation, construction in building would be given its proper role in the organism and, instead of being irreconcilable and authoritative as it is at present, it could again become a rich source of expression, in no way inferior to the human-spiritual role of construction in past building, be it Gothic or Japanese.

Yet, again, such scientific design is not to be considered a mere mathematical function that would solve all constructional problems and make structure expressive in the widest meaning. Instead, it is only the essential directive that guides the thought and action of the designer for an effective approach, and excludes the danger of either wasteful subjective searching or direct misuse. However, it requires the creative intuition of an artist to grasp this multiple potential of construction in its total scope and make it as well a unique expression of its spiritual significance. Only then will industrialized and mechanized architecture be the materialization of human life itself, as handicraft architecture has been before, and only then will it be able to stir in return the most varied human emotions. The constructional system of a building then would be no longer the inevitable result of a mere rational-mathematical equation. Instead, both the creation and experience of structure would possess features that are the characteristics of true art.

PLATE 1: The Japanese house. Its structure, organism, environment, and aesthetics are tradition for contemporary architecture.

番匠

我をもけとい
お国書
又め作里い
書て地
うり
うん
すゝ女

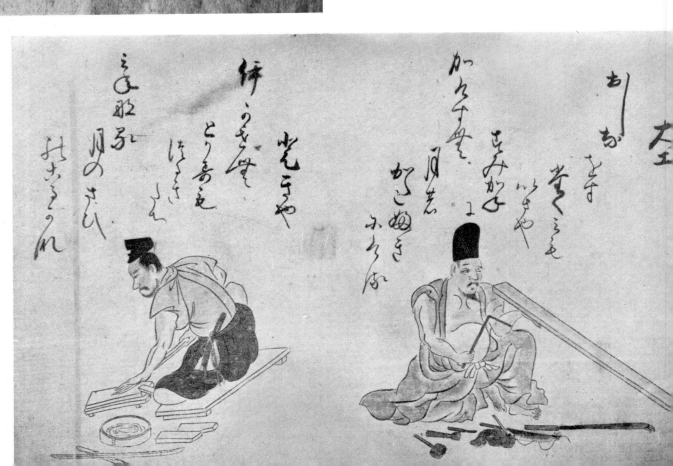

左

おしも
さす
覚くうそ
いちや
きみかよ
よ
加々井母
月さ
かこぬき
ふくゆ

絆
うさ庵
とり寿を
はささき
く

光子や
うさ那弘
月のさん
おほきの礼

PLATES 2–4: The carpenter. He is the master builder and
designer. He is the *daiku*, the great among the craftsmen.

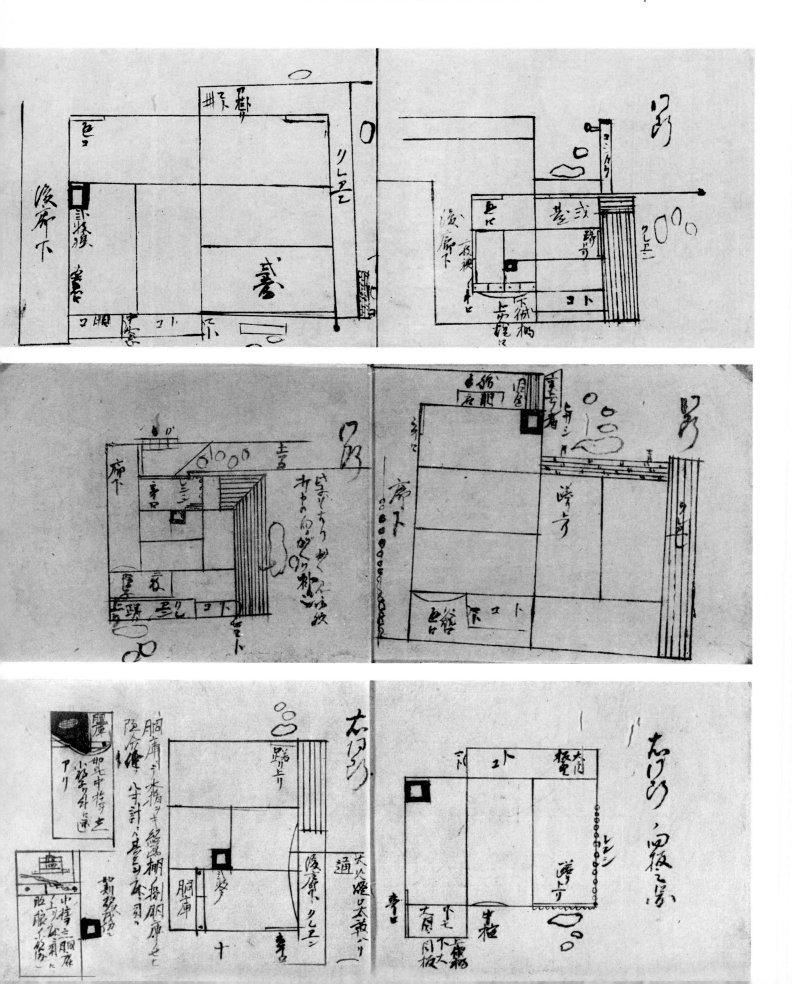

PLATES 5–7: The carpenter's sketchbook. Experiences, ideas, and prototypes are recorded with brush and ink. Shown here are floor plans of tearooms.

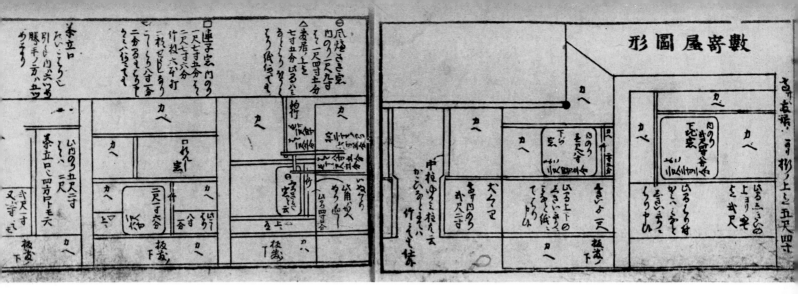

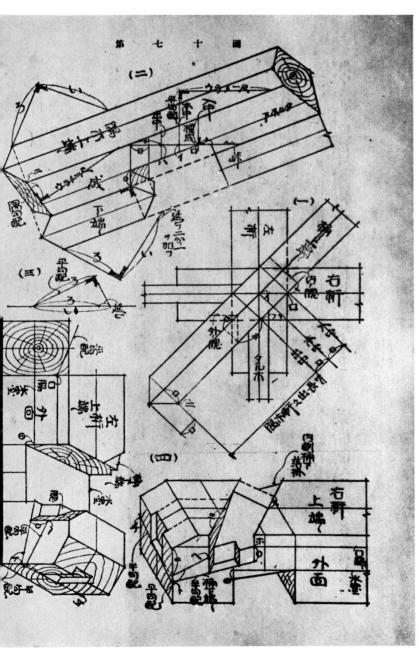

PLATES 8–9: Carpenter's manuals past and present. They contain rules, measures, proportions, and constructional details for all building types. Shown here are interior elevations of tearooms, details of joining of hip rafter and beam.

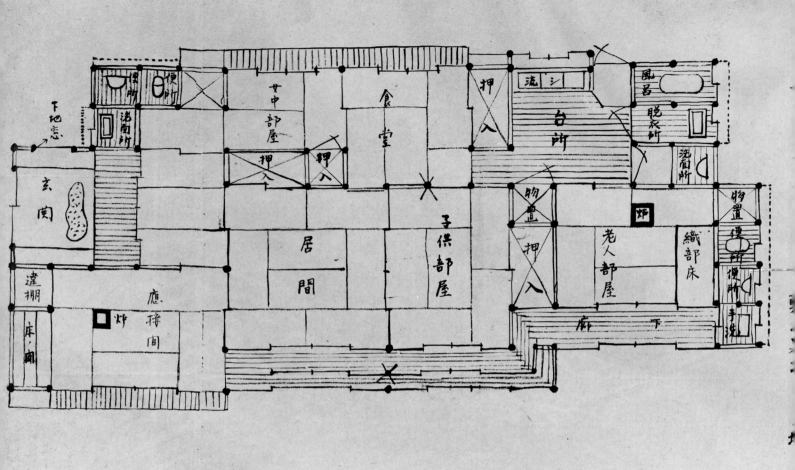

PLATE 10: *Tatami* layout sketch. The family itself sketches the floorplan, using the *tatami* as the ordering unit.

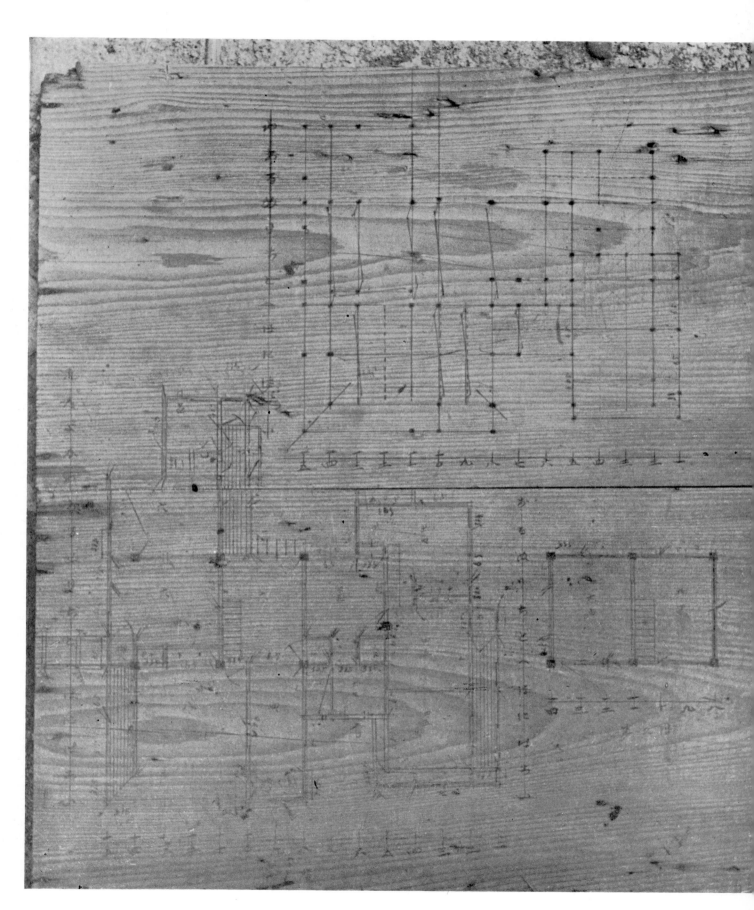

PLATE II: Contemporary working drawing of the carpenter. It indicates spacing of columns, placement of beams, and location of moveable and solid walls.

當世之矩尺　長一尺五寸横七寸五分幅五分色

カチ〱裡ニ尺四寸〉斜ニ尺四寸ニ毛四リ〱モ余ツモリ〱ケテ

用ルエニ一尺五寸ヲ足寸トス　矩術ミナ斜ニコモレリ

九天并ノアイタ一切ノ數ミナ是ニコモレリ

PLATE 13: Measure. It is the essential tool for understanding and creating building. This carpenter's manual shows the "ancient and current rules" of measurement.

PLATE 12 (right to left): Building in the past. This sequence shows modular layout, prefabrication of components, and a typical aristocratic residence (with couple, maid, guard, and dog).

PLATE 14: Building in the present. Carpenter's dress joints of roof beams.

PLATES 15–18: The structural framework. Houses with different floor plans are constructed with standard components (Plate 18 on following page).

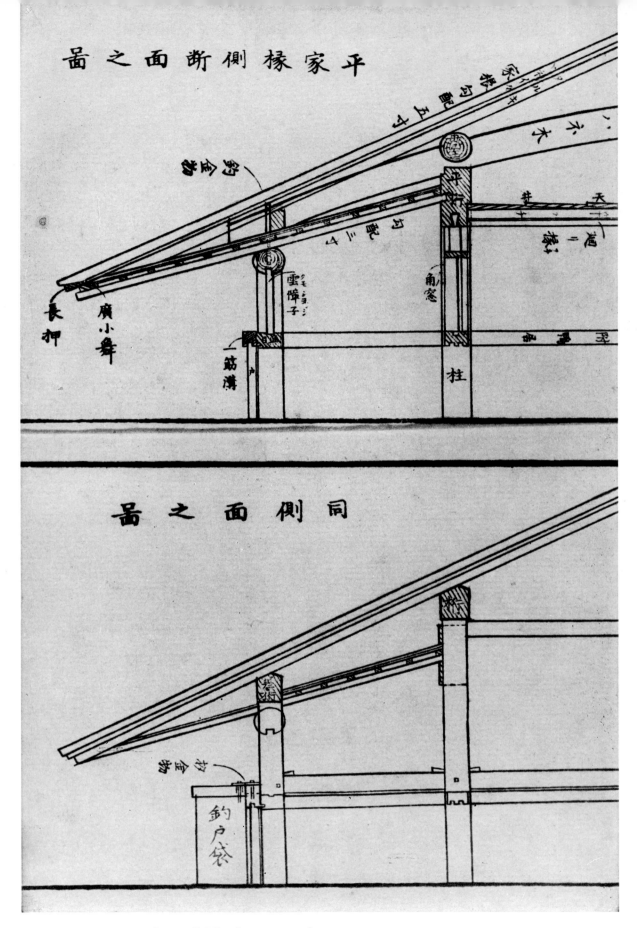

平家椽側断面之圖

同側面之圖

PLATES 19–20: Veranda roof. The lower set of
rafters originally concealed a cantilevered beam.

PLATES 21–23: House under construction. The prefabricated components are quickly assembled, and the framework is plumbed with a diagonal rope.

PLATES 24–25: Residences recently built. Using traditional forms, elements, and techniques, the houses have been freely designed, unhindered by site limitations.

PLATES 28–31: Small rural houses. Identical needs of each family have produced identical spatial requirements and consequently identical architectural plans and forms.

PLATE 32: Large rural house. It has literally grown out of one original structure.

PLATES 33–34: Merchant house. This building type effaced the distinctions between the different building-styles of the feudal classes.

PLATE 35: Ordinary city residence. The rigidity of city-block patterns imposed limitations on house design and produced distinct features in plan and façade.

PLATE 36: Extensive residence of a feudal lord. Because of the summer heat, the panels in one wing are removed in order to afford optimum ventilation.

PLATE 37: Stone. It serves as foundation and as the intermediate stage between house and environment.

PLATES 38–39: Wood, as raw material. Much of it is floated through shallow rivers, and, thus, the logs are cut into short pieces of standard length.

PLATES 40–41: Wood, as fabric. It is the dominant fabric in the Japanese house, both structurally and aesthetically.

PLATES 42–43: Roof tiles. They are imbedded in clay. Fabric and technique were adopted from Buddhist architecture.

PLATES 44–45: Bamboo. The material is used mostly in its natural form, being both practical and decorative.

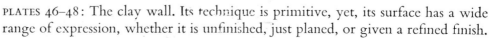

PLATES 46–48: The clay wall. Its technique is primitive, yet, its surface has a wide range of expression, whether it is unfinished, just planed, or given a refined finish.

PLATES 49–50: Translucent paper. Its qualities are
unique and have no equivalents in modern fabrics.

PLATES 51–52: The *tatami*. Originally only a portable element, it became the unique platform for Japanese living, serving as seat, bed, walkway, and table.

PLATE 53: Early room partition. The standing screen developed into the sliding panels.

PLATES 54–55: Opaque paper panel. The *fusuma* is the flexible interior room partition and at times also the canvas for paintings, calligraphy, or some other graphic art.

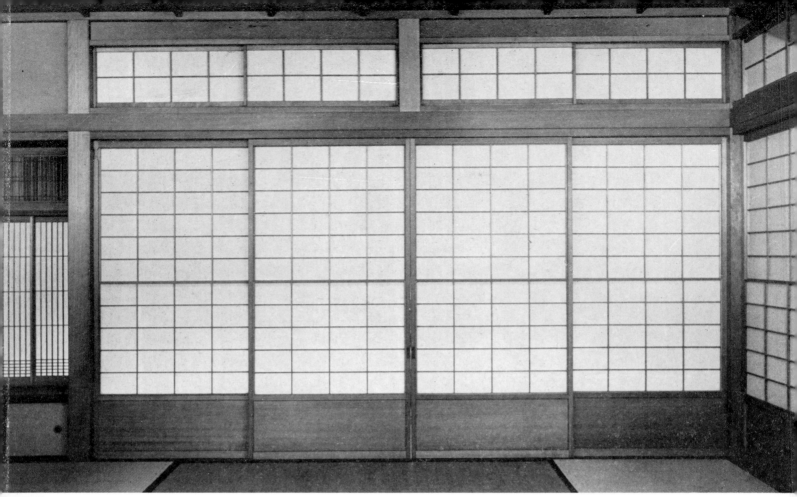

PLATES 56–57: Translucent paper panel. The *shōji* is the sliding screen
that admits light and serves as door, window, or space enclosure.

PLATE 58: Windows. In the tearoom the window is primarily for precisely controlling the interior light condition.

PLATES 59–60: Windows. In spite of extensive standardization, there is infinite variety in designing wall openings.

PART TWO organism

family
space
garden
seclusion

definition

FAMILY IN BUILDING is the collective body of persons who form one household under one roof. It consists of descendants of a common progenitor and includes servants.

FAMILY IN BUILDING is both cause and idea. As cause, it has initiated architecture because of the necessity of constructing shelter; as idea, it constitutes the essence of residential architecture.

FAMILY IN BUILDING, therefore, is man's individual and universal architectural image. As individual image, it expresses the personality of family; as universal image, it substantiates the ethics and concepts of society.

FAMILY IN BUILDING is not only exerting influence. It is also receiving influence in that progressive architecture frequently changes manners of living and, by creating new values of life, transforms the ethics of family.

FAMILY IN BUILDING is dependent on tradition. Most ethics and habits of the family have been handed down from the past, as much as many tastes and preferences are rooted in standards of the past.

FAMILY IN BUILDING, thus, is not always a stimulating agent. Adhering mainly to values of the past, it hinders progress and is the main cause for the lag of architecture behind the conceptions of pure arts.

FAMILY IN BUILDING manifests the culture of the epoch. For cultural level is characterized by the emotional relationship between man and man-made environment; hence, between family and house.

FAMILY IN BUILDING, then, is the essence that underlies residential architecture. Through family, building becomes house and through family the house lives.

Buildings are a means rather than an end. They are not themselves the purpose of architectural work, but they do fulfill a purpose. In the case of residential architecture this purpose is to provide adequate space for the family, space that is suited not only to satisfy the family's daily needs but to enrich their lives as well. Thus, for both architectural creation and architectural analysis, a study of the reality that underlies the family is essential.

The reality of family finds expression in three ways: first, in the manner in which the family unit is organized both morally and practically; second, in the position that each family member occupies in this organism; and, finally, in the resulting mode of living. Though these factors are of course partially dependent on individual values, their dominating motives are the principles of morality that control society and epoch as a whole. Since in the past no architect was needed in residential architecture to translate the values of a particular epoch into house, it was through the family itself that the morals of society were made manifest in building, a causality that lifted anonymous architecture (i.e., designed without a professional architect) above the level of mere practical device. Moreover, because of this direct creative process, residential architecture of the past is apt to give a better picture of the philosophies of society at that time than do the formalized and architect-designed buildings of ecclesiastic or aristocratic architecture.

This causality is clearly expressed in the Japanese house. As a matter of fact, many distinct features of the house as evolved from the 17th to 19th centuries can only be comprehended through knowledge of the ideals and morals that shaped family and society at that time. Much of this late medieval family system has changed rapidly in recent decades, especially in the cities. But there are rural areas where it still exists fairly unchanged so that investigation is concerned with both past and present.

In the following pages an endeavor is made to analyze the Japanese family order: its consistency, its underlying moral principles, and its practical manifestation through manners of living. An observation as to whether the characteristics of the Japanese family have influenced building, and to what degree such influence has been instrumental in the formation of Japan's residential architecture, should produce universally valid facts concerning the process of architectural creation, i.e., facts that are independent of time, locality, and race.

moral principles

There are four distinct characteristics of the Japanese family as it constituted the socio-economic unit from the 14th and 15th centuries to the present: disregard of the individual, absolutism of the head of the house, right of primogeniture, and subordination of the female. These characteristics, all in close relation to each other, have not only decisively molded Japan's history for centuries but, even more, have shaped what was both cause and effect of family: the house. Owing to this interdependence between man and shelter, "house" is not only conceived to be physical structure but also to be family—a truth that the fast changes in Western residential development have almost buried.

In medieval Japan no other value was placed on the individual than that of being a necessary component of an important whole. This was because the social order and its underlying ethics rested not upon the inherent worth of the individual, but rather on the strength of the family unit, just as in primitive times and countries preservation of the tribeal ways was the major basis for all of life's activities and values. There is hardly an instance in Japanese social and religious philosophy where the value of the individual was recognized other than by his rank in society. Still less has there been any indication of a movement for the individual's elevation and freedom. Rather, these teachings—and for that matter, those of all Oriental philosophies—have repressed and oppressed the individual insofar as the conservation and growth of the family has been the basis for all values. Even the Japanese Civil Code that has been in effect since the Meiji Reformation (1868) contains elements of this medieval notion: "The first duty of the man is to consider not his own individual interests, but those of his 'house.'"*

This conception of suppressing individual desires, if they are not in conformity with the idea of "house," is of course rooted in the Buddhist ideal of "salvation through self-annihilation." But, it must have received a strong impetus from the feudalistic form of society, the strength of which depended largely on this conception, for it was reasonable that the men in power emphasized all those concepts that reinforced their position, while suppressing all others. Therefore, the noted Japanese esteem for such virtues as sacrifice, obedience, patience, respect for age and authority is in essence less ethical than material. It has had, and still does have, a profound influence on the life and "house" of Japan, but frequently it has also been misused for the political ambitions of the men in power, even into recent history.

The other characteristic of the Japanese family, the absolutism of the head of the "house," in the sense of the subordination of all family members under one person, does not contradict what has previously been stated. For the head of the "house" in Japanese society was not primarily regarded as an individual with a distinct personality, nor was he viewed by the household as the caring father, loving husband,

* These rather general statements rest largely on the extensive studies by Sidney L. Gulick and George B. Sansom (see Bibliography).

or benevolent master. Instead he constituted the impersonal head of the "house," granting and securing existence, and was referred to as the *shujin* (important person), the *danna-san* (lord master), the *teishu* (importance of the house), expressions which also were used by his own wife. It was not through kinship that he held this position, but through his ability to maintain the family, to preserve its property, and to enhance its prestige. When he could no longer comply with his duties, he was replaced either by a son or some other kinsman, whoever was considered most capable of assuring preservation of the family unit. This position was so impersonal that the son, as authoritative head, was then obeyed by the father once he had abdicated, just as by all other members. Since the family and its shelter were simultaneously identified with its spiritual head, "house" had a profound symbolic meaning that incorporated the family, its shelter, and its head in a single concept. This very basic philosophic integrity of the word "house" is still evident today in the custom of referring to people in terms of building terminology. "Mister" in the polite form is *dono* (mansion), the warrior family is *buke* (house of strength), and the architect is *kenchiku-ka* (house of architecture). Similarly, individual members of the "house," having importance only insofar as their contribution to the family unit is concerned, are in many cases referred to either by the function they perform or the place they occupy in the house. The word *oku-sama*, used for the lady of the house, means (in the literal sense of its Chinese characters) the dark or inner chamber (of the house), while the husband simply calls her *kanai* (the house interior) or *tsuma* (the gable). In conversation, it is common to refer to oneself as *uchi* (house) and to a second person as *o-uchi* (honorable house) or *o-taku* (honorable dwelling). In the households of warriors or nobility there were many more instances of this architectural identification of people because function and position of the individual were more distinct.

These idiomatic peculiarities in the Japanese language must, of course, be understood as a means of avoiding direct reference to persons, the second and third person pronouns being customarily considered blunt and impolite. Yet, the fact that architectural designations are distinctly preferred shows that "house" in Japan has retained its original integrity—oneness of shelter, family, and man. On the other hand, it also leaves no doubt that the individual was of no worth in this family except as the representative of the "house" (the father), or was valued because of his contributions to the "house" rather than for his inherent attributes.

The major force that had shaped the order of the family as well as that of Japanese society in general was the moral and political philosophy of Confucius. The core of Confucian doctrine is the cult of the family as the basic component of the social and political organism. Its basic principle is filial piety, which finds expression in obedience to living parents and worship of departed ancestors. Some passages of a treatise on filial piety attributed to Confucius himself state: "The law of filial piety is that one should serve one's parents as one serves Heaven." "So long as one's parents are living, no enterprise must be undertaken without their counsel and approbation." "Parents must be obeyed during their lifetime, and after their death the son must do as they did." Here one realizes the source of the strong dependence on parents and the continuity of tradition in its negative, i.e., preservative, sense and also finds indication of worship of parents after their death, ancestor worship. In close relationship with Confucian doctrine is another feature of the Japanese family, the right of primogeniture. Yet, this expression is hardly appropriate to describe the system of succession because it implies inheritance of right and property by the eldest son. Instead, the head of the family always decided who was to be his successor, and this was not necessarily the first-born male unless he appeared promising enough. There are records which tell that occasionally even a person from another family—though preferably a kinsman—was adopted if none of the sons showed sufficient promise of being able to guarantee the continuation of the "house." While this attitude presents more proof of the indifference towards the individual human being and of the importance of the "house," such adoptions were exceptional. As a rule, the eldest son inherited the wordly goods and carried on the "house" while the younger sons left the family and set up their own "house," which would later be carried on by their eldest sons. Thus, succession of the "house," i.e., the continuity of family, as safeguarded by the right of primogeniture and the absolutism of the family's head, was the essence of the Japanese family system; and the presence of the head's parents was almost indispensable for family prestige. This order, then, has found visible expression in the residence and confirms the necessity of investigation.

The final and probably most striking contrast between the family system of the East and the West lies in the inferior value put upon the inherent nature of woman. This is not only expressed in the subordinated role the female plays within the "house" but also in her social position and moral relation to man. The three rules for obedience of the Japanese woman—"to the father when yet unmarried, to the husband when married, to the son when widowed"—strikingly demonstrate her inferior position. In the West, woman rather than man controls the expression of the house interior, and mother rather than father represents the family. But in Japan the wife is more a domestic than a helpmate, i.e., her position in the family is chiefly, if not entirely, valued on a utilitarian basis, that of bearing and rearing children for her husband, doing housework and farmwork and satisfying the comforts and pleasures of men, in short, of guaranteeing and facilitating continuity of family. This does not mean that the women are always miserable. Happiness, family joy, and marital affection can be found in many cases. But on the whole her position is low in relation to the man, a condition that still largely affects not only human relationship within family and society, but also the Japanese residence itself.

There are passages in the Confucian doctrine in which the inferiority of woman is quite distinctly expressed, but even stronger statements as to woman's low value may be found in the ethics of Buddhism: "She is the source of temptation and sin; she is essentially inferior to man in every respect; before she may hope to enter nirvana she must be born again as man." The attribution of such an explicit inferiority to woman, which, for that matter, is distinct in all Oriental beliefs, could easily lead to the conclusion that the cause of the low position of woman was ethical in nature. However, before the establishment of the distinct family system in the 14th century, the woman enjoyed a much higher esteem, even though Confucian and Buddhist views were already prevailing. This gives reason to believe that religious and social ethics were not alone responsible for this peculiarity of the Japanese family.

The 14th century was conspicuous for its continuous warfare and anarchy in which the men in power could no longer guarantee security to their subjects. It was, therefore, not accidental that from this time on masculinity was granted distinct privileges, and the custom of primogeniture was generally applied, while for the same reasons the subordination of the woman began. Thus, since the values of the Japanese family system came into existence in defense against environment and were maintained as an essential means for survival, it can be justly said that their character is also strongly material.

manners of living

Manners of living are essentially only a mirror of the moral principles to which individual, family, and society adhere, and the distinct manners of living of the Japanese family are no exception. In the case of any Occidental nation, manners of living could hardly be subjected to generalization because they vary in essence and performance, both locally and individually. By contrast, the major customs of the Japanese are universally practiced. This uniformity, however, is not due to the moral principles themselves, but to the influence of the social form at that time, feudalism, the existence of which depended largely upon preservation of the existing and prevention of the new. Regulation of the customs and demeanor of the individual family, making it conform to universal standards, was but one of many devices employed. The importance of this influence is by no means overestimated. For, at the time when the manners established themselves, the mass of the people was entirely uneducated and still unable to think in terms of moral principles. But this is not meant to challenge the existence of those principles as the basis of the Japanese family, its order, and manners, but rather to show that without such a form of society and government, ways of living unique for the whole of Japan never would have been established because of the more imperative local differences of climate and topography. Of course, in addition, other factors such as general poverty and tradition have shaped habits of living, as did also building itself, yet their influence is more indirect in nature.

The differences in the manners of living that distinguish the Japanese family from the average Western family (if such a generalization may be permitted) are numerous. All of them have architectural importance to a greater or lesser degree insofar as sensitive architecture will distinctly respond to even minute habits. A complete listing, however, would require a disproportionate amount of space. Therefore, only those phases of Japanese manners of living that appear to be essential for the thorough understanding of the Japanese house have been taken into consideration, i.e., height of sitting and sleeping, importance of bathing, esteem for visitor, and complexity of domestic work.

In the Western residence it is impossible to establish one eye-level height for human activity, or to even fix three separate eye-level heights for the postures of standing, sitting, and lying. While standing may still imply an absolute average eye-level, sitting and lying, being determined in each house by a variety of different base levels, are both impossible to identify with a particular eye-level because of the infinite number of resulting heights. Hence, an important medium for distinct architectural expression in interior design, orientation to eye-level, is excluded. In contrast, postures of standing, sitting, and lying in the Japanese residence are determined by a single base level, the floor, and have therefore produced three distinct eye-levels (Plates 70–73). However, since in the Japanese house itself standing is viewed as improper except when moving from one place to another, and since lying is a position used only when sleeping—and the eyes are then supposed to be closed anyhow— the eye-level of the sitting person is the only architecturally important orientation, and this orientation is so precisely made that in the Japanese house a standing person is alien to his environment.

The Japanese squats on the floor, either directly on the *tatami* or on a cushion; and thus he eats, reads, writes, and works. The polite form of squatting is that in which one sits on his heels with knees together on the floor, a type of kneeling. While for women this is the only method of sitting, a man may also sit directly on the floor with his legs crossed in front of him. Though the latter form is more comfortable, it requires much more space and is less convenient when arising. There is a tendency among writers, Western and Japanese alike, to furnish the Japanese way of sitting on the floor with religious or even philosophical motives. Yet, these and other allegations are not based on evidence but on the desire to eulogize rather than to admit a lack of facts. In countries the world over, the primitive form of sitting is squatting on the ground, and there is no evidence to sustain the belief that the Japanese squatting has some more noble foundation. Rather the Japanese form of squatting on the floor, though extremely graceful in appearance, is but primitive in essence. This deceptive contrast between primitiveness in basic concept and high refinement in detail is characteristic of many features of Japanese civilization. Indeed it is this discrepancy between appearance and underlying essence that is responsible for many of the misconceptions that exist about Japan, both about her people and her architecture.

The floor is also the supporting plane for sleeping. Mattresses and coverings, which during the day are kept in spacious closets, are spread out, and a very small and hard pillow supports, rather than comforts, the head. Thus the same level serves for all major forms of human posture, lying, sitting, and standing, it being equally convenient for playing the flute or making love. Therefore, it is only reasonable that the people, for their own good, strive for the utmost of cleanliness. Common sense, and not alleged respect for the house, has prevailed upon the Japanese to remove their shoes before entering the elevated part of the house, to use particular sandals for the boarded floor areas and again different ones for toilet and kitchen respectively. And common sense was also the reason for maintaining their characteristic floor mat so suitable for all different functions. Yet, the cleanliness of the mat is more apparent than real, for between carpet cover and straw underpart dust accumulates rapidly—much too rapidly in view of only two major cleanings per year as is customary.

Here a trait that is evident in so many aspects of Japanese life, the inability of grasping reality behind the obstructing subjectivity of both wish and emotion, comes to light. This becomes evident in many other instances. The device for heating during the winter, the charcoal brazier, suggests rather than produces heat; and the little wind bell out on the veranda in the hot summer months suggests an air draft hardly felt within the house itself. It is also evident in the structure of the house. Exposed braces *(nageshi)* and columns suggest rigidity where there is none; beams that span the house depth are made as heavy as possible, suggesting stability, but actually endangering it; and there is no doubt that basically the stagnation of building methods and ways of living are due to the same trait of not recognizing reality, or if doing so, then, escaping it.

A more realistic attitude, however, is manifested in the custom of bathing. During the summer months, the average family takes its bath every evening, as a rule before dinner and using such hot water that to any Occidental the bath must appear to be medieval torture rather than enjoyment. In the colder season some families reduce the number of baths to every other day. The prime reason for such frequent bathing, of course, is cleanliness. But an additional function of the hot bath during the humid summer is to temporarily overheat the body, thereby giving relief from continuous perspiration. During the cold winter months, in turn, the bath is very appropriate for providing additional warmth or, to speak more exactly, for thoroughly warming the continuously freezing body at least once a day, for neither a multitude of clothes nor charcoal brazier give effective protection against the draft and cold prevailing in the wintery Japanese house interior. Only the poorest do not possess a bath of their own and therefore use a public bath located within short walking distance. Yet, those with their own bath also go occasionally to public baths, because conversation in steaming water, with stark nakedness extinguishing all social barriers, and with sexes mingling freely, has always been a particular and understandable enjoyment for the Japanese.

The fact that all members of the family use the same water has often been mentioned by foreign observers, usually expressing both astonishment and disdain. What is not mentioned is that the Japanese, before entering the bath, squats in front of the tub on a wooden grating, dipping out water and soaping and cleaning himself thoroughly before entering the tub, where he then enjoys soaking in the clean steaming water. While such a method may not be ideal, it certainly is economical. By comparison, the Occidental procedure of soaping and washing within the tub and remaining thereafter for a while in the solvent of one's own dirt must appear strange, to say the least. The sequence of bathing is decided by rank in the family as explained earlier, i.e., the head of the house first, being followed by the other males, while the women are always last. As the temperature of the water is maintained by continuously feeding wood into a stove underneath the tub, it is very enjoyable squatting comfortably in the tub as in a kettle on a fire, especially in unfriendly weather with cold, rain, and wind; and it may take several hours until the last of the girls finally leaves the tub.

The sequence of bathing serves to demonstrate another of the differences between the Occidental manners of living and those of the Japanese: the esteem for the visitor. For if not merely a caller, the visitor will always have precedence. It is not an infrequent occurence that, even before the usual bathing hour, the bath is prepared just for the visitor; and occasionally a fresh kimono is also provided—a means of clearing mind and body for a quiet and thoughtful talk with the head of the house, which for this purpose is certainly more fitting than to cloud the mind, in addition to the body, with several cocktails, as is customary in the West.

The guest is the most honored person, and even the poorest house has provided one room in which to receive him. While the growth of this esteem is a matter of historical interest, only the fact of the voluntary subordination of the head of the house in his relation to the visitor should be mentioned here, because it constitutes a difference from the old patriarchal system of Western society in which the father maintains his superiority at all times and does not show such humbleness as long as he is within his own house. This difference is also clearly demonstrated by the seating arrangement in the reception room, where the guest, but of course not the female visitor, is given the most honored seat directly in front of the picture recess (tokonoma), enjoying a respect that is challenged only occasionally by the younger children who grow up without being reprimanded or punished and have not yet learned the fine gradations from inferior into superior, i.e., the secrets for a smooth social life.

Another distinction of the Japanese manners of living is the complexity of domestic work. It again mirrors only gross disconcern for the interests of the housewife, and is yet another expression of female subordination. Her role within the family is mainly on a utilitarian basis, i.e., at various times she is housekeeper and servant for the family in all matters of food, clothing, and cleaning, mother for her children, mistress of the house, entertainer for the guest, farmhand in the fields, and mate to the master; but never has she time or place to be herself. And if there is a maid in the house, she only shares the burden with the mother but can never free her from the complexity of her role within the "house." The many principles of residential design in the West, as derived from the esteem of the woman's place in the house, have been of no concern in the traditional Japanese residence. Here, the dominant principle for the arrangement of rooms is the differentiation according to inferior or superior position of the family member. If ever an improvement or enlargement of the existing dwelling is contemplated, no thought is given to relieve the complexity of domestic work but only to provide an even more distinct maintenance of order of rank.

influence on house

Manners of living, being shaped primarily through moral principles and secondarily through climate, tradition, and society (also through architecture itself), constitute a major cause for the evolution of characteristics in residential architecture. In fact, people everywhere have always revealed their true nature much more clearly by the way they have built their homes than by other products of the creative arts, which are always tied to the strong subjectivity of their creators and only seldom express the attitude of the people as a whole toward the world and life. This receptive-reflective nature of building should become particularly evident in the Japanese residence, for the Japanese manners of living are so distinct and so far different from those of other countries. Thus, an analysis of the physical response of architecture to these manners of living should have significance for contemporary building insofar as it may rediscover some media of interpreting life through architecture that have been lost in the process of rapid change and turbulent development of Occidental residences during the last century.

The mode of squatting on the floor has had the most visible effect on the residence interior. With chairs being superfluous, and thus less space being required for the individual and his movements, room sizes as a whole are distinctly smaller than those of comparable Western rooms. Moreover, the absence of sitting furniture, together with the fact that the few devices that are necessary, such as folding table and lamp stand, can be removed, allows the room to be easily transformed to suit all different human activities, including sleeping. The small size and sparsity of furniture are the decisive factors that made possible the noted multiusability of space in the Japanese residence.

Of even greater architectural influence has been the circumstance that only one eye-level prevails within the house for all major human activities, i.e., the eye-level of the squatting person. Accordingly, interior designs, such as ceiling, sliding panels, windows, objects of art, picture recess *(tokonoma)* and shelving recess *(tana),* the few pieces of furniture, and even the garden, are strictly orientated for a sitting posture, and such is the combined effect that standing within a room will cause a feeling of uneasiness and unrest in either the person standing or the one observing—as the Japanese express it *kimochi-ga-warui* (sensation is bad). The wide range of influence produced by this squatting mode of sitting includes not only the fact that the design of the kimono, has been determined thereby, but also the fact that the physique of the Japanese has been affected, though disadvantageously.

What serves as a base for sitting serves also as a surface for walking and sleeping. Thus, a particular floor material was necessary: one durable enough to sustain continuous use, soft enough for comfortable sitting and sleeping; a material both resistant and resilient—the floor mat, *tatami.* Since the particular manners of living already existed before the development of the *tatami* in its present form, there is reason to believe that its evolution as an architectural component has been strongly determined by the particular demands of the Japanese way of life. The multiusability of this traditional straw mat is the reason that, even in modern residences, it has not as yet been replaced by synthetic and more hygienic floor materials.

The habit of using living rooms as sleeping rooms during the night also had its distinct architectural response insofar as space had to be provided where the bedding could be conveniently stored. As a result all multipurpose rooms are furnished at one side with closets of 3 ft. (909 mm.) depth, called *oshi-ire,* which are closed by the same opaque paper panels *(fusuma)* that form the partitions between rooms. The proportional space provided for closets in the average house is as much as 15% of the entire floor area, while in small houses it even amounts to 17.5%.

Of not less profound influence on the features of Japanese residential architecture has been the particular Japanese family system. The Japanese residence is by form and function the house for the male and distinctly lacks a reflection of woman's presence. It has already been mentioned that the daily work of the mistress of the house is characterized by its complexity. What needs to be added is that her disposition, as well as her interest and taste as a woman, not only is ignored, but the places in which she works all day long are conspicuous by their architectural neglect. The kitchen that formerly was an unshaped huge space without floor or ceiling has but very recently, in new houses, been partly furnished with boarded floor and suspended ceiling and has also become more humanized.

Insofar as the living rooms are concerned, it is difficult to detect any female atmosphere as is so obvious in Western residence, except in the graceful arrangement of a flower placed in a vase on the platform of the picture recess. But even in this case, it is more as a gesture toward the husband or guest than for her own enjoyment, and, indeed, the flower arrangement itself and its appreciation, stemming directly from the tea cult, were originally more a male than a female concern.

Instead, all matted rooms breathe a spirit of male simplicity and convenience without attempting to hide the distinct traces of their succession from the warrior residence. It is not too unlikely to assume that only the nature of Japanese woman to identify herself with the preferences of her husband and master, and her incapability for developing a personality of her own, makes her appreciate the same values as those of the head of the house.

Importance of the man's interests and the high value placed thereon in preference to those of the woman is further demonstrated by the fact that his activity in the house, which includes the reception and entertainment of the guest, is clearly separated from all domestic affairs. Even the smaller house has not only a good sized entrance hall of about 1 tsubo (3.3. sq m. = 35.6 sq. ft.), but also an anteroom of 2 or 3 mats (3.3–5.0 sq. m. = 35.6–53.4 sq. ft.) interpositioned where both guest and host can comfortably kneel and bow to each other before they enter the reception room, giving exhaustive assurances of mutual respect. Of course, the custom of removing the shoes before entering the elevated part of the house required a particular entrance hall. However, its size, together with the arrangement of an anteroom for the mere purpose of extending a proper welcome to the visitor, is a "waste" of enclosed space that can only be understood when the high reputation any visitor enjoys is taken into consideration.

Significance of the daily bath and differences in bathing manners as described earlier are further factors that were instrumental in producing characteristics in the physique of the Japanese house. While in earlier residences the bath itself was separate from the main house and connected only by a corridor or veranda, the necessity of continuously kindling the flame through the bathing hours finally made way for a functionally more convenient arrangement adjacent to the kitchen. There is a record of the construction of a Buddhist monastery which describes how the monks completed the bathhouse and the hall for their religious exercises before beginning the construction of the temple itself—a practical attitude toward life, which, indeed, convincingly shows how highly the bath was considered.

Since the presence of the retired parents in the family is not only important for the prestige of the "house" but is also necessary because of lack of social welfare for the aged, a particular room is provided somewhat apart from the tightness of the other room cells, where the old parents can spend the rest of their lives; the grandmother still active in kitchen and house, the old master engaging in traditional pastimes such as calligraphy, music, or entertaining his friends. Because of its use for the latter, this room is frequently built to serve simultaneously as a tearoom.

There are other characteristics in the physique of the Japanese house that are due to the manners of living, but because they are based ultimately on either religion or tradition they will be subject to discussion in their respective chapters.

influence from house

The physique of building in its relationship to family life is usually assumed to be in essence receptive-reflective rather than causative-formative, i.e., it is commonly accepted that the house is but a mirrored image of the family therein. Yet, while this assumption appears to hold true for today's tendencies in architectural creation, which aim at confirming the existing rather than attempt to visualize the approaching, in the case of Japanese residential architecture there is ample evidence that, in a reverse manner, architecture has originally and directly produced some of the distinct features of the Japanese mode of living itself.

While Western civilization with its enormous technical achievements in building long ago succeeded in making life within the house independent of climatic changes, in the Buddhist world nature has never been considered as something to be fought against, conquered, and mastered. Consequently, little effort was made to realistically-creatively confront the architectural problems presented by nature, even less to use nature's forces for self-advantage. As a result, the living rooms in the average Japanese house during daytime are shielded against the outside only by light wooden frames covered with translucent paper, the shoji panels, which can easily be moved in their sliding tracks or can be entirely removed, as is the case in the height of summer heat (Plate 36). Their only function is to assure privacy while admitting light. But their consistency and construction is not such that, when closed, they can prevent cold, humidity, draught, or dust from penetrating into every corner of the house interior.

For this architectural reason the Japanese have come to adjust their manners of living distinctly to the changing climatic conditions of each season of the year. And this change is not only manifested in habits of eating, bathing, clothing, and bedding, but all movable parts of the house, such as interior and exterior sliding doors, the picture scroll in the picture recess, the floor covering and cushion, also undergo transformation with the change of season. It may be that the well-known respect of the Japanese people for nature has been strongly stimulated by this type of housing, which makes them directly experience the forces of nature, both the benign and the destructive.

Moreover, since the translucent paper panels do not keep out even the slightest sound, the Japanese from early childhood is accustomed to all kinds of noise from the outside, which need not necessarily be of the pleasant kind such as the ripple of a creek, the rustling of a tree, or the whisper of the wind. The result is that the average Japanese is more immune to obtrusive noise than the average Occidental, and so raises no objections against the loud-speakers at shrines, temples, and railway stations, the radios in university study rooms, and the hooting in the cities.

This, however, contrasts sharply with the self-control everyone exercises within his own house. As the partitions between the rooms are but opaque paper panels for the purpose of limiting sight, any conversation, music-playing, or less pleasant activities within the house have all members either as active or passive participants. Consequently, all activities within the house are conducted with a degree of mutual regard and respect among the family members that would be unusual in the individualistic West.

Further, the nature of room partitioning allows for no privacy of the individual. Since rooms serve also as corridors between one room and another, the sliding panels at any side can be opened or removed at any time. Nobody knocks before entering, for there are but paper panels against which audible knocking would have destructive consequences. No vices nor virtues can be hidden, for there is absolutely nowhere to hide them. Thus, everything about each member of the family, even the most private affairs, is known to all the other members, and decisions are never left up to the individual. True, such manner of housing has proven very successful in subduing those vices one may develop in solitude and has fostered a close family life in which the members are dependent on each other under the leadership of the head of the house. However, it certainly has also hindered development of individual personalities and has promoted the fatal dependence on opinions, decisions, and even ideologies of others rather than of self which is so apparent among the Japanese youth of today. Actually, the Japanese house, though divided by movable screens into smaller parts, is but one room, used by all the family at the same time and for all the different purposes of daily life. Naturally, it is only tolerable to live under these architectural conditions if all the family members submit themselves to a strict system of etiquette and unusual tidiness. And it is, therefore, not just an allegation to attribute the ceremony-like way of living in the Japanese house to the particular architectural situation prevailing.

Relationship between members of the family necessarily has to be very frank with little regard for the difference of sex, either in undressing or sleeping or in taking the hot bath. This may even account for the noted innocence and virtue of the Japanese woman, because the open and transparent atmosphere of the Japanese house, with rooms where every sound can be overheard by the entire family and that can be entered at any time from several sides, is hardly friendly to the growth of romance and would even less offer opportunity for adventurous love. Yet, the lack of privacy in the life of the individual, as it has been brought about by the particular construction of the Japanese house, is not limited to the confines of the family. Homes of the middle and lower classes open upon public streets and, whenever weather permits, the fronts and perhaps even the sides are literally removed, leaving the interior widely open to the air, the light, and the public gaze. It appears almost as if the exposure of private life, having been experienced from infancy on, has never made the individual feel a need for privacy, and it is therefore not surprising that no word exists for "privacy" in the Japanese language.

That this architectural peculiarity had further consequences is proven by the interesting fact that the Japanese is very indifferent to the exposure of the unclothed body. The nature of Japanese clothing makes for easy removal in the heat of the summer; and, due to the openness of the house both toward the outside and within, everyone has become well accustomed to the exposure of the other sex. Nobody is ashamed of the exposure of fellow man or fellow woman, and one not familiar with this practice may feel offended at so much indifference.

for contemporary architecture

It is seen, then, that the moral principles of family and society are practiced in the manners and customs of the family and substantiated in its shelter: the house. However, the Japanese house also gives example of the existence of a reverse order. Certain features of building that have been brought about chiefly by pressing environmental circumstances, such as weather, economy, or society, have unmistakably not only modified existing habits but have also produced new ones for the inhabitants, and thus, in the course of centuries, have caused the emergence of new values of life, i.e., new moral principles. This may even account for the emergence of characteristics that are commonly identified as innate features of the Japanese race. For although habits acquired by social heredity or architectural conditions are, in essence, psychical insofar as they determine diet, housing, clothing, education, and occupation they can result in acquired psychological or physiological, even anatomical, characteristics. In this respect, the Japanese house shows residential architecture in a role of forming rather than of reflecting habits of living, of producing rather than following moral principles, of creating rather than confirming psychical characteristics.

This phenomenon of Japanese residential architecture has a particular significance for the contemporary age insofar as it makes clear the noble and necessary mission of residential architecture: to *teach* the art of living, to *create* values of life. Always, the world over, the family lives, thinks, and likes in terms of yesterday, i.e., of the past. The creative artist can visualize the essence of the present and future, and among them the architect is qualified to comprehend the full significance socially, technically, economically, and ethically and to convey it to the family.

Thus, the causative role of the Japanese house actually demonstrates but a reality that underlies residential architecture, independently of time and place. It charges the architect with the imperative task of gaining comprehensive knowledge not only of the practical-technical aspect of building, but also of the intellectual and spiritual forces that control the epoch, which he is supposed to represent through building. It also shows that current educational methods have been inadequate in focusing attention on this essential content of architecture as an art, and in providing the intellectual basis for architectural philosophizing. Books that describe architecture as mere physical-material creation with distinct forms, and training programs that teach only the technical and practical aspect of design and building rather than architectural thinking, are largely responsible for the fact that building has become essentially a technical device of pleasant appearance, in no way different from any industrial product. Indeed, this educational deficiency is one of the factors that have caused the symptomatic and tragic indifference of contemporary man toward his own creations.

Unawareness of the universal values that distinguish the present and the resulting absence of such values in contemporary architecture not only have endangered the quality and potential of architecture as art, but are also the fundamental cause of the fact that the individuality in the architect's creations is no longer rooted in the anonymous order of the epoch. This individuality, in spite of excellence per se, has produced the chaos of the whole.

Another important lesson for contemporary architecture is the Japanese identification of family and its head with "house." The dual existence of house, that of being "image of the family" and "creator of family," is an architectural reality that today's rapidly changing living habits and building techniques have obscured. Thus, residential building has more or less become a functional-mechanical instrument that facilitates immediate human needs of eating, sleeping, working, viewing, enjoying, and may even exhibit visual-aesthetic qualities. But there is no philosophical depth because the reality of house and family is not comprehended and consequently not interpreted.

The emotional intimacy of the Japanese with their homes is actually but one among the many psychological associations with the physical objects of their total environment. Stimulated by the ancient nature religion of Shinto and by the Buddhist world view that integrates all inanimate and animate beings, the life of the Japanese is emotionally very rich in his continuous encounter with the spiritual meaning of his entire material environment. Here the essence of true culture is revealed. The criterion of culture is not a nation's works of art measured in comparison to that of other nations, it is instead the degree to which the summary of all creations of a nation, both the physical and spiritual, succeeded in stirring the emotions of the people, deepening their spiritual life, and sensitizing their feeling and taste. In this sense, Japanese culture, in spite of relative limitation of form, motif, and range in the arts, has achieved a very high level in that it provides a content and depth of living for the mass of the people that sharply contrasts with the physical commodiousness, intellectual complacency, and spiritual shallowness as brought about by contemporary Western culture.

On the other hand, Japanese residential architecture, as a valuable instrument for judging contemporary affairs, asserts itself not only in a positive role. The negative results of the Japanese interior space, as effected by the utter disregard of the woman's interest, confirm the importance of solving the complex position of the woman in contemporary domestic design everywhere. Certainly, the organization of design of the house interior is also by no means a simple rationalizing of communication and accommodation, but is basically a philosophic definition of the role that each individual should occupy within the organism of the family.

Naturally, the position of the wife and mother is the most diverse and multiple. With the current transformation of her place in wedlock, family, and society, it is in this sphere that decisive architectural progress is apt to take place. This cannot be brought about through merely simplifying and automatizing her daily chores, but will require a philosophical analysis of her place in the house as determined by present social ethics. Such realization will then provide the intellectual basis for efforts that will effect more essential progress than any technical or economical improvement possibly can: combining and rationalizing the housewife's functions in the house, incorporating rather than isolating her activities from the rest of the family, and making her presence a distinct architectural reality.

Yet, it is by no means intended to convey the impression that only the Japanese residence has substantiated the philosophy of its existence, or even that the Japanese had consciously aimed at such profound building, though in their case the signs are more obvious. In any residential architecture of the past, when the family did not yet require an alien interpreter, an architect, to pronounce its ethics and translate them into house, building was a direct creation of the family and craftsmen from its own ranks, and therefore became a strong and innocent statement of the period and its thinking. However, the increasing complexity of contemporary building no longer permits this organic order of architectural creation but requests intromission of an architect, who alone is qualified to substantiate the sublime significance of family and "house" with the complex instruments of contemporary building practice. The underlying reality of both family and "house" is manifested in the Japanese house more clearly than elsewhere. And its study, therefore, is of particular importance for the contemporary architect so that he may better understand the aim and source of his work.

definition

SPACE IN BUILDING is extension, purposefully controlled and clearly defined. It is not substantial matter but the void that exists between two points, between two lines, between two planes, between two moments.

SPACE IN BUILDING, therefore, has multidimensional quality. One-dimensionally, space is interval (linear space); two-dimensionally, space is area (planimetric space); three-dimensionally, space is volume (volumetric space); four-dimensionally, space is experience (traversed space).

SPACE IN BUILDING has a distinct character that affects man psychologically. This spatial quality is primarily dependent on actual dimensions, but is decisively tempered by light and shadow, line and contour, texture and color.

SPACE IN BUILDING, then, is an intrinsic medium through which the art of architecture asserts itself. Whereas other art forms express themselves by occupying and enriching human space, architecture is the art that, in fact, creates this space.

SPACE IN BUILDING is closely related to the scale of man. Man's struggle for survival and his subsequent striving for physical convenience was the fundamental reason for architectural space. Its limits were set by the properties of materials available and by methods of construction.

SPACE IN BUILDING is not only translation of human physical measurement, but is also increasingly determined by man's psychological requirements. Thus, spatial evolution in architecture more distinctly marks the progress of civilization than does the change in architectural technique or form.

SPACE IN BUILDING, in its role of enabling man to live and to work, is differentiated by purpose of the building. Accordingly, the character of residential space is distinctly different from that of commercial space, ecclesiastical space, or circulatory space.

SPACE IN BUILDING, then, is that void where the life of individual, family, and society unfolds. It is the very instrument that concedes a life different from that of animals and is the enclosement where all the instruments of mankind's progress, the arts, the science, the statecraft, were conceived.

Just as architecture has changed in its form and expression throughout history, so too has it changed in its concept of space.* While architectural form and expression was subject to abrupt breaks and sudden discontinuity, owing to technical discoveries, socio-political revolutions, or philosophical changes, space in building has experienced a steady and continuous evolution throughout architectural history. Indeed, space is the very element that links architecture of different epochs and different cultures and preserves continuity of architecture from the past to the present.

* Since it is difficult to conceive of space as a single entity that simultaneously constitutes linear distance, area, volume, or time, a limitation in use is necessary in order to avoid misunderstandings. Therefore, in all instances henceforth "space," if not otherwise specified, will denote the volumetric, i.e., three-dimensional space. The fourth dimension of participational time and the fifth possible dimension of participational effort, both of which are descriptive of architectural space, are excluded because they are, in fact, qualities of the three-dimensional form—subjective qualities, however, that depend on individual human capacity and disposition and therefore have no universal validity.

All architectural works—the primitive layout of early shelters, the intuitive construction of medieval cathedrals, as well as the scientific planning of contemporary cities and highways—can be identified with man's efforts to span space, enclose space, utilize space, and enrich space for the single purpose of serving man's physical and psychical wants. This includes also monuments from the Pyramids down to sculptures in modern plazas, which are architectural efforts to enrich space. Yet, space in monumental architecture had a development all its own, and while it may give some clue as to man's faculty of conceiving space, being the work of professional specialists, its concept must have been far removed from popular wish and idea. It is only since the professional architect has taken part in popular residential architecture that the achievements of the great tradition of monumental space have been made available to the common people. The influence of this tradition has provoked profound changes in the hitherto dormant concept of space in domestic architecture, and has disclosed more possibilities of fundamental progress than are possible through any improvement of constructional methods and mechanical conveniences.

Space in Japanese residential architecture is a phenomenon that has no equal in any stage of spatial growth in Western architecture. Its similarity to contemporary concepts is frequently mentioned by architect-writers and hailed as proof of progressive thought, but this analogousness is more seeming than real. There is even reason to doubt whether Japanese space, as distinct as it is, is the result of a real intellectual concept a priori, for there is no evidence at all that the spatial characteristics of the Japanese house were conceived in advance. Instead, it is very likely that the people, while struggling for existence, responded to immediate needs, technical possibilities, and climatic conditions with means that effected the characteristic Japanese space. This, however, does not deprive this space of its significance for contemporary architecture. Rather, since it contains certain features that have gained new interpretation and substantiation in contemporary architecture, the analysis of Japanese space is more than just an alien and abstract study of things past.

measure of man

The earliest and most primitive architectural space was the minimum volume required to contain the family. Its dimensions, therefore, were but human measurements in their multiple, modified by interior functional activities and by the limits that material and technique imposed. These basic factors of space in residential architecture have not essentially changed and are also prerequisite to adequate architectural space in contemporary design. This is not meant to challenge the importance of other less primitive-practical factors in the creation of architectural space such as its ideal or psychological aspect. No doubt, these are decisive for the quality of architectural space, but in residential architecture they can only be attributed secondary importance in comparison to the fulfillment of man's mere physical requirements for space, i.e., requirements for sitting, working, and sleeping.

The cause and idea behind space in residential architecture, therefore, is primarily functional-practical and only secondarily emotional-ideal. Of course, space may occasionally function to satisfy man's aesthetic-spiritual wants rather than his physical wants, but the dominant function of space in residential architecture is the fulfillment of man's practical requirements. Therefore, thorough knowledge of the measure of man's physique is essential for both analysis of the existing and creation of the new.

This is of even more importance in the case of Japan, where social conditions have imposed on the common classes the utmost of limitation and curtailment of space in building that has no equivalent in Western architecture. In fact, the relationship of human and architectural measurement is so immensely close that one may well speak of their being identical. It effects a strong interrelationship of man and house and is the major reason why the Japanese house appears dwarfishly small in compari-

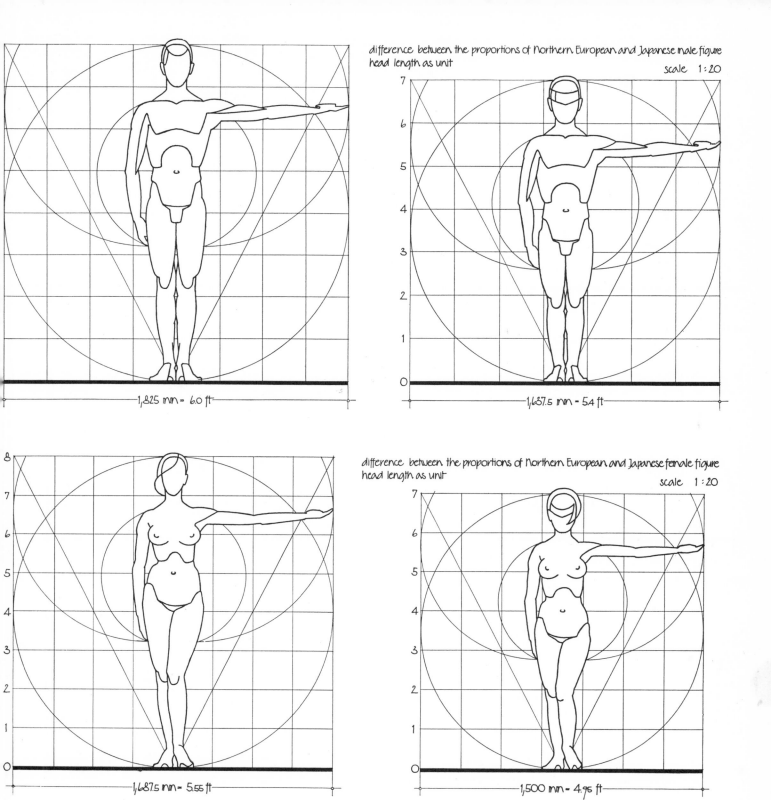

difference between the proportions of Northern European and Japanese male figure
head length as unit

scale 1:20

1,825 mm = 6.0 ft

1,637.5 mm = 5.4 ft

difference between the proportions of Northern European and Japanese female figure
head length as unit

scale 1:20

1,687.5 mm = 5.55 ft

1,500 mm = 4.95 ft

FIGURE 54: Comparison of standard human figures of Northern Europeans and Japanese.

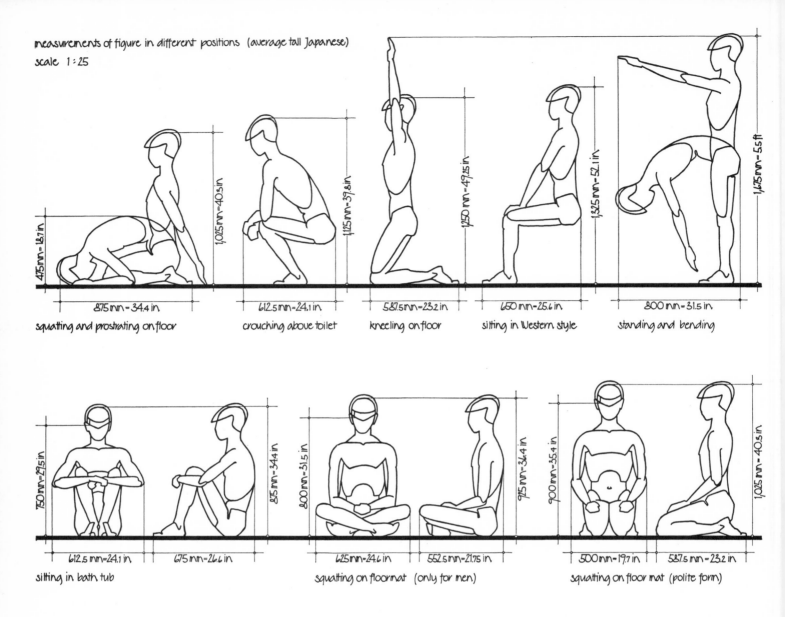

measurements of figure in different positions (average tall Japanese)
scale 1:25

475mm = 18.7 in

1,025mm = 40.5 in

875mm = 34.4 in
squatting and prostrating on floor

1,125mm = 39.8 in

612.5mm = 24.1 in
crouching above toilet

1,250mm = 49.25 in

587.5mm = 23.2 in
kneeling on floor

1,325mm = 52.1 in

650 mm = 25.6 in
sitting in Western style

1,625mm = 5.5 ft

800 mm = 31.5 in
standing and bending

750mm = 29.5 in

875mm = 34.4 in

612.5 mm = 24.1 in   675 mm = 26.6 in
sitting in bath tub

800mm = 31.5 in

625mm = 24.6 in   552.5mm = 21.75 in
squatting on floormat (only for men)

925mm = 36.4 in

900mm = 35.4 in

1,025mm = 40.5 in

500mm = 19.7 in   587.5 mm = 23.2 in
squatting on floor mat (polite form)

FIGURE 55: Space requirements of the Japanese figure in various postures.

son with Western residences, the difference being far greater than the difference between Japanese and Western figure would indicate.

Measurements of the average-sized human have little significance for architectural dimensioning. For building, no matter of what type, is not for the individual alone but for the majority of people. Consequently, architectural dimensioning has to prove adequate for all, i.e., it must be determined by the size of the average tall person so that convenience is provided for all others. Only the height measurements of furniture are exempted, because, here, the measurements of the average small person reversely prove adequate for all others. Therefore, the two extremes, the tall and the small human figure, have to be considered in architectural dimensioning. However, since furniture is very rare in the Japanese house, only measurements of the average tall Japanese are of value.

The dominant Japanese physical type is Mongoloid. In relation to the total figure height, the head is large and the limbs are short; also the face clearly manifests the Mongolian type. The main physical differences from the Caucasian type, having architectural importance, are the following:

1.   The average height is about 6 *sun* smaller (187.5 mm. = 7.4 in.).*

* The height difference between male and female is about 4.5 *sun* (137.5 mm. = 5.4 in.).

2. The whole body height is between 6 1/2 and 7 times that of the head height, while in Western countries the average is 7 1/2 to 8 times.

3. The body crotch is much lower than the middle of the body whereas the Caucasian type has the crotch about at half height.

4. This results in particularly short legs and other limbs, which are already shorter because of smaller body height.

5. Thus the torso has about the same height as the Caucasian counterpart, i.e., sitting on the same base, the eye level of both is about the same.

planimetric-functional space

To the architect, the compliance with man's physical requirements in architectural space is a matter of two-dimensional (planimetric) design. As the roof provides protection and adequate spatial height—as a rule beyond that of physical necessity—the space of functional efficiency is reduced to a two-dimensional one in the horizontal plane. Organization of horizontal planimetric space, and not volumetric space, is, therefore, decisive for the functional quality of building, and it is not against the nature of space in architecture to approach functional space, be it for analysis or design, on a two-dimensional basis.

The organization of functional space, as it is traditionally done by the Japanese family itself is but the arranging of standardized spatial units on a two-dimensional grid, using the mat as the ordering unit. It is primarily concerned with establishment of a simple circulation pattern and is influenced by considerations of site relationship, orientation to compass, and possible separation of "official" space from all "private" space, as has been described earlier. While utilitarian spaces such as bath, toilet, and kitchen, of course, are distinct in purpose and form, the physical similarity of all living spaces has given rise to the erroneous belief that the function of the individual Japanese living space is undefined and therefore alterable at will. The fact, however, is that each room has a distinct name relating to its major purpose, and that its use, though multiple, is well defined.

The smallest houses, of course, combine various functions in one or two rooms. Similar to Western practice, the larger the house is, the more distinct is the use of individual living space. Room designations, however, are difficult to translate into Western languages, for there are no equivalent words to describe rooms of double or triple function, nor are the Japanese designations distinct enough in themselves. Instead, at best the names permit only a clue to the original purpose of the room but hardly explain any later use. These names were traditionally maintained despite the fact that room usage changed and even varied from place to place—all adding to the difficulties in finding descriptive names for each room.

1. Bath unit, *ofuro* (literally honorable wind-fire place)

To begin the description of standard Japanese rooms with the bath must appear rather unusual, and yet, as has been noted, there is an old script which states that the very self-disciplined Zen monks, when building a monastery, completed their bathhouse and their hall for exercises before starting with the construction of the main temple and the rest of the complex.

The importance of the daily bath in the life of the Japanese has been mentioned earlier. The Japanese washes outside of the tub and, after having cleansed himself thoroughly, enjoys sitting in the reddening heat of the water in both summer and winter. Accordingly, the space in front of the tub is covered with a removable grating through which the water, after being splashed over the crouching body, trickles and then drains from the concrete or stone floor to the outside. Owing to the particular manner of squatting in front of the tub and inside, the minimum Japanese bathroom is much smaller than the smallest one in Western architecture.

The oldest type of tub is probably the one consisting of a simply coopered wooden box fitted onto a metal bottom which is a part of the stove underneath. To protect the feet from being burned, a wooden plank of the same shape as the metal bottom is

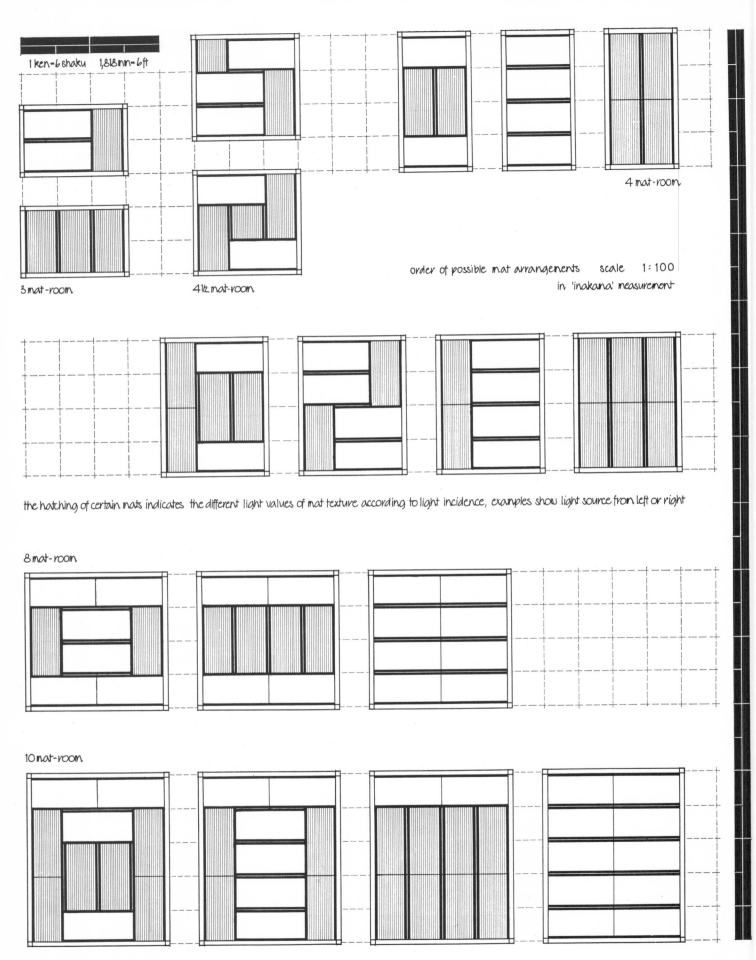

1 ken-6 shaku   1,818mm-6ft

3 mat-room

4½ mat-room

4 mat-room

order of possible mat arrangements   scale   1:100
in 'inakana' measurement

the hatching of certain mats indicates the different light values of mat texture according to light incidence, examples show light source from left or right

8 mat-room

10 mat-room

FIGURE 56: *Tatami* arrangements of standard rooms.

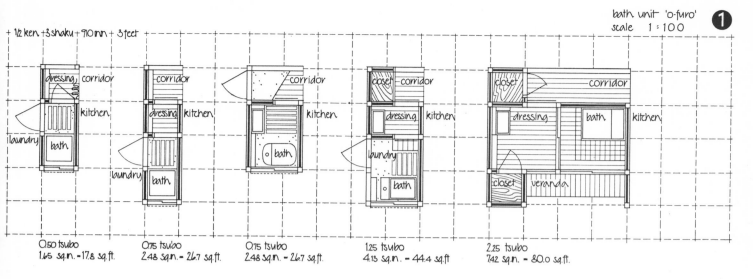

+ 1/2 ken + 3 shaku + 910 mn + 3 feet

dressing / corridor / kitchen / laundry / bath

corridor / dressing / kitchen / laundry / bath

corridor / kitchen / bath

closet / corridor / dressing / kitchen / laundry / bath

closet / corridor / dressing / bath / kitchen / closet / veranda

0.50 tsubo
1.65 sq.m. - 17.8 sq.ft.

0.75 tsubo
2.48 sq.m. - 26.7 sq.ft.

0.75 tsubo
2.48 sq.m. - 26.7 sq.ft.

1.25 tsubo
4.13 sq.m. - 44.4 sq.ft.

2.25 tsubo
7.42 sq.m. - 80.0 sq.ft.

FIGURE 57: Floor plans of standard room units.

used. It floats on top of the water and has two or three holes so the bather can easily force it down with his foot. It sometimes happens that the plank pitches in the last moment and all the fun of bathing may be spoiled for weeks to come. Thus the saying goes, that the timid enters this type of tub without removing his "shoes," the wooden clogs called *geta!* In another type of bath, the stove is built onto the side of the bathtub and is fed from the outside, making the water circulate continuously between the tub and stove. This system is actually similar to the type in which the water is heated in a separate furnace and is then piped to the tub. With the advent of gas, a portable tub is now frequently used with a burner that is operated from the bathroom itself.

2.   Toilet unit, *obenjo* (literally, place of honorable convenience)

Through contact with the West, many technical devices of Western origin have been added to the Japanese residence. Still, lack of public funds in both urban and rural communities has so far prevented general introduction of sewage systems. Thus, the toilet in the Japanese house has retained its primitive characteristics. And the Japanese, well familiar with the conveniences of Western sanitation, submit themselves to the inevitable, be it of the acoustical or the scented kind, just as they do to typhoons, earthquakes, or other supreme forces of nature. The only architectural measures that could be taken were to separate the toilet, if possible, from other utilitarian spaces such as bath and kitchen, to place it in a remote corner of the house, to furnish it with the best possible material and workmanship, to provide it with particular straw sandals, to furnish it with décor in the form of a flower and vase, and even to occasionally arrange a miniature garden outside it to be viewed from within in all leisure from the crouching posture—no doubt all these measures should compensate for other obvious disadvantages. Yet, in Japan the toilet has never been entirely separated from the house as is common practice in unsewered areas in the West. Instead, the toilet is a part of the house, easily accessible to both guest and inhabitant.

The toilet is usually divided into two compartments: one contains the urinal and sometimes a wash stand, the other has an oblong slot in the floor edged with a porcelain fitting above which one crouches to ease the human organism. Doubtless, this not too comfortable posture does have its advantages. As the body rests on the legs only with no other physical contact, the posture is very hygienic; moreover, becoming pretty tiring after awhile, it certainly shortens the procedure, which in spite of foul odors might be unduly extended because of so much architectural attractiveness! The sewage is directly collected in a vat of earthenware buried in the ground about 2 to 3 feet below the toilet floor (of course, the vat volume is also standardized according

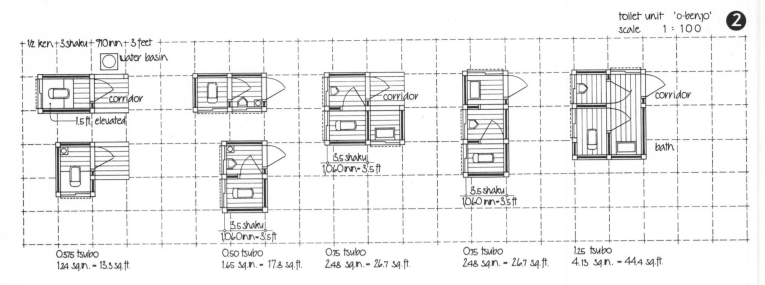

½ ken + 3 shaku + 710 mm + 3 feet
water basin

corridor

1.5 ft. elevated

corridor

3.5 shaku
1,060 mm - 3.5 ft

3.5 shaku
1,060 mm - 3.5 ft

corridor

bath

3.5 shaku
1,060 mm - 3.5 ft

0.375 tsubo	0.50 tsubo	0.75 tsubo	0.75 tsubo	1.25 tsubo
1.24 sq.m. - 13.3 sq.ft.	1.65 sq.m. - 17.8 sq.ft.	2.48 sq.m. - 26.7 sq.ft.	2.48 sq.m. - 26.7 sq.ft.	4.13 sq.m. - 44.4 sq.ft.

FIGURE 57 (continued): Floor plans of standard room units.

to average family capacity at three different periods of removal). At regular intervals, the farmer comes with cart and ox and removes the entire sewage, using it to fertilize his rice fields—a privilege for which he formerly paid his provider in field products. In small houses the wash stand is usually placed in the compartment containing the urinal, but in large houses either a third compartment is antepositioned or a tall stone basin that can be reached from the veranda with a scoop might be placed in the garden near the toilet (see Chapter VII).

3. Kitchen unit *daidokoro* (literally, place of basis)

The traditional kitchen, which even today is being built in farmhouses and can be found also in older city houses, is a huge unshapely space extending to the roof and without ground cover—a dark place where there is not the least protection from drafts and cold in winter and even less protection from all types of animals from domestic rats down to the various species of insects. More recently constructed city residences have eliminated this concept of the kitchen. Western influence may to a certain degree account for this change, but there is reason to believe that the actual inspiration came from the kitchenette, *mizu-ya*, adjacent to the ceremonial tearoom. Here utensils and cabinets are conveniently and neatly arranged to avoid any superfluous effort so as to enable harmony of movement, which is the dominant principle of ceremonial tea serving.

Nevertheless, the old type of kitchen receives dignity by way of its stove. As in ancient Western architecture, the kitchen stove is considered an important object and a symbol of prosperity in the "house." To the tutelary kitchen deity food and offerings are brought, but this devotion never goes so far as to provide the deity with a cleaner, better illuminated, and more dignified environment. The old stove consists of one big fire opening with three, five, or seven smaller fireplaces, each having a round hole on top on which to place a pot. All holes are plastered into the base structure and arranged in a circular form to facilitate their use from one spot in the middle. Smoke leaves at the other side of the fire hole and rises against the unceilinged roof. There it disperses gradually through an opening that is protected by a small raised roof or, in case of a thatched roof, through an opening in the gable. Inadequate lighting prevents one from becoming too aware of the dust and dirt above that mingle lustily with spider webs and smoke.

While this old kitchen in rural areas is also used as space for all kinds of indoor work, in the cities a more convenient type of kitchen that combines economy with hygiene and is dimensioned only for proper kitchen work has evolved. The greater part of the floor in this space is boarded, and the unboarded portion leads directly to

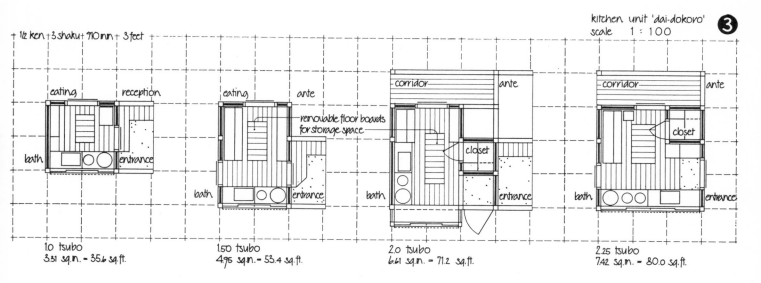

+ 1/2 ken + 3 shaku + 910 mn + 3 feet +

eating   reception

bath   entrance

1.0 tsubo
3.31 sq.n. - 35.6 sq.ft.

eating   ante

removable floor boards for storage space

bath   entrance

1.50 tsubo
4.95 sq.n. - 53.4 sq.ft.

corridor   ante

closet

bath   entrance

2.0 tsubo
6.61 sq.n. - 71.2 sq.ft.

corridor   ante

closet

bath   entrance

2.25 tsubo
7.42 sq.n. - 80.0 sq.ft.

FIGURE 57 (continued): Floor plans of standard room units.

the outside or to the entrance hall, enabling the traders to come directly into the kitchen without having to remove their shoes. This unboarded portion is either earthen or, more recently, concrete. From here a door occasionally provides a secondary access to the bath, which is also used as the laundry. Since there is no cellar in the Japanese house, frequently a portion of the floor boards in the kitchen is made removable, and a small storage space of brick or concrete is built underneath. The limited variety of cooking utensils and the simple wooden chopsticks do not demand much storage space, and a simple sink, a built-in stove, and a portable charcoal burner are all that is needed for kitchen work. The eating place, *chanoma,* is usually arranged adjacent to the kitchen, or separated only by an interior corridor. Smells of all sorts have never been of too much concern. Moreover, the natural ventilation is overly effective, both in summer and winter.

4.   Dining room, *chanoma* (literally, space of tea), *shokudo* (literally, hall of meal)

Neither the literal meaning "space of tea" nor the Western translation "dining room" adequately describes the function and significance of this room. True, it serves as a place where the family, though not the guest, takes its meals, and as such was never, until very recently, used for sleeping. In addition, it is also the family room where all gather around the charcoal brazier, *hibachi,* for a talk in their leisure time. Here the housewife carries on her domestic work when she is not engaged in the kitchen; here she also receives her own friends; and it is here that she keeps her utensils for all domestic work. This room is also the important junction between "official" space and "private" space. Being a junction, this room more than any other serves as a corridor. The cabinets in one corner, the drawers in the other, a low table in the third and the stand for writing equipment in the fourth, picture a room which, though "homey," is in essence and expression confused, undefined, and complex—a striking reflection of the wife's image in the Japanese house.

The room measures 4 1/2 or 6 mats in the average-sized house and is usually furnished with built-in closets. In the center of the room, sunk into the floor, is a fireplace, *kotatsu,* which during the summer months is covered up by board and mat. It is a square wooden cage about 1 1/2 ft. deep into which a charcoal brazier is placed during the wintertime. A table covered by a blanket is set on top of it, and the family enjoy hanging their legs into the warmth of the cage underneath with the blanket over their laps.

5.   Entrance hall, *genkan* (literally, mysterious gate) and anteroom, *hiroma* (literally, wide space)

The entrance hall plays an important part in the Japanese residence—so important

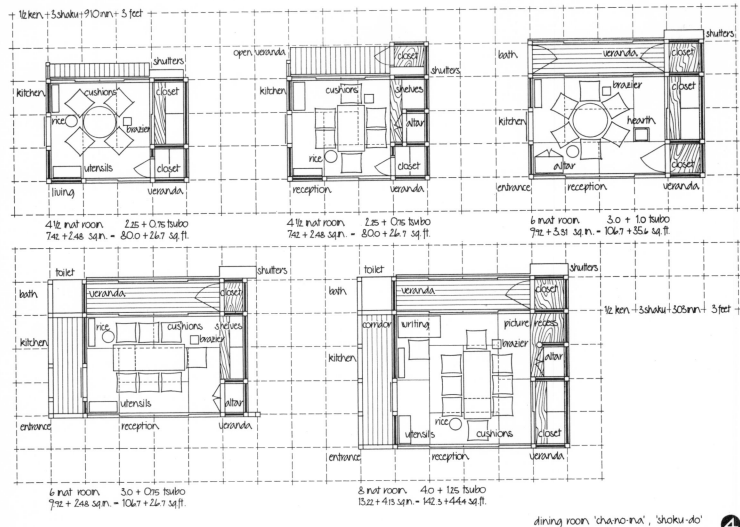

FIGURE 57 (continued): Floor plans of standard room units.

that even the smallest residences of 10 to 15 *tsubo* (33–50 sq. m. = 356–534 sq. ft.) have provided no less than 10% of the entire floor area for it. Investigation into its very interesting history reveals that the meaning of the entrance hall, *genkan,* has undergone various changes. Its appearance in the houses of the common people is fairly recent (since 1868) and its meaning today is entirely different from what it originally was (Plates 64–67).

The Japanese custom of removing the shoes before entering the house, no doubt, is the major reason why the entrance hall has maintained its place in traditional and modern dwellings alike. Usually the floor is of concrete or of pebbles set in cement, so that dirt carried in from the street can easily be removed. One or two broad steps of wood or a broad stone slab, rough or trimmed, bridge the difference in level between the entrance hall and living rooms. Yet, the mere need for a space in which to remove shoes cannot alone account for the importance of the entrance hall in the Japanese "house." Its obstinate retention in the house in spite of other less spacious possibilities for removing shoes, seems rather to suggest that the sentiments of the people are still governed, if only unconsciously, by concepts of the past society in which this formal entrance space was a privilege held only by the upper classes and forbidden to the general public. This concept of entrance hall has since taken on much human meaning as the space where man takes leave from an outside world which is increasingly indifferent or in contrast to his inner life. In this regard, the

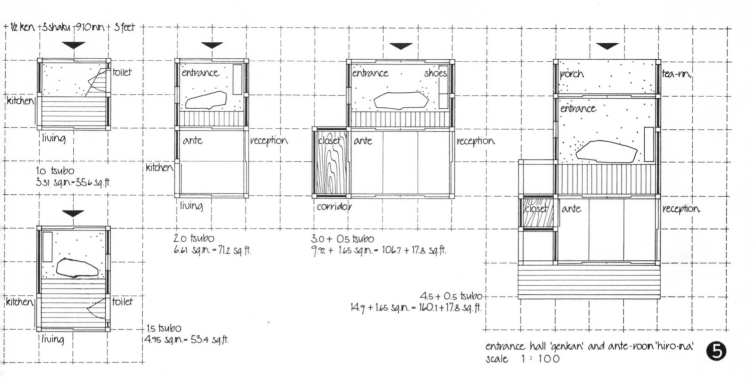

FIGURE 57 (continued): Floor plans of standard room units.

entrance hall symbolizes the first stage in removing this antithesis of man and his environment until both finally are reunited within the house and receive from each other confirmation and meaning of their existence.

Similarly, the anteroom, *hiroma,* can be considered as an intermediate stage in the process of integrating man into the house (Plate 68). The room is matted; its size in the average house is only 2 or 3 mats, but in larger residences it may even reach 8 or 10 mats. It is here that the wife welcomes her husband, and here that host and guest meet and prostrate themselves. The room usually has no walls that face to the outside and therefore receives only diffused light from the entrance hall through the translucent paper panels, *shōji.* Access is provided from the anteroom to any of the other rooms by sliding walls, the opaque paper panels, *fusuma.*

6. Reception room, *zashiki* (literally, seat spread); *ōsetsuma* (literally, responding and meeting space); *kyakuma* (literally, space for visitor)

The most important room, although the least used, is the reception room. While in smaller homes, this room is occupied by the parents as a bedroom, in larger residences it is reserved for receiving and entertaining the honored guest, who also sleeps there if he stays overnight. The historical evolution of this space is closely associated with the form of society. For in feudal society it was essential to provide one space where the head of the house could perform official functions and ceremonies while receiving a superior. This clearly indicates that the reception room in the house of the common people did not originate from a direct functional need of the family itself.

The traditional use of the reception room, even after the social reform of 1868, has actually preserved the purity of its original architectural expression. With the exception of electric lights and frequently glass inserted in the paper panels, none of the alien and unproportioned devices of Occidental convenience that have come to disturb the expression of other rooms have found their way into the reception room. The importance of this room is evident in the sheer size (8 mats and larger), but more so in the presence of the picture alcove, *tokonoma,* the ornamental shelving recess, *tana,* and occasionally the decorative study place, *shoin.* These three features form the spiritual core of the "house." Indeed, they may well be considered the

½ ken = 3 shaku = 910 mm = 3 feet

picture recess | closet

4½ mat room with open veranda
of width = 455 mm = 1.5 ft

picture recess | closet

6 mat room with open veranda
of width = 606 mm = 2.0 ft

closet | picture recess | shelving recess

study place 'shoin'

8 mat room with enclosed veranda
of width = 909 mm = 3.0 ft

picture recess

study place
'shoin'

veranda

enclosed veranda of width = 1,061 mm = 4.5 ft

veranda | ante-room | closet

closet

shelving

picture recess

study place 'shoin'

veranda

10 mat room with ante room (6 mat) and enclosed veranda
of width = 1,818 mm = 6.0 ft

reception room   'za-shiki', 'osetsu-ma', 'kyaku-ma'
scale   1 : 100

FIGURE 57 (continued): Floor plans of standard room units.

symbolic center of the entire dwelling site, because they adjoin the broad veranda and thus incorporate the most beautiful part of the garden into the harmonious ensemble of house, picture, flower, and man (Plate 69).

In larger residences, the reception room is adjacent to another room. The two rooms are merely divided by opaque paper panels, which for important gatherings can be removed, turning both spaces into one single room. Since the scale and proportion of any room in the house is subjected to the same order regardless of its use, this combining of room units can be accomplished without any visual discord. This internal metamorphosis, which occasionally also takes in other living rooms, is so complete that, if it were not for the wooden grooves imbedded in the floor and the tracks and transom above, the original state of partitioning could hardly be detected.

7. Living room, *ima* (literally, space of being)

While the rooms previously mentioned are the core of the Japanese house and have definite functions, there are other mat-covered rooms that refine this functional organism but do not add anything essentially new. Thus, a living room, *ima,* may take over a part of the function of dining room, *chanoma,* and provide space where the family gathers around a fireplace; another may be a day-and-night room for the children; and a third may be a room just for the parents, who otherwise use the reception room as their bedroom. Expression and size are fairly equal in all of these rooms. They usually face to the veranda and garden on one side and have one wall with 3-foot-deep closets. The other two walls consist of sliding panels, thus facilitating

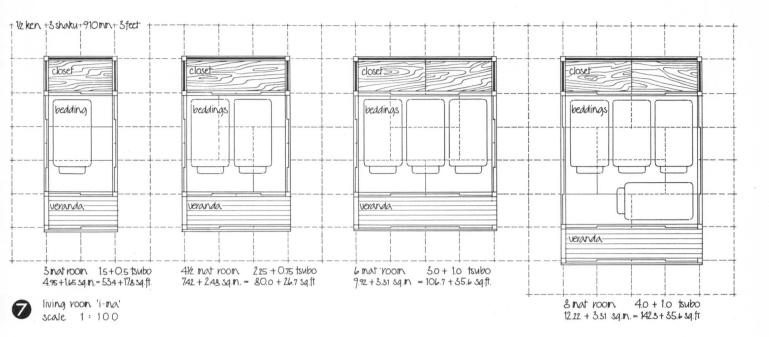

3 mat room   1.5 + 0.5 tsubo
4.95 + 1.65 sq.m. = 53.4 + 17.8 sq.ft.

4½ mat room   2.25 + 0.75 tsubo
7.42 + 2.43 sq.m. = 80.0 + 26.7 sq.ft

6 mat room   3.0 + 1.0 tsubo
9.92 + 3.31 sq.m = 106.7 + 35.6 sq.ft.

8 mat room   4.0 + 1.0 tsubo
12.22 + 3.31 sq.m. = 142.3 + 35.6 sq.ft

7 living room 'i-ma'
   scale   1 : 100

FIGURE 57 (continued): Floor plans of standard room units.

fusion with adjacent rooms and flexibility of the entire interior space. In larger houses, the maid may also have a room of her own, usually 3 or 4 mats in size. This room does not face to the garden but is situated near entrance and kitchen.

The living room for retired parents occupies a more distinct place in the house than do the other living rooms. Here the Japanese family order has found a clear substantiation as distinguished room for the husband's parents, whose presence is essential for the reputation and succession of the "house." The room is usually set somewhat apart from the compound of the other cells and is projected deep into the garden, so that the old, abdicated head of the house may enjoy his well-deserved days of contemplation in the midst of garden, unbothered by the vivacious growth of young life in the main part of the house. Usually the room has its own picture alcove, *tokonoma*, and shelving recess, *tana*, a suite of closets and a veranda that is frequently open. Since the retired father leads a life of leisure, he indulges in traditional Japanese arts such as calligraphy, music, and painting, in the seclusion of this room. Here he may also entertain his guests by serving them tea in a ceremonial manner and by showing them an object of art. Thus the space for the retired parents often functions as a tearoom, *chashitsu*, a very sensible combination in a country where the living standard does not permit any extravagant expense.

8. Tearoom, *cha-shitsu* (literally, room of tea); *chanoyu-no-ma* (literally, space for the hot water of tea)

Still, those who possess sufficient means have provided a particular room for the sole purpose of practicing the tea cult, either in the form of a separate house in the garden or a room which guests can enter directly from the outside. Such a room is usually arranged close to the reception room so that the visitors after ceremonial tea serving can go there for more substantial food and drink, or, if they have first come to the reception room, they can easily retreat to the tearoom for more substantial talk. Since the tearoom has its own historical background, expression, and spatial character, it will be analyzed separately.

space relationship

While the floor mat, *tatami*, is the most misunderstood tangible characteristic of the Japanese house, "Japanese space" can raise claim to being the most misinterpreted intangible characteristic of the Japanese house. There is hardly a book on Japanese architecture that does not discuss at length the "secret" of Japanese space, and there is equally no book that does not leave the reader in utter bewilderment as to the essence of Japanese space. Rather, after having gone through all insubstantial references with regard to its abstract, transcendental, philosophical, religious, natural, infinite, temporal, flowing, dynamic, and whatever other "realities," the reader is finally led to believe more firmly than ever in the "secret" quality of Japanese space.

Most interpretations have little significance for the contemporary architect, because they are based on subjective-emotional impressions instead of objective-factual observations; they profess the existence of only one unique Japaneses pace instead of distinguishing between residential and ecclesiastical space, urban and rural space, private and public space, even less between the different meanings of space in the various stages of its evolution; they constantly confuse universal (infinite) space, volumetric (three-dimensional) space, pictorial (two-dimensional) space, and even mental (philosophical) space; and they top the confusion by stating that the idea behind Japanese space was consciously conceived for architectural purposes.

In view of the uniqueness of Japanese residential space, a certain amount of enthusiasm on the part of the Occidental beholder, and of patriotism on the part of the Japanese, may be understandable. But if measured by the objective scale of architectural investigation, those interpretations are superficial and unfounded allegations, which largely account for the fact that Japanese architecture has not so far been found an appropriate lecture subject in Western schools. Since it is in architectural space rather than in the technique and material of building that architectural progress will materialize, an attempt will be made to analyze the reality that underlies Japanese residential space. The study is limited to space in its peak of development in the 18th and 19th centuries because each stage of its evolution would require separate study.

Physical convenience rather than necessity was the early reason for creation of "architectural space" in general, and was the motivation for moving life from the "universal space" that man shared with animals to "architectural space." Due to the ever increasing psychological sensitivity of man toward environment and his diminishing physical ability to resist climatic extremes, "architectural space" has long since become a prerequisite for human existence. The fact that "universal space" does not hold the same meaning for man is proof that there is an essential difference between "universal space" and "architectural space."

"Architectural space" is space captured by man from "universal space"; it is human space purposefully controlled in all dimensions: length, height, and width. "Architectural space" is defined in character and purpose according to man's wants; it is intentional. By contrast, "universal space" is uncontrolled space without distinct human purpose; it is accidental. Defined and enclosed spaces corresponding to man's wants may also exist in nature (caves, canyons, etc.), but since they do so by chance only and not by intention, they are not architectural spaces.

The essence of space is the void. In "architectural space" this void has distinct human character and human purpose. Yet, it is only through the tangible space demarcations that this character and purpose can be given to space. Only by means of material elements can space be captured and controlled; only through them can man perceive and experience architectural space. Architectural space, thus, requires *physical* control in all three dimensions. Significantly, however, this physical control does not necessarily mean physical enclosure. For even though one, two, or more enclosing elements may be absent, the eye accepts space architecturally, i.e., as being defined in character and purpose, as long as the remaining space-marking elements are pointed enough to optically suggest controlled space. This also holds true for spaces like a garden or town square which have no height enclosures.

This control of the three dimensions of space may assume different patterns according to the purpose of a particular interior or urban space. In certain types such as circulation spaces (streets, corridors, railway stations, exhibition halls, etc.), the control may even purposefully avoid enclosure in one dimension (usually horizontal) just as this "purposeful infinity" of one dimension is illusionally established in the Gothic cathedrals (vertical).

The prerequisite quality for residential space is finiteness. This is because of man's most fundamental psychological demand that house convey the feeling and awareness being of "in." Only the space, three-dimensionally finite, can convey this sensation. And it is neither an annulment nor an antithesis of the aforesaid that man psychologically also wants to be free from oppressiveness of enclosure in terms of permitting the eye to surpass the enclosure and experience depth from his dwelling. For the prerequisite for enjoying the surroundings from the dwelling is the feeling of being "in," i.e., inside of a three-dimensionally finite space.

Since life in the dwelling is essentially "immobile" (sitting, talking, working, sleeping, etc.) rather than "mobile" (walking, driving, carrying, shopping, etc.), sensitive residential space in its most appropriate substantiation is arresting rather than driving; it is static. As such it is characteristically different from other spatial concepts in architecture such as those of churches, railway stations, sports buildings, exhibition halls, aud others, each of which derives its spatial quality from its own architectural idea.

Paradoxically, the aim of contemporary design efforts in residential space is professed to be the creation of a flowing space, commonly referred to as "continuous space." However, "continuous" in the strict sense of the word has two meanings: first, that a matter is continuous in its "consistency," i.e., uninterruptedly extending; secondly, that a matter is continuous in its "movement," i.e., uninterruptedly flowing.

The first meaning of "continuous" in relation to space implies that space is extending, and presupposes that the consistency of space is continuous. This, indeed, is the case. For the quality of space is of continuous consistency anyhow, be it architectural or universal, interior or exterior, Japanese or Western. Therefore, this meaning of "continuity" in space cannot be a particular spatial concept as frequently is assumed, and consequently cannot become a subject of discussion at all.

Rather, the second meaning of "continuity of space," the flowing space, is a characteristic spatial concept and deserves to be considered more closely. The impression of "flowing space" can only be provoked when one dimension of a certain space volume is left infinite so that space can flow. The mere openness of one side of this volume can not create the feeling of spatial flow, but the infiniteness (real or illusional) of two directions from where space may come and to where it may go on. The resulting spatial quality, then, is no longer static, but moving. As such, it is contrary to man's psychological wants in residential architecture; it is antiresidential.

In many architectural publications "Japanese space" is referred to as the outstanding prototype of this concept of "continuous space" or "flowing space." These statements, however, are very superficial and cannot stand serious examination. Here, as so often is the case, apparent external similarities of the Japanese dwelling to contemporary phenomena obscure the internal basic differences and have resulted in misinterpretations.

The dominant members that form individual spaces and control the inter-room space relationship in the Japanese house are the opaque paper panels, They are arranged in double pairs between the columns, which are usually in the corners of rooms. Ceiling and floor, though complementing the definition of the individual space, have no part in the partitioning of interior spaces (Plates 152–153). The middle two of these paper panels can be moved to each side, opening the middle half of the wall area, or all of them can be easily removed if an occasion demands. In the former case, even though the panels are opened to two or more sides, the original spatial unit remains the same with only additional space being disclosed; space, though enriched, remains arrested. In the latter case, with all panels removed, two spatial units can be transformed into one new unit. This fusion is complete even though the grooves in the floor and tracks and transom above still indicate the original partition. However, this is not the case if two rooms are not aligned, but are staggered. Each room then maintains its separate identity because even after removal of the panels, a portion of the wall still remains, which, together with the partition above the upper sliding track, has a strong separating effect.

In contrast, the spatial relationship between exterior and interior is not controlled by the vertical partitions. Instead, floor and roof are so strongly set against the exterior space, that even the entire removal of the exterior wall panels never negates the feeling of being "in" (Plates 85–87). Though there is nothing but the slender columns to obstruct a view to the outside, interior and exterior space is nevertheless clearly defined. And yet, the slightly lower level of the veranda, its different ceiling, and the occasionally staggered placement of exterior room columns and veranda columns, all suggest a differentiation of space—a preparatory space to the exterior—and thereby prevent an abrupt change from interior to exterior (Plate 80).

This spatial effect of the veranda, which is characteristic of the Japanese residence, is largely responsible for the successful solution of exterior-interior relationship (Plates 90–92). For here the immense contrast between exterior space and interior space—the contrast between nature and technique, between living and dead substance, between organic and geometric form—is brought under control; not through the tangibles of glass, concrete, stone or brick, but through the intangible space 3 1/2 ft. deep (1,060 mm.). Thus, exterior-natural space is not separated and divorced from interior-technical space, nor are they intermingled. Never is an attempt to bring the exterior "in" or the interior "out" recognizable; and the small-scale interior gardens in larger residences are essentially different from their Occidental counterparts, where plants happily grow, protected by glass in fertile beds inside of the house, or where floor tiles inside and outside of the glass partition painfully and unsuccessfully try to efface the change from interior to exterior—all testimonials to the spatial confusion in the Western residence.

The two different orders of space definement and space control—the vertical planes for marking the individual rooms, the horizontal planes for marking the house interior—are the keys for understanding the Japanese space. In spite of all openness, the quality of space, though easily transformable, remains static and crystallinely defined. There is no interchange of space between exterior and interior, nor does space flow from room to room; there is no "continuity of space" ad infinitum in one direction. Instead there is either a succession of space with each spatial unit remaining a separate entity, or a fusion of space with two or more units being joined into one space. This, then, is the very reason why the Japanese open plan has been so successful psychologically and why by comparison the Western open plan has so frequently been unsuccessful. While Western residential architecture alleges to find in Japanese residential architecture confirmation of its efforts toward substantiation of "continuity of space," and fatally strives at an amorphous interflow of space elements, the fact is that Japanese space never has sacrificed the fundamental human need of being in limited and static space in favor of an openness at any cost. Rather, the clear spatial definition, room to room, interior to exterior, provided the very basis for appreciating openness and the outside and was the very means of liberation from oppressiveness of enclosure.

However, it is by no means contended that this refined method of space control was preconceived and consciously created. The study of historical precedence unmistakably shows that all features have developed in direct response to need and basically with only little imagination. Therefore, Japanese space cannot be termed a conception, i.e., something that had been purposefully conceived. It is rather an accidental phenomenon of the Japanese residence. However, there is no doubt that the Japanese really are very sensitive to the matter of space, maybe more so than the Occidental; they do feel, if only unconsciously, that a defined and enclosed space is the primary and fundamental prerequisite for human comfort within the house. This awareness is demonstrated by their habit of inserting in the heat of the summer either transparent cloth curtains or reed or bamboo blinds, *sudare,* at those interior wall parts where an entire openness would endanger the basic awareness of being in a static and defined space. There is no indifference toward space, and the Japanese never casually leaves a door open as is so common in the West.

physique of space

While it is through the character of the room-to-room and interior-to-exterior space relationship that the essence of space finds substantiation, the "physique" of space, i.e., the space-forming (walls, ceiling, floor) and space-occupying elements (furniture, utensils, people, etc.) functions as modifier of space, either as catalyst or as anticatalyst. In the Japanese residence, these tangible elements follow the very nature of residential space and do not obstruct, but confirm, its static essence. All living rooms, regardless of their size and function, are controlled by the same material, same treatment, same scale. Consequently, each room possesses the same spatial gravity that allows for both addition and fusion of rooms of different sizes without affecting the static quality of their space. The entire house is an addition of spaces of equal value. There is no physical accentuation of space that could suggest a direction or axial tendency, nor is there a culmination of space that could manifest a beginning or end. Thus, opening room to room is but setting equal to equal so that they either fuse completely or, if they remain separate, do not compete with each other; space, in spite of all flexibility of the partitions, remains in balance and static. It does not flow (Plates 152–153).

Likewise within the single room itself, the space-forming and space-occupying elements are not likely to produce any accentuation or one-sided emphasis that could bring about spatial tensions or flow. The space-marking and space-enclosing elements in the vertical plane, i.e., the columns and sliding panels, including those to the exterior, are related to each other in proportion and treatment, and the horizontal planes of floor and ceiling are but a projection of the geometric pattern imposed by the structural columns. There is no definite entrance or exit that would suggest an axial tendency, and furniture is not only scarce but again follows the same law of material, treatment, and form, which relates it to the space-forming elements. The only space-filling element that is alien to this common order is man. And yet, sitting on the floor, his contours become square and architectural; and the geometric kimono, then, executes the final unison of man and architecture. There is no longer antithesis of animate and inanimate and consequently the static quality of space remains unaffected.

Nevertheless, the spiritual center of the house is the reception room, and this is also physically expressed by a two-part recess 3 feet deep. One recess, called *tokonoma,* contains a hanging picture, and the other, called *tana,* holds the decorative shelving. These are features that do suggest architectural orientation and accent, but since their treatment, in the classic performance, is not different from that of the room itself, the spatial atmosphere of the reception room is in no way modified or changed.

This physical control of interior space, then, brings the Japanese residence in direct contrast to the Occidental substantiation of space. In the West difference in room usage is qualitatively expressed through scale, proportion, treatment, and decoration. Thus a succession of rooms becomes a differentiation from minor to major, and both fusion and addition of spaces can create tension and discord. Moreover, with distinct entrances and exits and with a window wall of essentially different proportions, the room inevitably is directed and orientated and its space is accentuated. This diffused state of spatial atmosphere is even further liable to disturbance from the many space-filling elements which the Westerner employs; and it requires both skill on the part of the architect and culture on the part of the inhabitant to create and maintain a unique spatial atmosphere.

Such a comparison, however, which so favorably contrasts the interior simplicity of Japanese space with that of Western multiplicity, has proven a source for gross misunderstandings in the West. The space unobstructed by furniture, the floor used as bed, chair, and walk, the rectangular kimono so easily stored, the wooden chopsticks instead of knives and forks, the square cloth instead of bag, brief case, or trunk, all these are praised by Western writers as superior products of Japanese civilization and are attributed profound philosophical significance. True, it was philosophy that taught that simplicity was an efficient means of grasping the more essential things of life, and that this was a form that would be rewarding, if not physically, at least psychologically. But this philosophy was not the cause for such simplicity. Japanese simplicity was not originally due to restraint, but was an expression of unwanted poverty, for there was nothing to be restrained. Though the belated philosophical interpretation of this simplicity succeeded in making a virtue of necessity by initiating the noted aestheticism of simplicity, it actually was a philosophy that taught resignation to existing conditions and contentment with what little there was. Far from seeking progress, the ideal was to do so as the fathers did. All those manifestations of simplicity, therefore, be it the space or its physical controls—and for that matter, the Japanese architectural achievement as a whole—are in fact but expressions of a passive attitude toward life. They had not been imagined and realistically conceived, but had been enforced by pressing environmental circumstances as the only means of existence. Once the existence was secured, no essential development took place from thereon; there was only agelong, subtle refinement of what already existed and the little basic progress that is recognizable was frequently due to importation or chance of accident.

Western architects and writers have repeatedly suggested to contemporary architects, Japanese and Western alike, to bring "Japanese simplicity" into the interior of contemporary architecture. Yet, however favorably the psychological quality of the Japanese space may compare with its modern counterpart, there is no doubt that the demands for man's physical comfort are more imperative. All conveniences of modern dwelling that are deplored by those writers as "impedimenta" that confuse living spaces, the sanitary equipment, the furniture, the heating and ventilating devices, the lighting systems, the labor-saving machines in the kitchen, the telephones, the radios and television, and many more, are actually important instruments of human progress. True, they are material devices, but it was through them that Western man could increase his health, his knowledge, his wealth, his comfort, his independence, his personal freedom; could develop his humanism. Indeed, the Japanese themselves have always felt the need for those material things that make modern interiors look inferior to Japanese interiors. With the exception of the houses of the wealthy who can afford to have one room used only for the entertainment of guests, there is no longer a room that has retained the pure, Japanese spatial atmosphere. Electric fixtures, glass, sanitary equipment, chair, tables, cabinets, sewing machines, radios, etc., are found now in most any Japanese house, and Western-style living rooms have increased markedly.

There is no possibility of simply converting the traditional Japanese house into an efficient modern dwelling without changing it radically; nor is there much value in transplanting external features of Japanese space from the past into the present. Instead, Japanese and Western architects alike face the same problem of creating an integrated architectural space descriptive of, and convenient for, contemporary living. This space should comply with all physical needs of modern man, yet should also preserve an atmosphere that can fulfill his fundamental psychological wants.

for contemporary architecture

Space in Japanese residential architecture thus differs essentially from spatial concepts developed in the West. Its defects lie in the lack of physical comfort and hygiene and also in the fact that it is not favorable to the unfolding of individual personalities. These defects of Japanese residential space should not be ignored, because they clearly show to both the Japanese and the Western architect that this form of spatial performance is a matter of the past. However, since in the Japanese house the elements of the early space enclosure did not undergo multiple changes and deflections as they did in Western residential architecture, the very essentials of architectural space are preserved in a clearer state than in the Western domestic forms, where a fast expansion of philosophy, the sudden discovery of new constructional methods, and the continuous transformation of society have covered up the fundamental cause and idea of original architectural space.

Whereas in Western architecture the emphasis on formation of enclosed space gradually changed to a preoccupation with those elements that control space, i.e., with construction, form, proportion, and decoration, Japanese residential architecture, owing to comprehensive standardization of component building elements and room sizes, used the three-dimensional void, space, as the primary stuff of architecture. Since the space-defining members are predetermined and prefabricated, Japanese architectural creation is concerned only with space, its demarcation by material elements, its inter-room organization, and its interior-exterior relationship. While in the houses of the West, expression generally is sought by means of the material elements of design, in the Japanese house, space itself is the major expressive medium.

Thus, Japanese residential design, being excluded from exploiting architecture's sculptural and pictorial potential, states the specific property of architecture in its pure and unadorned form, space. Architectural "substance" is space, and all space-forming elements become absorbed and immaterial through the supreme dominance of this void. Yet, any further attempt to analyze or describe this space discloses the astounding fact that current languages have failed as yet to establish a vocabulary that pertains directly to the distinctive property of architecture, space. Architectural terms such as balance, rhythm, proportion, light, texture, structure, contrast, emphasis, etc. obviously pertain to the material anatomy of building, and judgments as to the aesthetic qualities of building are made with analogies to painting, sculpture, music, or even poetry. Of course, architectural space is achieved by material means. However, just as in a poem, neither beauty of words nor harmony of meter per se but the poem's content and the form of expression are the criteria of judgment, so also the quality of a building is not to be found in the beauty of its material components per se but in the character of the space that is formed and controlled by them.

This illiteracy concerning space in architecture is actually but the result of a much deeper ill. Each word in a language is a symbol for a concept and hence presupposes an awareness of the nature of this concept. Whenever in the progress of civilization human consciousness captured one of the various phenomena of life and learned to distinguish each newly "realized" concept, inevitably this mental achievement was followed by a symbolic characterization through a new word. Thus, the development of language is but a reflected evolution of human consciousness, and the words therein are but external substantiation of man's intellect. Consequently, the absence of any vocabulary directly pertaining to architectural space demonstrates human unawareness of the essence of architecture, controlled humanized space. Therefore, even though the very importance of space is realized in contemporary architecture, thought, talk, and action in regard to space have remained vague, unscientific, and without conviction.

Such an absence of any vocabulary for architectural space has produced further consequences. Man is able to think only in terms of words, and if words are lacking, even the creative thinker is confined to comparisons and analogies that may encircle, but do not state the very core of the matter. Thus, the architect's inability to think and to act with a direct focus on space is not so much a matter of inadequate training, but the result of a lack of words that stand for concepts that constitute the essence of space. Doubtless, this has been the major reason that architectural science, architectural history, architectural practice, and architectural education are primarily concerned with the material aspect of building and not with its very essence, space.

Here, the inability to directly and precisely describe Japanese space—the void that even without any occupying objects is distinct in itself—uncovers the urgency for establishing a unique architectural language orientated to space. Based on a philosophic investigation into the nature of architecture, such a vocabulary could become the instrument that would coordinate history, science, education, and practice in building; it could facilitate communication between the professional, and it could even establish universal standards for judgment in architecture.

Japanese space performance is also instructive in disclosing certain basic elements that are intrinsic to architectural space. One such revelation is that man himself is an essential component of space. While in Western architecture the human element in space is represented by furniture and decoration, and human memories linger in photographs and paintings without requiring actual human presence, Japanese space obtains human significance only by man's immediate presence. Man is indeed an essential component of Japanese space itself.

This interdependence of space and man in the Japanese house points out the criterion that distinguishes architectural space from the space of other creative arts. For whereas the space in sculpture or painting leaves man outside, architectural space integrates man—a property which it shares with musical space. This realization may contribute to a more profound understanding of architectural space and is of value for a sound philosophy of design. It may also show the weakness of those approaches to contemporary interior design that make man the passive beholder of art and décor on display in architectural space—a visitor more than an essential component.

Equally meaningful for contemporary architecture is the technique of space demarcation that the Japanese have developed. Since the awakening of man's psychological sensitivity toward his environment, it has been the goal of architectural effort to liberate man from the oppressive enclosure in which he must take shelter. Only through fairly recent technological accomplishments have means been provided to achieve this goal without sacrificing the more basic physical comfort of man. As a result, the multiple exterior and interior solid wall elements that were formerly essential for structural reasons can now be largely dispensed with. The concept of such design is called the "open plan." The resulting spatial effect known as "continuity of space" has often been compared with the performance of Japanese residential space because of certain similarities and often is taken by Western observers as a confirmation of, and an equivalent example to, their theories. However, as the foregoing elaborations have shown, not only are the reasons for Japanese openness different, but, more important, Japanese architectural space has little in common with the idea of "space continuity" in contemporary architecture.

Japanese architectural space is distinctly defined from room to room and from interior to exterior, and this demarcation of space, both as cell and as an organism, retains clarity of distinction even if partitions are removed and room units are transformed. Therefore, as previously explained, space remains arrested and static in spite of its interior flexibility and openness to the outside. Though furniture, decoration, color, and personal garment be lacking, there is a very strong feeling of home and tranquillity, which cannot exist in a spatial atmosphere of movement or tension. It is, therefore, obvious that neither openness nor flexibility of space contradict the clear definition and limitation of space.

However, the Japanese house also shows that the success of spatial flexibility is not so much a matter of employing movable and removable screens for room partitions, but rests on a common order that produces rooms of equal spatial quality, completely fusible or harmoniously addible. The technical realization of spatial flexibility, of course, is brought about by the physical means of sliding panels, but the result would be confusion if each spatial cell and its physique were not subjected to a common order of scale, proportion, material, and treatment that creates an atmosphere unique to all of them. Order, then, in space definition and space physique is the very reason for the uniqueness of Japanese space performance.

The same unique order prevails in the planimetric-functional space (see definition) of the Japanese residence. It is characteristic that, here, architectural creation no longer is concerned with the development of individual room types. During the centuries all single-room units have become standardized in size, treatment, and equipment in strict accordance with man's minimum physical requirements. Consequently, design has become a matter of choosing between a few standard rooms and of arranging these units on a *ken* grid (1,818 mm. = 6.0 ft.), which insures constructional, aesthetic, and economic integrity. Standardization, then, is the reason that the Japanese are no longer entangled in the design of physical components or individual room units, but can focus their design on space relationship from room to room and interior to exterior.

So far the Western architect has not gained such a freedom in residential design. Each time he has to develop single room units anew, and he either has to sacrifice economy for the sake of construction or aesthetics, or make constructional or aesthetic concessions to maintain economy of the room cell, not to mention the time and labor required to achieve what can only be a compromise.

Whatever value the foregoing interpretation of Japanese space performance may contain for contemporary architectural design, it is to be taken as only one approach among several to reach the very essence of architecture, space. The thorough comprehension of space requires a total approach that encompasses not only residential space but all forms of spatial manifestations through architecture by which means alone universal principles can be established. And such an investigation is not a mere matter of intellectualism without purpose, but is a necessity in contemporary architecture. For the space-specialist in building, the architect, working on the basis of personal intuition and individual assumption, is unable to enforce his spatial ideas against science-based findings of the other specialists in building and thus faces increasing submission. In this sense, the foregoing treatise on space is intended to convey the realization of the necessity of a comprehensive study and also to provide substantial material for basic research into what, indeed, has made human life possible, architectural space.

CHAPTER SEVEN garden

definition

GARDEN IN BUILDING is the cultivated environment of building. It is not mere accidental nature but is the purposely designed space around the house by which man enriches his life.

GARDEN IN BUILDING, like all material creations of man, is one form of establishing human scale in the indifferent physical order of nature; of establishing a humanized environment. As such, garden is architecture and not nature.

GARDEN IN BUILDING is an integral part of building. It is related to the interior organism of house; it complements the indoors—functionally, economically, and aesthetically —and accentuates the architectural idea.

GARDEN IN BUILDING, being composed of natural components with natural forms, is in physical contrast to house. Architectural exploitation of this contrast is a rich source for architectural motif.

GARDEN IN BUILDING manifests man's aesthetic awareness of his environment. Complying with man's psychological wants and stimulating man's aesthetic senses, it performs the role of art.

GARDEN IN BUILDING reflects man's attitude toward nature, life, and the universe. As this attitude is distinct for cultural epoch and locality, cultures can be identified by the particular manner in which the people shaped their gardens.

GARDEN IN BUILDING depends on topographical, floral, and climatic conditions of the locality. Their peculiarities may either stimulate or prevent certain features in gardening and thus render garden architecture distinctive.

GARDEN IN BUILDING, then, is architecture that employs forms and products of nature. In the residence, it is the mediating space that brings together the contrasts of technical and organic substance, of geometric and natural form, and of human and infinite scale.

It is because of the more severe weather conditions of central Europe and the particular attitude of the Westerner toward nature, that the Western residential garden has, throughout the ages, had a fairly independent existence, regardless of whether the garden was attached to one side of the house or entirely surrounded it. Even though some gardens at best were related to interior room disposition, necessary insulating protection against the outside never permitted the garden to be more than a detached space, the use or appreciation of which was a matter entirely apart from indoor living. Only with the development of new building methods and materials, fostered by the new science of technique, technology, have means been provided for liberating man from oppressive enclosure and for making the surroundings of the house an actual part of indoor living. It is from that time on that the Western man has become increasingly sensitive to his environment in an appreciative rather than a defensive manner.

Thus, garden has become an integral part of house, providing a rich stimulus for architectural creation. Yet, this integration of environment is not, as is still frequently assumed, an architectural potential that one may or may not use, but has become an architectural factor to be necessarily dealt with. For gardening and landscaping affect the total physical environment of man as much as does the actual building itself and therefore fall within the responsibility of architectural work. Indeed, if the immediate surroundings of the house are not designed, but are neglected or left to chance, even the best architectural ideas and intentions may be defeated.

New technical means, then, of transparent space enclosure and perfected climatic control, have effected a basic change in the house-garden relationship by making the environmental garden an aesthetic object to be appreciated from within throughout the year. This change has heightened the importance of the garden in residential design, and many Western architects therefore have focused their attention on the Japanese garden, which seemed in many ways exemplary for their striving. Yet, it is as impossible to generalize on the Japanese garden as it is to do so on Japanese architecture or Japanese aesthetics. Not only has the garden at each stage of its agelong development produced features of its own, but also certain types of gardens have evolved, each of which is distinct in size, arrangement, and relationship to building, even though, in general, they are composed of the same component elements. Since this book deals with the dwelling of the common people, neither public park, temple, or palace gardens nor the extensive landscapes of the rich have been mentioned in particular; they have only been considered insofar as they influenced the ordinary residential garden.

The two Chinese characters that stand for home, *ka-tei,* mean "house-garden," and this ideographic phenomenon reflects the Japanese conception that only through the garden can mere house become a real home. Contrary to the West, where the non-utilitarian garden is considered a luxury rather than a fundamental component, in Japan even the poorest have at least one small garden. Generally, the garden is arranged in the front or the back, but in the long, narrow houses of tight metropolitan areas it may be enclosed by rooms on three or even four sides if there is no space left for the usual back yard. This garden space in the dwelling, favored by generally mild climate and stimulated by ancient beliefs, is an inseparable part of the dwelling due to the multiple interdependent links—the physical, functional, spatial, and the philosophical. It is for this reason that the study of the Japanese residential garden is not only essential for a complete analysis of the Japanese house, but also should produce facts that will shed light on the possibilities of the garden in contemporary residential design.

attitude toward nature

It is commonly held that the physical openness of the Japanese house toward its environment, the garden, with the resulting particular outdoor-indoor relationship, strongly stimulated, if not effected, the Japanese love of nature. While there may be room for discussion as to whether the Japanese house in its form is actually as closely adapted to environment of climate and nature as is commonly alleged, it is reasonable to assume that such physical openness has, in fact, made indoor life a part of the outdoors. But it was primarily the attitude of the Japanese toward life and nature, i.e., their philosophy, that provided the source for the psychological intimacy with nature* and largely influenced the house-garden relationship.

The topographical nature of Japan itself possesses captivating charm and suggestive depth and is, with the characteristic seasonal changes of weather and plants, impressive and engaging. But there are no grounds for the assumption that the early Japanese could have, even naïvely, been attracted to the beautiful things they saw around them. Rather, as was the case in all early beliefs, man's early respect for nature was brought about by his fear of nature. Exposed as man was to her incomprehensible forces, he

---

* The word "nature" in the following pages, if not otherwise mentioned, is to mean the system of all phenomena in space and time, or more specifically, both the environmental phenomena and their productive-controlling forces as far as they have remained unaltered by human activity. It does not pertain to other meanings of "nature" such as "inherent character" or "outdoor scenery."

FIGURE 58: Title page of a gardener's manual. It is descriptive of the function of the garden in the Japanese house, that of being an object to be seen and contemplated.

tried to please her with presents, supposedly in the same manner as he tried to avoid the scorn of his powerful neighbor. Since man was not yet able to conceive of the difference between the animate and the inanimate, between plant and creature, or to imagine things other than what he observed and felt within himself, he considered all things he saw around himself as possessing the same sensations that he felt within himself. Thus, nature worship, which regards all things in nature as being uniformly animated, was initiated. However, contrary to the West, where the teaching of Christianity dissolved nature worship and the discoveries of the Renaissance made nature an object of study and exploitation, in the East Buddhism refined the early identification of man with animal and nature and stated their absolute oneness. In Japan, it was especially the teaching of the Zen sect of Buddhism that tremendously stimulated the feeling for nature, not only by sharpening sensitivity to environment, but by providing the metaphysical and religious background that could also satisfy the growing inquisitiveness of man in his intellectual evolution.

Zen, just as all Buddhism does, conceives all physical forms upon the earth, both animate and inanimate, to be the material expression of a single force. The being of man is produced by the same force as is the being of a rock; the "life" that creates and controls both is the same. Thus, like the individual rock, nature as a whole is a fellowbeing of man and not an object to be conquered and wishfully exploited for man's physical convenience and profit. Indeed, as Daisetz Suzuki states, nature itself enables man to "be" by providing the means for his present and future existence. Nature is not man's enemy who continuously threatens his existence and obstructs his aims if he does not capture and force it into his service.

This attitude of Buddhism toward nature is characteristic of Buddhist philosophy in general. While feeling one with nature—with its total organism as well as with each individual element thereof—selfhood ceases to exist and "self" and "other" merge into one, this being the often misinterpreted Buddhist state of self-extinction. The result in Zen terms is an "absolute emptiness," an "utmost transparency" which transcends physical existence and merges man's objective world and his subjective mind. As long as man follows his conceptional systems, i.e., illusions which he constructs by separating subject and object, this "transparency" is obscured and love of nature is impaired by an artificial dualism. To love is to comprehend; to comprehend an object is to directly grasp its reality without intellectual media of any kind, to become one and feel one with the object. The addition of a third element always brings on complications, for it makes love dependent on comprehension of theories and concepts and thereby excludes those who are intellectually not capable of comprehending such concepts. Zen, therefore, rejects any medium and strives instead for living with and in the objects, whatever they may be. To respect nature is to love nature; it is to live nature's life.

This awareness of being one with nature, then, provides the philosophical basis for the rapport that the Japanese have with nature and causes them to experience beauty in nature beyond her mere outward appearance. Zen widens this experience further and points out that each single element in nature is related to the ultimate reason of all things: "all in one and one in all." The single grass stalk contains the essence of the universe as much as the universe contains the existence of the single grass stalk. This attitude has also been a principle of Japanese garden design, as is apparent in a passage from the book *Tsukiyama-teizō-den* (Making of Hillock Gardens) by Sōami in the 16th century: ". . . the ultimate aim of the landscape garden is to reveal the mysteries of nature and creation. This may be achieved by a simple flat garden with only few rocks. However interesting the pattern may be and however beautiful the scenes, the truth of the hills may be lost and even the heart of the master may appear ignoble, if the garden is lacking coherence. . . ."

To gain insight into the reality of all existence, Zen sees and experiences beauty not in outward form but in the meaning that the form expresses. Mere form has physical and thereby psychological limitations that hinder the beholder from associating himself with the inner meaning of the object. True experience of beauty cannot occur in the external world of limitations, but only where there is freedom of expression and freedom of feeling, i.e., in the infinity that only the meaning of an object and not its form can possess. Nature is to be loved by appreciating not its changeable and perishable appearances, but by understanding the greater significance behind them.

These, then, are the causes that effected the spiritual refinement of man-nature relationship, the noted Japanese "love of nature." But it would be an exaggeration of the intellectual-intuitional faculties of the Japanese in general to assume that there existed a keen awareness of these philosophical backgrounds among the mass of the people. Rather, due to the primitive nature worship, the general beauty of the landscape, and the exposed manner of building and living, nature obviously was very close to the people physically and spiritually and thus, quite understandably, evoked reactions of fear, respect, admiration, and compassion. This psychological-physical dependence on nature underwent subtle refinement and philosophical interpretation in Zen. It basically influenced all phases of life and thought and is especially apparent in the profound spiritual quality of Japanese art.

However, it should be understood that such a philosophy of life also had its adverse effect materially and, as an indirect result, spiritually. For it did not encourage exploitation of natural forces and opposed all opportunistic-materialistic thought such as is evident in science, industry, commerce, and other formative systems of the modern world. As a result, it did not instigate or encourage progressive development and essentially obstructed improvement in standards of living. Impeding the material improvement of life, this philosophy also prevented development of those means and devices that enable man to investigate, to learn, to know, and to give expression to his inner being, his freedom, and his personality.

house-garden relationship

This attitude toward nature, which constitutes the philosophical basis for the house-garden relationship in Japan, is convincingly expressed in the multiple ways in which the house is related to the environmental garden, functionally, spatially, and physically.

While the Occidental garden may occasionally stand in direct functional relationship to the house interior (such as is the case in service courts, patios, etc.), either the garden has lost its original character of employing natural forms and motifs, or the relationship between the two is so loose that either could exist separately without the other. By contrast, the functional house-garden relationship in Japan is intimate, basic, and necessary. Thus, especially in detached houses, the garden may constitute the outside "wall" that screens the openness of the house against south exposure in the summer. Seen from within, it is a "living picture wall," the greens of the trees, shrubs, and ground cover playing with sunlight and wind on bright open days or monotonously responding to raindrops or snowflakes on gray, low-clouded days (Plates 83–84). Broad roof overhangs prevent glare and expanse of sky from becoming dominant and thereby affecting the atmosphere of the "in" feeling, and the rigid limitation of garden depth assures the same human scale that controls the interior room partitioning. In the case of a court garden, which is common in metropolitan houses, the garden provides light for the interior rooms, which otherwise would be in complete darkness because of the tightness of city blocks and their houses. The garden may also function to provide shade and coolness or to absorb the heavy rainfalls of the country.

Yet, aside from all these practical purposes, the major function of the Japanese garden is to satisfy man's psychological need for beauty and to enrich his life by revealing the mysteries of nature and creation. The fact that even the houses of the poorest in Japan possess a garden solely for the delight of the eye makes the Japanese dwelling architecturally superior to those of the same class in the West, where immediate physical needs never let aesthetic concerns arise. To the Japanese, nature lives, and all components—the stones, the plants, the water—have a soul just as man has. They need care and respect just as a human does. Sitting on the mat and viewing them, guest and host may sense that in this small secluded garden the universe and the essence of their own being is present.

While Zen philosophy recognizes the integrity of man and nature, and the functional organization interlocks environment with house, it is the scale, or rather the extent, of the garden space that brings about the psychological intimacy of interior and exterior space. For, the extent is limited and the resulting space is not only three-dimensionally controlled, i.e., architectural, but its extent is of the same value as the spaces of the interior house organism. Thus, contrary to the large-scale Japanese garden with its infinite scale, the residential garden becomes but another additive space in the succession of spatial cells that constitute the constructed house and is thus incorporated into the dwelling organism. This fact indicates an awareness that interior living can experience its highest enrichment only through the controlled, i.e., archi-

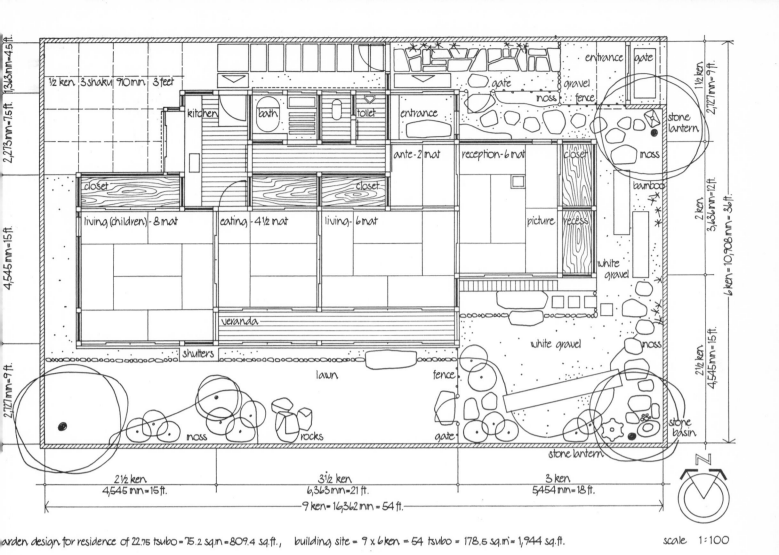

½ ken 3 shaku 910mm 3 feet

kitchen bath toilet entrance

closet ante-2 mat reception-6 mat closet moss

living (children)- 8 mat eating - 4½ mat living- 6 mat picture recess white gravel

entrance gate gravel moss fence stone lantern bamboo

veranda

shutters

lawn fence white gravel moss

moss rocks gate stone basin stone lantern

1,363mm=4.5 ft.
2,273mm=7.5 ft.
4,545mm=15 ft.
2,727mm=9 ft.

1½ ken 2,727mm=9 ft.
2 ken 3,636mm=12 ft.
2½ ken 4,545mm=15 ft.
6 ken=10,908mm=36 ft.

2½ ken 4,545 mm=15 ft.   3½ ken 6,363mm=21 ft.   3 ken 5454mm=18 ft.

9 ken= 16,362 mm = 54 ft.

N

garden design for residence of 22.75 tsubo = 75.2 sq.m =809.4 sq.ft.,   building site = 9 x 6 ken = 54 tsubo = 178.5 sq.m = 1,944 sq.ft.   scale 1:100

FIGURE 59: Representative examples of house-garden design.

tectural, garden space. Even on plots that would allow large-scale landscaping the size of the garden space is limited to "room-size" with rigid enclosure at eye-level height.

The small residential garden is built only to be seen from the interior house and not to be walked through and it thus stands in distinct contrast to the elaborate and independent garden with its walkways, bridges, lakes, rest arbors, and multiple trees. It receives its meaning and *raison d'être* from the house as also the house, in turn, receives much meaning as a home from the garden. There is no separate design of house and garden as in the West, where after the completion of the house construction, the garden is adapted to the structure. Instead, residential design is more a landscaping of conventionalized beauty in which the house itself in cases may have no other role than being shelter from which to view the garden. While such an approach to design is not always the rule, it is generally true that design of the house interior itself receives many an impulse from the garden, and characteristics of a house are in many cases due to the particular features of a site.

Since extent of garden is reduced to human scale and select features of nature are arranged in a meaningful order, the Japanese garden is no longer nature itself, as is frequently assumed. It is not even a miniature copy of real nature, but rather a symbolic abstraction that requires a certain knowledge of its terminology to be understood. About this role of the Japanese residential garden, Sōami has written in the book

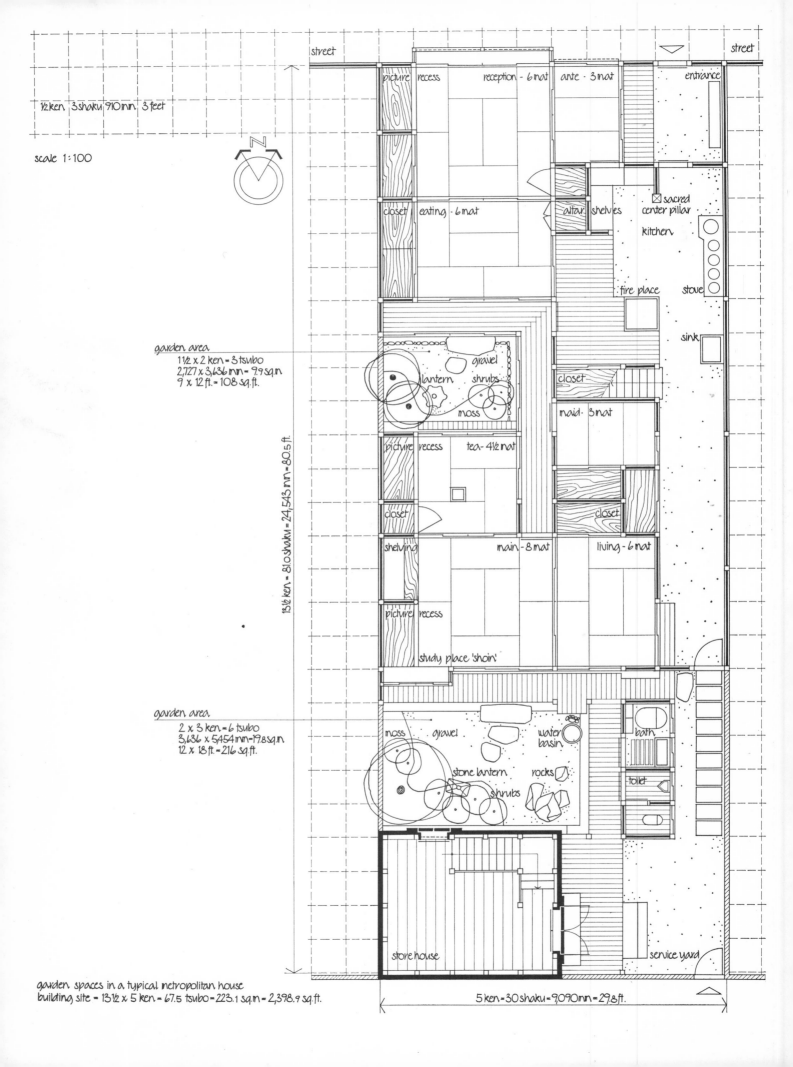

street   street

½ ken 3 shaku 910 mm 3 feet

scale 1:100

N

picture recess   reception - 6 mat   ante - 3 mat   entrance

closet eating - 6 mat   altar shelves   sacred center pillar

kitchen

fire place   stove

garden area
1½ x 2 ken = 3 tsubo
2,727 x 3,636 mm = 9.9 sq.m.
9 x 12 ft. = 108 sq.ft.

gravel

lantern   shrubs

moss

sink

closet

maid - 3 mat

13½ ken = 81.0 shaku = 24,545 mm = 80.5 ft.

picture recess   tea - 4½ mat

closet

closet

shelving   main - 8 mat   living - 6 mat

picture recess

study place 'shoin'

garden area
2 x 3 ken = 6 tsubo
3,636 x 5,454 mm = 19.8 sq.m.
12 x 18 ft. = 216 sq.ft.

moss   gravel

water basin

bath

stone lantern   rocks

shrubs

toilet

store house

service yard

garden spaces in a typical metropolitan house
building site - 13½ x 5 ken = 67.5 tsubo = 223.1 sq.m. = 2,398.9 sq.ft.

5 ken = 30 shaku = 9,090 mm = 29.8 ft.

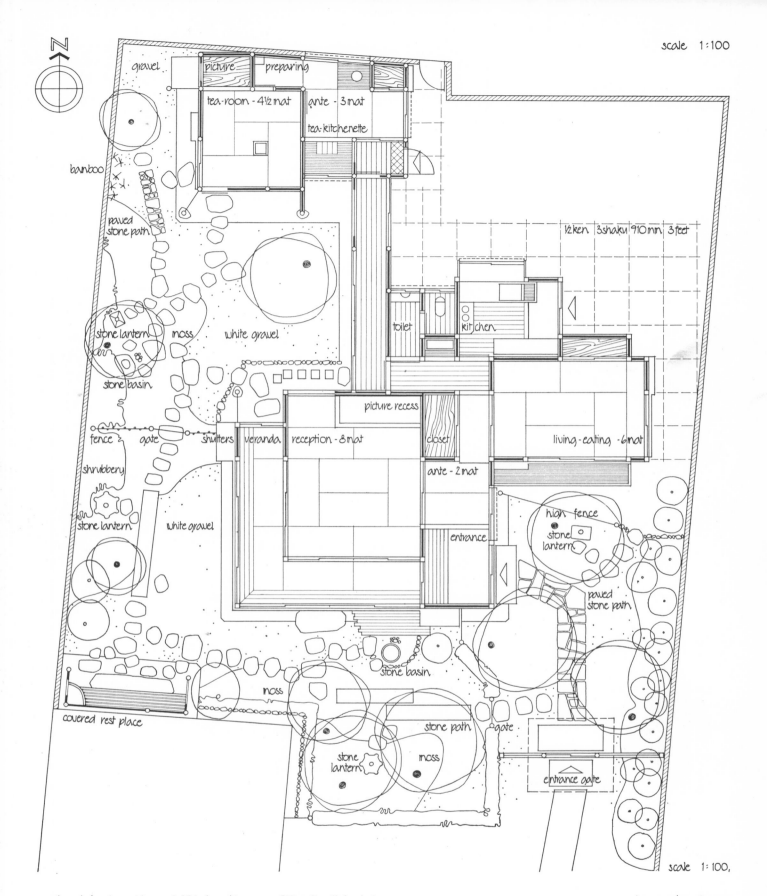

gravel

picture | preparing

tea-room - 4½ mat | ante - 3 mat

tea-kitchenette

bamboo

paved stone path

½ ken 3shaku 910mm 3 feet

stone lantern | moss

white gravel

stone basin

toilet | kitchen

fence   gate

shrubbery

picture recess

shutters | veranda | reception - 8 mat | closet | living - eating - 6 mat

stone lantern

white gravel

ante - 2 mat

high fence

stone lantern

entrance

paved stone path

stone basin

covered rest place

moss

stone path   gate

stone lantern | moss

entrance gate

garden design for residence of 20 tsubo = 66.1 sq.m = 720 sq.ft. with tea-hut

mizusawa komuten - co

FIGURE 59 (continued): Representative examples of house-garden design.

Tsukiyama-teizō-den (Making of Hillock Gardens), ". . . however small the garden may be, it can be made to include high mountains many miles away and to create waterfalls of tremendous height. There is a method of including distant waters and the vast expanse of the ocean. All this is possible by knowing how to handle water and rocks." In pursuit of this aim, no geometric pattern is employed as is customary in Western landscaping, except in the front yard (but here the garden fulfills an essentially different function). Steppingstones from veranda to garden in front of the major living rooms on the south side may indicate the beginning of a walkway, but, ceasing after two or three steppingstones, they give neither a definite direction nor do they terminate a walkway that is actually never used. Instead, they suggest only depth. As such, the garden stands in contrast to the building where brisk geometry and clarity of form produce an unmistakable counterpoint to the garden in its continuous seasonal change. Yet, this contrast, so frequently denied by writers, is neither in discrepancy with, nor in contradiction to, the spiritual integrity of man and nature in the Buddhist conception. To the contrary, it was this very conception of the integral life permeating all material forms that provided an encompassing order that stimulated rather than prevented clear and individual manifestation of distinct forms. Always, once an order of thought has established the important relationships within society, individual activity and creations are encouraged to become more independent and self-conscious than under conditions where the absence of universal principles invites individual adjustment and conformity.

This clear distinction of house from garden is very evident. As has been stated before, in spite of maximum openness, interior space is clearly separated from exterior space by roof and floor, the latter being no less than 2–2 1/2 ft. (610–760 mm.) above ground level. There is no flow of space, but only a succession of clearly defined spaces, both interior and exterior. The mediating agent from the interior is the veranda with the floor slightly lower than the matted room, but clearly conceived as interior space. From the outside, then, broad roof overhang and rising steppingstones provide a preparatory stage for the interior, but there is no mistaking this stage for exterior space (Plates 90–92). Even the small interior court gardens in the city houses are clearly separated from interior space and no attempt is made to intermingle and confuse the different qualities of natural and technical space as in the West. It is this clear distinction between interior and exterior that gives to each space its appropriate value and provides the very prerequisite for appreciation of garden with its natural forms (Plates 93–94).

While the minimum dwelling does not possess a front yard but is to be entered directly from the street, the average residences are recessed from the street, if only by 1 *ken* (1,818 mm.= 6 ft.) (Plate 63), and the only thing a passerby can see is the roof above the enclosure, which may be a solid wall or a compact plashing fence of natural stalk. Here the house-garden relationship is essentially different from that of the major garden (Plate 62). For the house, not possessing the openness it does to the south, is separated from the front garden, and the garden itself does not become a part of experience from within. Instead it functions as a mediatory space through which man walks, leaving behind the hurried world of profession and competition and entering the secludedness of his home. In this role, the front garden is but another stage in the gradual unification of man and house. Viewing while walking from the gate to the entrance off to the side, with the *geta* (Japanese wooden footwear) clattering against the hard stone pavement, is the experience of this space, and, accordingly, its spatial meaning is essentially different from that of all other spaces in the Japanese house, both garden and interior.

Clear distinction between interior and exterior spaces is further manifested in the motive of their origination. On the one hand, the features and forms of the Japanese house were essentially prompted by environmental pressures and not by imaginative ideas for man's progress. Being accidental in their origin, the forms were employed without aesthetic consideration, until they themselves had effected certain principles

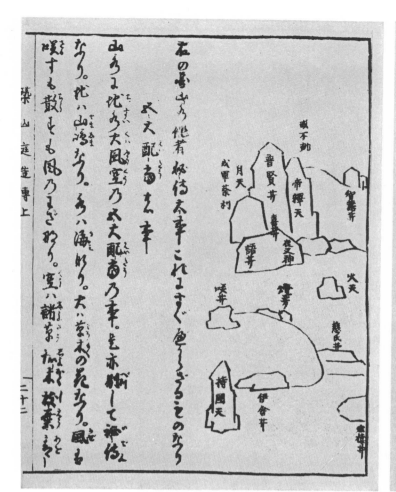
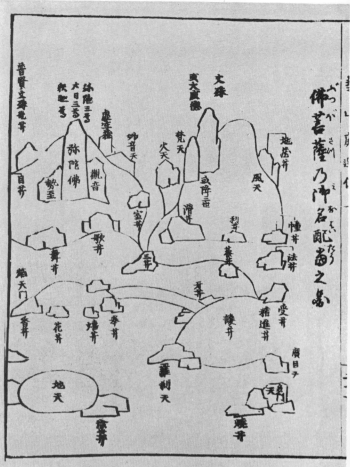

FIGURE 67: Pages from a gardener's manual. Stone arrangements and their symbolic meanings.

owner may associate with a particular shape. Although the aesthetic principles of rock grouping are set, the approach is empirical, i.e., stone placing is a matter of experimentation. In accordance with a preliminary design on paper, the rocks are carefully positioned in relationship to the house and are arranged in a group. They are shifted to different positions until the intended atmosphere is achieved. This process may eventually last for years, providing considerable material for both guest and host to think and talk about at the tea-cult gatherings and work for the master who enjoys such artistic, though heavy, labor. The standard rule is that in a stone grouping the center stone should be the largest while the two stones in front at left and right should, in character, be essentially different from each other, such as one stone standing and the other lying flat. Symmetry is considered opposed to nature and is to be avoided, and each individual stone by its posture should never raise doubt as to its stability.

The role of the steppingstones is entirely different. In extensive gardens the steppingstones provide the actual path (Plate 95) and the various stations from which to view parts of the building or garden. In the front yard of the smallest houses they also serve as pavement for the walk from the gate to the entrance, but in the private garden of the commoner they only suggest a path into the garden. Here their role is more symbolic than practical, for the garden is so small that it can be perceived with one look and does not need to be walked through. The steppingstones are arranged in front of the veranda, again following certain rules. Their discontinuity toward the depth of the garden symbolizes the infinity of nature and universe.

This tendency of expressing and suggesting infinity through the garden features is also obvious in the preference of water in its characteristic forms: as a waterfall, a small stream, a fountain, or a pond, both real and symbolized (Plate 96). Water,

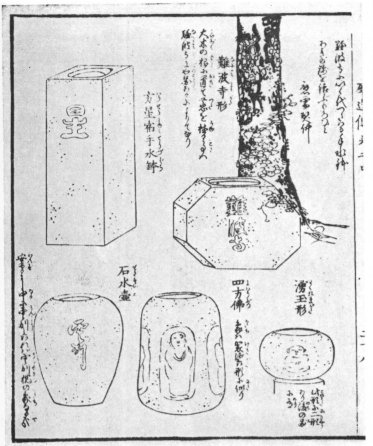

FIGURE 68: Page from a gardener's manual. Typical forms of stone lavers.

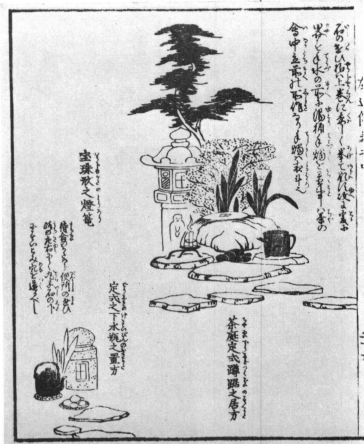

FIGURE 69: Page from a gardener's manual. Typical arrangement of stone laver with stone lantern–I.

in its many changing consistencies as rain, snow, fog, cloud, and ice has always been a source for contemplation of the universe. Water comes from the infinite skies, a gift of life to man, animal, and plant. A drop first, it forms streams and rivers, it merges into the immense ocean, and, finally, it is drawn back to the infinity of the skies, symbolizing an eternal cycle (Plates 150–151).

Ponds, *ike,* are of irregular, i.e., natural, shape, without any geometric affiliation as is the case in the West. The banks are protected by stones, and water is held by making the bottom impermeable with clay, or it is simply represented by white sand, which in larger gardens is raked to indicate a stream or waves. Also, the miniature stream, *yari-mizu,* is carefully patterned after nature and becomes a monotonously meandering broad river across a plain, or a swift mountain torrent shooting through narrow valleys and rocks. A waterfall, *taki,* in the flat-garden type is simply indicated by two large upright stones while in the hillock-garden type two stones in the slope symbolize a mountain recess where the water cascades down. More varied are the representations of fountains, *izumi.* In the form of a natural spring they convey remoteness at the foot of a mountain or in the depth of a forest; as a well, surrounded by stones with a dipping device, they suggest countryside and secludedness; and as water from a bamboo pipe they may create a feeling of a desolate mountainous area where a hermit monk has led the spring water to the solitude of his own simple dwelling.

To the Western eye these symbolizations are not always immediately conceivable. Rather, without knowledge of the symbolic vocabulary, one would be unable to identify the underlying meaning, and it appears that the Japanese himself would face the same difficulties if he were not familiar with the terminology of the garden. Yet, since the features are few and the performance standardized, he is, as a rule,

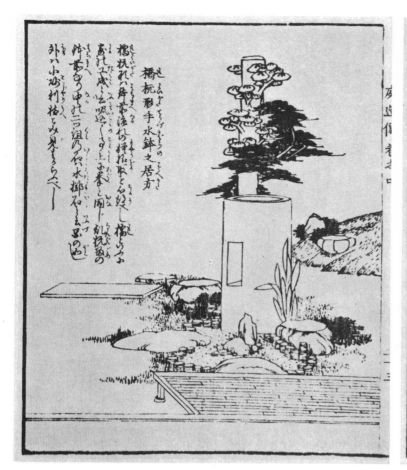

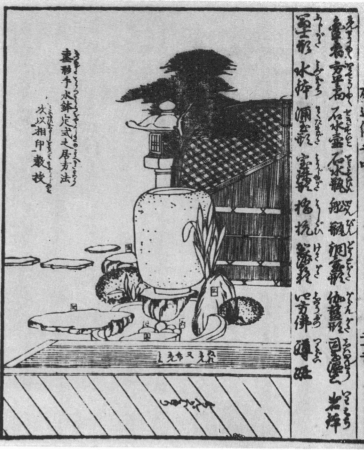

FIGURE 70: Page from a gardener's manual. Typical arrangement of stone laver with stone lantern–2.

FIGURE 71: Page from a gardener's manual. Typical arrangement of stone laver with stone lantern–3.

familiar with the symbolic identification and will conceive the symbols as if they were reality, contrary to the realistic mind of the Westerner, who in spite of detailed knowledge, will find it difficult to forget reality and to accept symbols in its stead. The faculty to surrender to suggestion, i.e., to see and feel things that are suggested and to overlook and neglect real things if told to do so, no matter how the senses have reacted, is a trait of the Japanese that becomes apparent in many instances, such as the suggestive wind bell in the veranda that "provides" coolness or the black-masked helpers on the open theater stage, who "do not exist."

Bridges are another device used to suggest water and large scale (Plates 97–99). Their most impressive performance is that of a simple unhewn stone slab that spans from shore to shore. The ends of the bridge are marked by two stones on each side. Yet, there are also bridges in which the stone slab is hewn; others are made of wood, consisting either of a straight plank with its weatherworn texture or of an archlike wood framework covered up by thick layers of earth and moss. Again there are others for which the garden builder may have used the natural roots of a living tree. There are no rails, and one not familiar with Japanese garden terminology may have difficulty in conceiving of it as a "bridge." Instead, the arched bridge of elaborate decorative design, painted blazing red, is much more familiar to the foreigner, but is nevertheless an imported feature that decorates, not always favorably, public parks, temple gardens, and Occidental films.

The trees in the Japanese garden are obviously shaped by human hand more than are the other natural components and they are continuously trimmed. For trees in their full natural growth would endanger the human scale of the garden and would be unproportionately large in comparison to the other components, which are miniature representations of nature. Yet, trimming of trees and shrubs in the residential garden is done in a manner that stresses the characteristics of the particular plant and rarely aims at pursuing unnatural geometric forms or at representing animals or ships as is done in the West. Of the needle-leaved trees, pine and cedar are used, and the small size to which they have been kept by Japanese gardening is almost miraculous, for they are otherwise strong and reaching trees. Of the broad-leaved trees, cherry and maple are liked because of their distinct colors in the various seasons; yet, they are frequently backed up by evergreens and shrubs so that the garden does not appear too bare in the wintertime. The placing of the trees and ground cover is patterned after nature. Thus, moss is found near the symbolic or real watercourse, as are all those plants and shrubs that like moist ground. The abundance of rain water throughout the year never lets the garden become a nursery for the sickly. Rather, fertile ground and rain allow the plants to grow in a minimum of space with hardly any direct sunlight, and moss does not only overgrow the back side of trees, but even covers stones, creating the particular feeling of *sabi* that permeates so much of Japanese thought and art.

Another standard feature of the Japanese residential garden is the stone laver. In contrast to previous elements of the garden, this feature fulfills a more obvious purpose than the others as a practical-decorative device. It also is different from other garden features because in most cases it is shaped in geometric forms. Almost every garden contains at least one or two of these water containers, which are provided with wooden or bamboo ladles and serve practically and symbolically as the place where one cleans both hand and heart. The one type, *tsuku-bai*, is arranged in the middle of the garden, most frequently in the tea garden, through which one proceeds toward the tearoom. Positioned low on the ground along the path of steppingstones, it is very symbolic of purifying the visitor before taking part in the ceremonial tea serving and is similar in this respect to the larger water basins in front of shrines and temples, from which this feature probably took its origin. Again, the arrangement of the stones adjacent to the laver is done according to prescribed rules, as is the case with the other type, the *chōzu-bachi,* which is placed near the toilet.

The *chōzu-bachi* type is fairly tall so that the ladle can be easily reached from the veranda after one leaves the toilet. Frequently, a particular platform is provided, slightly lower in level than the veranda, where one stands to wash the hands while water splashes down upon a drainage bed made of round stones and pebbles (Plates 100–101).

While the garden lavers, in spite of their geometric or even fanciful forms, are not really conspicuous because they are either attached to the house *(chōzu-bachi)* or purposely hidden in the uniqueness of the garden by stones and shrubs *(tsuku-bai)*, the stone lanterns, *tōrō*, do not attempt to hide their man-made quality; self-consciously they stand at such exposed positions in the garden as river bends, imaginary paths, or garden lavers. It is professed that the stone lantern is a genuine Japanese creation, originally dedicated to the Buddhist deity and placed in front of a temple in the courtyard. Yet, there are indications that it was originally introduced with Buddhism via Korea. Be this as it may, the stone lantern was adopted from the temple compound by the tea masters in the Momoyama period (1573–1603), and, set on a short base, serves to illuminate the path to the tearoom. From the tea garden, then, the lantern was incorporated into the garden of the ordinary dwelling and is used there now primarily for decorative purposes. The lantern, standing up on stone columns, consists of six parts, while the shorter type may have only a broad-legged base upon which the light container is placed. The forms are multiple and not always beautiful, and filling up the small gardens with many of these lanterns is a regrettable practice that is in contradiction to the original idea of Japanese garden design.

The physical component most important for the spatial quality of the Japanese garden is the enclosure. The forms of enclosure range from solid stone moats and tile-covered clay walls to all sorts of plashing fences, consisting of wood, bamboo, reed, or other stalk that is tied together with tendrils, stalks, or palm-fiber ropes.

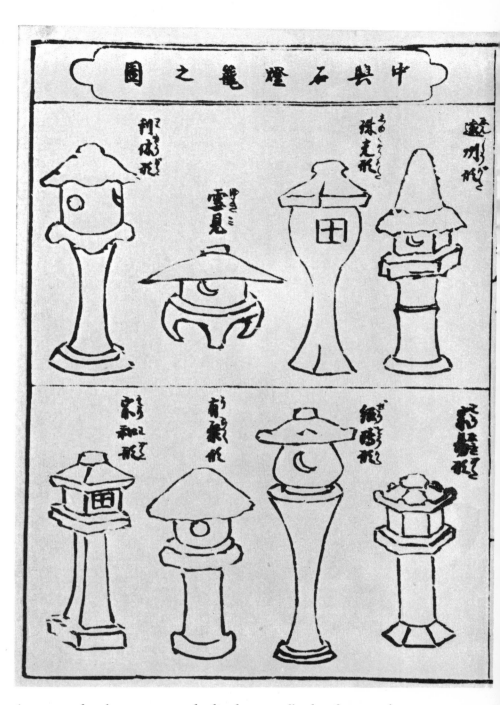

FIGURE 72: Page from a gardener's manual. Typical forms of stone lanterns, *tōrō*.

Though the major types of enclosures are standardized, as are all other features, there are innumerable ways of using patterns and materials within the given vocabulary. Imperative, in any case, is that the height of the enclosure be far above eye-level and that it separate the domestic space from the outside world. Of course, all measures of garden design, such as the suggestive ending of the steppingstone paths, the representation of rocks as high mountains, the symbolization of broad rivers, and the miniaturizing of trees, essentially aim at creating the infinity of nature and universe in a small space. This infinity can only be grasped and controlled by the enclosing fence—the Zen monk for a moment grasped the universe with his hands when the moon was reflected in the water that he took from the mountain spring: finiteness of space that turns infinity into architecture, finiteness of thought that turns infinity into comprehension! This seeming contradiction of infinity of nature in the finiteness of a small garden space is the very essence of the tremendous impact that the Japanese garden exerts psychologically. The forms of garden components, the expression of garden texture and color, the arrangement of garden features are not what give the

Japanese garden its uniqueness, but rather the concerted effort to represent the infinity of the universe, to bring it with direct-simple methods within human grasp, to deepen the conceptive faculties of man, and to enrich his spiritual existence. It is for this reason that the larger gardens of mansions, temples, or palaces, in spite of their elaborate features and their extensive publication, are aesthetically far less successful than those numerous unknown gardens of the small residences.

for contemporary architecture

The significance of the Japanese garden for contemporary architecture, then, does not lie in its form or feature or in the Japanese concept of nature. Adoption of form and feature, as it has become the fashion, is but imitation without any comprehension of its meaning. Adoption of the Japanese concept of nature, if possible at all, would be contrary to Western temperament and philosophy of life. Instead, the important lesson is that garden, like the house, can rise above the level of a merely visual and subjective device only when it succeeds in substantiating the ethics and philosophy of epoch and people as a whole. It is not so much what the Japanese have created or what were their spiritual grounds that is of importance for contemporary society, but how, and to what degree of perfection, they succeeded in materializing what they thought and felt. Since Western man has a different attitude toward nature, life, and the universe and since he lives in a different spiritual-intellectual environment, it is but a matter of course that the expression of a Western garden, even if aiming at enriching the spiritual life of the inhabitant as does the Japanese, must necessarily be essentially different from any form of the Japanese garden. And there are signs that the Japanese themselves will also have to re-create and re-enact their own gardens. For international communication and the exchange of education and thought have already brought about an essentially different attitude toward life among the younger generation, which requires a new interpretation of garden if it is not to become a dead relic from the past, alien to the contemporary age.

Japanese landscaping is the integral design of both house and garden, impartial attention being given to both interior and exterior spaces. Though the scale of this total approach is relatively small, it nevertheless uncovers the merits of total planning in architecture. Japanese residential design exhausts the full potential of building as an art, in that it employs all architectural media, the natural and the technical elements, the exterior and the interior spaces, in order to enrich the psychological being of man. Though in the case of the Japanese this total planning mainly concerns the aesthetics of living and, therefore, may not constitute a need, the increasingly complex form of present industrial society makes the total approach of planning an absolute necessity, because the many technical, practical, and economical problems involved can no longer be solved without comprehensive coordination. Also, if the architect, like any creative artist, considers himself responsible for the establishment of a unique culture, i.e., achievement of emotional intimacy between man and the man-made, he must concern himself with the whole of the physical environment of his time.

Unfortunately, the majority of architectural schools do not provide the intellectual basis for such a comprehensive approach toward architectural design, nor does the majority of architectural literature concern itself with this question of integrated planning. It is true the design of an individual building itself is a very complicated matter based on multiple agencies that can barely be covered by the present educational system, and it is also true that the principles of architectural planning involve areas of knowledge that require a comprehensive study of their own. However, the amount of study presently provided by the schools for the practical-technical aspect of building is inappropriately large, and this has meant that the architect in his preoccupation with individual structures only too often does not realize the more imperative laws of total planning.

It is reasonable, of course, in architectural training as in any other professional preparation, to approach the subject matter analytically, i.e., through the study of the smallest individual components of building, both material and conceptual. It must even be considered the only appropriate method of gaining the detailed knowledge that allows efficient work. But if those constituent cells of building are not brought into a precise relationship with the entity of total planning right from the start, and if there is not a profound initial understanding of the meaning of such planning within the activities of society, then all individual detailed knowledge is liable either to be used in contradiction to the objectives and meaning of the social organism or to become divorced and renegade.

With further expansion of science in building, specialization of the architectural profession is inevitable, and it is likely that comprehensive planning will become the concern of a separate profession. In fact, there already are schools that provide a particular curriculum for a specialized profession of planners. But it is obvious that the planner, as much as any other specialist-architect, can be effective only if he consciously serves the universal aims of contemporary man. Just as the specialist-doctor needs a comprehensive knowledge of the human organism in the whole for proper diagnosis and therapy, so too the specialist-architect, regardless of his particular field, needs to possess a thorough understanding concerning the basis that underlies his profession and work. Such a knowledge cannot be gained through history courses, because they commonly fail to establish a relationship with the present. It can be acquired only through the study of the science that deals with the spiritual basis of contemporary living and building, philosophy. It is in this realization that a major defect in contemporary architectural education is laid bare and the way for its removal shown.

Standardization of garden design, i.e., the selection of a concise vocabulary of feature, composition, and type for any garden design, is an outstanding Japanese characteristic that has not, if it exists at all, reached such high refinement elsewhere. Yet, in spite of universal standardization, each garden expresses a strong individuality. Indeed, the wide diversity in the expression of the Japanese garden prove that standardization by no means stifles creative design, but rather seems to stimulate it by confining design efforts to the more basic elements. If a nation as sensitive toward matters of taste and environment as Japan succeeded in finding a common language of creative expression, there is hope that in the individualistic Occident, also, the universal values and the unanimity of aesthetic sense may be acknowledged over and above personal preference and subjective taste. In this light it appears almost a paradox that in Japan, where labor is so cheap, standardization developed in all phases of the creative crafts while in the West, with its industrialized society, standardization is still confined to the mere mechanical devices of living.

Contrary to Western concept the residential garden is architectural space, i.e., three-dimensionally controlled space, in extent and proportion related to the interior rooms. It enriches interior space and is no more independent from the entire organism of the dwelling than is the individual room. As completely as the garden can be made visible from the interior, it also can be as completely shut off. With equal ease, the vista to the garden can be restricted to any given section. Such an exacting control of space allows for fine adjustments to the psychological wants of the inhabitant and never lets garden become a picture that continuously imposes itself upon the inhabitant. Liberation from oppressiveness of enclosure, is one of the slogans in contemporary architectural design—a liberation that only too frequently has led to anarchy of spatial values. Here, Japanese residential architecture manifests unmistakably that only clear and rigid space definition, room to room and room to garden, is the very factor that allows openness and freedom from enclosure without sacrificing other more basic psychological needs of man.

The second of the two Japanese ideographs for residential garden, *tei-en,* contains the meaning of enclosure; it indicates that the enclosure is one of the original and basic elements of the Japanese garden. Since the Japanese generally show a remarkable indifference concerning the exposure of their private life to neighbor or passerby, one cannot but attribute to the high enclosure of the garden a function other than just of "defensive" character. Rather, its function is "offensive" in that it captures space, makes it architectural, and integrates it as another spatial unit into the ensemble that constitutes the dwelling. This stands in contrast to the large-scale Japanese garden and to the better of the contemporary Western gardens, where the house becomes a part of the landscape, but the garden never a part of the house. Here, the Japanese residential garden holds the important lesson that the successful incorporation of garden into house is not a physical, functional, or climatic problem, but a spatial and dimensional one. All attempts at making the infinity of nature a part of experience from within will be unsuccessful as long as the spatial quality of the exterior remains universal, i.e., three-dimensionally uncontrolled and non-architectural.

From all this it is evident that Japanese gardening is never left to chance; it is designed, and design implies conscious use of motif, purposeful composition of elements, and meaningful order of the whole. Though it may be true that the design is aimed at symbolizing or even imitating nature, the result is no longer nature or natural. Indeed, the environment cherished from the house interior has, in essence, nothing in common with nature except that its motifs and components are taken from nature. It is obvious that this "unnaturalness" of the garden has been acknowledged by the designers and no attempt is visible to disguise the artificial basis of its composition or to hide the abstract-intellectual orientation of its idea.

In this light, it must be questioned whether the Japanese appreciation of such architectural-human space can really be identified with "love of nature" as is customary. For it is one thing to aesthetically appreciate certain aspects in nature and another to like and to love nature as a whole. Rather, it seems probable that the Japanese did not actively love, but passively submitted themselves to, the destructive elements of nature as represented in the seasonal typhoons, the frequent earthquakes, and the torrential rains that each year bring death and destruction.

Thus, it appears that the noted Japanese "love of nature" is one of those sweeping generalizations that only too often obscure the very issue of the matter. It has added much to the confusion that exists about the relationship between architecture and nature in contemporary architectural design. The confusion stems from the superficial contention that nature is beautiful. But if beauty is that quality of object or matter that elicits a pleasant reaction from the human senses, then, evidently nature with its incomprehensible and often destructive forces, being entirely indifferent to human affairs, is certainly not beautiful, not to speak of nature's many unsightly features. Indeed, it is this continuous adversity of nature toward man's physical and psychical being that engaged man to build, i.e., to create a human environment as opposed to the environment of nature.

Nature is indifferent to human life; it does not protect human life. In fact, man could not survive in nature without his "unnatural" conveniences. Nature is unpredictable and accidental; though in detail functional and beautiful, it is without comprehensive order that would comply with human thinking. Nature is without scale; there is a microscopic world in a drop of water and there is another immeasurable world beyond the earth, both unrelated to man's physique and psyche. Nature is also opposed to the very human distinction of withdrawing into the self and contemplating the self. In fact, nature is inhuman.

Therefore, to live a natural-human life is a contradiction because natural living, i.e., following instincts and biological drives alone as all creatures do, would deny the very achievement and distinction of humanity: ethics and morals. It would be inhuman living. Also, to design and to build like nature, to make house and garden as if it were naturally grown, would disguise the very human element. It would obscure the fact that designing and building are an intellectual and purposeful process, that their means and methods are artificial, that they are based upon a definite human scale, and that they aim at establishing order and meaningful composition.

The Japanese garden, contrary to most interpretations, unmistakably is not natural. Though elements and motifs—but only the beautiful ones—are taken *from* nature as abstract or natural symbolization of a significant aspect *in* nature, these elements are reduced to human scale, are ordered in a meaningful composition, and are precisely limited. Garden is but extension or component of the main design, a mediating agent that bridges the enormous gap between the opposites of humanized and natural environment. Yet, there is no question that the Japanese garden is architecture and not nature.

Such a concept of garden design can be of great benefit for contemporary landscaping. The important message is that, as in building itself, it is not the external form that renders the garden distinctive, but the underlying idea. Selecting a certain phenomenon from nature, capturing it symbolically or actually, and integrating it into an architectural-human space, i.e., a vase, an alcove, or a garden, is apt to awaken the human senses to the beauty in nature more than any indiscriminate imitation of, or romantic pretense for, nature as a whole. From there, then, may spring a new consciousness of the value of things in the worlds of both man and nature; a clear and direct psychological intimacy between man and environment that may produce a more true culture than any vague and misty-romantic worship of nature.

CHAPTER EIGHT seclusion

definition

SECLUSION IN BUILDING is both the state of and the place for being in solitude within the house. It is the physical and psychological isolation of the individual from both his fellow man and his environment.

SECLUSION IN BUILDING is introverted and self-existent. It is a microcosm in which man can search and unfold his personality, unobstructed by his demanding fellow man or by an obtrusive environment.

SECLUSION IN BUILDING is the space where man is sole content. It is a neutral environment that becomes meaningful only through man's presence.

SECLUSION IN BUILDING is an essential instrument for establishing, or preserving, the freedom of man. For only in solitude can man escape from the coercion to which he is subjected when among the masses.

SECLUSION IN BUILDING was the dominant quality of early architectural space. It was closely associated with the sensation of being protected against the hostility of environment, both weather and animal, and thus was prerequisite for psychological comfort.

SECLUSION IN BUILDING, both as the withdrawn room and as the hidden house, is not antisocial. Instead, it is the affirmation that man is primarily individual rather than component of family and, again, that ties within family are stronger than those to society.

SECLUSION IN BUILDING is expression of humanity. For solitude, being withdrawal from environmental concern, is the very requisite for the human distinction of taking a stand within the self: thinking.

SECLUSION IN BUILDING, then, is manifestation of residential architecture as an art. For it is in solitude where man can experience spiritual elevation and inner perfection, to which finally all technical and philosophical progress of mankind serves.

In the West, seclusion in building had been an inevitable condition dictated by unfavorable weather and limited technical means rather than a condition prompted by an awareness of man's psychological need for solitude. That is to say, seclusion was not an intentional creation, but an accidental circumstance. It is for this reason that progressive Western architecture has never fully recognized the psychological implications of seclusion in building and, consequently, has frequently done away with a room separable from other rooms, as soon as technological achievement made the use of solid and opaque walls superfluous for structure or insulation. As a result, contemporary houses, like city and landscape as a whole, generally lack the seclusion where man can be with himself. Life has become exposed because transparency is fashionable; it has become stereotyped and shallow, and the one who creates seclusion by erecting a high fence around his house risks being considered antisocial.

Thus, seclusion of house in the community, and of room in house organism, has obtained the stigma of being backward and old-fashioned. It is not realized that the ultimate goal of architectural progress—and for that matter the goal of all progress in science, technique, and education as well—is not wealth, health, comfort, and amusement of living as manifested in the efficiency, practicality, and openness of contemporary housing, but is the spiritual elevation of man and the perfection of his inner self.

In contrast, the Japanese residence, unless it is just the barest minimum for existence, has materialized its awareness of seclusion in building through one of the very distinct achievements of Japanese architecture: the tearoom. While all living rooms in the ensemble are psychologically extraverted, the tearoom in its pure form is inwardly orientated and shuns external experience other than bringing the microcosm of the room into precise relationship to the macrocosm of the universe by a limited picture-like glimpse of a small tea garden or by a simple flower in the vase. It is the humble space solely provided for aestheticism, self-reflection, and spiritual elevation within a meager dwelling, where economic poverty and hardship of living has barred anything that could not prove its continuous necessity and has limited room size and house extent to the very minimum possible. It is this astounding esteem for the seemingly "unnecessary" tearoom that calls for a deeper interest than that which any other Oriental oddity may arouse.

Yet, seclusion in building as manifested in the tearoom is but an expression of a much more universal and profound spiritual aestheticism: the cult of tea. This cult can be outlined as being an expressionism that consciously aimed at responding to the life and ideals of the poverty-stricken general public and the farmer and at recognizing the humanistic and artistic value contained in poverty. As such, its influence was not only prevalent within the realm of the tearoom but embraced residential architecture as a whole and decisively shaped and articulated the art, life, and ethics of Japan in their totality.

Much disagreement exists, however, as to the degree of that influence, its causes, its importance, and even its meaning, value, and spiritual basis. It seemed necessary, therefore, not to limit this treatise to describing the content of the tea cult and the expression of the tearoom, but to attempt an interpretation of all factors that directly or indirectly have been instrumental in the growth of the tea cult. For, most likely, such an investigation will not only provide a better understanding of this extraordinary cult of Far Eastern aestheticism, but will also be the one way to bring out into the open those facts of formative forces in architecture that are universal and timeless.

necessity of tea

The reality of the tea cult as it evolved in the 16th century is multiple and diverse; its influence is comprehensive and unique. As to its origin, there can be little doubt that it was the architecture and the life of the ordinary farmer from which both motif and form of "tea" were taken, and that again it was architecture that provided the space and the medium through which the spirit of "tea" could express itself clearly and directly reach the broad masses of the population, who lacked the intellectual training to comprehend verbal interpretations. It is this general acceptance by the poor classes which raised the value of the tea cult above that of a refined amusement and fanciful entertainment for the rich, which would have had little meaning for contemporary architecture.

Thus, residential architecture was both the source and manifestation of the spirit and the form of the tea cult, and the outstanding properties of the Japanese residence—and for that matter of Japanese art in general—such as simplicity of function and form, restraint of motif and color, preference for the natural and inconspicuous, intimacy with the asymmetric and imperfect, already existed in house and in art long before tea drinking took the form of an aestheticism. These properties of the Japanese residence were the logical, yet accidental, results of efforts to cope with environmental pressure by methods that suggested themselves and were unconsciously used by the lower classes, until the "cult of tea" elaborated the inherent beauty in them and effected a conscious application. As such, the tea cult did not create a new language of expression, but detected and interpreted the principles of aesthetics behind an existing and well-established form of life and house.

The evolution of "tea" as a cult shows again a trait of the Japanese that repeatedly asserted itself throughout their cultural history: adoption of a foreign achievement and its basic transmutation into something essentially different which had but the name in common with what had been its germ. And the tea, both its seed and its significance as being more than a mere medicine or beverage, is no exception. For it was an import from the Chinese T'ang dynasty, when Buddhist monks of the Southern Sect used to drink tea from a single bowl before a sacred Buddha image in ritual formality. Japanese scholars, who had participated in these elaborate ceremonial tea gatherings while studying on the Chinese continent, brought this custom back as early as in the 8th century. Consequently, ceremonial tea drinking in its early stages was practiced only in Buddhist monasteries, though it may be assumed that the court also engaged in tea drinking, for it is recorded that in the year 729 the emperor gave tea to one hundred monks in Nara, the capital at that time.

In the 12th century, again following the development on the continent, the "tea ritual" and "tea ideal" of the Chinese Sung dynasty were adopted, bringing a different conception of life along with novel forms in the preparing of tea (tea from whipped tea powder instead of that brewed from tea leaves as before). While in the monasteries "tea" maintained its solemn character, at the court it took the form of gay social entertainment and poetic exercise with colorful and pompous expressions, which in turn led in the 15th century to the creation of *cha-suki,* a kind of tea play. Besides the Zen sect's tea ritual and the court's tea play, the common people also had their "tea ceremony," a kind of party in the villages called *cha-yoriai,* and all three of them, Buddhist ritual, aristocratic play, and popular party, provided the tradition for the unique tea cult, which, as it emerged in the 16th century, was to decisively influence Japanese life, art, and building.

There is a decidedly historic logic in the emergence of the tea cult on the Japanese scene, which definitely contradicts the common assumption that Zen Buddhism was the only, or at least the major, formative factor. For not only are there numerous examples of Zen architecture that do not manifest the aesthetic principles of "tea," but the ritual of tea drinking, as it was practiced since the early 13th century in all Zen temples, also shows little evidence of the later principles of "tea." Instead, there is good reason to believe that several socio-environmental circumstances were directly responsible for the rise of the particular tea cult, as well as for the universal appeal to all classes in the feudalistic society, for the different interpretation by each of them, and for the multiple meaning of the final form of "tea."

One decisive factor in the rise of the Japanese tea cult, its timing, and its form, was architecture and art itself. The current residential style of the ruling classes was the *shoin* style, with its colorful, gorgeous interior, its impressive scale, and its rigid standardization, all of which were, in their social and emotional content, far remote from their counterparts in the houses of the commoners. As any contrast stimulates comparison and any comparison leads to mutual evaluation, this difference between abundance and scarcity, between colorful gorgeousness and natural rusticity, between multiplicity and simplicity, must have at one time awakened the imagination of one sensitive to matters of aesthetics and familiar with both worlds of life. And it is, therefore, by no means an accident that a tea master uncovered, rather than discovered, a valuation of the things that was entirely independent from that of their material worth.

Already in the 15th century, Shukō, a Buddhist priest in Nara (1422–1502), had exercised an independent tea ceremony different from the traditional practice of the monks, which he called *cha-no-yu,* wherein he set forth its principles as harmony, *wa,* reverence, *kei,* purity, *sei,* and tranquillity, *jaku,* principles that were in marked contrast to the gay and loud amusement of the court. Yet, it was Sen-no-Rikyū (1518–

91) who perfected the idea and form of "tea." To teach the art and the beauty of a simple life, he built a hut to symbolize a remote farmhouse and used the practice of tea serving to demonstrate the aesthetics of life in its most common aspect.

The fact that Sen-no-Rikyū came from a wealthy mercantile family of Sakai (a part of present Osaka) is very revealing indeed. For the other factor of tea's historic necessity was the rise of a new progressive class, the citizen class, consisting of merchants and artisans. Although this class was increasingly gaining in economic power and thus political influence, it was not yet able to decide its own form of living; even less was it able to shake off the yoke of the ruling classes. Rising pride and class consciousness prompted them to show their wealth in their houses. Yet, the nobility and the military, fully aware of the growing challenge, increasingly and forcefully restricted all those features of living and building (clothes and children's toys included) wherein the citizen class could imitate the life of the nobility and thus demonstrate their material wealth. Therefore, since the current *shoin* style of the aristocratic architecture was not available for their use, there was a want for a different style that would not only be out of the reach of governmental control but that would also satisfy their pride in possessing something of their own. For this want the aesthetic principles of Shukō and their manifestation through Sen-no-Rikyū provided the answer and offered infinite ways of displaying wealth through a refined and costly appreciation and execution of sophisticated simplicity in art and architecture. From the wealthy citizen class, then, the Japanese "cult of tea" reached the various classes of the late-feudalistic society, the nobles, warriors, and commoners, and each of them adopted "tea" for essentially different reasons.

To the ruling classes, who lived a life of abundance, the remoteness of the tea hut and the simplicity of tea serving must have had a great appeal, just as contemporary man, enjoying an advanced civilization, longs, if only subconsciously, for a more primitive life, apart from all the conveniences and mechanisms of modern life to which he has become a slave rather than a master. The tea cult provided this refuge from the extravagant life the nobles were leading and thus found willing acceptance by them. And here, the spirit of "tea" did not remain confined to the tea hut and the activities performed therein, but, by permeating the thinking of the nobility and the military, effected the hitherto gorgeous style of their houses to become more quiet and restrained in color, form, and motif.

Especially to the warrior class, the samurai, who were in fact of peasant ancestry, the simple ritual of tea serving in the tea hut offered refuge from their life of continuous vigilance and warfare. Ceaseless engagement in their bloody profession did not leave them much time for intellectual training. Rather, in those years of war and strife, intellect must have been an actual detriment to swift and effective work with the sword. Thus, the soothing gathering in a tea hut, the simple ritual of serving and drinking tea, and the easily intelligible content of its spirit, provided both relief and enjoyment in those rare moments of relaxation. Separated from all wordly struggles and superficialities, the warrior for once was able to forget the very cruel reality of his life and find the refuge that his own house could seldom offer.

Entirely different was the interpretation of "tea" by the lower classes, who lived in bitter poverty. For them "tea" gave some meaning to the pitiful life they were leading and caused them to view their existence not as a continuing hardship and injustice but as a form that had a beauty all its own. Moreover, since the ceremonial serving of tea could be executed with the most common kind of tea and with the most ordinary utensils, not only were the poorest able to engage in artistic activity and thereby experience beauty, but even the uneducated could grasp the meaning, for the act was one of daily experience, the understanding of which did not require an intellectual medium. Thus, with the lower classes gradually performing art, the level of the people as a whole was enormously elevated, not materially but spiritually, and it is here that the tea cult transcended the realm of an extravagant pastime.

There is one other architectural factor that no doubt contributed to the emergence of the tea cult and that accounts for many of its particular features. The *shoin* style, in which the mansions of nobleman and warrior were built, had become standardized in a manner that froze any development. Not only had dimensions and room disposition been fixed, but unalterable rules had also been set for kind, treatment, and form of material. Since any individual alteration would have provoked a chain reaction of other changes, development had come to such a standstill that it did not leave any possibility for expressing personality in a society of growing individual self-consciousness. Against this impersonal and rigid system of the *shoin* style, the tea cult introduced its *sukiya* style, in which the individual taste and disposition of the owner could express itself in any possible form.

Thus, the causative reality of the tea cult, its materialization in *sukiya,* the "abode of fancy," and its performance in the ceremonial tea serving, is in essence socio-environmental. While originally having different meanings for each class of society, it provided the answer to the prevailing conditions and problems. Its substance, therefore, was of multiple and contrasting nature—counteraction to extreme trends in architecture and art, resistance against the ruling authorities, resignation to prevailing conditions of society, refuge from the troublesome life of continuous warfare, amusement with something different and fanciful, and demonstration of solidarity with poverty. As such, it was confirmation of an existing situation rather than formation of a new progressive thought.

Yet, although all of these multiple factors in one way or another were instrumental in producing favorable conditions for the birth of "tea," it was the merchant class that caused and carried the aestheticism of "tea." Through them, however, the meaning of the "tea spirit," i.e., symbolization and embodiment of the life of the poorest class and appreciation of its inherent beauty, has experienced a basic deviation from the original ideal, for it actually took over only the form without learning the bitter truth that had caused this form.

The life and shelter of the poor farmer, which served as models for the "tea spirit," were formed as a result of the farmer's daily fight against poverty, suppression, exploitation, and nature; they were shaped by his homely wisdom of life and by the naïve and animated simplicity of expression. Secluded from the outer world with the interior in semidarkness, the old farmhouse manifested a healthy simplicity and a very real naïveté and rustic directness. This inherent quality was called *wabi* by the tea master Sen-no-Rikyū and was considered to be the essence of "tea." Yet, its reproduction as a tearoom or tea hut and its performance in the tea serving in the houses of the merchant class was inevitably something entirely different. While the true *wabi* was an expression acquired through a continuous fight against poverty, the *wabi* of the *sukiya* was an expression of affirmation of poverty. As such, it was not an active attitude but a passive-submissive one that accepted poverty and conformed to it. Thus, *wabi* of the tea cult obtained a meaning of "noble poverty," i.e., a sophistication of poverty that has but its form in common with the *wabi* of the old farmhouse, which was an expression of real poverty.

And even form underwent a delicate refinement in the course of the *sukiya*-style development. For the ostentatious desire to be simple, naïve, and rustic became the dominant expression of form rather than the quality of simplicity itself. Moreover, as to the actual participation in the tea cult, there is an essential difference between real confrontation with the limitations of poverty and occasional experience of poverty in "tea," with the full awareness of one's own wealth and readily available comfort. With life being secure, it was only too easy to beautify poverty and to derive from it aesthetic ideals. However, solidarity with poverty is true only when poverty is actually lived and shared or when an attempt is made to help others overcome poverty. There was, in fact, no desire on the part of the merchants to participate in the struggle of the poorest classes, much less to become one of them. In this sense, the tea cult was more a fashionable entertainment and amusing pastime than a deep awareness of the tragic beauty of poverty. The fact that the tea masters were associated primarily with the ruling classes, not even yet with the merchant class, and that the more famous of them like Yūraku, Oribe, and Enshū were themselves of the highest nobility shows that there was actually little understanding of real poverty and that the cult of appreciating poverty was more fashionable than real.

This inherent paradox of the tea cult, namely, that of being essentially the appreciation of poverty and at the same time having been developed by the classes of wealth and power, did not deprive "tea" of its stimulating influence on Japanese life, art, and architecture, nor of its significance for contemporary architecture. Yet, it is only through a thorough knowledge of all circumstances and background factors that the essence of "tea" can be grasped. Without such knowledge, not only "tea" itself but Japanese art, life, and architecture will also remain obscure; only form will be realized, and not reality, which alone can uncover universal truths of architectural creation both in the past and in the present.

philosophy of tea

While the causes for the rise of the tea cult were socio-environmental and many, and its performance in the houses of the wealthy was a paradox, it was in the acceptance of "tea" and its practice among the common classes that it reached its noble destination and performed its high ethical task. Yet, Zen Buddhism, which earlier had been instrumental in importing from China "tea" as plant and cult, was the very source that gave "tea" its profound philosophical meaning and ultimate perfection as a cult of aestheticism and enlarged its sphere of influence to include all phases of life. As in the case of the garden, where Zen Buddhism not only philosophically confirmed an existing intimacy with the natural environment but also deepened and enriched an originally unconscious feeling, so too in the case of "tea" it uncovered a significance for life and thus related the life of the individual to the infinity of the universe. "Tea" and Zen, therefore, through history and philosophy, are closely related to each other, as is evidenced by the fact that all tea masters of the past were students of Zen.

The limited meaning of the tea cult is the active appreciation of the aesthetic qualities inherent in poverty, such as simplicity, naïveté, imperfection, insufficiency, discomfort, and primitivity. Yet, Zen does not consider this poverty as a cause or an effect of limitation. Instead, Zen aims at seeing poverty as a mental state of being independent from things worldly such as wealth, power, and reputation and of being self-satisfied with what is given. In order to grasp the essence of life, one must liberate oneself from continuous concern with material values, which only obscure reality; one should live the barest life possible, which is the life of poverty.

Zen states that only the spirit of a thing is important, and not its outward appearance. Conspicuous form only too often calls attention to itself rather than to its meaning. In other words, neglect of form through utmost restraint of motif and through ultimate simplification of performance is more apt to lay bare the essence of all things than is the perfected form, which only too easily diverts attention from its inner truth. In more concrete terms, as to the construction of the tearoom, the most ordinary inconspicuous material will display inherent beauty and purpose better than the costly one in which expensiveness of purchase distracts from its true value.

It is through this interpretation and attitude of Zen that the tea cult, as manifested in the tearoom and tea serving, becomes more than an appreciation of outward form. The mere visual beauty in poverty is transcended, and "poverty" becomes the very prerequisite to realizing the inner wealth and truth of life. Stripped of all unessentials, the tearoom becomes the abode of emptiness where man's spirit can move freely; restricted to simple utensils and most rational movements, the tea serving symbolizes the fact that living is art. By performing the most basic activity of living, drinking, life is consciously and directly experienced and grasped in its aesthetic meaning. For such an experience, as the tea master Shukō has pointed out, feelings of harmony, reverence, purity, and tranquillity are prerequisite. These feelings are also principles in the life of Zen monks, as much as the practical serving of tea, no doubt, is a pure demonstration of Zen methods of spiritual teaching through immediate experience rather than verbal interpretation or instruction.

Also, the notions of *wabi* and *sabi,* which are considered the emotional essence of the tearoom and tea life, have had their precedence in Zen Buddhism. *Wabi* actually means "poverty," not a state of deficiency but a state that liberates man from external concern and makes him aware of a more essential inward value. As a cult, *wabi* is the aesthetic appreciation of the expression of this "poverty," the primitive simplicity. Through insufficiency of means and through inability to fulfill each of one's desires, self-sufficiency is achieved (Plates 141–142). *Wabi* thus sees beauty in the imperfection of life and in this transmuted meaning becomes almost synonymous with the other term *sabi. Sabi* is related to the Sanscrit term, *santi,* which means "tranquillity" or "peace." It is frequently used in Buddhist scripts to designate the ultimate liberation from worldly passions and sorrows, which is a state called *nirvana.* The Japanese identified this ultimate tranquillity of *sabi* with a place of loneliness and solitude. Since in the tea cult, this place was conceived to be one that showed signs of age or even decay, *sabi* as aesthetic concept received the connotation of something that had gracefully grown old and was no longer perfect. It is in this meaning that *sabi* and *wabi* in their association with imperfection and insufficiency are no longer distinguishable as separate concepts.

This multimeaning of the terms *sabi* and *wabi,* their occasional sameness and their frequent differences, have given rise to an almost mystical regard for these notions among the Japanese, as either lack of knowledge or vagueness of concept always invites mystic speculation. Most likely, instead of coining new terms for the various new aesthetic qualities that arose from the tea cult, the terms *sabi* and *wabi* were relied upon because both were already significant terms of Zen Buddhism, and were somehow related in their meaning to the new properties they were to describe. Each tea master, then, true to his individualistic life conception, had his own subjective interpretation without exercising an objective discipline of intellectual thinking. This trait can be evidenced also in the word "tea hut," *suki-ya,* which was to designate a particular architectural style. Its original meaning is "abode of fancy," yet, written with different Chinese ideographs, *suki-ya* may also mean "abode of vacancy," "abode of the unsymmetrical," "abode of imperfection," "abode of nothingness," and the like.

As with Zen, in "tea" external and earthly distinctions are also considered unessential. This feeling was so strong that even in the feudal society, the existence of which depended on precise class distinctions and careful distribution of privileges, the spirit of equality and fraternity during the time of tea serving let commoner and nobleman sit together and share the same experience. In this, the latent ethics as to the equality of man and reverence to fellow being, so much obscured in Japan by the particular form of society, has found an unmistakable manifestation.

The emphasis that "tea" places on purifying the senses from contamination and the methods used to accomplish it are remindful of the importance that Buddhism attributes to "purity." In the words of a tea master (Nakano Kazuma): "The idea of the tea cult, *cha-no-yu,* is to cleanse the five senses from contamination. By seeing the picture scroll, kakemono, in the alcove and the flower in the vase, one's sight is cleansed; by smelling the burning incense, one's sense of odor is cleansed; by listening to the boiling water in the iron kettle and to the dripping of water from the bamboo pipe, one's ears are cleansed; by tasting tea one's mouth is cleansed; and by handling the tea utensils one's sense of touch is cleansed. When thus all sense organs are cleansed, the mind itself is cleansed from defilements. The tea cult is after all a spiritual discipline, and my aspiration for every hour of the day is not to depart from the spirit of the tea cult, which is by no means a matter of mere entertainment."

And again the spirit of Zen Buddhism is evident in the attempt to relate this substantiation of an ideal life to the universe. The roots of this effort, which is more a preservation of, than a striving for, the unity of life, lie in the doctrine of the Chinese Taoists, who claimed that the secret of success in the mundane drama was to maintain the geometric proportions of the phenomena of life, i.e., never to lose the conception of the whole because of that of the individual. The flower in the vase and the small opening to the enclosed garden not only bring nature and universe within reach but establish the precise relationship of life and universe by demonstrating that nature is a part of life, as life is a part of nature. Thus, within a small enclosed space the art of life is practiced very conscientiously, free of all artistry and being just the minimum of an everyday activity. Simplification and elimination of all unessentials bring the values of life to the open in their most basic and pure form and thus give evidence that life is art. It is not the media, such as skill, material, form, or technique, that are art, but rather the revealing of a pure, innocent, and simple spirit. Thus with media being most simple and basic, the lowest classes were also able to create art on their own, to feel beauty, and to somewhat comprehend the meaning of life, thus lifting the Japanese as a whole toward a high spiritual level of architecture and life, in spite of, or rather because of, their material poverty.

physique of the tearoom

As much as Zen Buddhism has fostered the ceremonial drinking of tea and has given depth and spiritual esteem to the tea cult, as much has Zen permeated and spiritualized the physique of the tearoom. The first architectural measure toward an independent space for exercising the tea serving was the partitioning of a space called *kakoi* (enclosure) within a main room through portable screens. The name *kakoi* later came to designate those tearooms that are integrated or physically attached to the main house. Partitioned space, thereafter, became enclosed space, and it was Sen-no-Rikyū who created the independent tea hut, *sukiya,* the "abode of fancy." This was usually a detached, hermitage-style structure called *sōan,* available mainly to the wealthy classes. Its forms were so unique that a new architectural style was initiated, the *sukiya* style, but its thorough investigation is beyond the scope of this paper. Instead, the analysis will concern itself only with the spatial and expressional features in the tearoom *(kakoi, cha-shitsu)* that were incorporated into the houses of the common people.

The dimensions of the space for the classic tearoom, as elaborated by Shō-ō, a tea master of the 16th century, are determined by an area covered with 4 1/2 mats, which is a square room of about 2,700 mm. or of 9 ft. width. This size is said to be symbolically linked with the room in which a legendary Buddhist figure welcomed a saint and 84,000 disciples of Buddha as a manifestation that conceptual limitations such as space do not exist for the truly enlightened. Yet, in the world of material reality, the classic 4 1/2-mat tearoom is dimensioned to accommodate not more than five persons. The interior features of the tearoom aim at suggesting the atmosphere of a faraway farmhouse with its remoteness, poverty, humbleness, simplicity, and semidarkness, and many motifs have, therefore, been taken directly from the old farmhouse.

However, what set out as an aestheticism that attempted to uncover the humanistic and artistic values of poverty gradually became an aestheticism of poverty's forms and features alone, to a degree that it no longer had anything in common with the very real and direct poverty of the farmers and general public. Thus, in their wish to manifest solidarity with poverty, the wealthy class engaged the best craftsmen, used the most exquisite material, employed the most elaborate techniques, prepared the most costly tea, served with most precious utensils, and wore the most expensive clothes, thus making the teahouse and tea drinking an elaborate and very costly art— a paradoxical attitude, indeed, in an aestheticism that claims to be an appreciation of the values in poverty. Only, when the tearoom was adopted into the houses of the commoners was the discrepancy of the tea's existence solved, and tea became the very humble cognizance of the reward and value of poverty, not only in its physical manifestation as tearoom but also in its symbolic performance as tea serving.

In contrast to the openness of all living rooms in the Japanese house, the tearoom, as created by Sen-no-Rikyū, is a hermitage, enclosed on all four sides by solid clay walls of a particular rough, earthen texture, with no visible attempt to compensate for unevenness in the handicraft technique (Plate 103). The lower part is pasted with gray or white paper, *koshi-bari,* to a height of about 1–1.5 ft. (300–450 mm.). The leaves of old letters are also frequently used to create a feeling of insufficiency. While in the ordinary rooms of the Japanese residence the functions for door, window, and partition are performed as a rule by identical sliding units, *shōji* and *fusuma,* in the tearoom these functions are given separate treatment. There is even a distinction made between the window which provides light and that which permits a limited view to the garden, in case the latter exists at all. For, frequently its function may be fulfilled by the low entry through which the guests crawl while entering from the garden. Also, the entrance, direct from the house interior or indirect from the veranda or the tea kitchenette, is clearly marked by a frameless sliding panel pasted with white opaque paper and is thus in physical contrast to the dark-colored clay wall. Frequently, a third entrance from the house interior is provided, differentiating the entries for tea serving and meal serving. Another difference from the ordinary living room is the use of logs in their natural shape as columns. The frieze rail, *nageshi,* in the tea cult's continuous attempt at simplification, is also absent, as is the clerestory window for ventilation, *ramma.*

The forms of windows vary individually, yet, certain conventional forms that effect a certain uniformity for these wall openings have developed as well. Thus, for the illumination of the room a rectangular window with high sill, *taka-mado,* is used. It is furnished with translucent paper panels and usually receives a bamboo lathwork on the outside, in which case the window is called *renji-mado.* Equally common is the clay-wall window, *shitaji-mado,* which, though not being submitted to formalistic rules, is preferred in a circular shape or as a rectangle with the corners cut off or rounded. It is said that this motif has been taken from the old farmhouse, where ventilation was provided by simply laying bare the bamboo skeleton of the wall from its wall clay. Though the positioning of the windows appears rather free, it again follows certain principles that allow no arbitrary measures. One of them is that the place of the host is effectively illuminated so that the guests can properly observe the host's art of preparing tea. Another is that the recess with the hanging picture scroll receives sufficient light. Frequently the light is tempered by bamboo curtains attached to the windows from the outside, which in the latter part of the tea gathering, are removed, thus creating an entirely different light condition that enriches the experience of "tea."

The presence of the picture recess, *tokonoma,* in the tearoom indicates the strong relationship of "tea" with Zen Buddhism (Plate 79). For the Zen temple itself was but a college room for the monk students, with one wall slightly recessed to contain a Buddha statue or sacred picture, in front of which the monks held their discussions and meditational practices, burning a censer and drinking ceremonial tea. One may still find a censer in the tearoom next to the flower vase—a remnant of the original form of *tokonoma.* For the recess post, *toko-bashira,* a natural stem of irregular form, different from the material of the columns in other rooms, is preferred. The hearth, a square hole of 1.4× 1.4 (also 1.3× 1.3) *shaku* (430× 430 mm.= 16.7× 16.7 in.) sunk into the floor, is located in a particular relationship to the two entrances and to the picture recess—a consequence of the exacting rules of the tea-serving procedure. Here the water is heated in an iron kettle, which is frequently suspended from the ceiling by an iron chain. The ceiling is much lower than in ordinary rooms; it may have a pattern of bamboo wicker or of interwoven wooden strips and is divided with one part sloped, as if to suggest the underside of a roof or attic space.

This sloped part may have a skylight with a movable cover, as in the kitchen of the old farmhouse, and, with rising or sinking daylight, it is mainly through this window that the room receives the fast-changing light of the rising or sinking sun. Such a control of room illumination, together with the single flower and the picture scroll in

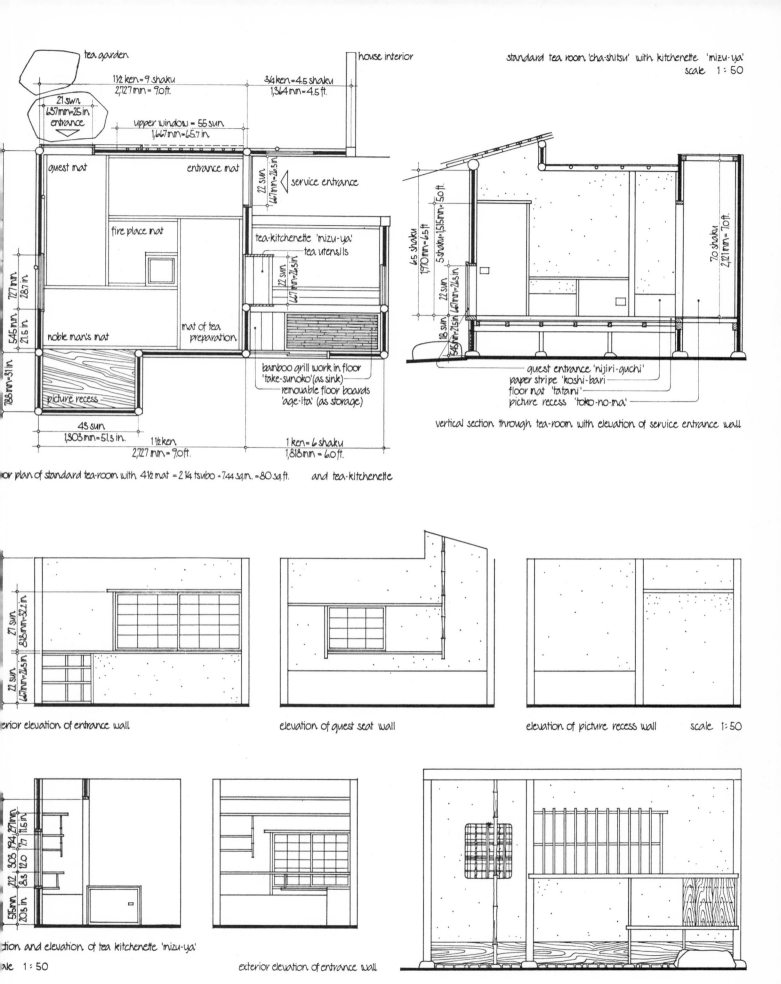

tea garden

1½ ken = 9 shaku
2,727 mm = 9.0 ft.

¾ ken = 4.5 shaku
1,364 mm = 4.5 ft.

house interior

standard tea room 'cha-shitsu' with kitchenette 'mizu-ya'
scale 1:50

21 sun
637 mm = 25 in
entrance

upper window = 55 sun
1,667 mm = 65.7 in

guest mat

entrance mat

22 sun
667 mm = 26.3 in

service entrance

fire place mat

tea-kitchenette 'mizu-ya'
tea utensils

22 sun
667 mm = 26.3 in

727 mm
28.1 in

545 mm
21.5 in

noble man's mat

mat of tea
preparation

788 mm = 31 in

picture recess

bamboo grill work in floor
'take-sunoko' (as sink)
removable floor boards
'age-ita' (as storage)

43 sun
1,303 mm = 51.3 in.

1½ ken
2,727 mm = 9.0 ft.

1 ken = 6 shaku
1,818 mm = 6.0 ft.

plan of standard tea-room with 4½ mat = 2¼ tsubo = 7.44 sq.m. = 80 sq.ft.   and tea-kitchenette

4.5 shaku
1,970 mm = 6.5 ft.

5 shaku = 1,515 mm = 5.0 ft.

7.0 shaku
2,121 mm = 7.0 ft.

22 sun
667 mm = 26.3 in

18 sun
545 mm = 21.5 in

guest entrance 'nijiri-guchi'
paper stripe 'koshi-bari'
floor mat 'tatami'
picture recess 'toko-no-ma'

vertical section through tea-room with elevation of service entrance wall

27 sun
818 mm = 32.2 in

22 sun
667 mm = 26.3 in

interior elevation of entrance wall

elevation of guest seat wall

elevation of picture recess wall   scale 1:50

27 mm 7.7 in
303 12.0
212 8.3
515 mm 20.3 in

section and elevation of tea kitchenette 'mizu-ya'

scale 1:50

exterior elevation of entrance wall

FIGURE 73: Plan of prototype tearoom, *cha-shitsu,* with kichenette, *mizuya.*

the alcove, provides infinite possibilities to adapt the emotional quality of the tearoom either to the weather or to the disposition of the house master, making the architecture of the tearoom not only physically but also psychologically a true image of man himself. To exploit these possibilities, of course, presupposes an awareness of the potential of light in architecture, and in the tearoom it appears as if the Japanese understood very well the importance of light in the art of living.

In this role, the spatial character of the tearoom is basically different from that of all the other rooms. The tearoom is a seclusion, boldly isolated from the outside world, be it house interior or garden—a space free from any outside intrusion, both actually and suggestively. It is significant that the rigid enclosure was not created as a defensive measure, such as the defense against weather which caused the isolation of the interior of Western buildings; nor was it an inevitable circumstance brought about by constructional methods. Instead, this solid enclosure was effected by the realization that seclusion in building is essential in order to create a maximum atmosphere of introversion in building.

In the classic tearoom of 4 1/2 mats, the mats are arranged around the half mat in the middle, which contains the hearth. Each mat has its particular name that corresponds with the procedure of tea serving. Thus, the half mat in the middle is called "hearth mat"; the mat in front of the picture recess, i.e., the most honorable seat, is called "mat before the alcove" or "nobleman's mat"; the mat at the guest entrance, where the guests take their seats, is called "guest mat"; the mat upon which the host prepares the tea is the "mat of tea preparation"; and the mat in front of the service entrance from the house interior is called "entrance mat." Smaller rooms have only the "guest mat" and the "mat of tea preparation," the latter then containing the fireplace. The variety of room sizes, according to mat numbers, is enlarged by the use of a 3/4 mat called *daime*, which is liked very much because it creates an alcove owing to the shorter length of the mat. Even in rooms with only normal mats, this spatial effect of an alcove is purposefully produced by projecting a stub wall 1–2 ft. (300–600 mm.) into the room at the mat joint. This clay wall directly joins the hearth and is terminated with a natural round stem, *naka-bashira*, of frequently irregular shape which has a strong sculptural effect. Through this manipulation, a place for tea preparation of no more than 3 × 4.5 (6) ft. (900 × 1,350 mm.) is spatially, yet not visually, separated, allowing for an arrangement of shelves behind the stub wall without interfering with the simple austerity of the tearoom.

While in ordinary houses the utensils for the tea serving are kept in another room, usually the dining room, *chanoma*, the tea ceremony being prepared in the kitchen, in more extensive houses a particular kitchenette called *mizuya* is provided for this purpose. Its size is not larger than two mats (1,818 × 1,818 mm. = 6 × 6 ft.), yet, it contains all facilities necessary for the preparation of the tea ceremony. One part of its floor along the exterior wall is perforated with a bamboo grill that serves as a sink for cleaning the tea utensils. The wall shelves are designed along both practical and aesthetic lines, and all other features of this room are determined by the same principles as those of the tearoom. It was the exemplary convenience and practicality of this kitchenette that influenced the unhygienic and inconvenient kitchen in old houses to become more efficient and human.

These, then, are the physical components of the tearoom. The motifs were features of the old farmhouse and, to a limited degree, of the primitive city dwelling, complemented by characteristics of the Zen college. Their execution, however, is subjected to the principles that were proclaimed by the tea masters to be the essence of tea feeling and the prerequisite for a profound tea experience. Their psychological implications are infinite; they not only make the tea cult an ever new experience, but they will also respond to the particular state of mind of each individual. While the restrained decoration in the form of a hanging picture scroll, *kakemono*, and a single flower or branch changes according to the season, weather, or disposition, and thus is ever new, the permanent component of the tearoom's physique is also ever new. For it contains many symbolic meanings that may be perceived differently according to the mood of the individual beholder.

Thus, the irregularity and roughness of a natural wood column may suggest poverty in all its humbleness and simpleness. It may also be conceived of as a bold demonstration that form is to be neglected if the spirit behind the matter is to come to the open. Conspicuous and unnatural form may direct attention to itself rather than to inner truth. The same column may convey the notion of something imperfect that engages the imagination to complete it. The experiencing of beauty is not passive beholding but active partaking. Therefore, Zen asserts that perfection of beauty lies in its imperfection, in which the emphasis rests upon the process through which perfection is sought, rather than upon the perfection itself. Symmetry and geometry are to be avoided because they express not only completion and perfection, but also repetition. Again, the frailty of the slender columns may transmit the awareness that all material is perishable. House is only a temporary refuge for the body, as the body is for the soul. Eternal only is the spirit behind the phenomena, and spirit has mastery over matter. The suggestive power of this natural-irregular column, in the subdued light of the intimate tearoom, may even carry one to the desolateness of the rugged mountains, where the life of a daring young pine tree has come to an untimely end because of cold and lack of food among the vastness of rocks, while the singing of the teakettle may be heard as the tremendous howl of the storm that brings the tree's final downfall.

Also, the single flower in the vase in the picture recess is infinite in its spiritual content. Never placed in the center of the alcove, it affirms that nature is asymmetrical, as is life and existence. There is beauty everywhere, but it must be sought and brought out. Simplicity is set against multiplicity; a single flower is apt to reveal its inherent beauty much more clearly than a whole bouquet. Just as two different themes of music may nullify each other's beauty, so too two strong motifs of color, form, or meaning, if not in precise harmony, may nullify each other's aesthetic value. Moreover, the flower is taken from nature. Brought into the realm of architecture, flower becomes architecture, and architecture is made by man, is human. Nature unfolds true beauty if brought into the human sphere. Human interpretation of nature, humanization, produces beauty. Flower may suggest humanity. When primitive man offered the first flower to his maiden, he transcended his existence as a brute subjected to raw drives, and became human. Again, it may reflect mood and temperament of the house master. *Sukiya* is the "abode of fancy" and, as such, is very personal. Shelter is built for man and not man for shelter. Adjustment to temporary psychological disposition is a function of art, and, as such, art must be true to contemporaneous life. And, finally, the lonely flower, brightly shining in the darkness of the room, may appeal very much to one's emotions: sacrifice for beauty. And it appears as if the flower itself were aware of this. For more than in life, it offers its beauty at the time of its death.

Equally, the tearoom, as space, is an infinite, ever changing source for spiritual experience through its manifold symbolic manifestations. Rigidly enclosed, it suggests separateness from the outer world: seclusion. Only in seclusion can the mind free itself from the continuous entanglement with everyday life and its selfish aims and material values, and strive for the spiritual elevation to which all life should serve. It may create a feeling of loneliness—eternal loneliness, different from that which man feels in his longing for something greater and better than himself. Rather, it is the solitariness of an absolute being that arises when the soul leaves the world of space, time, and causation behind. Except for flower and hanging picture scroll that respond to a temporary aesthetic mood, the room conveys a feeling of being vacant and empty. The reality of the room is its void, not its walls, ceiling, and floor, even less its furniture or decoration; and the reality of a teacup is its hollowness, not its material form. Vacuum is all-potent because it grants infinity of use and freedom of movement, both in spirit and material; only in vacuum can the full extent of man's aesthetic emotion unfold, and only through making oneself a vacuum can man's physical and intellectual, moral and spiritual limitations be overcome.

The semidarkness of the tearoom may suggest remoteness and refuge. It tempers all features of the room and blends them into harmony. Sometimes there is a limited view to the garden. But this produces neither glare of light nor a distraction of the contemplating mind. Rather, this glimpse of the macrocosm, by symbolically establishing a relation between man's moral proportions and the universe, leads man toward "innerliness," where the true life takes place.

Also, one may be captivated by the spirit of purity and cleanliness prevailing in form, feature, and motif. Cleanliness is not newness, and so everything that might suggest recent acquisition is avoided. Purity of mind and body is the moral quality of man; it is comprehensive and inconspicuous. Cleaning of the room is an art as is the cleaning of the tea utensils.

Simplicity and primitivity of the tearoom may symbolize the "original abode," i.e., *the* human space. Zen asserts that elaborate and sophisticated object forms are likely to obstruct the realization of the subject matter behind the object. Consequently, Zen aims at simplification to the very point where subject and object can no longer be dualistically conceived. In order to uncover the very basis of man's life, representation and performance of dwelling has to be reduced to the barest essentials: the hut and the drink, the tearoom and the tea.

Thus, the physique of the tearoom, both as a whole and in detail, is infinite in its spiritual perception, an immense source for the exercise of art in living. It reveals abundant richness by substantiating humble poverty. To build a simple hut is as much an art as to drink a cup of tea. For true art is perfected only when it ceases to appear as "art"; it is perfection of the artlessness when the innermost sincerity of man's own being asserts itself. To live this life of *wabi* is to free oneself from the continuous enslavement to man's material wants and comforts and to follow the very basic longing of going back to the simple and true, to be one with the universe.

art of living

According to Sen-no-Rikyū, the art of tea consists of nothing more than boiling water, making tea, and sipping it. This is meant to demonstrate that the simple and commonplace life in its most trivial aspect can become art. For art is not a matter of skill and training but a matter of inner attitude. Painting, sculpture, literature, music, and theater are only particular techniques or media through which the spiritual essence of man's being asserts itself; it enriches life by elevating the psychological sensitivity of fellow man and disclosing new areas of man's existence. In this sense, the art of tea is the art of living. For it makes man's everyday activities of living an instrument for experiencing the beauty of existence. Indeed, unlike the other arts, it is a "craft" whose mastership can be obtained by all, even the underprivileged classes, and thus it can also lift the poorest from the level of a mere basic existence to a life of art.

"Tea," therefore, in both its practice and its expression, aims at stimulating the awareness of beauty in everyday life by limiting it to its most fundamental activity, drinking, and by symbolizing and refining each of the constituent acts that lead to, and culminate in, the cup of tea. Its theme, as Okakura Kakuzō said, is man himself. For it is he that relates god to the world, distinguishes yesterday from tomorrow, establishes the difference of things. Man is the relativity of all things. In him relativity experiences adjustment and becomes art, and if this adjustment is concerned with man's immediate environment, it becomes the art of living or building. In this is revealed the fundamental truth that the art of building and of living are in their causations one and the same.

The guests, after resting for a while in the portico, *machiai,* enter the low entrance, dimensioned at: height × width = 2.3 (2.2) × 2.1 ft. (702 × 640 mm.), in an order previously agreed upon (Plate 102). This order disregards any social standing, a remarkable attitude at a time when the existence of society depended on strict observance of class privileges and separate class living. Moreover, the size of the entrance literally forces the proud warrior to leave his sword, the symbol of superior standing, behind on the rack beneath the eaves and requires that both high- and low-ranking guests bend low, thus actually and symbolically effacing the difference of social standing and the discrimination of the social order. In the tearoom, worldly considerations are no longer valid, and basic matters of life ask for equal reverence from nobleman and commoner alike.

The guests take their seats in silence, while giving quiet attention to the flower and the picture in the alcove. The host is not immediately present, thus giving the guests time to adjust themselves to the new environment without being distracted by any need for polite attentiveness, which the presence of the host would demand—evidence of the refined art of a tactful living. And this adjustment takes physical forms. For the eyes gradually adapt to the prevailing semidarkness and the room itself becomes lighter and more familiar to the guest, while the sound of the boiling water kettle fills the air unobtrusively so that the silence of the guests does not become in itself disturbing. And then the host appears in order to prepare the tea for his visitors. His movements are performed simply and naturally, yet with a minimum of effort—the beginning of a drama, the theme of which is life interwoven with tea, flower, and painting.

How rich the experience of such a simple act can be is expressed in a comment of the tea master, Takuan (1573-1645): ". . . when visitors are greeted with due reverence, we listen quietly to the boiling water in the kettle, which sounds like a breeze passing through pine needles, and become oblivious of all the worldly woes and worries; we then pour out a dipperful of water from the kettle, reminding us of the murmuring waters of mountain streams, and thereby our mental dust is wiped off. This is truly a world of recluses, saints on earth. . . ."

Harmony and purity prevails in the host's preparation of tea. All utensils are within comfortable reach when the host kneels before the singing iron kettle, a symbolization that economy in living is not only a necessity but also an art. The teacup is of earthenware, handmade, and irregularly shaped with perhaps infinite spiderweb-like cracks in the glaze, an expression of *wabi,* the charm of the rustic-primitive. Of contrasting expression are the minutely dressed, immaculate bamboo utensils used for the preparation. Exacting workmanship has turned the most ordinary material into a sensitively shaped tool, a piece of art. They are handled with care and precision, with love. Yet, all movements are natural and harmonious. There is "awareness" in every part of it and, as with the captivating, speechless acting of a great stage play, one may be fascinated by this drama that has no other theme than the daily chores of living. Thus, the tea is prepared and offered to each guest, who again symbolizes purification by wiping over the edge after having emptied the cup. Subdued light from the small window, gentle odor from the incense burner, suggestive sound from the iron water kettle, unobtrusive colors of picture and flower—they all blend with man and his activity into a harmonious and integrated whole, where thought can become free.

In such an environment, the mind is lifted above the perplexities of life, and while the guests sip their tea, one of them asks the host's permission to examine the tea utensils, showing a tactful interest in the host and recognition of his efforts to serve the guests. Thus conversation is initiated, and the friends talk freely about the black-ink drawing in the alcove or discuss thoughts that have been suggested by the tea utensils; or the host may even provide on occasion an interesting story as to their unusual origin or pathetic past. One of the guests himself may have brought along a piece of art, old or new, which may become the center of thought and talk; or the host may ask again, as he has so often done before on other gatherings, how his guests like the recent changes in the rock grouping, which during the years in his small garden has been in continuous "growth," as much as it has been the subject of profound thought and talk in the tearoom. Thus, time passes and the guests take their leave. Their presence has been appreciated and often the host symbolically expresses his humble thanks by presenting each a single biscuit, wrapped in white paper. For their presence has enriched his life and brought art into his house.

The tearoom is a refuge from the outer world with its continuous struggle for material wealth and superficial reputation. Its democratic-liberal spirit and simple-honest performance allows an undisturbed and free adoration of the beautiful. Here the warrior of the 16th century, a time of war and strife, could for once lay down his strenuous readiness to fight; here the merchant of the 17th century, a time of formalism in art, could keep art alive and save it from stagnation; here the noble-man and commoner of the 18th century, a time of rigid class enforcement, could communicate freely.

Life has not become simpler since then. Rising technology, instead of freeing man in his struggle for life, has come to make him a slave to his own achievements, and the material standard of living has risen as much as its spiritual quality has sunk. Modern man does not know what the destination of his existence is nor what leisure hours are for, because neither society nor the architect has provided a space where man can be alone and where he can strive for the more essential values of life as the Japanese can in the seclusion of the tearoom.

tea garden

As the residential garden is an integral constituent of the Japanese home, so the tea garden is a necessary requisite for the tearoom. Though its motifs and components are not different from those of the residential garden, its function and character, never-theless are essentially different. For, in contrast with the house garden, the tea garden is a preparatory space that has to be walked through in order to enter the tearoom. This role becomes apparent in one of the Japanese terms for tea garden, *roji,* which simply means path, while the other terms, *chatei* and *chaniwa* (tea garden), are more exacting, yet less descriptive. Again, a distinction must be made between the large-scale tea garden and the residential tea garden. The former is divided into an outer garden, *soto-roji,* and an inner garden, *nai-roji,* and usually contains a detached tea hut, while the residential tea garden is but a small separate access space to the tearoom. The limitations of this paper dictate that only the latter be made an object of consideration.

The tea garden, *roji,* emphasizes the atmosphere through which tea seeks the spirit-ual elevation of man: creation of an introverted world of purity, separated from the extroverted world of superficiality. In this role, the tea garden is subjected to the same fundamentals which control the tearoom and tea ceremony, namely, to prepare man psychologically and physically for a pure experience of art and beauty. The tea garden is the first act in this drama. The connection with the exterior world is broken; man enters a new world of different and more eternal values. This new world is also physically separated by high fences and, once the door is closed behind, man must fol-low a path, both actually and symbolically, until he has reached both in body and in mind the entrance to "tearoom" and "tea mood."

The path is exactly prescribed by steppingstones carefully placed for a leisurely walk, and determined by a sensitive anticipation of the walker's psychological reaction. The fairly small steppingstones, protruding above the mossy ground, direct attention to the ground rather than to the general environment; and here the visitor's mind is carefully guided as if in a captivating theater play, in order to liberate it from the entanglements of everyday life. At certain spots, the irregular flagstones may widen to a platform where inevitably the guest is tempted to interrupt his slow walk for a break and an all-around view; and it is from here that he will experience surprising and significant views of the garden or the teahouse. One of these places may also uncover a small water basin, *tsuku-bai,* which has been hidden from view up until this time. It is furnished with a bamboo dipper to wet mouth and hands as a symbolic

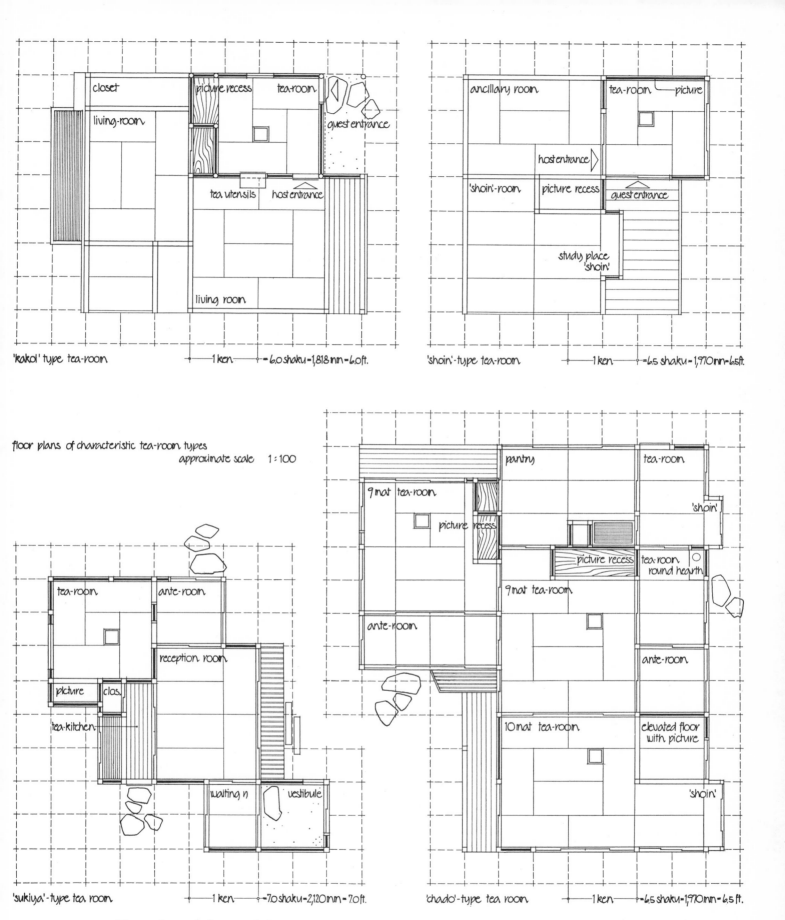

'kakoi' type tea-room   ⊢—1 ken——⊣ = 6.0 shaku = 1,818 mm = 6.0 ft.

'shoin'-type tea-room   ⊢—1 ken——⊣ = 6.5 shaku = 1,970 mm = 6.5 ft.

floor plans of characteristic tea-room types
approximate scale   1 : 100

'sukiya'-type tea room   ⊢—1 ken——⊣ = 7.0 shaku = 2,120 mm = 7.0 ft.

'chado'-type tea room   ⊢—1 ken——⊣ = 6.5 shaku = 1,970 mm = 6.5 ft.

FIGURE 74: Floor plans of characteristic tearoom types.

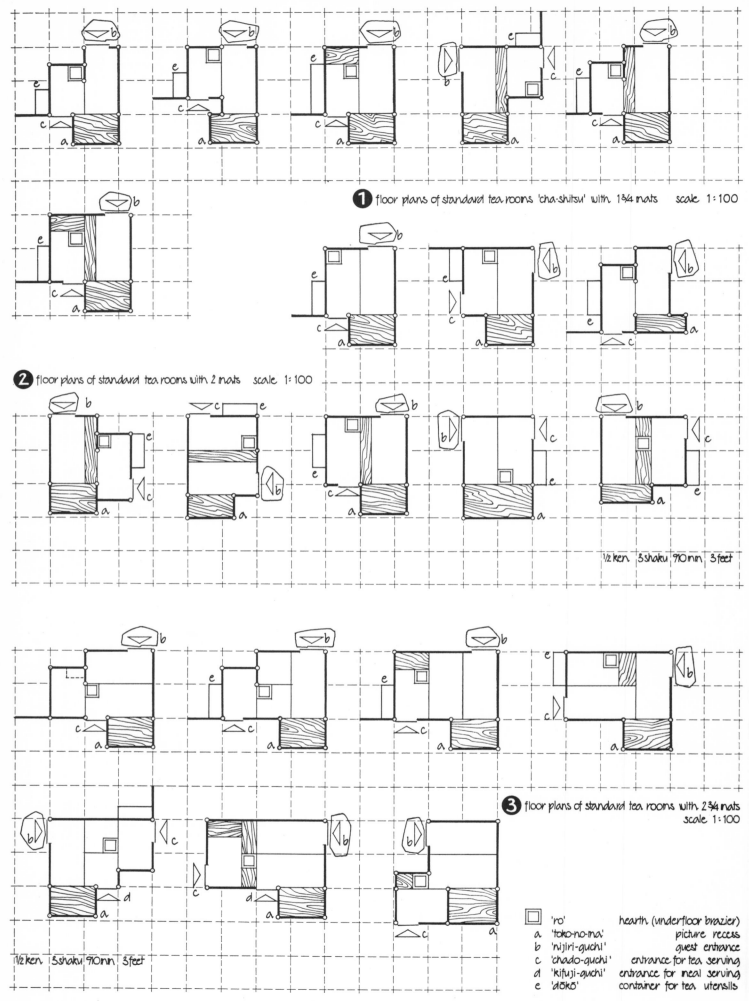

1 floor plans of standard tea rooms 'cha-shitsu' with 1¾ mats   scale 1:100

2 floor plans of standard tea rooms with 2 mats   scale 1:100

½ken   3shaku 910mm 3feet

3 floor plans of standard tea rooms with 2¾ mats
scale 1:100

½ken   3shaku 910mm 3feet

	'ro'	hearth (underfloor brazier)
a	'toko-no-ma'	picture recess
b	'nijiri-guchi'	guest entrance
c	'chado-guchi'	entrance for tea serving
d	'kifuji-guchi'	entrance for meal serving
e	'doko'	container for tea utensils

FIGURE 75: Floor-plan diagrams of standard tearooms showing variations in size and arrangement.

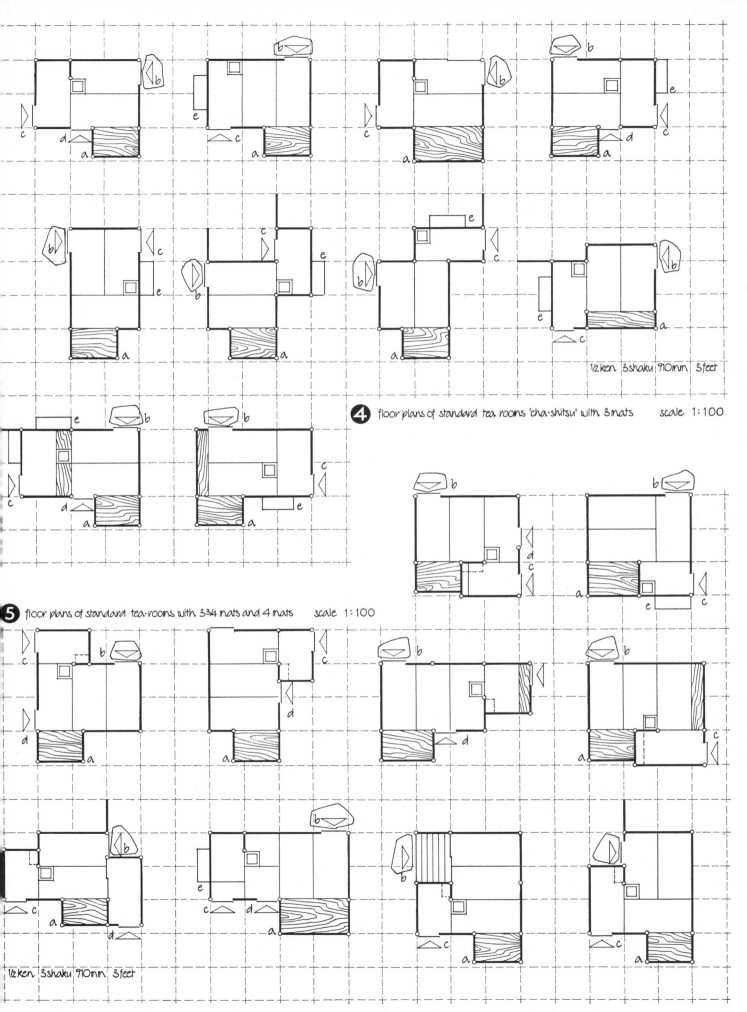

④ floor plans of standard tea rooms 'cha-shitsu' with 3 mats   scale 1:100

½ ken 3 shaku 910mm 3 feet

⑤ floor plans of standard tea-rooms with 3¾ mats and 4 mats   scale 1:100

½ ken 3 shaku 910mm 3 feet

FIGURE 75 (continued): Floor-plan diagrams of tearooms showing variations in size and arrangement.

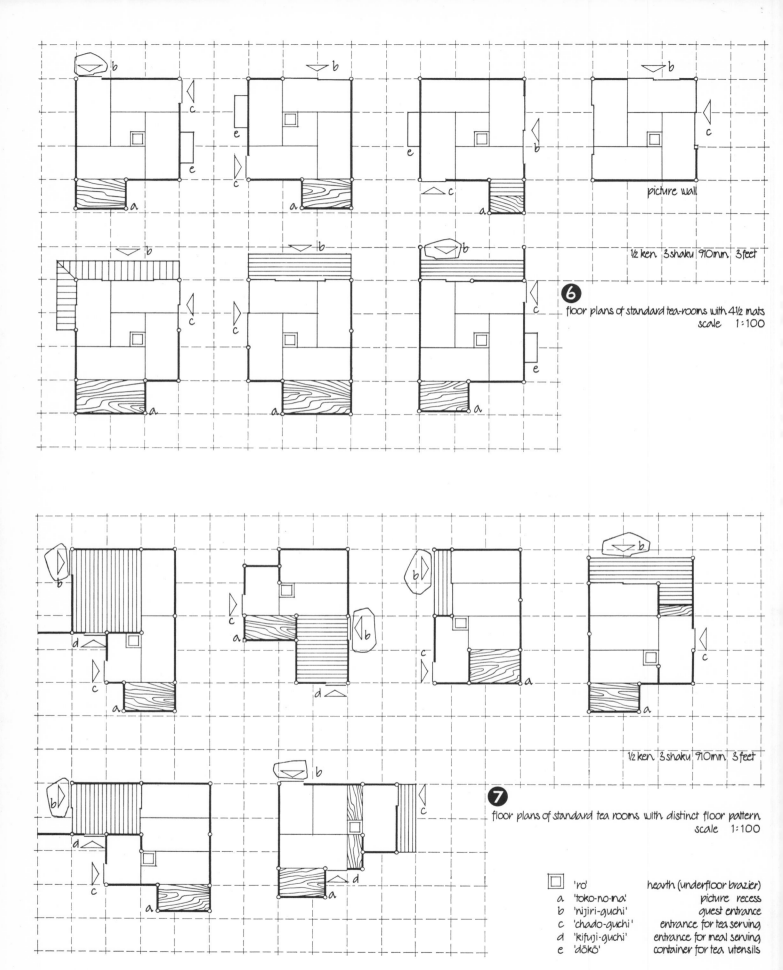

½ ken 3 shaku 910mm 3 feet

6
floor plans of standard tea-rooms with 4½ mats
scale 1:100

picture wall

½ ken 3 shaku 910mm 3 feet

7
floor plans of standard tea rooms with distinct floor pattern.
scale 1:100

□	'ro'	hearth (underfloor brazier)
a	'toko-no-na'	picture recess
b	'nijiri-guchi'	guest entrance
c	'chado-guchi'	entrance for tea serving
d	'kifuji-guchi'	entrance for meal serving
e	'dōkō'	container for tea utensils

FIGURE 75 (continued): Floor-plan diagrams of tearooms showing variations in size and arrangement.

gesture of purification. To reach dipper and water, the guest has to crouch down and as he brings the first dipper of water to his lips, he may catch, through a small opening in the thicket, a view of a hidden pond or even a faraway lake—the water in his pitcher, the water of the lake, . . . for a moment man may grasp the universe in his hands.

Thus, treading along the tea path, between the dark-green moss with its remoteness, between the colorful leaves in their decay, between the weathered stone lanterns in their serenity, between the shadowy shrubs in their evergreenness, between the dark rocks in their unchangeableness, a feeling of *sabi,* of aloofness and remoteness, is created, and the mind is gradually removed from concern with everyday thoughts. One may feel as if in the depth of a dark forest or in the remoteness of a rugged mountain, far away from the shallowness of civilization, while in fact being in the midst of a bustling city.

Thus prepared, the guests one after another arrive at the portico, *machiai,* a bench protected by a roof overhead, which in larger gardens may be a separate structure from which to view the tea hut. In common residences it is but a porch connected to the tearoom where the guests assemble, exchange greetings, and look back to the path that led them from the outer world.

standardization

Use of the floor mat, *tatami,* and, even more so, the incorporation of the tearoom into the house structure based on the *ken* grid, have subjected the tearoom as well to the common order that controls the planimetric space of the Japanese house. Yet, the use of a three-quarter mat, called *daime,* and of an exposed floor board (mostly pine) of varying widths inserted between the mats, together with a picture recess that is not submitted to the *ken* system, has provided more varieties of room size than is the case for the other rooms in the house. Still, the tea hut, *sukiya,* could not quite escape the formalism of the Tokugawa period (1600–1867), and what originally was a demonstration against uniformity and a conscious expression of subjective taste became largely a repetition of motif, form, and measure, copied and recorded from the famous individual works of the tea masters in that creative period of the 16th and 17th centuries.

It is true standardization of *sukiya* architecture, as brought about by the distribution of woodblock-printed manuals, *sukiya-hinagata,* among the carpenter guilds, made an otherwise very costly creation available to the poorer classes, but it should be understood that because of such standardization, *sukiya* architecture also became a contradiction to the original idea of its creators insofar as it was no longer an expression of individuality. Not only was the physique of the tearoom standardized, but also the performance of tea serving was subject to strict rules. These rules, though, are by no means arbitrary, yet deviate not only from the basic idea of "tea" but also from the principles of Zen Buddhism's teaching, which are against all formalism. As the tea master, Takuan, has remarked: ". . . the principle animating the tearoom from its first construction down to the choice of tea utensils, the technique of service, the cooking of food, wearing apparel, etc. is to be sought in the avoidance of complicated ritualism and ostentatiousness. . . ."

This paradox of standardization of what was intended to be a manifestation of personal taste, together with the paradoxical nature of "tea," namely, that of being an aestheticism of poverty performed by the wealthy class, is the reason that tea is of a very contradictory nature and frequently is grossly misinterpreted according to the particular viewpoint. However, these standards for building the "tearoom" and performing the tea serving brought to the common people an awareness of the beauty in their most ordinary activities, and here standardization showed its most noble influence. And it is interesting to note that among the lower classes the rules themselves were never applied in a rigid formalism as was the case in the educated circles, where even the verbal appreciation of the tea utensils and the hanging picture scroll became a matter of mere conventionality and formality, without any attempt at being critical and, thus, honest.

Actually, no less than four different types of tearooms have to be distinguished: *kakoi* style, *shoin* style, *sukiya* style, and *chadō* style. The *shoin*-style tearoom, an individual room originally used in the *shoin*-style mansions of the nobility and military, closely resembles the ordinary living room with its square columns, ceiling height, and openness to the garden and to the house interior through movable wall panels. The *sukiya*-style tearoom is an independent tea hut separated from the main house with anteroom and kitchenette. And in the *chadō* style, the tearoom serves for more official gatherings and thus is larger than 4 1/2 mats. These three types bear no direct relationship to the Japanese residence and to contemporary evaluation, or, as in the case of *shoin* style, are not distinct enough to be treated in particular. Instead, the *kakoi*-style tearoom not only manifests the characteristics of the distinct *sukiya* style but is also incorporated as an essential spatial unit into the organism of the main house. As such, it is this type rather than the others that is intimately related to the day-to-day living in the Japanese house, and, consequently, has a particular significance for the contemporary West. Therefore, only this type has been considered in this chapter.

The standardization of tearoom size is expressed in the number of mats, *tatami,* the smallest room being not larger than 1 3/4 mats (2.9 sq. m.= 32 sq. ft.). The arrangement of the mats in relationship to the entrance and the picture recess follows patterns set by famous tea masters, and accordingly is identified as Rikyū-konomi (*konomi,* literally, taste), Oribe-konomi, Yūraku-konomi, Enshū-konomi, Senke-konomi, etc. Each of them has standard measurements and standard features that encompass the smallest details of wood dimensioning and joinery, yet their differences are not essential. It appears that these prototypes were at one time created sensitively and individually along certain general principles dictated by the spirit and procedure of tea serving, and that the later generations, no longer possessing such an intuitive grasp, preferred to rely on the types developed by their ingenious forefathers.

Sukiya-style tea huts had already been mentioned in the manuals of carpenters, such as in the Shōmei scripts of the carpenter family Masanobu. Although these scripts contained wood dimensioning and timber allotment for each structure of the warrior residence, significantly for the *sukiya* no measurements are given. Thus, judging from the scripts of noted tea masters themselves, it appears very likely that the design of tea huts was a matter solely of the tea master and not of the carpenter, in spite of the latter's high reputation among all other craftsmen. Only after the 18th century, when the creations of the tea masters, although not their knowledge, were made available to the carpenters through woodblock prints, did they too engage in the design of tea huts—a design, however, that was no longer a creative activity, because tea huts were already standardized.

for contemporary architecture

As paradoxical as the background and even the evolution of the tea cult is, its influence on Japanese culture, architecture, art, and life is comprehensive and profound. The most unique accomplishment of its cultural mission is to be found in its influence upon the common classes, where it brought art and beauty into the most impoverished building and living. Contrary to commonly accepted opinion, the universal contribution of the "tea" is not evidenced in the sophisticated tearooms of the monasteries and wealthy residences, nor in the formalistic tea servings of the tea schools; even less in the eclectic nature of the modern *sukiya* style in contemporary Japan, all of these repeatedly being represented as the most outstanding substantiation of tea culture. Their individual artistic excellence is by no means contested. However, it should be understood that in spirit and performance they have little in common with the very truth of "tea." Deriving idea and motif from imitative and compassionate observation and not from comprehension of reality, these outstanding examples of tearoom architecture did not provide a solution for the social problems of the time and thus must be considered in essence masterpieces of fashionable art rather than architecture itself.

Yet, these works in the past have been instrumental in the rise of a comprehensive and profound tea culture insofar as they set standards and thus prompted the acceptance of "tea as art" among the lowest classes. And it was here that the true tea culture unfolded and produced results that have so much significance for contemporary architecture. For it raised the awareness that living can be art, that each trivial activity or feature of life can be art, and that each human is capable of creatively practicing this art. While in the upper classes "tea" was from its early beginning a fashionable device of entertainment that soon became encrusted in rigid formality, in the unskilled, yet conscious, tea serving of the common classes "tea" always remained a living, organic, and ever new art. Through "tea" the poorest became conscious of aesthetics in living and were inspired to aesthetic activity. Through "tea" the poorest farmer learned how to arrange flowers artistically, the lowest laborer how to appreciate rocks and waters. Through "tea," therefore, the cultural level of living has been raised to a standard superior to that of any comparable form in the West, where architecture and architects have so far failed to raise the interest of the common classes beyond that of satisfying their mere physical needs and comforts.

Residential architecture in the West, in its preoccupation with reflecting at best the ethics and morals of the family, with stimulating man's awareness of nature, with relieving the complexity of the woman's role in the house, with bringing the life of the individual into the family and that of family into society, and with liberating the individual from those multiple domestic chores, seems never to have become aware of the ultimate purpose that all these laudable architectural efforts serve. For there is hardly any attempt to provide that space and environment in the house where man can be introverted and can seek a personal world, the development of which should be the cause and effect of all human efforts. Extroversion and transparency of building, with little possibility for being separated and of being in solitude, cannot create psychological conditions conducive to contemplating one's inner self and the more profound matters of life that lie behind such phenomena as art, science, technique, and building. And it may very well be possible that man's trend toward spiritual superficiality and emotional indifference is in no small part due to a society wherein the facilities of sensitizing his awareness of life are either not regarded or are considered an end in themselves.

By contrast, the Japanese residence does contain a space solely provided for man's aestheticism, self-reflection, and spiritual elevation: the tearoom. It is significant that this space is rigidly isolated from the exterior world in spite of a climate and tradition that distinctly asked for openness toward environmental nature and fellow man. For the sensitive Japanese tea masters were aware that only in seclusion could man find the stage where his thought could leave the superficiality of wordly life and where he could experience spiritual elevation. It is in seclusion that residential architecture transcends the level of mere physical-psychical convenience to become an interpretation of life in its highest aspirations, and it is but a characterization of the disintegration of human values in the modern age that contemporary houses lack this seclusion.

It would, however, be misleading to say that the profundity of the influence of the "tea" is only substantiated in the tearoom, for many of the common houses do not possess a particular tearoom. Instead, soon after the principles of tea culture were established, they controlled the residential architecture as a whole, and, while the colorful architecture of the nobility and military became, under its influence, more restrained, simple, and integrated, the common classes for the first time consciously applied the features that in essence had determined their buildings since early times. "Tea" thus uncovered architectural values encompassing the entire residential architecture and, with this, imparted a unique morality to Japanese residential architecture. It is this morality that differs favorably from that of any contemporary architecture in the West, which as a whole lacks such morality. And it is here that an important lesson is to be learned.

It is noteworthy that while the source of "tea" was architecture and life itself (namely, that of the impoverished farmers and the general public), architecture and life in turn were the objects that were spiritually-ethically elevated through this morality to such an extent that both the building of houses and the living in houses became art. And this art was not the privilege of a particularly trained class, but was exercised by each and every one. Not only were farmers their own builders, but the nobility and clergy as well engaged in the art of building and exercised the art of living in "tea."

That living in its most common aspect can be art is a notion unheard of in the West. Here, living and dwelling is conceived as a summary of daily chores highlighted by meals, leisure, and entertainments. The chores vary from family to family and so do the highlights; and architecture, being concerned only with the sheltering of such activity, consequently does not possess any encompassing morality. Therefore, the reasons for the West's non-morality and spiritual disorder in contemporary building are not the multiplicity or variety of climate, topography, tradition, custom, or religion, but the absence of any awareness that living and dwelling itself is art. This art is infinite in expression and application and encompasses multiple possibilities of architectural creation in contemporary residences, provided the truth is realized that even the smallest utensils and objects of daily use can be created in such a way that they have a spiritual existence of their own and thus are able to enrich man's being.

Here, the culture of "tea," as it is substantiated in the seclusion of the Japanese house and life, shows the most human role of architecture, as the environment that protects the maintenance of human distinctions: withdrawal into the self, contemplation, thought.

For the faculty that distinguishes man from the animal is his ability to think.* That is to say, whereas any other creature is controlled in its actions by fear of, or hunger for, its environment, both of which function without any possible restraint, man is able to temporarily detach himself from the immediate concern with his environment and to take a stand within himself, to meditate, to think. Yet, these human powers of intentionally withdrawing from the environmental world, the other, and of entering the inner being, the self, are not innate. That is to say, the ability to think is not simply given to man by nature, but is a faculty that man is in continuous danger of losing.

Indeed, the human distinction "thought" is a very unstable acquisition, and the extinction and retrogression of highly developed cultures in history are evidence that "thought" in fact has frequently been lost. Without retreat to the inner self, no human life is possible. The human who can no longer liberate himself from environmental concern is governed by the things in this surroundings. As recent history has shown, he will then act without previous thinking, not unlike the animal creature, and in doing so he may lose his human distinction. There are obvious signs that in the industrial societies of the West the exposure of living and the continuous entanglement with a multiplicity of entertaining (and advertising) devices has, in fact, endangered the basis of an existence that is human.

All this is to a great extent due to the failure of architecture to provide an environment contributive to man's self-reflection. Certainly, contemporary architecture shelters and interprets the life of modern man, but it must be doubted whether it protects and stimulates the human distinction of man's existence.

Here the Japanese residence states clearly the fundamental task of architecture: creation of that residential and urban space that allows man to free himself from his continuous concern with the material world and helps him to come to terms with the self; to form ideas and to reappear with a plan for action; to act in accordance with that plan upon the material environment and upon other men: the destiny of man. This would be granted by a space of seclusion, of solitude, of retreat. And its absence in contemporary architecture uncovers the almost tragic truth that while man learned to master the art of building he forgot the art of living.

* This and the following statements are based on the philosophy of Ortega y Gasset (see Bibliography).

PLATE 61: Site enclosure. It is the fence between public life and private life, between exposed world and secluded world.

PLATE 62: Front garden. It is the preparatory space for the unification of man and house.

PLATE 63: City-residence entrance. Even under limited site conditions, a small front garden is considered a minimum requirement in order to bridge the gap between the "out" and the "in."

PLATE 64: Family entrance (left) and official entrance hall (right). In order to visibly manifest the esteem for the visitor, frequently the entrance hall, *genkan*, is projected—a remnant of feudal days.

PLATE 65: Interior of entrance hall. Here the separation from the "outer" world takes place.

PLATES 66–67: Welcome. The proper greeting of the visitor is an important function of cultured living.

PLATE 68: Ante room. Here host and guest meet and exchange courtesies.

PLATES 70–73: Indoor life. The *tatami* is the universal platform for indoor living—for work, leisure, art, entertainment. It is the key for understanding the organism of the Japanese house.

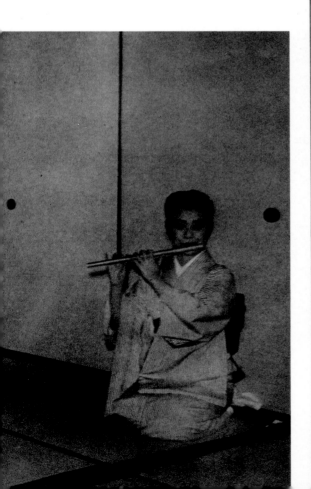

PLATE 74: Predecessor of the *tokonoma*. This section from a picture scroll depicts a niche (upper right) with scripts and a flower vase in front.

PLATES 76–77: Picture recess, *tokonoma*. It is the place where heaven, nature, art, and man meet.

PLATES 78–79: The *tokonoma* in *sukiya* style. In spite of the standardization of the *tokonoma*, personal taste and ingenuity can manifest itself in new design forms.

PLATE 80: The veranda of the warrior residence.
It served both domestic and official functions.

PLATES 81–82: Veranda. It is the space that mediates between the contrasts of the "out" and the "in." It is the space that affords both work and leisure out of doors in the midst of the garden.

PLATES 83–84: Indoor-outdoor relationship. The garden enriches indoor living. It is the "picture wall" of the interior space.

PLATES 85–87: Indoor-outdoor relationship. Complete control of both interior and exterior spaces allows openness without infringing upon the feeling of being "in."

PLATES 88–89: The study place, *shoin*. It was originally a feature of the Buddhist priest's residence, a projected bay window with enough light and seclusion for contemplating, studying, and writing.

PLATES 90–92: Steps to the garden. The break between house and garden is distinct, yet, often a mediating stage is interpositioned.

PLATES 93–94: House front from the garden. The narrowness of the ordinary garden permits only a partial view of both the house and the garden.

PLATE 95: Walkway. While the ordinary residential garden is but an object to be seen and not to be walked through, larger gardens have carefully planned walkways.

PLATE 96: Stone and water. The stone is the module of the garden design. Water, either symbolic or real, suggests the multiform and regenerating universe of Buddhist conception.

PLATES 97–99: Bridges. Though typical forms have evolved, bridges have always remained objects of creative design.

PLATES 100–101: Stone lavers. The *chōzu-bachi* is placed near the toilet, it being reached directly from the veranda. The *tsukubai* is in the midst of the garden and serves to purify, symbolically, the visitor on his way to the tearoom.

PLATE 102: Tearoom entrance. It symbolizes complete separation of man from worldly standards and concerns.

PLATE 103: Tearoom. It is the space of seclusion. A limited opening to the garden serves to establish the relationship between man's self and the universe.

PART THREE environment

geo-relationship
climate
philosophy
society

CHAPTER NINE geo-relationship

definition

GEO-RELATIONSHIP IN BUILDING is the geographic relationship between one architectural region and another. Closeness in this relationship has decisively influenced architectural growth, just as geographic isolation has affected architectural evolution.

GEO-RELATIONSHIP IN BUILDING is both state and quality of an architecture being influenced by another regional architecture. It manifests the interdependence of architectural development in regions that are in geographic-communicational contact.

GEO-RELATIONSHIP IN BUILDING, thus, is dependent on regional communication. It may assert itself through the migration of people with their entire cultural pattern, or through the importation of individual foreign ideas and cultural achievements.

GEO-RELATIONSHIP IN BUILDING asserts itself as both direct and indirect influence. Directly it is the adoption of architectural features; indirectly it is the introduction of foreign thought or custom, which will then be substantiated in building.

GEO-RELATIONSHIP IN BUILDING is an incentive for architectural development. In many great architectures of both the past and present, essential impulses have been received from abroad, and geographic proximity has often effected analogous development.

GEO-RELATIONSHIP IN BUILDING in the contemporary epoch has undergone decisive change owing to communicational improvement between regions and continents. This change diminished its primary dependence on immediate neighborhood, but not its importance.

GEO-RELATIONSHIP IN BUILDING, though, is not only a result of geographic coincidence. Often politics are responsible for establishing intimate geo-relationship between geographically separated regions, just as they may also interrupt geo-relationship of neighboring regions.

GEO-RELATIONSHIP IN BUILDING, then, is an important factor of architectural growth. While in the past it depended on geographic closeness, modern communication has brought all regions into close geo-relationship with each other.

In the architectures of the past, geographic proximity of two cultural regions has often decisively affected architectural development of one or both of them. For not only have "spiritual goods" such as religion and philosophy of one cultural region exerted their influence on life, thought, and action of the other, but "architectural goods" such as constructional techniques, symbolic-idealistic forms, productional methods, decorative devices, and even entire systems of dwelling have also frequently been adopted from another region and incorporated into the existing native culture.

The fundamental role of geo-relationship in building is unmistakably evidenced in the growth of Western architecture from ancient times to the present. There is no doubt that without this geographic possibility of close exchange between Greece and Rome in ancient times, between Italy, France, Germany, and England in the Middle Ages, between France, Belgium, Holland, Germany, and Austria in the Modern Age neither Western architecture nor its culture as a whole would have developed to a level and variety that is unparalleled in all the world. In contrast, regions in geographic isolation both spiritually and architecturally have been steady in their cultural growth and exempt from the violent eruptions and abrupt changes that the contact and exchange with other cultural patterns produces. Once a certain cultural level was achieved, these isolated regions remained nearly immobile until Western technology conquered and "annihilated" their geographic isolation and more or less brought all countries into close geo-relationship. Indeed, it was this change in geo-relationship that upset the existing international balance and greatly disturbed the contemporary political scene, as the rise of new world powers in Asia exemplifies.

This improvement in interregional communication has provoked revolutionary changes in countries that until recently possessed a unique but relatively static culture spiritually, socially, and physically, and has accelerated development in all fields of life, art, and science throughout the world. This is especially true in regard to Asian regions which, though previously engaged in some cultural exchange among themselves, are now experiencing basic changes in their patterns of culture and life. On the other hand, the West is now for the first time able to perceive the Orient other than through the perspective of the occasional and casual traveler; indeed, only since the beginning of the 20th century has Western culture received important stimuli from the Far East.

In the case of Japan, geo-relationship has been a decisive factor in the nation's growth. And this to a degree that permits this conclusion: without Japan's particular geographic locality, the course of events would have differed essentially. This, however, may hold true for the cultural development of any European region, as Japanese scholars emphatically point out. However, Japan is indebted to both China and the West not only for the stimuli that eventually provoked genuine creations, but also for a good deal of creations per se that became content and essence for her own form of life and thought. Nevertheless, the contemptuous opinion of many foreigners that the traditional Japanese culture is but a branch of the Chinese is erroneous, as is also the eulogistic assertion in so many books by Japanese authors that Japanese culture is thoroughly Japanese. Some cultural achievements of China as well as of the West were taken over unmodified just as others were developed independently within the country without the least aid from abroad.

This unique trait in Japanese culture is in direct affinity to Japan's geo-relationship. For, owing to her closeness to the Chinese mainland and Korea, knowledge of the cultural achievements of the continent could easily be gained, but, conversely, owing to her insular location, it was also easy to shut off the whole nation from any external communication. Both features of Japan's geo-relationship have been decisive factors throughout her history, culturally and politically, and knowledge thereof becomes imperative for an evaluation of the Japanese achievement in both art and architecture.

racial migration

Architectural creation is in essence one form of comprehending the reality of environment. The resulting architecture, then, is a substance that both mirrors and enriches this reality. Consequently, the quality of any architectural work can be fairly well measured by the degree to which environmental reality has been met and how greatly it has been enriched. It follows then that for both contemporary creation and historical evaluation of architecture, attempt must be made to comprehend the reality of time and locality in which the particular architecture was, or is to be, created. This becomes more difficult the farther the observer is separated in time and locality from his object. If Japanese residential architecture of the 17th and 18th centuries is viewed with a mind geared only to the Western reality of the 20th century, it must necessarily lead to misinterpretations. This can be evidenced in many recent comments by Western writers who indiscriminately identify external similarities between Japanese and contemporary architecture as the result of an analogous or even identical conception toward architecture.

One misconception concerns the origin and meaning of the elevated floor of the Japanese house raised on stilts. Here, allegations run as far as to identify this particular feature with the contemporary "piloti," i.e., a system of exposed supports that raises the building shell above the ground a full story high. The purpose of the "piloti" is not only to provide additional sheltered space for the users of the building but also to allocate private space for public use, i.e., to combine practicality with morality. In this respect, the "piloti" differs basically from the structure that raises the Japanese floor above grade. Although the space underneath is occasionally used for storage of material or is occupied—though without consent of the house master—by all sorts of unwanted animals, the reason for general use of the elevated floor all over Japan seems to be its appropriateness for the prevalent damp ground condition.

This probability, however, does not permit the conclusion that the high-floored dwelling had developed logically from the early pit dwelling, by way of the ground-level dwelling, as a realistic answer to environmental conditions, as is frequently assumed. Archeological evidence indicates that the high-floored dwelling and pit dwelling (the ground-level dwelling is a variation of the latter) did exist side by side, and that they were essentially different in their constructional system and practical qualities, even in their general purpose and interior organization (Plates 108–112). Also, the fact that the constructional system of the high-floored dwelling was by far more susceptible to the seasonal typhoons than that of the pit dwelling clearly contradicts the widespread misconception that the high-floored dwelling represented a realistic and novel response to prevailing environmental conditions (Figure 33). Moreover, the high-floored dwelling actually gave far less protection against cold than the pit dwelling in a climate where the winter, though relatively mild, is still in large parts of Japan very cold and snowy. Indeed, all these factors must raise doubts as to the realistic attitude that allegedly caused the elevation of the floor above the ground.

Instead, all evidence suggests that the high-floored type of dwelling was a building form characteristic of warmer areas with fewer or no typhoons, probably southeast Asia. It is likely that this dwelling system reached the Japanese islands in prehistoric times along with the migration of southern people, and distinct characteristics of Japanese racial features would indicate that these people must have migrated either directly or indirectly from Polynesia, Malaya, Indonesia, the Philippines, or south China. This assumption gains probability from the fact that by contrast the pit dwelling in many respects manifests appropriateness for local environment. Being realistic in the response to environmental conditions, it remained fairly unaffected by the evolution of the high-floored dwelling. It was the dwelling type of the farmers and general public exclusively until, in comparatively recent times, it incorporated features from the high-floored dwelling, the residential system of the nobility.

True, there may be room for question in these theories, but the particular features of the high-floored dwelling clearly indicate that this form originally belonged to a different geographic-climatic region. There is no evidence throughout the centuries that this prehistoric system of dwelling was realistically re-created in full compliance with Japanese environment, either climatically or constructionally. Though a refined adaptation to Japan's locality took place in the smaller details of the dwelling, and features were elaborated to high standards, the high-floored dwelling never quite lost its unrealistic character. This fact strongly suggests that the essential form of the common Japanese residence of the 17th and 18th centuries owes its existence to migration of a people from the southern parts of Asia, i.e., to accidental chance rather than intentional creation.

While such reasoning appears to have but significance for measuring the absolute value of Japanese residential architecture, i.e., an inherent value without direct relationship to the present, it still contains valuable information for the contemporary approach to architecture. Certainly, the basic inappropriateness of the high-floored dwelling for the Japanese environment is evidence of the Japanese inability to transcend the forms of custom and inheritance. It shows that even a people as sensitive toward their environment as the Japanese did not realize, in their subjective state of mind, the basic and primary demands of environment. These facts may call attention to the likelihood that contemporary architecture everywhere is also strongly guided by principles of the past—principles that are simply accepted as universal truth and are hardly ever examined as to whether they still constitute a realistic answer to contemporary conditions and their problems. It follows that origins and causes of architectural form are not finite, but must be continuously investigated.

Also, investigation into the racial origins of a nation may shed light on the backgrounds of architectural features, even though conclusions will be frequently based on assumptions. In the Japanese case such investigation lends support to the theory that the high-floored residential prototype was of southern origin, because the Japanese show characteristics of southern races such as Malayan, Polynesian, and South Chinese. It also confirms the likelihood of the pit dwelling's northern background by the existence of distinct Mongolian features in the Japanese race. There is also a Caucasian element existent, stemming from the Ainu, who seem to have been the earliest inhabitants of Japan and were once scattered over the entire archipelago. Yet, their dwelling form seems to have had hardly any influence on the evolution of the Japanese residence. While in continuous warfare with the newly arriving races, the Ainus were largely absorbed, and only as small groups have survived, fairly unmingled, in the northern island of Hokkaido. There is no archeological evidence as to whether those two racial elements from south and north arrived separately and at different times, or whether they reached the islands already as a mixed group from a common center of the Asiatic continent. The earliest findings in Japanese soil indicate only that there already was a unique culture throughout Japan long before the Christian era.

Architecturally, however, the two different dwelling forms of north and south maintained their independent existence for a long time; the pit dwelling in the two forms of the farmhouse and the house of the early common citizens (both almost stagnant, with the floor gradually being raised above ground), the high-floored dwelling in the form of the aristocratic mansion. Only much later did both types exert influence on each other and produce the noted residence of the commoners in the 17th and 18th centuries. Although this residence appears to have sprung from the aristocratic mansion by way of the merchant house, there are many features incorporated therein, both spiritual and physical, which were derived from the Buddhist priest's abode as well as from the early farmhouse and primitive citizen dwelling.

Thus, the ancestry of the Japanese residence shows a direct affinity between racial migration and cultural pattern, which not only confirms theories based on archeological findings, but also sheds light on cause and motive of certain features of the Japanese residence and permits judgment as to their architectural value. Since these migrations took place at a time of most primitive communicational means, direct geo-relationship to the region of origin was prerequisite. Its earliest architectural product, the high-floored dwelling, has essentially influenced all successive developments of the Japanese residence and delivers a convincing example of the importance of geo-relationship in building.

closeness to the continent

On the other hand, the importance of geo-relationship not only for Japan's architecture but for her culture as a whole can be evidenced even more by the cultural contact that Japan, owing to her proximity to the Asiatic continent, was able to maintain with China. This contact was so intimate, continuous, and decisive that without it the present Japanese cultural-political evolution, as it stands, is unthinkable.

The extent and depth of this cultural dependence has always been the subject of argument and one-sided interpretation. For a long time ignorant Western writers and self-conscious Chinese scholars considered Japanese culture merely a branch of the Chinese. However, since the beginning of the 20th century there has been an increasing tendency of writers on Japan to either stress the independence of Japanese culture or to minimize the essential impact of foreign influence by making analogies to the various culture transfers that have taken place in the Western world, such as from Crete to Greece, from Greece to Rome, from Rome to Middle Europe.

However, these transfers differ basically from the Japanese case. In the West the cultural achievement of one region, when adopted by the other, was but an incentive that caused a sequence of chain reactions that produced something essentially new, surpassing and transcending the foreign impulse. Unlike that of the Japanese, the culture of medieval European countries was not borrowed, but was inherited in direct succession from antiquity. Except for interruption due to war or pestilence, intellectual and cultural development of Western Europe was continuous, and for this the intimate geo-relationship, supported by a common language of the educated classes, Latin, was decisively instrumental. The particular geo-relationship enabled the rising Humanism to benefit directly and profoundly from the ancient sources such as the Greek, Roman, Byzantine, Hebrew, and Arabian; it made any individual discovery in the sciences simultaneously available to the entire Western civilization; it stimulated competition among the nationalities for the benefit of all.

This cultural evolution differs essentially from the Japanese. Owing to her particular geo-relationship to the Asian continent, Japan could seize cultural achievements only from the almost static culture of China. Of course, among these were also elements from other cultural regions, but they had already been transformed or at least modified by passing through China. While this was an accidental circumstance that could not be helped, the Japanese attitude toward foreign influence differs essentially in two aspects from that of medieval European nations. The first difference is that throughout her history Japan has adopted entire social institutions and cultural achievements intact from abroad. The second and even more decisive and characteristic difference is that the Japanese, in their multiple borrowings from China, most frequently failed to adopt the spiritual essence or intellectual basis in which those cultural products were rooted.

Thus, Chinese forms, rather than the more intangible sources of these forms, were adopted unmodified; they were copied. As they were disassociated from their original and true meaning, these imports could so easily be adapted and transformed to suit the different physical and psychological environment. However, they could hardly set the spark for something essentially new and progressive, which in return would have been of benefit to that culture from which the impulse had come. Yet, for the same reason, they also did not affect, even less transform, the very core of the Japanese soul. While cultural importation in Western countries provided the basis for something new, cultural importation in Japan remained, always and only, a subject of transformation and transmutation that eventually left only the name in common with its original state. Although in the case of architecture, an adopted feature very often reached a perfection it never possessed in the country of its origin, there is hardly evidence that it incited Japanese ambition to pioneer beyond the existing and to transcend by creative efforts the already given scope, to become contributive instead of consumptive.

These foreign imports, coming from China as long as immediate geo-relationship was dominant, but from Europe after technology "annihilated" geographic distances, encompass all phases of life: the arts, social institutions, moral standards and manners of living, educational systems, writing and language, technique and industry, the military, and, of course, architecture. Since architecture itself also reflects all the other aspects of life, it is obvious that the Chinese influence upon Japanese architecture took place in many ways and through many forms. Least affected by this influence was the residential architecture of the common people, the farmers and the general public, because here bitter poverty excluded any deviation from traditional methods, unless such measures provided immediate economical advantage or, at bottom, did not produce disadvantage. More so than the residential architecture of the nobility and the military, the anonymous architecture of the masses maintained its essential integrity. Only after the rise of the wealthy citizen class, the *chōnin,* which coincided with the adoption of the style of official architecture by the architecture of the common people, did essential elements from the Chinese continent, though already Japanized, come to characterize also the residences of the commoners.

There is no definite knowledge as to when cultural contact with China first began, yet the long sequence of continuous and substantial adoption of Chinese culture actually started in the 7th and 8th centuries, when Buddhist scholars on their return from China introduced not only Chinese writing but also cultural institutions in their entirety. Thus, Japan's government was administratively centralized as in the Chinese system, and a social order was set up according to the civil code *Taihō-ritsuryō,* by name, the "code of the great treasure," which was a copy of the Chinese civil code. Architecturally this code is of importance insofar as it contains volumes on city organization and measure systems and also notes on individual city dwellings. Yet, more concrete evidence as to the extent of Chinese influence in this sphere is given by the fact that the entire Japanese capital of Nara, laid out in 710, was a model of the Chinese capital at Hsi-an with its characteristic street pattern in relationship to the Imperial Palace (Figures 111–112). Moreover, it is very probable that the Imperial Palace itself and the mansions of the nobility were to a large extent patterned after Chinese models. Indeed, the first residential style of the aristocracy, as evolved in the 10th and 11th centuries, the *shinden-zukuri* (literally, sleeping-hall style), must have been entirely, or at least partially, of Chinese origin (Plates 119–120).

This style, the main feature of which was the organization of individual halls around a central main hall with interconnection through corridors, eventually lost its rigid symmetry and transformed into another residential style, the *shoin-zukuri* (literally, study-bay style) (Plates 121–122). Yet, even the latter can hardly be called a genuine Japanese achievement, for some of its distinctive features, such as picture recess, *tokonoma,* and study-bay, *shoin,* were taken from the Zen Buddhist priest's house, which was itself traditionally patterned after Chinese scripts. And along with them went a number of Chinese details such as the curved roof, the roof tiles, the portable screen that eventually was transformed into sliding panels, plus many others. They all were modified in the course of decades and centuries and frequently retained their original meaning only by name. Yet, they never essentially transcended the scope of their original theme, even less set the basis for fundamental progress either in technique or in feature.

Tea drinking, both its esteem and its seed, had also originated in China, but the tea drinking as a cult was thoroughly Japanese. Under its influence, the native Japanese element also became dominant in the aristocratic residences. This development was in close affinity with the incorporation of the farmhouse simplicity into plan and detail of the warrior houses. Temporary political break of all communication with the Chinese mainland then helped this native element grow, undisturbed by foreign influence. Aided by the simultaneous decline of the rank distinction of the feudal society, this isolation fostered the exchange of form and idea between the building styles of the various social classes within Japan. The result was the emergence of a new residential type that incorporated and coordinated all the multiple influences and counterinfluences: the dwelling of the ordinary citizen.

The specifics of all these influences from abroad and from within are a matter of historical concern and are of less importance than the general realization that Japan's geo-relationship to a continent with a permanently advanced civilization had brought her cultural growth in very close affinity to that of China. Yet, while other nations might have very easily been overwhelmed and basically transformed by the impact and strength of such a superior civilization, the Japanese could maintain their identity owing to a particular racial distinction of a hard center element non-adaptive to, and unaffected by, influence from the outside. It is because of this impenetrable core that Japanese culture, in spite of its great intellectual and spiritual debts to the successive Chinese dynasties of Han, T'ang, Sung, and Ming, can be called essentially Japanese.

insular isolation

While closeness to the Chinese continent is a feature of Japan's geo-relationship, the importance of which in her cultural evolution can hardly be exaggerated, another peculiarity of her geo-relationship, her insularity, was a circumstance of no less far-reaching consequences. Not only did it essentially help the Japanese to remain free from any conquest and domination, which inevitably results in successive imprints of alien patterns upon the native, but it also allowed the Japanese rulers to control the flow of foreign influences at will.

Thus, from about the beginning of the 17th century, at a time when many popular uprisings began to shake the absolute power of the feudal system, the exclusionists among the military dictatorship of the Tokugawa family gradually gained strength for their policy by associating uprisings with influence from abroad, especially from Europe. By the middle of the century the country was virtually sealed off from all contact with the outside world, both China and the West. Only a small group of Dutch and Chinese traders was allowed to stay in confines at Nagasaki. No Japanese was allowed to leave the country; the mere attempt to do so meant a certain death penalty.

This self-inflicted isolation of Japan, which was to last more than two hundred years, was of immense significance for the nation as a whole. Before, there was great cultural activity by obtaining and utilizing wealth from abroad. Yet, when cut off not only from China's static culture but also from Europe's new and dynamic source of learning, the creative instinct of the Japanese, maybe for the first time in history, had to rely only upon itself; and it is significant to note that there evolved in that period but elaborations, refinements, and interplacements of what had been created before.

This isolation affected Japan's cultural development also in another respect. In the West the Renaissance was prompted, to no small degree, through foreign trade and through the subsequent wealth that accumulated in those countries, but Japanese economy, already in transfer from an agricultural to a mercantile system, was isolated from foreign trade and could not improve its low standards. Therefore, it was also incapable of providing the material means for cultural growth.

All measures taken by the military rulers were directed to arrest rather than stimulate progress, to conserve rather than to fully use resources, and to reduce rather than to expand society in terms of population, trade, or art. Naturally, residential architecture was also decisively affected by those measures, both in its physique and in its development; and it is certain that the noted Japanese "economy in matter and spirit" that is commonly ascribed to a voluntary choice of the Japanese owes much to this socio-economic situation as brought about by Japan's isolation.

Also directly Japan's insularity had distinct implications for architecture throughout history, as became particularly evident during her long period of political seclusion from the rest of the world. Since the new and different was no longer provided from the foreign country, each individual class of the feudalistic society looked to the other classes for novelty and inspiration. Thus, to a varying degree, architectural features were exchanged between the ecclesiastic, aristocratic, and popular architectures, and architectural forms and devices that originally had characterized the building of but one class began to appear in the buildings of all the others. It is for this reason that there is in Japanese architecture no morphological distinction between dwelling, palace, shrine, and temple.

Before severing all contacts with the outside world, the Japanese had never really been impelled to employ their own inventive genius. Thus, when they lapsed into isolation, they turned their interest upon the existing. With all strata of society—the nobles, warriors, priests, merchants, farmers, and townspeople—living in close proximity, it was only natural that an enormous exchange took place between the differing cultural patterns of the various classes, both in thought and in form. It is, therefore, not too farfetched to assume that the evolution and refinement of the Japanese residence during those years is in no small part a product of Japan's insularity, which brought together the architectural achievements of the aristocracy, clergy, and commoner.

The Japanese trait of adopting from Chinese culture form rather than content, as mentioned earlier, is also very much connected with Japan's insular geo-relationship to the Asian continent. Though both countries were actually in very close geographic proximity, the sea between them prevented immediate intercommunication. Therefore, the Japanese could not directly pattern their copies after the Chinese originals themselves, but only after descriptions of these prototypes. And these descriptions were in a language which not only was not their own, but which also could not be translated due to the fact that the Japanese did not at that time possess a system of writing based on their own native language. It is, therefore, not astonishing that most of the Chinese cultural imports reached Japan in form only and without the very content that had produced that form.

A further architectural effect of Japan's insular geo-relationship that became apparent during her self-willed isolation was the necessity to economize and ration her own products. Of course, necessity is said to be the mother of invention, but it is also true that where means are lacking the inventive spirit can be fatally handicapped. Moreover, many of the great discoveries of mankind were due to the grace of accident, perhaps during the leisurely hours of a gifted rich man or during the studies of a well-patronized explorer, yet without the presence of necessity. A great part of Western culture was made possible only through the sponsorship of the rich nobility, i.e., through material wealth, but Japan, isolated from the outside world, was confined to her own resources, which were not such as to produce wealth. The only architectural virtues that could spring from such a state of affairs were those of economizing, rationing, and standardizing, which presupposed an exact and comprehensive planning and a tight control of the entire economy, including building activity. In this respect, no doubt the Japanese have gained mastership.

The reasons for the comprehensive order in Japan's residential architecture were not an inbred sense for organization of social building on the part of the Japanese or an inherent grasp of the ethical value in economical building; even less did they represent an innate awareness of the beauty in a coordinated and harmonized architecture. Rather, this unique physical order in building was due to the environmental pressure of insularity and of political isolation that left the Japanese no choice but to rigidly control consumption and application of existing resources and to avoid any essential change that could upset the precious balance established to safeguard a social order in which the nobles and warriors were supreme. As such, the motivations behind the comprehensive physical order in Japanese residential building are of essentially different nature than those behind the contemporary attempt to subject all building activity to universal principles and to set up regional planning committees that would coordinate the multiple concerns of building in an industrial society.

imitation

In tracing back the cause and motivation of Japanese cultural evolution from early history until modern times, including Japan's miraculous emergence as a modern world power, it is apparent that adoption and absorption of foreign cultural achievements is a distinct feature of Japanese evolution. This distinction has given rise to the general opinion that in the present, as in the past, the Japanese have continuously imitated and copied advanced civilizations and that most, if not all, of their cultural achievements have in fact originated elsewhere.

As unimportant as the question of "authorship" appears for the evaluation of a past architecture, if "imitation" was the essential requisite by which Japan was able to benefit from the combined achievements of advanced societies, and if it was the distinctive method by which Japan within only one generation could transform a medieval society into a modern nation that could even challenge the leading industrial and military power of the world, then, indeed, the discussion of imitation becomes important insofar as it should provide answers as to how to transform other underdeveloped areas with equal rapidity into self-sufficient organisms that will enjoy similarly high living standards and that may even become contributive to the family of nations.

That is to say, if "imitation" is measured by the role it played in Japanese cultural evolution, transforming primitive Japan into Japan of the early and later feudal ages and then into Japan of the 20th century, such practice must definitely be commended rather than frowned upon as is usually done. Already in 1903 Sidney L. Gulick had realized that a nation able to discriminate and to adopt certainly must have an advantage over nations that are so wrapped up in self-content and self-conviction as to not see what else in the world is good, advantageous, and worth imitating.

A comparison with the development of other nations, however, shows that though imitation was the method employed, an inherent instinct of discriminating between the suitable and unsuitable, combined with an intuitive gift for adapting foreign products to the native situation, was in fact the decisive and distinct Japanese qualitiy that made these "imitations" produce results that no other nation past or present has been able to do. Unquestionably, modern Japan owes as much to the cultures of the West (and she continues to adopt achievements of science and technique without inhibition or scruple) as she does to the Chinese and Korean cultures, which she imitated for more than a thousand years. However characteristic for the Japanese such multiple and comprehensive adoption of things foreign must appear, if the test of originality were given to any other nation, their tendency to adopt would no longer seem so characteristic. No European nation can claim that its art, method of writing, architecture, science, or even language, is its "own" by right of origination.

Not imitativeness, but intuitive discernment is the singular quality that characterizes Japanese evolution. And this gift manifested itself not only in material-technical adoptions from the continent but also, and with more profound effect, in the importation of religion and philosophy. Thus, the Japanese cultural evolution reveals distinctly that imitation of advanced societies, in the sense of adopting the progressive achievements of other civilizations, i.e., cultural exchange, is the most effective method for fostering progress to an enormous extent. It also leaves no doubt that the essential requisite for making such an exchange bear fruit is the power to discriminate between what is good and what is not.

for contemporary architecture

The distinctiveness of Japan's geographic locality, i.e., closeness to the Asiatic continent and insular isolation and, probably, maritime contact with the southeast Asian islands, has produced results that clearly show the importance of geo-relationship for the architectural development of Japan. Since this distinct situation existed without human wish or intent, the effects of geo-relationship in building are accidental in nature. However, the Japanese example shows that this accidental state does not necessarily procure architectural benefits. It shows, rather, that it is but a potential that, only if exploited thoroughly, can become a tremendous stimulus for architectural progress. A comparison with other nations in similar geo-relationship demonstrates that in the case of Japan the architectural benefit gained by this geo-relationship was no longer accidental or inevitable, but was a very conscious act of cultural policy, which in a good architectural sense made use of a given situation.

Of course, since geo-relationship is essentially dependent upon actual distance and its conquest through communication, the nature of geo-relationship in building underwent decisive changes with the "annihilation of distance" by modern technology. Owing to improved transportation and communication, goods both in material and in thought are available everywhere in the world, and any technological progress serves all countries at the same time. However, this shift has, in fact, only widened the range of possibilities while leaving architectural exploitation of them up to the far-sightedness and insight of the nation. Japanese residential architecture not only proves, by its positive achievements, the high standards to which architecture can develop through borrowing from other architectural regions, but also clearly shows, by certain negative results, that for such cultural adoption comprehension of essence is more important than mere imitation of form.

In contemporary competitive society it is a necessity to expand geo-relationship in building by investigation and study of foreign trends and developments in architecture. The unparalleled rise of Japan from medieval society to an industrialized nation within seventy to eighty years (a process by no means yet completed), the emergence of the Soviet Union as a first-rank military and scientific power within less than forty years, and, last but not least, the fabulous social, industrial, and philosophical transformations that are taking place within China show how immense the benefit of such scientific-cultural interchange can be. This broad sense of applied geo-relationship necessarily will bring enormous advancement in architecture due to the combined mental contributions of the nations. The success in each individual case, however, will continue to depend on the ability to realize and decide which of the foreign goods, both material and spiritual, are contributive to a nation's own development. In this respect the Japanese have throughout history proved themselves as unrivaled masters in that they retained only those foreign institutions and achievements that suited their own society and rejected those that were not likely to conform to their own way of living and thinking.

Yet, direct geo-relationship, i.e., the immediate proximity of architectural regions with distinct characteristics, will also continue to remain a stimulating factor of contemporary architectural creation. There are signs that the lasting presence of regionalism in building is due not only to climate, geology, topography, material, socio-economic structure, academic orientation, or tradition of locality but also to the geo-relationship to another architectural region with its particular features. Thus, without doubt a distinct Japanese influence is visible in the architecture of Hawaii and of the American West Coast; in contemporary southern France a distinct North African influence is evident; and many motives of contemporary architecture in the southwest United States have been taken from her Mexican neighbor. The rise of the "new architecture" in the Middle European countries at the end of the 19th century provides an even more striking example of how decisively the factor of geo-relationship can influence the course of architecture.

The architectural utilization of geo-relationship by the Japanese bears a lesson for the contemporary in still another sense. For, since form rather than content was imported, in many instances the Japanese failed to realize the fundamental factors that underlie creation of form in general. Consequently they often did not succeed in freeing themselves from the form itself, whether it was that of custom, tradition, construction, or ornament. Even less were they able to re-enact it creatively by themselves. Contemporary Western architecture has also not remained free from such a trend. For example, in the United States not only do the traditional European styles still exert their influence, but, even more important, the whole of society everywhere is encumbered by concepts, ideas, and traditions of the past that obscure recognition of reality and obstruct substantiation of reality, both recognition and substantiation of reality having but one identification in English, realization. Knowledge of precedence, not comprehension of reality, characterizes residential design today, on the part of both patron and architect, and it is for this reason that the motivation and causation behind the many features, concepts, and devices that are commonly taken for granted must be continuously re-investigated, both for appraisal of the past and for creation in the present.

The realization of the enormous potential of geo-relationship for architectural growth, as evidenced in the evolution of the Japanese dwelling, makes it imperative to think and work on an international level. The purpose is the utilization of man's architectural accomplishments the world over, and this can be done by means of evaluating research, combining efforts, assimilating education, and coordinating programs. Yet, in order to make such an undertaking efficient, an international body that would guarantee a comprehensive coverage of all progressive thought, a complete exhaustion of all potentialities, and an optimum range of their dissemination is needed. It would function as an incentive to inventive research, as a means for testing new ideas, as a sponsor of promising projects, and as a catalyst for architectural growth.

Such an attempt has already been made in international organizations such as UNESCO (United Nations Educational, Scientific, and Cultural Organization) and, especially, CIAM (Congrès International d'Architecture Moderne). The latter has for more than thirty years accomplished substantial work in this area both practically and theoretically. Still, there is much lethargy within each separate nation, in her politicians, her architects, and her people, and much of her rich achievements have remained unused or even unnoticed by others.

In view of the rapidly increasing world population and the extreme difference of living standards between the nations, both of which are the hidden agents for political tensions and actual warfare on the international scene, the exploitation of geo-relationship by means of the internationalization of research is not a mere economic advantage but a moral and ethical necessity. The effects of Japanese geo-relationship convincingly demonstrate the importance of international exchange for building and may provide valuable material for judgment of the potential of international collaboration in building.

CHAPTER TEN **climate**

definition

CLIMATE IN BUILDING is the architectural response to the particular local weather condition. It is man's measure to adapt house to the prevailing climatic environment.

CLIMATE IN BUILDING, therefore, reveals man's insight into his environment. Through awareness of climatic characteristics and by intelligent countermeasures man made the first step toward utilization of natural forces.

CLIMATE IN BUILDING was the earliest agent in the formation of architecture, for the first shelters were constructed to protect human life against the forces of nature and were therefore essentially a response to climatic pressures.

CLIMATE IN BUILDING is closely related to construction techniques. Certain climatic characteristics dictate distinct constructional measures and thereby become cause and source of form in building.

CLIMATE IN BUILDING reflects man's sensitivity toward environment. While in the early forms of shelter man separated himself from the climatic environment, in the contemporary house he seeks to integrate climate into the house interior.

CLIMATE IN BUILDING is most apparent in areas with extreme climates, for it is the extreme form of climate, and not the mild form, which impairs man's existence and therefore exerts compelling pressures upon architecture.

CLIMATE IN BUILDING is not only directly formative. It also influences the house indirectly. For climate either fosters or hinders the growth of certain natural materials. Climate also molds the manners of living and it even tempers man's mentality.

CLIMATE IN BUILDING, then, is an important factor of architectural creation. While family is the causation of early building, climate supplied the motivation for the beginning of architecture.

It appears to be the accepted procedure to begin a treatise on Japan's architecture with general notes on her climatic and geological characteristics, presumably in order to help the layman on Japanese architecture achieve a better understanding of an architecture so different from the Western. This procedure, however, has only added to the many misconceptions that already exist about Japanese architecture. For although some features of the Japanese residence have been shaped by climatic-geological circumstances, actually the neglect of many of these environmental pressures in the house structure far outweighs the positive responses to them. Therefore, it seems appropriate to present the house–climate relationship after the main elements of the Japanese residence have already been analyzed so that the reader will be capable of judging for himself the alleged "climatic nature" of the Japanese house.

Japan's climate has many particular features, and writers on Japanese architecture in one way or another have succeeded in relating them to the various characteristics of the Japanese residence, closing their arguments with the statement that the Japanese house is a very realistic response to climatic environment. Taking for granted that the value of architecture can be measured in one sense by the degree to which the particular conditions of its environment are coped with, Japanese architecture would fall very short of the mark, for among all the extremes of Japanese climate it is just the most dangerous ones that have not found any architectural response at all. This fact must raise doubts as to whether the architectural precautions against other and less extreme features of the local climate have really sprung from a realization of the environment. For it is unlikely that the Japanese, if they wanted to protect themselves against the adversities of nature, would have preferred to fight only some of the minor ones while submitting themselves to the major ones.

Therefore, a comprehensive knowledge of the local climate is prerequisite to any judgment of the realistic value of the Japanese house as far as coping with environmental conditions is concerned. In the following discussion about climate, Japan's topography and seismography (which in a strict sense are a part of Japanese geography) are included because their impact on architecture is of the same nature as that of the climate.

characteristics

Regional climate is primarily dependent on latitude and on relationship to seas and other continents and secondarily on topographical formation. Japan is an archipelago consisting of a main island, Honshu, two smaller islands, Shikoku and Kyushu, in the southwest, another island, Hokkaido in the north, and innumerous tiny islands spread in between and around these. Its main stretch is in a northeast-southwest direction, slightly curving toward the Asiatic mainland and coming close to it at both ends, in the southwest to Korea and in the northeast to Sakhalin (USSR). In between lies the Sea of Japan with Manchuria opposite. The southeast coast of the main island faces the Pacific Ocean, which leads into the beautiful Inland Sea, between the main island and the islands of Shikoku and Kyushu. The latitudinal range is from 27° to 45°30′ North, corresponding with the respective latitudes of Port Said (Egypt) and Milano (northern Italy), a remarkable range of difference for a country as small as Japan. Six-sevenths of the archipelago is hilly and mountainous, with the major mountain range following the northeast-southwest stretch of the islands.

Accordingly, Japan's climate is influenced by her closeness to the Asiatic mainland, by her contact with the Pacific Ocean, and by her exposure to a warm current, the Kuroshio (literally, black stream), from the south and also, at certain times, to a cold current from the north, the Oyashio (literally, parent stream). It could be expected that these strong influences would effect a climate unique to the whole of Japan. But both the great difference in latitude and a mountain range that separates those very opposed influences from the Asiatic continent and the Pacific Ocean have caused a variety of differing micro-climates that hardly permit generalizations to the degree usually employed. Of course, since the metropolis of Tokyo—now as in feudalistic days—functions as the dominant voice of Japan in all internal and external affairs, it is no wonder that the Western student inevitably concludes that the climate of Japan is unique, or, more exactly, that the climate of Tokyo is the climate of Japan. Although it is true that the political, scientific, and economic "climate" of Tokyo, as well as her cultural "climate" to a lesser degree, is valid for the rest of Japan, there is substantial proof that the meteorological climate of the different regions of Japan, even in the days of the most rigid feudalism, has gone its own way and so far has withstood the centralistic domination of Tokyo.

The weather during the cold season is determined mainly by the monsoons. Owing to the extreme cold in north China and east Siberia, the barometric pressure rises and cold air flows over all the Far Eastern countries. The air, being originally dry, absorbs much vapor from the Sea of Japan and, somewhat tempered, reaches the main part of Japan from the northwest. Rising over the mountain chains, it forms clouds, resulting in gloomy weather with heavy snow in all parts of Japan that face the Asiatic continent. Yet, because of extreme differences in latitude, the snow does not remain on the ground very long in the southern island, Kyushu, nor in the southern provinces of the main island, Honshu, as it does in the more northern provinces of

FIGURE 76: Map of Japan and neighboring lands.

Aomori, Akita, Niigata, Toyama, Ishikawa, and Fukui, and on the island of Hokkaido, where the snow reaches depths of more than 10 feet (3 m.) and covers the ground throughout the winter. The average temperature of Aomori, the northernmost prefecture of the main island, Honshu, during the winter months, for example, is the same as that of Chicago and Warsaw, while in central Hokkaido temperatures as low as −30° F (−35° C) are not uncommon.

Owing to the shielding influence of the central mountain chain, weather conditions in the half that faces the Pacific Ocean are essentially different. Usually fine weather prevails throughout the cold months and the humidity is the lowest of the year. This part of Japan is not only protected from the cold and wet winds from Asia but is also tempered by the Pacific Ocean with the warm equatorial current Kuroshio. Therefore, in contrast with the northwestern half of Japan, the southeast in general has very mild winters with much sunshine. However, the more northern provinces and especially the northern island of Hokkaido, including their Pacific shores, are under the influence of the Asiatic climate with overcast skies and heavy snowfall. Even Sendai and its vicinity, situated much further south on the Pacific Coast, has chilly winter months while in Tokyo, still further south, the temperature often falls several degrees below the freezing point. Osaka has very mild winters, but Kyoto, the ancient capital only 30 miles inland from Osaka, has an almost continental climate with a great range of temperatures. Kii Peninsula, with the city of Shionomisaki, has winter temperatures comparable to those of Marseilles or Geneva, while in the southern islands almost tropical climate prevails.

In the summer, temperatures in north China and Mongolia rise excessively, due to intense insolation and arid soil condition. The high-pressure zone of the cold season disappears and a low-pressure area builds up. Consequently, air flows in from all portions of the Far East. This system of air currents is the summer monsoon that blows over the Japanese archipelago mainly in a south-to-east direction. It is weak and intermittent compared to the forceful winter monsoon, in fact too weak to dispel the sultriness of the summer days or to effect a marked difference in climate on either side of the Japanese archipelago.

Neither does the great range in latitude make any particular difference in the height of summer. In the daytime the temperatures in Hokkaido rise as high as they do in Kyushu, yet remain that high for only a few hours. Thus, in August, the hottest month of the year, mean maximum and minimum temperatures in Sapporo (Hokkaido) are 79° and 61° F respectively (26° and 16° C), while in Kagoshima (Kyushu) they are 87° and 75° F (30.5° and 23.3° C). Osaka, much further north, has mean extreme temperatures of 90° and 74° F (32° and 23° C) and Tokyo, which is still further north, has mean maximum and minimum temperatures of 86° and 72° F (30° and 22° C), which are almost identical to the August mean temperatures of Kagoshima in the south. Contrary to continental climate, the hottest months have the highest humidity of the year (similar to New York). The summer, therefore, is most uncomfortable and unhealthy.

With fair regularity each summer, the Japanese experience a rainy season called *bai-u* (literally, plum rain) or *tsuyu*, which is so very important for a good rice crop. And yet, the wettest season is the winter. In the provinces facing the Sea of Japan snow falls almost every day and railway traffic is maintained only through mile-long "snow tunnels." The summer rainy season begins early in the second fortnight of June and continues for about four weeks. It is caused by the expansion of the Pacific high-pressure area toward the Japanese east coast, in the course of which it is cooled by the cold ocean current, Oyashio, which comes from the northeast. This cold air undercuts the warm air stratum over Japan and thus causes gloomy, rainy weather all over Japan with air almost at a standstill, because the low-pressure zones coming from the Yangtze Valley are halted by the high-pressure areas on traveling east. The amount of precipitation in this rainy season is not too heavy in spite of the fact that it lasts for a month or so. This is because most of it is in the form of a fine, drizzling

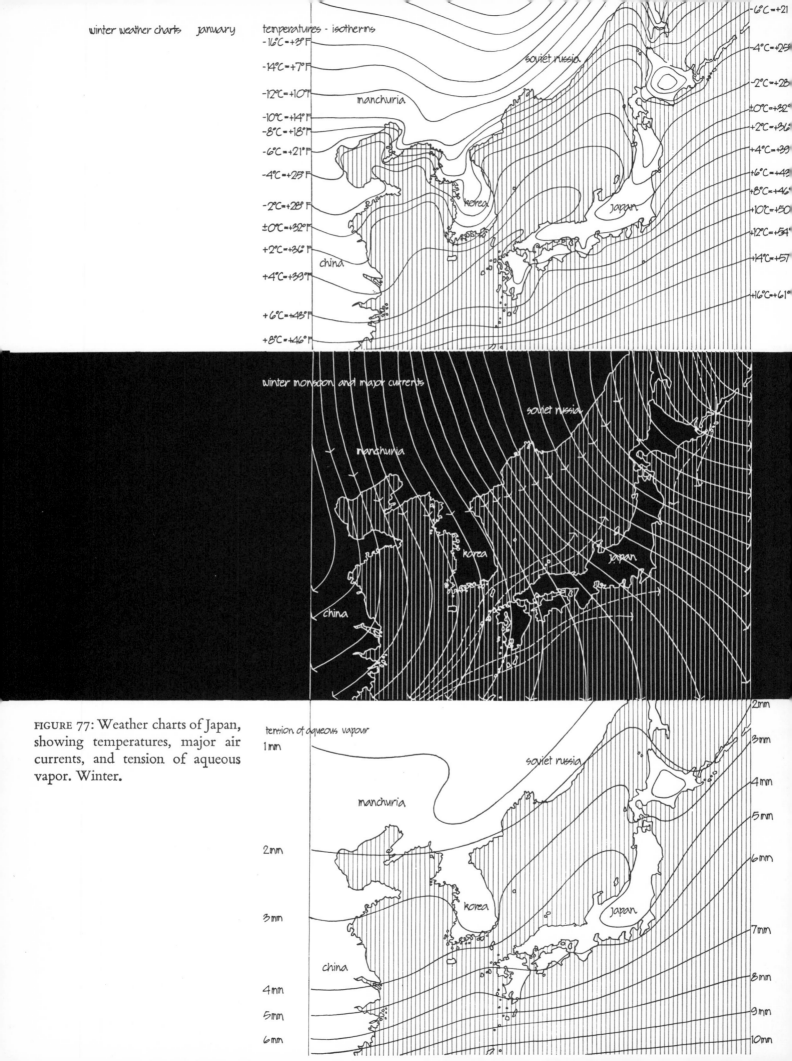

winter weather charts   january

temperatures - isotherms

-16°C=+3°F
-14°C=+7°F
-12°C=+10°F
-10°C=+14°F
-8°C=+18°F
-6°C=+21°F
-4°C=+25°F
-2°C=+28°F
±0°C=+32°F
+2°C=+36°F
+4°C=+39°F
+6°C=+43°F
+8°C=+46°F

-6°C=+21
-4°C=+25°
-2°C=+28°
±0°C=+32°
+2°C=+36°
+4°C=+39°
+6°C=+43°
+8°C=+46°
+10°C=+50°
+12°C=+54°
+14°C=+57°
+16°C=+61°

soviet russia

manchuria

korea

japan

china

winter monsoon and major currents

soviet russia

manchuria

korea

japan

china

FIGURE 77: Weather charts of Japan, showing temperatures, major air currents, and tension of aqueous vapor. Winter.

tension of aqueous vapour

1mm

2mm

3mm

4mm

5mm

6mm

2mm
3mm
4mm
5mm
6mm
7mm
8mm
9mm
10mm

soviet russia

manchuria

korea

japan

china

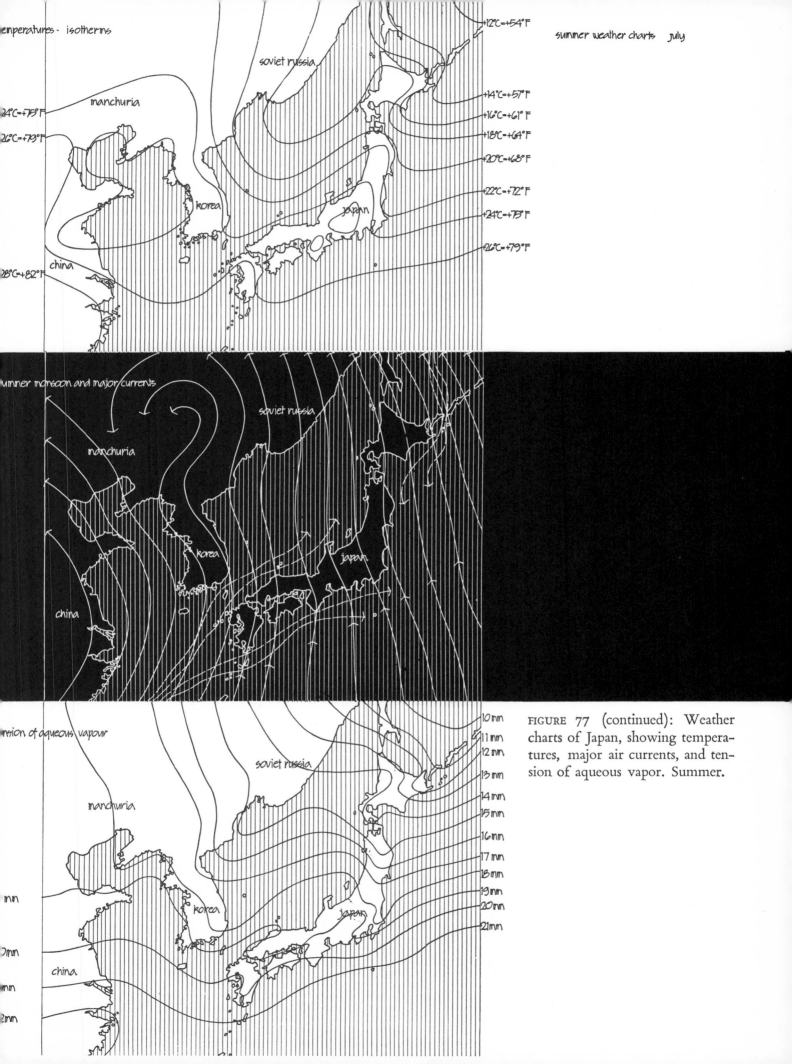

temperatures - isotherms

soviet russia

manchuria

+12°C=+54°F

+14°C=+57°F
+16°C=+61°F
+18°C=+64°F
+20°C=+68°F

24°C=+75°F

26°C=+79°F

korea

japan

+22°C=+72°F
+24°C=+75°F

+26°C=+79°F

china

28°C=+82°F

summer monsoon and major currents

soviet russia

manchuria

korea

japan

china

tension of aqueous vapour

soviet russia

manchuria

10 mm
11 mm
12 mm
13 mm
14 mm
15 mm
16 mm
17 mm
18 mm
19 mm
20 mm
21 mm

korea

japan

mm

china

mm

mm

mm

summer weather charts   july

FIGURE 77 (continued): Weather charts of Japan, showing temperatures, major air currents, and tension of aqueous vapor. Summer.

rain that does not necessarily fall every day. Still, the amount of annual rainfall is about two to three times as great as that of northern Europe and is a distinctive feature of the Japanese climate. Again, there are considerable local differences of precipitation within Japan herself, which is evident in the following comparative statistics of annual precipitation.

Hokkaido	(northernmost island)	1,000 mm.	39 in.
Tohoku	(northern part of main island)	1,000–1,500 mm.	39–59 in.
Tokaido	(middle part of main island)	1,500–2,000 mm.	59–79 in.
Kyushu	(southern island)	2,000–2,500 mm.	79–98 in.

Since architecture is likely to be influenced by the extreme rather than by the mild form of local climate, it would seem that a description of winter and summer would suffice when examining the climatic quality of the Japanese house. Yet, spring and autumn also have climatic extremes that must be included in the discussion. In the northern part of Japan these seasons are very short; snow covers the ground from the middle of November until the middle of April and often into May. Yet in the middle and southern sections of Japan the intermediate seasons are distinct and most pleasant owing to moderate temperatures and clear skies.

The period from late August until the middle of October, mainly the month of September, is the season for typhoons. Each year these destructive cyclones successively approach the Japanese archipelago from the south or southeast and roll over the islands in a north to northeast direction, with torrential rains, leaving devastation and death in their wake. The regularity of their annual recurrence and the inability of the Japanese to cope with their awesome impact, unmistakably contradicts the usual description of the Japanese climate as being moderate.

earthquakes

With similar power, yet with less regularity, Japan is haunted by earthquakes. Strictly speaking, earthquakes are not meteorological but are of geological nature. But since they afflict man and his buildings in a manner similar to that of the seasonal storms, they are, in an architectural sense, of the same environmental nature and are examined in connection with the Japanese climate.

Seismic shocks that range anywhere from harmless tremors to violent rockings that make buildings collapse visit the islands irregularly, but frequently. They strike without warning and not only damage buildings directly, but they also topple braziers and stoves, and, therefore, because of the high inflammability of the Japanese house, they are often the cause of conflagrations that lay entire city sections into ashes before they can be brought under control. The power of these seismic shocks differs locally and there are areas that seem to be entirely immune. How close to the surface this activity of the earth's interior must be is further evidenced by the existence of no less than approximately 190 volcanos (many of them still active, others newly erupting), of countless hot springs, and of many outlets for sulfide gases that, like safety valves, seem to relieve the tremendous powers that reside not too far underground in this part of the earth.

As the susceptibility to earthquakes varies locally, further differences are added to the regional distinctions of the Japanese climate, and the wide range in topographical elevation means differentiation of climate even within one region. Consequently, Japan must be termed a country, if not with distinct micro-climates, yet, one with greatly varying climatic conditions.

However, there are some distinct climatic features that have architectural significance for all, or at least the greater part, of Japan. If measured according to the severeness of their impact on architecture, i.e., as to whether they threaten the very existence of building or whether they affect only man's physical comfort, they must be listed in the following order of importance:

1. Seasonal typhoons, mainly in September, for all of Japan.
2. Irregular earthquakes, with areas of particular susceptibility.

3. Heavy precipitation throughout the year for all of Japan.
4. Heavy snowfall and severe cold in the regions facing the Asiatic continent, in the entire northern section, and in the higher altitudes during the winter months.
5. Humidity and heat for all of Japan during the summer months.
6. Fairly mild winters in the middle and southern parts of Japan that face the Pacific Ocean.

These features of Japanese climate and their respective architectural importances need to be borne in mind when considering the question of how realistically external forces have been perceived and how efficiently they have been met through building. For the primary criterion for judging a dwelling is the degree to which it shelters its inhabitants from the elements.

climatic architecture

The particular climate of a locale has always been one of the main forces for prompting an architecture with locally distinct features, a regional architecture. The marked difference in daily temperatures in the Mediterranean coastal region and India, the heavy snowfall in Scandinavia and the Alps, and the trade winds in the Pacific islands, all demanded counteracting architectural measures in order to protect human existence and to grant freedom of life within the home. Just how exactly this role of shelter is performed and how sensitively climatic change has been architecturally met, is one of the many scales for measuring quality of building. In other words, good architecture, both past and present, needs to be a climatic architecture, i.e., an architecture that either counteracts climate by basic measures and features or adapts itself to it.

Such an evaluation is difficult in Japanese residential architecture. Although it appears that some charcteristics of the Japanese climate were sensitively met, there are others that have simply been disregarded. No effective architectural precautions have been taken to guard against the seasonal cyclones, the typhoons. It is true such measures as tying the ridge tiles to the roof with wire or cement and loading the roof plane with heavy stones may be considered architectural responses, but considering the forces involved, these measures are utterly unrealistic. The entire framework, owing to lack of any diagonal bracing members, is susceptible to the slightest horizontal stress, the danger of which is aggravated by a fatally high point of gravity due to the overly heavy roof. Indeed, the Japanese house in a typhoon is like a house of cards in a draft.

Constructional inefficiency is similarly apparent in the absence of any measures to counteract the effects of earthquakes. While it is true that the use of wood as structural material is very appropriate in such geological conditions, or at least is superior to the use of stone or brick material because of its elasticity and tensile strength, the lack of lateral stability in the framework certainly must raise doubts as to whether the Japanese chose wood material because they realized its advantages in the face of earthquakes. Rather, it seems that the Japanese actually were never really aware of the structural advantages of wood, for during the early adoption of Western techniques, materials such as stone and brick were employed without hesitation, though with dire consequences. Until very recent times there is no evidence that the Japanese have ever tried to pioneer in residential building with materials (with the exception of paper) and techniques, other than those adopted from the modern West or handed down from primitive times.

In spite of continuously recurring earthquake damage, the over-dimensioned roof construction and heavy roof load of clay tiles and clay joinery have been maintained, without any visible attempt to reduce the dangerous top weight or to increase the dimensions of the undersized vertical members, or to brace the latter by rigid diagonal members. Even minor horizontal earthquake shocks, thus, may easily become fatal because the upright framework fails to transmit the shocks to the roof. The roof, then, with its unmoved enormous load pushes the supporting members out of their vertical position, causing them to break or collapse with its tremendous weight. The widespread theory that the sheer weight of the roof braces the column against minor shocks has no structural logic and probably has been motivated by the desire to eulogize.

In the light of such an unrealistic attitude toward meeting horizontal seismic stresses, doubts must also be raised as to whether the loose connection between the house framework and the stone layer foundation—as appropriate as it is to reduce the impact of seismic shock on the structure—is actually due to an awareness that flexibility is one means of guarding against sudden stress just as reinforced rigidity is the other. For, paradoxically, modern techniques using continuous concrete foundations in Japanese residences tie the whole framework rigidly to the ground with bolts, thereby transferring every slight tremble into the upright members. Of course it may be possible that this type of flexible ground-house connection had been realistically created at one time, but if so, then later generations forgot its structural advantages.

A better climatic adaptation is evident in the architectural response to the heavy rainfall. The roof eaves project far beyond the exterior wall and, in addition, the veranda and all the wall openings are provided with separate canopies, ranging from a single board to a post-supported rafter roof. Garden "furniture," such as stone lanterns, fences, gates, wells, and posts, all receive a small roof, adding up to the "roofiness" of the Japanese residence. This multiplicity of roof planes rather than dominance of the main roof is characteristic of Japanese residental architecture, and though these planes never deviate from their horizontal emphasis, their multiplicity may become obtrusive and may efface the general geometry and simplicity of the ground plan.

A stereotyped statement of writers on Japanese architecture is that the Japanese house is "built" mainly for the Japanese summer. Strictly speaking, it should merely be stated that the dwelling is "appropriate" for the summer, because the words "to build" imply an intentional design and a conscious act of creation. There is no evidence that the Japanese house was really "planned" for the hot summer, nor is it likely that the Japanese would build their houses with just those one or two summer months of humidity and heat in mind and would ignore those three to four winter months of uncomfortable cold. In the greater part of Japan the winter is cold, and the many fussy devices that the Japanese employ to heat themselves during the cold season also prove that this cold is uncomfortably felt. The cold of the winter does not merely bother them. It actually affects the Japanese to such a degree that the proportional death rate of winter over summer is the highest in comparison with other countries. Also, in more recent buildings for public use such as schools and offices (without air conditioning) priority is given to heating rather than to ventilating facilities, i.e., to winter rather than summer.

Of course, there are many features in the Japanese house that have been influenced by adaptation to local climate. The movable and removable wall panels facilitate ventilation; the raised floor gives protection from dampness; the elevated stone foundation prevents essential wood parts from decaying; and the veranda toward south and east shields the interior from the high solar incidence in the height of the summer, allows sitting in the sun during the intermediate and pleasant seasons of spring and autumn, and still lets the sun's rays reach into the depth of the room during the cold weather.

However, the presence of these features in the Japanese house was not due to climatic reasons, i.e., a realistic response to environment. There is substantial evidence that features such as the elevated floor and the openness of enclosure were in essence imported from abroad (see Chapter IX), while the veranda was created for different purposes than climatic control and at one time was antepositioned on all four sides of the dwelling.

By contrast, the old-type farmhouse that has directly descended from the primitive pit dwelling reflects a much more realistic attitude toward local climatic conditions. The elevated floor, partial openness, sliding panels, and veranda were adopted much later in a very limited application without sacrificing the solidness of the rigid walls that offers protection against winter storms. Its early predecessor, the pit dwelling, was primarily a result of realistic efforts to shield human living from the major adversaries of local climate, i.e., from earthquakes and typhoons, from rain, snow, and cold. Throughout the centuries, there is no evidence that the oppressiveness of the heat and humidity of the summer ever became a major concern in its climatic adaptation.

Therefore, it is but a lyric allegation that the Japanese house, in its appropriateness solely for the few summer months, constitutes a good example of climatic architecture. For more fatal extremes of Japanese climate did not receive any architectural response whatever, and those architectural features that are appropriate for the summer season owe their existence primarily to non-climatic reasons. In the evolution of the Japanese residence there is no evidence of any measure dealing realistically and boldly with the major climatic pressures, and the basic sameness of the residential architecture throughout a country with such greatly varying climatic conditions and such greatly differing topographical formations shows only too obviously that the Japanese residence in essence is not climatic.

Sensitive architecture reacts minutely to environmental differences and, in spite of a common cultural background or even local proximity, produces distinct features. There are, of course, regional differences in Japanese residential architecture, but these differences are in nature additive (adaptive) and not primary (essential). They show that the Japanese themselves were fully aware of the climatic deficiency of their houses and, yet, that they failed to introduce basic and realistic-radical changes. The reasons for this are various and have been mentioned in part at an earlier time. The general poverty that excluded any experimenting and the increasing rigidity of standardization that obstructed any basic change were partly responsible, as was also the feudalistic control that forbade any deviation from the old. However, the understandable desire of the common masses to imitate the nobles and warriors, who themselves in the Middle Ages of Japan were far from comprehending the reality of their environment, has, no doubt, also been a stifling factor. And the carpenter-architect had long since worked from inherited scripts and therefore designed less creatively with each generation. There is also room for the belief that the Buddhist world view hindered any decisive opposition to the forces of nature, for it taught one to live in harmony with the natural environment and to submit oneself to the inevitable rather than to fight it.

It is, therefore, obvious that the Japanese residence of the 17th and 18th centuries was not a realistic climatic reaction, for it did not actively counteract climatic extremes with efficient architectural measures. Its appropriateness for the humid summer months is accidental as is its inappropriateness for other more dangerous characteristics of Japanese climate such as cyclone, earthquake, and cold. However, being unable to radically change the inherited form and system of their dwelling, the Japanese creative instinct turned to minute adaptations of existing features to local climate, and it is in the detail that the Japanese house experienced climatic adaptation and took on certain local differences.

climatic adaptation

This climatic adaptation in the detail is comprehensive, subtle, and unique. The main part of the house, if it is not subjugated to a rigid city-block pattern, extends in an east-west direction, an orientation that must have been common practice for a long time because the Chinese ideograph for ridge pole is composed of symbols for "east" and "wood," denoting that the ridge is pointing east. Accordingly, the "good side" of the house faces to the south (southeast). Here, the 3 1/2 ft. (1,220 mm.) deep veranda is prepositioned so that it checks the sun incidence in the hot months, while letting the rays penetrate deep into the room during the cold season.

The major orientation of the house to the south is also favorable because it permits an optimum of through ventilation during the summer. Of course, the mountainous topography does not permit generalizations as to the prevailing summer winds, yet the summer monsoon, as weak as it is, reaches Japan from south to east and the houses are built so air can pass freely through. Very often the living room, facing south, has an anteroom on its north so that both can be turned into one single room. While in the summer months interior activity generally takes place in the northernmost room, with the change of season this activity then moves to the rooms facing the south. The east side of the house is open and in most cases has a veranda. The evening sun in the height of the summer, from the west and northwest, is uncomfortably hot and as a rule requires that the western front of the Japanese house be closed up by solid clay walls and shaded by trees.

More interesting, however, is the adaptation to the different seasons of the year. It is true that in the West life within the house also changes with the seasons to a certain degree in terms of food, clothing, and bedding and that it does so in spite of climatic control of the interior. Yet, these changes hardly affect the architecture itself. Paradoxically, Japanese inefficiency in architecturally counteracting the climatic extremes is the very reason that on its surface the Japanese house reacts so sensitively and efficiently to all changes of weather in such a manner that can be called a unique architectural phenomenon. Since, climatically speaking, the Japanese house is essentially but a roof for protection against rain, snow, and sun, but not against cold, heat, draft, humidity, and dust, the Japanese lives the year around practically under the same climatic conditions that prevail on the outside. It was only natural, therefore, that he not merely adapted himself to the seasonal rhythm, but also that he figured out devices that made such living conditions as comfortable as possible.

This contrast between the utter inefficiency of the Japanese in coping basically with the adverse forces of nature and their high efficiency in developing a flexible system of climatic adaptation has brought about the many misunderstandings as to the quality of the Japanese residence. The fact is that disregard of, or submission to, the primary climatic pressure actually was prerequisite for the elaborate architectural reaction to season change, and it is here that Japanese residential architecture has again achieved distinction.

To meet the cold of the winter inside the house, the Japanese wears thickly padded clothes and woolen underwear, i.e., essentially the same clothes that he wears outside, because there is little, if any, difference between interior and exterior temperatures. As the Japanese sit on their feet there is no problem of keeping them warm, although solid shoes are not worn and only cloth footwear, the *tabi,* which are tightly buttoned around the ankles, is used. However, the Japanese do not appear to be very sensitive to cold feet, for one can often see people walking in deep snow with only wooden clogs on their bare feet. Their hands, however, seem to be more sensitive to cold, because everyone wears gloves, even on mildly cold days, and the traditional *hibachi,* a charcoal brazier used for heating, in fact, serves only to warm the hands held over it.

For such limited usage the portable charcoal brazier, *hibachi,* is very suitable. It is 1–1 1/2 ft. (300–450 mm.) in height, made of earthenware or porcelain, frequently with an artistic design, and is so heavy that it cannot be toppled easily by carelessness or by earthquakes. Indeed, the *hibachi* is an economical and practical device, for with only a few pieces of charcoal properly buried in the ashes, a family of five or six, squatting around with hands stretched out, is not only supplied with sufficient heat for several hours but also with ready hot water for the esteemed green tea. Naturally, from such a position no substantial work can be accomplished within the house, but a chat in the evening with the family while sipping steaming tea eventually may prove more rewarding than any business transaction in the office in town. And even in the office, activity slows down during the winter months; gathering around the coal stove, with hands brought close to it, is an ideal setting for discussion of the latest political events on the domestic or foreign scene.

Though at least once a day the entire body is thoroughly warmed up by a hot bath taken before or shortly after dinner, its pleasant effect as a rule does not last until bedtime. Thus, a small charcoal container is placed between the bed quilt and the mattress on the floor, providing the necessary heat for a well-tempered sleep throughout the night. With the room temperature far below the freezing point, this arrangement indeed provides a cozy place that is difficult to leave in the morning. This "night heating device" consists of a small oblong container of earthenware, called *kotatsu*, in which glowing coals are buried under fine ashes to slow down the burning process. The container is then placed in another box of wood or earthenware with various openings, large enough to let the heat out, but small enough not to admit an average human foot. It is positioned at the foot of the bed and held between the legs (couples and children sometimes have one *kotatsu* between them). The arranging of the glowing charcoal pieces in the ash, as well as the proper placing of the legs during sleep, individually or as a pair, is an art that is taught very efficiently in a Zen-Buddhist-like method, i.e., by experience rather than by verbal instruction. A sleepless night with cold feet is as apt to refine this art as are any sudden interruptions from pleasant nightly sleep, dreams, or other pastimes, when a foot comes in contact with an overheated box or even a big toe somehow manages to penetrate right to the source of the supposedly comforting heat.

A similar type of brazier is also used in the daytime. Here the small charcoal container, *kotatsu*, is set into a somewhat bigger wooden cage, which has a top plane that is large enough to serve as a table. A heavy quilt is spread over it to store the heat, and when taking a seat, one covers his legs on top and tightens the quilt on the sides so that no warmth gets lost. In more recent constructions, a wooden grating is built below the floor under which the *kotatsu* is placed. Above the 3 × 3 ft. (900 × 900 mm.) floor opening a table of slightly larger dimensions is placed, and this, again, is covered with a heavy quilt. Sitting around the table on the mat, one conveniently lets the feet rest on the grating below and covers oneself with the quilt up to the hips.

Still, life in the Japanese house in the wintertime is most unpleasant; less so for the man, who after his return from work enjoys sitting at the brazier or spending considerable time in the hot bath, than for the woman, who in all that cold has to prepare wood and fire for the daily bath and carry on her multiple domestic chores in a kitchen where the biting northwest wind makes itself felt and the water freezes in the sink. It might very well be true that for the man who spends each day in a heated office and comes home to a lengthy bath, a meal, or a chat at the brazier, and to a properly heated bed, the winter is not as uncomfortable as the summer, when oppressive humidity and heat disturbs his nightly sleep. But for those who have to carry on work in the Japanese house, no doubt the winter is by far the most inconvenient, most unhealthy, and most unpleasant season. And since it is primarily the female, of course, who works in the house, it is no wonder that discontent hardly ever comes to the open, even less is mentioned in print.

After all the unpleasant winter months, the arrival of spring is celebrated with understandable enthusiasm and, with changing mood and manners, the house interior also undergoes adjustment. The small braziers for the night, *kotatsu*, are stored away and the sunken floor grating is neatly covered up by a half-mat 3 × 3 ft. (900 × 900 mm.). When the days become hot and humid, the opaque paper panels, *fusuma*, are exchanged for panels with a reed pattern that lets air freely pass through. The floor is also adapted to the changed season, being covered with a separate reed carpet, which is cool to feet and body. A hanging bamboo screen on the veranda gives protection from the low afternoon sun and the public view, while the exterior wall panels are literally removed to allow even the slightest breeze to enter the interior.

The result of this sensitive adaptation to weather conditions is that the inhabitants are in emotional rapport with nature and live in full awareness of the great rhythm of the seasons. This intimate relationship is strongly symbolized by the display in the picture recess, *tokonoma*. The hanging picture scroll in the alcove, which may be but a few Chinese ideographs or a depiction of nature, together with the flower in the vase below, has meaning only if associated with a particular season; and the foreigner is bewildered because of his inability to comprehend the principles of such an association that seems to be keenly felt even by the youngest children in the family.

for contemporary architecture

Though technology has succeeded in making the interior of Western houses largely independent from the exterior climate, it is a misconception to assume that the influence of local climate has been diminished thereby. The external forces that work on the building have remained the same, while only the shielding efficiency of the building has been improved to such an extent that the interior is increasingly unaffected by exterior changes in temperature, light, humidity, wind, and precipitation. Therefore, even contemporary progressive architecture, in spite of the efficient technical devices for interior climatic control, cannot ignore the compelling pressure of local climate and will remain subjected to local climatic conditions. Therefore, climate, now as before, is instrumental in the appearance of regional features in architecture, and thorough knowledge of climatic characteristics, their changes and extremes, is imperative for the architect, both in analyzing and creating building.

In residential architecture of the past, protection against local climate was the chief factor in architectural work. Left to simple techniques and materials, architecture reacted more grossly to climatic differences than it does today and very obviously reflected those differences in its physique. Climate, therefore, was the primary reason for local characteristics, for regionalism in architecture. Yet, in Japan the Buddhist-inspired, standard-encrusted, and government-enforced passivity toward the adverse forces of nature has molded a dwelling type that is basically inefficient at meeting the major extremes of Japanese climate and that is, therefore, primitive in its protective devices. However, it was this passivity and the resulting exposure to climatic environment that led the Japanese to develop a highly refined climate control within the realm of the existing. Thus, the Japanese house breathes in simultaneous pulse with the seasons and is in continuous organic change. Life is consciously experienced in its multiple forms and changes, and the beauty inherent in the change itself is keenly felt.

By contrast, houses in the West are designed to meet and to fend off the most oppressive occurrences of local climate. Finely-graded climatic control is limited to interior temperature and humidity, or to adjustable sunshading at best. Otherwise the house remains physically unchanged and unaffected by the changing seasons. Accordingly, for the average Occidental citizen, the particular seasons of the year have become distinct only for their particular sports, concerts, entertainments, vacations, etc. and are hardly experienced as the gigantic rhythm of nature, life, and universe. In Japan, passivity to climatic pressure and subsequent exposure to the weather have actually produced a high emotional sensitivity to climate and nature, but, paradoxically, the opposite architectural reaction to climatic pressure, i.e., the efficient shielding of human activity from climatic changes, has made the modern Westerner even more sensitive to all minor climatic changes than the primitive man. In addition, while early man, being exposed to nature, feared her incomprehensible violence, contemporary man, being well protected (well fed, well clothed, well conditioned), has become also emotionally sensitive to his environment, mainly due to the influence of art, which raised awareness of the beauty in nature. Therefore, in a reverse trend, man again wishes for, if not necessarily physical, then psychological, participation in the inherent beauty of the changing weather.

Architectural progress, then, was responsible for climate gradually losing its stigma of hostility to human life. It provided through building a well-protected space that enabled man for the first time to conceive of nature other than defensively. Yet, even though modern technology has provided the possibility to visually appreciate the exterior change of seasons from a well-conditioned and well-protected space, it has not yet made use of the architectural possibilities of physically expressing climatic changes within the house interior or of employing artistic adaptations to the different seasons in décor and furniture.

The Japanese house shows that beauty of living is not merely a passive awareness of of certain values, but is the sensitive reaction to them and the practical participation in them. Therefore, in accordance with the change of weather, the manners of living change just as does building itself, resulting in a closely synchronized pulse of nature, house, and man. Also, for contemporary houses such flexibility of climatic control would provide an additional expressional motif in architecture, such as adjustable sunshading or, even more obviously, southern solar houses. It would also provide physical comfort due to minute reaction to climate and would effect spiritual elevation by bringing the gigantic rhythm of nature into the house.

Culture is measured by the degree of emotional delight that man is capable of deriving from the many forms of his physical and spiritual environment. The psychological indifference of contemporary man to most expressions of his surroundings —the arts, architecture, science, and nature—is symptomatic of the level of contemporary culture, in spite of infinite psychological stimuli and communicational means. Architectural response to the pulse of nature by integration of distinct seasonal expressions into living is one means of removing man's indifference to his environment. Through rapport with the phenomena of nature, awareness of the supreme being can be stimulated and a regard for nature can be won, which is more than the casual esteem for nature of the "outdoor-type" people such as skier, swimmer, climber, or sight-seer. It would mean sensitizing man's appreciation of his total environment and could become instrumental in promoting culture in contemporary society, the final purpose that all learning, all working, all creating should serve.

definition

PHILOSOPHY IN BUILDING is the spiritual content of house that lies beyond its meaning of physical-psychological shelter. Due to this content, architecture transcends the realm of technical product to become interpretation of human life.

PHILOSOPHY IN BUILDING is man's conception of the universe, his *Weltanschauung* substantiated in architecture. It is the spiritual substance of building that makes man's daily living a part of the supranatural life in which he believes.

PHILOSOPHY IN BUILDING reflects not only man's personal principles of life but also the philosophy of the epoch and its society. Architecture, therefore, is substantiation of the spiritual evolution of mankind.

PHILOSOPHY IN BUILDING is the image of man's religion in the house. It asserts itself in the space and furniture for worship, meditation, and religious service at home and in the influence of religion on architectural principles.

PHILOSOPHY IN BUILDING, yet, is not only reflective in character. Oftentimes building form is impulsively created rather than consciously thought out, and the philosophic interpretation or religious alignment is established thereafter or even derived therefrom.

PHILOSOPHY IN BUILDING, thus, is in effect instructive. Due to its direct and continuous contact with living, it is apt to convey the spiritual values of the epoch to the people more effectively than can any of the sophisticated verbal interpretations.

PHILOSOPHY IN BUILDING is fundamental to architecture as an art. For the art of building is to translate the spiritual values of human life into material form, i.e., values that are interpreted and uncovered by philosophy and religion.

PHILOSOPHY IN BUILDING, then, manifests the highest aspirations of man and is therefore the criterion of humanity in building. Architectural creation thus requires thorough knowledge of the universal philosophical values that characterize the contemporary epoch and its society.

It is characteristic of Japan that her three great religions, Shintoism, Buddhism, and Confucianism (the latter two not indigenous) have been closely associated with her secular philosophy. In fact, there was no difference between the religious and philosophical interpretation of life until the introduction of Western thought at the end of the 19th century brought different learning and an end to this unity. The reason for this congruity of religion and philosophy is that the religious beliefs, especially those of Buddhism and Confucianism, were concerned not only with man's spiritual life, but also very much with the practical everyday life of the individual and with the morality of society as a whole. Since the speculative ambitions of the Japanese philosophers were also mainly devoted to the solution of practical problems, it was in the interest of all concerned to integrate religion and philosophy into one system of an organized religion. Therefore, when Japanese religions as a whole are spoken of, it is to be understood that they also encompass Japanese philosophy with regard to moral conduct and world view.

Shinto, literally meaning "the way of the gods," can hardly be called a religion since it has no dogmas, sacred book, or moral code. Rather it is a form of mythology which, not unlike early Western beliefs, conceived of all natural things as being animated by supernatural beings that either controlled, or themselves were, the forces of nature. Even though noble families liked to claim descent from one of those deities, Shinto is not an ancestor worship as is so often assumed, but essentially a nature worship in which the major ritual was to propitiate the changeable and evil deities and show gratitude to the good ones. Ancestor worship actually was instigated by Confucianism imported from China. The basis of Confucius' metaphysical and ethical doctrine was the cult of the family as the essence of the state. Teaching submission to parents and rulers, this doctrine was only too appropriate to bolster the feudalistic system during the Middle Ages of Japan, and hence found much favor among the ruling classes.

Both Shintoism and Confucianism had great influence in molding Japanese thought and life throughout history, and even at present the Japanese still adhere to many of its principles, even if only subconsciously. In architecture also, this influence of Shintoism and Confucianism is obvious, both directly and indirectly. As has been mentioned earlier, it was especially Confucianism that shaped the Japanese family system and thus proved a decisive factor in the evolution of the Japanese dwelling. However, the third great religion, Buddhism, was by far more influential on all phases of Japanese life. As in the fine arts, crafts, social institutions, etc., so also in architecture was this religion strongly formative, as already has been evidenced in the previous chapters that dealt continuously with the direct or indirect influences of Buddhism. Yet, it would be difficult to clearly separate the influences of each religion. For Shintoism and Confucianism have exerted influence on Japanese Buddhism just as Buddhism has on them.

In the following treatise an attempt is made to show how a comprehensive religion-philosophy affected the Japanese residence in various ways. It is hoped that from such a study conclusions can be drawn that may help in understanding the philosophic meaning of "dwelling," and that thereby direct insight can be gained into the more profound problems of contemporary design. For this reason, it seemed more appropriate to confine the following elaborations to Buddhism alone, even though Shintoism and Confucianism have been formative in architecture too, if only to a lesser extent. Such limited and specific investigation should more conclusively disclose universal truths regarding the relationship between architecture and philosophy than can general statements.

And a further limitation has been exercised. There have developed a multitude of Buddhist sects, each of them adhering to different methods of attaining Buddhist salvation, i.e., through practice, through intellect, or through intuition. Thus, one group emphasizes ritualistic or magical means; another group believes that salvation can be attained through worshipping Amida, a deity who deferred his own salvation in order to further the salvation of others; a third sect, Nichiren, identifies salvation of the individual with establishment of a Buddhist state; and, finally, the Zen sect denies the efficacy of intellectual and contemplative means to gain salvation and instead maintains that enlightenment can only be directly attained without conceptual medium by one intuitive grasp of the reality that underlies life and its multiform appearances.

Zen philosophy, because of its particular methods on the one hand and its universal approach on the other, has, from Japan's Middle Ages on, influenced all phases of Japanese life more profoundly than has any of the other sects and was closely associated not only with the arts, social institutions, government, and all classes of society, but also, particularly, with architecture and landscaping. Therefore, the following study is focused primarily on Zen and its role in residential architecture, even though general statements on Buddhism as a whole must also be made.

zen-buddhism

Buddhism in general is the religion-philosophy that has developed out of the teachings of Gautama Siddhartha, 563–483 B.C., who later became the "Buddha," i.e., the Enlightened One, the Awakened One. Ultimate enlightenment, the state of Buddahood, is the goal of Buddhist teaching and is attained by studying, by perfecting self, and by exercising morality. The core of the Buddhist doctrine deals with the conception of this enlightenment and with the methods for its attainment. And in this sense it equally encompasses religion, philosophy, metaphysics, mysticism, psychology, magic, and ritual. Too extensive and too difficult to describe comprehensively, too distinct and too important to generalize upon, the only possible way within the scope of this paper seemed to be to take up some of the major characteristics of this profound school of thought, especially those that contrast with other philosophies, with no other purpose in mind than to give an introduction to a world of thought so different from the Western.

The Buddhist view conceives of a universe that evolved by itself, not one that was created by a supreme being. The universe itself, then, is the ultimate reality, self-creating and self-governing, and thus controls man's affairs. Ultimate reality is beyond concepts and verbal interpretations with their inherent limitations, and thus a god cannot be the absolute being or, if a god is conceived of, this god is only a symbol and is not reality itself. Therefore, Buddhism sees in the existence of gods in other religions a confirmation of the Buddhist reality. It consequently does not oppose any of the other existing religions but embraces them all, and it is for this reason that the indigenous cult of Shinto, with its many deities of nature, can exist side by side with Buddhism, simply being integrated into the great framework of Buddhist thought as one of the expressions of the universe.

The essence of the universe is law, for the universe is subjected to law and functions according to law. This law is the "logic of causation," named "Karma": each effect has its cause. Existing conditions, i.e., effects, then, are the results of past causes, just as future conditions will be determined by causes prepared in the present. The merits and demerits of the causes establish the merits and demerits of the effects. Man will, therefore, experience in the future only the effects of causes that he prepares in the present, just as he presently experiences the effects of causes that he himself has prepared in his past (or in his past forms of existence). Thus, man is not only responsible for his present state but also is able to shape his future by himself. He will be reborn again and again until he attains the absolute wisdom, and will be absorbed into the ultimate to become the enlightened one, Buddha himself. All forms of "life," the animate and the inanimate, are destined to reach Buddhahood.

"Life" is conceived as one; only the forms in which "life" is embodied are multiple and varied. Since this "one-life" in its recurring and changing forms will never cease; there is no death; only the forms will disappear. Such a conception of "life" unifies all different forms in which "life" appears and elicits compassion for beings other than human, inanimate as well as animate. Nothing is permanent except "life," or else change itself is permanent. As there is only one "life," the aims of each form of "life," such as man himself, should serve the whole. If man, therefore, strives only for his own interests, it will necessarily lead to conflicts and difficulties for himself and others. Ignorance as to the essence of "life" is the cause of these difficulties, and it is necessary to remove the cause in order to put an end to them. The sources of man's ignorance of "life" are his personal concerns, his desires for pleasure, his attachment to things material. Freedom from one's earthly desires and absorption into the universal life that is independent of time and space, thus, is the aim of all existence. Therefore, man should strive to overcome the limitations of selfhood and to attain "loss of self." This is called with a Sanscrit term *nirvana,* which literally means "extinction." It is the ultimate Buddhist enlightenment and the self-salvation of man.

The methods of attaining this state of self-extinction, *nirvana,* differ according to the sect, and most unique among them is the teaching of Zen. Zen questions the value of intellect as a means of reaching the ultimate enlightenment. Sole dependence on intellect excludes the intellectually less gifted; also, since the intellect expresses itself only in words, concepts, and theories, with their inherent human limitations, it causes a separation from the direct and comprehensive grasp of ultimate reality. Intellect is never able to completely express what man actually knows; it can only be a part, instead, of a whole or a concept instead of an idea, or theory instead of a reality, i.e., it is apt to obscure and limit knowing. Zen, thus, concentrates on attempting to know directly, without learning, praying, or ritual, and hence its emphasis on meditation, *dhyana* in Sanscrit, which in Japanese is *zen*.

Enlightenment in Zen terminology is *satori*. It is conceived of as a state of becoming one with the universe. Man transcends the individual world of limitation in feeling and thinking, in time and space, and "knows," i.e., he grasps the one-life permeating himself and all other forms. Zen conceives of one absolute state where the beholder and his object, the thinker and his subject matter, merge into one; a state of an "absolute emptiness" or "utmost transparency" where no barrier between the self and other exists: the "ultimate oneness." Even though such intuitive grasp may come in the flash of a moment or after tedious periods of meditation, Zen, in the attempt to bring it about, considers facts and impulses of direct experiences very highly. For it is not the reasoning of the intellect but the active response to immediate experience that sensitizes intuition.

This Zen approach to attainment of *satori*, the enlightenment, has strongly influenced those phases of Japanese life where comprehension of reality is fundamental: the swordmanship and archery as well as all the arts. "Draw bamboos for ten years; become a bamboo; then forget all about bamboo when you are drawing. In possession of an infallible technique, the individual places himself at the mercy of inspiration. . . ." Here, the characteristic Zen approach is clearly expressed. Artist and product, man and object are one, selfhood is extinct, and the genius can unfold without limitation.

Such a *Weltanschauung* has penetrated deep into the minds of the Japanese. However, it would be misleading to assume that each Japanese is fully conscious of such philosophy of life. For the average Japanese hardly knows what Zen is, even less could put it into words. He actually lives Zen in unawareness and therein differs from the Japanese scholar who realizes Zen analytically and critically. To live Zen is to value facts of experience higher than concepts and theories. To analyze and explain Zen means to descend to the realm of words and definitions with all their inherent limitations; and it is here that it seems very appropriate to put an end to inadequate verbal explanation.

buddhist features

Owing to the close association of Buddhist philosophy with art, cultural activity was tremendously stimulated in all countries where Buddhism reached, from Ceylon to Tibet, from India to Japan. As the prevailing philosophy, religion, or *Weltanschauung* always strongly influences man's thoughts and emotions and consequently all creative art, it was only natural for the countries of Buddhism to produce an art manifesting the common spiritual basis from which it had sprung. It is for this reason that Buddhist art can be spoken of in a general sense, even though great local differences are obvious in its expression. Yet, not only did Buddhism exert indirect influence by providing a common conception of the universe; it also directly furnished each country with Buddhist achievements such as techniques, expressions, systems, materials, and motifs for all arts.

In the case of Japan, such a direct adoption was almost continuous, owing to her intimate geo-relationship to the advanced Buddhist culture of China. In architecture, this influence was only imitative or adoptive during the first stages, and the adopted existed side by side with the indigenous architecture. But due to the integral development of the religious, artistic, and utilitarian life, for which Japan is noted, this influence did not remain confined to ecclesiastic architecture (the temples, monasteries, and the houses of the priests), but was adopted by, and adapted to, residential architecture of all classes of society. Most of the Buddhist features that were incorporated into the Japanese house have been mentioned earlier in a different context, yet a brief reference to them at this place is appropriate in showing the extensive physical influence that ecclesiastic architecture exerted upon popular architecture—an influence that is unusual by Western standards.

It is understood that the many novel techniques, forms, and materials that came successively to Japan from China along with Buddhism in the 7th and 8th centuries remained for centuries of benefit only to ecclesiastic architecture and, at best, to that of the aristocracy. This was caused by the general poverty of the masses, their lack of technical knowledge and equipment, and the rigid class distinction that was also enforced in building. Yet, there is evidence that the technique of the clay wall was adopted by all classes of society. Before that time the nobility used wooden planks and the people a knit work of branches, methods less efficient than the Chinese import. Roof tiles were another product which, together with Buddhist temple architecture, was brought from China. Yet, both general poverty of the common classes and the sectionalistic attitude of the clergy for a long time prevented the use of tiles for popular houses. In fact, it was only because the high inflammability of the straw and bark cover endangered also the houses of the military and nobility that the men in power were inclined to remove their restrictions on the use of roof tiles.

Yet, whereas the clay wall and roof tile are components that could simply be adopted without adjustment to different localities, the modular standardization that reached Japan in the form of procedural scripts for construction of temples and attached buildings needed essential transformation before it could be used for the ordinary residential architecture. Ingeniously re-forming and re-enacting these building rules, the Japanese produced a standardization for residential building that justly can be called unique in the architecture of the world (Figures 7–14). While it is true that the outstanding modular order of *kiwari* for both ecclesiastic and domestic building is an achievement of Japanese architecture alone, it nevertheless ·should also be understood that in residential architecture the idea and system were derived, by way of the warrior's residence, *shuden,* from the Buddhist mansion, which itself had been unquestionably modeled after Chinese types.

Another characteristic of Japanese residential architecture—and the most dynamic expression of Japanese aestheticism—the picture recess, *tokonoma,* is in more than one way closely associated with Buddhist architecture (Plates 74–79). Though it is professed that the origins are still in dispute, there is reason to believe that the controversy over the *tokonoma* is not concerned so much with its origins as it is with the question of deciding as to which of the various prototypes should be given the major credit, a matter, indeed, of importance only for the competitive spirit of the archeologist.

The sacred meaning of the picture recess, as is still evidenced by the frequent presence of an incense burner, can be traced back to the houses of the Zen monastery, where on one wall a sacred Buddhist picture scroll was hung, with flowers and incense burner placed on a shelf underneath. The Zen monks gathered in front of this wall for spiritual exercise or meditation, and here, in a profound ritual, they drank tea from one bowl. Both ritual and picture wall had been introduced by monks returning from the Chinese monasteries in the 13th century, and there should be little question that this was the earliest and most basic source for the form and sacred meaning of the later picture recess, the *tokonoma.*

Also, the role of the picture recess to display art in the form of a hanging picture scroll, *kake-jiku,* is, if only indirectly, due to Buddhism. For it was the Buddhist monks that imported famous paintings from China, and it is very likely that the nobility in their search for a proper place to appreciate them took to a similar form used by the

Zen monks. Documents of the early 15th century show that three or five picture scrolls were hung side by side above a broad board that projected from the wall. It stretched the entire width of the room and was not more than 1.7–2.0 *shaku* (about 500–600 mm.= 1.7–2.0 ft.) deep. There was not yet a recess in the strict sense of the word, nor was the word *tokonoma* employed. Instead, the board is referred to as *oshi-ita* (the push board), which suggests that this board originally was portable and removable.

The name *tokonoma*, literally "space for platform," or shortened, *toko*, actually came from the main hall of the warrior's residence, *shuden*, or *hiroma*, built in the so-called *shoin* style. In this building, a portion of the main room, called *jōdan* (literally, upper step), was elevated one step, with a shallow picture recess and shelving recess on the long wall, and a study place on the wall facing to the outside, the latter having the form of an elevated bay or a projected window. The *shoin* style, then, gave to the *tokonoma* its name and also the significance of being the place for the honored guest. Also, in this instance, as it appears, Buddhism was in a way involved. For the system of construction in the *shoin*-style residence, its modular order, and its physical appearance all indicate that it was strongly modeled after the Buddhist priest's dwelling.

While the role of the *tokonoma* as the place of meditation and art was derived from the Zen Buddhist hall and obtained its additional meaning of official place for the honored guest through the Buddhist-modeled warrior residence, it was in the tearoom that the architectural-physical potentials of the picture recess were fully explored. Here the various types of *toko* were developed, and it was mainly from this time on that the picture recess was also used in the houses of the common people. Yet, again, as has been described earlier, the tea cult, tea master, and tea hut were intimately related to Zen Buddhism, so that the final stage in the evolution of this singular achievement of Japanese architecture was also strongly determined by factors emanating from Buddhism.

Another distinct feature of the Japanese residence, the study place, *shoin*, also owes its existence in the dwelling to Buddhism (Plates 88–89). For the *shoin* originally was the study room of the Zen priest, with a projected window whose sill served as a desk for study. Originally, it was an independent private room, reaching over the veranda into the garden, and was pictured in the documents of the Kamakura period (1185–1336) with a monk studying. But later it became a small elevated bay or simply a projected window and was attached to the picture and shelving recesses, *tokonoma* and *tana*, in the representative reception room of nobility and military. Here it no longer served a primarily utilitarian purpose, but assumed a decorative character. As the study place, *shoin*, was distinctive for the official residential style of the 16th to 18th centuries, the term *shoin-zukuri* came into use, designating a building style with characteristic ground plan and form. The rising merchant class, then, in the 17th and 18th centuries, increasingly defying prohibitive regulations of the feudalistic government, adopted among other features the decorative study place, *shoin*, and thus also made it accessible for the common people. Here, the *shoin* in junction with *tokonoma* has the form of a mere window with high sill, either flush or projected, and frequently again serves its originally utilitarian purpose as a study place.

There are other features in the Japanese residence that are directly or indirectly related to Buddhist architecture and they have been noted at the respective places in previous chapters. Their individual mention at this place, though, has been omitted because the foregoing evidence seems sufficient to demonstrate how intimate the relationship between Buddhist ecclesiastic architecture and popular residential architecture has been, and how strongly the Japanese residence has borrowed in motif, form, technique, and material from the rich source of Buddhist architecture (Plate 105). Though the features of Japanese Buddhist architecture were essentially modeled after Chinese prototypes and were largely standardized, they gradually withdrew from these patterns and took on forms with a strong Japanese sentiment.

No doubt with such an overwhelming and superior architecture as that of the

Chinese in immediate proximity, it was only too reasonable to draw from this abundant source on the continent for improvement of building rather than to pioneer into the unknown with its inevitable failures and questionable results. Yet, this has been a fateful trend in Japanese history. For, the Japanese being accustomed to simply adopting cultural achievements from the superior civilization of China and later from Europe, it was inevitable that the achievements of their own culture were hardly realized, and even when they were recognized at all were only attributed an inferior value. Moreover, this trend of simply adopting from superiors also became the functioning agent of progress within Japan herself. Far from realistically meeting environmental circumstances and advancing on the basis of native achievement, the upper classes relied on the Buddhist architecture as much as the lower classes preferred to look up to the superior class for inspiration and improvement, which was so much easier, less costly, and not at all risky.

But when those Buddhist features were finally incorporated into the houses of the common people they were no longer Chinese. For not only had the imports gone through the prism of simplification and transmutation when re-enacted on Japanese ground, but also they were newly interpreted in the houses of the nobility and military, from where, in fact, the lower classes had borrowed them.

Modern Japanese technology and science largely follow the same pattern of merely improving on foreign achievement instead of using them as a basis for essential advancement, even less as a stimulus to independent venture. But it is important to note that in the case of the Japanese residence these adoptions were subtly refined and eventually transmuted. Although they never quite left the scope of their original theme and form, they reached a perfection and purification that can be called singular in the world.

religious expressions

While the common masses in contemporary Japan are quite unreserved in their religious devotion, the intelligentsia, by comparison, appear to be indifferent to matters of religion. However, the latter attitude is more seeming than real. It is true that Buddha himself was an agnostic and that the Confucian doctrine, which largely regulated the thought of the Japanese for more than three hundred years, discards the active belief in supreme beings. But the educated Japanese, even though he is familiar with Western science and philosophy, adheres to a humble observance of his somewhat vague traditional beliefs as soon as he is in the secluded world of his dwelling, where the environment no longer demands pretense. There is room for argument as to how much superstition is involved, but there is no question about the seriousness of his faith. Japanese religion is not a matter confined to the church or temple as is largely the case in the West, but is actually a part of daily living.

That this religious faith is sincere and universal for the whole nation is evidenced in the presence of the *butsu-dan,* the Buddha altar, and of the *kami-dana,* the Shinto god shelf, in most dwellings (Plates 106–107). Those who adhere exclusively to Shintoism have only the latter, but they are very rare indeed, and as a rule the Japanese family possesses both—obvious proof of the indiscriminative and absorbent nature of Buddhism. The Shinto god shelf is very simple, as is Shinto architecture in general; the Buddha altar is very ornate, elaborate, and splendid. The altar is kept either in a particular cabinet or is built into a closet behind sliding panels. Here the memorial tablets of the ancestors are placed on the altar, here each day the mother makes food offerings in the form of rice and tea, and here at certain intervals a Buddhist priest performs a simple mass.

While the picture recess, *tokonoma,* though by origin the sacred place of Buddha worship, constitutes the representative-official center of the Japanese house, where aesthetics and intellect and formality prevail, the Buddha altar is often withdrawn from the official atmosphere of the reception room and placed in the privacy of family rooms where it is concealed from the eyes of the visitor. Humble devotion, religious service, and daily care for the Buddha altar are not a matter of public demonstration nor a "confession" limited to the time and place of a church. Rather, it is the conscious and continuous living and practicing of a profound religious belief in the house.*

It may be argued that these phenomena in the Japanese home are mere custom and formality performed without much sincerity and belief, as often form alone continues in religion while its very essence is no longer recognized or felt. Yet, the continuation of the daily services in spite of all Western learning among the majority of the Japanese people, proves that the presence of ancestors and the "life" of the universe, even in the most primitive dwelling, is keenly felt at all times. Another proof of this honest faith of the simple man are the frequent pilgrimages. Significantly, in prosperous years rather than after a bad crop, entire villages visit noted Buddhist temples and Shinto shrines or climb sacred mountains. From there they bring back many charms, *o-mamori,* honorable safeguard (protector), or *o-fuda,* honorable ticket, and nail them at the front door or place them on the god shelf, to bear witness of many a tedious pilgrimage that had been made faithfully to the ancestors and the gods.

It is the house to which this evidence of the pilgrim's worthiness is brought, and it is the house that preserves it for the children as proof of, and reward for, the religious life of the parents. Though the house may afford only little physical protection to its inmates against the elements of nature, it yet harbors the ancestors and gods and thus gives spiritual safeguard, which is considered a more efficient protection of the inhabitants than a reinforced house structure. In this instance, the Japanese house has distinctly substantiated the religion-philosophy of its time and people. In fact, if the house is measured by the degree of its response to the physical requirements of man and environment, it must be conceded that Japanese residential architecture is more philosophical than it is practical.

zen and house

It is characteristic for the Zen sect that it has not limited the range of its influence to the religious aspect of the people, but has concerned itself with all phases of life. Zen rejects the intellect as the sole means of attaining knowledge into the ultimate reality of things and considers immediate experience in an active life as the most direct and thereby the most powerful method of reaching wisdom. Experience is the encounter with environmental impulses. Continuous encounter stimulates intuition, and intuition fosters knowledge. Intuitive response to an environmental impulse is likely to reveal the true nature of the impulse; it is, as well, evidence of man's insight into the reality of the impulse. Especially, art, both as object and creation, should reach man's inner being more effectively than any theories and principles of morality. For not only is art, as creation, a direct expression from within, but art, as an object, also communicates directly with man's heart, contrary to a code of morality that is constructed by the intellect and thus remains imposed from without. Thus, Zen considers expressions and impulses of art as more basic than those of morality and, therefore, was particularly closely associated with all forms of art—painting, poetry, sculpture, theater, music, and architecture.

It could be expected that Zen in particular would seize upon residential architecture in order to demonstrate the unique Zen approach and to promote Zen ideas of life, especially since Zen's unsophisticated methods and its non-discriminative attitude also found particular favor among the intellectually and materially less fortunate classes such as the warriors, farmers, and the general public. In fact, as has been elaborated earlier, the tea cult was in one sense but a bold, realistic method of Zen to raise an awareness of living through direct encounter with the most basic essentials of life, shelter and drink. However, Zen did not invent shelter and drink any more than it

* Similar spiritual content can be evidenced in the traditional European houses. There the "god corner" with crucifix, flowers, and Bible, together with the other corners for the crib and the coffin, formed a trichotomy that revealed the mystery of life in building.

invented the form and expression of the Japanese residence. If obvious causes of a form are lacking, it is only too simple a method to credit them to the one who gives symbolic meaning to that form.

Thus, the noted simplicity of Japanese residential architecture was originally the very real expression of lack of means and poverty, not that of wise restraint. The merit of Zen is that it showed the beauty inherent in conscious simplicity, dissolved the stigma of simplicity as being the accidental result of unwanted circumstances, and instead made simplicity an intentional expression of profound significance. Through Zen, then, not simplicity but the aestheticism of simplicity was discovered, and herein lies an essential contribution to the world's civilization.

Simplicity as a visual expression is the result of continuous elimination of the superfluous, is reduction of form, space, motif, construction, function, and material to the barest minimum necessary to comply with the purpose of existence. The result is that the purpose will experience its most pure substantiation. In fact, what is left no longer allows a differentiation between form and essence, container and content, expression and spirit. Such a simplicity effects a very close psychological intimacy with the object. No artificiality or sophistry covers up the very essence of the matter, and nothing therefore needs to be overcome in order to associate with the true meaning of the matter. The emotional response is immediate and profound.

Such a simplicity—the art of making things simple—made the overhanging roof a dominant element that hovers protectively above the family, the living and the dead, and that shields against rain and creates sheltered space. "It" gave to the roof supporting columns, slender, square, and in natural texture, visible from both inside and outside. "It" placed them where they were needed and not where questionable visual concern would want them. "It" made them balance on round stones that protrude from the ground lest the dampness from underneath should reach them, leaving the weight from above the only connection. "It" hung the floor between the uprights and covered it with the mat to make it a universal stage for living, being simultaneously bed, seat, and walk. "It" prepositioned a veranda toward the midday sun and the garden, and thus provided a platform that grants both protection from summer sun and enjoyment of the garden. "It" inserted panels between the uprights to create room, expand room, shield room, and lighten room. "It" also provided an alcove where nature, man, house, and heaven meet. And this simplicity did not forget to designate a sacred place for tending the ever present spirit of the ancestors and for holding a simple Buddha mass. "It" even separated a space, where in seclusion and semidarkness, aloof from the material world, man could become aware of life and himself. "It" thus substantiated the mystery of human life by means of building under one roof, while giving each element of the house its distinct place and an expression that clearly stated its *raison d'être*.

Such a simplicity is but a system of cause and effect, of action and reaction, of problem and response, both practically and spiritually. The resulting form, however, can hardly be described with Western concepts in which "form" is a separate quality of a building independent from motivations other than the visual. For "form" of the Japanese house is no longer the primary concern and even less the idea of architectural creation, but is only the necessary and unconscious expression of something more essential: construction, utilization, religion, tradition, philosophy. To compare, as Western interpreters do, the "form" of Japanese architecture with the forms of, for example, Greek or Gothic architecture is actually a misleading practice, because the "form" in the ordinary Japanese residence was hardly consciously conceived along visual principles, as were the forms of these examples of Western architecture, but was the simple substantiation of the various form-giving factors. It is important to note that the effect of this unsophisticated expression has such a strong appeal for contemporary architects, because it must raise the question whether preoccupation with outward proportion, balance, rhythm, composition, harmony, contrast, and the like for the sake of visual beauty in building is not an approach too one-sided to address the full range of human emotions.

Pursuing simplicity of external form is also a demonstration of the Buddhist assertion that the phenomena of the material world are unreal and temporary and are only expressions of the one-life that permeates them all. For in order to reveal this "life" in concrete matter its form has to be unobtrusive and simple; overly conspicuous form is to be rejected because it draws attention to itself rather than to its content. From this, Zen derives another principle for "form" in art and architecture and states that symmetry be avoided at any cost. Instead, asymmetry is to be consciously sought. This, though, is not merely substituting one arbitrary principle for another, but is a successful measure to make the least out of form in order to lead directly to the very spirit behind all form.

The Zen interpretation of Buddhist ideals produced still another principle for the control of external form. This principle is derived from the realization that comprehending and appreciating an object is not a passive reaction, but an active process, i.e., the act of becoming one with the object. For this act the completed and perfected form—no matter how simple and inconspicuous—is not appropriate, because it hardly leaves room for imagination and hence excludes the beholder from participation. Though an object is apt to disclose its inner meaning by simplicity of form itself, it does not invite participation if its theme is already fully exhausted.

Zen, therefore, attempts to provoke a strong association between object and beholder less by "what is" than by "what is not." The most captivating form is the one that is left uncompleted and imperfect so that the beholder is stimulated to either imaginarily or really complete the form. This trend is quite obvious in Japanese arts. The stimulative blank of the painting, the suggestive end of a poem, etc., all demand active participation and exclude passivity. Indeed, imperfection in form, expression, thought, or performance not only suggests a continuation of growth, but also makes art appreciation a creative activity.

As to Japanese architecture, such aestheticism is most obviously expressed in the tearoom. Here apparent imperfection and incompleteness of the wall texture, column floor, or tea bowl produce a very intimate psychological response, because man's insufficiency is revealed and the pathos of human life is experienced. Yet, these principles did not remain confined to the tearoom, but gradually determined all living rooms in the Japanese residence. It is from this time on that the features of simplicity in the Japanese house, such as the rough wall texture or the asymmetrical picture recess, became a very conscious artistic creation.

Not only the individual components of the house, but also the architectural space— clearly defined as it is both inside and outside—received a philosophical interpretation through Zen. Zen does not distinguish between the "all" and the "one." The world contains infinite drops of water, as each water drop contains a world of its own; the 4 1/2-mat room has as much infinity as has the small fenced garden. In the midst of a succession of individually defined spaces from room to garden to universe, house becomes but a transient station for life, a material form that temporarily shelters human life. Therefore, there is no reason to build a house for eternity, stable to withstand the violent forces of nature, resistant to bear the wear of weather. The unpainted wood exposed to rain and decay demonstrates the perishableness of all material form more convincingly than could any verbal instruction.

Also, the individual interior room that had originally been the expression of poverty in its lack of décor, form, motif, and color becomes, through Zen's interpretation, the very vehicle of man's aesthetic experience. For it provides an environment that requires man's presence and participation to fill the void. Room in the Western residence is human without man's presence, for man's memory lingers in the multiple devices of decoration, furniture, and utility. Room in the Japanese residence becomes human only through man's presence. Without him there is no human trace. Thus, the empty room provides the very space where man's spirit can move freely and where his thoughts can reach the very limits of their potential.

Yet, contrary to frequent allegations, such a spatial concept of the material world was never identified by Zen as the "philosophical space" of the Buddhist salvation, where the one-life was conceived of as moving self-creatingly. There is no evidence that Zen, in its attempt to teach with realistic methods, used the spatial concepts of architecture to raise cognizance of this "philosophical space," which, free of earthly limitation and devoid of any physical attachment, was thought by the Buddhist mind to be the state of ultimate realization and salvation. Nor is it likely that Zen would want to relate the "ultimate space of enlightenment" to architectural space and thereby lead back to the realm of human conceptions and their inherent limitations on the full comprehension.

Life is one, and all phenomena, both the animate and the inanimate, are but different expressions of the one-life. Their relative value, thus, is equal and cannot be discriminated. No distinctions are made between the costly and the inexpensive, the rich and the poor, the noble and the common, for these are material valuations that are not real. Zen goes beyond that and realizes that it is just the inexpensive, poor, and ordinary matter that is most successful in showing the real value of the matter, because there is less danger of the material valuation interfering. In building, the most ordinary material will bare the inherent aesthetic value of its substance more plainly than the costly one, because only too often the mere amount of cost is taken as an aesthetic standard. The result of such conception is that the most ordinary materials, their simple use, and their plain treatment are no longer an expression of poverty but become the very prerequisite to reveal the intrinsic value of *all* things and to raise awareness of the *one* value that permeates them *all*—as Zen asserts: "All in one and one in all."

for contemporary architecture

Japanese residential architecture, then, presents an outstanding example of philosophical architecture. For the spiritual environment has been successful in raising the ordinary dwelling above the level of a mere technical device that responds only to man's physical-psychological needs and has made the house a true expression of the religious faith and the philosophical conception of the people and their epoch. Here architecture has assumed its most profound spiritual role. Such religious-philosophical materialization has been attained by the adoption of features from religious architecture, by the provision of sacred space for religious worship, and by the adjustment of expression in all components to religious-philosophical principles. It needs particular mention here that this house was the dwelling of the poorest class of the people, who lived under suppression in the bitterest of poverty, because it shows not only that even these people vigorously demanded a place to satisfy their supranatural and mystic aspirations, but also that it was economically possible without upsetting a building system that had to work with the minimum of expense.

Western architecture, in its continuous quest for improvement of physical comfort, no longer acknowledges this fundamental need of man. Or it may be that man himself, in his increasingly material orientation of values, has ceased to be aware of what is fundamental to his being. Consequently, most of contemporary residential architecture has come dangerously close in its essence to being a mere technical product, such as the automobile, radio, or furniture, which, while exactly complying with man's physical needs, does no more than combine efficiency with an aesthetically pleasing appearance. Contemporary architecture no longer manifests its role of spiritual shelter, for it does not reflect the philosophy of its inhabitants, even less the spiritual values of the era. Contemporary architecture has become dehumanized in the sense that it no longer architecturalizes the most distinctive and noble of human aspirations: the faith in, or the imagination of, the invisible world.

No doubt, since the mechanical revolution has largely taken residential building out of the layman's hand, the responsibility for this state of affairs rests with the architect, for it is he who sets, or should set, the standards of living, both materially and spiritually. There is an urgent necessity for the architect to concern himself with the reality of the contemporary epoch and its controlling currents of thought. He will realize that in the Western world the Christian religion no longer possesses the dominant position in the spiritual life of man as it did in the Middle Ages. Instead. Western philosophy has brought forth other ideologies of contemporary mankind that are not necessarily contrary to Christian values but are essentially different. Though they have frequently produced conflicts, they nevertheless have created a new and unique picture of *Weltanschauung* that demands a fresh architectural interpretation.

In Buddhism there is no dualism of religion and philosophy. For the world of realities is the spiritual world and not the material world, which is only the visible and ephemeral expression of the former. This cognizance of life is manifested in every Japanese house by the Buddhist altar, the regular masses, and the food offerings to the departed ancestors. Yet, far beyond merely reflecting the existing, Zen sought and found a human answer to the life of late medieval Japan and made architecture an honest statement of the epoch and its dominant forces. It did not create novel forms as is often assumed, but newly interpreted what already existed and from this derived aesthetic and moral principles.

Thus, Zen revealed the truth that conscious simplicity is a discipline of art. The aesthetic meaning of this simplicity, though, differs much from the narrow functionalist concept of "form follows function," as it differs also from the simplicity of contemporary design. For unlike modern simplicity, which in matters of aesthetics still works intuitively, disorderly, vaguely, and without any comprehensive code that is philosophically founded, Zen succeeded in establishing the "art of simplicity" by providing simplicity with universal principles. These principles have given morality and "style" to the residential architecture and have turned the ordinary house into a piece of art. They may also provide stimulating ideas for similar attempts in contemporary architecture in its quest to overcome the alienation between contemporary structures and man.

Zen asserts that simplicity is the quality inherent in the most direct response to an impulse. As to architecture, simplicity is manifested in the most immediate and most effective measure to cope with an architectural problem. There are always many ways of solving such problems elaborately and artistically, but there is only one simple way, and this way alone will reveal the problem itself in its most pure expression. No building will be alien to man if it exercises such a simplicity but, rather, will become a part of man. He will be able to feel and know the building directly and thus experience a beauty different from that of a picture or sculpture. In such simplicity, form no longer is an intermediary that needs interpretation; form no longer exists of its own right.

Zen has thus provided a morality of architectural values that has significance not only for Japan but for contemporary international architecture with its prevalent ideological confusion. For simplicity in contemporary architecture, if it is backed aesthetically only by visual-external factors, is as shallow a form as the multiplicity of eclectic architecture that was also determined by mere surface principles unrelated to the organisms behind the façade. The forms and structures of the architectural styles in the past have been an expression of an ideology that characterized the epoch and nation as a whole and consequently evoked emotions of truly ethical value. Contemporary architecture is lacking any forceful spiritual idea or philosophical conception, and it is very well possible that in this ideological vacuum of the present the aesthetic-philosophical principles of Zen Buddhism, timeless and inclusive as they are, could provide the basis for a new morality in architecture.

It is an important fact that one of the major sources from which Zen drew new impulses was architecture itself. In the houses of the common people Zen realized confirmation of its own philosophy. It discovered that the house could provide excellent media for demonstrating Zen principles directly to the masses. Zen thus gave a new philosophical interpretation to an existing architectural order, dissolved its meaning as inescapable expression of poverty and suppression, and made it a forceful instrument of architectural creation with a profound spiritual meaning.

This belated establishment of a philosophical "motive" for an existing architectural phenomenon (which has been the source of much misunderstanding as to the role of Zen in Japanese residential architecture) holds a strong suggestion for contemporary architecture. For it shows that an architectural ideology can be derived from an architecture that already exists. In Japan the architectural standard of the epoch and society had not been primarily conceived through abstract reasoning but through observation and interpretation of features that distinguished the dwellings of the poorest people. Through philosophical interpretation, thus, an emotional relationship between house and man that made the most primitive shelter meaningful and a true instrument of art was established.

It may be argued that contemporary buildings are no longer a direct expression of their owner's wisdom of life due to the intercession of the architect and thus do not permit direct derivation of ideological fundamentals from existing buildings. But it cannot be denied that contemporary architecture, if it is not too encumbered with romantic relics, manifests a common spirit in forms unprecedented and distinct for the present age. Though it appears as if the expression of industrialized building had come about without human intention or even over human objections, it nevertheless states the dominating element in contemporary physical and intellectual endeavor of man: technique and science.

It is the imminent task of contemporary architects to concern themselves academically with philosophy. A comprehension of the intellectual basis of man's contemporary existence will induce universal values in their works. It will give them the tools to rationalize their often intuitive designs and to defend them against other agencies of pure material orientation. It will also qualify them to elicit, through verbal interpretation, understanding, and sympathy among a general public that so far has remained psychologically aloof from the form expression of the new architecture.

The contemporary architect needs to be a philosopher, and architecture needs to be philosophical. That is to say, the architect, as the one charged with translating man's life into building, needs to comprehend the spiritual basis of human existence; he must philosophize. And architecture, as the instrument destined to guarantee human life, needs to manifest the spiritual reality of man; it must be philosophical. It is true that the emotional alienation of progressive building from the taste of the general public is due to the fact that the novel forms of architecture no longer move, nor even reach, the emotions of the people. But this is so not because the new forms have no emotional potential, but because the architect, himself, has neither consciously analyzed this potential in his works, nor has he educated the people. In matters of aesthetics, the architect still works intuitively rather than consciously and remains individual where he should be universal. Thus, the fundamental reason for the alienation of architecture from popular sentiment is that the architect, not comprehending intellectually the reality of contemporary life, is not a philosopher and that, consequently, his buildings are not philosophical.

Formerly, architecture was philosophical; it was expressive of its epoch in both technique and spirit and was congruent with the beliefs and knowledge of the people. But expression in contemporary architecture has evolved so fast that the receptibility of the general public can no longer follow this development. Its forms have departed too far from the accepted to be reached by the sentiment of the masses. It is no longer possible in contemporary society to educate people through direct material creations, be they art or architecture, or to set new perspectives through pace-setting masterpieces, because the aesthetic delight in modern creations is no longer a question of liking or disliking, but a matter of comprehension. Disliking, while yet understanding, gives a feeling of superiority and induces a conciliative spirit; but disliking due to the failure of understanding results in a feeling of humiliation and hence provokes indignation and antagonism. It is for this reason that modern architecture is essentially unpopular.

The only way of equipping the masses with the ability to comprehend and, thus, to appreciate the new architectural expression is to enlighten them verbally and intellectually. This means that the architect must descend from the throne of the aloof individual artist and concern himself with public opinion and the means of influencing it. For among all artists it is the architect who has the privilege to work with the conscious intention of addressing the sentiments of the masses, as is the mission of all art.

Such a task presupposes that the architect is fully aware of the philosophic basis of his work, and it is here that a basic need for the contemporary architect and his education is uncovered: the imperative to concern himself with the science of philosophy. And he also cannot be released from this imperative by the philosophic profession, because the total comprehension of building requires previous experience as an active participant in the creative process, and it is unlikely that one aloof from any practical work can comprehend the full range of architectural creation, especially in view of the particular ideological implications brought about by the mechanical revolution.

While the professional philosopher investigates the reality of the present epoch and analyzes the major spiritual forces that bear upon society, it is primarily the task of the architect to derive therefrom general values of living and universal principles of architectural creation. These, then, may again give building the ideological content that alone distinguishes architecture from the mere technical product and may provide the spiritual basis of a comprehensive order, which contemporary architecture is lacking. That is to say, the major task of contemporary architecture is not so much a matter of economical, social, hygienic, or technological improvement, but is essentially a matter of philosophic search.

definition

SOCIETY IN BUILDING is the social order manifested in building. It is the architectural response to the particular rules under which society is organized in pursuit of its ideals.

SOCIETY IN BUILDING is the architectural substantiation of the ordered community, which, though composed of individuals, possesses innate characteristics of its own that, in turn, act upon the individual.

SOCIETY IN BUILDING, therefore, can be of restrictive consequence. Since the rules of community life set limits on the freedom of the individual, such a system may narrow the possibilities for architectural creation.

SOCIETY IN BUILDING can also be of an incentive nature. Since society combines and directs individual efforts and organizes development, individual architectural ingenuity is likely to be utilized to the optimum.

SOCIETY IN BUILDING is effective both directly and indirectly. Directly, it subjects building to the common order of an organized communal living; indirectly, it affects building through its influence upon ideals and morals of the individual.

SOCIETY IN BUILDING is increasingly important in contemporary architectural development. Since nobility is ceasing to be the patron of art and architecture, society itself has become the sponsor of cultural progress.

SOCIETY IN BUILDING is closely connected with politics. For it is the government that represents society, deciding economic policy, promoting art, and influencing architectural development.

SOCIETY IN BUILDING, then, is a major force in the development of contemporary architecture. It is manifested in the coordinated planning of cities, the systematic layout of surface communication, the organized support of social housing, and the accurate supervision of hygienics and security in building and it is increasingly concerned with the aesthetics of city and community.

In addition to geo-relationship, climate, and religion-philosophy, society itself, through its organizational structure, governmental policy, rules of behavior, and universal ethics, is another environmental factor of architectural formation, both in the past and in the present. Though society is influential in almost every aspect of cultural activity everywhere, its extent and importance for architectural growth have generally found only little attention. It is true that society is a heterogeneous organism composed of, and created by, individuals, but it is also an autogenous organism that, in reverse, influences the life and thought of the individual within it. Thus, the development of art and architecture has always been in close affinity with the form of society. In fact, in many cases society itself, and its political organization, has been the decisive factor in architectural progress, and many cultural epochs are linked as much with the name of a particular political form or its leading statesman as with the names of the individual artist creators.

In the past, society was organized in such a way that material wealth, intellectual knowledge, and executive power were in the hands of only a few. Consequently, only these few possessed the potential, both spiritual and material, to patronize art and architecture. Now, with the shift of this potential from the individual nobleman to the impersonal bourgeoisie (industrial corporation, school board, church congregation, etc.) decisive changes have taken place. The patron, whose individuality together with the artist's ingenuity constituted a distinct and generating polarity of creation, has been replaced by a collective representative body, overly powerful because of its anonymity, indistinct because of its multiplicity, and changeable because of its political dependence.

As a result, the former creative polarity between architect and patron, a harmonious interdependence, has been set off balance or has been dissolved altogether. It has made the architect and artist either subservient to the collective government or has relegated them to independence at the price of non-support. The so called "autonomy" of the "new architecture," as hailed by architects themselves, has ironically limited the influence of architecture upon other creative professions and has, in fact, brought architecture into another much greater dependence on forces it can no longer control.

Moreover, building in contemporary society has increasingly become a field for political demonstration that has little esteem for architecture itself, only considering it as one of the means to either win popular support for political issues or to manifest political ideologies. The fatality of these tendencies was very evident in the governmental pressure put upon the creative arts in Germany during 1933–45, which resulted in the exodus of the strongest protagonists of progressive architecture and art and caused German architecture to lapse back into a neoclassic-nationalistic style; they are apparent in the monumental scale of the official architecture of the Soviet Union; and they are also manifested in the planning committees for cities, communities, or provinces, whose existence and activity are often bound to politics rather than to architectural principles.

In this light, it is an urgent task for contemporary architecture to study the interdependence between society and architecture and precisely define the competence and the role of each within the other. Growing cities with their increasingly complex functions require central organization and control. Yet, unawareness of the consequences of this centralization upon the sphere of the individual has left both the architectural layman and the specialist disinterested in the setup of these central bodies and in many countries has caused central planning to be controlled mainly by administrators and economists, with the result that the political-partisan issues have become more dominant than the architectural-social ones.

From this viewpoint, the example of Japanese residential architecture, because of its close association with the evolution of its society throughout history, has a direct relationship to contemporary architecture. It will show the factors involved more objectively, because its happenings belong to the past; more clearly, because the social structure was simple; and more instructively, because the interdependence of architecture and society was so intimate.

In the following pages the various ways in which society, its organization, and its policy have influenced the Japanese house and its evolution are given particular attention. The influences have been manifold and profound, and their effect upon each phase of Japanese cultural evolution cannot be stressed enough. They have been referred to frequently in the foregoing chapters and thus may be taken as evidence of the encompassing imprint society itself leaves upon the growth of architecture.

policy

The cultural development of Japan is conspicuous by its dependence on governmental initiative. In Europe, also, art and architecture were very often fostered by the farsightedness of a statesman or by the patronage of an aristocrat. But it was, primarily, either from the genius of individual creators or from the wisdom of anonymous communities that decisive impulses were received (though never without affinity to the political scene). Japan too has produced great personalities in all fields of creative art. However, it is important to note that the essential stages in her cultural growth as a nation can be, in one way or another, traced back to governmental policy. In this sense one may very well speak of a "state culture" in its good meaning. And the sudden transformations that proved so decisive for Japan's culture until very recent times permit the conclusion that without the particular governmental policies that mark Japanese historical development the culture of Japan would have gone an essentially different way—a statement that could not possibly be extended to the development and achievement of Western culture.

In fact, the establishment of an intimate and continuous cultural contact with China, which throughout history brought the achievements of China's superior civilization to Japan; the isolation from any external communication during Japan's late Middle Ages, which allowed undisturbed evolution of national traits; and the adoption of Western civilization, which turned Japan into a modern world power were obviously all political measures. They demonstrate the immense consequences of governmental policy on cultural growth. That such policies that determined cultural matters were altogether possible was again due to a political decision. For, when the relationship with the Asiatic mainland had opened the eyes of the ruling classes to the fact that China had a governmental system superior to theirs, the brilliant prince regent Shōtoku Taishi (ca. 570–621) adopted it as a basis for his own administration and that of the following rulers. It was this Taika Reform and the resulting central government that enabled a cultural policy that summarily decided on matters of religion-philosophy, art, and architecture and made the whole country follow suit. Without it, the cultural consistency throughout Japan would have never reached such a conformity, nor would the national achievement have been as great as it is.

As to Japanese residential architecture, it could hardly be expected that governmental policy would in particular concern itself with the houses of the commoners at a time when the value of the lower classes was measured only in terms of their material capacity, as farmers for production or as soldiers for destruction. In fact, the early forms of the ordinary residence, the pit dwelling and the subsequent farmhouse, were indigenous forms and remained unaffected by authority. However, not only did this form of dwelling show hardly any progress throughout history but its influence on the later dwelling, the subject matter of this paper, was also minor by comparison to the influence of the aristocratic mansion. The fact that the prototype of the aristocratic dwelling, the *shinden* style, was basically Chinese and that many of its later changes were direct adoptions of features from Buddhist architecture or were stimulated indirectly through the influence of Chinese philosophy demonstrates how such political measures as contact with China and the patronage of Buddhism were instrumental in the evolution of the Japanese house.

The influence of governmental policy upon culture, then, culminated in the feudalism of the Tokugawa clan (1600–1867), who, in spite of their non-cultural motives, effected, probably quite unintentionally, the development of Japan's distinct and unique residential architecture. During that period, the ruling classes, in an attempt to retain their declining power, shut off the archipelago from any communication with the outer world for more than two hundred years (1639–1854). Laws were issued to arrest any progressive movement that could provoke a change and endanger the *status quo,* covering even such minute details of life as material, color, and form of clothes and the time to wear them. Infanticide was not only practiced but was officially encouraged—successfully encouraged because it stabilized the population during those centuries of political isolation.

Before that time there already existed particular regulations that substantially controlled the residential architecture of the cities. But the policy of isolationism had an even stronger effect upon the building activity of the common classes. In order to both economize and control residential building, rules were set up for the system and detail of house construction, and these were woodblock printed and distributed to all carpenters. Thus, while the farm population continued dwelling in their primitive way because of inhuman suppression, all other building activity was masterfully organized, economized, and simplified, resulting in a unique building order such as the West has as yet to reach. It was a comprehensive organization of building through government, with a materialistic and despotic aim, but with social and aesthetic rewards.

However, this initiative of government in cultural matters from early history until the present, together with the feudal order of society, has produced a trend among the people that has not always been of benefit for Japan's growth. With the dependence of inferior on superior being absolute (the children on the parents, the wife on the husband, the followers on their lord, the lord on the rulers), the people were trained to implicit obedience. Individual initiative and independence was frowned upon, or even forcibly repressed, and it was, therefore, only natural that the habit of imitation was strongly stimulated.

Moreover, the particular social system allowed the rulers to impose any change upon the mass of the people, be it in thought, religion, philosophy, or art, and to compel them to employ the new even though they might not comprehend it. In other words, the people were made to imitate. The policy toward China must have had a similar effect, for the continuous borrowing by the government from the advanced Chinese culture set the example for a long sequence of imitative adoptions of architectural features between the various styles of the feudal class-architecture within Japan herself. Rather than trying to set out independently and explore on their own, craftsmen and artists essentially relied on types employed by the more fortunate classes of their own society or on the superior civilization from without. And the story of Japan's Westernization of life, science, industry, and society after the Meiji Reformation (1868) until the present is convincing proof that the Japanese succeeded in developing a positive trait out of what was for centuries only a circumstance imposed upon the people by the government and its policy.

social order

The structure of society itself, the feudalism—with lord-vassal relationship, class system, and fine gradation into superior and inferior—also had decisive architectural consequences. It indirectly influenced the formation of the Japanese residence by regimenting the life and thought of the people and it also provoked direct and immediate architectural response by requiring certain spaces and features for the performance of official functions.

It has been mentioned earlier that the "official space" in the Japanese house generally is clearly separated from the private space and that the guest is bestowed with particular honors. These principles, different from the general Western conception, are clearly reflected in the ground plan and room appropriation and have been prompted by the class society. Paper scrolls with illustrations of *shinden* mansions, the early aristocratic style of the 10th to 12th centuries, show that in the early stages of residential development no separate space for reception of the official guest was provided for (Plates 119–120). Rather, the visitor was received on the veranda, *hisashi,* though there are examples indicating that frequently a certain part of the veranda was portioned off for this particular purpose. But with the expansion of the ceremonies, a separate house was provided for this purpose, the guest hall, *kyaku-den.* This building, the interior of which was partitioned for the various ranks, gradually transcended its sole function as guest hall and became the standardized main residence, *shuden,* of the warrior caste, in which the reception room then became the most important feature (Plates 129–131). Here the vassals gathered, and here at times the lord also was entertained. Order of rank was precisely manifested in the seating of the guests, and even a separate anteroom was provided for the lower ranks.

As to the houses of the commoners, it of course hardly ever happened that a superior entered and, consequently, no such distinction existed originally. But when the rising merchant class and other commoners, in spite of all preventive measures by the government, gradually patterned their houses after the prototype of the warrior residence, not only did they incorporate the physical features of the reception room, such as picture recess, *tokonoma*, shelving recess, *tana*, and study place, *shoin*, but they also took over the particular order of seating and the esteem for the guest. This adoption was not merely prompted by the understandable wish to possess these symbols of social standing, but was an almost necessary measure. For the visits of warriors to the houses of rich merchants were no longer so rare because of the mounting financial difficulties of the warriors. It is from this sociological peculiarity that the reception room and the visitor obtained their pronounced importance within the Japanese residence.

Similarly, the feature of a spacious entrance hall, *genkan*, which is distinct for the Japanese residence, is closely interrelated with the social order, and the evolution of this feature reflects the development of society. In the early residential form, the *shinden* style, the entrance consisted of two central gates, *chū-mon*, each arranged in a covered walkway, *chū-mon-rō*, which extended in south direction on the east side and the west side of the main hall, *shinden*, and which linked the separate buildings of the aristocratic mansion together (Plates 119–120). In the succeeding *shoin* style, the east walkway was incorporated into the main hall, *shuden*, as an expanded veranda with a separate roof and combined with the broad veranda on the south toward the garden to become the actual and most impressive center of the entire compound. This extended veranda, still called *chū-mon*, i.e., the central gate, merged with a particular carriage stop, *kuruma-yose*, that was accentuated with a curved roof, and became the distinct entrance hall, *genkan*.

In the late medieval society of Japan, this entrance hall was attributed a special significance as the expression of social rank, and commoners were strictly forbidden to construct such a hall. This regard of the entrance as an expression of power in the social order went so far that in 1843 the shogunate, *bakufu*, had to issue an explicit interdiction against the construction of entrance halls by the commoners under threat of severe punishment. It is, therefore, understandable that when, finally, in the reformation of 1868 those class manifestations were declared invalid, even the poor citizen constructed a particular entrance hall for his own, although he probably still continued to use his former inconspicuous family entrance.

So strong has been the memory of the house attaining distinction by the entrance hall that this feature has successfully maintained its existence until the present day in spite of all measures of rationalizing and economizing. It is true that the entrance hall serves a very practical purpose, because space is required for removing the shoes and overcoming a level difference of about 2 ft. (600 mm.) between the ground and the matted floor. However, there is a high probability that in the meantime the Japanese have come to realize that an abrupt change from exterior world to interior space is uncomfortable and brutal and that the compensation for this contrast by a mediatory and well proportioned space is just the minimum requirement for cultured living and is, therefore, more imperative than any economic-rational objective.

city community

While the terms "village" and "city" in contemporary usage indicate difference of size rather than difference of consistency, in the past the two terms had more than quantitative implications. Until the beginning of modern times the village was a community which, for mutual protection and assistance, loosely tied together independent farming families that still led an autonomous life. The village thus remained a multiplicity of individual organisms even though as a rule they had some sort of common leadership. By contrast, the city was a being unto itself in which individuals or families were only constituent elements, i.e., organs that depended on each other for their existence. In the city, the various functions of existence, securing of food, shelter, and protection, were no longer performed by each single family, but separately by particular groups. Cause of the city was the realization that specialization into single trades provided advantage; result of the city was organization, both socially and politically.

Therefore, it was mainly the environment of the cities that was conducive to stimulating progressive forces, and the subject matter of this paper, the Japanese residence of the 17th and 18th centuries, was essentially a product of the organized community in the city, that is, a citizen house. The farmhouse has also profited greatly from this architectural achievement of the city, but, as the rural population lacked the means for education, material, and time to concern themselves with architectural improvement, no basic changes of living and building in the rural areas have taken place through the centuries except for an occasional adoption of architectural features.

Japan is conspicuous for the frequent transfer of the imperial site or even of the entire capital to a different locality. Some theories have been established as to the causes for these transfers. One theory maintains that the cause is the ancient ontology that death would defile the house; another theory attributes the move of the capital to more practical reasons, such as indicating a different political course or escaping the local influences of monasteries, clans, and the like. But, even though true in one or the other case, these theories do not bear general validity and are significant only insofar as they suggest that the transfer of capital or imperial palace was made for diverse reasons.

No doubt, the structural deficiency of the houses also made such a change, with the subsequent new erection of the entire capital, very desirable, and the very simple social system and uncomplicated governmental apparatus in early history did not yet provide any substantial obstruction. If cities were systematically laid out before the 7th century, no traces of them are known. In the 7th century, however, the capital Naniwa-kyō (present Osaka) was constructed on a grid-like pattern according to a model plan, which was taken from China as also was the system of the society as a whole. Thereafter, the capital was moved for the period of two emperors to Otsu on Lake Biwa, and again newly constructed in Fujiwara (Nara Prefecture). Late in the 7th century the capital Heijō-kyō in Nara was laid out, modeled after the capital Chang-an of the Chinese T'ang dynasty, and was completed in 710.

By that time, the quality of architecture had improved considerably and Nara remained the capital under seven emperors. After, in a sudden move, the capital had been transferred to Nagaoka for a short time, a new capital was erected in present Kyoto. It was called Heian-kyō, the "capital of peace." Heian, or Kyoto as it later was named, remained the capital until 1869, when the emperor moved to Edo (Tokyo). But, long before that time Kyoto had lost its meaning as executive locale, because for centuries the actual political decisions were essentially made by the military leaders, the shoguns, and the family clans in Kamakura and Edo. As could be expected, other rising cities of the growing nation took advantage of the planning experiences gained in these frequent transfers and adopted similar systems of regular layout for their own, thus greatly contributing to the spread of progressive features from the old cities.

Certainly, this relatively rapid transfer of the metropolitan site in early history and the subsequent enormous building tasks to be accomplished within the shortest time must have stimulated a systematic building of houses just as did those frequent fires that only with some luck might occasionally spare a minor part of the city on the windward side. Though the extent of this stimulus cannot be exactly measured, there can be little doubt that it contributed greatly to the development of standardization in residential building, for which Japanese residential architecture is so famous. But of more consequence in generating architectural creation and development was the environment of the city community itself, both physically and spiritually, and

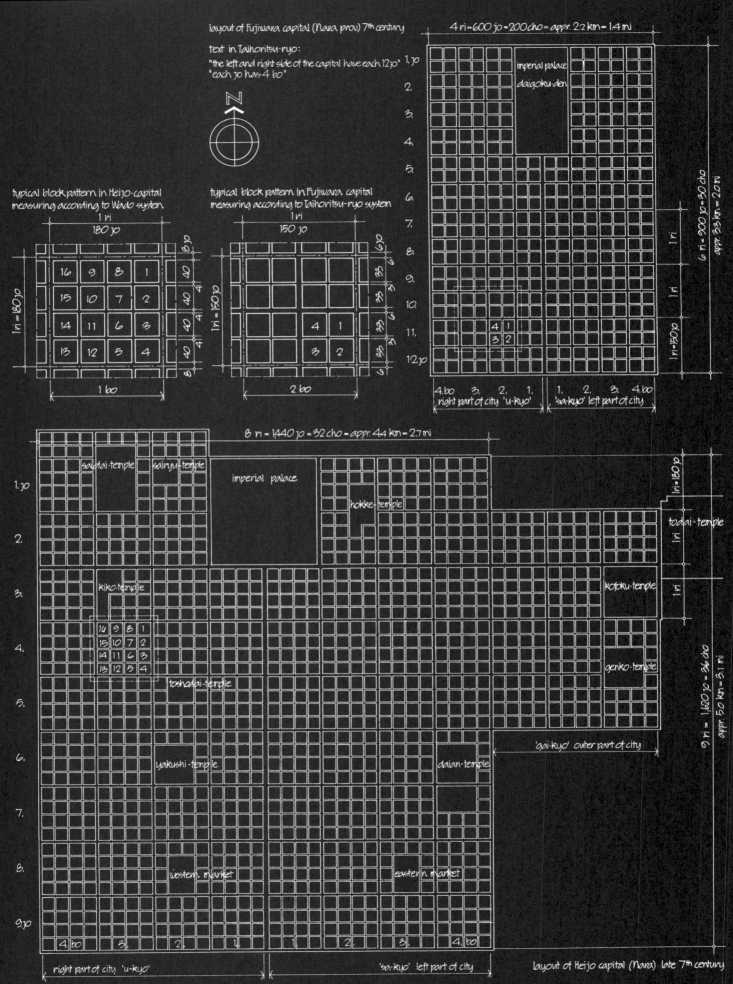

layout of Fujiwara capital (Nara prov.) 7th century

text in Taihoritsu-ryo:

"the left and right side of the capital have each 12 jo"
"each jo has 4 bo"

typical block pattern in Heijo-capital measuring according to Wado system.

typical block pattern in Fujiwara capital measuring according to Taihoritsu-ryo system

4 ri = 600 jo = 200 cho = appr. 2.2 km = 1.4 mi

imperial palace
daigoku-den

right part of city 'u-kyo'   'sa-kyo' left part of city

8 ri = 1440 jo = 32 cho = appr. 4.4 km = 2.7 mi

saidai-temple   sairyu-temple

imperial palace

hokke-temple

kiko-temple

todai-temple

kofuku-temple

toshodai-temple

genko-temple

yakushi-temple

daian-temple

'gai-kyo' outer part of city

western market   eastern market

right part of city 'u-kyo'   'sa-kyo' left part of city   layout of Heijo capital (Nara) late 7th century

FIGURE 78: Layout of ancient capital cities. Fujiwara and Heijō.

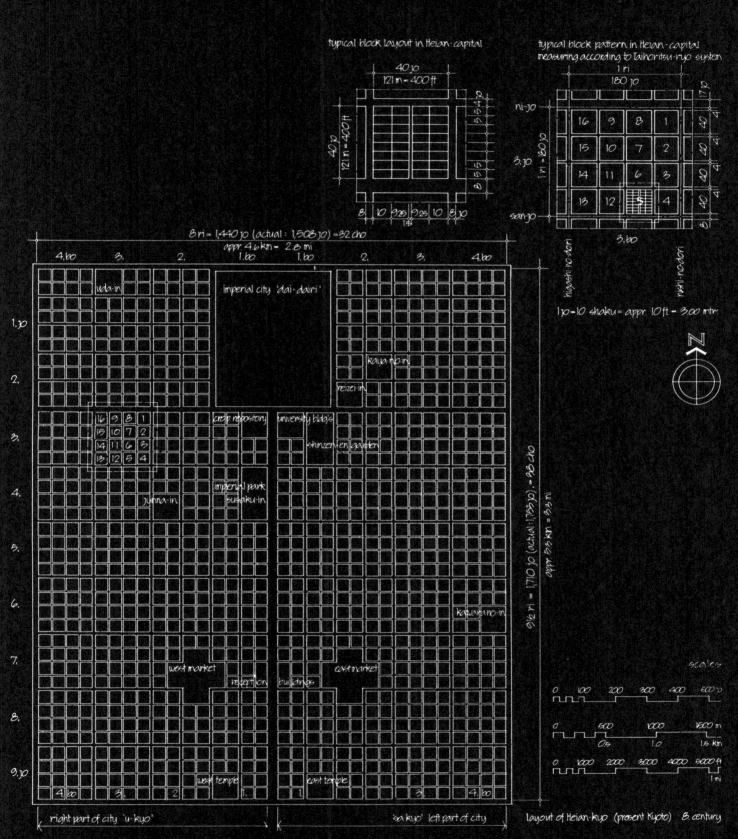

typical block layout in Heian-capital

typical block pattern in Heian-capital
measuring according to Taihoritsu-ryo system

40 jo
121 m = 400 ft

1 ri
180 jo

40 jo
121 m = 400 ft

ni-jo

16	9	8	1
15	10	7	2
14	11	6	3
13	12	5	4

3 jo

1 ri = 180 jo

san-jo

3 bo

higashi no dori

nishi no dori

1 jo = 10 shaku = appr. 10 ft = 3.00 mtr.

8 ri = 1,440 jo (actual: 1,508 jo) = 32 cho
appr. 4.6 km = 2.8 mi

9½ ri = 1,710 jo (actual: 1,753 jo) = 38 cho
appr. 5.5 km = 3.3 mi

4 bo   3   2   1 bo   1 bo   2   3   4 bo

1 jo

2

3

4

5

6

7

8

9 jo

uda-in

imperial city 'dai-dairi'

kaya-no-in

reizei-in

16	9	8	1
15	10	7	2
14	11	6	3
13	12	5	4

crop repository

university bldg's

shinzen-en garden

imperial park
susaku-in

junna-in

kawakano-in

west market

east market

reception   buildings

4 bo   3   2   1   1   3   4 bo

west temple

east temple

right part of city 'u-kyo'

'sa-kyo' left part of city

scales

0   100   200   300   400   500 jo

0   500   1000   1500 m
0.5   1.0   1.5 km

0   1000   2000   3000   4000   5000 ft
1 mi

layout of Heian-kyo (present Kyoto) 8. century

FIGURE 78 (continued): Layout of ancient capital cities. Heian.

the outstanding features of the Japanese residence are in more than one way linked to the city and its community.

Here, the merchant class established themselves and patronized the cult of tea, an aestheticism that permeated all Japanese architecture and art and made them distinct from anything in the West. Here, upon orders from the rulers, the ablest artists and craftsmen of the nation gathered and competed with each other in developing the best new designs and methods of building. Here, the superb carpenters of Japan set up their guilds and developed their secret manuals of building technique. Here, collaborative forces made building an entirety that related house to site, site to block, block to street, street to palace and temple, thereby creating a universal order of architecture. Here, the unique Japanese measure system emerged through fusion of the constructional column distance in residences with the measure unit of city planning, the *ken* unit in *kyō-ma* measurement, and provided the world with a metric phenomenon in architecture that has no equal. Here, narrowness of city lots and restrictive regulations of the rulers imposed the exercise of restraint and economy and stimulated recognition of its ethical and aesthetical values. Here, the proximity of the social classes inspired the noted exchange of architectural features between all classes and made it possible for the Japanese residence to incorporate features from the architecture of the clergy, nobility, military, peasantry, and merchantry and, in fact, to become the very materialization of the dominant traits of all those classes: the religiosity of the priest, the delicacy of the nobleman, the austerity of the warrior, the simplicity of the farmer, and the practicality of the merchant.

In this sense, the community of the city was the laboratory where the material and spiritual essentials of the Japanese residence were prepared and were then "assembled" by the most proficient craftsmen. The mere physical environment of the city community, however, also stimulated a direct architectural response. A result of one such response is the window with latticework, *kōshi-mado,* which is so characteristic of the Japanese dwelling. For the dense order of vertical battons enabled the inhabitants to open the house toward the street for light and air and for the pleasant pastime of observing street life, without necessarily having to put up with the public gaze, which could prove quite embarrassing at times if the house was one in the geisha quarters. Also, there is reason to believe that the systematic layout of the city street pattern, with resulting identical width for the individual lots, has encouraged the standardized building of residences. And the paper scrolls depicting street scenes among the common citizens in ancient Heian (Kyoto) show that the post distance *ken* (which later was to become an official measure unit) had already at that time been fairly standardized for each house unit; probably at about 8 *shaku* (2,400 mm. = 8 ft.).

Also, the straight, gently sloped roof of the Japanese residence apparently was derived from the ancient citizen house. For contrary to the steep slope of the thatched roof of the farmhouse and also different from the curved slope of the tile or shingle roof of Buddhist and aristocratic architecture, the roof of the early citizen house, covered by simple boards, already possessed the straightness and inclination of that of the future Japanese residence.

There are many more individual features that owe their existence to the environment of city community. Yet, their mention would only emphasize and not alter the fact that the ordinary Japanese dwelling, which is the subject of this paper, is essentially a house that evolved in the city and is not the house of the farmer, who constituted the major portion of the population. Yet, since the city house increasingly influenced the architecture of the farmhouse also, it has seemed appropriate to term this city house generally as "the Japanese house" even though it was originally the house of a minority living in the city.

prohibition

It has been mentioned earlier that the concept of simplicity, a distinct quality of Japanese residential architecture, originally was the pure expression of poverty, which only later was elevated through the cult of tea to a medium of profound aesthetic expression. Here also society has been instrumental, because the rise of the tea cult was mainly the result of certain circumstances and tensions provoked by the class system of the feudalistic society. This indebtedness of Japan's noted simplicity in architecture to the prevailing socio-environmental conditions is further authenticated by the numerous restrictive laws issued by the Tokugawa shogunate (1600–1867), which, though hardly for ethical reasons, forced the rising citizen class to exercise simplicity in building, apparently against their own will.

With the intention to retain the *status quo* of the existing socio-political situation, the activities of the citizen, both public and private, were prescribed in all details during the Tokugawa period and were controlled to such a degree that it made the life of the individual a stereotyped compliance with numerous rules—rules that did not even exempt children and their toys or the letters of young lovers. Yet, there is reason to believe that actually many more regulations were in force than those that have been preserved in the form of written public announcements or ordinances. For, as requests to the military government, the *bakufu,* in Edo indicate, local officials issued their own laws to suit the prevailing circumstances without interference from the central government as long as they were in conformity with the general policy.

Most of these prohibitions, as the existing documentary evidence shows, were concerned with the citizen class, *chō-nin,* i.e., the merchants and artisans who politically and also culturally had become increasingly influential. For they alone among the commoners possessed the means, both financially and intellectually, to think about improving their conditions and to become a challenge to the ruling classes. The farmers, however, who constituted the mass of the people, did not require such restrictive regulations. For it was the efficient and therefore wise practice of the lords to simply tax them beyond their ability to pay. Mounting debts were found to be most conducive to hard labor and to a total mobilization of manpower that also took children and the aged into the production process. Continuous work at the brink of physical capacity had proven an appropriate method to keep the farmers from concerning themselves with the possibilities of eventually improving their living conditions, which necessarily would be at the expense of their superiors.

It is no accident, indeed, that the noted characteristics of Japanese living and building took distinct form just at this time when the enormous, and for the contemporary Westerner hardly conceivable, pressure of the feudal regime minutely controlled all phases of life in society and suppressed any tendency toward demonstration of material wealth by the people. It is reasonable to assume that the very narrow limits set by the government were decisively instrumental in the rise of the famed spirit of restraint, simplicity, and rationalism that characterizes the Japanese residence and distinguishes it from its Western counterparts.

A study of the known ordinances for residential building reveals the following motives:

1. Many regulations concern fire preventive measures. Issued right after the instructive experience of one of those devastating fires that periodically swept Edo (Tokyo), they prescribe building materials, house distances, eaves projections, access to water supply, length and depth of houses, surface finish, etc.

2. Other regulations, mostly of a restrictive nature, aim at preventing the wealthy citizen class from extinguishing visible class differences by imitating the residential style of the nobility and military, or from perhaps even surpassing them in material or decorative quality. Accordingly they deal with building materials, interior features, décor, room sizes, house depth, etc.

3. Less numerous are the regulations for the military that were made in order to

retain their rapidly deteriorating economic power and to prevent their financial dependence on the merchants. Not only did they restrict any extravagance in their official life (for example limitation of the quantity of food to entertain visitors), but they also issued ordinances for simplicity and restraint in house construction and room appropriation, though with fewer threats of penalty for non-compliance than in the case of the merchants.

4. The fewest regulations in fact, were instigated directly by architectural factors. Being mainly concerned with the functional efficiency of the cities, they prescribe street width, setback of house from the street, maximum projection of roof eaves, and building depth; and there is a possibility that in these measures they followed but a customary rule that no longer held meaning for that time.

The absence of any rules that were prompted primarily by the aesthetics of architecture and life, though not astonishing at all, is significant insofar as it shows that not only were the ruling classes hardly concerned with the aesthetic quality of their subjects' life, but also the exercise of simplicity and restraint in many cases was as much imposed upon the people as it was supposedly disdained by them. It can be assumed that the classes that were actually able to concern themselves with the aesthetics of life did not tend toward simplicity at all but, quite naturally, wanted to express their material wealth in the style, size, material, and décor of their buildings. Otherwise no prohibitive law such as the following would have been necessary:

" 'Regulations concerning residences, weddings, funerals, etc.,' March 1668.

"When constructing a city house, it should be plain and simple. Frieze rails, *nageshi*, doors of cedar, *sugi-do*, projected study window, *tsuke-shoin*, fine wood carving, *gushi-kata horimono*, elaborate wood profiles, *kumi-mono*, are forbidden. It is further not allowed to lacquer the wooden strips, *toko-bushi-san*, and sill of the picture recess, *toko-gamachi*; also the use of *kara-kami* (Chinese paper) for the opaque paper panels, *fusuma*, is not permissible. . . .

"Chinese paper, *kara-kami*, with sprinkled gold leaves, decorative bows, rackets for children's games, *hago-ita*, equipment with gold decoration for the doll festival, *hina-matsuri*, and for the boys' festival, *tango-matsuri*, are forbidden. . . .

"If a person fails to follow those rules the superintendent will be held responsible. . . ."

Also, the warrior residences became increasingly subjected to such control, as is apparent in a later announcement of the shogunate, *bakufu*. In this ordinance, after issuing similar restrictions in material and décor already imposed upon the ordinary citizen, the text continues:

"There has been previously an announcement that houses should be built as small as possible, and in general this was correctly understood. To emphasize it, even if one wants to build a room of 10 mats, one rather should limit it to 5–6 mats. Especially, houses and rooms that are not immediately needed should not be built at all. It is important that the height of the house should be as low as possible. . . .

"The ordinance to build tile roofs does not mean that all tiles have to be imbedded in clay. Only if one uses flat tiles, *hira-gawara*, or pan tiles, *san-gawara*, a clay bed is necessary. It is not permitted to make a tile roof just for better appearance. The building with walls at the outside entirely coated by plaster can only be encouraged. . . ."

In the latter part, no doubt concern for fire security was instrumental, and it was not the hygienics of living nor any sort of consideration for the welfare of the lower classes that prompted these fire preventive measures. Instead, experience had taught that fire with its destructive mood did not recognize any distinction between the classes of society and wiped out all buildings regardless of aristocratic privileges. Thus, the upper classes took extreme care that the ordinary citizens also observed these measures lest their own homes be endangered. This attitude was certainly instrumental for the issuance of the following announcement concerning the city slums which was made public right after a devastating fire in the capital on January 18, 1657, when fire fighting had been essentially hampered by the density of building on each city block where the formerly open back yards had increasingly been built with houses.

"At the construction it is understood that the living space (room) of the tenement houses facing to the street, *naga-ya,* and those in the back yard, *ura-dana,* should not exceed 3 *ken* (about 6,500 mm. = 19.5 ft.) in depth. . . ."

The yielding of authority to the increasing pressure of the citizen class is evident in the edict of April 1720, after a fire in the previous month.

"Until now, in the city plaster-built enclosures and houses were not permitted for the citizen class, *chō-nin,* but from now on the use of plaster and clay tiles is also set free for the ordinary citizen. Besides, anything is permitted if it serves fire prevention and protection against fire spreading. . . ."

And it appears that the farming population also became increasingly defiant of the imposed authority of feudalism and occasionally challenged the hereditary right of professional monopoly that was granted by the social order. For in 1803 the feudal lord of Sado inquires of the shogunate in Edo (Tokyo):

"In the domain of Sado the farmers who thus far on their own had built only minor structures such as toilets, shacks for fertilizer, barns, etc., are lately engaging also in constructing entire residences, even temples, shrines, and pagodas. They were ordered to stop by the master carpenter of the 'town below the castle,' but did not follow the order. It is asked in the name of the feudal lord whether it is right to forbid the farmers such activity."

The shogunate then answered back: "If the unprofessional work endangers the activity of the hereditary handicraft, it is all right to strictly forbid such activity. . . ."

Without any doubt, as the authorities controlled and regulated any and all phases of living and building, not only did customs emerge that were stereotyped and without inner truth, but also the taste of the people must have been essentially molded by restrictions that told them what to like and what not to like. Although the famed Japanese simplicity in architecture, art, and life is based to a great extent on genuine tradition, there is no question that the prohibitive influence of the feudal regime was an essential factor which, hardly for noble reasons, reinforced that tradition and prevented the rise of any deviation. Wherever the authoritative power did not reach, the opposite trend of colorful and demonstrative beauty became dominant among those who could afford it, providing convincing evidence that even aesthetic conceptions are neither inherited nor racially linked, but are in essence due to environmental factors, one of which is the form of society itself.

for contemporary architecture

Residential building in the medieval Japanese society, thus, presents an example of integrated planning in the sense that the small was subjugated to the large and clearly manifests an obvious and essential dependence of the individual house on society, its rulers, its organization, and its aims. Yet, it should be taken into account that, in comparison to the contemporary West, the structure of society was simple and clearly defined, the problems of planning were few, and the right of the individual was of no concern. It is for these reasons that the dependence of house upon society is substantiated in terms more easily readable and more instructive than in any modern society.

The long period of unchanged feudalistic order allowed the house to respond sensitively even to subtle social pressure. The reactions show that society provided a common denominator not only for the physical-external aspects of housing but, more important, also for the spiritual aspects of life and house. In origin it was an order that had been imposed by the rulers, who had not always had noble motives. But, in the end, the individual had the reward of living in a society that through a universal order of living and building yielded him a share in each accomplishment of the community.

In the West, after a long period of organic growth of the medieval towns and villages, the newly achieved freedom of the individual together with the rapid growth of cities after the industrial revolution brought about a misunderstanding as to the role of architecture in society which has led to the physical and spiritual disorder of contemporary cities in the West, as it has also done in modern Japan. The awareness seems to be lost that the relationship of man-society, or of house-city, is one of mutual dependence. Society serves man as much as man serves society; the city affects the house as much as the house affects the city.

Only a system of organized society allows man's existence and individual freedom. But it simultaneously imposes upon each individual a continuous tribute that earns him the right of living in society. It is a dangerous notion of the contemporary age to think that the material price alone is sufficient for such a tribute and at the same time to expect unlimited freedom of action and thought as long as it does not physically conflict with others. For not only does this eliminate the individual as an element that shapes society, but it also degrades society to a mere material-opportunistic association without any ethical and aesthetic values of its own. There is little evidence of the architect's willingness in general to cooperate with planning committees, even less to submit his individualism to more general principles of which he himself might not always approve. Much less is the citizen willing to sacrifice even one of his personal likings for the sake of the whole.

While morality and aesthetics of "human behavior" are anchored in the civil code, no attempts have been made to analyze the morality and aesthetics of "human building," even less to subject it to a common law. It is true that in most countries rules have been established in the form of building codes. But the guiding principles of these rules are more concerned with security, stability, practicality, and hygiene of building than with conceptions of aesthetics. The public boards that promote these principles usually have only little executive power and are, as a rule, opposed by the architect himself. The deeper reason for this phenomenon is that city and society are not conceived of as an entity with its own laws and principles, but are regarded as an accidental assemblage of independent elements, each with its own personal morality. Consequently, the planning boards of cities generally do not have the right to interfere with the aesthetic notions of the individual. There is no awareness that order is an essential element of art and, even less, that the organized planning of cities is an art.

Here, the Japanese residential architecture as a whole shows the aesthetics of a metropolitan order owing to submission to general rules of society just as European medieval towns do owing to their faithful adherence to a common belief. The contemporary West, however, is lacking in both absolute rulers and unique beliefs. What increasingly determines present life in all its phases, independent of race and place, is intellect, i.e., science. Education, politics, family life, even the arts and architecture, have become strongly influenced by science rather than by intuition, emotion, or faith—not because of man's wish but because of his belated recognition that only science will enable his survival. All cities are liable to undergo tremendous physical transformations owing to the increase in population, industrialization, automation, and their inevitable effects, and only through science can the media be provided to successfully cope with this challenge. In the course of events, it can be expected that science will give further substantial evidence not only that the psychological well-being of man depends very much on his physical environment, but also that this environment constitutes the individual house as much as it does the whole of society.

Yet, Japanese residential architecture shows also the negative aspect of rigid regulating and planning of building through a single body. For with decisions of the ruling men not always being guided by ethical reasons, but frequently serving only their own political or at best patriotic-nationalistic ambitions, the welfare of the people and the fate of the individual have often been utterly neglected. Rigid and inflexible rules of both government and trade guilds froze all creative spirit and, in the end, virtually killed any progressive tendency. Even when such measures actually stimulated and inspired one or the other potential that brought about cultural achievement, such positive results were purely accidental and should not obscure the defective character of the motive.

The development of Japanese residential architecture, thus, shows the drawbacks of city planning if it is primarily dependent on political issues. Of course, the planning of cities, development of surface communication, aid to public housing, etc. are themselves political issues of contemporary society, but they are so by their own right and must not be subordinated to other political issues of a partisan program. It points out the deterioration of the ethical values of the present, when social elements such as education or architecture have been degraded to objects of political bargaining, while by the same reason political association frequently has become the vehicle for gaining architectural influence and commissions.

Yet, aside from the controversy of political affiliation, which varies with each nation and government, Japanese residential architecture gives proof that society and its organization, especially a comprehensive policy in building, is not a matter outside of the individual's life but will directly and lastingly affect the personal sphere of each individual, whether in his architectural relationship he is the creator or the beneficiary. Such an influence has been felt in Japan in many different ways and its convincing manifestations are very well apt to raise an awareness of the far-reaching consequences that an organized planning of building in society, a comprehensive architectural policy, will have upon the individual building.

There is an intimate and mutual dependence between the individual and society. The individual, though being the constituent element of society, is not just an unimportant part thereof, for society performs the task of protecting the rights of the individual and thus does serve him. Yet, society is not merely a secondary device of practicality either, because, ideally, the individual works for the benefit of society. This interdependence is generally not acknowledged. Indeed, the major difficulties in urban and regional planning are rooted in the absence of principles that would define this interdependence, the issue being the rights of the individual versus the rights of society.

The causes for this dilemma are twofold. First, there is the emergence of specialization in all creative fields, brought about by the mechanical transformation of society. Although doubtlessly this is one of the greatest achievements of the present, it is, however, followed by an ever increasing inability to conceive the whole. As a result, the role of the social organism in the evolution of mankind and its importance for human progress are not understood. Secondly, there is the evolution of a strong individualism, brought about by the spiritual-scientific transformation of society. Though this personal freedom is likewise one of the greatest gains of civilization, it is accompanied by an egocentric conception of life. As a result, personal freedom is overemphasized and idealistic-voluntary surrender of individuality for the benefit of the greater whole is frowned upon.

Since it is through ethics and morals that the spiritual foundation is established for the practical relationship of the individual to others and to society, the realization is gained that the major problem of building for contemporary society is not so much one of technical, economical, or political bearing, but is in essence a question of moral and ethical conception. Philosophy, then, is the very issue and the level at which a solution can be found.

In the past decades the scope of human conception and action—scientifically, philosophically, politically, and also architecturally—has expanded beyond any foreseeable proportion. In the same pace, the task and responsibility of each professional has expanded. Mechanization of living, improvement of communication, and increase of population have brought regions and peoples into an ever thickening concentration, with intrinsic problems and new problems yet to anticipate.

To the architect, this concentration has brought on a task and responsibility that may well be called the major challenge of contemporary architecture: regional planning and redevelopment of the cities. It is characteristic that the available data for this architectural task are not constants but are values that rapidly change along with the advance of science, automation, and the standard of living. As a result, both architectural practitioner and educator are often overwhelmed by the continuous emergence of new factors and problems and in coping with them frequently fail to realize the ethical fundamentals of total planning for the human society and the individual therein.

Japanese residential architecture discloses these fundamentals very clearly, in spite of the fact that their objectives no longer conform with contemporary ethics. It shows that it is possible to translate social ethics and objectives directly into building, both in planning cities and in designing houses and it may, therefore, inspire a reassessment of the values that represent the present state of civilization, i.e., the unique relationship that exists between contemporary man and contemporary society.

PLATE 104: Shinto. It taught respect for nature and her forms and stressed purity.

PLATE 105: Buddhism. It integrated the house into a universal philosophy and thus gave spiritual meaning to a dwelling that had been a mere expression of necessity.

PLATES 106–107: Buddhist altar. The Japanese house is also a house of worship.

PLATES 108–112: Pit dwelling and high-floored dwelling, the pre-decessors of the Japanese house. The pit dwelling was the dwelling of the common people. The house on stilts was that of the aristocracy.

PLATES 113–114: High-floored dwelling. This prototype already contained the major constructional features of the Japanese house.

PLATES 115–116: The farmhouse. It is the descendant of the pit dwelling.

PLATES 117–118: The farmhouse. It influenced the evolution of the Japanese house both directly and indirectly.

PLATES 119–120: The *shinden* style. It was the residential style of the aristocracy. It consisted of individual halls connected by covered walks and originally had a symmetrical layout.

PLATES 121–122: The *shoin* style. It developed from the *shinden* style and was to provide decisive stimuli for the evolution of the Japanese house.

PLATES 123–125: The *shuden (hiroma)* style. It is the residential style of the warriors in the late Middle Ages of Japan. It is a simplified form of the *shoin* style and integrates architectural features of the residences of the farmer, the clergy, and the nobility.

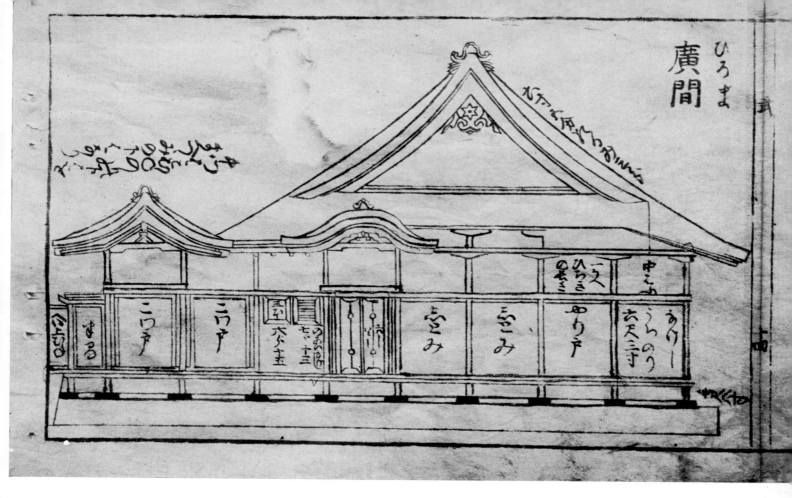

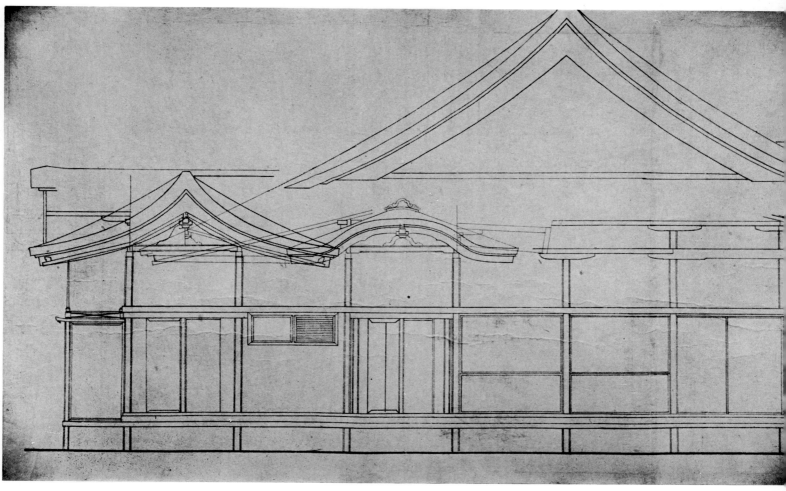

PLATES 126–128: Interior of the *shuden* style. From this style of interior design the Japanese house adopted the distinctive combination of picture recess, *tokonoma,* shelving recess, *tana,* and study place, *shōin.*

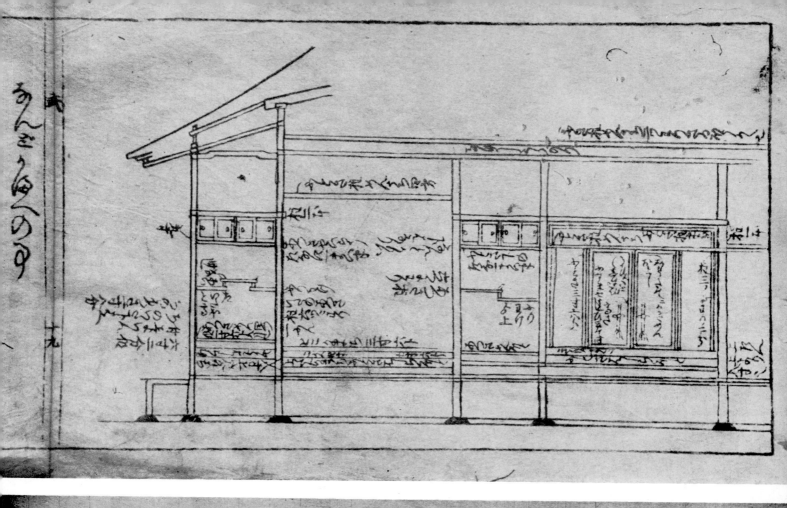

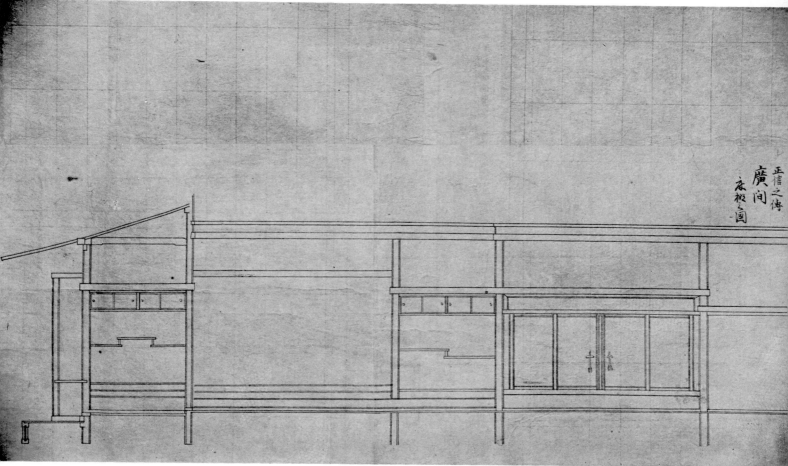

正信之傳
廣間
床板之圖

PLATES 129–131: Plan of the *shuden* style. A distinct feature is the clear separation of official space from domestic space. This feature was adopted by the common Japanese residence.

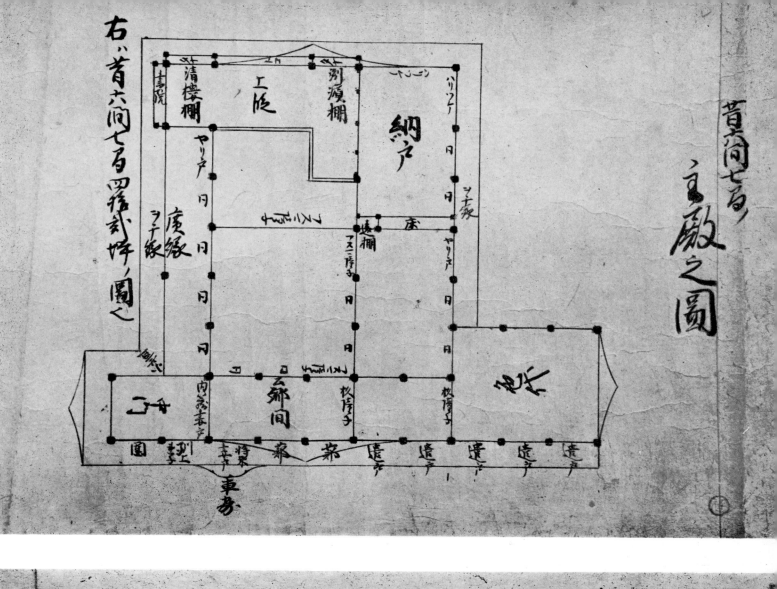

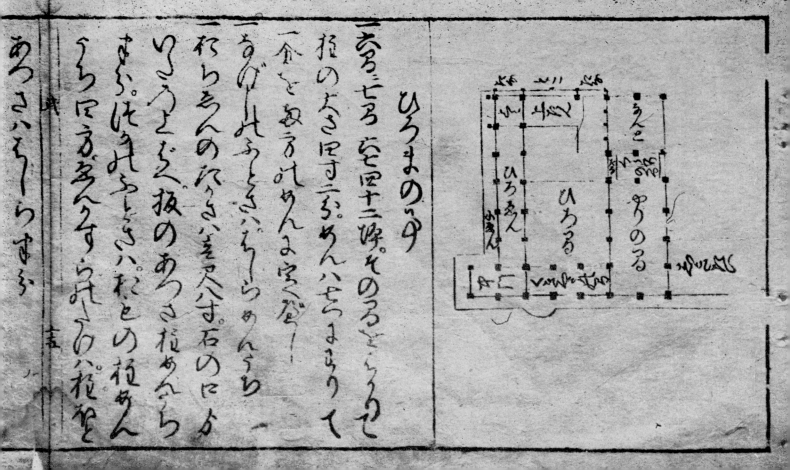

PLATES 132–133: The city community. Building in the city was subjected to limitations of floor plan because of the particular site conditions prevailing in the cities. On the other hand, it was exposed to an environment that fostered progress.

PLATES 134–135: The rural community. The struggle against continuous poverty and exploitation taught the wisdom of simplicity in living and building.

PLATE 136: The fishing village. In spite of the high density of housing on an irregular coastal strip, the universal order for building form and building fabric has established harmony of expression.

PART FOUR aesthetics

taste
order
expression

definition

TASTE IN BUILDING is the manifestation of a certain conception of beauty in architecture. Responding to man's psychological need for beauty, it is a documentation of his idea of architectural aesthetic.

TASTE IN BUILDING, yet, is not a reflection of individual liking in architecture, but is the conscious materialization of a particular set of aesthetic values to which a region or epoch adheres. As such, it asserts itself not only in décor and surface but also in essence and substance.

TASTE IN BUILDING is not an unvariable factor of architectural design, but is dependent on locality and time. Different people and different ages possessed different aesthetical conceptions and demanded different physical forms.

TASTE IN BUILDING, though dependent on region and epoch, still is bound by timeless and universal values. For taste is rooted in man's psychological-physical reaction to sensuous impulse and is, therefore, subjected to biological law.

TASTE IN BUILDING is the criterion of humanism in architecture. Not being prompted by practical demands but directly addressing man's feelings, it establishes emotional relationship between man and his environment.

TASTE IN BUILDING, however, is not merely reflective in cause and affirmative in character. Being substantiated through architectural creation, it can set new values of aesthetics and sensitize man's aesthetic capacity with its infinite expressional possibilities.

TASTE IN BUILDING varies in proportion to other factors that contribute to architectural creation. Not only is each building type distinct in its particular degree of aesthetic influence but also the cultural epochs of the past can be identified according to their particular esteem for aesthetics, including the extremes of neglect and preoccupation.

TASTE IN BUILDING, then, is an important demand of man from architecture and as such is a decisive factor of architectural creation. It is the psychological link between man and building and is the agent that humanizes architecture.

The most difficult task of architectural analysis is to judge the aesthetic quality of an architecture, especially if this architecture is distant in both time and place. While any other aspect of building can be fairly well evaluated through sound reasoning, the aesthetic quality of architecture cannot be approached in the same manner, for cause and aim of beauty in art and architecture is not man's reason but is his delight.

Aesthetics is a branch of philosophy that attempts to uncover the elements and factors of the beautiful. Aesthetics in architecture, thus, is the theory of the principles that underlie beauty in building. Since beauty is the quality that gives pleasure to the senses or delightfully exalts the mind and spirit, it is apparent that beauty in architecture is not confined to the visible and physical aspects, but comprehends all those elements of building that may provide such pleasure. Aesthetics in building, therefore, depends essentially on the particular pleasures that are, or in the past have been, felt. To like one thing and to dislike another is but an assertion of taste.

Thus, just as aesthetics in contemporary building reflect but the prevailing taste, i.e., the dominant preference for a particular beauty, so also the aesthetic quality of a past and distant architecture is to be understood only through knowledge of the aesthetic taste of that time and place.

That is to say, any judgment of the aesthetic quality of Japanese residential architecture of the 17th to 19th centuries that directly applies only Western and contemporary thought will inevitably result in gross misinterpretations, as is always the case when, upon measuring, the wrong scale is employed. The consequences of such misjudgment are evident not only in the fancy for, and the indiscriminate appreciation of, Japanese form in architecture, as is apparent in most contemporary architectural literature, but also by the imitation of this form in both contemporary Japan and Western America. The only appropriate procedure, therefore, is to try to understand those aesthetic pleasures that have actually been felt at the time, while simultaneously attempting to refute the many preconceptions, slogans, and misuses that beset the discussion of contemporary aesthetics in architecture.

Aesthetic standards of the time and locality are the criteria of beauty in man's physical and spiritual environment, for they determine the relationship between environment and the human mind. Such standards do not exist a priori but are established through man's discriminative power, which is taste. Therefore, in order to properly appreciate aesthetic quality in building, a thorough understanding of the current taste is prerequisite—for contemporary architecture the taste of the present, for Japanese architecture the taste of Japan.

However, it is by no means intended to give the impression that such analytic approach could in any way convey the aesthetic impact of the Japanese residence. For architectural beauty is a matter that cannot be described, but can only be experienced. Thus, the following elaborations are limited to providing but the basis for viewing the Japanese residence aesthetically and for evaluating a record of actual sensations and emotions as compared to the infinity of truly "mixed feelings" that the sight of contemporary architecture provokes. It should be clearly understood, however, that actual proof can be found only through direct encounter with Japanese form and space, for which pictorial and verbal representations are no substitute.

Such an understanding, then, if confronted with the aesthetic expressions of the contemporary West, may well allow certain conclusions to be drawn or even universal laws to be established, which in turn may bring order into the confusion of contemporary ideas of architectural aesthetics. For these ideas, not having been scientifically investigated, are not thoroughly understood. Although separate studies have laid the groundwork, the ideas have not been precisely incorporated into the total framework of architectural factors. They are but half-truths and are by no means the solid standards that could pave the way for a visual order in contemporary building. Instead, these ideas on architectural aesthetics have become a two-edged weapon whereby there is no building so bad that it could not, with a little dexterity, be effectively defended, and none so good that it could not, with a little manipulation, be successfully attacked.

Thus, this treatise on the aesthetics of the Japanese residence begins with an analysis of Japanese aesthetical taste in the late middle ages. "Taste" in the architectural meaning, however, is not that very personal, inconsistent, fashionable, and changeable preference for which, as a proverb says, there is no accounting but which is, nevertheless, the very object of violent argument. Taste, rather, is the aesthetic sense in man through which he is able to discern the beautiful and the ugly. Since architectural taste manifests itself as physical-psychological response to sensual perception and since those reactions are, in fact, submitted to biological law, there is reason to assume that man basically possesses a unique taste that differs as to individual, race, locality, and time only insofar as environmental factors and personal temperament always modulate but do not reverse the universal conceptions of "good" and "bad."

Yet, the study of the aesthetical aspect of the Japanese residence in a separate chapter by no means represents the opinion that the aesthetic quality of building is, or ever could become, an independent factor of architecture. For aesthetics in building is not only its visual-geometric aspect, but, rather, and even more important, the total qualities in building that can stimulate emotional pleasure. Since mere physical comfort and utilitarian convenience also have their own emotional consequences, all architectural efforts in their highest aspirations are, or at least should be, of aesthetic nature.

Any measure that improves a given situation in man's physical environment enters the realm of conscious aesthetic creation. Consequently, the previous chapters have actually dealt with the aesthetics of the Japanese residence, and have analyzed the essential elements where Japanese aestheticism has asserted itself. If in the following treatise the aesthetic principles of Japanese building and their backgrounds are studied once again, but with focus on architectural taste, it was prompted not only because the appreciation of a prior and distant architecture requires such knowledge, but also because controversies about the aesthetics in contemporary building makes such comparative analysis truly rewarding.

theory of genesis

It is beyond any doubt that architecture has not come into existence due to a desire for beauty. It has been brought about by man's instinct for survival in the face of a hostile environment, both animal and weather, and by his subsequent attempts to evade its causality by creating a human environment. House, thus, was prompted by the basic needs of man. Satisfying such needs was, and still is, the first concern of architectural effort. Since in the construction of early dwellings there was not a variety of materials, techniques, or forms from which to choose, architectural taste could not assert itself. Consequently, these dwellings do not reflect aesthetical awareness, no matter how attractive or stimulating they appear to contemporary eyes.

Yet, man's continuous struggle with nature for existence taught him very early to distinguish between inferior and superior quality of weapons, tools, and shelters. He also learned that this difference in quality was directly dependent on the skill and the ability of those who created these "instruments." As a result, the concept of skill and ability as a prerequisite for superior quality entered human consciousness. This faculty to discern between differing skills, and the admiration for superior quality, provided the basis for man's first aesthetic assertion in building, just as it long before had given birth to art in the manufacture of weapons and tools—a causation that the origin of the word "art" (from Latin *ars,* meaning "skill") still affirms.

Discernment of varying degrees of skills, thus, was the earliest manifestation of architectural taste. Though in the meantime many new motivations for man's aesthetic pleasure in building were disclosed—through differentiation of early architectural taste rather than by evolution of new discriminative abilities—the earliest criterion of aesthetic taste in building, i.e., display of superior skill, remained the primary source of aesthetic delight. It was, therefore, only natural that art products of all forms aimed primarily at demonstration of skill, thereby initiating an aestheticism in which the masterly handling of color, motif, and form was the essential factor. And there is evidence that also in both ancient and contemporary Japan, one major branch of aesthetic consciousness found delight in such multiplicity, in no way different from the aesthetic taste of man everywhere.

Inseparable from man's early sensitivity to evidence of superior skill in building must have been his preference for things that were strong and secure. For man's continuous quest for improving the quality of construction and attaining superior performance in building was in reality but an effort to increase the security of his existence. Thus, he must have been aware not only that superior skill meant increased safety, but also that certain forms were more likely to give security than were others. Experience had taught him that the man who had lost a hand in fight, the tree situated on a steep mountain slope, the boat one-sidedly loaded, did not convey such sensation of security, but that the physically healthy man, the tree growing on level ground, and the equally loaded boat did.

Thus, through trial and error, man's taste must have come to distinguish very early the appearance of the stable and the unstable, the secure and the insecure, and as a result aesthetic preference for symmetry came into being. Once consciousness of symmetry was reached, the realization that any deviation from symmetry had to be compensated for was but a subsequent development, and thus the important principle of asymmetrical balance in composition was established.

Most likely man's struggle for security also stimulated other criteria of early architectural taste. Skill, as requisite for the quality of any product, could already be evidenced while the product was being made, and consequently the building of houses became a matter where taste of both observer and performer could assert itself. Since for a particular repetitious action (digging, hammering, sawing, etc.) only one distinct time interval provided the highest efficiency, man became aware of advantages in rhythmical action, he became sensitive to the rhythmical character of the product, and, finally, he felt aesthetic pleasure in rhythm itself. Transcending the action, then, this taste asserted itself in the rhythms of static décor and later also in the character of building itself.

Yet, consciousness of the beauty in rhythm provoked another early aesthetic principle in architecture. For rhythm, being in fact but repetition of the familiar, of the known, of the previously experienced, allowed anticipation of the known and therefore lent the feeling of security, just as the unexpected and unknown was the source of fear and discomfort. Especially due to the realization of rhythm in the seasons, man was able to anticipate and, therefore, encounter the extremes of seasonal climate —a consciousness that must have provided considerable psychological comfort. Presumably, it is because of this observation of nature's pulse that man's aesthetic instinct for order was stimulated. Order, then, in the sense of regular succession and conformity to law could be understood and could be depended upon. And it is conceivable that this awareness of rhythm and order was the very basis for the growth of a taste that derives pleasure from the purely intellectual understanding of a building, the "intellectual taste" that strongly determines the aesthetic experience of modern man.

While the previous elaborations are but theories based on fragmentary evidence and contemporary psychology, there is no evidence that human taste in architecture, like aesthetic sensitivity as a whole, did evolve as an independent human instinct. Instead, it has crystallized through man's struggle for survival, i.e., it was provoked by necessity. Continuous experimentation, then, raised consciousness of the strict interdependence between the appearance of building and its protective quality, and thus sensitized man's discriminative ability, his architectural taste. Its early characteristic was the preference for skill, symmetry, balance, rhythm, and order, which afforded the very basis for the psychological and mental structure of all aesthetic taste independent of time and place.

zen aestheticism

Taste in the field of aesthetics is, in fact, inevitable. In architecture the eye perceives, and both body and mind react to the impulse, effecting sensations and emotions of comfort or discomfort. It is from this biological reaction, which varies in strength individually, that man obtains his taste, i.e., the ability to discern between the good and the bad, the beautiful and the ugly, the fit and the unfit, the orderly and the chaotic. Taste, thus, is inevitable—a fact that is proven by the unanimous agreement existing about the beautiful in the past, without which there is no true culture.

On the other hand, there is also evidence that not only do different regions and ages show a marked difference of aesthetic appreciation, but also each of these manifests a very distinct language of aesthetic expression. This evidence indicates that, if not the functioning of taste, then certainly the creative manifestation of taste is dependent also on agents other than those inherent in the human organism. Since it has always been a particular time or locality that produced a characteristic taste, the possibility that such distinction is due to difference in basic psycho-physical reaction of the individual can be safely dismissed. Nor can racial difference be the cause, for not only were regions of distinct architectural taste inhabited by people of varying racial origin, but also one and the same race often went through varying periods of distinct and often contrasting architectural tastes.

Instead, environmental influences, the elements that distinguish different localities and periods in time, especially religion-philosophy and society itself, and, to no smaller degree, the cultural leadership of an individual artist, priest, or aristocrat were the actual generators of architectural taste. While the formative influence of these environmental factors upon living and building has been mentioned in previous chapters, their effect upon the evolution of Japanese aestheticism is given separate attention here in spite of occasional restatement of facts. Because an examination of the aestheticism of Zen and the tea cult in its role as modulator of the characteristic Japanese taste will provide material for a better understanding of a subject so important and controversial as taste in architecture.

In discussing aesthetics of a past architecture, it is only too common an error to conceive of a "taste of the epoch" as one aesthetic consciousness possessed by an entire society. The fact is that in the class societies of the past each class had a distinct taste within the scope of things it could create and possess. For in the past, as in the present, discriminative ability, i.e., taste, requires previous actual experience and knowledge. Thus, the aesthetic quality of the architecture of the nobility and the clergy did not in the least reflect the taste of the common masses, nor is it likely that the lower classes were able to aesthetically appreciate this architecture other than in the sense that the less learned always tend to admire the works of the learned, without being able to judge them.

In Japan, as in Europe, active exercise of aesthetic taste was confined to a very small group of artists, priests, and aristocrats, i.e., to a cultural elite. The broad mass of the people had hardly anything by means of which taste could be practiced, except for the few tools and utensils of daily use and very minor details of house construction. Building—its idea and design—was determined exclusively by physical need and material economy, and had no other aesthetic quality than that which mere physical comfort and utilitarian convenience provided. It is, therefore, a fallacy to assume that the simplicity of the early Japanese house prior to the 17th century was the expression of a particular aesthetic taste. Like primitive houses everywhere, the dwellings of the farmer and general public in Japan were but the result of crude necessity and only the expression of bitter poverty. By contrast, the architecture of the nobility and clergy was elaborate, colorful, and demonstrative. It responded to an architectural taste that was strongly influenced by the Chinese.

It was the teaching of Zen Buddhism and the tea cult, after its transformation in the 16th and 17th centuries, that for the first time positively pointed out the aesthetic quality inherent in simplicity, economy, and restraint. This aestheticism, however, did not change the existing physical characteristics of the dwelling, but merely changed their psychological effect. Heretofore, external form in the simple dwelling either was without any relationship to the human mind or had only a depressing effect insofar as it continuously reminded the inhabitants of their inhuman and sorrowful life. The new aestheticism, then, gave the same form a different meaning and made it a source of aesthetic delight. And it was only thereafter, in the course of refinement, that this aestheticism influenced the existing form.

The major theme of this aestheticism was derivation of emotional pleasure not merely from external and visible appearance but from the internal and invisible meaning indicated by that appearance, i.e., aesthetic sensation achieved through understanding and sympathizing with the themes underlying outward appearance.

Beauty should not be displayed and pronounced but should be hidden humbly behind the surface of things, to be discovered and brought forth by the beholder himself.

Responding to the socio-environmental state of the nation, the practical and unsophisticated teaching of Zen demonstrated that material poverty, with its expressions of the unadorned, simple, unsophisticated, imperfect, and limited, possessed a beauty of its own, more profound and more rewarding than the ostentatious beauty of wealth. Through this interpretation of the features of the most simple houses a conscious architectural taste was raised for the first time among the broad mass of the people, an aesthetic taste that the lower classes were able to appreciate and practice with the material and intellectual means at their disposal.

This new architectural taste differed essentially from the aesthetic taste of the cultural elite and was also different from the conventional aestheticism in the Western world. Its effect on architecture was a devaluation of external appearance, both real and allusive, and an avoidance of the trite, obtrusive, and emphatic. The taste can be well paraphrased by a paradox through which Zen likes to speak: "Great mastery is as if unskillful." It reached a state of sensitivity where obvious form, obtrusive color, and pronounced motif, because of their continuous demand on the visual-emotional senses, were felt to be obstacles in associating with the very meaning that this outward appearance represented. Instead, restraint, allusion, and suggestion in physical appearance were considered the most powerful stimuli for aesthetic experience.

This increasingly refined demand on architecture to reveal meaning and essence was, in fact, the cause for the aestheticism of simplicity, which is Japan's outstanding contribution to the field of architectural aesthetics. For in order to uncover the essence of a function the physical form had to be simplified to the point where a discrepancy between form and essence, between container and content, and between expression and spirit no longer existed. The result was a serene expression that permitted an optimum of intimacy between man and object, while both satisfying and sensitizing man's taste.

Architectural creation, thus, employed visual impulses only as media to convey meaning and significance. Since the human mind is more qualified to vividly re-experience a previous understanding than to recall a visual pattern, such a system affords the most profound and lasting impression. Form, as the only communicating agent, though, could not simply be ignored, yet, it did not possess existence for its own sake, but was simply the expression of a particular function. However, this attitude has only little in common with the functionalistic theory in contemporary architecture, "form follows function." For function in the Japanese interpretation was not limited to material structure, utilitarian space, human physical convenience, and monetary economy, but also included human psychological comfort, religious faith, philosophy of life, and, in rare instances, mere visual-geometric necessities.

This taste for simplicity, i.e., the aesthetic delight in doing things simply, expressing things simply, and feeling things simply, was an essential deviation from the previous emphasis in art expression. For taste no longer asserted itself in the demonstration of superior skill, but in the most effective, because the most direct, expression of function ("function" in the broad meaning as described before) in architecture as well as in art generally. This meant that excellence of technique or even the type of technique employed were no longer prerequisite for "art," both as performance and product. Full mastership of technique, though, was essential in order to grant unhindered expression of "function," but any trivial activity or any ordinary utensil could become art if performed or used in full awareness of its meaning. In fact, with the supremacy of skill and virtuosity being broken, the way was open for everyone to exercise art and to be an artist.

Thus, through the cult of tea, Zen brought art into the houses of the lowest classes. Through practice, it taught them that just as the preparing and serving of tea could be performed in a manner that would provoke aesthetic delight, so too any phase of life contained its own aesthetic aspect. The writing of a letter, the arranging of a flower in a vase, the welcoming of the guest, the mode of speech provided an infinite variety of actively exercising art in the house. The result was the awareness that a proper life, itself, was art.

traditional trait

However, in stating that Zen and tea initiated the taste for simplicity and created an aestheticism of such great significance for the present, it is not meant to say that all this has been without precedence. Even before the teaching of Zen Buddhism exerted its influence, there was in other art forms, especially in literature and painting, an undercurrent that tended toward a very direct and informal language of expression. Yet, this taste, the forms of which were strongly influenced by their Chinese prototypes, was not a "national" taste, but a taste confined to artists, priests, and aristocrats, who alone had the ability, both material and intellectual, to appreciate art.

Also, the distinct aestheticism of Zen itself obviously had its roots in the ideals of the Chinese Taoism, the religion-philosophy of Lao-tsu (604–531 B.C.). The aestheticism of Taoism, in accepting the world with all its realities, seeks beauty not in the supranatural but in the mundane and commonplace; it has often been called the art of "being in the world." Its art favors the most simple form of expression and considers allusion or suggestion as the most powerful impulse to instigate the beholder's participation. The vacuum, being marked by substance, yet not being substance itself, was considered the aim of artistic creation, which would allow the exercise of the full range of emotions. Here principles are stated that make Zen aestheticism appear a successor of Taoism.

This aesthetic tradition, however, did not entirely remain confined to those few who could afford to exercise and appreciate art. For these few were also the ones that initiated the rise of aesthetic consciousness among the mass of the people, and it was inevitable that in this process much of the conceptions of the cultural elite also entered the aestheticism of the lower classes. That is to say, the taste of the common people in the late Middle Ages of Japan also inherited elements from the aesthetical conceptions of the past and was in many ways linked to tradition.

However, just as such a tradition provided the profound aestheticism of simplicity, so also it led to a trend that prevented the full use of aesthetic sensibility. The active search for the pure, simple, and direct became but a passive denial of the complicated, multiple, and diverse, and paradoxically resulted in an escape from the very reality that had originally been the source for beauty. Now, man no longer sought delight in the world of realities, but in the calmness of his own microcosm. Being contented with imperfection, deficiency, and insufficiency in his physical environment, he felt intimate compassion for his environment to the degree of identifying himself with the objects in his surroundings. He sometimes even purposefully created such a condition in order to painfully sense and contemplate the pathos of man's existence. Such architectural taste, then, did not instigate the Japanese to search and struggle for beauty. Often dangerously close to a pseudo-romanticism, it did not embody a spirit that made them wrest beauty from nature. While Western art and architecture, by means of discovery and exploitation of new mechanical laws and also through spirited pursuit and consistent study of aesthetics, greatly contributed to both physical improvement and psychological sensitization of mankind, Japanese taste resigned itself to contemplating immutable meanings instead of ever new forms and appealed to a pioneering and active spirit as little as the Buddhist view of nature, man, and universe did.

This tendency is obvious in an early-10th-century collection of poems called *Kokin-shū* (Collection of Poems Old and New), which contains about 1,100 poems, in form generally short and exquisite, in expression delicate and not without artificiality, and in content limited both emotionally and themewise. In these poems it appears that the sentiment of the higher classes must have been already strongly moved by a sort of resignative compassion for the small things of life. This concept was called *mono-*

no-aware, which might be imperfectly translated as "compassion with the pathos in man and nature" (Plate 138). The consistent recurrence of this sentiment permits the conclusion that the dominant taste of the aristocracy at that time was to contemplate the individual small world with secluded and often narrow subjectivity. True, this taste showed awareness of the tragedy in this transient world in a sentimental and melancholic manner, but it was entirely unconcerned with the realistic themes of the time as presented by the many pressing problems within society. The taste asserted itself in a subjective and resignative refinement of art with an inclination toward finesse, an aesthetic quality that was called *miyabi.*

In a later collection of poems, the *Shin-kokin-shū* (New Collection of Poems Old and New), recorded in the early 13th century, the tendency toward a taste of resignative contemplation of life became even more pronounced. Here, the trait of finding delight in the somewhat sentimental compassion for one's own subjective conception of the world took the form of an escape from the world of material realities. This taste is called the beauty of *yūgen,* i.e., the beauty of the mysterious and unreal (Plates 139–140). Beauty was thought not to lie in the contaminated material existence of the individual, but in the purity of the abstract universe. Yet, *yūgen* at the same time meant a departure from the occasional playful sophistication of *miyabi* toward a more serene, unpretentious theme in which overcoming of the egoistic "self" was thought essential for the experience of beauty.

Against this mode of playful and class-confined taste, Zen Buddhist standards of aesthetics set their austere simplicity. Through profound philosophical interpretation, this traditional taste achieved a more comprehensive value and, as a result, became universally accepted by the broad mass of the people. However, this incorporation into a philosophical framework did not essentially alter the traditional concept of a calm retreat from wordly cares into a secluded microcosm of quiet and serene beauty. The concepts of *suki* (literally, "fancy") and of *sabi* (literally, "rust," "look of age"), so difficult to explain in words, which had been brought forth as aesthetic principles by the tea masters, actually symbolized the conscious withdrawal into a personal sphere from where all phenomena of the external life were viewed with gentle melancholy through the mirror of individuality.

It has been stated that doubtlessly Zen's emphasis on allusion, suggestion, and restraint provided art impulses far more powerful, lasting, and engaging than those of obvious and emphatic display of beauty and thus prompted a taste in building and art characteristic of the Japanese and without exact counterpart elsewhere. However, such a tradition, which found deepest satisfaction in contemplating the meaning symbolized in, or suggested by, external form, did not provide incentive to explore the infinity of aesthetic pleasures to be derived from experimentation with these forms.

Moreover, the *mono-no-aware* of the 9th and 10th centuries, the *yūgen* of the 12th and 13th centuries, the *suki* and *sabi* of the following centuries, though professing to be concepts of direct and immediate expression, after a short bloom lapsed into artificiality and finesse that actually defeated their own *raison d'être.* The tea cult, essentially an aestheticism of honest simplicity and conscious restraint, also took a turn toward a formalistic and expensive ritual in the circles that could afford it and therein became a paradox to its very purpose.

The foregoing comments, though, are not meant to give a thorough analysis of Japanese aesthetic taste, but only to present a short summary with the intent to show the causes and consequences of a traditional trait that produced the unique Japanese taste for an architectural simplicity in Japan's Middle Ages.

taste of the townspeople

Though in all previous references Japanese taste has been rationalized and set apart both from the art product in which taste could manifest itself and from the society for which this art was performed, it would be wrong to assume that Japanese architectural taste arose only as a result of theoretical thought. The formative stimuli for architectural taste in general are multiple. The *avant-garde* design of the artist may be as influential as religion, philosophy, tradition, and social ethics, and the artist himself is in turn influenced by his spiritual and physical environment, irrational habits, and even the technique of his media, although he himself might obey a mere desire to create.

In the case of Japan there is a high probability that the particular architectural taste that determined residential building in the late Middle Ages of Japan was not only prompted by the abstract reasoning of Zen, but also owed its essential impulses to those prototypes of applied simplicity that had been created by individual artists or by anonymous artisans. It is, therefore, an oversimplification to consider Japanese architectural taste but the result of a set of values provided by current metaphysical ideas or determined by material and technique. Rather, there is considerable evidence that the existing residential building, itself, was the very source from which architectural taste was derived.

Moreover, as previously mentioned, society itself was strongly instrumental in the formation of Japanese taste in the late medieval Japan. For centuries the ruling classes had dictated the cultural growth of the nation according to their "official taste," which was strictly dependent on Chinese standards, while at the same time they prevented the lower classes—sometimes by force—from practicing any such "official taste" in their homes. It was, therefore, understandable that with the emergence of the bourgeoisie, the *chōnin* (a class of self-conscious merchants and strong-willed artisans), an ideological-aesthetic spirit of defiance against aristocratic supremacy and of opposition to anything old arose.

This spirit that emerged among the cultivated bourgeoisie in the early 18th century, called *iki* (literally, "high spirits"), became apparent in all fields of art (Plates 146–147). It even disclosed new forms of art, especially in the fields of literature and painting where it created the renowned *haiku* (literally, "joking verse"), short, epigrammatic verses without the severe canons of classic poetry, and the famed *ukiyo-e* (literally, "picture of the floating world"), colorful-bold pictures—in painting or print form—of life and amusement in the cities. This spirit of the townspeople, *iki,* was a rare phenomenon in Japanese cultural evolution. Vivacious, comic, polemic toward the old customs and restraints, sometimes ironic, occasionally vulgar, colorful and energetic, never losing its bold directness, and deriving aesthetic delight from the material world of realities, it was an entirely new concept of Japanese taste.

Strictly speaking, the idea of *iki* was "to be contrary." It was a spirit of opposition rather than a theory of aestheticism, for it did not establish distinct principles for its art forms. Yet, its influence upon Japanese aesthetic taste is beyond question. Before that time the lower classes had looked for aesthetic inspiration and patterns of living to the cultural elite of the aristocracy and clergy. But when the spirit of *iki* broke through they challenged for the first time this "official taste" and set their own standards against it, standards that certainly more truly expressed the native sentiment than did the aesthetic standards of previous periods.

Therefore, the Japanese aestheticism of serene simplicity no doubt owes much to this spirit of defiance and opposition *(iki)* that incited the common people to boldly counteract the delicate multiplicity and colorful extravagance of the "official taste" with their opposites of rustic simplicity and serene restraint. In a reverse order, then, the aristocracy adopted this taste in a more refined version as a pattern for their own life, thus making it a universal aestheticism for the entire society.

Of course, architecture—its reaction to the new always lagging behind the pure arts—never really came to manifest this sentiment purely, and it is tempting to imagine what the consequences would have been if this vivacious and challenging spirit in its full power had reached building. However, as had happened with earlier concepts, before building could react to the new, the townspeople had already organized themselves so rigidly into guilds with sanctioned privileges that healthy and stimulating competition could not possibly take place.

The subsequent rise of a new concept of aesthetics each time a former concept had lapsed into formalism and passivity, shows that there is an element in the Japanese taste that, inspired by individual artists, sought and found delight in the new. This spirit of *karumi* (literally, "light") expressed itself in leaving all conventional forms and lightheartedly rising above earthly limitations and personal worries (Plates 143–145). It permeated each new idea and was especially prevalent in the taste of *iki*. Yet, before it could ever transform architecture in its very substance, it lost its gay strength and, in fact, never did effect any essential deviation from the traditional pattern. Social, traditional, and national pressures and economic limitations always proved in the long run stronger than ambitions and revolutionary ideas.

Only after the feudal system was abolished by the Meiji Reformation of 1868 and after traditions were shattered by the defeat of Japan in World War II did the Japanese achieve a physical-psychological environment that for the first time in history allowed them to give unhindered expression to their taste. However, this taste, which is unique due to its consistent striving for simplicity of form and purity of expression, does not consistently assert itself. It is true that in the feudalistic society there was a unique taste because the nation was educated, or often just was told what to like, how to behave, and what to do. However, with restrictions removed and traditions discredited, a vacuum was created which the ordinary people, due to lack of initiative, were unable to fill with values of their own.

At the present time, it is very apparent that the average Japanese is confused and uncertain in his aesthetic taste. He is positive in his aesthetic judgment only in an environment such as already existed when the feudal government had laid down the rules for proper conduct and appreciation. In unfamiliar situations brought about by absorption of Western civilization, the taste of the average Japanese has as yet failed to assert itself. As a result, contemporary Japan is characterized by a seemingly inconsistent and contradictory environment in which the beautiful and the ugly, the pure and the dirty, the simple and the complicated, the holy and the sinful, coexist in immediate proximity. It is yet to be seen whether the element of lightheartedness, *karumi,* and the spirit of self-confidence and defiance, *iki,* are strong enough to overcome certain outdated notions of the past, as well as those many fashionable and half-true conceptions of so-called modern building and living. These modern conceptions, imitated from the industrial societies of the West, so far have hindered the expression of a unique architectural taste corresponding with the sentiments of the Japanese and, as a result, have delayed the development of a residential architecture that would be a realistic answer to the problems that face contemporary Japan.

for contemporary architecture

Japan's contribution to aesthetics in architecture is the discovery and development of an aestheticism in which the primary impulses for delight are derived not from direct experience of form and space, but from the understanding of, and the sympathizing with, the meaning that each of these two tokens of architectural creation represents. Austere simplicity in the design of form and space is only the external result of this aestheticism.

There is an essential difference between the simplicity manifested in contemporary architecture and that apparent in Japanese residential architecture. Simplicity in modern building came into existence as a reaction against the eclectic trend of the 19th century, as a result of the machine technique, and as a principle of convenience and economy. As it expresses only these origins, i.e., its own existence, or at best conveys its own beauty (geometric proportions), it is an end in itself. It is also true that the forms of simplicity in the Japanese house have originated as a result of the technique and socio-economical circumstances of the time, but, by contrast, this simplicity has been realized as the quality most effective for expressing a content of any nature—utilitarian, religious, traditional, social. Simplicity in the Japanese house is not an end in itself but is a medium. It is the key, for which there is no duplicate, for understanding the meanings underlying form and space and for the delight in contemplating these meanings.

The difference of contemporary simplicity in building could not be greater. While contemporary architecture always expresses the same content with infinite means, Japanese residential architecture expresses an infinite content always with the same means. It is because of this difference that modern simplicity in building can hardly be identified with the Japanese aestheticism of simplicity. Both are essentially different and so are the psychological reactions that they evoke in the unbiased observer.

The fact that simplicity in contemporary architecture is largely met with indifference shows that the dehumanizing effect caused by mechanization of building has not as yet been overcome. Simplicity in building still remains an expression imposed by mechanical law and is unrelated to human psychology. Here, the evolution of Japanese taste for simplicity holds an important suggestion for contemporary architecture in its attempt to reconcile the present opposites of "technicality" and humanity. For simplicity in the Japanese house was also not originally the result of a preconceived theory of aesthetics, but was actually an expression of crude necessity. The conscious appreciation of, and the aesthetic delight in, this simplicity were brought about through posterior association with current religion and philosophy. That is to say, the unique Japanese taste for simplicity in architectural expression has been prompted by education and not by an aesthetic impulse a priori.

This is an important observation because it shows that the distinct architectural taste of any region and epoch is not due to a certain racial-biological constitution but to a particular set of environmental factors. It follows, then, that the multiplicity of architectural tastes manifested by the layman, and to a certain degree also by the professional, is not an inherent biological phenomenon of the contemporary age, but is due to a difference in environmental influences; and that through guiding and controlling those influences by means of education, a unique architectural taste, no doubt, could be achieved. And such education is an urgent need for a society whose environment is without relationship to the human psyche (as evident in modern art, science, technique, and building) and therefore dehumanized. For only education can bring this environment back within the range of human emotions and thereby establish a unique emotional intimacy between man and his total creations, which is the distinction of culture.

The basis for such an attempt should be a scientific analysis of the sources of contemporary form and the laws of human psychological reaction. Once the facts of the interrelationship between architectural form and human psyche are known, light also would be shed on the potential in "simplicity of expression." Of course, true simplicity results when the utmost of restraint is exercised. Yet, in the case of the Japanese, it is significant that restraint is exercised not on the content but on the medium of expression. Through this restraint, the highest efficiency in clearly stating the underlying meanings is achieved.

Therefore, in the Japanese house form closely follows function. Yet, this function is not confined to constructional or utilitarian needs, but includes social, philosophic, and religious themes as well. It is this broad meaning of function that humanizes the austere forms of simplicity in the Japanese house. It discloses that real simplicity of form expression will lose its inhuman character only if the conception of function in building is expanded to include the psychological needs of man also. And this expansion of "function" is very necessary for an architecture that attempts true simplicity of expression. For without the broad meaning of "function" little can be manifested in building that directly relates to the psychological needs of man. Although those needs may be modified by the environment, in essence they are fundamental and permanent.

The value of such utilization of Japanese aesthetic concept in contemporary building may be questioned on grounds that the Japanese sense of beauty is different from the Western due to an inherent difference in the temperament of the Japanese race and that the Westerner simply would not possess the mental constitution to aesthetically appreciate the invisible. It is true that a distinct mentality innate to a race may express itself through a distinct architectural language. Nevertheless, the end product will elicit basically identical aesthetical sensations in all races provided they have the intellectual key, i.e., an understanding of the local aesthetic taste and its conditioning thought. There is essentially an identity of human taste for architecture the world over, and knowledge of the factors that modulate this taste toward distinction will allow the appreciation of art objects of any locality, race, or epoch. Oriental art may provoke positive emotions within an Occidental just as Western art may raise deep sensations within the Oriental's mind, provided that both are familiar with the taste that has been instrumental in their respective developments. Even the Japanese themselves have to learn the vocabulary of landscaping in order to appreciate the beauty of their own gardens.

Two possibilities, then, are indicated here that can humanize modern simplicity, i.e., can remove man's indifference toward simplicity of contemporary architectural expression and make it aesthetically appreciated. The first is to instruct the general public in the motivations for modern form language. Once the factors underlying contemporary structural forms, such as machine production, economy, structural stresses, and beauty of geometry are known, a relationship with man's intellect is established and thereby an emotional response can be assured.

The second possibility of humanizing modern simplicity is to furnish expression in contemporary building with broader and more profound themes and to consciously exploit them. The concept of "function" for architectural form and space should not be confined to practicality, economy, stability, or external geometry alone. Instead, the human psychology, the philosophical-spiritual values, and the moral aims of the 20th century should become the sources of form, expressed in the language most easily understood: simplicity. This expression of simplicity would no longer remain outside of human comprehension and sympathy but would appeal directly to the intellect and thereby leave a profound and lasting emotional impact. Man's intellect, then, would be in both instances the important link between modern form and human psyche, and intellect would be the criterion for an aestheticism of simplicity.

In the present age such a development seems inevitable. For contrary to previous ages, human living, feeling, thinking, and building are no longer determined by religious faith, romantic emotions, or traditional heritage, but are increasingly controlled by intellect, as is apparent in the arts, education, statesmanship, and even in the religions themselves. Already there are obvious tendencies toward intellectualization in contemporary architecture, for this is not only the sole means for humanizing industrialized building, but also because it presents the strongest impulse for stimulating the aesthetic senses of modern man. The resulting building would be an expression of the contemporary age in its most decisive feature: science. It would possess the infinite possibilities encompassed by science and thus would multifariously respond to individual intellect and emotion. And if the word "style" signifies a unique trait of a new movement in architectural creation, then, this aesthetic trend should be properly called the "intellectual style." It is the merit of Japanese aestheticism to have delivered its early, if only incomplete, prototype.

CHAPTER FOURTEEN order

definition

ORDER IN BUILDING is the agent that effects physical and spiritual coherence in building. It establishes organic unity in building whereby all individual factors become an intelligible whole—related, harmonious, balanced, proportioned.

ORDER IN BUILDING is the discipline that both physically and spiritually subjects building to an encompassing law. This law relates building to man and man to universe and effects human environment, which is distinct from both natural and technical environment.

ORDER IN BUILDING as physical principle is the dimensional relationship between the individual components of a structure and their dependence upon one basic size element. Its conscious application is modular coordination. Its basis is a standard unit that is both technical and human measurement.

ORDER IN BUILDING as physical principle, however, is expressed not only in metric or formalistic terms. The relationship between colors, textures, materials, and surface treatments is as important a factor of physical order in building as is the relationship between buildings, blocks, streets, and landscape.

ORDER IN BUILDING as spiritual principle is the subjection of building to a major ethical concept. It relates architectural order to the order of society and incorporates both into the encompassing order of religion and philosophy, which is the spiritual basis for man's existence.

ORDER IN BUILDING is response to human psychology. For order is the pattern of the human mind, and all of man's effort in life, both in art and science, is directed toward establishing his order in the natural environment of non-human order.

ORDER IN BUILDING aims toward giving each element in building its proper place and an expression that clearly states its *raison d'être*. It relates those elements functionally and aesthetically and establishes a meaningful and intelligible organism.

ORDER IN BUILDING integrates the three distinct orders of man, nature, and machine and relates them to ethical principles. Therefore, it is the prerequisite to humanism in architecture and to the physical, spiritual, and, hence, aesthetical unity of all human work.

If simplicity—that is, meaningful simplicity—is the distinct quality of aesthetic expression in the ordinary Japanese house, then order—that is, comprehensive order—is the very medium that makes this simplicity understood and appreciated and that also integrates it into an organic unity wherein all formative factors, the physical and the spiritual, are "ordered" (are brought into order) as elements that constitute the whole. In fact, it is this comprehensive order of values that is the distinctive characteristic of Japanese residential architecture.

Human order is a self-willed discipline, intellectual by origin and rational in its purpose. In architecture it achieves aesthetical meaning by means of the distinct physical expression it provokes. This aesthetic role of order is most evident in the "orders" of the Greek temples. However, contrary to these "orders" in which the visual result of order is beautiful, in the Japanese residence the order itself, i.e., its consistency and its integrating range, is beautiful. It is not so much the association with the expression of this physico-spiritual order that will provoke aesthetic delight as the very realization of a consistent and harmonious discipline that integrates all constituent elements.

While in all previous chapters the individual components of Japanese physical and spiritual order have been examined in detail and system, the following pages will attempt to show how this order has attained aesthetic quality. For, though it is true that order is an essential element of aesthetics because it grants unity to diversity, each order is not necessarily aesthetical nor does it always turn the ugly beautiful. It is this undefined role that has made order in contemporary architecture a very controversial topic. As it affects the fundamentals of architectural creation, investigation into the nature of order in building is imperative.

Of course, the ever increasing use of prefabricated parts has already imposed a certain physical order in contemporary building, but in the discussion on the future of architecture there is disagreement as to whether unconditional acceptance of this trend will really effect an order of organic-human unison or, just the opposite, an order of technical-inhuman uniformity. The question also arises whether any degree of physical order in building is feasible in Western contemporary society with its overemphasis on individual freedom, its preoccupation with personal integrity, and its contempt for mental discipline. And this absence of unanimity exists not only among the general public, but also in professional circles, where it is even more apparent. For the architect himself, firmly believing in his own principles, is not willing, understandably, to sacrifice his individuality for the benefit of a universal order that he does not acknowledge.

It appears that the only promising road to the acceptance of, and the submission to, a comprehensive order in building by both professional and layman would be an investigation into the causes, contents, and effects of physical and spiritual order in general. This would give the architect a basis for architectural creation and would remove the many preconceptions, and misconceptions, of the layman. For such an undertaking the comparative analysis of the Japanese comprehensive order in residential architecture will provide substantial material, because the houses of the common people in Japan embody a unique order of human, natural, and technical values—an order that is Japan's outstanding contribution to the architecture of the world.

theory of genesis

While attempting to uncover the principles of an architectural order that is beautiful, it is a rewarding effort to contemplate the possibilities of how the notion of "order" first might have entered human consciousness and how it might have achieved its aesthetic significance. Such a study should provide hints as to where, and which, the hidden agents are that make order an element of beauty. It likewise should show in which direction order in building should be developed in order to increase man's aesthetic sensation through the encounter with architectural order.

Order is the distinct pattern of the human mind. In fact, "thinking" is but an "ordering" (setting in order) and relating of notions attained by previous experiences, and if the faculty of thinking distinguishes man from animal, this very difference must have been brought about by man's consciousness of order. It is true the animal also recognizes and may even remember environmental experiences, but it is not able to bring order into these notions. Though it may appear that the behavior of animals follows a certain order, this is achieved through instinct rather than consciousness.

Thus, the faculty of conceiving order is man's alone, as is the faculty of creating order, because creation presupposes conception. From perceiving certain repetitions in the environmental nature—of order in nature—man was able to anticipate the seasonal extremes and to prepare himself in advance. It is reasonable to assume that this realization of order in nature also very early made man conscious of the fact that this order was indifferent to him, i.e., was non-human. Therefore, all human work was, and still is, aimed at establishing a human order in an indifferent environment.

Order could be understood, and understanding increased man's security, giving him psychological comfort and hence aesthetic delight. Through the perception of order, therefore, man's natural environment became intelligible and architectural environment became possible.

Once the concept of order had entered human consciousness, it was reasonable that man in his artistic creations should search for forms that would convey this feeling of intelligible order, while avoiding forms that seemed to obstruct such sensation. At the roots of this early form vocabulary was doubtless the twofold desire to make matter both comprehensible and reliable, but owing to the increased preoccupation with form, this very reason for aestheticism of order became less and less pronounced and finally was no longer imperative. Instead, the order of physical appearance became the subject of aesthetic delight, regardless of whether a certain pattern or ornament still possessed its intended meaning.

From this physical order, then, principles of balance, rhythm, harmony, and unity entered human aesthetic consciousness. Yet, while these were aesthetic principles that were hardly any longer connected with the practical-functional meaning of order when it first entered human aesthetic awareness, the original character of architectural order is most strikingly manifested in one of man's earliest intellectual achievements, the awareness of measure. In fact, without such a consciousness, principles of scale, proportion, symmetry, and asymmetric balance could never have arisen. Measure, therefore, the most efficient and practical criterion of physical perception, was the early basis for order in building, and it is by no means just a coincidence that the standard for measure was man himself. Because, in man the order of physical environment is perceived, in man the orders of heaven and earth meet. Man, in fact, is measure of all things.

Thus, all activities that aim at establishing order in the environment are basically acts of measuring, i.e., acts of dimensioning the environment according to human standards, at first only physically but later also psychologically. And, here, the concrete difference between architecture and nature comes to the open. Architectural environment is created according to human scale, while natural environment does not possess any scale related to man. In fact, it was the latter circumstance that instigated man to establish his own order by means of building. Architectural order, therefore, as architecture itself, is in contrast to natural order as architectural form is in contrast to natural form, and the present intermingling of these clear distinctions speaks for the confusion in contemporary concepts and ideas.

physical order

The feature that distinguishes Japanese residential architecture from any other architecture, past and present, is order. This order is comprehensive, it is both physical and spiritual. True, each noted style of past European architecture possessed unique and profound order, but this order was confined mainly to monumental architecture and by comparison was not nearly as comprehensive and universal as that of the ordinary Japanese house.

The Japanese order of material (see Chapter I) is not concerned with the number of materials employed as is contemporary architecture, which attempts to achieve unity in building either by limiting the number of materials, or by creating aesthetic effect through the use of many contrasting materials. Instead, the Japanese order is based on the nature and expression of the material itself. Unity and coherence, both the aim and effect of architectural order, is achieved by the limitation to natural products, employment of only handicraft techniques, and expressional articulation of the inherent nature of each material in the fabric of building. Thus, the choice, technique, and treatment of material is not determined by considerations of their juxtapositioning, nor by how many materials are used, but by subordination of all under a common denominator. The result is expressional harmony.

The Japanese order of measure (see Chapter II) is even more unique. All the minute components of the house are standardized in size and form, as are also the major units composed of those elements. Yet, standardization itself does not yet achieve unity, and it is the module of *kiwari* (literally, wood proportioning) that brings each measurement into mutual ratio and proportion (Figures 7–14). Actually, there are two units that serve as moduling agents: the cross-section of the standard column for dimensioning of the other individual wood sections, and the standard distance between the main columns for dimensioning of the major building elements such as posts, beams, sliding panels, mats, etc. Both units originally had been the keynotes of an aesthetic canon and varied relatively with size of building, yet, for practical and economical reasons, the column section for the ordinary residences was very early established at 4 *sun* (121 mm. = 4.8 in.), while the column distance, the *ken* of 6 *shaku* (1,818 mm. = 6.0 ft.), became an actual unit in the official Japanese measure system, lending itself in its multiple or its fraction to a variety of column spacing without upsetting the modular order. Thus, the controlling order of measure brings all dimensions of the house into a geometric relationship that combines aesthetics with economy. The result is structural unity.

The Japanese order of design (see Chapter III) is no longer concerned with the individual building component or the room unit, nor even with the constructional system or the expression of building. Instead, design is but the composition of standardized form and space. It is characteristically free from visual-external concern and follows only practical-functional principles. And, yet, the pure logic of organizing space and form has a strong aesthetic impact. The unit for establishing order in the interior space is the rigid, thick floor mat, *tatami,* in size about 3 × 6 ft. (900 × 1,800 mm.). The mat not only designates individual room size but also takes up the vertical order of tangible construction and translates it into the horizontal order of the intangible space. As such, the mat is more an integral element of the space itself than of the physical space enclosure, and though it does designate size of interior space, it does not function as module for the space-enclosing elements as is often assumed. Instead, the mat is the "ordering" agent for the void of the interior space. It permits diversity in both room size and room usage, without changing its own size or expression. The result is spatial coherence.

The Japanese order of construction (see Chapter IV) employs principles that allow the free addition of spatial cells without problematic consequences in structural feasibility, regardless of how irregularly the standardized space units are added to one another. Also, this freedom of space organization does not have any aesthetic disadvantages. For, with design being subjected to the order of measure with the standard unit *ken* of 1,818 mm. or 6.0 ft., unity in scale and congruity of structure and space are preserved. Further, as the structural members for the main part are visible both from without and from within, the exposed structure makes both the order of measure and that of design boldly visible and thereby constitutes an essential factor of architectural expression. Order of construction allows assemblage of identical parts, i.e., standardized elements, for interior space organizations of any size, proportion, relationship, or taste, without ever diverging from its structural integrity or losing its simple and organic coherence. The result is physical unity in diversity.

Such physical order, as a very simple principle, permeates material, measure, design, and construction. It produces unity of the total building physique and harmony among individual building components. But the aesthetic quality of this order is not achieved primarily from these physical effects. For unity and harmony in building expression do not alone create aesthetic sensation. Rather, this order is beautiful because, characteristically, it bears direct relationship to human proportional senses and permits immediate perception and distinction of the individual forces, both physical and spiritual, that shaped the house. Indeed, this order allows man to plainly "read" the house and to learn its history. As a result human emotions will respond, and man will feel such an intimacy with the house that building will become a part of himself. No architect is needed to interpret "house." The simplicity of the order permits everyone to not only understand "house" but to also be familiar enough with its technical aspect to be his own architect.

With all elements of the house being submitted to the same order, another source of aesthetic delight is tapped. For human emotions react pleasantly if expectancy is fulfilled and react uncomfortably when anticipation remains unfulfilled or when it is upset by the entirely unfamiliar. With all houses and all rooms basically being determined by identical principles, architectural anticipation never remains unanswered, and experience with the different manifestations of this consistent order produces a continuous stimulus for aesthetic response.

Japanese physical order in residential architecture shows that order becomes aesthetical only when it is distinctly and immediately related to man, i.e., when it is human, physically, emotionally, and intellectually. Humanism, therefore, is the criterion that makes physical order aesthetical; humanism is the requisite for beauty in building. Indeed, it is because of the absence of humanism in the expression of many modern buildings, that even the better ones often remain unaesthetic and without delight, in spite of a comprehensive physical and intellectual order of their own.

spiritual order

However, the physical order of Japan's domestic architecture receives its most powerful aesthetic impulse by its relationship with, or rather identity to, the spiritual order of Japanese living as expressed in the ethics of family and society, in the religious faith, and the philosophic interpretation of the world. In the case of the Japanese, both the physical order and the spiritual order are actually one and exist as a duality only in the analytic Western mind because of lack of one concept that would integrate both. Still both orders originated independently, and it was not until the late Middle Ages of Japan that fusion took place. The physical order of house was not only adapted to the spiritual order of living, but the spiritual order of living also obtained new momentum from the physical order of house.

This influence through architecture, as through art in general, upon the growth of spiritual order in society is too often minimized or simply denied. It is common practice to conceive architecture and art as merely reflecting a certain pattern of spiritual values rather than generating them. However, the Japanese house does show that the outstanding architectural features and expressions existed long before their spiritual interpretation through, and their alignment with, the existing religion-philosophy. Also, as has been shown in earlier chapters, the code of ethical value and proper conduct became very much crystallized through building itself. It was this mutual interchange of values between both the physical and spiritual orders that finally effaced all contradicting elements between them and produced the unity of the whole.

The Japanese order of family (see Chapter V) is distinguished by four features. Positively interpreted, emphasis on family unit, responsibility of head of the house, right of primogeniture, esteem for malehood. Negatively interpreted, disregard of individual human being, subservience to head of the house, underprivilege of the postgeniture, inferiority attributed to femalehood. The aesthetic quality of such an order may be questioned from the viewpoint of the present pattern of thinking. However, measured against the standards of the late Middle Ages of Japan, it was not only a very practical order that was best suited to maintain this socio-economic unit, but it was also the only form that could protect the life of the individual in those troubled times. Even in this day, due to lack of institutions for social welfare in Japan, this order of family is a necessary and appropriate form of living, and though in cause it is less ethical than material, in effect it provides psychological comfort, hence aesthetic delight. Consequently, the Japanese house is characterized by a strong interdependence of the order of family and the physical order of house. In fact, the Japanese house is but the materialized order of family. The result is humanity in building.

The Japanese order of society (see Chapter XII) during the time when the Japanese residence evolved, was that of a class structure, with the strict subordination of the lower classes by those in superior ranks. It was modeled after the Chinese system and was spiritually supported by the Confucian doctrine. A strict order it was, indeed, for each class was given its exact position in the social organism in the form of duties and privileges, and this confined position was so rigidly guarded that distinct class cultures developed within the same nation. The rise of a new class, the progressive and wealthy townspeople, late in the Middle Ages of Japan, prompted a residential architecture that incorporated those differing patterns and brought about a unique architectural-cultural taste for the entire nation. This social order is also physically expressed in many ways in the Japanese house, as has been mentioned earlier. The architectural manifestations of the social order were often imposed, but in the end they produced aesthetical sensation and awareness, and understanding of the social order. In such a role, the Japanese house, apart from being shelter for the individual family, puts the order of society into material form and functions as interpreter of social ethics; the result is social spirituality in building.

The Japanese order of religion-philosophy (see Chapters VIII and XI) is characterized by an identity of religious belief and philosophic thought. Moreover, differing from Western tendencies, this unified spiritual endeavor of religion and philosophy is not a practice confined to temples or schools, but is a daily exercise and a part of life within the home. The house, then, is also the place of worship and meditation and provides the space in which man pursues his spiritual aspirations; and this role of the house is clearly manifested in many physical forms. However, of even stronger aesthetic meaning for the inhabitants is the spiritual interpretation of the physical components in the Japanese house, especially the many symbolic meanings that Zen Buddhism and the tea cult gave to individual parts and features of the house structure. These features were in existence long before Zen and "tea" became influential in Japanese cultural life and so was the expression of simplicity. But the new identification turned this unwanted and poverty-born simplicity of living and building into a simplicity that thereafter was consciously sought because of its profound aesthetic meaning. This order of religion-philosophy universally permeates each component, technique, and expression of the house and constitutes the encompassing spiritual order of residential building from the 17th to the 19th century. It provokes a stronger aesthetic response than the physical discipline of the house itself. Indeed, it is this spiritual order that gives the physical order its aesthetic philosophy. It makes the tangible but expression of the spiritual and the individual a part of the universe as the Japanese conceive it. Its result is morality in building.

While the physical order, of course, is confined to the dwelling and the life therein, the spiritual order is the controlling agent for building and encompasses and permeates life and art in general. Thus, Japanese residential architecture is not autonomous and, therefore, does not possess independent ethics and laws, but is integrated into the greater order of the entire physical and spiritual environment. Identical spiritual standards control living, building, thinking, and believing and thus satisfy the inquisitive human mind and the searching soul. They effect a total coherence of all values. The result is profound aesthetic delight.

for contemporary architecture

Such a profound and encompassing order, then, stands in marked and favorable contrast to either the pronounced individualism or the inhuman uniformity of contemporary residential architecture. It is also essentially different from the occasional geometric-visual order in contemporary commercial and industrial building.

Architectural order, briefly stated, exists when individual elements of an organism are in conformity with a dominating principle, be it of physical, spiritual, or intellectual nature, so that each element is designated its proper place and thus becomes intelligible and meaningful. Order, therefore, is not only prerequisite for unity of an organism but is also the agent that makes the organism function.

This analytic definition shows that order can instigate aesthetic feeling in two different ways. First, by satisfying the desire of the human mind for order as such order may create aesthetic sensation and itself become beautiful. However, the realization of order per se, i.e., the mere discovery of regular relationships, patterns, in physical form or spiritual meaning is not necessarily beautiful. In fact, order can even become appalling, as the monotony of mechanized structures (especially, curtain walls) or the ideological discipline under totalitarian governments (especially, Nazi Germany, the Soviet Union) proves. The reason is that these orders are distinctly lacking in any human element; they are non-human orders. Therefore, order can stir aesthetic emotions only if controlled by human factors.

Secondly, as order makes the elements it organizes functional and intelligible, it can also effect aesthetic sensation by disclosing content, i.e., meaning or purpose of an object. Of course, such role of order can then provoke aesthetical response only if the content disclosed bears an intimate relationship to the psychology of man.

In both instances, the Japanese order differs markedly from contemporary order (the contemporary does have an order, since disorder is also a particular state of order). First, in its potential of being itself aesthetical, present architectural order is at best confined to the visual-physical qualities of building except for that part that is a result of the directives and codes of the building authorities. Contemporary order in building is one of geometry that relates the appearance of building to the proportional senses of man, i.e., to his aesthetic taste. By comparison Japanese order relates the orders of building to the orders of individual, family, and society and integrates them all into the universal order of religion-philosophy and epoch. It thus exhausts its full potential and is capable of stirring the most varied and most profound human emotions.

In the second aesthetic role of order, namely that of functioning as transmitter of architectural content, the difference between Japanese and contemporary Western order is even more pronounced. Order in modern commercial and industrial building (for there is hardly as yet any physical order in residential building) discloses but the physical aspect of building, such as structural system, constructional stresses, and utilitarian purpose, but not the spiritual-human aspect. In contrast, the order of the Japanese residence not only gives each physical element its proper place and an expression that clearly states its function, but also lends expression to the entire nation's religious and philosophical concepts. Order in the Japanese house rather than any sophisticated and abstract education, renders intelligible to the mass of the people the spiritual forces that guide their lives, and establishes a profound and intimate relationship between man and house. It is in this capacity that order in Japanese residential architecture achieves another aesthetical quality.

Japanese order, as compared to that of contemporary architecture, very distinctly states the requisites that make order a true instrument of architectural aestheticism. Physical order in contemporary building is inevitable because of increasing industrialization and because the complexity of contemporary living requires a comprehensive order for smooth operation. However, such an order, if devoid of any human element, is apt to turn environment into a non human uniformity and cold functionality that does not possess any aesthetic quality. The only agent that has so far produced order in contemporary architecture is the machine technique. It is, therefore, the imminent task to humanize present industrial technique by integrating it into the great framework of contemporary thought. Only then will present architectural order be understood, appreciated and wanted. Only then will it become aesthetical.

The Japanese order of architecture contains still another lesson for contemporary architecture. Although integrated into a universal order of *Weltanschauung*, it possesses its own innate standards of architecture that are markedly and consciously set against those of nature. True, Buddhist beliefs conceived of a one-life permeating all existence, both animate and inanimate, and provided the spiritual order that preserved the unity of the whole, but Buddhism was also the instrument that, under the protection of its integrating order, allowed individual thought to be freely expressed and to be rendered in independent and often contrasting form. By spiritually establishing the basic oneness of man and nature, it encouraged rather than prevented the realization that, physically, nature is indifferent toward human matters. Although the same belief was responsible for the Japanese not aggressively exploiting the potential forces of nature, but rather submitting themselves passively to them, it seems to have stimulated a keen awareness that the order of nature was non-human and that any human environment had to be essentially different.

Such awareness is clearly demonstrated in the Japanese house. Although elements in their natural shape are occasionally employed for individual visual effect, generally no expression of nature is taken as a pattern for architectural form, and technical house is clearly and unmistakably separated from natural environment. This consciousness of the physical incoherence and the inhuman scale in nature is even better evidenced in the residential garden. For the Japanese garden, though strictly patterned after nature, is thoroughly architecturalized, i.e., it has limitation of extent, meaningful composition of feature, coherent organization of elements, and reduction in scale; in short, it has a human order. Only some of the constituent parts are still nature-like, but the whole itself is distinctly architecture and not nature.

Conventional tendencies in Western residential architecture that attempt to make the house look as if naturally grown, that imitate the structure of nature, or even look to nature for architectural inspiration and legality, are based on the fallacious assumption that nature is beautiful and that beautiful architecture, consequently, has to look "natural." However, nature, meaning the physical environment not changed by human hands, is not always beautiful. In fact, it is unsightly more often than it is truly beautiful. Thus, nature in its physical disposition is aesthetically inconsistent, i.e., it does not possess any aesthetic order. Therefore, to build "like nature" would mean abolishment of aesthetic order, and, since building is creation with artificial means, would be a contradiction to the very essence of architecture itself.

By comparison, the Japanese house, in spite of consistently employing natural materials and of keeping their unfinished surfaces, has never belied its artificial-human creation and has never become "like nature." Probably in no other nation is nature loved and appreciated as it is in Japan, and yet there is an awareness that architectural order is intellectually and emotionally in contrast to nature. The beautiful *in* nature is realized and made use of. The grain of the wood, the texture of the clay wall, the flower in the vase, the steppingstones to the veranda, the shrubs and pebbles in the garden, etc.—they no longer express the inconsistency and incoherence of nature's order, but have become architecture. The result is that humanized nature, i.e., the garden, can be fully appreciated and human order in the sphere of the home can remain unaffected. By means of this order a morality is established that contains an important message for contemporary architecture, with its confusion of human, mechanical, and natural orders.

And, finally, Japanese order in residential building dispenses with the commonplace preconception that material order in residential building, i.e., subordination of all building under physical or spiritual principles, will necessarily lead to non-human uniformity. As the previous chapters have shown, the physical standardization of the individual elements in the Japanese house has actually liberated the Japanese from stifling concern with detail and has allowed them to concentrate solely on organization of interior and exterior spaces—the very art of architecture. Individuality in residences, therefore, is not distinguished by elements of color, form, light, and décor, but by the distinctive property of architecture, space. This primary concern with space itself not only expresses individuality much more profoundly and architecturally, but also allows unlimited diversity without sacrificing unity in the total architecture.

All human efforts aim at establishing a physical and spiritual human order in an indifferent and non-human world. The task of architecture is to establish order in the total physical environment of man, order that is aesthetical because it is human. Japanese residential architecture shows the elements of such an order and constitutes an architectural precedence, knowledge of which may well inspire contemporary and future architecture.

CHAPTER FIFTEEN expression

definition

EXPRESSION IN BUILDING is the element in building that communicates with the psyche of man. It conveys as content either mere visual-external form, or spiritual meaning represented in form.

EXPRESSION IN BUILDING, with external form as content, is a pattern or arrangement of sensuous materials, colors, shapes, lines, and masses. It appeals directly to the senses of the beholder and establishes psycho-physical harmony.

EXPRESSION IN BUILDING, with meaning as content, is the architecturalization of ideas, concepts, emotions, images, or customs. It appeals to the intellect, imagination, or emotions of the beholder and establishes spiritual harmony.

EXPRESSION IN BUILDING reflects the taste of the epoch and of the region. Responding to a particular aesthetic liking, it is manifestation of a people's culture and life.

EXPRESSION IN BUILDING indicates not only disposition of the creator and his time, but also manifests destination of building. The distinct purpose of a building directly influences idea and form of design and, hence, intimately its final expression.

EXPRESSION IN BUILDING, yet, is not only reflective but also educative. With building being the most immediate and continuous physical environment of man, architectural expression strongly shapes man's psychology and influences his aesthetic sensitivity.

EXPRESSION IN BUILDING, though, is not always conscious and intentional architectural measure. Often, and especially when economical considerationsa lone condition architectural creation, expression of building is not premeditated and hence is accidental.

EXPRESSION IN BUILDING, then, is the element that gives aesthetic quality to architecture. It is the area where building assumes the role of art, and is, therefore, an important concern of architectural creation in all its constituent factors.

In order to fully understand the aesthetic quality of Japanese residential architecture, and for that matter, that of any building or art object, three things must be studied. First, the form or material object as perceived by the senses; second, the idea, content, or spiritual significance of the object; and, finally, the psychological subject of aesthetic experience, i.e., the contemplating human. All these three, in fact, have been the subject matter of the previous chapters. The form and idea of the Japanese house have been analyzed, the harmony between both has been described, and their relationship to the psyche of the Japanese has been stated. That is to say, all previous chapters have actually dealt with the aesthetics of the Japanese house; all architectural measures are essentially aesthetic.

Yet, in order to gain the proper perspective for the aesthetic quality of the Japanese house, it is necessary to distinguish between those expressional features that owe their existence to mere coincidence and those that have been prompted by aesthetic intent and, further, to point out those seemingly modern features that please the contemporary Western eye but that neither in their cause nor effect have had any relationship to the aesthetic taste of the Japanese in the 18th and 19th centuries. For much confusion has been created by aesthetic judgments that do not make these distinctions and that analyze all expressions of Japanese residential architecture by the subjective standards of contemporary Western disposition. The assumption that all seemingly "modern" features of the Japanese house are due to an attitude toward building identical with that of modern man is as fallacious as the supposition that all detail expression had been originally prompted by mere practical reasons.

This analysis also intends to state clearly and in context the very causes that make the expression of the ordinary Japanese residence so aesthetically profound and rich, in spite of the exercise of utmost restraint in material, form, color, and space. The findings will not be merely of archeological value, but will bear a direct relationship to the controversial subject of aesthetics in contemporary architecture. For the aesthetic expression of simplicity in the ordinary Japanese dwelling contrasts favorably with the ostentations and demonstrative "taste" of contemporary Western residences. It is also fundamentally different from that simplicity in contemporary building that is effected alone by emphasis on function, economic restriction, or assimilation to modern technology.

In this light, a summary consideration of the elements that have a direct bearing on the specific expression of the Japanese house, together with an analysis of their causes, may well stimulate an overdue re-evaluation of aesthetic standards in contemporary society and inspire new aesthetic values for an architecture that seems to lack the possibilities of profound and varied aesthetic expression.

interior

It has become a generally accepted procedure to begin description or judgment of the aesthetic quality in a particular building with analysis of its external features. Emphasis is placed on physical form as seen from without—a tendency that is quite obvious in the majority of books on architectural history, in magazines of contemporary building, and in the drawings of the architect. In other words, both the creation and the experience of aesthetic expression are mainly concerned with architecture's role as sculpture, i.e., the material three-dimensional form as can be seen from without.

In deliberate opposition, this treatise begins by analyzing the aesthetic expression of the Japanese house interior. For not only is the design of the Japanese house primarily concerned with interior spaces, their organization among themselves, and their relationship to the environmental garden, but also the architectural taste of the Japanese has predominantly asserted itself in the features of the house interior. The exterior façade is only an inevitable result thereof, and the garden serves only to enrich the interior space and to provide the ultimate wall that encloses the total world of the Japanese home.

Moreover, placing the Japanese house interior before the external, i.e., the pictorial-sculptural aspect, is meant to represent the conviction that architecture, both residential and non-residential, is predominantly a matter of enclosing space, i.e., creating and shaping human space. Consequently, aesthetic expression in architecture, different from that of sculpture or painting, does not lie so much in the material components but in the space. The expression of the material elements has architectural meaning only insofar as it gives character and expression to space—the interior walls, ceiling, and floor to the domestic space, the façade of the building to the urban space.

Generally, expression in architecture is conceived similarly to that of sculpture, namely, as a quality that radiates *from* an object in space, and not as a force that is predominantly directed *toward* a focal space, be it domestic or urban. This trend is very much related to the inadequacy of current methods to pictorially represent enclosed space, or for that matter, to represent the effect that the combined space enclosures (walls, ceiling, floor, façade, paving, planting, etc.) will have on the final architectural space. The result is, in fact, the disunity of contemporary architecture not only in the interior spaces of homes, offices, or stores but, with even more fatal consequences, in the urban space.

The tendency to consider aesthetic expression in architecture to be of the same nature as that of sculpture has resulted in having the design of interior spaces in building —dimensioning of ceiling height, proportioning of wall plane, amount of window area and its placing in the wall, etc.—predominantly determined by the external aspect of building. For the same reason, the expression of the façade itself in most cases remains an isolated statement, unrelated to adjacent façades in the ensemble of elements that form urban spaces. Many of them may exhibit a high expressional quality as individual sculpture, but in the total picture, they only add to the confusion that characterizes the expression of the contemporary urban spaces.

By contrast, the external appearance of the Japanese house is unconditionally subjected to its interior organization. It is not a conscious creation but an inevitable result of the interior design. And the expression of the interior itself, insofar as its basic elements—the mats on the floor, the exposed columns of the wall, the sliding panels, or the clay wall in between, i.e., both entity and form—had come into existence out of necessity, is no less accidental in its causation. Through the tea cult, however, these features were aligned with the current religion-philosophy and then employed as a conscious expression of an aestheticism that is distinct for Japan.

The basic expression of the Japanese house interior is standardized, i.e., the principles for interior form, order, texture, and color are the same for each house (Plates 152–153). Keynote is the modular unit, *ken* (1,818 mm. =6 ft.), expressed through the exposed columns. The function of the columns is essentially structural. Their placement is determined by room partition, but the form of the columns in their contrast to the movable and fixed wall panels, is also decorative. All horizontal members of the structural framework are either above the ceiling or below the floor, or are concealed in the solid wall. Yet, horizontal braces, *nageshi,* that no longer have a structural necessity are exposed on both sides. They provide the necessary horizontal differentiation, tying the upper sliding track of the panels together and providing the visual "support" for the clay wall above.

This order of the vertical space enclosure based on the modular spacing of columns, is translated into the two horizontal planes of floor and ceiling as a rigid geometric pattern of rectangles, which in the case of the floor obtains a particular accentuation from the black ribbon, *heri,* at the long sides of each mat. Thus, the discipline of the *ken* encompasses all planes that form the interior space both horizontally and vertically and subjects them to a common standard. Nevertheless, each individual component in the composition is distinctly differentiated from all the others, the columns, the wall, the individual sliding panels, the ceiling rods and ceiling boards, and the individual mats—a system of sharply defined elements tied together through the structural beat of the *ken*.

And this coordinating role of the column is further fortified by its modular influence upon the dimensions of other wood members. For not only are they sized in direct ratio to the section of the standard column, but the standard distances for elaborate millwork are also often derived from column clearance. Generally, all wood sections are rectangular, the pieces being butted together without casing trim. The resulting forms consist of straight lines and right angles, making up a geometric linear space description that, with rare exception, is conspicuous through the absence of curves. Measure and proportion are no longer subject to alteration, but are in subtly calculated dependence upon the order of the *ken*.

contrast

Since the traditional Japanese house is not equipped with furniture in the Western sense, and since the items used are low in height and rectangular in shape, it could be expected that such a rigid geometric formality would create a very technical and impersonal environment that, except for scale, would not establish a harmonious relationship with the inhabitant because of its austerity. Technical and impersonal it is, however, three factors are instrumental in effacing formal rigidity and establishing human warmth: texture, color, light.

All materials are employed in their natural texture without any surface finish other than that which would stress the inherent structure of material. The wood shows its irregular grain and the wear of age; the clay wall shows its individual ingredients as well as the imprint of handicraft; the translucent paper panel shows the fiber of its pulp and the repeated patching of its damaged parts; and the floor mat shows the braided work of the natural grass and the wear from usage. Such natural and human irregularity within the regularity of technique is a contrast that not only attracts attention to each of the opposing elements, but also reconciles the human senses with man's own unnatural creation, technique. While rigidity of form addresses the intellect and only indirectly stimulates sympathetic response, the natural-human imperfection within this system effects direct and immediate emotional harmony.

Color of materials, too, is instrumental in effacing the rigid formality of expression. In fact, color establishes another contrast in the composition of space definition. For all individual components of the space enclosure are sharply differentiated from each other, each of them clearly stating its individual function. But, on the other hand, they all have colors of the same category, which counterbalance this intellectual clarity of distinction and contrast with the formality. The yellowish pale brown of the wood, the yellowish pale green of the floor mat, the cream-yellow of the opaque paper panels, *fusuma,* also the white of the translucent paper panels, the yellowish dark brown of the clay wall, etc.—they are all of similar color value and establish harmony and unity in the composition of clearly differentiated individual members.

The third factor that functions within the ensemble of compensating forces is light. While in contemporary Western dwelling the discrepancy of linear and technical structure versus multiform furniture and abundant decoration is painfully accentuated by a glaring light with pronounced shadows, the light in the Japanese house is subdued by the antepositioned veranda with its broad roof overhangs, and diffused by the translucent paper of the exterior sliding panels. Harshness and rigidity of geometric expression under such an influence become softened, and stern severity turns into serenity.

Texture that contrasts geometry, color that contrasts differentiation, light that contrasts distinction, all establish a harmonious atmosphere of opposites that, doubtlessly, is one of the reasons for the successful expression of the interior space enclosure. Its distinction is that each pair of these contrasting elements produces a new homogeneous expression that no longer has any direct relationship to the original character of either of its two constituents. This aesthetic quality, in fact, is the expression that the Japanese term *shibui* (Plates 148–149). It may be insufficiently rendered into English as sweet-bitter, soft-hard, light-dark, simple-refined, or similar opposites, shunning a simple and comprehensive translation that no doubt is a major reason for the many and gross misinterpretations of the meaning of *shibui* by Western writers.

Although the Japanese are conscious of this aesthetic quality and intentionally strive for it in all forms of creative art, it is understood that this strange coexistence of austere classicism and emotional romanticism has not been intentionally designed, nor does it manifest a particular original taste of the Japanese. Rather, these characteristic expressions of the Japanese interior space were basically the inevitable and thus accidental result of architectural measures dictated by technique and material and the rigid limitations imposed by low economic standards. Realization and appreciation of the aesthetic value of these expressions followed much later. After this, however, the interplay of form with texture, color, and light was further refined and consciously applied. There is a high probability, therefore, in the assumption that the architectural taste of the Japanese crystallized and asserted itself through an architectural expression that had come into being by necessity and practicality.

individuality

With the expression of the Japanese house interior thus being minutely determined and universally performed, the question arises as to whether such uniformity does not stand in contrast to a strong human sentiment. For, with or without reason, man desires individual expression in his shelter or, if genuine personal taste is lacking, at least an expression different from the house of his neighbor. Such an urge for individuality is regrettably apparent in contemporary building, where for the sake of being different and new it has caused a physical disorder in both residential and commercial architecture.

The Japanese also possess these human inclinations toward individual expression. However, as the physical character of residence is beyond any personal influence, individual expression is shifted to an area that not only is the distinct property of architecture but that also decides predominantly the quality of building, space itself. Again, since not only the physical space enclosure but also the individual space volume are exactly standardized in size, individuality finds expression in a most architectural criterion, space relationships.

In the Japanese house, space—the invisible, the intangible, the void—is not confined to its common role as the aim or result of architectural efforts, but is used also as a primary instrument for expressing personal aesthetic preference. It is less the simplicity of physical form than this design with space that is the outstanding feature of Japanese aesthetic expression. Thus, individuality asserts itself only in organizing the total interior space and in relating it to the environmental garden space. The result is not only a genuine appreciation of space relationship by the mass of the people but also an unrivaled mastership in its handling.

Of course, there are other ways of expressing individual taste such as the type of wood latticework for the translucent paper panels, the color and pattern of paper for the opaque paper panels, and the type of clerestory window above the panels. Yet, in all these cases it is but a selection from forms contained within the narrow limits of a singular expression. Also, a particular combination of those standard forms may effect a certain individual expression. But all these manifestations of individuality are less strong by far than that which is gained through space relationship, in spite of the physical identity of component parts.

Of more potential for an expression of individuality is the picture recess, *tokonoma,* and the shelving recess, *tana,* which usually decorate the room where the guest is entertained, the reception room (Plates 76–79). Although these features as an integral part of the house are minutely standardized in scale and proportion, the central column, *toko-bashira,* which divides the two recesses, allows unlimited freedom to exercise individual taste. Here the house master may manifest his preference for the stem's shape, texture, color, polish, and even its fragrance and thus tangibly express his individuality. This singular instance in the Japanese house interior where individuality can express itself freely in physical-architectural form is highlighted by the presence of the only additive decoration in the Japanese home, the picture scroll on the recess wall and the flower in the vase on the elevated floor, a homogeneous fusion of nature, technique, art, and man through architecture.

And this personal display of décor is not a static expression, but a dynamic exercise of aesthetic taste. For the arranging of the flower or simple branch is a daily care of the housewife, and the picture scroll is changed according to the season or the occasion. The picture, the theme of which may be a simple motif of nature or a few characters of profound meaning written artistically by a famed priest or artist, is never an inevitable and continuous object of experience, liable to be overlooked or virtually not even seen with passing time, but is an ever changing expression of the Muses that asks for attention and appreciation.

association

Generally, these characteristic expressions of the house interior have been acknowledged by writers and critics on Japanese architecture or, at least, have never really been contested. However, there is considerable unawareness as to why these expressions, then, have such a great appeal to contemporary Western man, a beholder who in taste, temperament, belief, and philosophy is so very different from the Japanese to whom this residence has meant physical and spiritual shelter.

Disregarding the many publications in the West which, because of their superficial-pictorial content, have but the appeal of the unusual-exotic and considering only those that attempt a serious analysis of Japanese architecture, it appears that "simplicity of expression" is held to be the agent that so strongly addresses the senses of contemporary man. However, no explanation is provided as to why, then, the simplicity in most contemporary building does not produce the same effect. Evidently, "simplicity of expression" cannot be the reason for the appeal of the Japanese house to the Westerner. It is not recognized that it is not Japanese simplicity itself, but the idea it expresses that has such a strong impact. Without a forceful idea to express, simplicity has no purpose, for simplicity is only a method of expression, not its content. The frequent failure of contemporary simplicity is that it either conveys a content that denies human acceptance or it has no content to express at all. It is for this reason that simplicity of expression in contemporary architecture will often remain outside human sympathy and will not provoke emotional reaction.

All aesthetic pleasure in architecture and art can be said to stem from man's ability to associate himself with the form or idea of the object. In the case of the Japanese house this association is achieved by form expressions that all ask for man's participation, physically, intellectually, and emotionally. Unlike the Western art and architecture in which the elaboration of an idea and its representation in physical form is carried to the best possible completeness and thereby forces the beholder to assume a passive role, in Japan man himself is an essential component of the interior space. Without the beholder's presence and participation, Japan's architecture, as well as her art in general, would be incomplete. Through him, the enclosed space attains human scale and atmosphere. Man himself, not the objects created by him, is the only element that can remove the "horror vacui." Here, pleasure in art is not the passive contemplation of objects, but is the action of arranging a flower, unrolling and choosing a picture, serving tea to the guest, and carrying on conversation. This engaging quality of Japanese architectural expression is in fact the reason why the house is aesthetically so impressive to Western man also, even though he is not familiar with the vocabulary of the religious-philosophic meaning of its form and feature.

Yet, the expression of the Japanese house interior demands not only man's physical but his intellectual participation as well. For all forms in the interior composition are but expressions or symbols of a more profound meaning, a material vocabulary for concepts that unveil the religion-philosophy of the nation. In fact, without man's serious attempt to associate himself with the philosophic thought behind form, the expression of the material space enclosure would remain but a statement of rational-practical functionality without any other appeal to the Western beholder than that of its strangeness. Through man's intellectual participation in analyzing and interpreting symbols, communication is established between inhabitant and his immediate physical environment.

Thus, the translucent paper panel, *shōji*, is aesthetically appreciated not only because of its delicate form, contrasting light, compensating colors and warm texture, but also, and even more so, because the functional, practical, constructional, economical, and visual-geometric motives represented in these expressions are understood (Plates 56–57). It is comprehended that they manifest a state of unstable equilibrium. Strength and heaviness for constructional rigidity versus lightness for ease of operation, or reduction of component members for material savings versus insertion of members for visual-geometric effects. Overemphasis of any one of those factors will topple this unstable and therefore intricate state of equilibrium, a true expression of Japanese refinement in building.

Through both physical and intellectual association with the material space enclosure the most varied feelings are stirred. They are further deepened by the direct delight gained in seeing and contemplating the visual order—the single flower in the vase, the single picture in the recess, and the environmental garden—and thus establish a very strong emotional relationship between man and house. This intimate association, which inevitably makes man a part of building, both physically and intellectually, is the very reason why contemporary Western man is aesthetically so strongly moved and feels so closely associated with a residence whose profound philosophic background he may not as yet know.

exterior

There is no evidence that the exterior expression of the Japanese dwelling has been prompted by visual concern, nor that the external characteristics, except for mansions and tea huts of the wealthy, have been molded by reasons other than those of necessity or practicality (Plates 24–36). In fact, the exterior form of the house is but a result of the interior space organization, as much as the individual features of the house are but the result of technique and construction prompted by material and tool. The external expression of the Japanese house, therefore, is accidental and not intentional.

Such an indifference toward the exterior appearance of building only too easily could be misinterpreted as evidence of a defective inner attitude. Always, the disregard of form in all human affairs is not merely an external matter but also, because such attitude lacks social understanding, manifests a defective internal-basic conception. Certainly, negligence of the exterior shape of a building would deny architecture's definite potential as sculpture and thus would produce physical chaos and aesthetic dissatisfaction, both as individual building or as a component of the urban space.

Not so, however, in Japanese residential architecture. Although the appearance of the house is not designed in the strict sense and thus is free of visual-external concern, the structural rhythm of the *ken* in the façade and its moduling influence upon all constituent parts maintains coherence of building and establishes unity of expression. Further, since material, scale, technique, and construction are uniquely standardized for all building, such expressional order exists also on an urban scale, in spite of the individual differences in spatial concept of building or organization of site.

Still, every so often when the size of the individual site is not very limited, the free organization of interior spaces, especially the preference for interior courts and for steplike patterns and the frequent expansions in later years, produces disorder. Unhindered by concern for the resulting building mass, this designing from within frequently results in a building physique that lacks sculptural unity, especially due to complicated roof shapes, the multiplicity of which is further emphasized by separate roofs for veranda and for each wall opening. Although in many such cases even the moduling influence of the *ken* and the unifying effect through standardization fail to establish coherence of the building, the garden wall, 6–8 ft. high (1,800–2,400 mm.) toward the street actually discloses only the major roof of the house, while in the garden the narrowness of separate garden spaces prevents an overall view of the house with its sculptural multiplicity.

Here evidently, Japanese residential architecture of the common people differs distinctly from Western conception. The house, except for separate farmhouses and residences directly on the street, cannot be seen as a whole from without like a sculpture, but can only be seen in part. In this partial perception of the house, however, because of the direct connection of one room with one garden space, the inter-relationship of house-environment is more intensely felt than in the Western case where the entire façade with so many and diverse rooms behind it, does not allow such immediate identification. In part and detail, no doubt an awareness of architecture's role as sculpture does exist but no attempt is visible to conceive the house as a whole externally, nor to exploit the sculptural possibilities of the total building mass and façade.

The disregard for the design of the building exterior is most strikingly evident in the instance of two adjacent rooms of different width, for example, 2 *ken* (3,636 mm. = 12 ft.) and 1 1/2 *ken* (2,727 mm. = 9 ft.), coming together in one façade. No doubt, in Western architecture in order to maintain "order" in the façade and to establish continuity of proportion, in spite of the different column spacing of each room, the larger unit would have been furnished with four panels and the smaller with three panels, each of about 1/2 *ken* (909 mm. = 3 ft.) width. Not so in the Japanese residence. Because the system of four panels is more practical than that of three, regardless of visual consequences from without, each opening is provided with four panels, resulting in two types of panels with essentially different proportions.

At the sight of such discontinuity of proportion, separated only by a slender column, the critical Western observer—and these are few since most tend to praise everything indiscriminately—will feel uneasy, as a disharmony of form or motif will always effect displeasure. But at the same time, whereas harmony only too often fails to attract the pronounced attention of the observer and may even escape his attention altogether, disharmony unquestionably acts more strongly, although in a negative manner, upon the receptive senses of man. Once this attention has been aroused, the question about the motive of such a discrepancy arises and the beholder will easily comprehend the reason behind such an architectural measure. There will no longer be displeasure.

Through intellectual comprehension, then, this discrepancy of proportion loses its unaesthetic quality. In fact, through the logic of its architectural motivation it becomes a medium that makes the beholder feel much more intimately related to the organism of house than he would from any visual harmony. And such association of human intellect and emotion with house is fortified through all the other physical components by means of which the eye perceives building. The expression of the house—structural framework, screening panels, protecting roof overhang, shading veranda, the house on stilts, etc.—is such that the beholder not only immediately comprehends the various components of building and their function, but is also able to analyze, without detailed examination, the constructional process, the accurate dimensions, and the arrangement of the interior rooms.

Thus, if it is agreed that the dominant function of sculpture is to convey the idea of its cause and existence, then, the expressional quality of the Japanese house must be called that of true sculpture. For its external form discloses the idea of house, namely, that of being an *interior* space—shelter for human living, seclusion for human contemplation, structure to capture interior space, organism of different spatial cells, stage to experience beauty.

Westerners accustomed to perceiving the exterior of building as an abstract composition of lines, masses, textures, materials, and forms to be judged separately from the interior function, may find the external expression of the Japanese house lacking in coherence and even in sculptural quality altogether. But if its appearance is valued as to how well it expresses the idea of house, then, the exterior of the Japanese house is sculpturally very successful in that it convincingly expresses its inner cause and existence. It constitutes a bold interpretation that the idea of house and home is the enclosed space, and that all other factors must be uncompromisingly subordinated under this idea.

for contemporary architecture

The foregoing study of the aesthetic expression of the Japanese house is instructive for contemporary architecture. It provides substantial material for gaining insight into the problem of "expression in architecture." But it should be well understood that it does not provide the ultimate answer in the controversy of modern aesthetics, Japanese or Western. Present living has its own values, forms, and principles, and their architecturalization must be essentially different. With this understanding, however, the analysis of Japanese expression in building gains in importance. For it is apt to unveil the sources of human aesthetic sensation through building and to directly stimulate contemporary architectural creation.

One such stimulus is contained in the unique role that art objects play in the life and house of the Japanese. Art objects—and even the poorest people possess picture scrolls or woodblock prints—are kept in closets or in particular fireproof storehouses. Hidden from everyday sight and indifference, they are chosen according to season or occasion and brought forth for the attention of both host and guest. Literally, the picture is unrolled in the picture recess, *tokonoma,* the teacup is offered at the ceremonial tea drinking, the ancient script or the woodblock print is handed to the guest to be examined and to become the subject of lengthy conversation. That is to say, individual art pieces are selected, arranged, viewed, contemplated; art is not a static "furniture" but a dynamic, ever new, aesthetic exercise.

By comparison, the interiors of contemporary Western houses increasingly look like a museum. Art pieces of any period and region are crowding mantelpieces and walls. Unrelated in their motif and expression, they are fighting an even battle among themselves and a losing one against the jazzy colors of modern furniture, which, in turn, is already engaged in a successful combat with the few pieces of "style furniture." And in between are spread fertile beds for cactus and other exotic plants, lustily creeping over wall shelves that are loaded with books, photographs, petty souvenirs, and pseudo art. As much as the intellectual alignment of many art objects, displayed side by side in a museum, excludes any spiritual association with, and submergence into, the theme of any single work, so too in modern homes the proud display of the ambitious art hunter no longer permits that intimate dialogue by which art reaches and may elevate the heart of man, the very mission of art.

The Westerner may disapprove of the simultaneous performance of several musical works, even if they are the creations of one and the same composer, and yet may feel entirely at ease if confronted with such a chaotic assemblage of visual art. Moreover, even though the inhabitant himself may have carefully considered the composition of the interior art décor, its continuous presence will make him no longer aware of them. Usually such décor remains unchanged or only further multiplied, and thus deprives man of the continuous joy of aesthetic exercise in his own home. It arrests the aesthetic expression of the room once and for all, and degrades art to a neutral element of the material space enclosure.

Here, the example of Japanese architecture has direct meaning for the contemporary. Not only could a *tokonoma,* the unique place for appreciating art objects, find acceptance in the Western house, but also the idea of art objects, i.e., its being a changing experience in the house, could restore the significant and rewarding role of art in living and building. To let a guest decide what paintings he would like to decorate the room with during his presence could be as much of an aesthetic experience for both guest and host as is the daily task of the wife to arrange flower and vase and to select the picture at the wall according to season, weather, or particular occasion.

The Japanese room, with such austere yet ever regenerating décor, is void of any element that could channel thought or arrest aesthetic expression. Its emptiness is the very state that grants greatest possible freedom to personal imagination and intellect and needs both man's presence and his direct participation as the essential elements that humanize an impersonal room. Whereas in the Western house man remains passive in creating and decorating his own physical environment, even remains an alien element in the architectural composition, in the Japanese house man himself determines the spatial atmosphere by his presence, his thought, and his choice of décor and constitutes himself a component of architecture.

This realization, evaluated for contemporary architectural design, strongly suggests to the architect to abstain from prescribing each and every piece of furniture and from freezing the emotional atmosphere of the room. Instead of designing and architecturally deciding the maximum in order to create space as is usually done, he should engage in finding the very minimum necessary to designate architectural space, while leaving the rest to the imagination of the inhabitant.

Such an approach toward creation in residential architecture, of course, is novel and not without problems. For interior design would largely withdraw from the controlling influence of the architect only to be subjected to the inexperience of a non-professional. On the other hand, however, the often too personal "handwriting" of the architect would lose its ambitious imprint. Instead, the unbiased layman may not only produce more direct expressions of his own concept of life but will also feel much more a part of the house than one who has remained outside of the creative process. Actual practice and direct experience are more apt to regain a lost culture of living than could any controversial interpretation through words.

Also, the expression of the Japanese house, both exterior and interior, distinctly shows the importance of contrast in architecture. It is true that man becomes aware of objects through contrasts, and architecture as perceived by the senses is but an intricate composition of contrasts—the voids and solids, the light and shadow, the straight and curved, the heaviness and lightness, the natural and artificial, the rough and smooth, the transparent and opaque, the skeleton and screen. But only too often these contrasts are applied with an unawareness as to their potential in the aesthetic expression of building.

Contrasts attract the attention of the beholder to both opposing elements. At the same time contrasts may compensate for the dominance of one or both of the opposing elements. In the Japanese house contrasting elements are not effaced but are pointedly set side by side, resulting in an architectural expression of immense clarity that immediately discloses the functions of the individual parts and makes the whole intelligible. Thus, through contrasts of the many, awareness of the individual is raised, awareness of its functional meaning, its aesthetic quality, and its material consistency, and varied aesthetic emotions are stirred.

Doubtlessly, in contemporary building a similar distinction between individual components, i.e., a conscious usage of contrasts, contains an inexhaustible source of architectural expression. Modern man increasingly experiences aesthetic pleasure through purely intellectual comprehension of an organism, be it of animate or inanimate nature. It is not so much the beauty of the external shape of a radio that will effect joy as the understanding of its complicated mechanism. Consequently, if beauty is the quality of an object to which the senses react pleasantly, then an expression that makes the understanding of building possible must be called beautiful; i.e., mere logic of expression highlighted by bold contrasts already possesses aesthetic quality.

Contemporary architecture could greatly benefit from such awareness, because only too often clarity of definition is effaced and expressional values are confused. Thus, structural members of the skeleton are literally "screened" with tiles, mosaics, metal sheets, or concrete coat; screening members are treated in their finish as if they were solid walls; mullions and external ducts are dimensioned and shaped as if they were structural columns. And such expressional deterioration exists also on a larger scale. Schoolrooms tend to look no longer like places for learning but places for entertaining and viewing environmental nature; bank and insurance buildings look like palaces where wealth needs to be displayed instead of institutes that economically administer and handle values; and house interiors look like exhibition pavilions rather than shelter where man is content.

Here, the congruence of expression and idea, of form and content in the Japanese house is apt to show the beauty in logic of architectural expression and to purify the confusion of values in contemporary architecture. This is by no means meant to dismiss the definite aesthetic potential of architecture to compose the façade separately from its interior organism. Certainly, contemporary design should exploit this potential and should also shape building like a sculpture in which aesthetic delight is derived from association with its external material surface. The Renaissance architecture gives evidence of how profound such aesthetic experience can be. But, since the feelings of inquisitive modern man are increasingly determined by intellectual comprehension of interior organism rather than by mere visual appreciation of external form, the demand for logic in architectural expression is due to become the strongest factor in both aesthetic creation and aesthetic appreciation of building. In Japanese residential architecture such an aesthetic interpretation has been exploited to its fullest and has produced effects the study of which has direct meaning for contemporary architecture.

PLATE 137: Form. Man perceives buildings through their forms. Buildings express their meanings through their forms.

PLATE 138: Taste of *mono-no-aware*. It can be described as a sophisticated compassion with the small things of man and nature.

a pine tree,
many years it stood
the sound of wind,
became pure
as life grew old.

my hands
sore with pounding rice,
tonight again
the lord's young son
will hold them and sigh.

. . . although
I should be weary of that life
and feel ashamed of it,
as I am no bird
I cannot fly up and escape . . .
[*from the Manyōshū*]

PLATES 139–140: Taste of *yūgen*. In a simplified interpretation it is the beauty of the mysterious and unreal.

no one left
at the border post.
the autumn wind blowing.
[Sadaie Fujiwara]

PLATES 141–142: Expression of *wabi*. It is the form produced by insufficiency or self-sufficiency, and it is thus associated with expressions of the simple, the rustic, the unpretentious, the imperfect.

PLATES 143-145: Spirit of *karumi*. It can be compared with a disposition of lightheartedness that overcomes the burden of the past and consciously ignores the shortcomings of the present while doing the unconventional.

dewdrops limpid small
and such lack of judgement shown
in where they fall.
[Sōin]

PLATES 146–147: Spirit of *iki*. It expresses itself in the intention to be contrary. It is thus the conception of opposing the existing, of wanting to be different from others, and of doing the unexpected.

I sleep, I wake,
how wide
the bed with none beside.
[Buson]

they spoke no word,
the host, the guest,
and the white chrysanthemum.
[Ryōta]

PLATES 148–149: Expression of *shibui* (epitomized in *shibui* form, i.e., as an understatement). It is the characteristic expression of two opposites in a precarious but meaningful balance, such as in a pronounced understatement of meaning, in a refined primitivity of form, in a severe lightness of manifestation, in an irregular order of pattern, or in a perfected artlessness of technique.

PLATES 150–151: Symbolism and abstraction. They contain the power of immeasurable and ever-new suggestion.

PLATES 152–153: Expression of the void. The space, open to all sides and empty, yet static and controlled, allows optimum freedom for both mind and body.

PLATES 154–155: Appeal of the natural. Elements of nature brought into the human realm and composed in a meaningful way become beautiful.

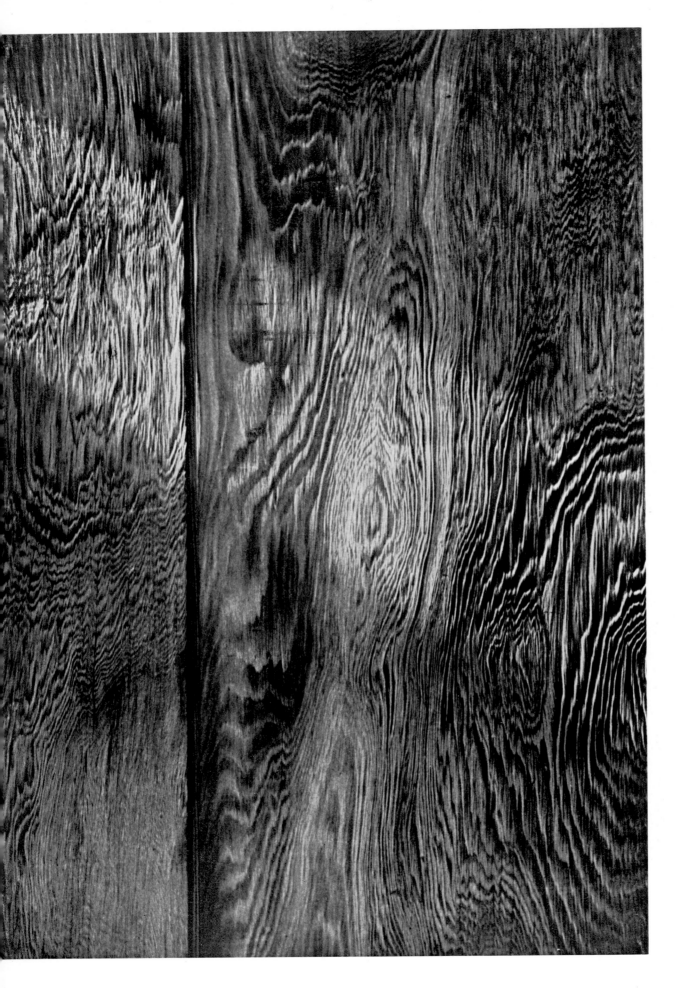

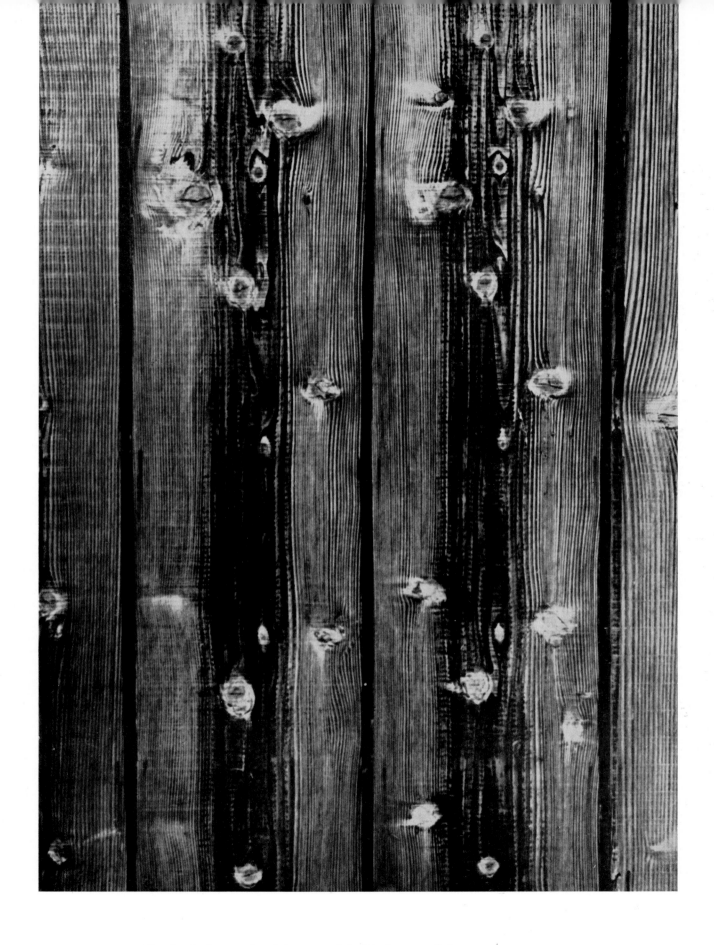

PLATES 156–157: The intrinsic worth of the material. Disclosure of the character of the material removes its anonymity and effects expression.

PLATES 158–160: Integration. Art (painting) that is integrated in utilitarian devises (door panels), and utilitarian devices (door handles) that are integrated in art are fortified in their expressional impact.

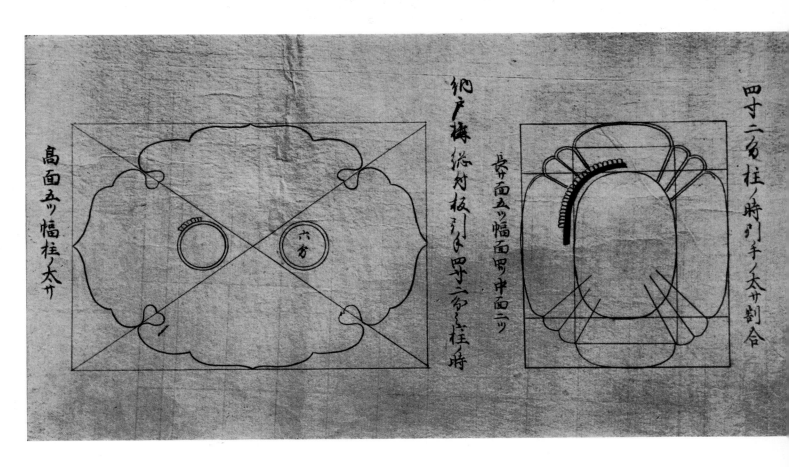

四寸二分柱ノ時引手ノ太サ割合

納戸棚　総対板引手ノ面四寸二分〈キ柱ノ時

長サ面五ツ幅面四ノ中面二ツ

高面五ツ幅柱ノ太サ

六方

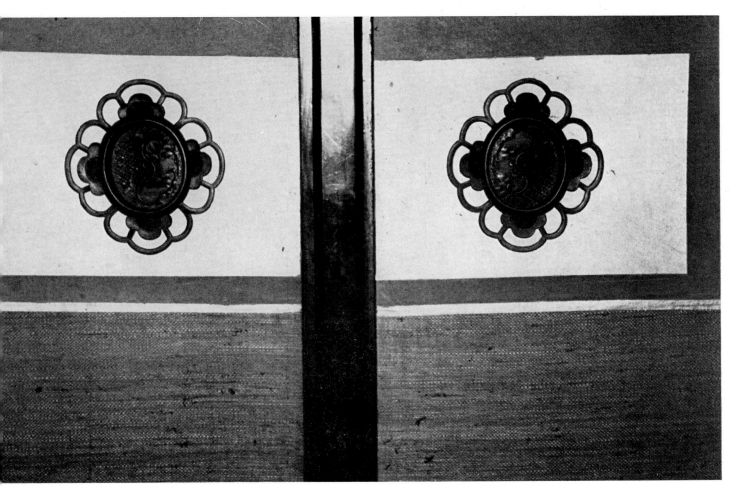

PLATES 161–162: The refined form. It maintains its strength of expression only as long as the basic-primitive prototype is not obscured. It will gain additional impact when the original form is further purified.

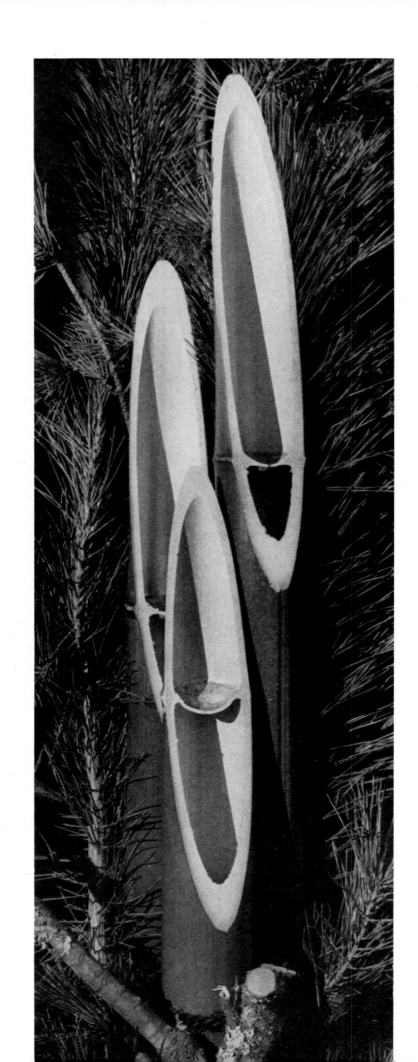

PLATES 163–164: Organic and technical form. The impact of the intrinsic form of the material can become immensely intensified by bringing natural material in contact with technical form.

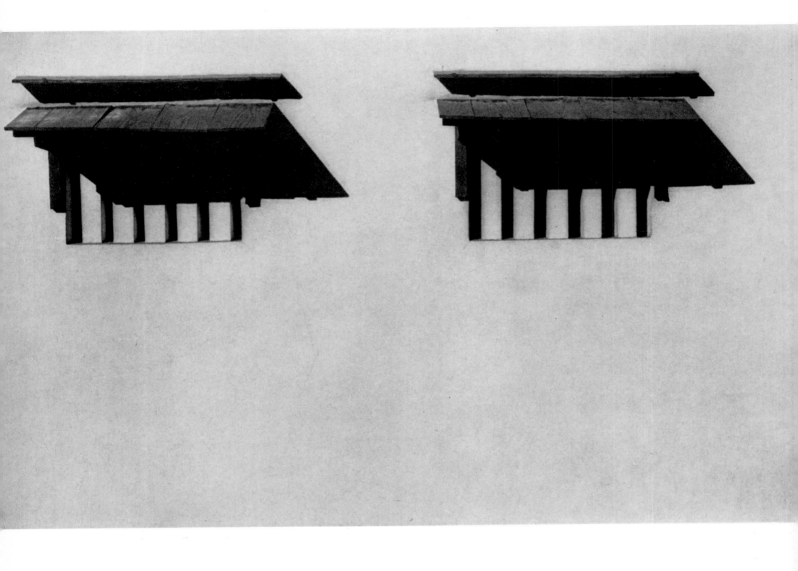

PLATES 165–166: Simplicity. It is the most direct method of responding to an architectural problem or of stating an architectural content. It is the ethical economy of expressing the most with the least.

PLATE 167: The Japanese house. A tradition for contemporary architecture.

CONCLUSION
for contemporary architecture

influence and eclecticism

The foregoing research has shown that the significance of the Japanese house for contemporary architecture does not lie so much in its form expression or its space substantiation as in the unique relationship that its form and space, the two interrelated keystones of any architecture, have with their cause and motivation. The projection of the sources of Japanese form expression and space substantiation against present conception of architectural form and space has proven truly instructive for almost any aspect of contemporary building.

The unique circumstance here is that in any one Japanese house those primary and secondary forces that comprehend the total scope of formative factors in architecture, past and present, have been active. This circumstance makes each ordinary Japanese house an ideal study case where the interdependence and interaction of individual factors in building can be seen and also where the integral unity of all active forces can be comprehended.

The Japanese house, therefore, qualifies as a primary medium to acquaint the student of architecture with the full range of architectural forces, their character, and their effects. Moreover, by providing a comparative scale for judging contemporary trends and by uncovering universal principles of architectural creation, the Japanese house is a unique reference case and a rich stimulus for any creative architect.

In view of this potential, it is unfortunate that the influence of Japanese traditional architecture, in the West as well as in modern Japan, has so far remained only decorative, imitative, or, at its best, adoptive in character, but by no means essential. Mere form and feature have been transplanted to different time or location, ignoring the fact that their *raison d'être,* and hence their aesthetic meaning, bears no relationship to contemporary living and thinking.

Japanese traditional architecture like any other architecture is but the expression of a particular epoch, and the epoch that produced the noted Japanese house does belong to the past. Modern *sukiya* style in Japan and current pseudo-Japanese style in America's West are but forms of eclectic architecture, fashions that cease to be fashionable from the moment they have become fashion. It constitutes a lapse into a formalism comparable to that of the past century, and is expressive of the present age only insofar as the rapid appearance and disappearance of fashionable forms seem characteristic.

The architect who attempts to demonstrate his esteem for a cultural achievement of the past, be it Gothic or Japanese architecture, by merely imitating its form is lacking two qualities essential for esteem: knowledge and respect. He, more than any other creative professional, artist or scientist alike, is in a position to grasp the essence of the present in its total aspect—socially, politically, technically, economically, ethically. He should, therefore, realize that materialization of the present through building necessarily must be as distinctly different from that of other eras as is contemporary industrial civilization itself.

While the Western architect-writer usually deplores the changes that are taking place in contemporary Japan, the Japanese architect seems to have understood that the architectural epoch in which he is living and working has a philosophical basis essentially different from that which produced the distinct residential architecture of Japan. His ethics, and those of the society for which he provides the human environment, are liable to be increasingly influenced by recognitions universal to all nations, regardless of how strong the ties to the past still are.

science and art

One misconception that exists about the Japanese residence, and for that matter a misconception that is akin to similar ones that exist about most cultural achievements of the past, is the assumption that the emotional response of the Japanese to his simple dwelling, both exterior and interior, is identical to the aesthetic pleasure that the uninitiated Western observer feels when experiencing Japanese form and space. The fact is that the emotional reaction in each case is essentially different.

However, it has been revealed that the contemporary Westerner is also able to experience identical sensation provided he is made familiar with the social, philosophical, and religious background. This possibility of identical aesthetic appreciation (of course, within the tolerance of individual physiological differences) by beholders so vastly apart in time, location, race, and culture delivers proof that man's psychological reaction to sensuous impulse, his aesthetic taste, is submitted to legality.

That is to say, the aesthetic response to the material and spiritual environment—architecture, art, technique, as well as science, religion, or education—is basically the same for all men. It follows, then, that aesthetic sensation, which is but a mechanical process of physico-psychological interaction within man, can be predicted. Since it is visual design that endeavors to evoke aesthetic sensation through form, scale, light, color, and space, it can be concluded that visual design has a scientific basis.

This realization means that visual design, at present still a matter of subjective search and intuitive grasp, can be based on principles that acknowledge the scientific facts of physico-psychological reaction to visual phenomena, i.e., the aesthetic factor of architectural design has an exact science at its disposal just as the structural, mechanical, physical-chemical, economical, functional, and social factors have.

Utilization of the scientific facts of sensuous perception for the aesthetics of architectural design will be of great value to the architect in contemporary industrial society, who is in danger of losing his leadership in the creation of buildings. Due to necessary specialization of contributive activity in building, the architect has been irrevocably deprived of the structural, mechanical, economical, and social elements in large-sized architectural projects, even of the landscaping. His activity here is confined to the spatial composition and the visual design of the building or, at best, consists of a coordination that is supposed to creatively integrate all individual efforts in the architectural team to produce a homogeneous and aesthetic entirety.

The findings of the specialists in this team are hard and substantial facts, based on a concrete science. They are impossible to object to and are difficult to alter, not in the least by a coordinator-architect who is *not* a scientist. By contrast, the spatial-formal ideas of the architect are backed by nothing but the vague standards of his "feelings." Unawareness of the scientific foundation of visual design imposes right from the start a serious handicap on any strong aesthetic idea of the architect and certainly will prove fatal in a head-on clash of interests between the various formative agencies of contemporary architectural design.

Only the acknowledgment of science in the aesthetic aspect of architectural design, i.e., the disclosure of the scientific laws of psychological reaction to form, scale, light, color, and space, can give the architect and planner the solid basis for realizing his aims in a society where individuality is indiscriminately surrendered on grounds of science, but obstinately defended on grounds of taste.

Such utilization of science can provide the encompassing basis for a common visual order in the contemporary environment. It would secure in all form creations a suprapersonal element that would fulfill the demands of psychology in general. It would also function as the controlling agent for giving optimum freedom to the creative potential and personal liking of the individual, while preserving the unity of all physical expression. It would establish a universal aesthetic standard, the maintenance of which alone would guarantee that each man-made form would be within emotional reach of all individuals.

However, this application of the facts of science (psychology) in design is not meant to replace any intuitive approach and to reduce the aesthetic aspect of design to a mathematical function. As is evidenced in the material, structural, economical, social, and hygienic aspects of building, the increased influence of science has never arrested but has always stimulated artistic imagination and creative thought. Therefore, it is plausible that also in the aesthetic aspect of building the intimate knowledge of the scientific facts of visual design will liberate the architect from tentative and empirical designing. It will enable him to directly and efficiently exploit the full range of human sensation through building and thus will make architecture a true instrument of art.

The mission of art is to give expression to feelings, to translate the infinity of human emotions into forms that in turn will evoke these emotions in the beholder. Art, then, stimulates human feelings and sensitizes them. Due to its immediate appeal to man's inner life, art raises awareness of what is right and what is wrong, and thus has functioned through the ages as the controlling standard of morality. Formerly, all creative manifestations of man provoked emotional response and were, in fact, art. But with the abrupt change of creative expressions owing to the sudden progress of science and technique, human emotions were no longer able to react to the novel forms of the environment. As a result, art withdrew from the major creative forces in the industrial civilization, science and technique, and retreated to specialized and narrow fields to become "the arts."

This absence of art in most of contemporary science and technique is, in fact, the reality behind all major problems in the contemporary civilization. Without art there is no controlling moral agency left in the creative activities with which man shapes the face of the earth, in architecture as well as in politics.

By contrast, the study of the Japanese house reveals the presence of art in every aspect of building and living. The "practice" of tea serving is as artistic as the "art" of tea serving is practical. There is no separation of the practical, technical, and artistic, and, consequently, living is a continuous aesthetic experience with a high morality.

This observation clearly defines the task facing the industrial society. The two separate sources of creative expression in human life, science and art, need to be brought into immediate proximity and reconciled; a science that is art in that it stirs and elevates human emotions; an art that is science in that it recognizes and utilizes the laws of human psychology. An integral concept encompassing all creative forces of the industrial civilization is needed—as the ancient Greek called it, a "techne" (characteristically the origin for the word "technique"), meaning all forms of "*real*-izing-life" in its significantly dual English meaning of today, recognition of life and materialization of life, i.e., science and art.

philosophy and architecture

The analysis of the Japanese house has not only illuminated the dilemma of the present but has also disclosed the basic method by which the solution of this dilemma can be approached.

The physique of the Japanese house, both interior and exterior, was originally prompted by necessity, i.e., its shape was simply that of a necessary tool for man to survive in a hostile environment. Only much later did the current religion-philosophy integrate and interpret this technical device and make it a source for profound aesthetic experience. But the religion-philosophy did not in the least change the basic form of the house, it only intensified, directed, and refined the growth of its existing features. In fact, by this integration a new aestheticism was born that took its forms essentially from what had been the most simple instrument for protecting the most basic living.

The contemporary situation is not much different. A new architecture has come into being with forms that are essentially expressions of necessity as dictated by productional methods, economic restrictions, and modes of living of the industrial society, and also by its political decisions. The mass of the people, due to education as well as the dissecting effect of scientific development in general and of philosophy in particular, have for a long time been trained to separate thinking from feeling, and do not have any relationship toward this new architecture other than that which they have toward any product of the machine industry. The result is man's general indifference toward the physical forms of his environment, and hence the danger of their unchecked and chaotic growth.

Here, the example of the Japanese house is very instructive. For the investigations have delivered proof that it is possible to incorporate an existing architectural form through post-interpretation into an existing framework of religion-philosophy and thereby essentially change its aesthetic meaning without necessarily altering its external shape. Through integrating both science and technique into an encompassing philosophy, a human application of technical-scientific products would be guaranteed and an emotional relationship between man and the mechanical environment established. The fatal emotional indifference of modern man toward his own scientific achievements and technical products could be removed; the artificial gap between thinking and feeling could be closed; awareness of the aesthetic quality, positively or negatively, in each material object of the industrial civilization could be raised; and a unique aesthetic relationship between man and the man-made could be established, which, in fact, is the prerequisite and distinction of true culture.

The necessity for philosophy in architecture, technique, and science (philosophy not in its meaning as summary of personal principles but as the science that attempts to disclose the facts and principles of reality) that would integrate all material creations of man into contemporary ethics is further highlighted by the vagueness, and hence the misuse, that distinguishes present social, political, scientific, and architectural concepts and actions.

Without an encompassing philosophy, the purpose of human life and work remains clouded, the aims of progress obscured, and the function of society undefined. No accurate relationship can be established between the individual and society; neither can the competence of the individual professional groups within this society be clearly marked out. No interpretation as to the function of architecture within the social organism is possible; consequently, no definition as to the role of the architect—his tasks, rights, and responsibilities—can be established. Even less is it possible to precisely define his relationship with other creative professionals such as the artist, scientist, engineer, or politician. And as long as all this is not known, appropriate training and education in the architectural profession will never come about.

In the contemporary age, with energies given into man's hand that can become means of construction or destruction with equal efficiency and completeness, it is no longer possible to re-establish a unique culture by adjusting the obsolete bit by bit, correcting the defective one after the other, and deriving new ideas from observation of shortcomings in the small range of subjective daily experiences. That is to say, it is no longer possible to merely improve upon the existing.

Instead, the contemporary industrial society requires an integral concept that will coordinate its major formative forces, science and technique, as well as architecture and art, economy and politics. Such reappraisal of the spiritual basis of contemporary existence is imperative for all professions that play key roles in the shaping of man's world. The frequent failures of international conferences of scientists, artists, politicians, or architects, show that the main issue in the contemporary world scene is less the individual problem that may have prompted such a gathering than it is the absence of, or disregard for, a universal philosophy for all human thought and action.

Therefore, as is the case in all creative fields of industrial society, the major problem of contemporary architecture is essentially one of a philosophical nature. With a knowledge of the spiritual values and aims of man, the scientific and technical forces of the industrial civilization could be orientated; the means of progress, technique and science, could be humanized; and the nucleus for a unique culutre could be formed.

culture and tradition

The studies on the interrelationship of the Japanese and their homes have produced evidence that architecture is not only reflective of existing culture but is also a primary instrument for establishing culture. The part that the ordinary Japanese house had in bringing about a unique culture prompted a definition of culture that clearly discloses the fallacies that beset contemporary conceptions of culture.

The commonly accepted interpretation is that culture (not the culture of the individual but that of a nation or region) is the artistic-technical and philosophic-spiritual activity, and that its standard is the achievement in art, technique, philosophy, religion, and science measured comparatively among nations or regions. That is to say, works of art, products of technique, recognitions of philosophy, teachings of religion, and discoveries of science per se are considered to be evidence of the presence of culture.

This definition reflects a trend that also characterizes contemporary human striving in general: preoccupation with perfection of the means of human progress and neglect of the aims of human progress. Creative accomplishments are taken as an end in themselves but not as a means toward a goal. There is little awareness that any creative activity earns its right of existence only when it serves man collectively as a group, nation, region, or even epoch.

It is for this reason that Europe, as well as China and India, prides itself as ranking very high culturally because of a rich tradition, whereas for the same reason, America excuses herself with being culturally less fortunate because of lack of any sizable tradition. The fallacy is twofold. First, the mere existence of separate creative products is taken as a sign of culture, regardless of whether they are successful in their mission of reaching and elevating the masses. And, secondly, the summary of regional or national cultural achievements of the past is taken as tradition, regardless of whether those achievements still constitute a living force in the formation of contemporary society.

The Japanese experience a rich emotional intercommunication with their total environment, and consequently humanism permeates all the physical and spiritual creations by means of which they shaped or interpreted their world. Here the essence of culture is uncovered. The criterion of culture is not a nation's or a region's works of art, technique, or science, measured in comparison to that of other nations or regions; it is instead the degree to which the summary of all creations of a nation or region succeeded in spiritually enlightening and emotionally enriching the lives of the collective people.

Japanese residential architecture, measured by the international standards of technical, economical, aesthetic, social, and scopewise achievement is doubtlessly very much inferior to the architectural accomplishments in the West. And yet, this Japanese dwelling has proven more efficient by far in its mission of establishing culture than has any form of architect-designed contemporary residential architecture equipped with the latest achievements of modern technology. Even though it provides insufficient physical comfort and protection against the extremes of weather, the Japanese house is a forceful and meaningful environment that stimulates philosphic thought, religious belief, artistic activity, and emotional sensation of its inhabitants.

The result is a distinct type of human being, unique and clearly distinguishable, and as easily defined as for example the Italian of the Renaissance, *one* attitude toward life, *one* idea of ethics, *one* interpretation of law, *one* standard of aesthetics, *one* disposition toward family and society, *one* belief into the supreme being, i.e., culture.

Here the formative role of Japanese residential architecture unveils the reality of culture: formation of a distinct type of human being, ethically, intellectually, spiritually, and aesthetically. That is to say, culture exists when the man-made spiritual and physical environment is such that it shapes or creates a unique type of human being distinct for a nation, region, or epoch.

This oneness, however, is not one of "con-formity" or "uni-formity," i.e., of qualities that pertain to external form and not to internal idea, but is on that very deep level where the intrinsic humanism relates man to fellow man and where the spiritual oneness of the family of man is to be found. To awaken this fundamental oneness of man's inner being should be the goal of all human efforts. Its attainment is culture.

Though such realization seems to possess but the value of a mere intellectual exercise, it yet has the merit of clearly marking out the task of contemporary society: reappraisal and reorientation of the total creative activities according to the fundamental objective of human progress, sensitizing the moral, aesthetical, and emotional consciousness of man. It means that the creative professional, especially the architect and artist, should concern himself seriously with the prevailing sentiment of the collective people instead of only expressing, developing, and satisfying his own "ego." With such an approach, art and architecture could again become the primary instruments for creating an ethical imperative in man, which is fundamental for culture and progress.

Still another very important concept of architectural and artistic creation that is presently both misused and misunderstood has been given a novel and precise definition by the foregoing studies: tradition. The potential of the Japanese residential architecture of the past to positively influence contemporary design is evidence that building undoubtedly will benefit from creatively using achievements of different time and location, i.e., it will progress by being traditional.

But the discovery of such a potential on the level of cause and motive rather than on that of effect and form unmistakably proves that traditional disposition does not simply mean continuation of, or reliance on, the achievements of the past, but is the successful application or new interpretation of creations and experiences of prior epochs for establishment of a culture that would give the present its own significance. Tradition in this sense is the formative presence and constructive force of previous attainments in present creation, both physical and spiritual. Form or product preserved from the past is not tradition; it is instead that which has been recognized for its timeless merit and has been introduced as a regenerating force in establishing a culture that is contemporary.

Strictly speaking, it is simply impossible to conceive of any of the present achievements that do not have direct ties with the past and thus must be termed as "handed down," that is to say, traditional. Indeed, tradition is necessarily a matter of the present and not of the past. For only the present can establish traditions, and what has been created today becomes tradition tomorrow, provided its quality is of lasting and universal validity. It is deplorable that much of contemporary architecture is lacking in any such traditional quality and has so far been unsuccessful in becoming tradition for a new and unique culture.

The direct value that Japanese residential architecture of the past contains for building in the contemporary West shows that creative tradition is by no means bound to locality, nor is it inevitably the property of the nation of its origin. Whatever prior generations have created, no present society has the right to claim as its own merit or contribution. Tradition is not simply given, but must be attained. Each society, each epoch, chooses its own traditions that become the crystallizing agents in the growth of a genuine culture, and there is no question that Japanese residential architecture qualifies to become one of the traditions for contemporary architectural creation in its efforts to establish culture.

history and present

This treatise, then, has been an attempt to establish a link between an architecture distant in time and locality and contemporary architectural creation. This link was not found in external form or in interior space designation, which time and again have served as material for proving the alleged "modern" quality of the Japanese house. Regardless of how closely these features resemble contemporary expression in building, they do so only by coincidence, because the causes and motivations of these expressions were of an essentially different nature.

The significance of Japanese architecture has been found on a much deeper level, in the discussion of cause rather than effect, of motivation rather than reaction, of source rather than product. Through confrontation with the respective phenomena in contemporary building, the validity of current theories has been put under test, a clearer perspective as to the major problems in contemporary building has been gained, and suggestions for architectural progress have been derived. Even predictions as to the course of future architecture have been indulged in unreservedly, because no discussion on the intellectual situation of today is of any value if it does not mark out the way toward tomorrow.

Although it is true that Japanese residential architecture, through its distinct features as well as through its unique evolution, bears a more instructive relationship to contemporary architecture than any other residential architecture does, it is contended that the confrontation of almost any cultural achievement of the past with present problems will enable a keener insight into contemporary affairs, provided that such confrontation is not one of external aspects, but of conditions and causes that effect architectural form, past and present. This is meant to express the conviction that knowledge of architectural history is not only essential for a more profound understanding of contemporary architecture but also constitutes a contributive element to architectural progress.

This realization has been followed by another, namely, that most of the current works of architectural history, being mainly assemblages of facts, have not exploited their enormous potential for the present with its search for universal principles of architectural creation. Of course, mere finding and recording of detailed fact is important, because only through comprehensive knowledge can any substantial conclusion be drawn. But of even more importance is the interpretation of those facts in the light of the contemporary situation in building.

Indeed historic research becomes meaningless if it is not brought into precise relationship to the present. Thus, the awareness of the fast flux of development in the contemporary society, of the solution of old problems and the rise of new problems, has given conviction that history is not absolute and finite. Rather, as man himself and the reflection of the environmental world within him continuously change, so also the image of the record of the past is ever changing. History needs to be rewritten along with the progress of man. There are no standard works of history.

In this sense, the foregoing interpretation of Japanese architecture should not be considered a finality. Rather, it is a transient reflection based on the present state of research as projected against the present situation in building. Both are expected to change. Not only will further research bring light to those many features of which the cause and motivation are still obscured, but the current scene in the architectural theater will also be followed by another. Architecture, after all, is a manifestation of life and, therefore, is in continuous growth, and thus should be the verbal interpretation that deals with it.

epigram

by EDWARD E. KIRKBRIDE

Sit
alone,
cross-legged, static, and immobile.
Think
in seclusion
unchecked, active, and flowing.

Sit
upon a mat.
The mat is three by six.
Think
disciplined
of the immeasurable and infinite.

Sit
between paper screens
and see the world within, the Self.
Think
of the unseen,
the without: The out is in, the in is out.

Sit
after bath
to wonder at the peace and order.
Think
when clean.
In purity is truth, and truth is beautiful.

Sit
with tea
lovingly prepared and thus presented.
Think
with scented potient.
Understanding enters the ordered mind.

Japan
and architecture:
How very beautiful their marriage.
Moderns
and architecture:
man estranged from the world he created.

Japan,
its architecture
scents the air with thoughtful beauty.

Modern
architecture
empty when naked, searching ashamed for a leaf.
Japan
finds architecture:
Each facet ordered and full of meaning.
Moderns
lose architecture:
a labyrinth of coin and thoughtlessness.
Japan
knows architecture:
Each home, the palette and canvas of man's life.
Moderns
lack architecture:
no depth or search, just surface pleasure.
Japan
is architecture:
Man is house, and house is life.
Modern
architecture:
Sit and listen and think and profit.

What
is architecture?
O Zen and hosts, your message we beseech.
It is
thoughtful living,
necessity softened by history, intellect, and life.
What
is necessity?
A roof, thatched or china-tiled, creator of interior.
It is
a platform
shielded against rain and sun, man's world.
What
causes necessity?
Nature: adversary, master, and mystic.
It is
Man's desire
to survive, be Self, and understand the unknown.
What
tools for necessity?
Nature's yield: wood, earth, bamboo, rice paper.
It is
space,
Nature's essence, captured, measured, and cared.
What
lesson, architecture?
The space: image and envelope of human life.
It is
humanity,
architecture's cause and destiny, its alpha and omega.

bibliography

IN JAPANESE

Banshō-shiki-shaku (Master Builder's Ceremony and Measure), medieval copy script

Buke-hinagata (Standards for Samurai Houses), script from the 17th–18th centuries

Fujiwara, Giichi. *Shoin-zukuri no Kenkyū* (A Study of the Shoin Style Architecture), Kyoto, 1946

Gokyōgoku (Fujiwara), Yoshitsune. *Sakutei-ki* (Notes on Garden Making), 12th century

Heinouchi, Masanobu. *Shōmei* script (Builder's Explanations), 1608

Kitao, Harumichi. *Chashitsu Kenchiku* (Teahouse Architecture), Tokyo, 1941

——. *Shoin Kenchiku Shōsai-zufu* (Shoin Architecture in Detailed Illustrations), Tokyo, 1956

——. *Sukiya Shōsai-zufu* (Teahouses in Detailed Illustrations), Tokyo, 1956

Kon, Wajirō. *Nihon no Minka* (Japanese Rural Houses), Tokyo, 1954

Ōta, Hirotarō. *Kenchiku-gaku Taikei* (Manual of Architectural Research), Tokyo, 1954

——. *Zusetsu Nihon Jūtaku-shi* (Illustrated History of the Japanese Residence), Tokyo, 1952

Saji, Yasuji. *Nihon Seikatsu-shi* (History of Japanese Living), Kyoto, 1952

Sakuma, Tanosuke. *Nihon Kenchiku Kōsaku-hō* (Construction Methods of Japanese Architecture), Tokyo, 1930

Sasaji, Shōjirō. *Kaoku Sekkei no Junjo to Shikata* (Procedure and Method of Residential Design), Tokyo, 1942

Sekino, Katsumi. *Nihon Jūtaku-shōshi* (Short History of the Japanese Residence), Tokyo. 1954

Sōami. *Tsukiyama-teizō-den* (Conventions of Hillock Garden Design), 16th century

Sukiya-hinagata (Standards for Tearooms), script from the 18th–19th centuries

Taihō Ritsuryō (Code of the Great Treasure), 8th century, original lost, references to it found in the *Shoku Nihongi* (A.D. 707), published in 2 vols. (1956 & 1957) in the *Kokushi Taikei*, Tokyo

Tanaka, Kazuhiko. *Kenchiku Zairyō* (Building Materials), Tokyo, 1953

IN ENGLISH

Blaser, Werner. *Temple and Tea-House in Japan,* New York, 1957

Borissavliévitch, M. *The Golden Number,* New York, 1958

Drexler, Arthur. *The Architecture of Japan,* New York, 1955

Engel, David E. *Japanese Gardens for Today,* Rutland & Tokyo, 1959

Gropius, Walter. *Scope of Total Architecture,* New York, 1953

Gulick, Sidney L. *Evolution of the Japanese,* London, 1903

Henderson, Harold G. *An Introduction to Haiku,* New York, 1958

Humphreys, Christmas. *Buddhism,* London, 1954

Kirby, John B. Jr. *From Castle to Teahouse: Japanese Architecture of the Momoyama Period,* Rutland and Tokyo, 1962

Liu, Wu-chi. *A Short History of Confucian Philosophy,* London, 1955

Okada, Takematsu. *A Sketch of the Climate of Japan,* Tokyo, 1936

Okakura, Kakuzo. *The Book of Tea,* Rutland and Tokyo, 1956

Ortega y Gasset, José. *The Dehumanization of Art,* New York, 1956

Perry, John. *The Story of Standards,* New York, 1955

Sadler, A. L. *A Short History of Japanese Architecture,* Rutland and Tokyo, 1962

Sansom, George B. *Japan: A Short Cultural History,* London, 1938

Scott, Geoffrey. *The Architecture of Humanism,* New York, 1956

Suzuki, Daisetz Teitaro. *Essays in Zen-Buddhism* (First Series), London, 1949

——. *Essays in Zen-Buddhism* (Second Series), London, 1950

——. *Essays in Zen-Buddhism* (Third Series), London, 1953

——. *Living by Zen,* Tokyo, 1949

Suzuki, Daisetz Teitaro. *Zen-Buddhism and its Influence upon Japanese Culture,* Kyoto, 1938
Taut, Bruno. *Houses and People of Japan,* Tokyo, 1958
Tsuda, Sokichi. *What Is Oriental Culture,* Tokyo, 1955
Yoshida, Tetsuro. *Gardens of Japan,* New York, 1957
——. *The Japanese House and Garden,* New York, 1956
Zevi, Bruno. *Architecture as Space,* New York, 1957

IN GERMAN

Baltzer, F. *Das Japanische Haus* (The Japanese House), Berlin, 1903
Berliner, Anna. *Der Teekult in Japan* (The Tea Cult in Japan)
Bohner, Hermann. *Shotoku Taishi,* Tokyo, 1940
Giedion, Siegfried. *Architektur und Gemeinschaft* (Architecture and Society), Hamburg, 1957
Heidegger, Martin. *Vorträge und Aufsätze* (Lectures and Writings), Tübingen, 1954
Malraux, André. *Psychologie der Kunst* (Psychology of the Arts), Hamburg, 1957
Ortega y Gasset, José. *Betrachtungen über die Technik* (Thoughts on Technology), Stuttgart, 1949
Scheidl, Leopold. *Die Geographischen Grundlagen des Japanischen Wesens* (Geographical Backgrounds of the Japanese Character), Tokyo, 1937
Sotei, Akaji. *Zen-worte in Tee-raum* (Zen Aphorisms in the Tearoom), Tokyo, 1943
Yoshida, Tetsuro. *Japanische Architektur* (Japanese Architecture), Tübingen, 1952

NOTE: *Numbers in italics indicate pages on which plates appear; all other numbers indicate text pages.*